KEVIN SMITH
Writer

PHIL HESTER
Penciller

ANDE PARKS
Inker

GUY MAJOR
Colorist

SEAN KONOT
Letterer

MATT WAGNER
Original Covers

GREEN ARROW

QUIVER

GREEN ARROW: QUIVER
Published by DC Comics. Cover, introduction and compilation copyright © 2002 DC Comics. All Rights Reserved.

Originally published in single magazine form as GREEN ARROW 1-10, cover of Wizard Magazine 113 (February 2001) Copyright © 2001, 2002 DC Comics. All Rights Reserved. All characters, their distinctive likenesses and related indicia featured in this publication are trademarks of DC Comics. The stories, characters, and incidents featured in this publication are entirely fictional. DC Comics does not read or accept unsolicited submissions of ideas, stories or artwork.

DC Comics, 1700 Broadway, New York, NY 10019
A division of Warner Bros. — An AOL Time Warner Company
Printed in Canada. First Printing.
HARDCOVER ISBN: 1-56389-802-0
SOFTCOVER ISBN: 1-56389-887-X
Cover illustration by Matt Wagner.
Publication Design by Maria P. Cabardo.

GREEN ARROW: QUIVER

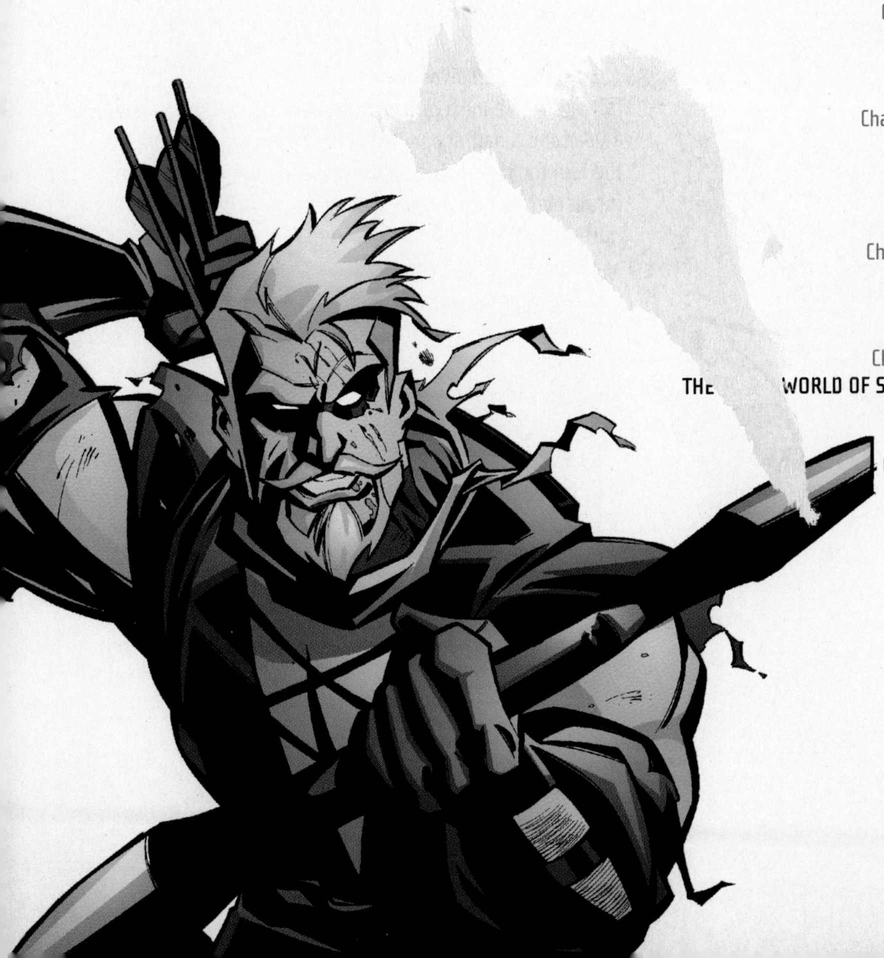

INTRODUCTION by KEVIN SMITH

Anyone out there ever try to actually use a bow and arrow?

It's one thing to *read about* the exploits of a guy who can nock and let fly with the shafts so rapidly (yet artfully) that he can disarm goons with guns, but try hitting the range yourself and not struggling to pull back that catgut. You need chest muscles like a circa mid-'90s Rob Liefeld drawing to draw on a longbow, and it doesn't stop there. Archery requires more than just upper-body strength; it requires grace and fluidity of motion. And anyone who's ever gotten a good look at me knows that I've got none of that going on.

You can figure out a lot about yourself by picking up a longbow. And that's what I did prior to writing word one on GREEN ARROW. It was a rare move for me, as I've never been a "method" kind of writer. Yes — I *did* work at the convenience and video stores where we shot *Clerks,* but that wasn't research for my writing; that was how I paid my bills. I didn't sign on for that minimum wage gig with the intention of jockeying the register in an effort to cultivate fodder for an indie film; I took that job because it was physically nontaxing and I could watch TV while I was doing it. I am, by nature, very lazy. Especially when I write.

So I surprised myself when I asked Byron, my wife's step-father, to give me a primer in archery in our backyard about a year and a half ago, with the express purpose of getting the feel for the quiver. It was research you couldn't put in for many other super-heroes. Were I to write AQUAMAN, the likelihood of me dunking my head in the aquarium to get a feel for how fish spoke was low, but as I was only going to be writing GREEN ARROW, I figured I should at least familiarize myself with the draw of a bow. It was one of the rare occasions when I could engage in even the slightest investigation of a character I was writing, and it might actually *inform* the story I was going to tell.

So Byron, an accomplished amateur archer, set me up with his longbow, put up a target, took me within five feet of it, and said "Go ahead." Naturally, being so close to the target initially felt insulting. However, after my first attempt at drawing back the bow, I realized the wisdom in my proximity to the hay bale.

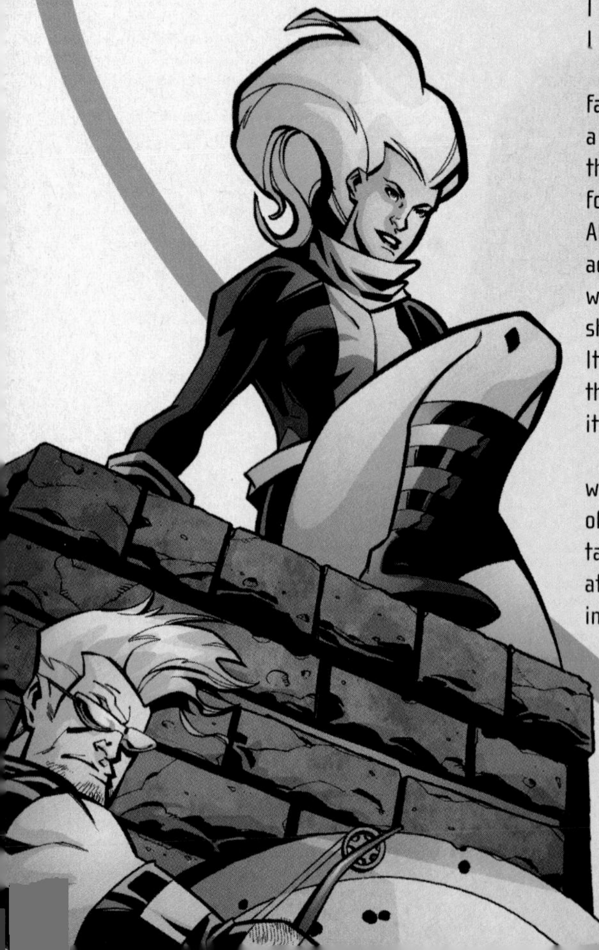

This simple act took the upper-body strength of an Olympian. My chest was on fire, my jelly-arms were suddenly jam. I was shaking like Gotham during the Cataclysm (wow — a ham-fisted comic-book reference; imagine that). I, who have faced down death threats on *Dogma* and gotten Affleck to openly deride his post-*Amy* career in *Jay and Silent Bob Strike Back* (all available on home video, plug-plug), suddenly felt powerless and small.

That is, until the nay-sayers weighed in with their judgments of QUIVER.

I knew I was in trouble from the get-go, because I wasn't writing a jump-on comic. My run on GREEN ARROW didn't invite the average noncomics fan into the medium; it almost chased them off. At least, that's what some folks told me when they read issue one.

"Too mired in continuity!" they bitched.

"Too many references to history of the DC Universe!" they moaned.

"All the characters do is talk!" they wept.

"You should've written a story the casual, non-GREEN ARROW fan could jump into more easily!" they back-seat drove.

And, who knows? Maybe they were right.

Granted, the entire ten-issue run of the QUIVER storyline sold about a million copies, but who knows? Maybe they were right.

Or were they the powerless and small?

My defense? Well, I have none. I just wrote a story I would've liked to have read myself, had it been written by someone else. This was a GREEN ARROW tale that paid deep, deep homage to all the other great Arrow-heads of the past: from O'Neil and Adams, to Maggin, to Grell, and even to Dixon. And beyond those gents, this was a GREEN ARROW story that tipped its pointed cap to Alan Moore's fantastic non-Arrow romp through the DCU of the mid-to-late '80s (with the lone exception of his handling of the Emerald Archer in the pages of SWAMP THING during a JLA appearance). This was a GREEN ARROW story about second chances, and how bad-ass Batman is. This was a GREEN ARROW story about costumed derring-do, and outdated liberalism in a largely liberal world.

But really, this was a GREEN ARROW story about how much I love GREEN ARROW and the rest of the DCU.

So ultimately, there's not a whole lot of text in QUIVER that relates the tremendous effort it takes to nock and fire an arrow (it's only mentioned once, by Mia), but who wants to read about that anyway? When I pick up GREEN ARROW, I want to read about a guy for whom nocking and firing ten arrows in ten seconds is a breeze, but owning up to being a father is difficult. I want to read about how that guy interacts with a bunch of folks in costumes who are under the distinct impression that he's dead. I want to read about whether it's the identity or the soul that defines a man...

And I want to read about ten issues that're filled with *twenty issues* worth of dialogue.

By the end of QUIVER, I'd done all of that. I wrote the exact story that I wanted to write, and it sold like Batman T-shirts, circa 1989. And not only was it fulfilling and fun; it was also easy.

A hell of a lot easier than shooting a bow and arrow, I assure you.

A few shout-outs are in order to those without whom there is no QUIVER: Phil "You Want How Many Panels on a Page?!?" Hester, Ande "He Wants How Many Panels on a Page?!?" Parks, Sean "My Hand Fell Off at Issue Two" Konot, Guy "I Don't Care What Color They Say the Feather Is!" Major, and Bob "I Had the Name First" Schreck. Honorable mentions go out to Michael "I'd Rather Be Working on Batman Books" Wright, and Nachie "Yes — That's My Name" Castro. Without all these fine gents (notice the disturbing lack of estrogen on this book?), there'd be no wildly successful GREEN ARROW relaunch.

Each turned in their best work to date, I feel, and for that, I'm slobberingly grateful.

And let me toss you, the readers, a shout-out. You catapulted a third-tier character into the top ten with your voracious consumption of the book — so much so that DC went to a first-time-in-ages Fourth Printing of Issue One. Keep that up, and folks might have to stop prophesying the death of the industry.

But my final shout-out goes to Matt Wagner. This man not only turned in stunningly beautiful covers that enticed many a reader into giving the title a shot, but he then sold me said covers for a fairly reasonable price. Each is already framed and hanging at my comic-book store in Red Bank, New Jersey, Jay and Silent Bob's Secret Stash (plug-plug), where they serve as constant reminders of my first foray into the DCU. I'll keep them forever...

Or at least until I run out of cash.

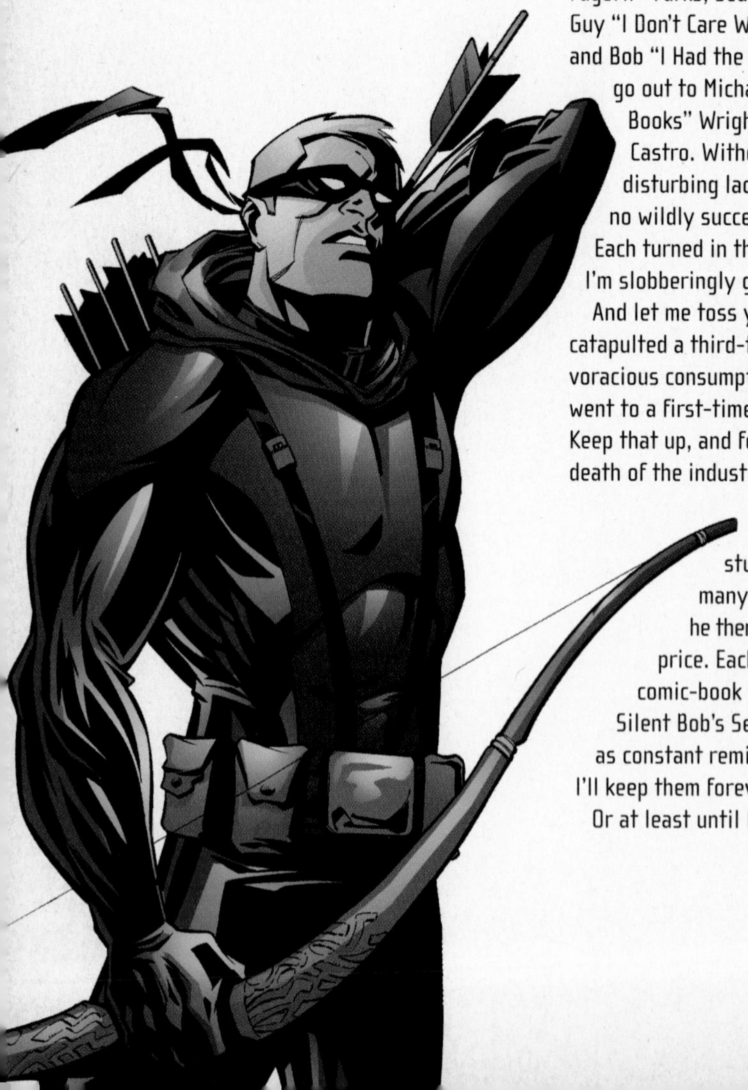

— Kevin Smith
January, 2002

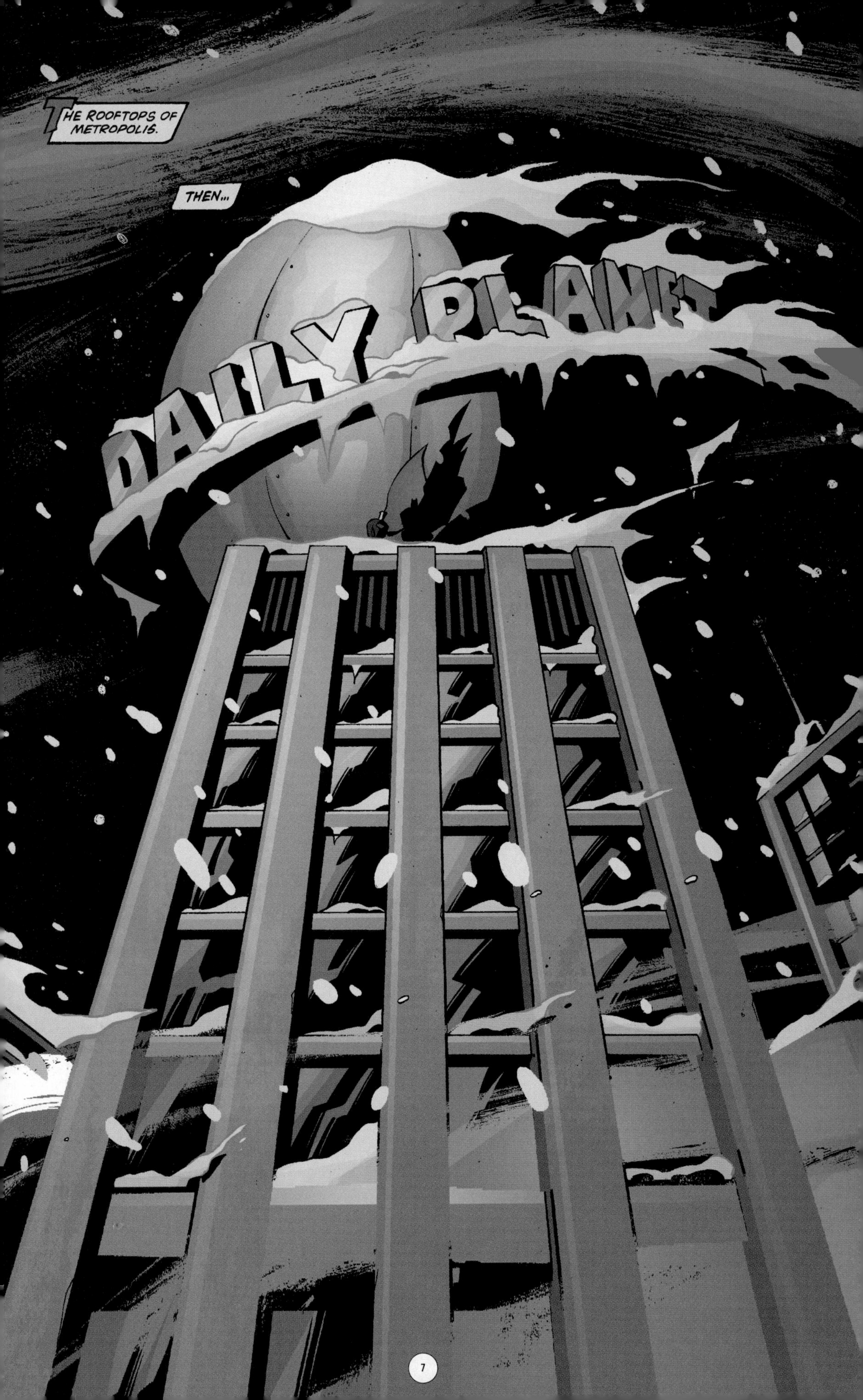
THE ROOFTOPS OF METROPOLIS.
THEN...
DAILY PLANET

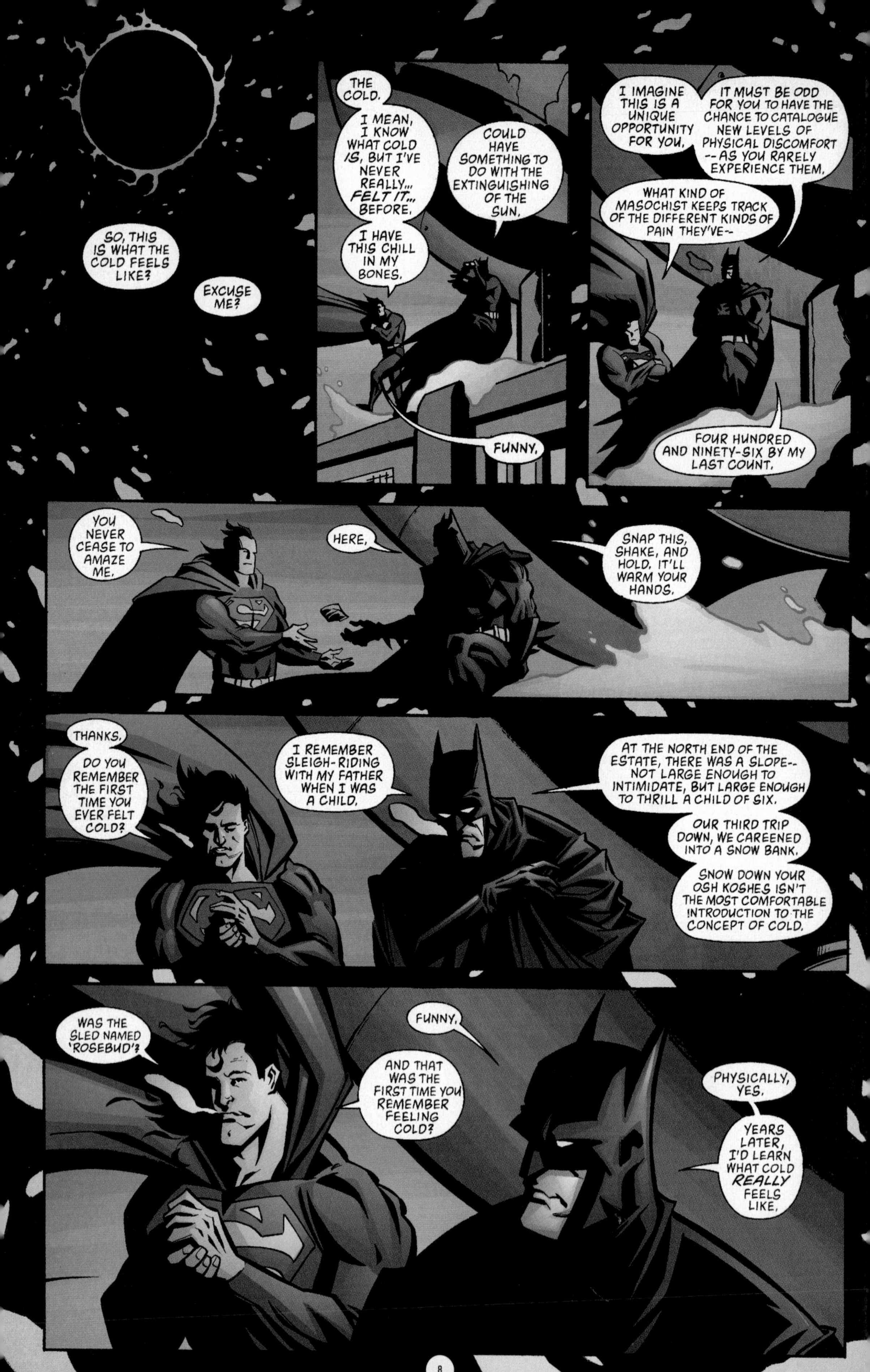
SO, THIS IS WHAT THE COLD FEELS LIKE?
EXCUSE ME?
THE COLD.
I MEAN, I KNOW WHAT COLD IS, BUT I'VE NEVER REALLY... FELT IT... BEFORE.
I HAVE THIS CHILL IN MY BONES.
COULD HAVE SOMETHING TO DO WITH THE EXTINGUISHING OF THE SUN.
FUNNY.
I IMAGINE THIS IS A UNIQUE OPPORTUNITY FOR YOU.
IT MUST BE ODD FOR YOU TO HAVE THE CHANCE TO CATALOGUE NEW LEVELS OF PHYSICAL DISCOMFORT --AS YOU RARELY EXPERIENCE THEM.
WHAT KIND OF MASOCHIST KEEPS TRACK OF THE DIFFERENT KINDS OF PAIN THEY'VE--
FOUR HUNDRED AND NINETY-SIX BY MY LAST COUNT.
YOU NEVER CEASE TO AMAZE ME.
HERE.
SNAP THIS, SHAKE, AND HOLD. IT'LL WARM YOUR HANDS.
THANKS.
DO YOU REMEMBER THE FIRST TIME YOU EVER FELT COLD?
I REMEMBER SLEIGH-RIDING WITH MY FATHER WHEN I WAS A CHILD.
AT THE NORTH END OF THE ESTATE, THERE WAS A SLOPE-- NOT LARGE ENOUGH TO INTIMIDATE, BUT LARGE ENOUGH TO THRILL A CHILD OF SIX.
OUR THIRD TRIP DOWN, WE CAREENED INTO A SNOW BANK.
SNOW DOWN YOUR OSH KOSHES ISN'T THE MOST COMFORTABLE INTRODUCTION TO THE CONCEPT OF COLD.
WAS THE SLED NAMED 'ROSEBUD'?
FUNNY.
AND THAT WAS THE FIRST TIME YOU REMEMBER FEELING COLD?
PHYSICALLY, YES.
YEARS LATER, I'D LEARN WHAT COLD REALLY FEELS LIKE.

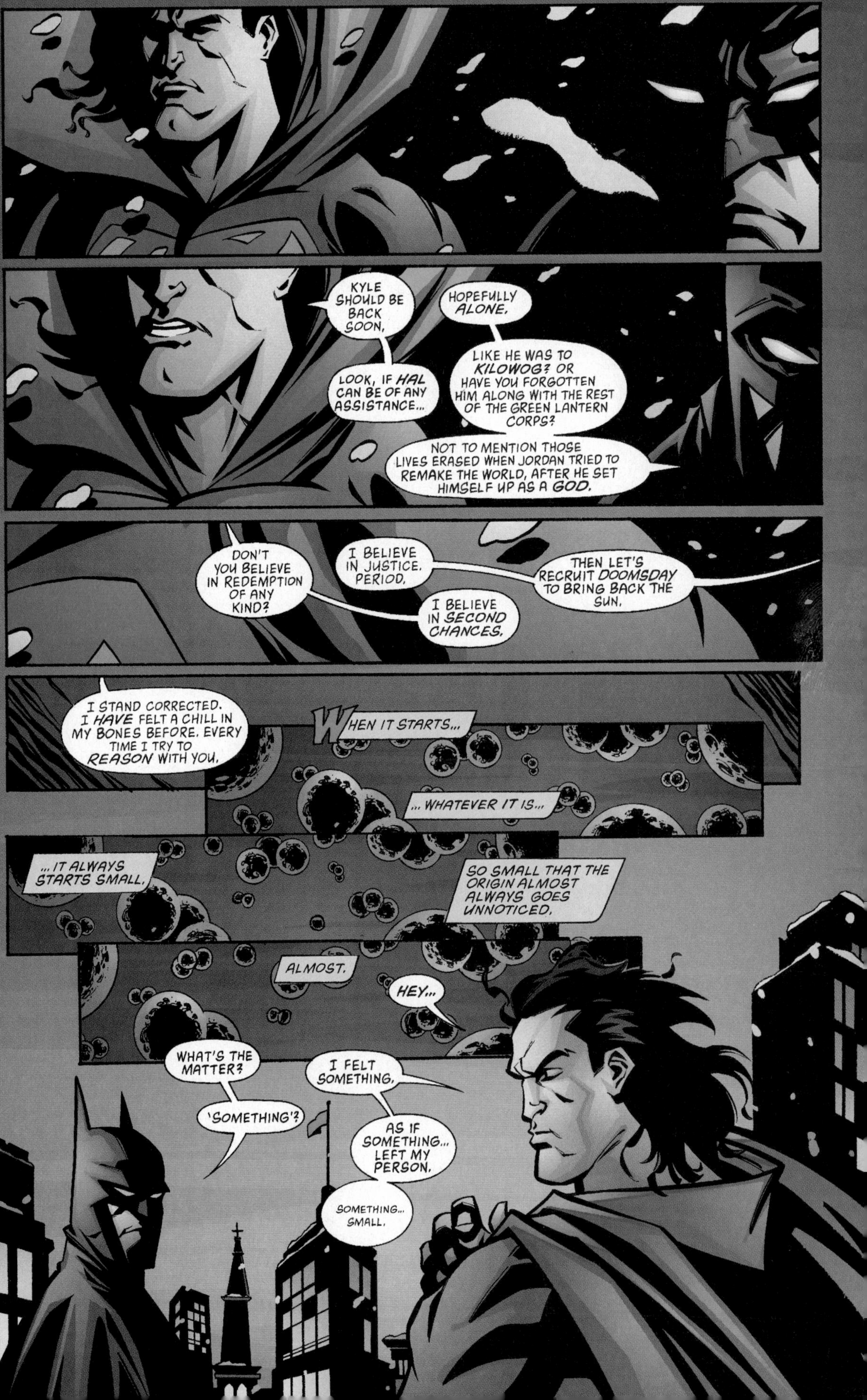
KYLE SHOULD BE BACK SOON.
HOPEFULLY ALONE.
LOOK, IF HAL CAN BE OF ANY ASSISTANCE...
LIKE HE WAS TO KILOWOG? OR HAVE YOU FORGOTTEN HIM ALONG WITH THE REST OF THE GREEN LANTERN CORPS?
NOT TO MENTION THOSE LIVES ERASED WHEN JORDAN TRIED TO REMAKE THE WORLD, AFTER HE SET HIMSELF UP AS A GOD.
DON'T YOU BELIEVE IN REDEMPTION OF ANY KIND?
I BELIEVE IN JUSTICE. PERIOD.
I BELIEVE IN SECOND CHANCES.
THEN LET'S RECRUIT DOOMSDAY TO BRING BACK THE SUN.
I STAND CORRECTED. I HAVE FELT A CHILL IN MY BONES BEFORE. EVERY TIME I TRY TO REASON WITH YOU.
WHEN IT STARTS...
...WHATEVER IT IS...
...IT ALWAYS STARTS SMALL.
SO SMALL THAT THE ORIGIN ALMOST ALWAYS GOES UNNOTICED.
ALMOST.
HEY...
WHAT'S THE MATTER?
I FELT SOMETHING.
'SOMETHING'?
AS IF SOMETHING... LEFT MY PERSON.
SOMETHING... SMALL.

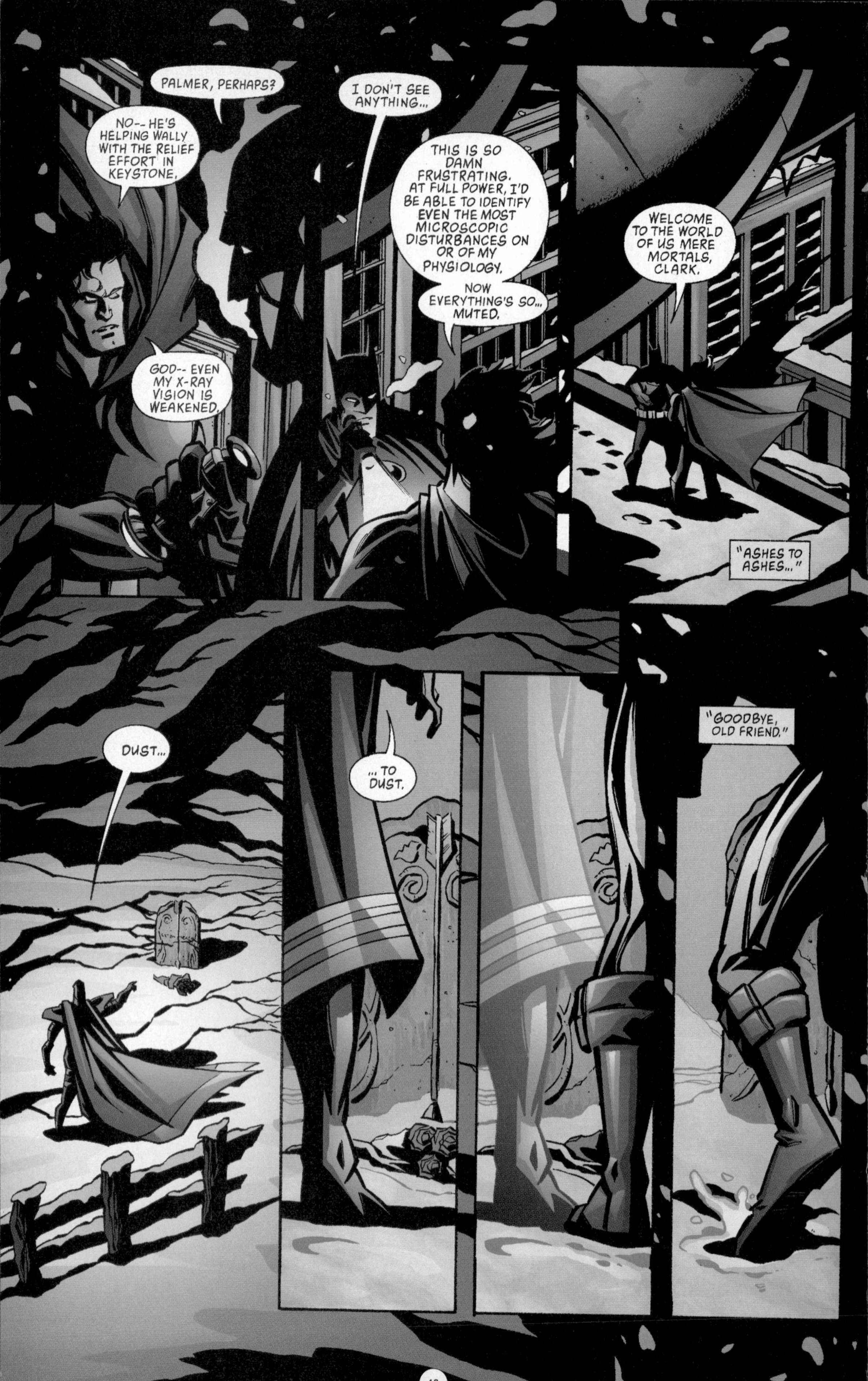
PALMER, PERHAPS?
NO-- HE'S HELPING WALLY WITH THE RELIEF EFFORT IN KEYSTONE.
GOD-- EVEN MY X-RAY VISION IS WEAKENED.
I DON'T SEE ANYTHING...
THIS IS SO DAMN FRUSTRATING. AT FULL POWER, I'D BE ABLE TO IDENTIFY EVEN THE MOST MICROSCOPIC DISTURBANCES ON OR OF MY PHYSIOLOGY.
NOW EVERYTHING'S SO... MUTED.
WELCOME TO THE WORLD OF US MERE MORTALS, CLARK.
"ASHES TO ASHES..."
DUST...
...TO DUST.
"GOODBYE, OLD FRIEND."

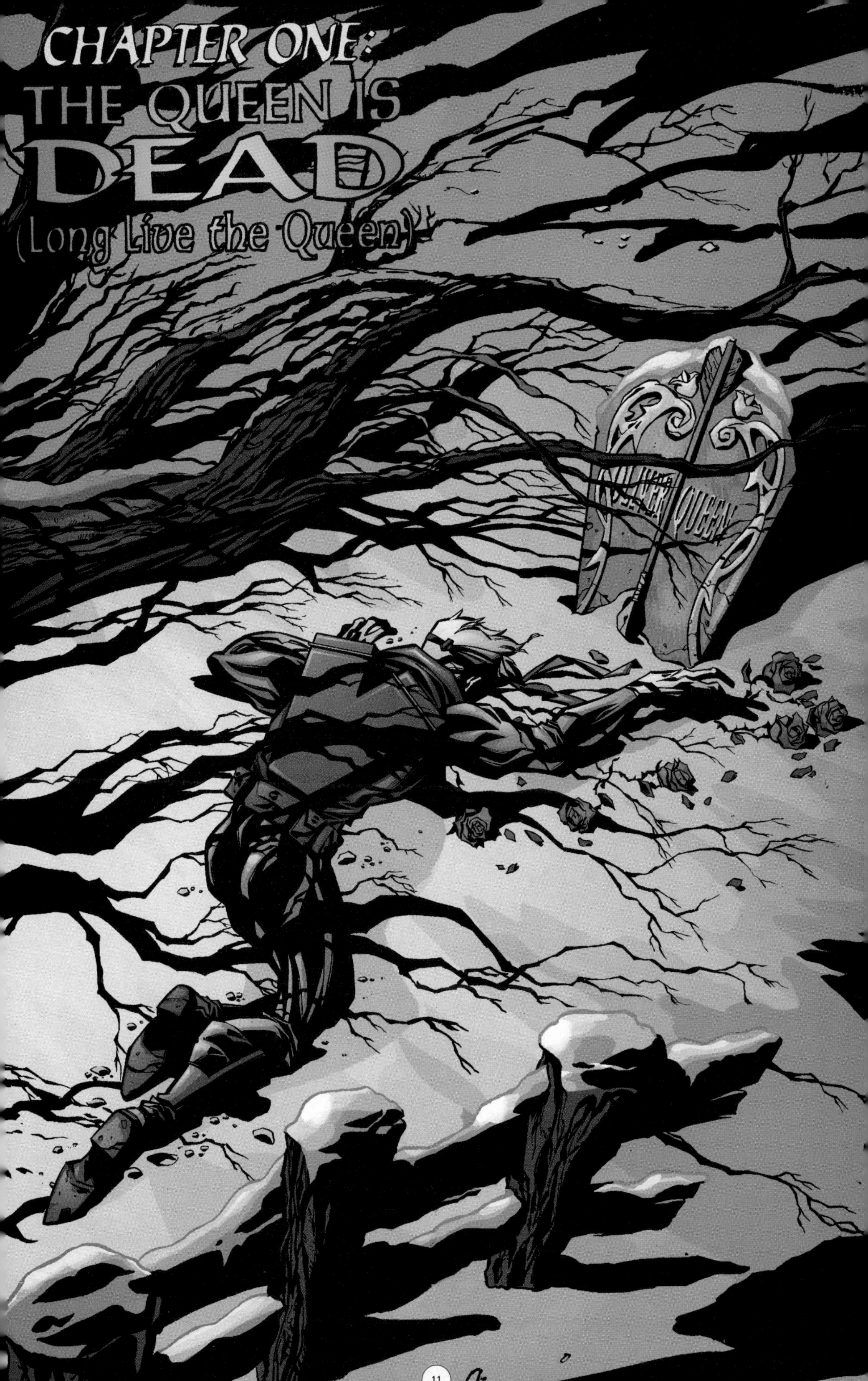
CHAPTER ONE:
THE QUEEN IS
DEAD
(Long Live the Queen)
QUEEN

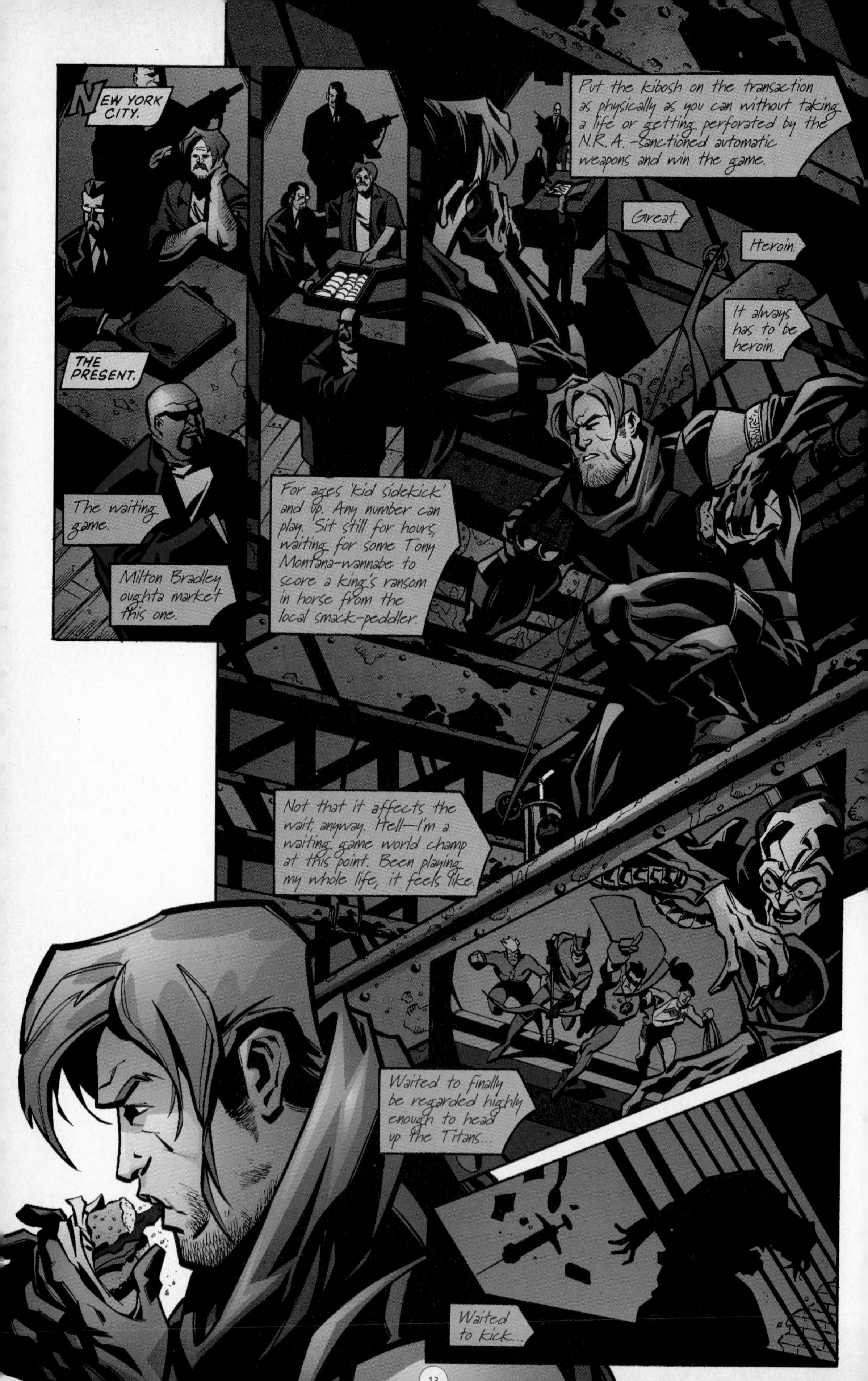
NEW YORK CITY.
THE PRESENT.
The waiting game.
Milton Bradley oughta market this one.
For ages 'kid sidekick' and up. Any number can play. Sit still for hours, waiting for some Tony Montana-wannabe to score a king's ransom in horse from the local smack-peddler.
Put the kibosh on the transaction as physically as you can without taking a life or getting perforated by the N.R.A.-sanctioned automatic weapons and win the game.
Great.
Heroin.
It always has to be heroin.
Not that it affects the wait, anyway. Hell—I'm a waiting game world champ at this point. Been playing my whole life, it feels like.
Waited to finally be regarded highly enough to head up the Titans...
Waited to kick...

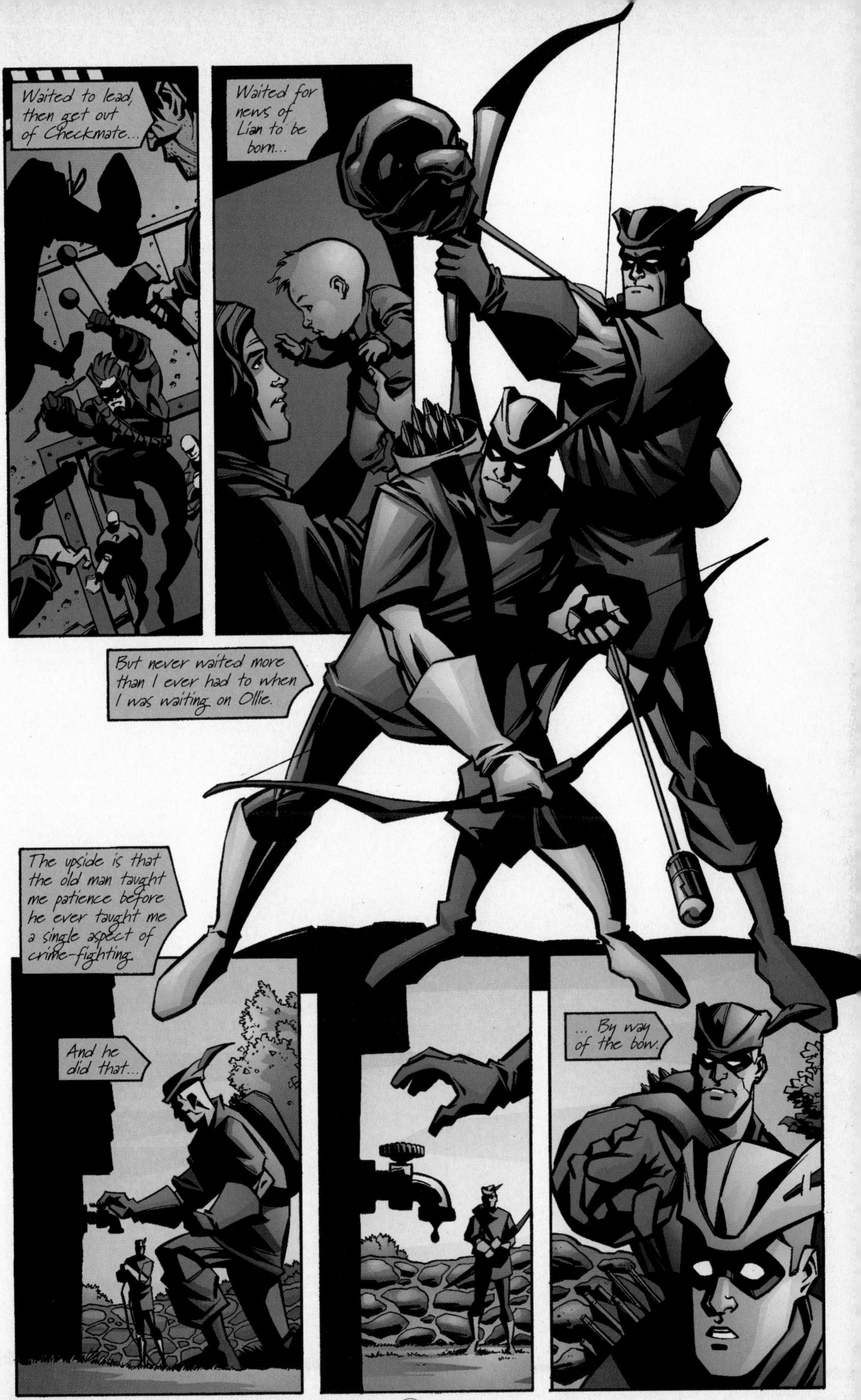

Waited to lead, then get out of Checkmate...
Waited for news of Lian to be born...
But never waited more than I ever had to when I was waiting on Ollie.
The upside is that the old man taught me patience before he ever taught me a single aspect of crime-fighting.
And he did that...
...By way of the bow.

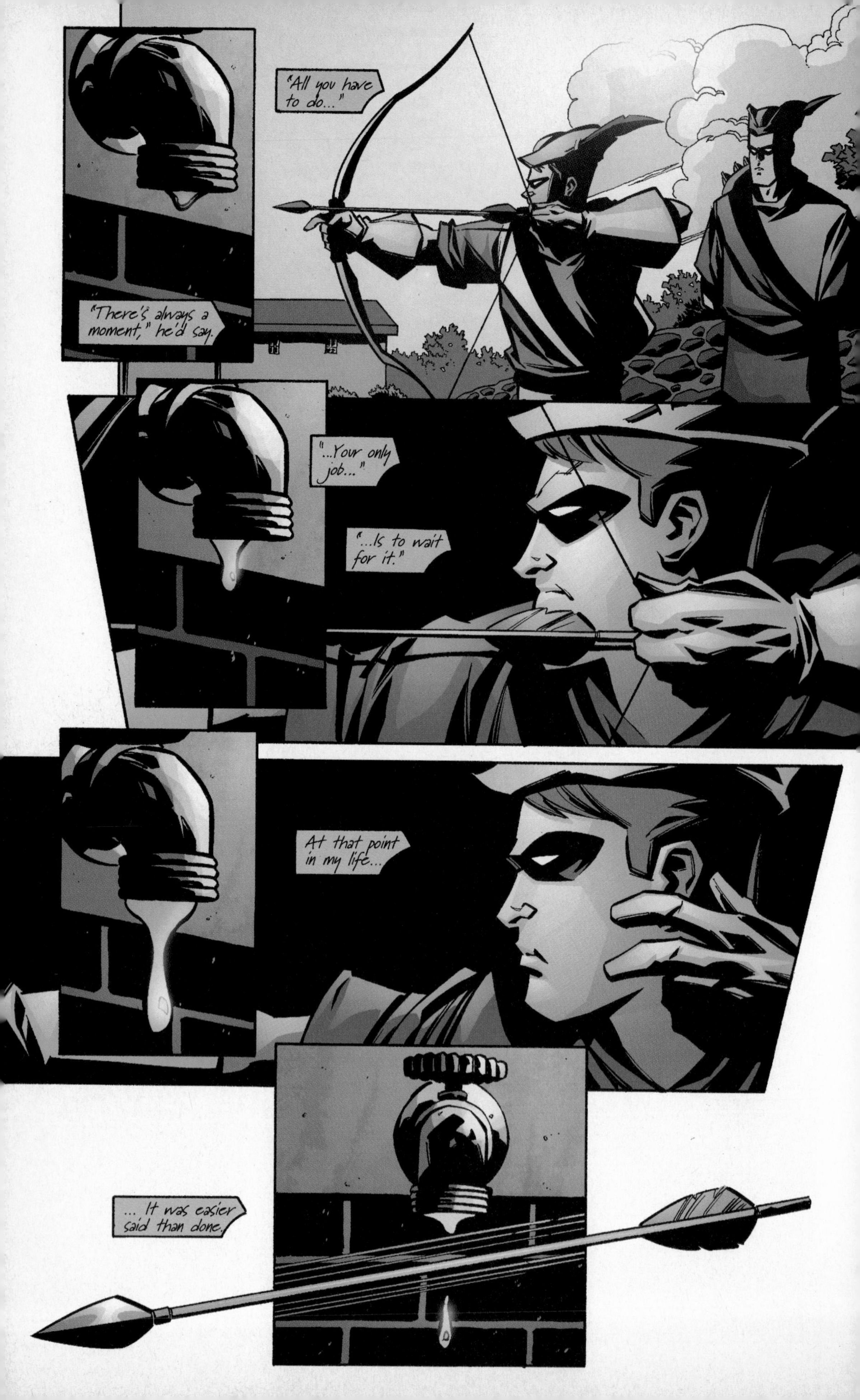
"All you have to do..."
"There's always a moment," he'd say.
"...Your only job..."
"...Is to wait for it."
At that point in my life...
... It was easier said than done.

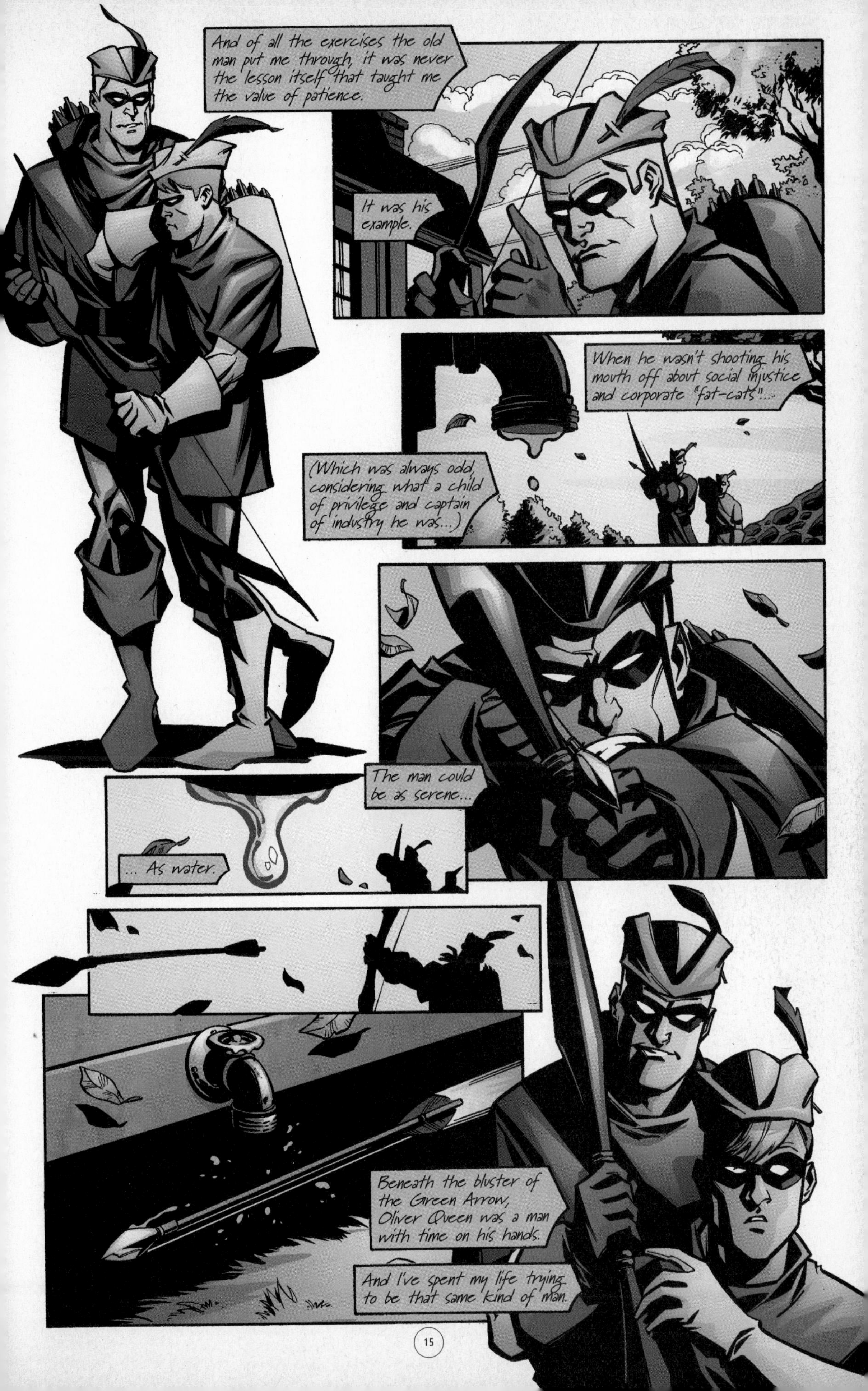
And of all the exercises the old man put me through, it was never the lesson itself that taught me the value of patience.
It was his example.
When he wasn't shooting his mouth off about social injustice and corporate "fat-cats"...
(Which was always odd, considering what a child of privilege and captain of industry he was...)
The man could be as serene...
... As water.
Beneath the bluster of the Green Arrow, Oliver Queen was a man with time on his hands.
And I've spent my life trying to be that same kind of man.

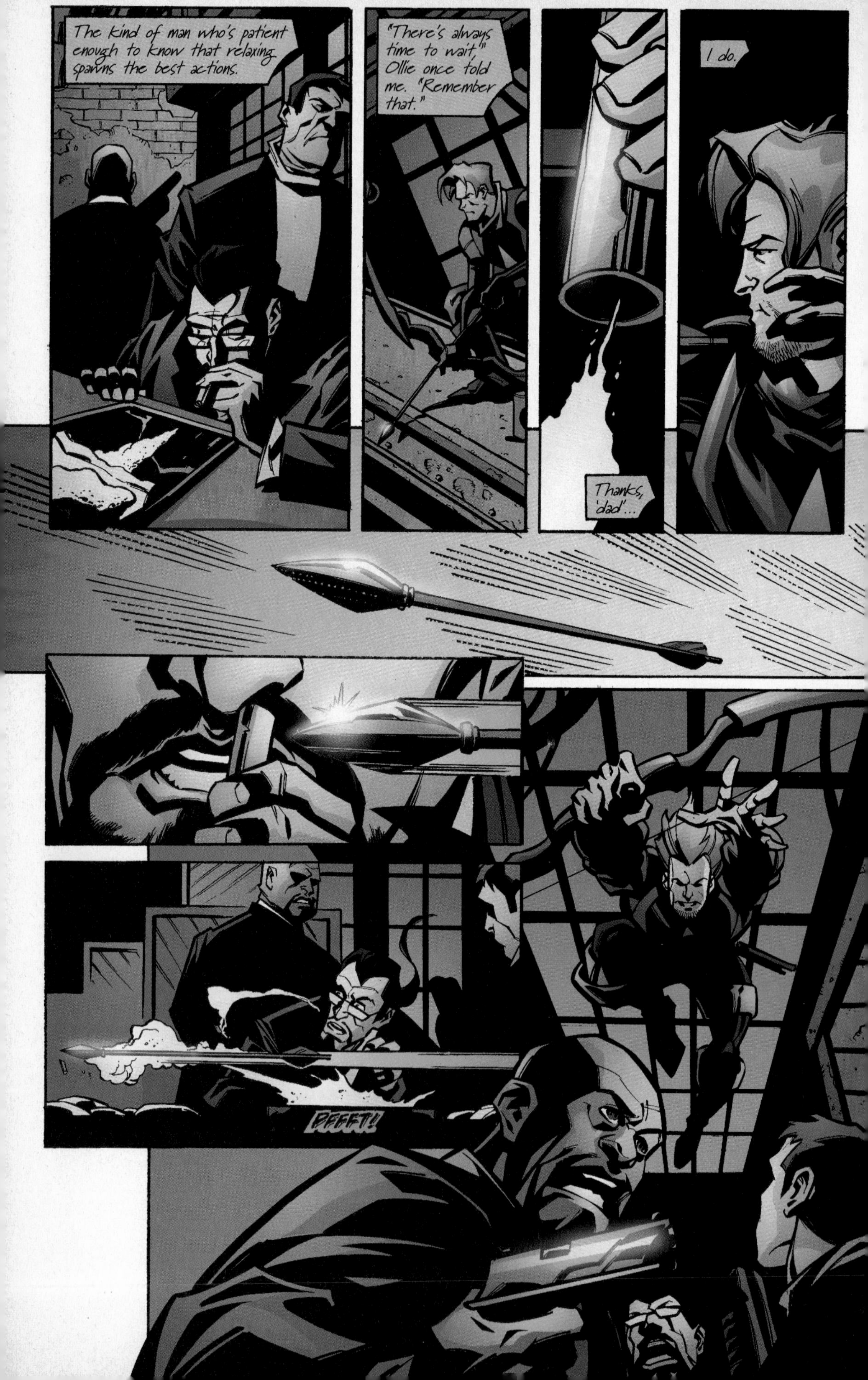

The kind of man who's patient enough to know that relaxing spawns the best actions.
"There's always time to wait," Ollie once told me. "Remember that."
I do.
Thanks, 'dad'...
PFFFT!

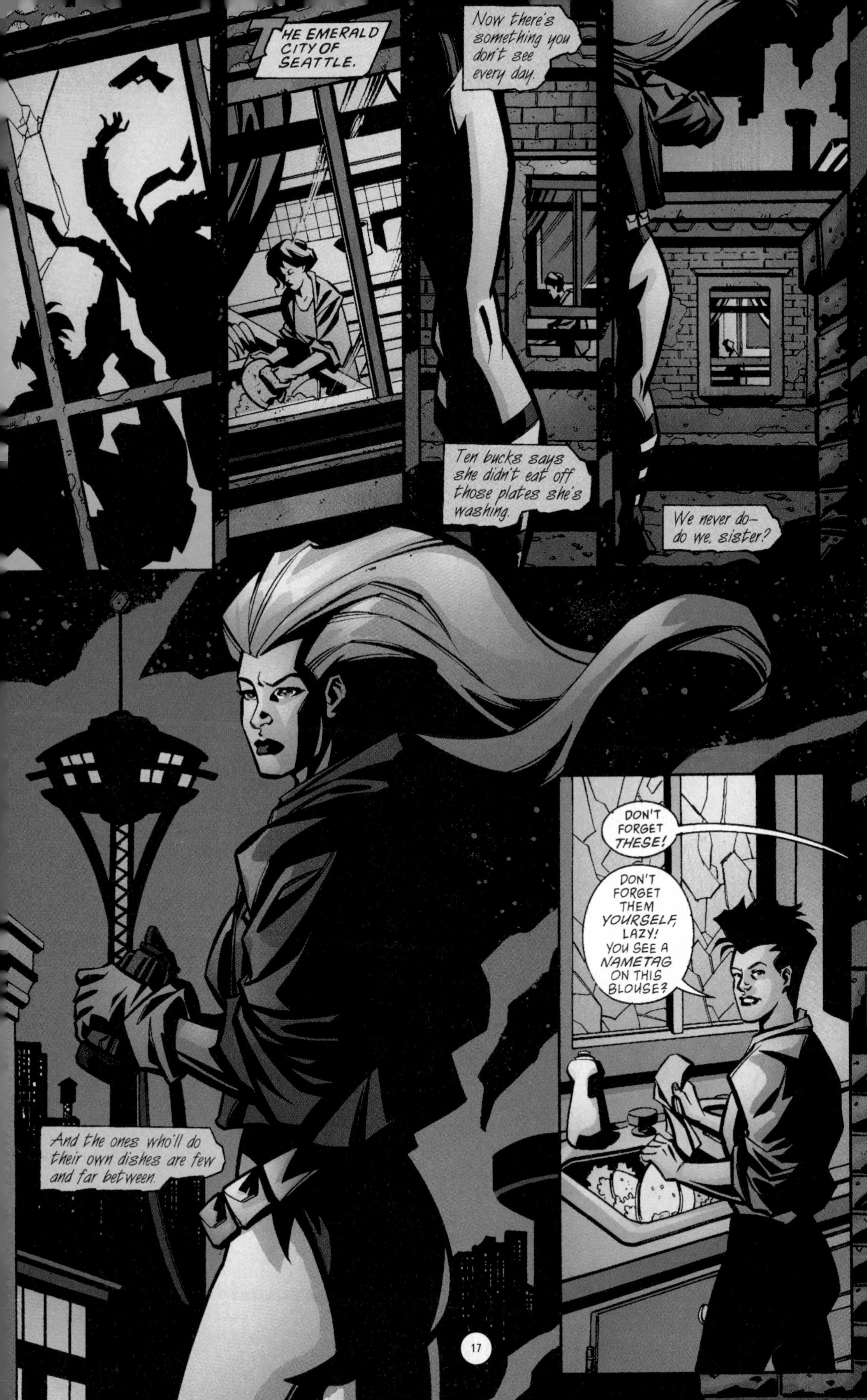
THE EMERALD CITY OF SEATTLE.
Now there's something you don't see every day.
Ten bucks says she didn't eat off those plates she's washing.
We never do-- do we, sister?
And the ones who'll do their own dishes are few and far between.
DON'T FORGET THESE!
DON'T FORGET THEM YOURSELF, LAZY! YOU SEE A NAMETAG ON THIS BLOUSE?

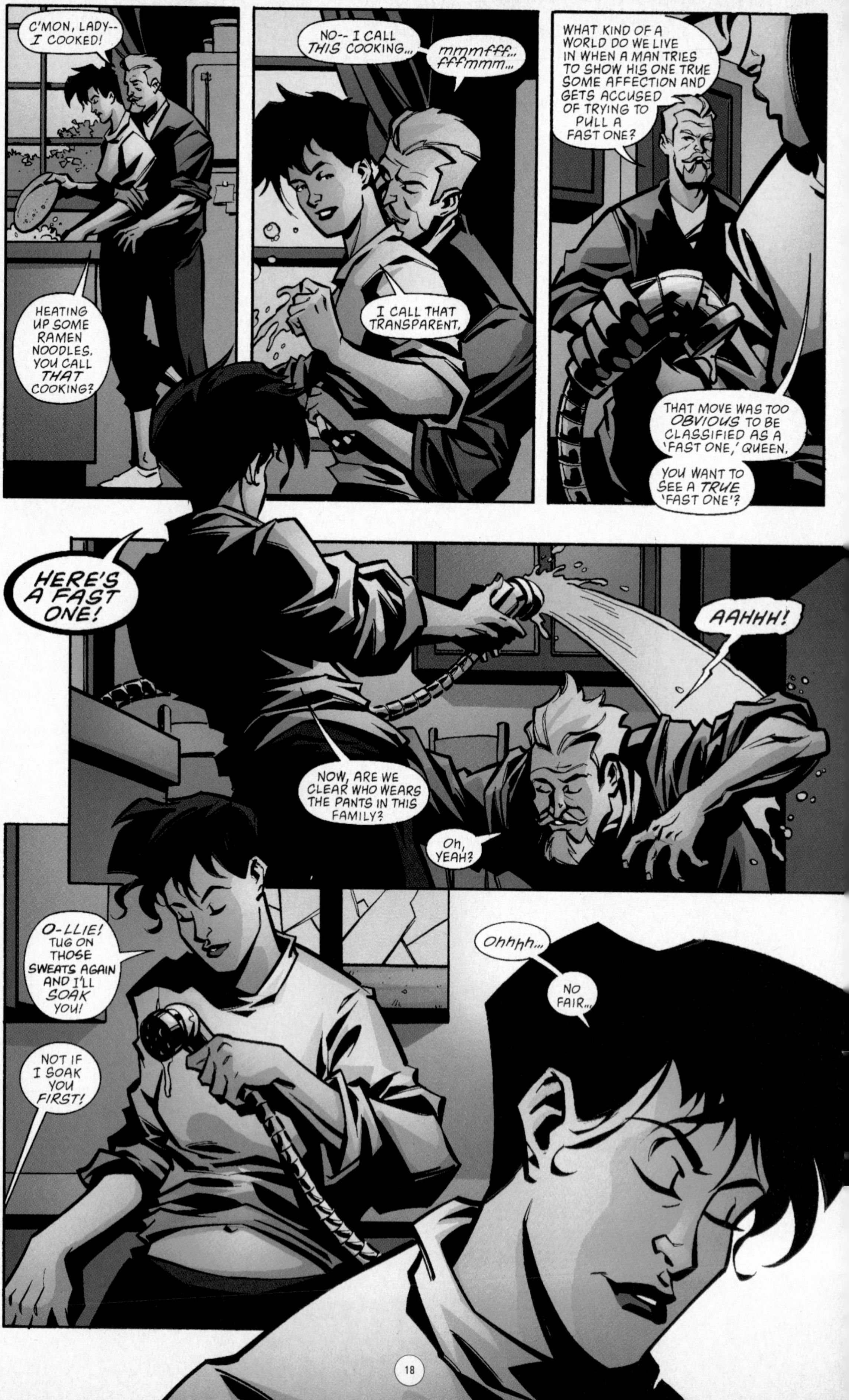
C'MON, LADY-- I COOKED!
HEATING UP SOME RAMEN NOODLES. YOU CALL THAT COOKING?
NO-- I CALL THIS COOKING...
mmmfff... fffmmm...
I CALL THAT TRANSPARENT.
WHAT KIND OF A WORLD DO WE LIVE IN WHEN A MAN TRIES TO SHOW HIS ONE TRUE SOME AFFECTION AND GETS ACCUSED OF TRYING TO PULL A FAST ONE?
THAT MOVE WAS TOO OBVIOUS TO BE CLASSIFIED AS A 'FAST ONE,' QUEEN.
YOU WANT TO SEE A TRUE 'FAST ONE'?
HERE'S A FAST ONE!
AAHHH!
NOW, ARE WE CLEAR WHO WEARS THE PANTS IN THIS FAMILY?
Oh, YEAH?
O-LLIE! TUG ON THOSE SWEATS AGAIN AND I'LL SOAK YOU!
NOT IF I SOAK YOU FIRST!
Ohhhh...
NO FAIR...

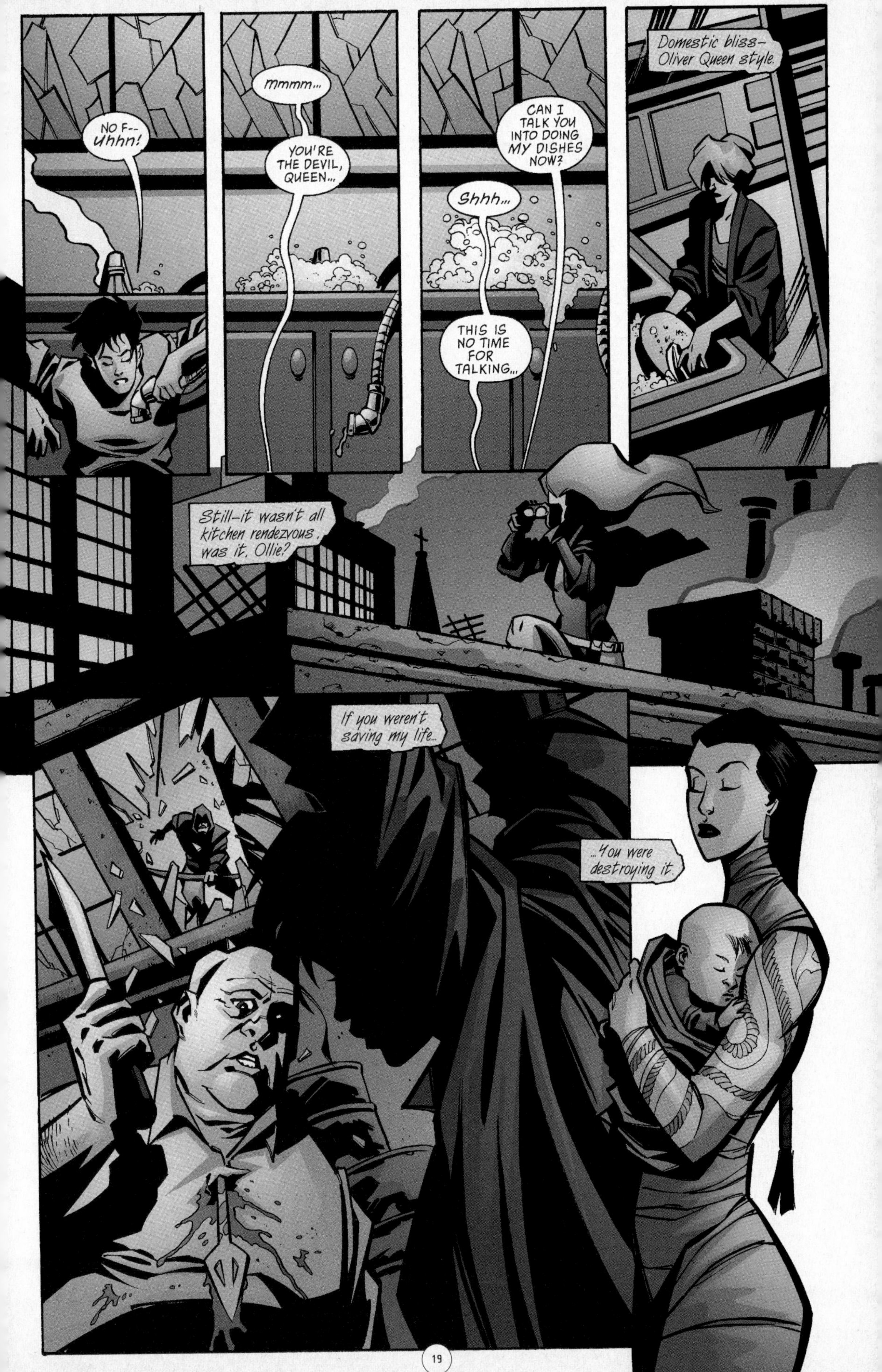
NO F--
UHHN!
mmmm...
YOU'RE THE DEVIL, QUEEN...
CAN I TALK YOU INTO DOING MY DISHES NOW?
Shhh...
THIS IS NO TIME FOR TALKING...
Domestic bliss--
Oliver Queen style.
Still--it wasn't all kitchen rendezvous, was it, Ollie?
If you weren't saving my life...
...You were destroying it.

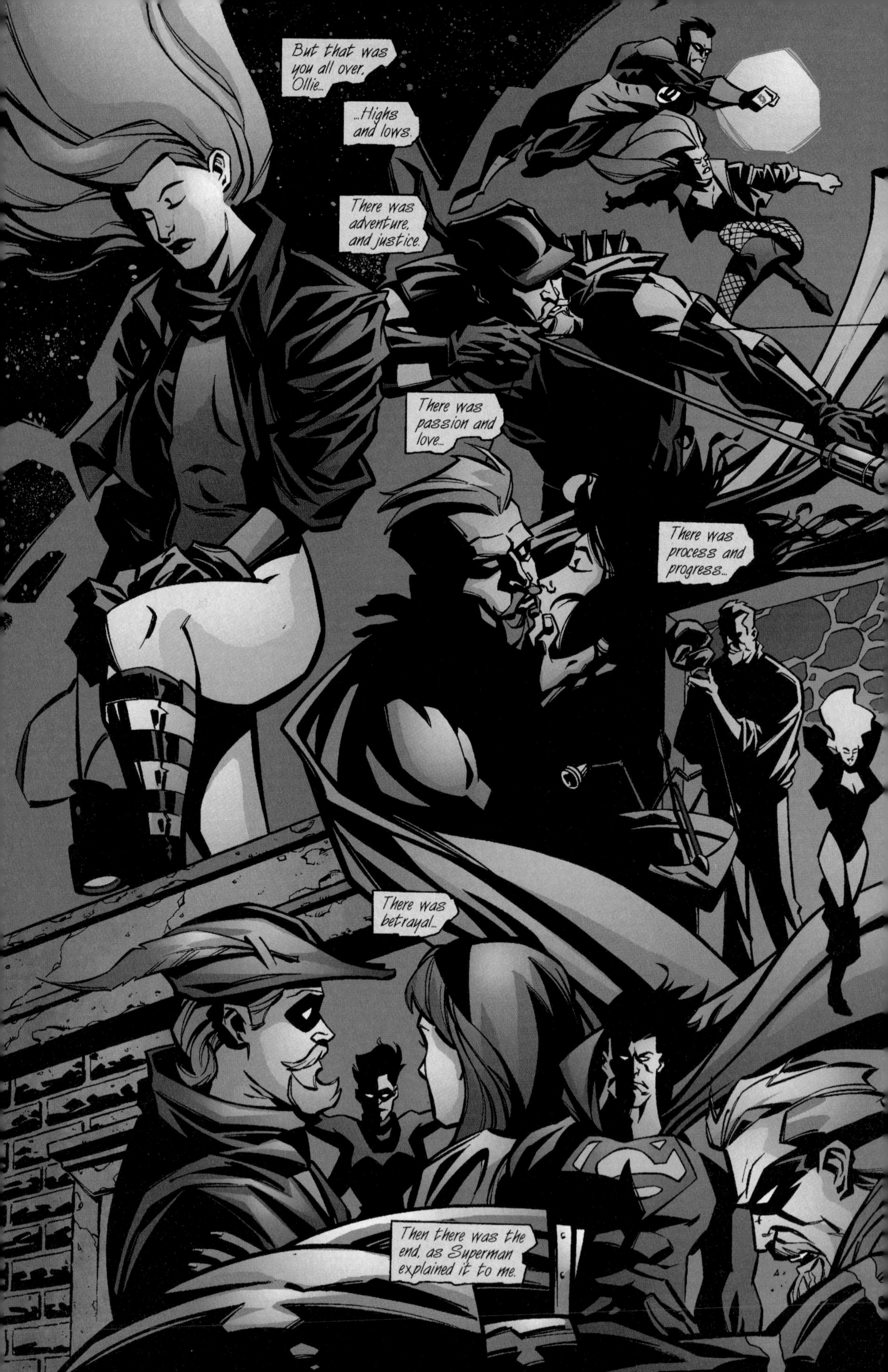
But that was you all over, Ollie...
...Highs and lows.
There was adventure, and justice.
There was passion and love...
There was process and progress...
There was betrayal...
Then there was the end, as Superman explained it to me.

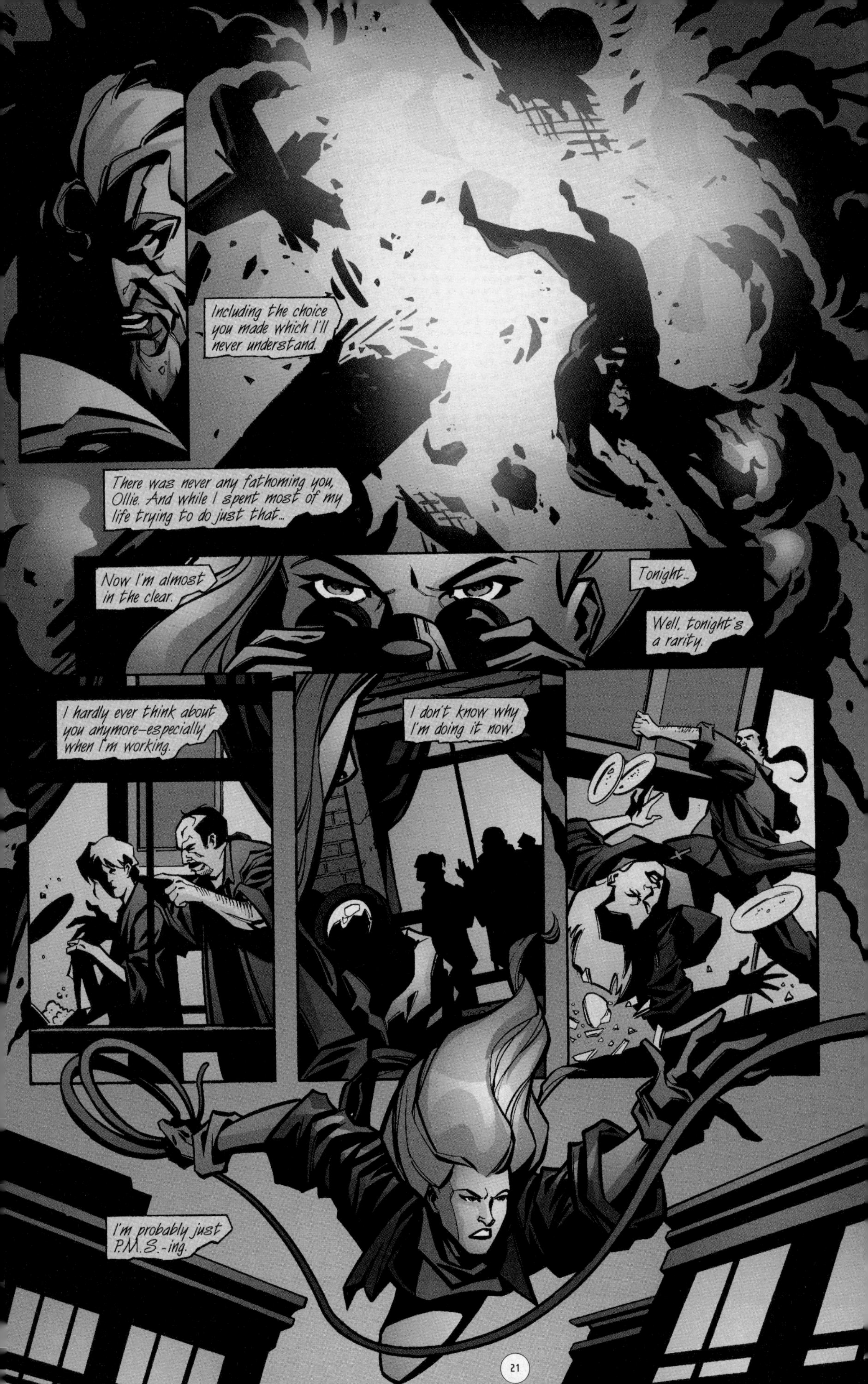
Including the choice you made which I'll never understand.
There was never any fathoming you, Ollie. And while I spent most of my life trying to do just that...
Now I'm almost in the clear.
Tonight...
Well, tonight's a rarity.
I hardly ever think about you anymore–especially when I'm working.
I don't know why I'm doing it now.
I'm probably just P.M.S.-ing.

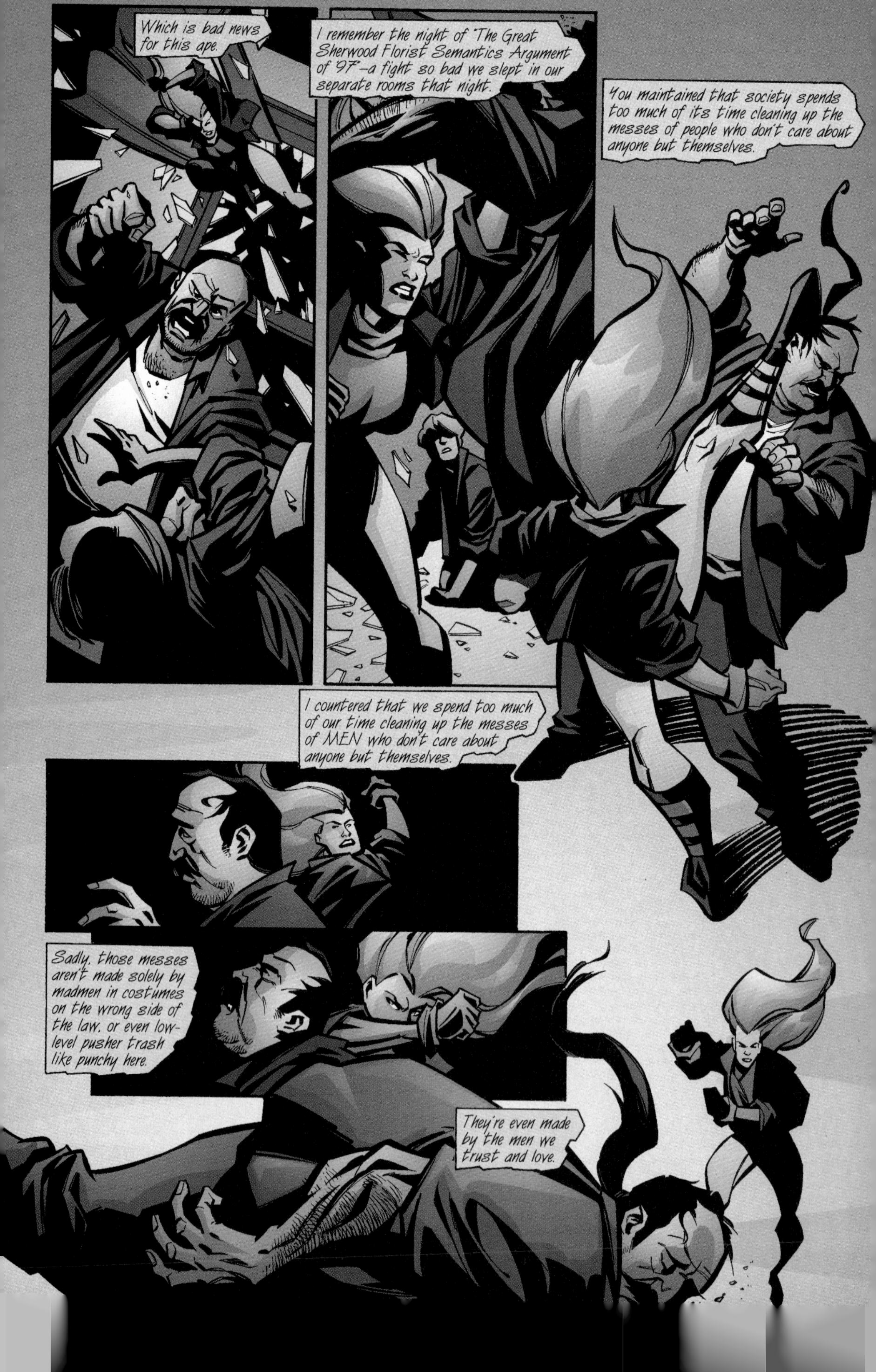
Which is bad news for this ape.
I remember the night of "The Great Sherwood Florist Semantics Argument of '97"—a fight so bad we slept in our separate rooms that night.
You maintained that society spends too much of its time cleaning up the messes of people who don't care about anyone but themselves.
I countered that we spend too much of our time cleaning up the messes of MEN who don't care about anyone but themselves.
Sadly, those messes aren't made solely by madmen in costumes on the wrong side of the law, or even low-level pusher trash like punchy here.
They're even made by the men we trust and love.

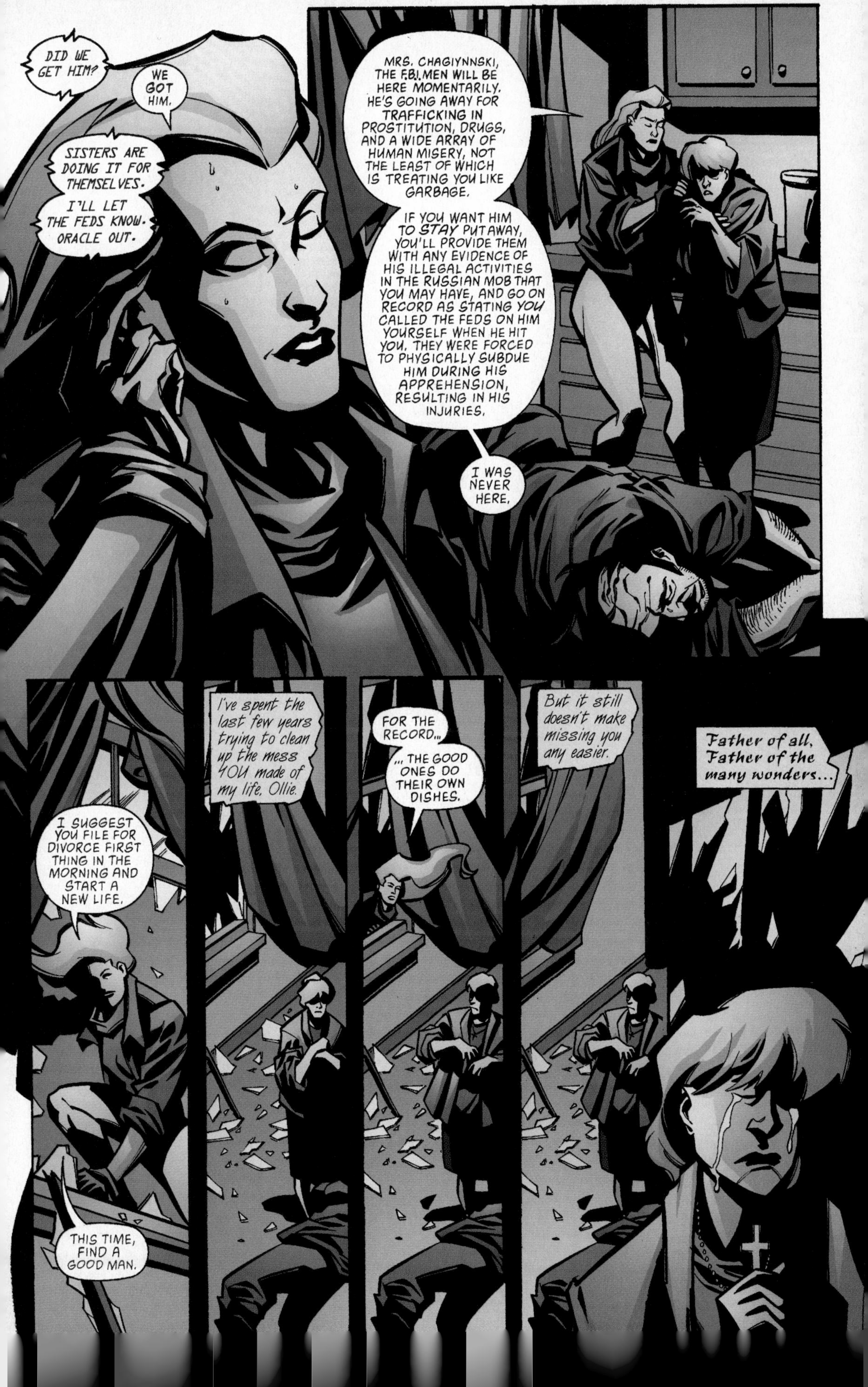
DID WE GET HIM?
WE GOT HIM.
SISTERS ARE DOING IT FOR THEMSELVES.
I'LL LET THE FEDS KNOW. ORACLE OUT.
MRS. CHAGIYNNSKI, THE F.B.I. MEN WILL BE HERE MOMENTARILY. HE'S GOING AWAY FOR TRAFFICKING IN PROSTITUTION, DRUGS, AND A WIDE ARRAY OF HUMAN MISERY, NOT THE LEAST OF WHICH IS TREATING YOU LIKE GARBAGE.
IF YOU WANT HIM TO STAY PUT AWAY, YOU'LL PROVIDE THEM WITH ANY EVIDENCE OF HIS ILLEGAL ACTIVITIES IN THE RUSSIAN MOB THAT YOU MAY HAVE, AND GO ON RECORD AS STATING YOU CALLED THE FEDS ON HIM YOURSELF WHEN HE HIT YOU. THEY WERE FORCED TO PHYSICALLY SUBDUE HIM DURING HIS APPREHENSION, RESULTING IN HIS INJURIES.
I WAS NEVER HERE.
I SUGGEST YOU FILE FOR DIVORCE FIRST THING IN THE MORNING AND START A NEW LIFE.
THIS TIME, FIND A GOOD MAN.
I've spent the last few years trying to clean up the mess YOU made of my life, Ollie.
FOR THE RECORD...
...THE GOOD ONES DO THEIR OWN DISHES.
But it still doesn't make missing you any easier.
Father of all, Father of the many wonders...

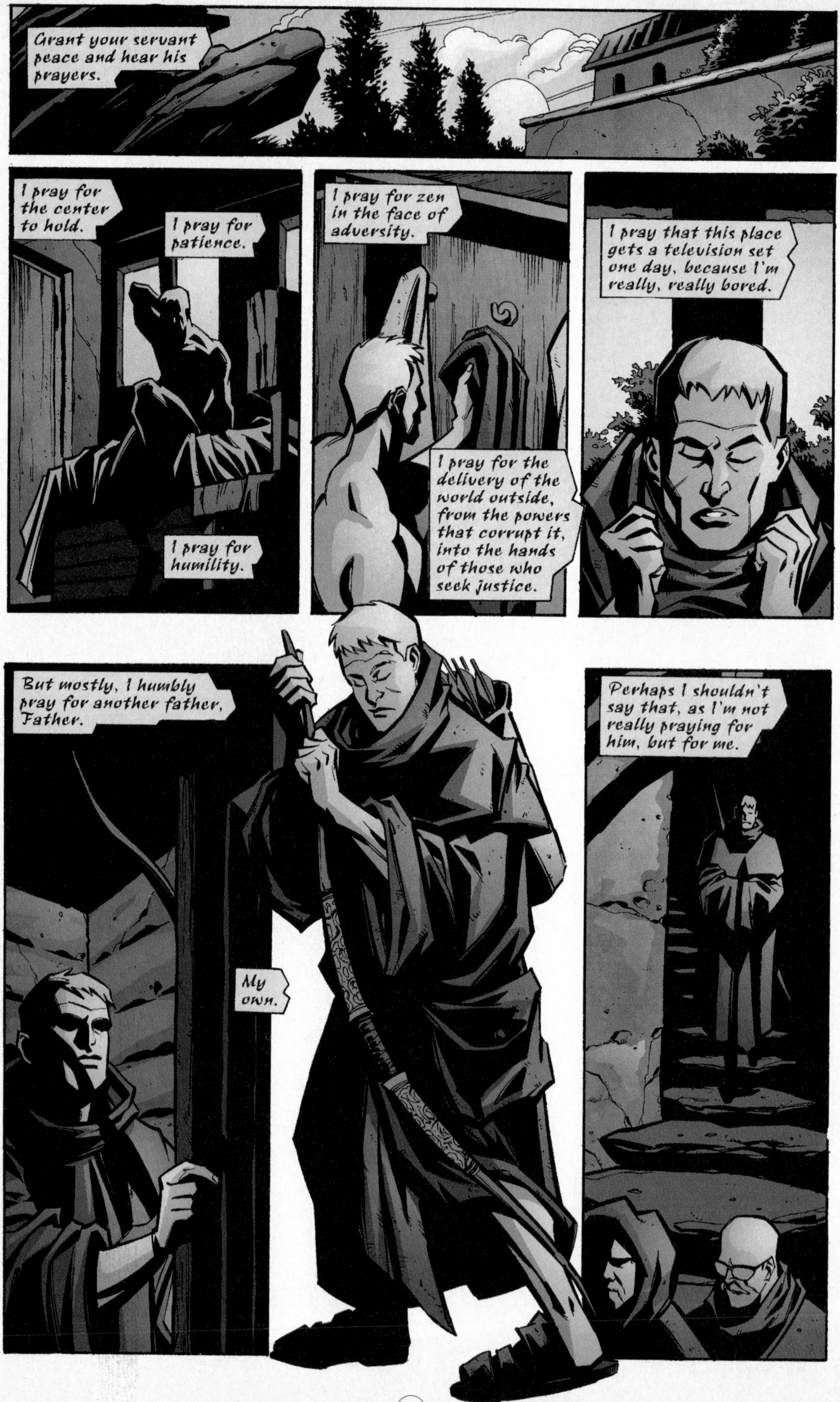
Grant your servant peace and hear his prayers.
I pray for the center to hold.
I pray for patience.
I pray for humility.
I pray for zen in the face of adversity.
I pray for the delivery of the world outside, from the powers that corrupt it, into the hands of those who seek justice.
I pray that this place gets a television set one day, because I'm really, really bored.
But mostly, I humbly pray for another father, Father.
My own.
Perhaps I shouldn't say that, as I'm not really praying for him, but for me.

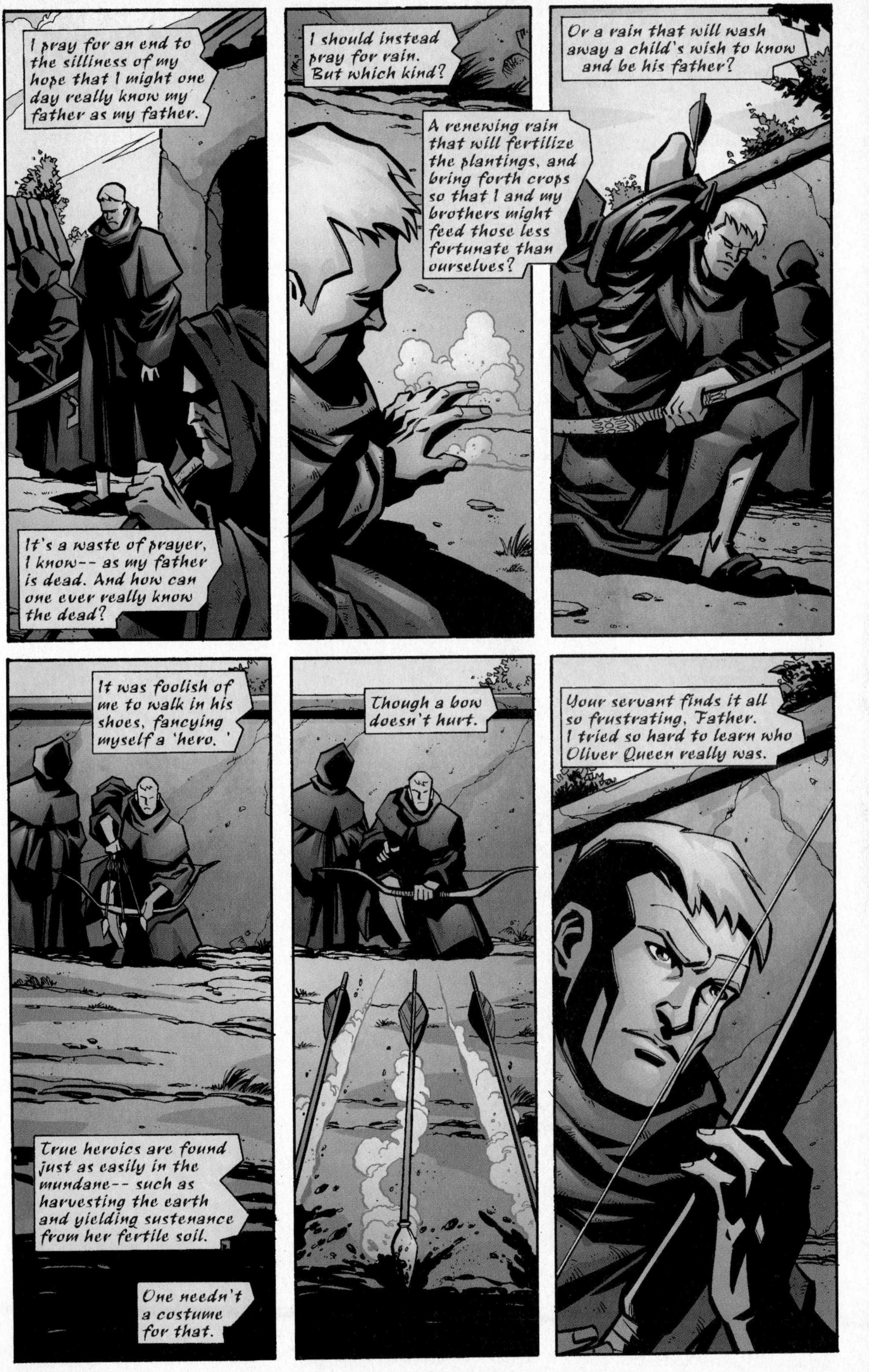
I pray for an end to the silliness of my hope that I might one day really know my father as my father.
It's a waste of prayer, I know-- as my father is dead. And how can one ever really know the dead?
I should instead pray for rain. But which kind?
A renewing rain that will fertilize the plantings, and bring forth crops so that I and my brothers might feed those less fortunate than ourselves?
Or a rain that will wash away a child's wish to know and be his father?
It was foolish of me to walk in his shoes, fancying myself a 'hero.'
True heroics are found just as easily in the mundane-- such as harvesting the earth and yielding sustenance from her fertile soil.
One needn't a costume for that.
Though a bow doesn't hurt.
Your servant finds it all so frustrating, Father. I tried so hard to learn who Oliver Queen really was.

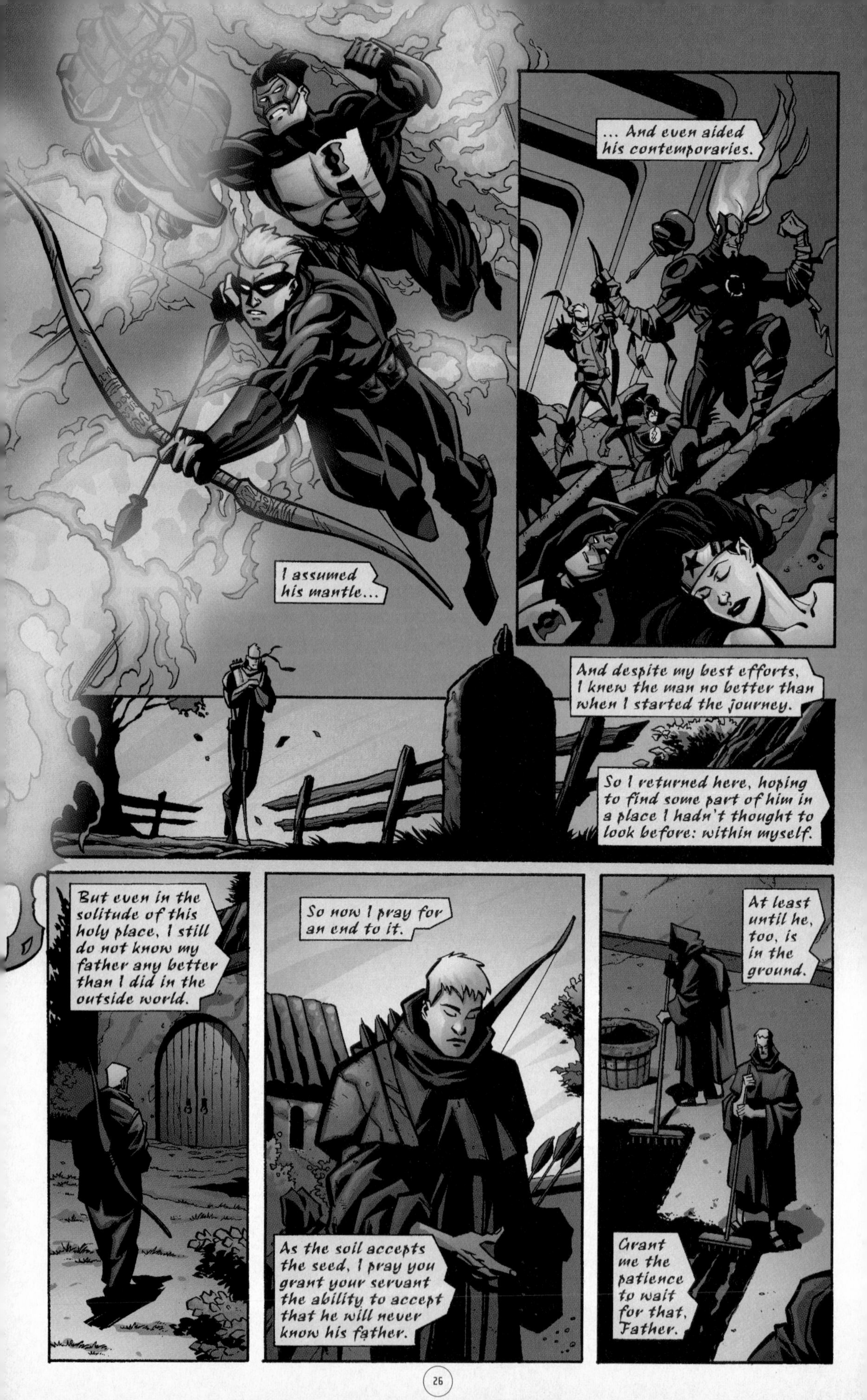
I assumed his mantle...
... And even aided his contemporaries.
And despite my best efforts, I knew the man no better than when I started the journey.
So I returned here, hoping to find some part of him in a place I hadn't thought to look before: within myself.
But even in the solitude of this holy place, I still do not know my father any better than I did in the outside world.
So now I pray for an end to it.
As the soil accepts the seed, I pray you grant your servant the ability to accept that he will never know his father.
At least until he, too, is in the ground.
Grant me the patience to wait for that, Father.

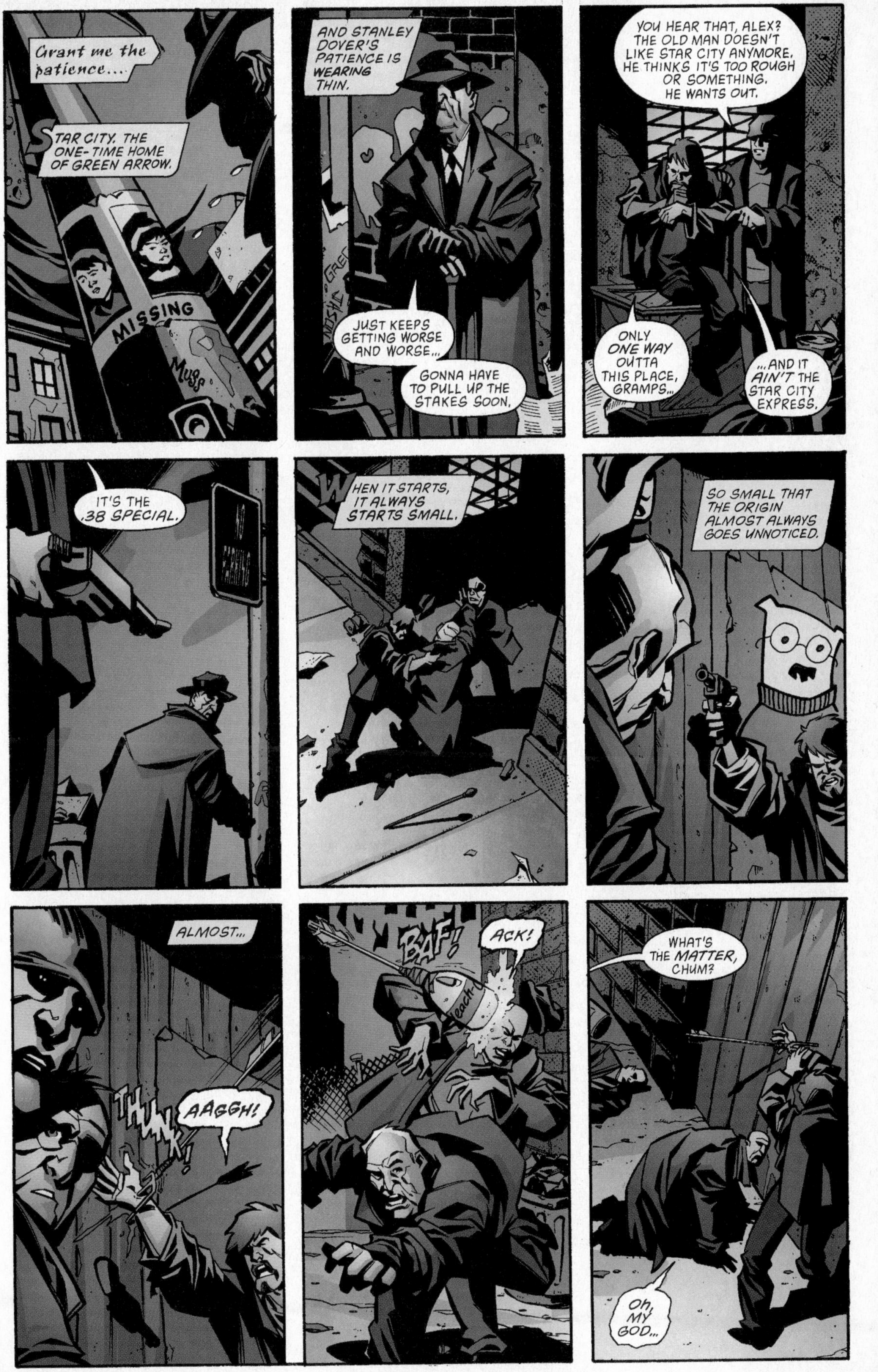
Grant me the patience....
STAR CITY. THE ONE-TIME HOME OF GREEN ARROW.
MISSING
AND STANLEY DOVER'S PATIENCE IS WEARING THIN.
JUST KEEPS GETTING WORSE AND WORSE...
GONNA HAVE TO PULL UP THE STAKES SOON.
YOU HEAR THAT, ALEX? THE OLD MAN DOESN'T LIKE STAR CITY ANYMORE. HE THINKS IT'S TOO ROUGH OR SOMETHING. HE WANTS OUT.
ONLY ONE WAY OUTTA THIS PLACE, GRAMPS...
...AND IT AIN'T THE STAR CITY EXPRESS.
IT'S THE .38 SPECIAL.
WHEN IT STARTS, IT ALWAYS STARTS SMALL.
SO SMALL THAT THE ORIGIN ALMOST ALWAYS GOES UNNOTICED.
ALMOST...
THUNK!
AAGGH!
BAF!
ACK!
WHAT'S THE MATTER, CHUM?
Oh, MY GOD...

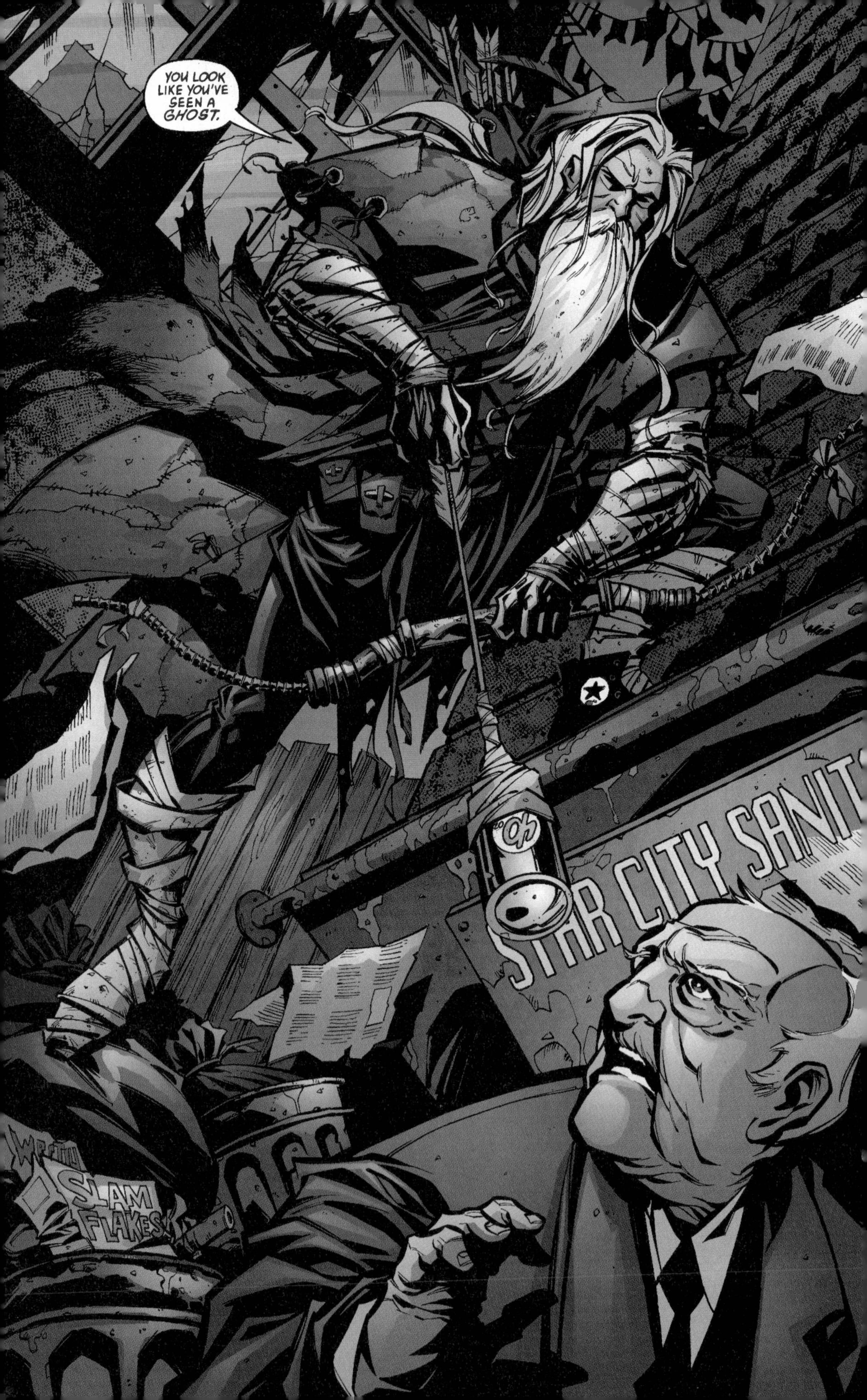
YOU LOOK LIKE YOU'VE SEEN A GHOST.
STAR CITY
SLAM FLAKES

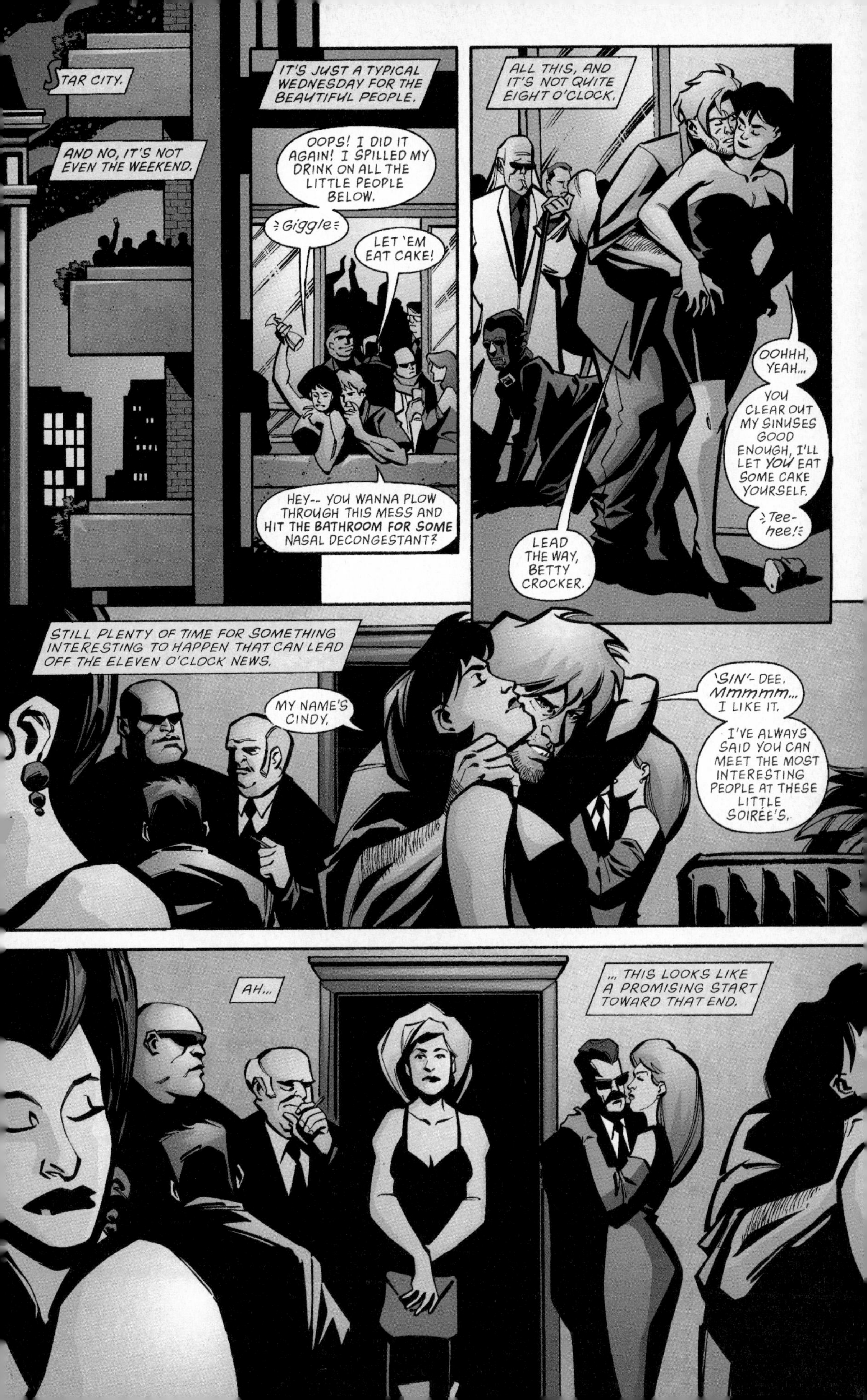
STAR CITY.
AND NO, IT'S NOT EVEN THE WEEKEND.
IT'S JUST A TYPICAL WEDNESDAY FOR THE BEAUTIFUL PEOPLE.
OOPS! I DID IT AGAIN! I SPILLED MY DRINK ON ALL THE LITTLE PEOPLE BELOW.
Giggle
LET 'EM EAT CAKE!
HEY-- YOU WANNA PLOW THROUGH THIS MESS AND HIT THE BATHROOM FOR SOME NASAL DECONGESTANT?
ALL THIS, AND IT'S NOT QUITE EIGHT O'CLOCK.
OOHHH, YEAH...
YOU CLEAR OUT MY SINUSES GOOD ENOUGH, I'LL LET YOU EAT SOME CAKE YOURSELF.
Tee-hee!
LEAD THE WAY, BETTY CROCKER.
STILL PLENTY OF TIME FOR SOMETHING INTERESTING TO HAPPEN THAT CAN LEAD OFF THE ELEVEN O'CLOCK NEWS.
MY NAME'S CINDY.
'SIN'-DEE. Mmmmmm... I LIKE IT.
I'VE ALWAYS SAID YOU CAN MEET THE MOST INTERESTING PEOPLE AT THESE LITTLE SOIRÉE'S.
AH...
...THIS LOOKS LIKE A PROMISING START TOWARD THAT END.

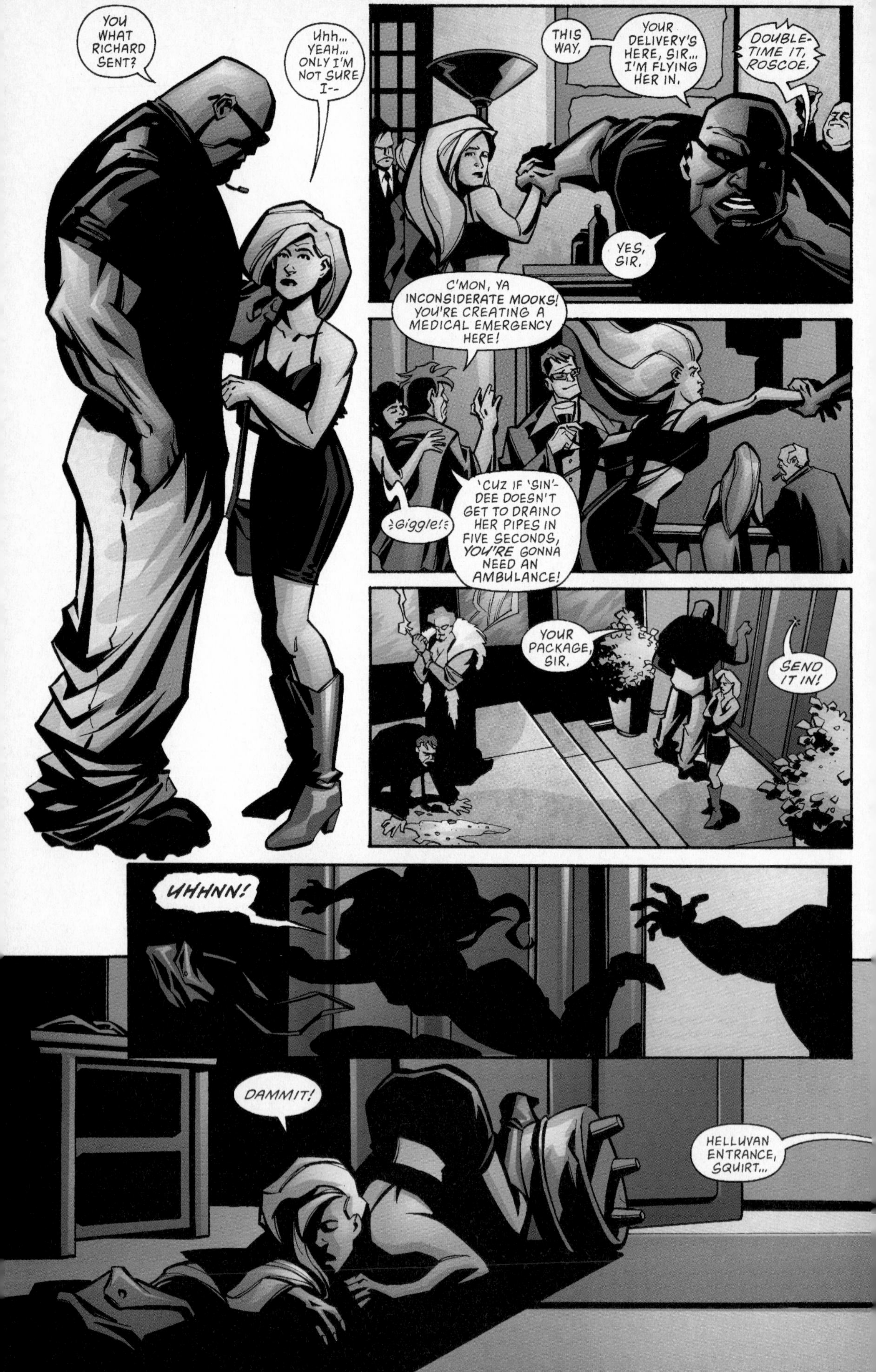
YOU WHAT RICHARD SENT?
Uhh... YEAH... ONLY I'M NOT SURE I--
THIS WAY.
YOUR DELIVERY'S HERE, SIR... I'M FLYING HER IN.
DOUBLE-TIME IT, ROSCOE.
YES, SIR.
C'MON, YA INCONSIDERATE MOOKS! YOU'RE CREATING A MEDICAL EMERGENCY HERE!
'CUZ IF 'SIN'-DEE DOESN'T GET TO DRAINO HER PIPES IN FIVE SECONDS, YOU'RE GONNA NEED AN AMBULANCE!
Giggle!
YOUR PACKAGE, SIR.
SEND IT IN!
UHHNN!
DAMMIT!
HELLUVAN ENTRANCE, SQUIRT...

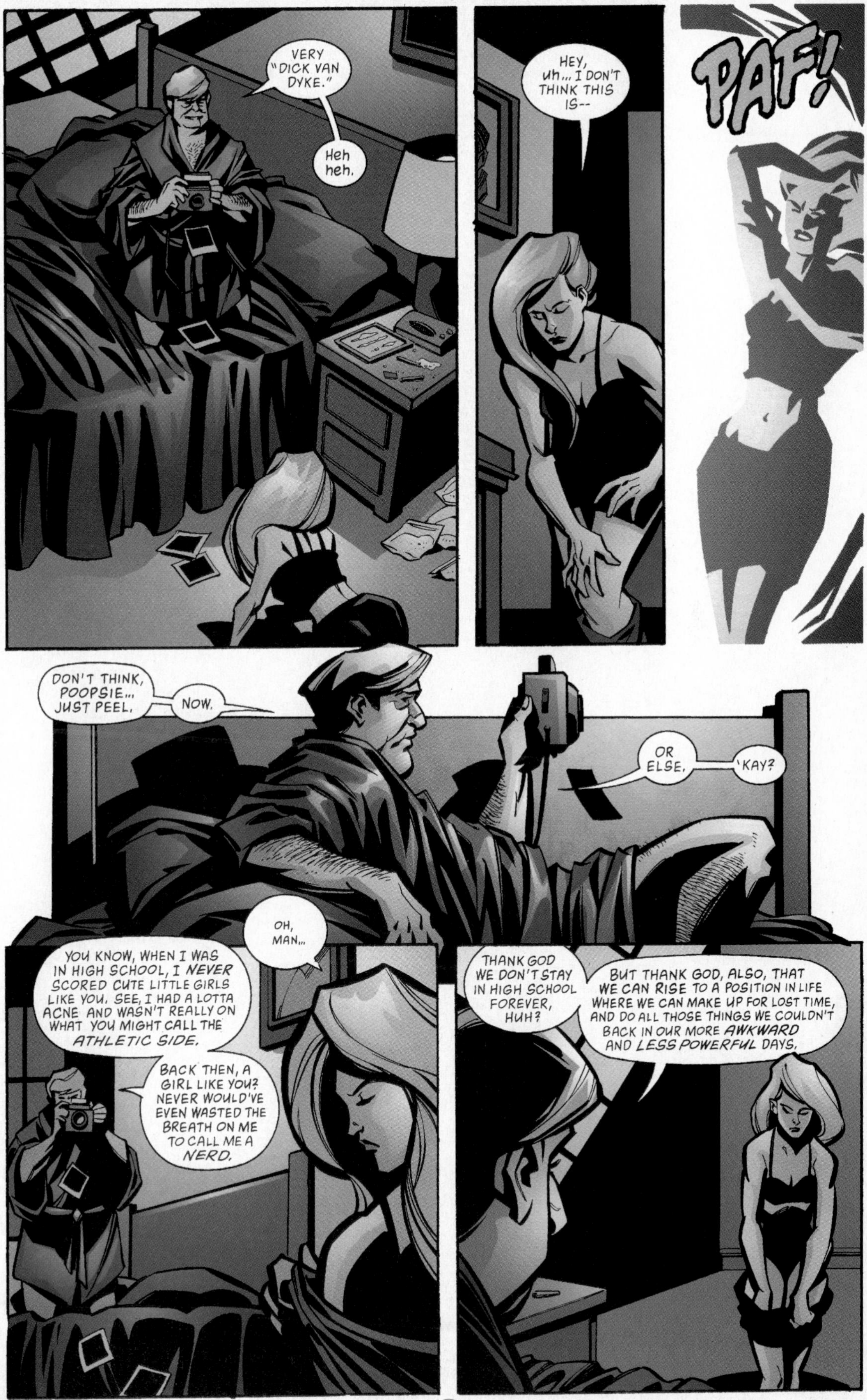
VERY "DICK VAN DYKE."
Heh heh.
HEY, uh... I DON'T THINK THIS IS--
PAF!
DON'T THINK, POOPSIE... JUST PEEL.
NOW.
OR ELSE.
'KAY?
OH, MAN...
YOU KNOW, WHEN I WAS IN HIGH SCHOOL, I NEVER SCORED CUTE LITTLE GIRLS LIKE YOU. SEE, I HAD A LOTTA ACNE AND WASN'T REALLY ON WHAT YOU MIGHT CALL THE ATHLETIC SIDE.
BACK THEN, A GIRL LIKE YOU? NEVER WOULD'VE EVEN WASTED THE BREATH ON ME TO CALL ME A NERD.
THANK GOD WE DON'T STAY IN HIGH SCHOOL FOREVER, HUH?
BUT THANK GOD, ALSO, THAT WE CAN RISE TO A POSITION IN LIFE WHERE WE CAN MAKE UP FOR LOST TIME, AND DO ALL THOSE THINGS WE COULDN'T BACK IN OUR MORE AWKWARD AND LESS POWERFUL DAYS.

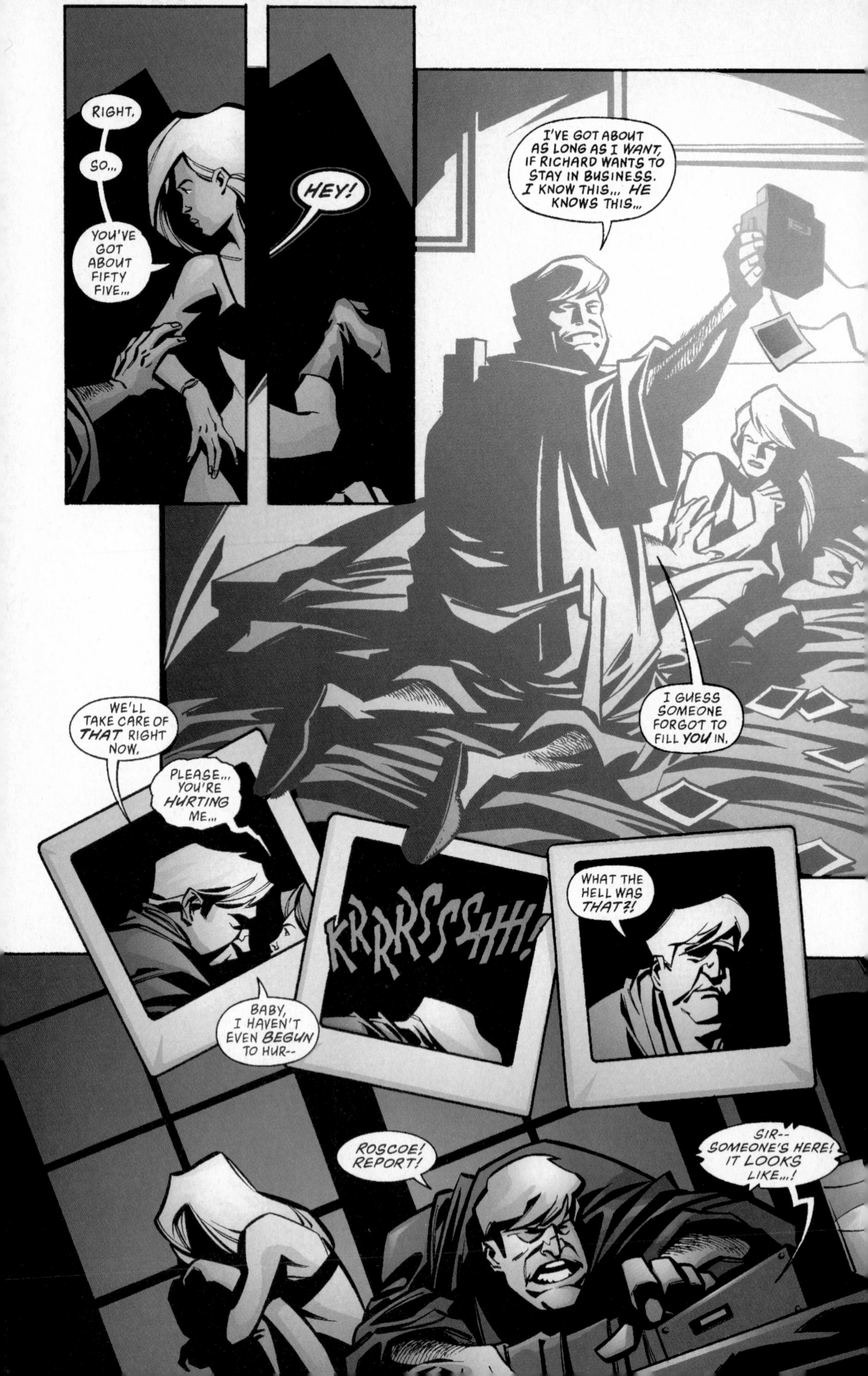
RIGHT.
SO...
YOU'VE GOT ABOUT FIFTY FIVE...
HEY!
I'VE GOT ABOUT AS LONG AS I WANT, IF RICHARD WANTS TO STAY IN BUSINESS. I KNOW THIS... HE KNOWS THIS...
I GUESS SOMEONE FORGOT TO FILL YOU IN.
WE'LL TAKE CARE OF THAT RIGHT NOW.
PLEASE... YOU'RE HURTING ME...
BABY, I HAVEN'T EVEN BEGUN TO HUR--
KRRRSSSHHH!
WHAT THE HELL WAS THAT?!
ROSCOE! REPORT!
SIR-- SOMEONE'S HERE! IT LOOKS LIKE...!

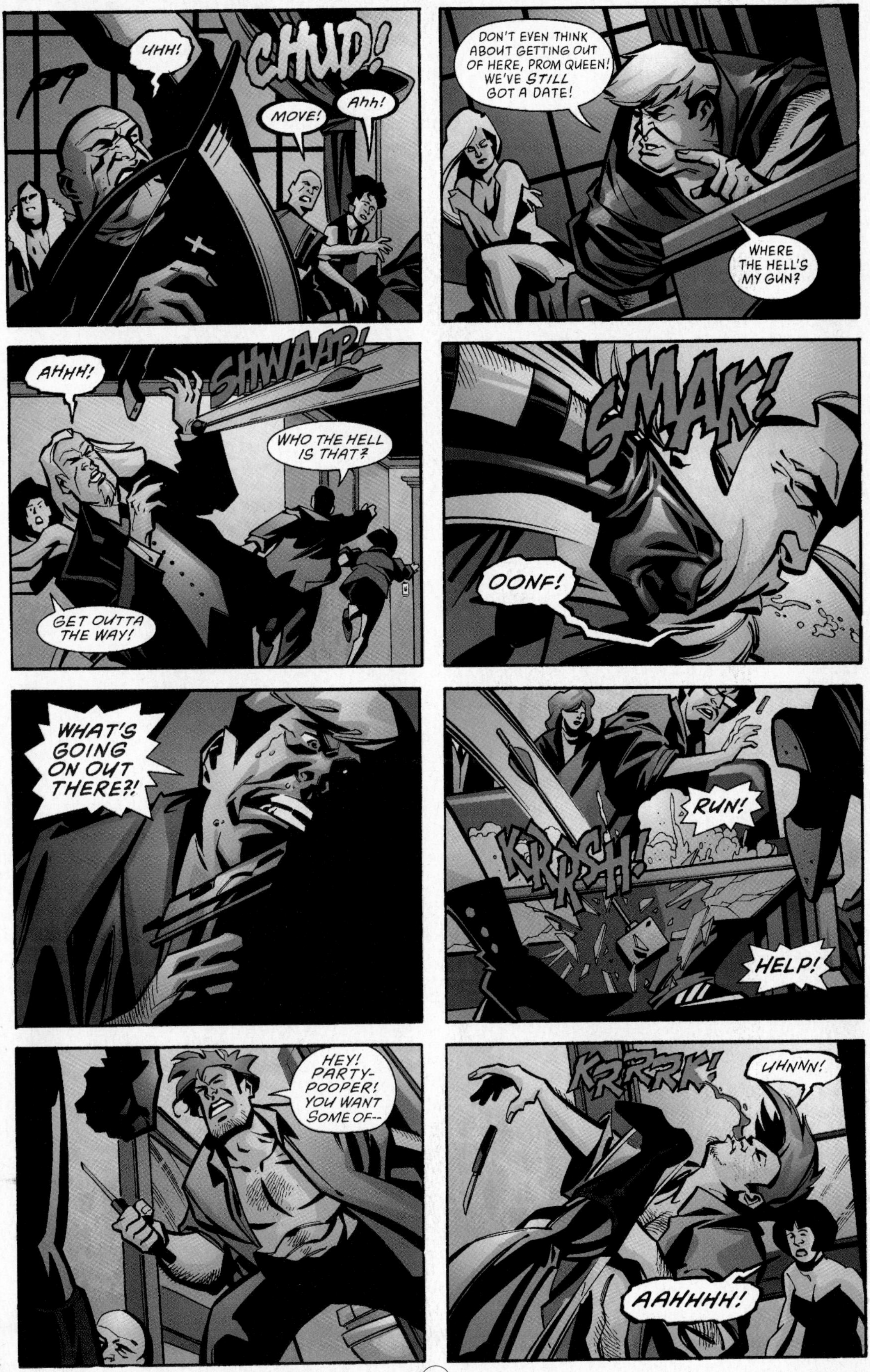
UHH!
CHUD!
MOVE!
Ahh!
DON'T EVEN THINK ABOUT GETTING OUT OF HERE, PROM QUEEN! WE'VE STILL GOT A DATE!
WHERE THE HELL'S MY GUN?
AHHH!
SHWAAP!
WHO THE HELL IS THAT?
GET OUTTA THE WAY!
SMAK!
OONF!
WHAT'S GOING ON OUT THERE?!
RUN!
KRRSH!
HELP!
HEY! PARTY-POOPER! YOU WANT SOME OF--
KRRRK!
UHNNN!
AAHHHH!

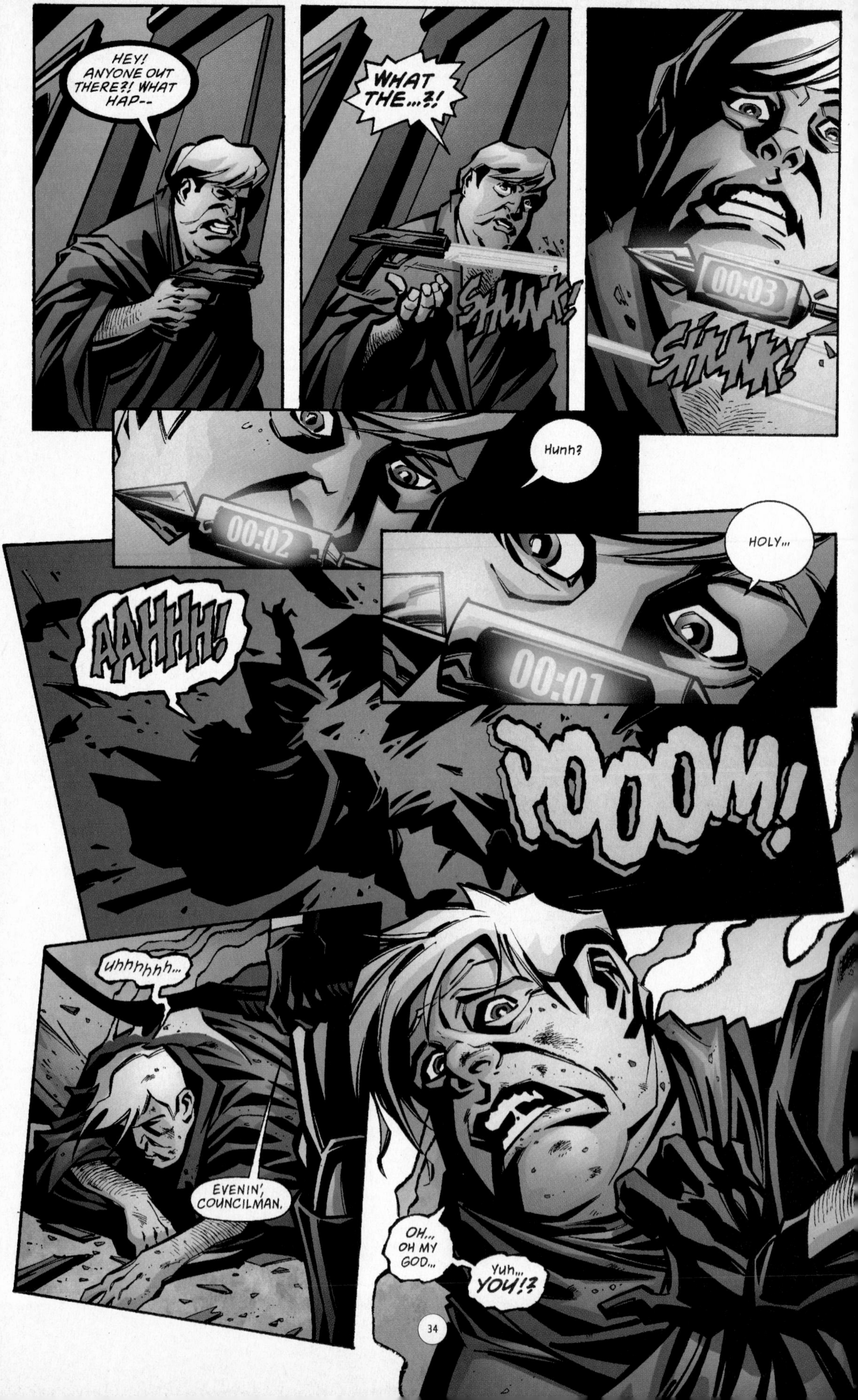

HEY! ANYONE OUT THERE?! WHAT HAP--
WHAT THE...?!
SHUNK!
00:03
SHUNK!
00:02
Hunh?
HOLY...
00:01
AAHHH!
POOOM!
uhhhhhh...
EVENIN', COUNCILMAN.
OH... OH MY GOD...
yuh... YOU!?

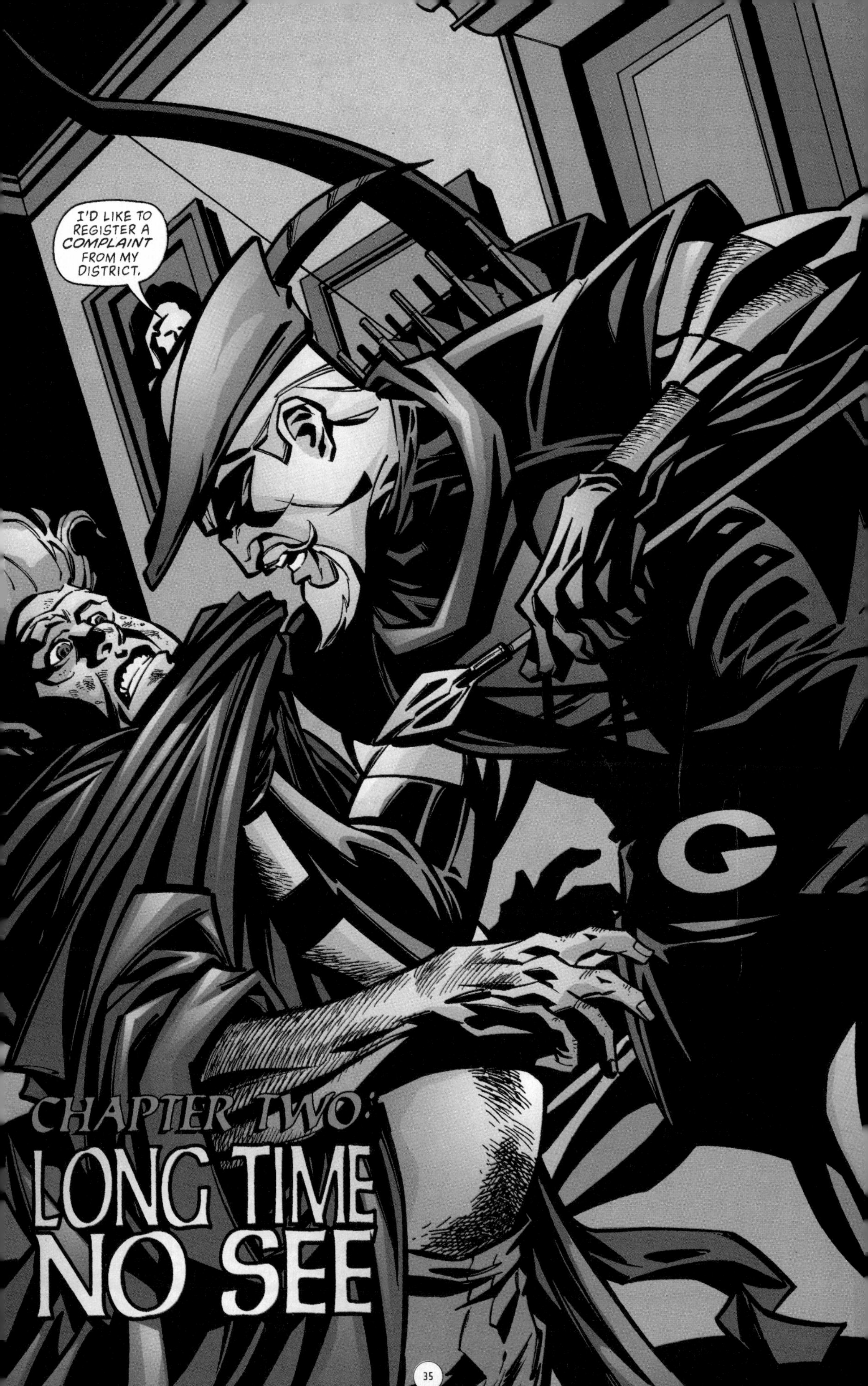
I'D LIKE TO REGISTER A COMPLAINT FROM MY DISTRICT.
CHAPTER TWO:
LONG TIME NO SEE

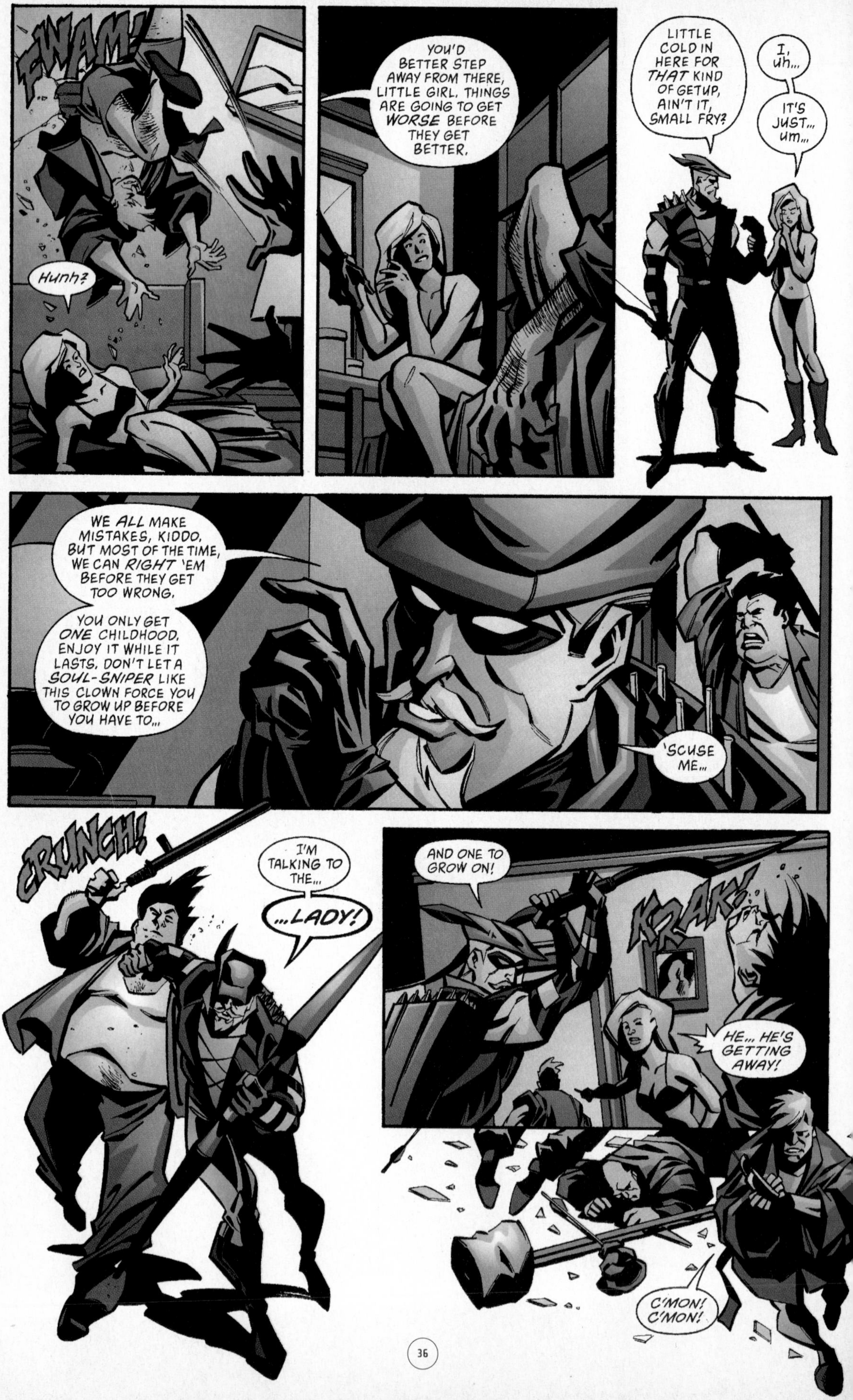
FWAM!
Hunh?
YOU'D BETTER STEP AWAY FROM THERE, LITTLE GIRL. THINGS ARE GOING TO GET WORSE BEFORE THEY GET BETTER.
LITTLE COLD IN HERE FOR THAT KIND OF GETUP, AIN'T IT, SMALL FRY?
I, uh...
IT'S JUST... um...
WE ALL MAKE MISTAKES, KIDDO, BUT MOST OF THE TIME, WE CAN RIGHT 'EM BEFORE THEY GET TOO WRONG.
YOU ONLY GET ONE CHILDHOOD. ENJOY IT WHILE IT LASTS. DON'T LET A SOUL-SNIPER LIKE THIS CLOWN FORCE YOU TO GROW UP BEFORE YOU HAVE TO...
'SCUSE ME...
CRUNCH!
I'M TALKING TO THE...
...LADY!
AND ONE TO GROW ON!
KRAK!
HE... HE'S GETTING AWAY!
C'MON! C'MON!

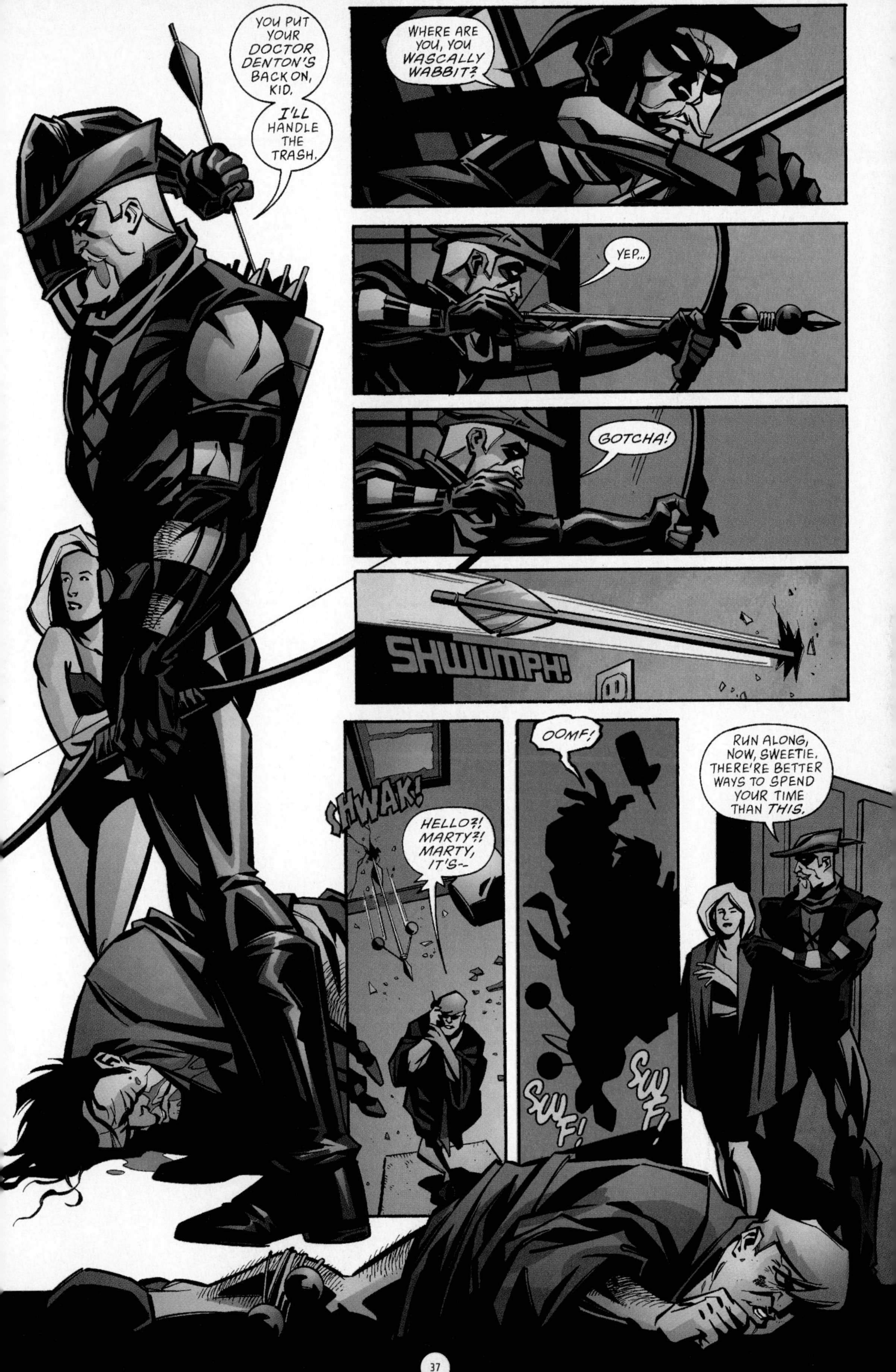

YOU PUT YOUR DOCTOR DENTON'S BACK ON, KID.
I'LL HANDLE THE TRASH.
WHERE ARE YOU, YOU WASCALLY WABBIT?
YEP...
GOTCHA!
SHWUMPH!
SHWAK!
HELLO?! MARTY?! MARTY, IT'S--
OOMF!
SWF!
SWF!
RUN ALONG, NOW, SWEETIE. THERE'RE BETTER WAYS TO SPEND YOUR TIME THAN THIS.

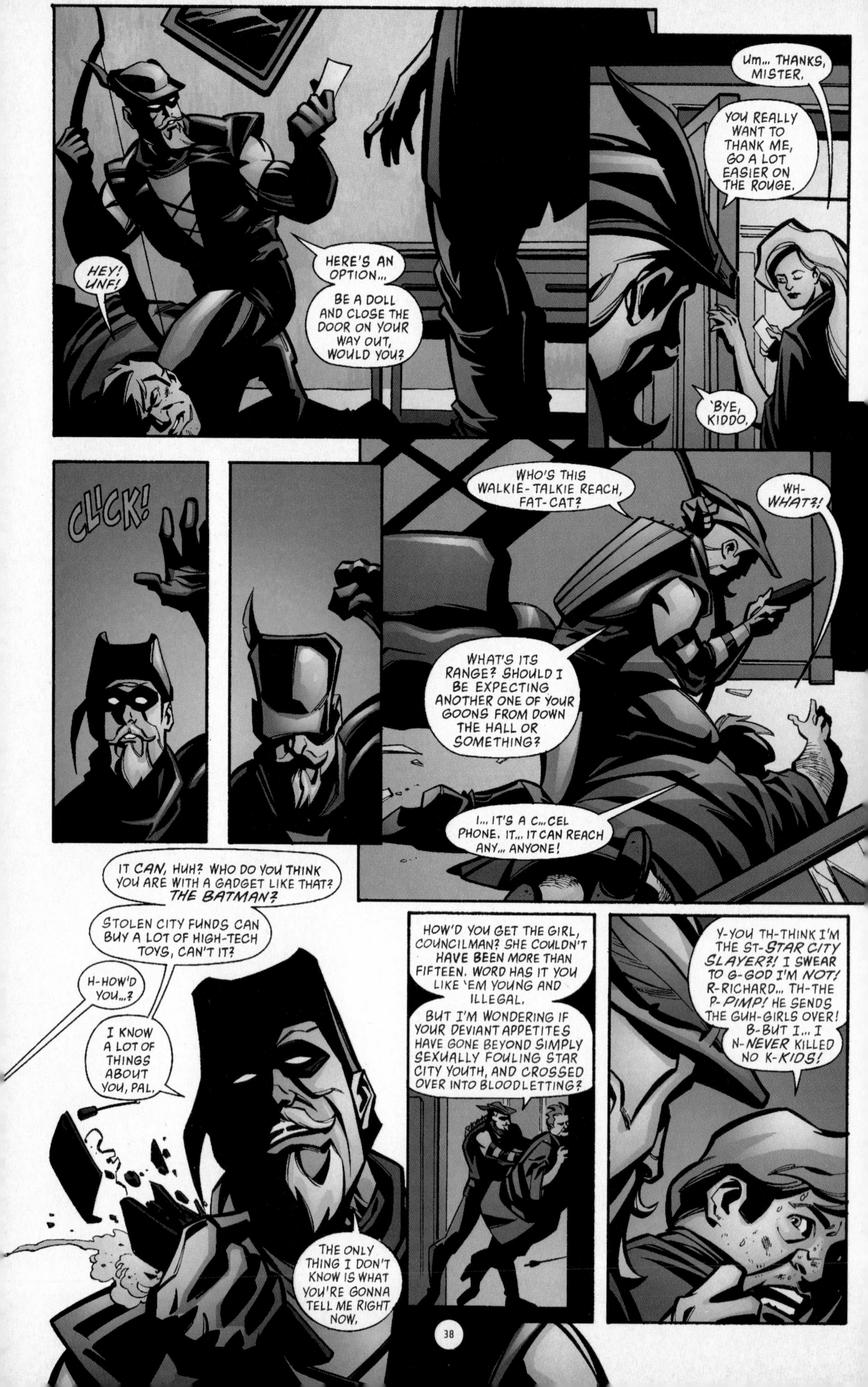

HEY! UNF!
HERE'S AN OPTION...
BE A DOLL AND CLOSE THE DOOR ON YOUR WAY OUT, WOULD YOU?
Um... THANKS, MISTER.
YOU REALLY WANT TO THANK ME, GO A LOT EASIER ON THE ROUGE.
'BYE, KIDDO.
CLICK!
WHO'S THIS WALKIE-TALKIE REACH, FAT-CAT?
WH- WHAT?!
WHAT'S ITS RANGE? SHOULD I BE EXPECTING ANOTHER ONE OF YOUR GOONS FROM DOWN THE HALL OR SOMETHING?
I... IT'S A C...CEL PHONE. IT... IT CAN REACH ANY... ANYONE!
IT CAN, HUH? WHO DO YOU THINK YOU ARE WITH A GADGET LIKE THAT? THE BATMAN?
STOLEN CITY FUNDS CAN BUY A LOT OF HIGH-TECH TOYS, CAN'T IT?
H-HOW'D YOU...?
I KNOW A LOT OF THINGS ABOUT YOU, PAL.
THE ONLY THING I DON'T KNOW IS WHAT YOU'RE GONNA TELL ME RIGHT NOW.
HOW'D YOU GET THE GIRL, COUNCILMAN? SHE COULDN'T HAVE BEEN MORE THAN FIFTEEN. WORD HAS IT YOU LIKE 'EM YOUNG AND ILLEGAL.
BUT I'M WONDERING IF YOUR DEVIANT APPETITES HAVE GONE BEYOND SIMPLY SEXUALLY FOULING STAR CITY YOUTH, AND CROSSED OVER INTO BLOODLETTING?
Y-YOU TH-THINK I'M THE ST-STAR CITY SLAYER?! I SWEAR TO G-GOD I'M NOT! R-RICHARD... TH-THE P-PIMP! HE SENDS THE GUH-GIRLS OVER! B-BUT I... I N-NEVER KILLED NO K-KIDS!

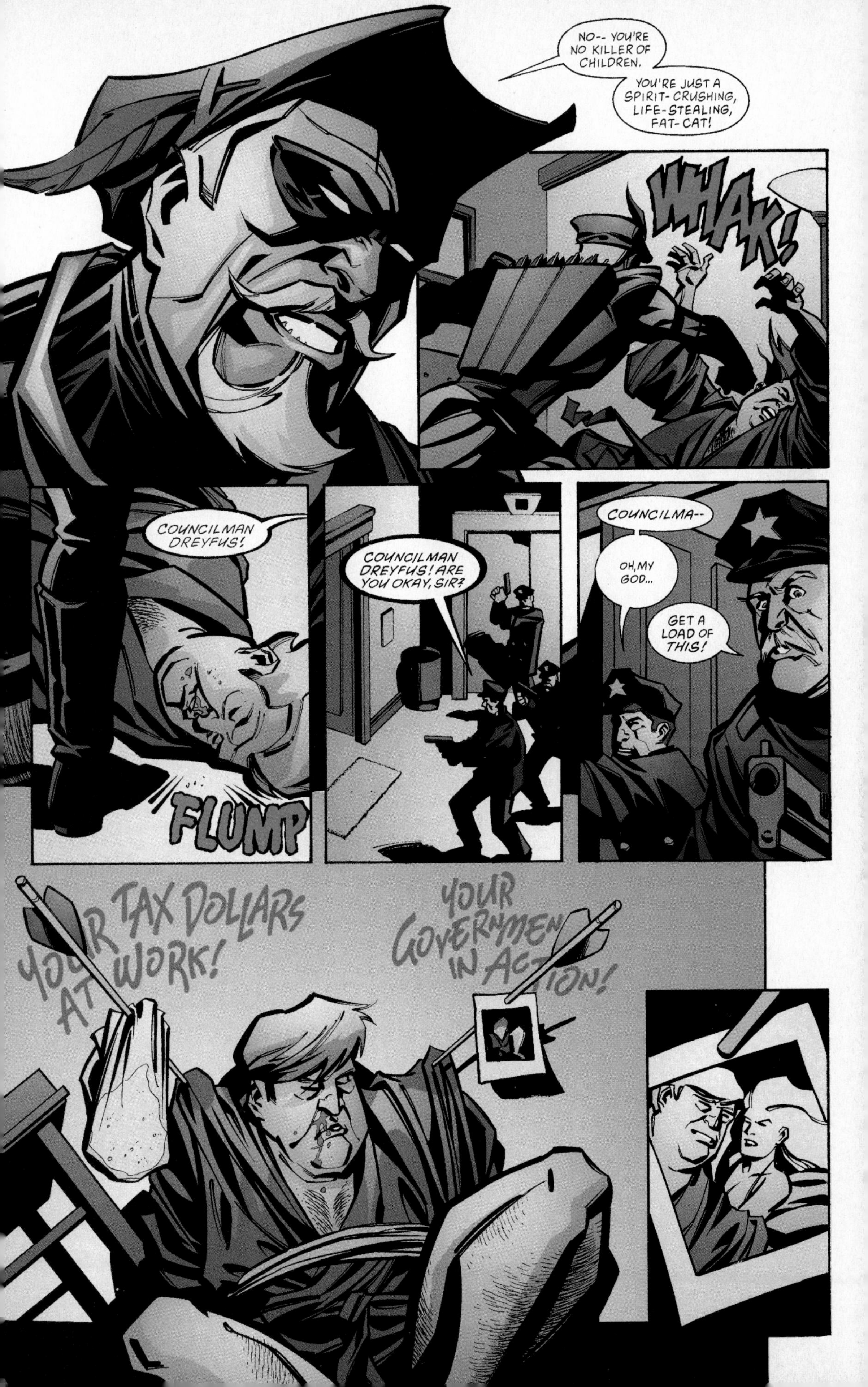

NO-- YOU'RE NO KILLER OF CHILDREN.
YOU'RE JUST A SPIRIT-CRUSHING, LIFE-STEALING, FAT-CAT!
WHAK!
COUNCILMAN DREYFUS!
FLUMP
COUNCILMAN DREYFUS! ARE YOU OKAY, SIR?
COUNCILMA--
OH, MY GOD...
GET A LOAD OF THIS!
YOUR TAX DOLLARS AT WORK!
YOUR GOVERNMENT IN ACTION!

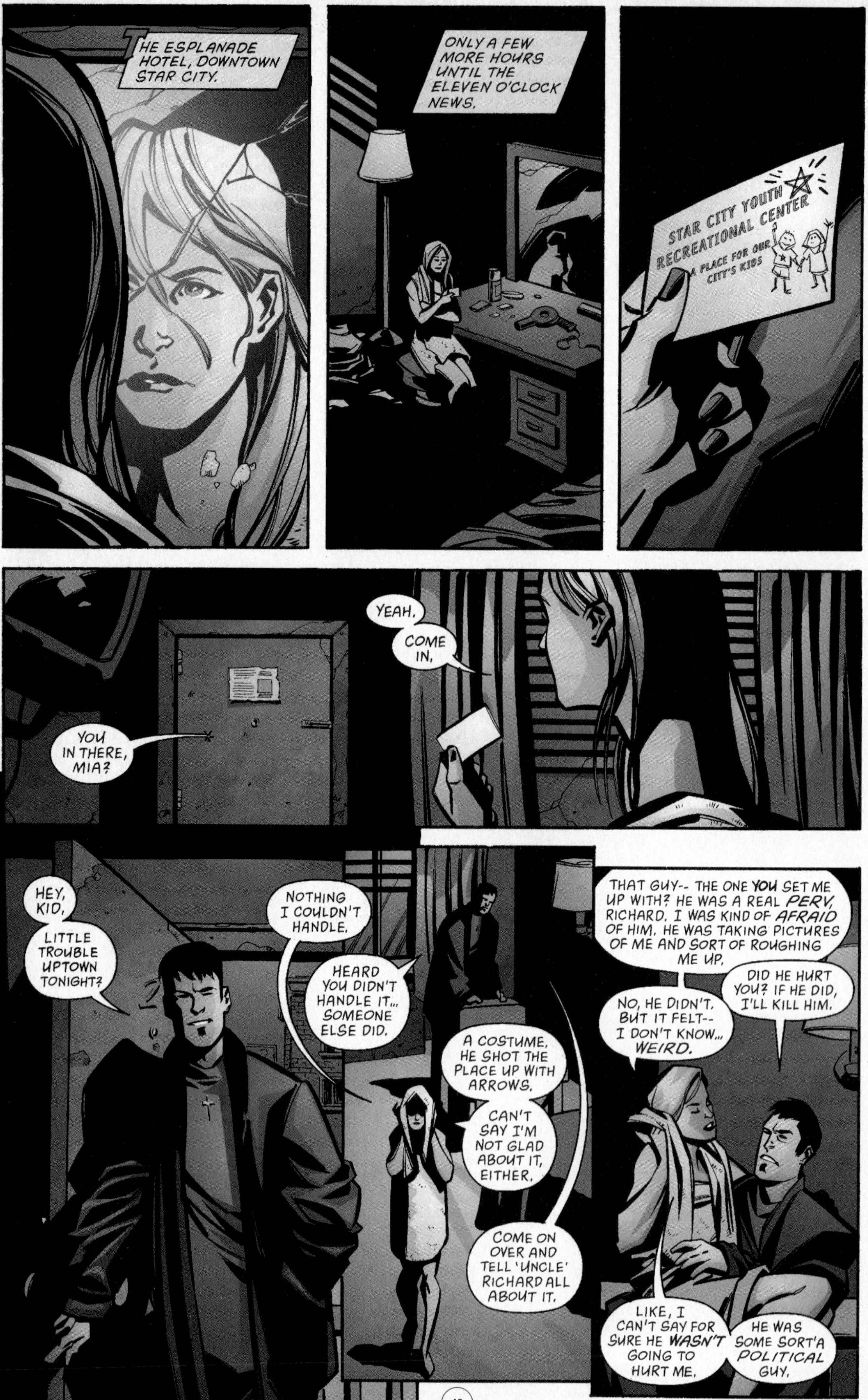
THE ESPLANADE HOTEL, DOWNTOWN STAR CITY.
ONLY A FEW MORE HOURS UNTIL THE ELEVEN O'CLOCK NEWS.
STAR CITY YOUTH RECREATIONAL CENTER
A PLACE FOR OUR CITY'S KIDS
YOU IN THERE, MIA?
YEAH,
COME IN.
HEY, KID,
LITTLE TROUBLE UPTOWN TONIGHT?
NOTHING I COULDN'T HANDLE.
HEARD YOU DIDN'T HANDLE IT... SOMEONE ELSE DID.
A COSTUME. HE SHOT THE PLACE UP WITH ARROWS.
CAN'T SAY I'M NOT GLAD ABOUT IT, EITHER.
COME ON OVER AND TELL 'UNCLE' RICHARD ALL ABOUT IT.
THAT GUY-- THE ONE YOU SET ME UP WITH? HE WAS A REAL PERV, RICHARD. I WAS KIND OF AFRAID OF HIM. HE WAS TAKING PICTURES OF ME AND SORT OF ROUGHING ME UP.
DID HE HURT YOU? IF HE DID, I'LL KILL HIM.
NO, HE DIDN'T. BUT IT FELT-- I DON'T KNOW... WEIRD.
LIKE, I CAN'T SAY FOR SURE HE WASN'T GOING TO HURT ME.
HE WAS SOME SORT'A POLITICAL GUY.

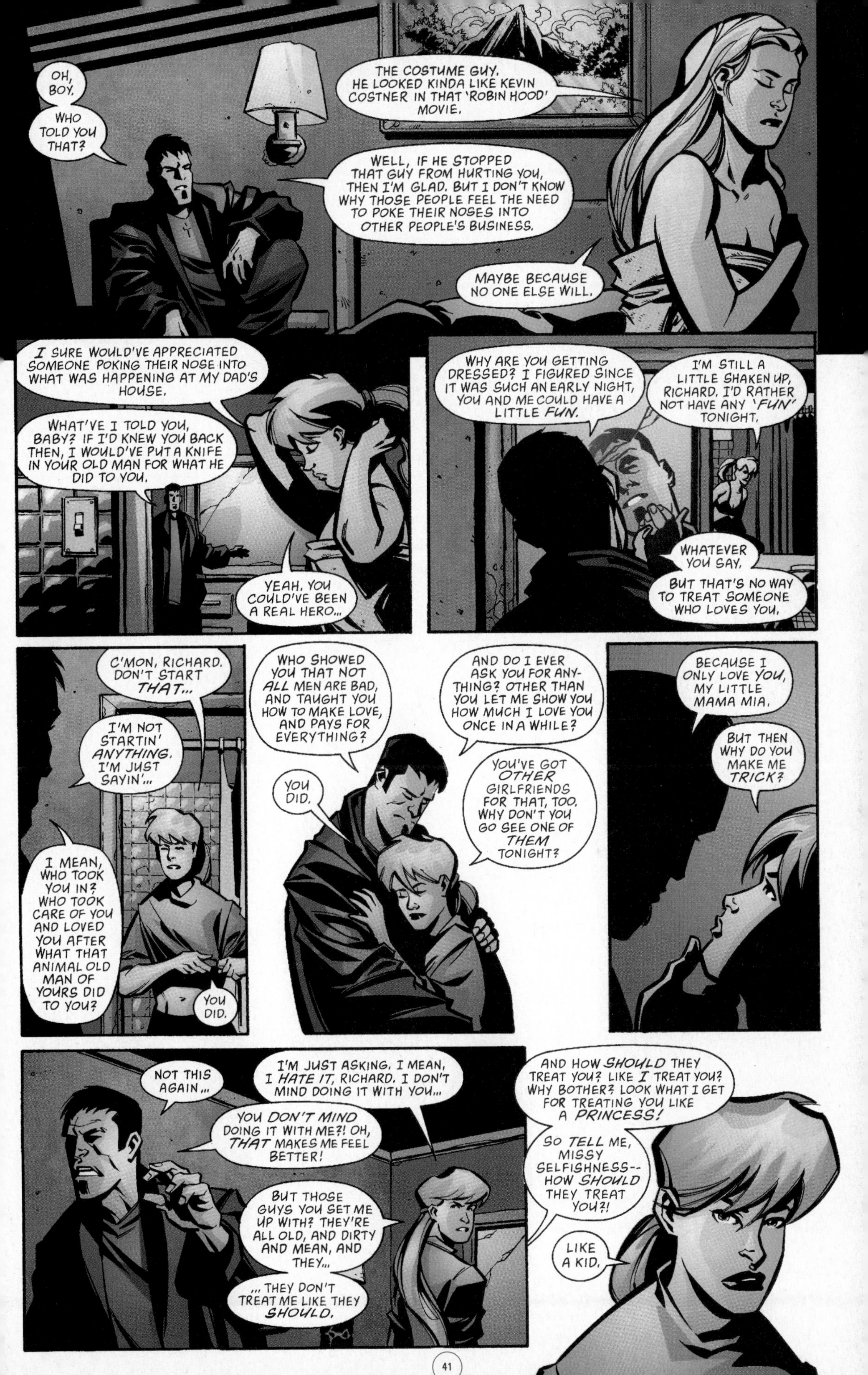
OH, BOY.
WHO TOLD YOU THAT?
THE COSTUME GUY. HE LOOKED KINDA LIKE KEVIN COSTNER IN THAT 'ROBIN HOOD' MOVIE.
WELL, IF HE STOPPED THAT GUY FROM HURTING YOU, THEN I'M GLAD. BUT I DON'T KNOW WHY THOSE PEOPLE FEEL THE NEED TO POKE THEIR NOSES INTO OTHER PEOPLE'S BUSINESS.
MAYBE BECAUSE NO ONE ELSE WILL.
I SURE WOULD'VE APPRECIATED SOMEONE POKING THEIR NOSE INTO WHAT WAS HAPPENING AT MY DAD'S HOUSE.
WHAT'VE I TOLD YOU, BABY? IF I'D KNEW YOU BACK THEN, I WOULD'VE PUT A KNIFE IN YOUR OLD MAN FOR WHAT HE DID TO YOU.
YEAH. YOU COULD'VE BEEN A REAL HERO...
WHY ARE YOU GETTING DRESSED? I FIGURED SINCE IT WAS SUCH AN EARLY NIGHT, YOU AND ME COULD HAVE A LITTLE FUN.
I'M STILL A LITTLE SHAKEN UP, RICHARD. I'D RATHER NOT HAVE ANY 'FUN' TONIGHT.
WHATEVER YOU SAY.
BUT THAT'S NO WAY TO TREAT SOMEONE WHO LOVES YOU.
C'MON, RICHARD. DON'T START THAT...
I'M NOT STARTIN' ANYTHING. I'M JUST SAYIN'...
I MEAN, WHO TOOK YOU IN? WHO TOOK CARE OF YOU AND LOVED YOU AFTER WHAT THAT ANIMAL OLD MAN OF YOURS DID TO YOU?
YOU DID.
WHO SHOWED YOU THAT NOT ALL MEN ARE BAD, AND TAUGHT YOU HOW TO MAKE LOVE, AND PAYS FOR EVERYTHING?
YOU DID.
AND DO I EVER ASK YOU FOR ANYTHING? OTHER THAN YOU LET ME SHOW YOU HOW MUCH I LOVE YOU ONCE IN A WHILE?
YOU'VE GOT OTHER GIRLFRIENDS FOR THAT, TOO. WHY DON'T YOU GO SEE ONE OF THEM TONIGHT?
BECAUSE I ONLY LOVE YOU, MY LITTLE MAMA MIA.
BUT THEN WHY DO YOU MAKE ME TRICK?
NOT THIS AGAIN...
I'M JUST ASKING. I MEAN, I HATE IT, RICHARD. I DON'T MIND DOING IT WITH YOU...
YOU DON'T MIND DOING IT WITH ME?! OH, THAT MAKES ME FEEL BETTER!
BUT THOSE GUYS YOU SET ME UP WITH? THEY'RE ALL OLD, AND DIRTY AND MEAN, AND THEY...
...THEY DON'T TREAT ME LIKE THEY SHOULD.
AND HOW SHOULD THEY TREAT YOU? LIKE I TREAT YOU? WHY BOTHER? LOOK WHAT I GET FOR TREATING YOU LIKE A PRINCESS!
SO TELL ME, MISSY SELFISHNESS-- HOW SHOULD THEY TREAT YOU?!
LIKE A KID.

HAHA HAHA HAHA!

WHY'S THAT SO FUNNY?

BECAUSE YOU'RE *NOT* A KID, BABY DOLL! YOU'RE A *WOMAN!* A HOT-BLOODED, FULL-BODIED WOMAN WHO DOES THINGS THAT WOMEN *DO* IN BED!

BUT I DON'T WANT TO. I NEVER WANTED TO.

MEN FORCE THAT ON ME,

SO NOW I *FORCE* MYSELF ON YOU, IS THAT IT?

I DIDN'T MEAN IT LIKE THAT,,,

NOW I'M NO BETTER THAN YOUR OLD MAN, IS THAT IT?

I'M SORRY, RICHARD. DON'T--

THIS IS THE *THANKS* I GET, RIGHT?! I TREAT YOU LIKE A DAMN QUEEN AND FEED YOU AND CLOTHE YOU AND GIVE YOU A PLACE TO LIVE, AND I'M NO BETTER THAN YOUR RAPIST FATHER, IS THAT IT?!

RICHARD! PLEASE--!

I WAS TRYING TO DO THIS *NICE*, MIA! I WANTED TO CUDDLE YOU BEFORE I HAD TO DO WHAT I GOTTA DO-- BECAUSE I *LOVE* YOU!

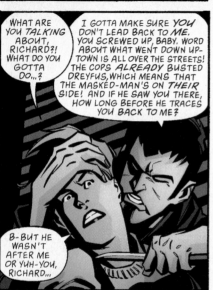

WHAT ARE YOU *TALKING* ABOUT, RICHARD?! WHAT DO YOU GOTTA DO,,,?

I GOTTA MAKE SURE *YOU* DON'T LEAD BACK TO *ME.* YOU SCREWED UP, BABY. WORD ABOUT WHAT WENT DOWN UPTOWN IS ALL OVER THE STREETS! THE COPS *ALREADY* BUSTED DREYFUS, WHICH MEANS THAT THE MASKED-MAN'S ON *THEIR* SIDE! AND IF HE SAW YOU THERE, HOW LONG BEFORE HE TRACES YOU BACK TO ME?

B-BUT HE WASN'T AFTER ME OR YUH-YOU, RICHARD,,,

I'M SORRY, MAMA MIA, BUT I CAN'T TAKE THAT *CHANCE.* I CAN'T DO NO TIME FOR NO LITTLE *GIRL'S* STUPID MISTAKE.

NO!

NOW THIS...

...THIS COULD LEAD OFF THE ELEVEN O'CLOCK NEWS...

...BUT MIA DEARDEN HAS JUST REALIZED THAT SHE HAS NO DESIRE TO BE ON TV.

OW!

OOF!

HURK!

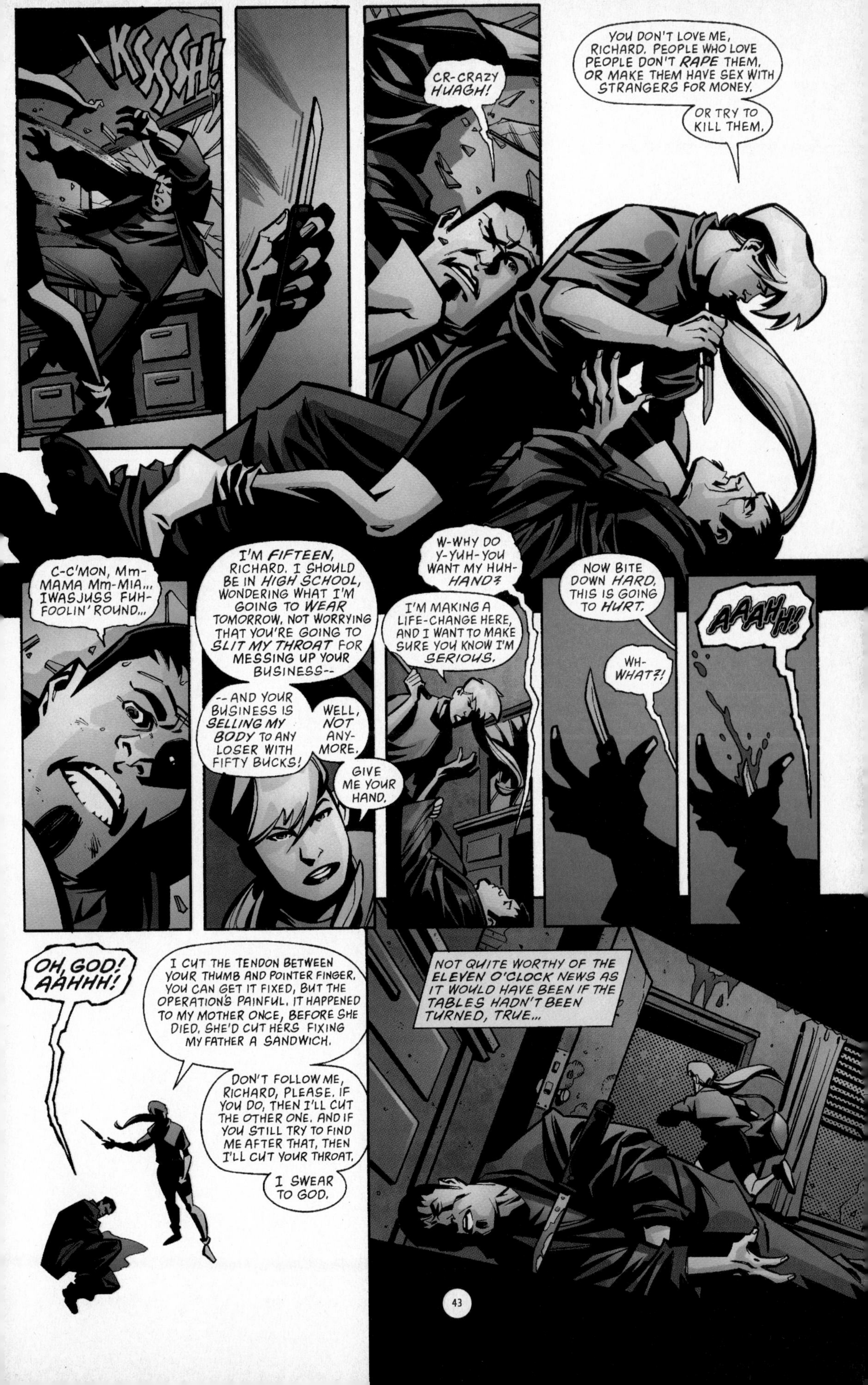
KSSSH!
CR-CRAZY HUAGH!
YOU DON'T LOVE ME, RICHARD. PEOPLE WHO LOVE PEOPLE DON'T RAPE THEM, OR MAKE THEM HAVE SEX WITH STRANGERS FOR MONEY.
OR TRY TO KILL THEM.
C-C'MON, Mm-MAMA Mm-MIA... IWASJUSS FUH-FOOLIN' ROUND...
I'M FIFTEEN, RICHARD. I SHOULD BE IN HIGH SCHOOL, WONDERING WHAT I'M GOING TO WEAR TOMORROW, NOT WORRYING THAT YOU'RE GOING TO SLIT MY THROAT FOR MESSING UP YOUR BUSINESS--
--AND YOUR BUSINESS IS SELLING MY BODY TO ANY LOSER WITH FIFTY BUCKS!
WELL, NOT ANY-MORE.
GIVE ME YOUR HAND.
W-WHY DO Y-YUH-YOU WANT MY HUH-HAND?
I'M MAKING A LIFE-CHANGE HERE, AND I WANT TO MAKE SURE YOU KNOW I'M SERIOUS.
NOW BITE DOWN HARD. THIS IS GOING TO HURT.
WH-WHAT?!
AAAHH!
OH, GOD! AAHHH!
I CUT THE TENDON BETWEEN YOUR THUMB AND POINTER FINGER. YOU CAN GET IT FIXED, BUT THE OPERATION'S PAINFUL. IT HAPPENED TO MY MOTHER ONCE, BEFORE SHE DIED. SHE'D CUT HERS FIXING MY FATHER A SANDWICH.
DON'T FOLLOW ME, RICHARD, PLEASE. IF YOU DO, THEN I'LL CUT THE OTHER ONE. AND IF YOU STILL TRY TO FIND ME AFTER THAT, THEN I'LL CUT YOUR THROAT.
I SWEAR TO GOD.
NOT QUITE WORTHY OF THE ELEVEN O'CLOCK NEWS AS IT WOULD HAVE BEEN IF THE TABLES HADN'T BEEN TURNED, TRUE...

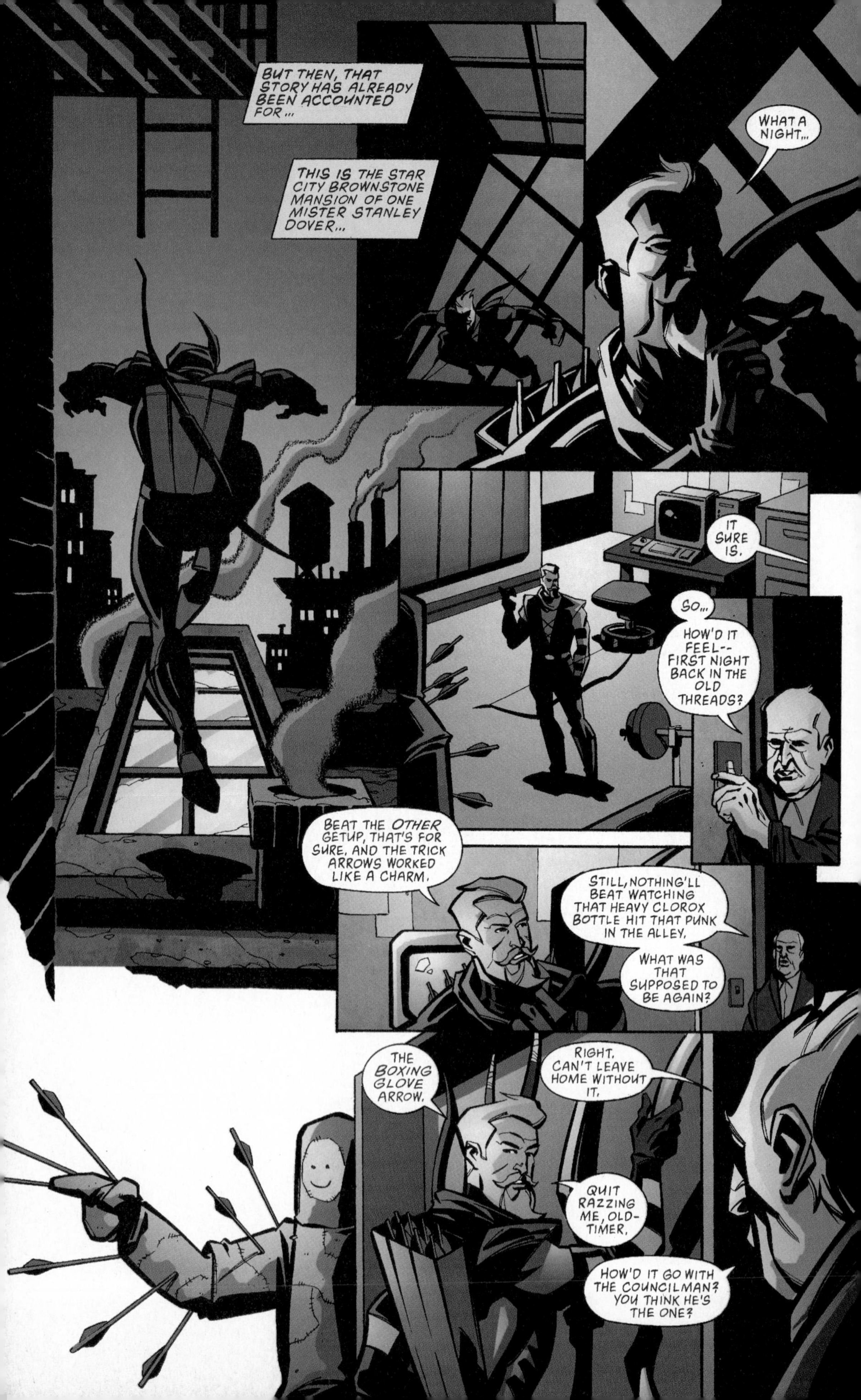
BUT THEN, THAT STORY HAS ALREADY BEEN ACCOUNTED FOR...
THIS IS THE STAR CITY BROWNSTONE MANSION OF ONE MISTER STANLEY DOVER...
WHAT A NIGHT...
IT SURE IS.
SO... HOW'D IT FEEL-- FIRST NIGHT BACK IN THE OLD THREADS?
BEAT THE OTHER GETUP, THAT'S FOR SURE, AND THE TRICK ARROWS WORKED LIKE A CHARM.
STILL, NOTHING'LL BEAT WATCHING THAT HEAVY CLOROX BOTTLE HIT THAT PUNK IN THE ALLEY.
WHAT WAS THAT SUPPOSED TO BE AGAIN?
THE BOXING GLOVE ARROW.
RIGHT, CAN'T LEAVE HOME WITHOUT IT.
QUIT RAZZING ME, OLD-TIMER.
HOW'D IT GO WITH THE COUNCILMAN? YOU THINK HE'S THE ONE?

HE'S A SCUM-LORD OF THE HIGHEST ORDER, BUT HE'S NOT THE STAR CITY SLAYER. REGARDLESS, I LEFT HIM GIFT-WRAPPED FOR THE BLUE FASCISTS TO DEAL WITH.

LIKE FINDS, I GUESS.

THIS INTELLIGENCE CAME IN WHILE YOU WERE OUT. THERE'S RUMOR OF A CHILD SLAVERY RING THAT'S BEING RUN OUT OF STAR CITY.

COULD HAVE SOMETHING TO DO WITH THE SLAYER, NO?

AS GOOD A PLACE TO CHECK AS ANY. THAT'S ON TOMORROW'S MENU.

THANK GOD *YOU* KNOW HOW TO HANDLE THAT GLORIFIED TOASTER, IT'S BEYOND *ME*. THEY USED TO HAVE STUFF LIKE THAT ON THE SATELLITE, BUT I STAYED AS FAR AWAY FROM IT AS I COULD.

THERE'S NOTHING WRONG WITH A LITTLE TECHNOLOGY, OLIVER. PROGRESS IS THE WAY OF THE WORLD.

NOT *MINE*, THANKS. GIVE ME A BOW AND ARROW AND A GOOD RIGHT HOOK, AND I CAN GATHER ALL THE INTELLIGENCE A SCARED SECOND-STORY MAN CAN BLAB BEFORE PASSING OUT AND WETTING HIMSELF.

I TAKE IT YOU USED A LOT OF THE NEW ARSENAL TO EMPTY BLADDERS *TONIGHT*.

I SEE THE *BOLO-ARROW'S* ALREADY GONE. THE *TIME-BOMB* ARROW, TOO.

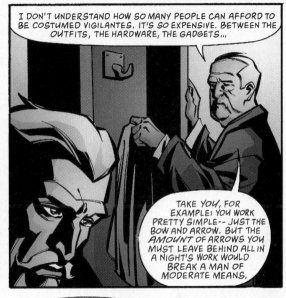

I DON'T UNDERSTAND HOW SO MANY PEOPLE CAN AFFORD TO BE COSTUMED VIGILANTES. IT'S SO EXPENSIVE. BETWEEN THE OUTFITS, THE HARDWARE, THE GADGETS...

TAKE *YOU*, FOR EXAMPLE: YOU WORK PRETTY SIMPLE-- JUST THE BOW AND ARROW. BUT THE *AMOUNT* OF ARROWS YOU MUST LEAVE BEHIND ALL IN A NIGHT'S WORK WOULD BREAK A MAN OF MODERATE MEANS.

I HAVE *YOU* TO THANK FOR THAT, STANLEY. AND I DO THANK YOU-- FROM THE BOTTOM OF MY HEART. YOU PUTTING ME UP, LAYING OUT THE JACK FOR ALL THE EQUIPMENT AND THE SUITS, LETTING ME OPERATE OUT OF THIS ROOM...

WELL, DON'T EVER THINK A DAY GOES BY THAT I DON'T APPRECIATE YOU HELPING ME GET BACK ON MY FEET.

WHAT'D I TELL YOU? YOU DON'T OWE ME NOTHING. YOU SAVED MY LIFE, OLIVER, AND IN THAT MOMENT, I REALIZED THAT A FORTUNE SITTING IN THE BANK COLLECTING INTEREST COULD BE PUT TO BETTER USE EQUIPPING AND AIDING THE ONLY *HERO* THIS CITY EVER HAD.

AND AS IF THAT'S NOT ENOUGH, HELPING YOU GIVES AN OLD, RICH MAN'S LIFE SOME NOBLE PURPOSE HE MIGHT'VE DIED WITHOUT KNOWING.

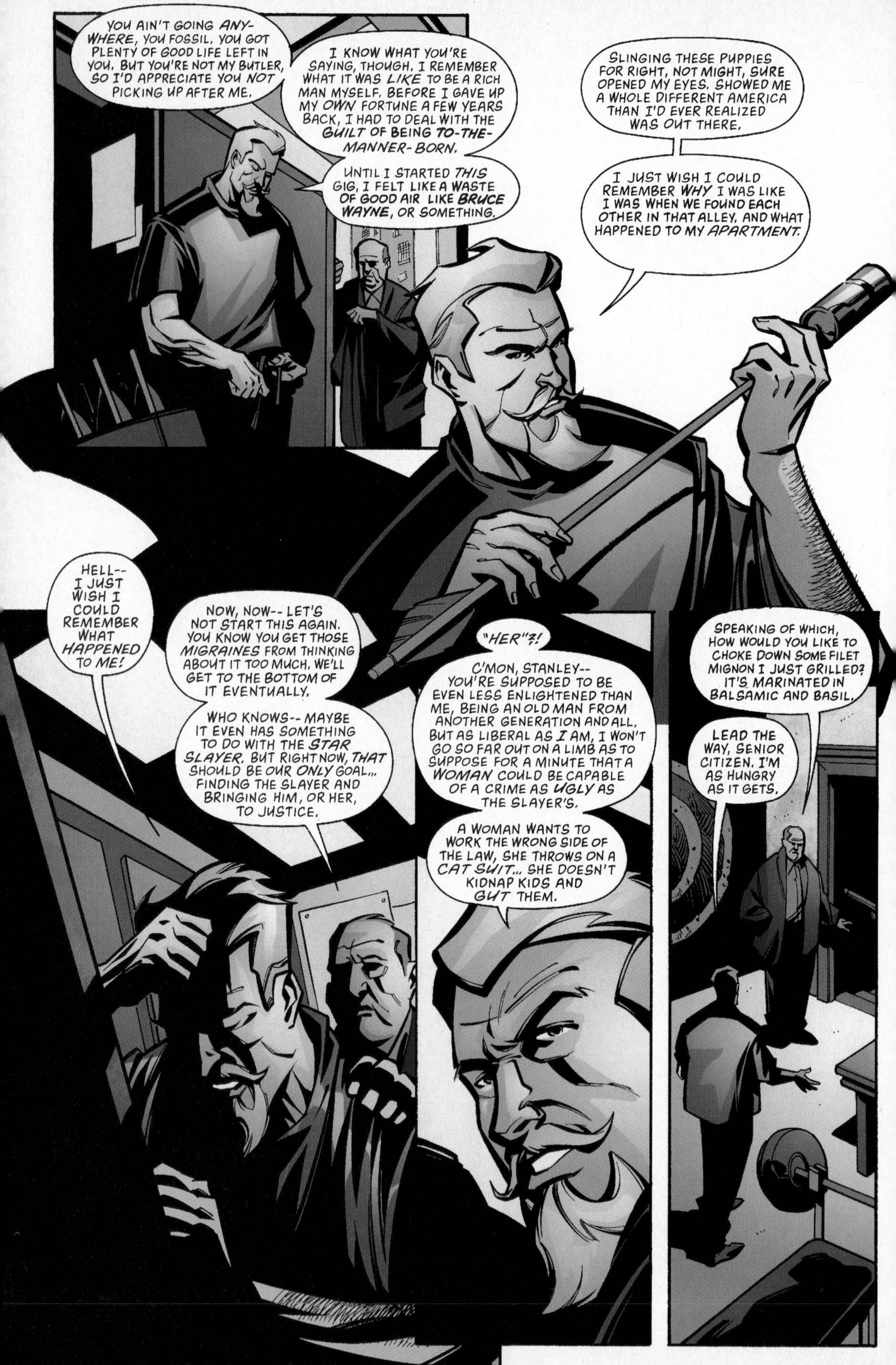

YOU AIN'T GOING ANY-WHERE, YOU FOSSIL. YOU GOT PLENTY OF GOOD LIFE LEFT IN YOU. BUT YOU'RE NOT MY BUTLER, SO I'D APPRECIATE YOU NOT PICKING UP AFTER ME.
I KNOW WHAT YOU'RE SAYING, THOUGH. I REMEMBER WHAT IT WAS LIKE TO BE A RICH MAN MYSELF. BEFORE I GAVE UP MY OWN FORTUNE A FEW YEARS BACK, I HAD TO DEAL WITH THE GUILT OF BEING TO-THE-MANNER-BORN.
UNTIL I STARTED THIS GIG, I FELT LIKE A WASTE OF GOOD AIR LIKE BRUCE WAYNE, OR SOMETHING.
SLINGING THESE PUPPIES FOR RIGHT, NOT MIGHT, SURE OPENED MY EYES. SHOWED ME A WHOLE DIFFERENT AMERICA THAN I'D EVER REALIZED WAS OUT THERE.
I JUST WISH I COULD REMEMBER WHY I WAS LIKE I WAS WHEN WE FOUND EACH OTHER IN THAT ALLEY, AND WHAT HAPPENED TO MY APARTMENT.
HELL-- I JUST WISH I COULD REMEMBER WHAT HAPPENED TO ME!
NOW, NOW-- LET'S NOT START THIS AGAIN. YOU KNOW YOU GET THOSE MIGRAINES FROM THINKING ABOUT IT TOO MUCH. WE'LL GET TO THE BOTTOM OF IT EVENTUALLY.
WHO KNOWS-- MAYBE IT EVEN HAS SOMETHING TO DO WITH THE STAR SLAYER. BUT RIGHT NOW, THAT SHOULD BE OUR ONLY GOAL... FINDING THE SLAYER AND BRINGING HIM, OR HER, TO JUSTICE.
"HER"?!
C'MON, STANLEY-- YOU'RE SUPPOSED TO BE EVEN LESS ENLIGHTENED THAN ME, BEING AN OLD MAN FROM ANOTHER GENERATION AND ALL. BUT AS LIBERAL AS I AM, I WON'T GO SO FAR OUT ON A LIMB AS TO SUPPOSE FOR A MINUTE THAT A WOMAN COULD BE CAPABLE OF A CRIME AS UGLY AS THE SLAYER'S.
A WOMAN WANTS TO WORK THE WRONG SIDE OF THE LAW, SHE THROWS ON A CAT SUIT... SHE DOESN'T KIDNAP KIDS AND GUT THEM.
SPEAKING OF WHICH, HOW WOULD YOU LIKE TO CHOKE DOWN SOME FILET MIGNON I JUST GRILLED? IT'S MARINATED IN BALSAMIC AND BASIL.
LEAD THE WAY, SENIOR CITIZEN. I'M AS HUNGRY AS IT GETS.

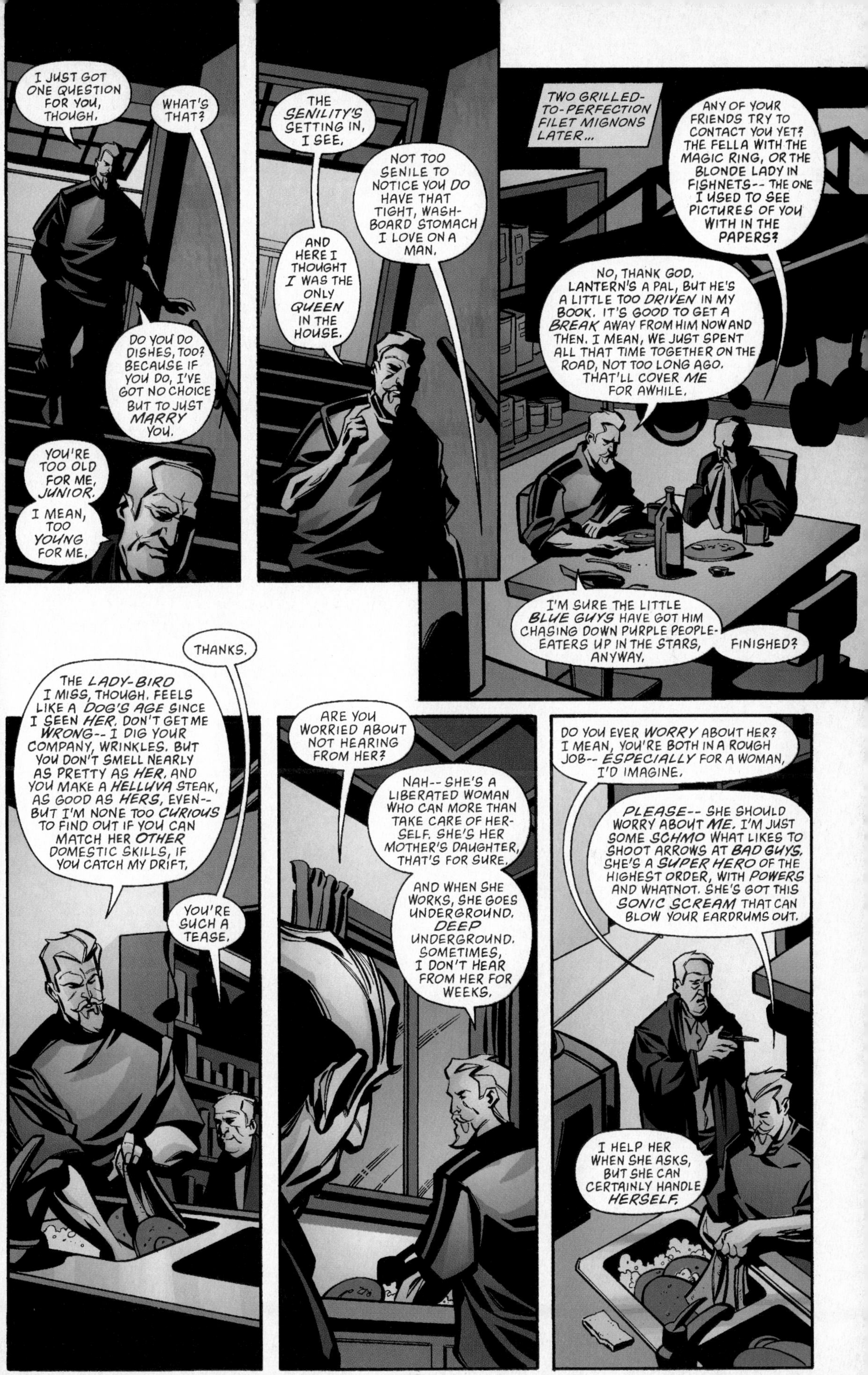
I JUST GOT ONE QUESTION FOR YOU, THOUGH.
WHAT'S THAT?
DO YOU DO DISHES, TOO? BECAUSE IF YOU DO, I'VE GOT NO CHOICE BUT TO JUST MARRY YOU.
YOU'RE TOO OLD FOR ME, JUNIOR.
I MEAN, TOO YOUNG FOR ME.
THE SENILITY'S SETTING IN, I SEE.
NOT TOO SENILE TO NOTICE YOU DO HAVE THAT TIGHT, WASH-BOARD STOMACH I LOVE ON A MAN.
AND HERE I THOUGHT I WAS THE ONLY QUEEN IN THE HOUSE.
TWO GRILLED-TO-PERFECTION FILET MIGNONS LATER...
ANY OF YOUR FRIENDS TRY TO CONTACT YOU YET? THE FELLA WITH THE MAGIC RING, OR THE BLONDE LADY IN FISHNETS-- THE ONE I USED TO SEE PICTURES OF YOU WITH IN THE PAPERS?
NO, THANK GOD. LANTERN'S A PAL, BUT HE'S A LITTLE TOO DRIVEN IN MY BOOK. IT'S GOOD TO GET A BREAK AWAY FROM HIM NOW AND THEN. I MEAN, WE JUST SPENT ALL THAT TIME TOGETHER ON THE ROAD, NOT TOO LONG AGO. THAT'LL COVER ME FOR AWHILE.
I'M SURE THE LITTLE BLUE GUYS HAVE GOT HIM CHASING DOWN PURPLE PEOPLE-EATERS UP IN THE STARS, ANYWAY.
FINISHED?
THANKS.
THE LADY-BIRD I MISS, THOUGH. FEELS LIKE A DOG'S AGE SINCE I SEEN HER. DON'T GET ME WRONG-- I DIG YOUR COMPANY, WRINKLES. BUT YOU DON'T SMELL NEARLY AS PRETTY AS HER. AND YOU MAKE A HELLUVA STEAK, AS GOOD AS HERS, EVEN-- BUT I'M NONE TOO CURIOUS TO FIND OUT IF YOU CAN MATCH HER OTHER DOMESTIC SKILLS, IF YOU CATCH MY DRIFT.
YOU'RE SUCH A TEASE.
ARE YOU WORRIED ABOUT NOT HEARING FROM HER?
NAH-- SHE'S A LIBERATED WOMAN WHO CAN MORE THAN TAKE CARE OF HER-SELF. SHE'S HER MOTHER'S DAUGHTER, THAT'S FOR SURE.
AND WHEN SHE WORKS, SHE GOES UNDERGROUND. DEEP UNDERGROUND. SOMETIMES, I DON'T HEAR FROM HER FOR WEEKS.
DO YOU EVER WORRY ABOUT HER? I MEAN, YOU'RE BOTH IN A ROUGH JOB-- ESPECIALLY FOR A WOMAN, I'D IMAGINE.
PLEASE-- SHE SHOULD WORRY ABOUT ME. I'M JUST SOME SCHMO WHAT LIKES TO SHOOT ARROWS AT BAD GUYS. SHE'S A SUPER HERO OF THE HIGHEST ORDER, WITH POWERS AND WHATNOT. SHE'S GOT THIS SONIC SCREAM THAT CAN BLOW YOUR EARDRUMS OUT.
I HELP HER WHEN SHE ASKS, BUT SHE CAN CERTAINLY HANDLE HERSELF.

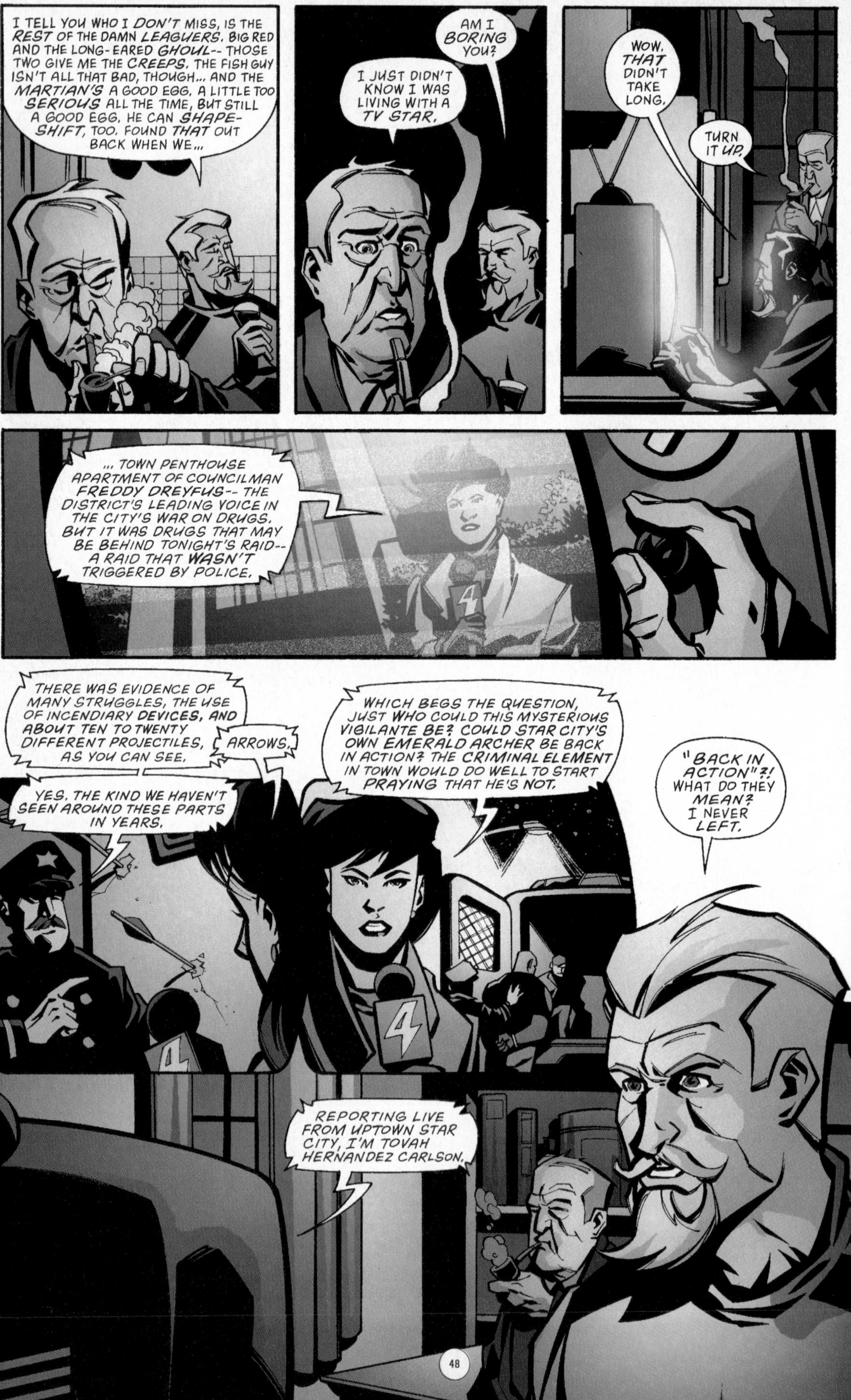
I TELL YOU WHO I DON'T MISS, IS THE REST OF THE DAMN LEAGUERS. BIG RED AND THE LONG-EARED GHOUL-- THOSE TWO GIVE ME THE CREEPS. THE FISH GUY ISN'T ALL THAT BAD, THOUGH... AND THE MARTIAN'S A GOOD EGG. A LITTLE TOO SERIOUS ALL THE TIME, BUT STILL A GOOD EGG. HE CAN SHAPE-SHIFT, TOO. FOUND THAT OUT BACK WHEN WE...
I JUST DIDN'T KNOW I WAS LIVING WITH A TV STAR.
AM I BORING YOU?
WOW. THAT DIDN'T TAKE LONG.
TURN IT UP.
... TOWN PENTHOUSE APARTMENT OF COUNCILMAN FREDDY DREYFUS-- THE DISTRICT'S LEADING VOICE IN THE CITY'S WAR ON DRUGS. BUT IT WAS DRUGS THAT MAY BE BEHIND TONIGHT'S RAID-- A RAID THAT WASN'T TRIGGERED BY POLICE.
THERE WAS EVIDENCE OF MANY STRUGGLES, THE USE OF INCENDIARY DEVICES, AND ABOUT TEN TO TWENTY DIFFERENT PROJECTILES, AS YOU CAN SEE.
ARROWS.
YES. THE KIND WE HAVEN'T SEEN AROUND THESE PARTS IN YEARS.
WHICH BEGS THE QUESTION, JUST WHO COULD THIS MYSTERIOUS VIGILANTE BE? COULD STAR CITY'S OWN EMERALD ARCHER BE BACK IN ACTION? THE CRIMINAL ELEMENT IN TOWN WOULD DO WELL TO START PRAYING THAT HE'S NOT.
"BACK IN ACTION"?! WHAT DO THEY MEAN? I NEVER LEFT.
REPORTING LIVE FROM UPTOWN STAR CITY, I'M TOVAH HERNANDEZ CARLSON.

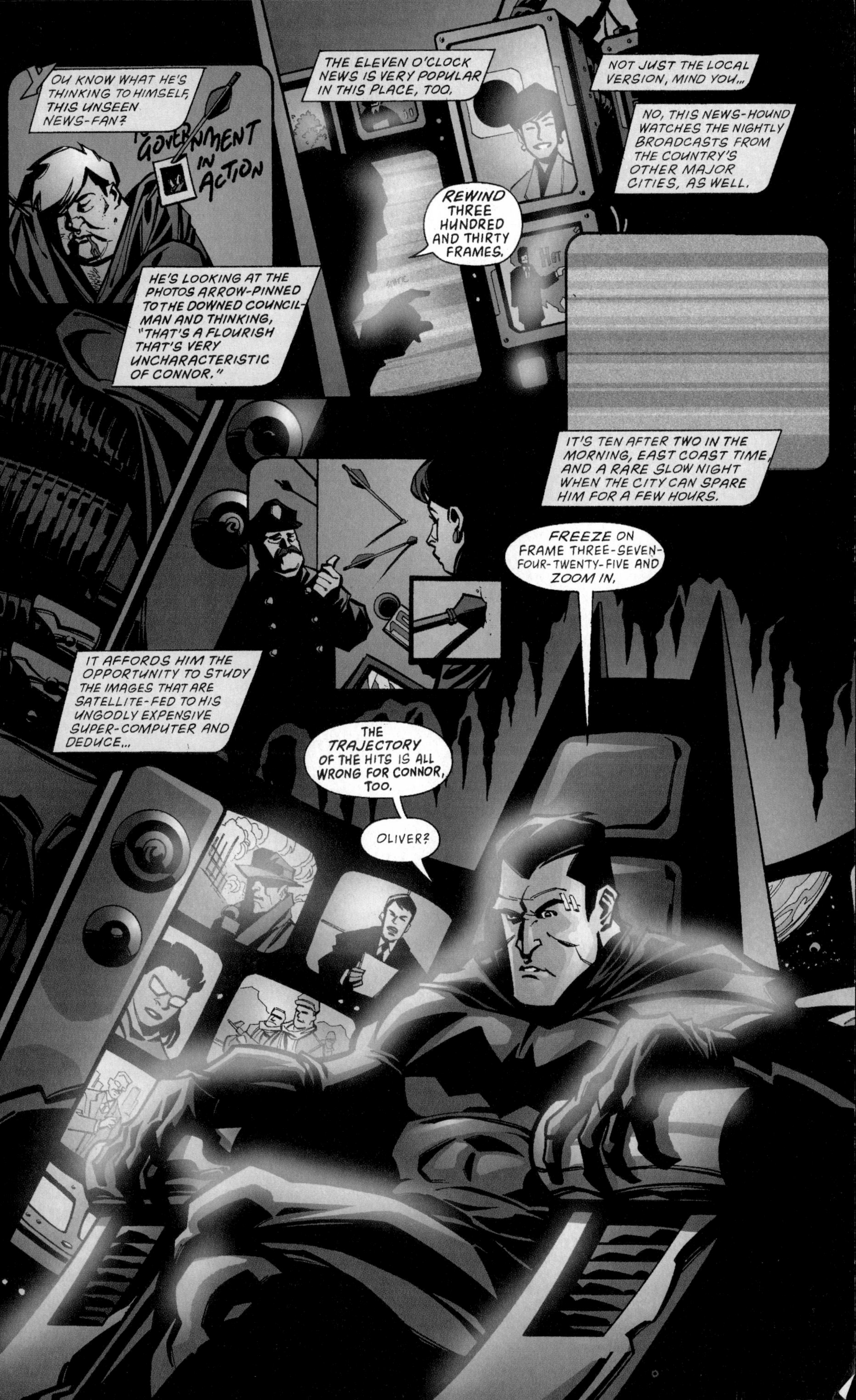
YOU KNOW WHAT HE'S THINKING TO HIMSELF, THIS UNSEEN NEWS-FAN?
GOVERNMENT IN ACTION
THE ELEVEN O'CLOCK NEWS IS VERY POPULAR IN THIS PLACE, TOO.
NOT JUST THE LOCAL VERSION, MIND YOU...
NO, THIS NEWS-HOUND WATCHES THE NIGHTLY BROADCASTS FROM THE COUNTRY'S OTHER MAJOR CITIES, AS WELL.
REWIND THREE HUNDRED AND THIRTY FRAMES.
HE'S LOOKING AT THE PHOTOS ARROW-PINNED TO THE DOWNED COUNCIL-MAN AND THINKING, "THAT'S A FLOURISH THAT'S VERY UNCHARACTERISTIC OF CONNOR."
IT'S TEN AFTER TWO IN THE MORNING, EAST COAST TIME, AND A RARE SLOW NIGHT WHEN THE CITY CAN SPARE HIM FOR A FEW HOURS.
FREEZE ON FRAME THREE-SEVEN-FOUR-TWENTY-FIVE AND ZOOM IN.
IT AFFORDS HIM THE OPPORTUNITY TO STUDY THE IMAGES THAT ARE SATELLITE-FED TO HIS UNGODLY EXPENSIVE SUPER-COMPUTER AND DEDUCE...
THE TRAJECTORY OF THE HITS IS ALL WRONG FOR CONNOR, TOO.
OLIVER?

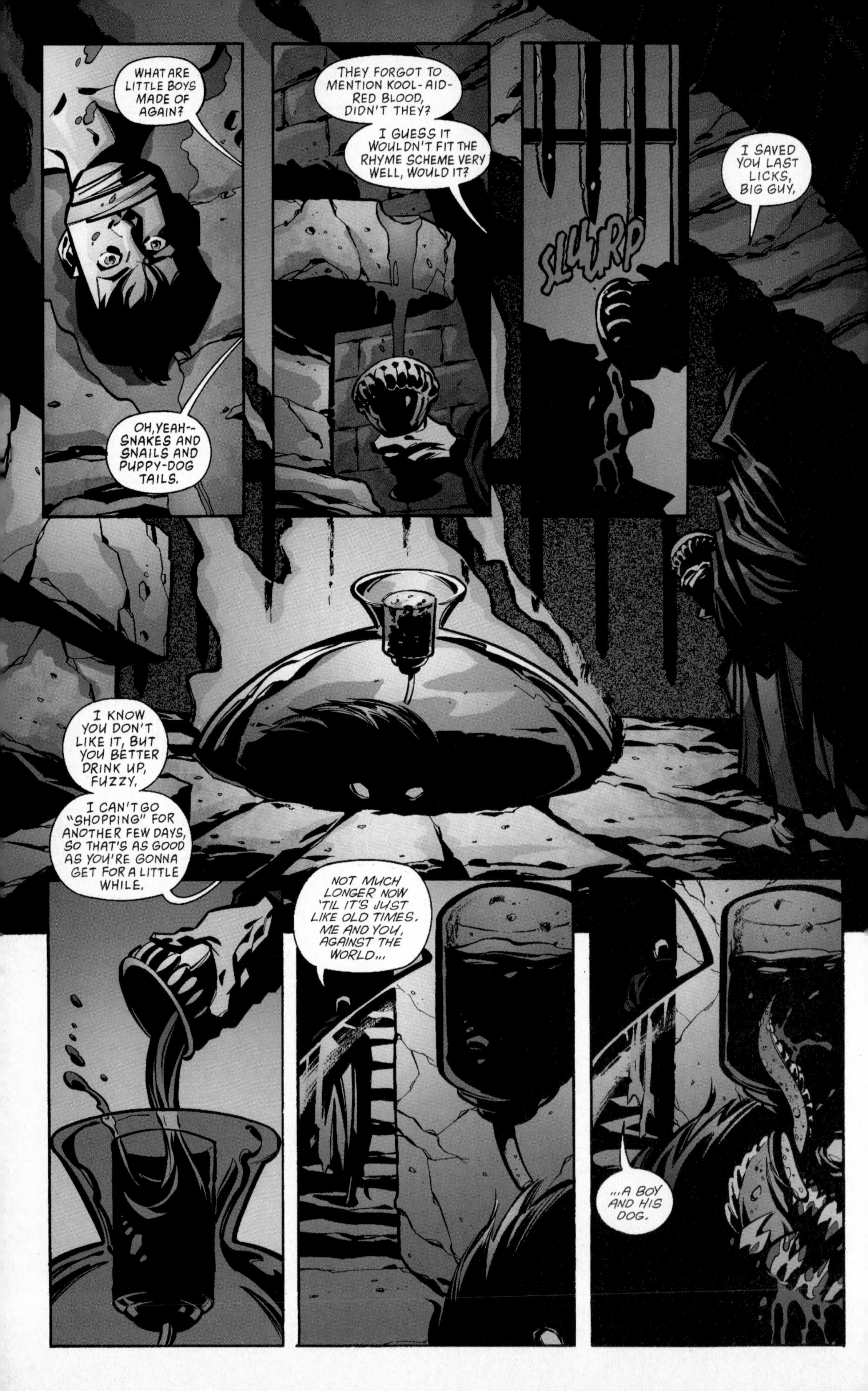
WHAT ARE LITTLE BOYS MADE OF AGAIN?
OH, YEAH-- SNAKES AND SNAILS AND PUPPY-DOG TAILS.
THEY FORGOT TO MENTION KOOL-AID-RED BLOOD, DIDN'T THEY?
I GUESS IT WOULDN'T FIT THE RHYME SCHEME VERY WELL, WOULD IT?
SLUURP
I SAVED YOU LAST LICKS, BIG GUY.
I KNOW YOU DON'T LIKE IT, BUT YOU BETTER DRINK UP, FUZZY.
I CAN'T GO "SHOPPING" FOR ANOTHER FEW DAYS, SO THAT'S AS GOOD AS YOU'RE GONNA GET FOR A LITTLE WHILE.
NOT MUCH LONGER NOW 'TIL IT'S JUST LIKE OLD TIMES. ME AND YOU, AGAINST THE WORLD...
...A BOY AND HIS DOG.

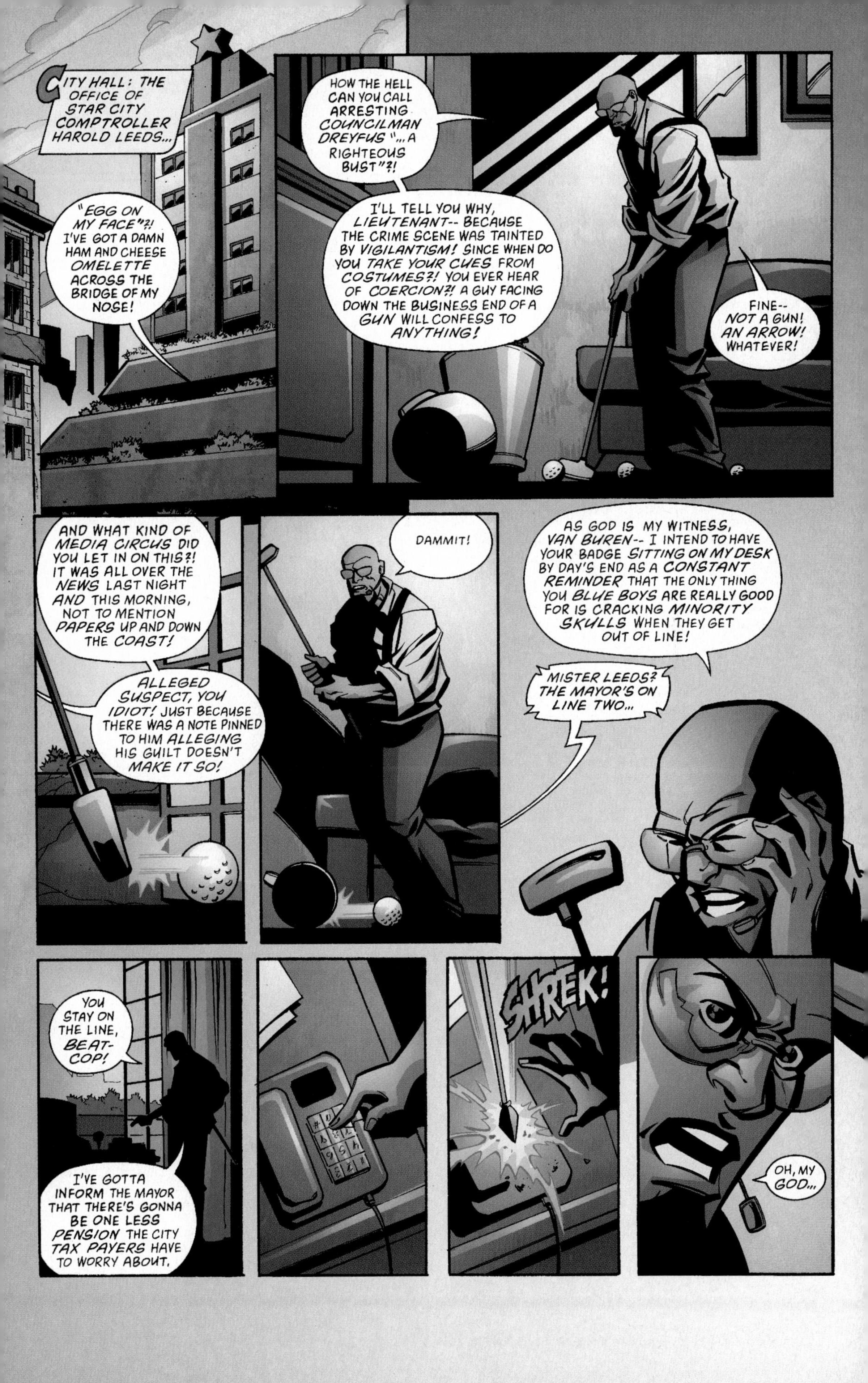
CITY HALL: THE OFFICE OF STAR CITY COMPTROLLER HAROLD LEEDS...
"EGG ON MY FACE"?! I'VE GOT A DAMN HAM AND CHEESE OMELETTE ACROSS THE BRIDGE OF MY NOSE!
HOW THE HELL CAN YOU CALL ARRESTING COUNCILMAN DREYFUS "...A RIGHTEOUS BUST"?!
I'LL TELL YOU WHY, LIEUTENANT-- BECAUSE THE CRIME SCENE WAS TAINTED BY VIGILANTISM! SINCE WHEN DO YOU TAKE YOUR CUES FROM COSTUMES?! YOU EVER HEAR OF COERCION?! A GUY FACING DOWN THE BUSINESS END OF A GUN WILL CONFESS TO ANYTHING!
FINE-- NOT A GUN! AN ARROW! WHATEVER!
AND WHAT KIND OF MEDIA CIRCUS DID YOU LET IN ON THIS?! IT WAS ALL OVER THE NEWS LAST NIGHT AND THIS MORNING, NOT TO MENTION PAPERS UP AND DOWN THE COAST!
ALLEGED SUSPECT, YOU IDIOT! JUST BECAUSE THERE WAS A NOTE PINNED TO HIM ALLEGING HIS GUILT DOESN'T MAKE IT SO!
DAMMIT!
AS GOD IS MY WITNESS, VAN BUREN-- I INTEND TO HAVE YOUR BADGE SITTING ON MY DESK BY DAY'S END AS A CONSTANT REMINDER THAT THE ONLY THING YOU BLUE BOYS ARE REALLY GOOD FOR IS CRACKING MINORITY SKULLS WHEN THEY GET OUT OF LINE!
MISTER LEEDS? THE MAYOR'S ON LINE TWO...
YOU STAY ON THE LINE, BEAT-COP!
I'VE GOTTA INFORM THE MAYOR THAT THERE'S GONNA BE ONE LESS PENSION THE CITY TAX PAYERS HAVE TO WORRY ABOUT.
SHREK!
OH, MY GOD...

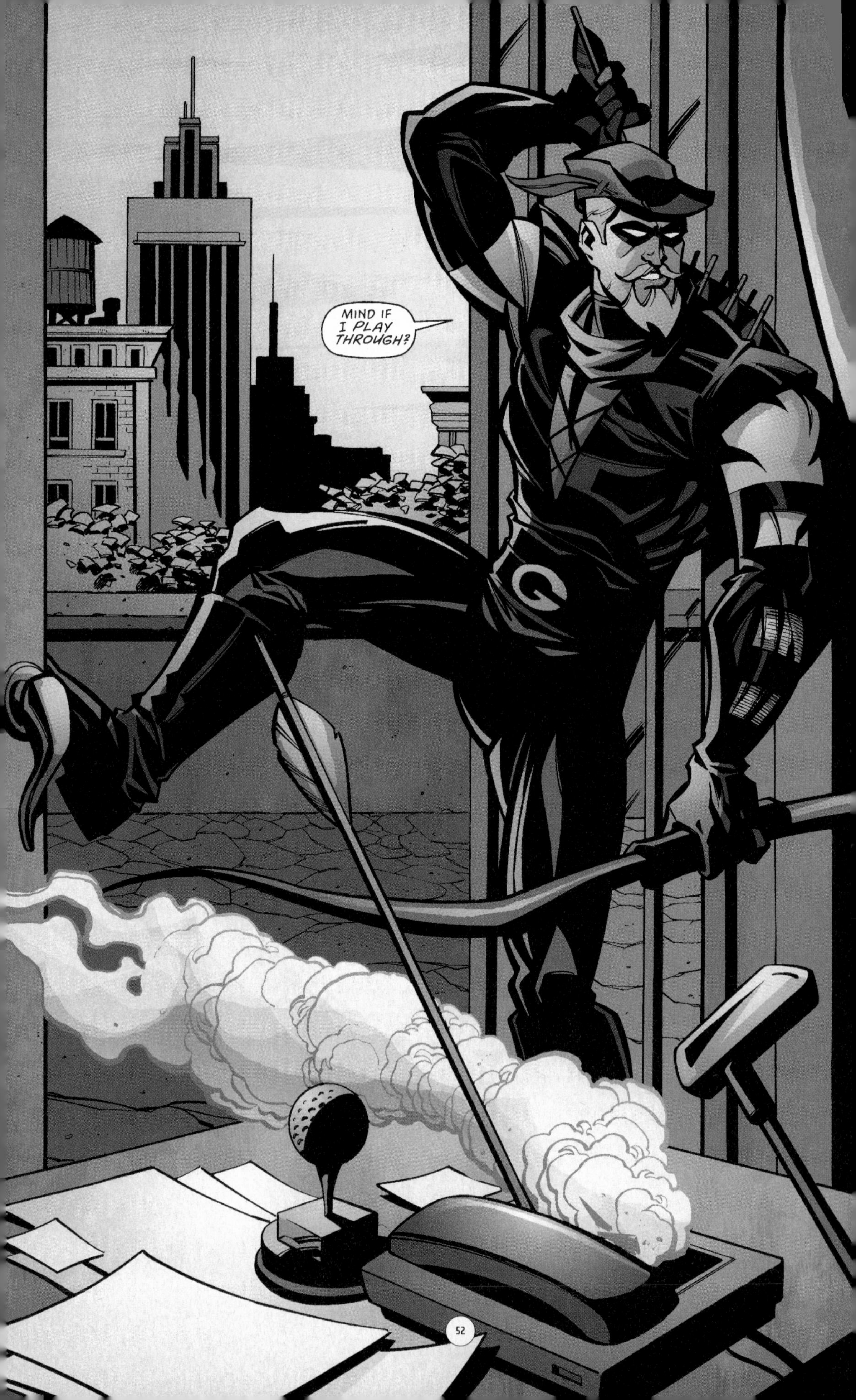
MIND IF I PLAY THROUGH?

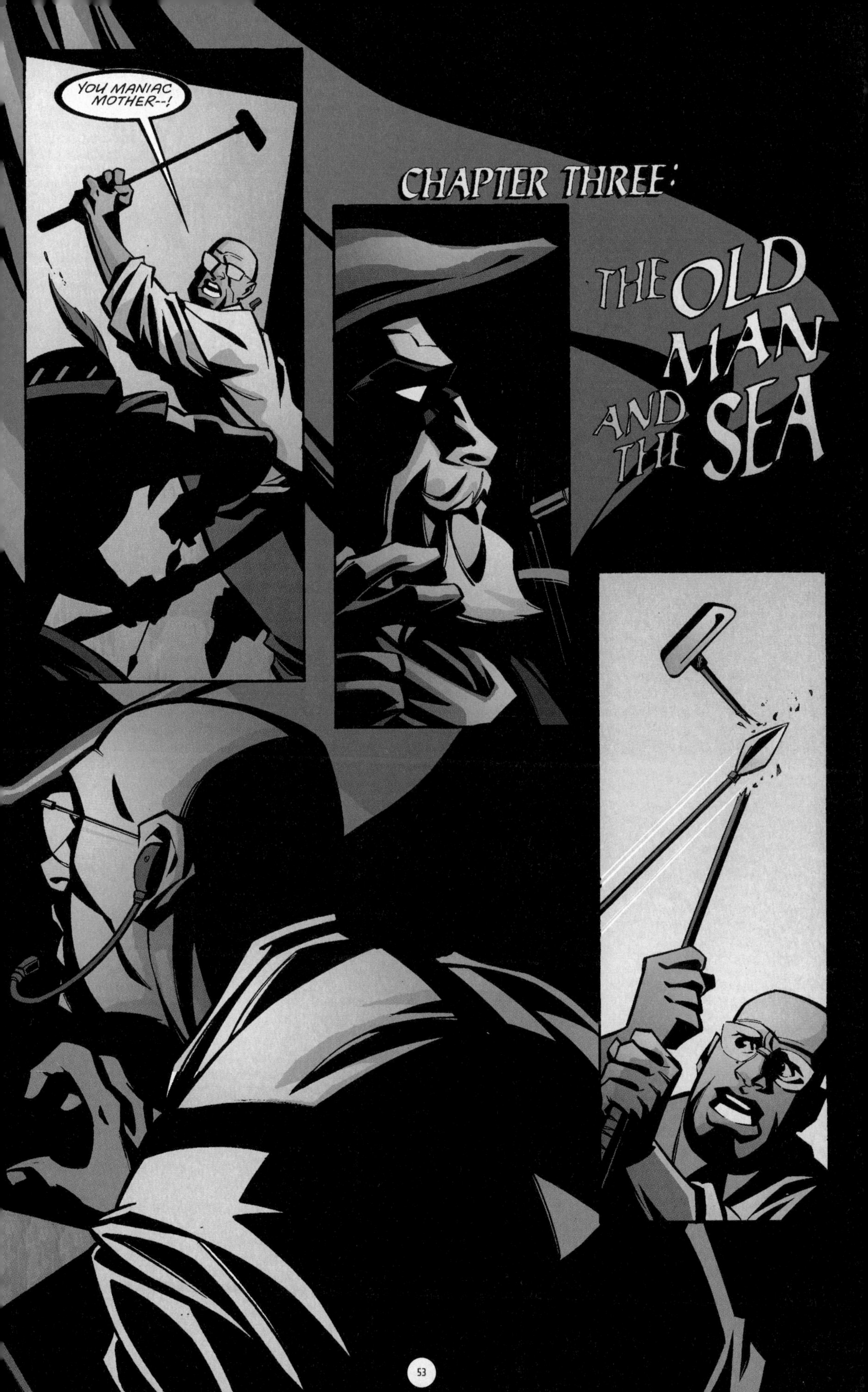
YOU MANIAC MOTHER--!
CHAPTER THREE:
THE OLD MAN AND THE SEA

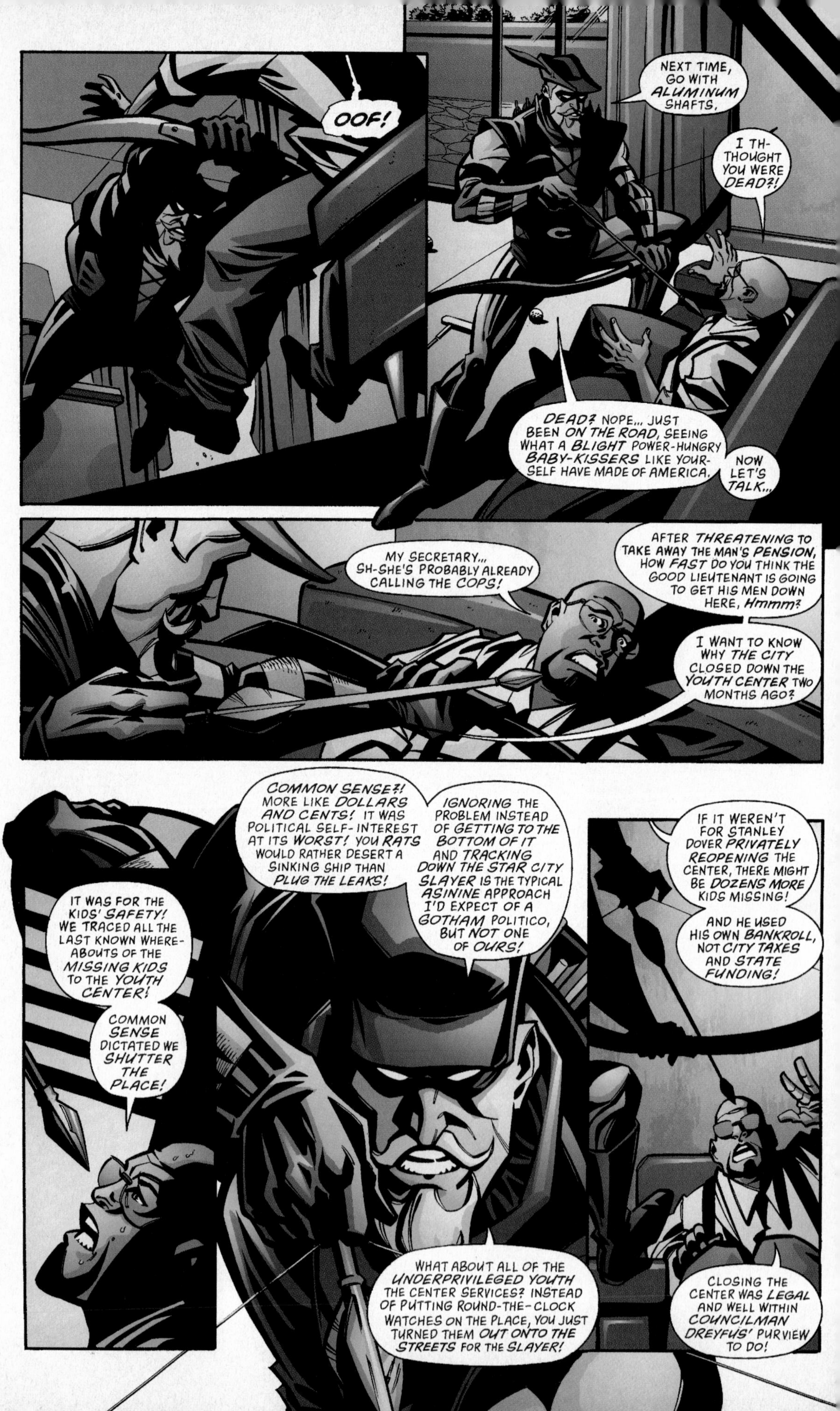
OOF!
NEXT TIME, GO WITH ALUMINUM SHAFTS.
I TH-THOUGHT YOU WERE DEAD?!
DEAD? NOPE... JUST BEEN ON THE ROAD, SEEING WHAT A BLIGHT POWER-HUNGRY BABY-KISSERS LIKE YOURSELF HAVE MADE OF AMERICA.
NOW LET'S TALK...
MY SECRETARY... SH-SHE'S PROBABLY ALREADY CALLING THE COPS!
AFTER THREATENING TO TAKE AWAY THE MAN'S PENSION, HOW FAST DO YOU THINK THE GOOD LIEUTENANT IS GOING TO GET HIS MEN DOWN HERE, Hmmm?
I WANT TO KNOW WHY THE CITY CLOSED DOWN THE YOUTH CENTER TWO MONTHS AGO?
IT WAS FOR THE KIDS' SAFETY! WE TRACED ALL THE LAST KNOWN WHERE-ABOUTS OF THE MISSING KIDS TO THE YOUTH CENTER!
COMMON SENSE DICTATED WE SHUTTER THE PLACE!
COMMON SENSE?! MORE LIKE DOLLARS AND CENTS! IT WAS POLITICAL SELF-INTEREST AT ITS WORST! YOU RATS WOULD RATHER DESERT A SINKING SHIP THAN PLUG THE LEAKS!
IGNORING THE PROBLEM INSTEAD OF GETTING TO THE BOTTOM OF IT AND TRACKING DOWN THE STAR CITY SLAYER IS THE TYPICAL ASININE APPROACH I'D EXPECT OF A GOTHAM POLITICO, BUT NOT ONE OF OURS!
WHAT ABOUT ALL OF THE UNDERPRIVILEGED YOUTH THE CENTER SERVICES? INSTEAD OF PUTTING ROUND-THE-CLOCK WATCHES ON THE PLACE, YOU JUST TURNED THEM OUT ONTO THE STREETS FOR THE SLAYER!
CLOSING THE CENTER WAS LEGAL AND WELL WITHIN COUNCILMAN DREYFUS' PURVIEW TO DO!
IF IT WEREN'T FOR STANLEY DOVER PRIVATELY REOPENING THE CENTER, THERE MIGHT BE DOZENS MORE KIDS MISSING!
AND HE USED HIS OWN BANKROLL, NOT CITY TAXES AND STATE FUNDING!

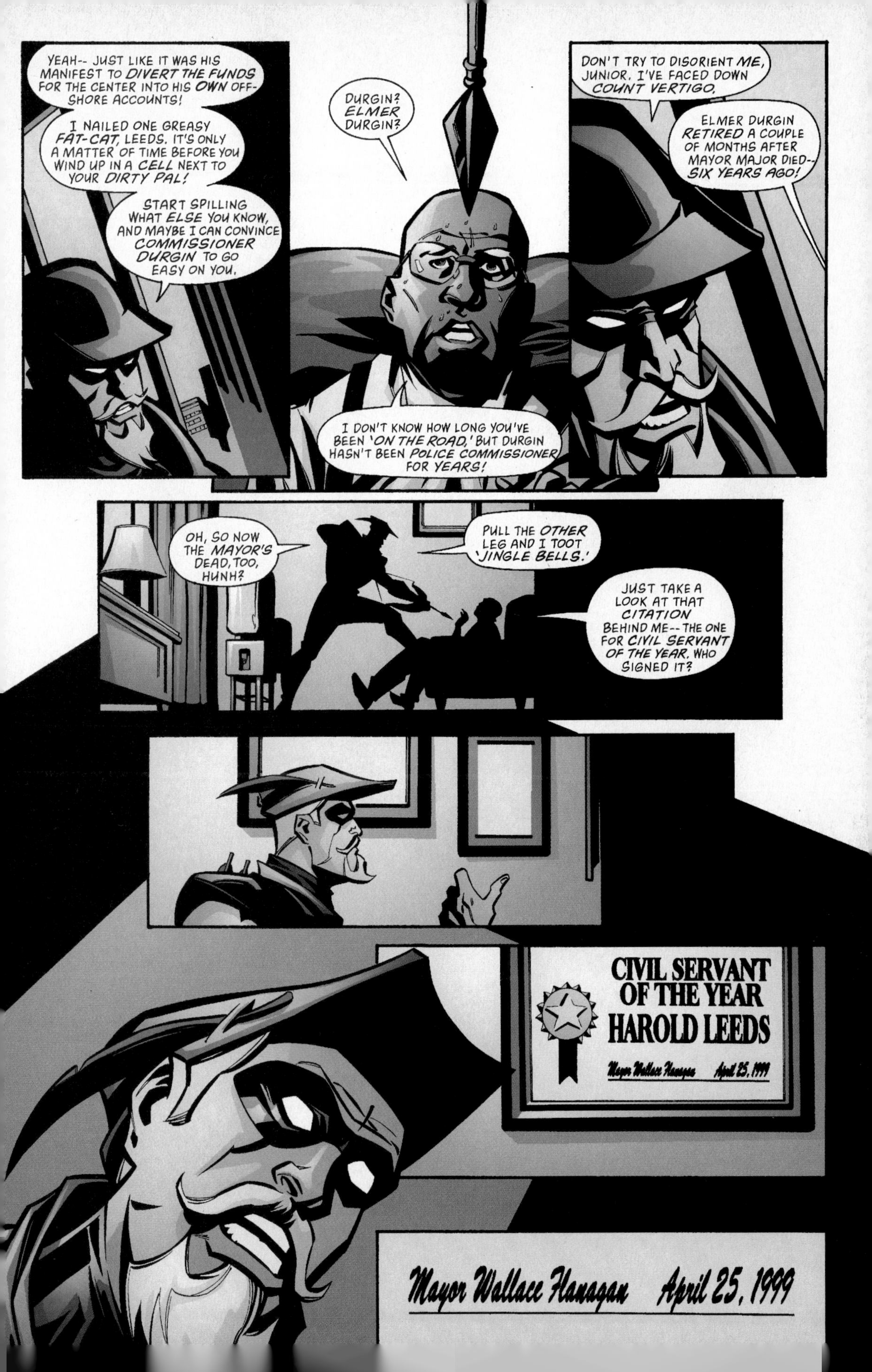

YEAH-- JUST LIKE IT WAS HIS MANIFEST TO DIVERT THE FUNDS FOR THE CENTER INTO HIS OWN OFF-SHORE ACCOUNTS!
I NAILED ONE GREASY FAT-CAT, LEEDS. IT'S ONLY A MATTER OF TIME BEFORE YOU WIND UP IN A CELL NEXT TO YOUR DIRTY PAL!
START SPILLING WHAT ELSE YOU KNOW, AND MAYBE I CAN CONVINCE COMMISSIONER DURGIN TO GO EASY ON YOU.
DURGIN? ELMER DURGIN?
I DON'T KNOW HOW LONG YOU'VE BEEN 'ON THE ROAD,' BUT DURGIN HASN'T BEEN POLICE COMMISSIONER FOR YEARS!
DON'T TRY TO DISORIENT ME, JUNIOR. I'VE FACED DOWN COUNT VERTIGO.
ELMER DURGIN RETIRED A COUPLE OF MONTHS AFTER MAYOR MAJOR DIED-- SIX YEARS AGO!
OH, SO NOW THE MAYOR'S DEAD, TOO, HUNH?
PULL THE OTHER LEG AND I TOOT 'JINGLE BELLS.'
JUST TAKE A LOOK AT THAT CITATION BEHIND ME-- THE ONE FOR CIVIL SERVANT OF THE YEAR. WHO SIGNED IT?
CIVIL SERVANT OF THE YEAR
HAROLD LEEDS
Mayor Wallace Flanagan April 25, 1999
Mayor Wallace Flanagan April 25, 1999

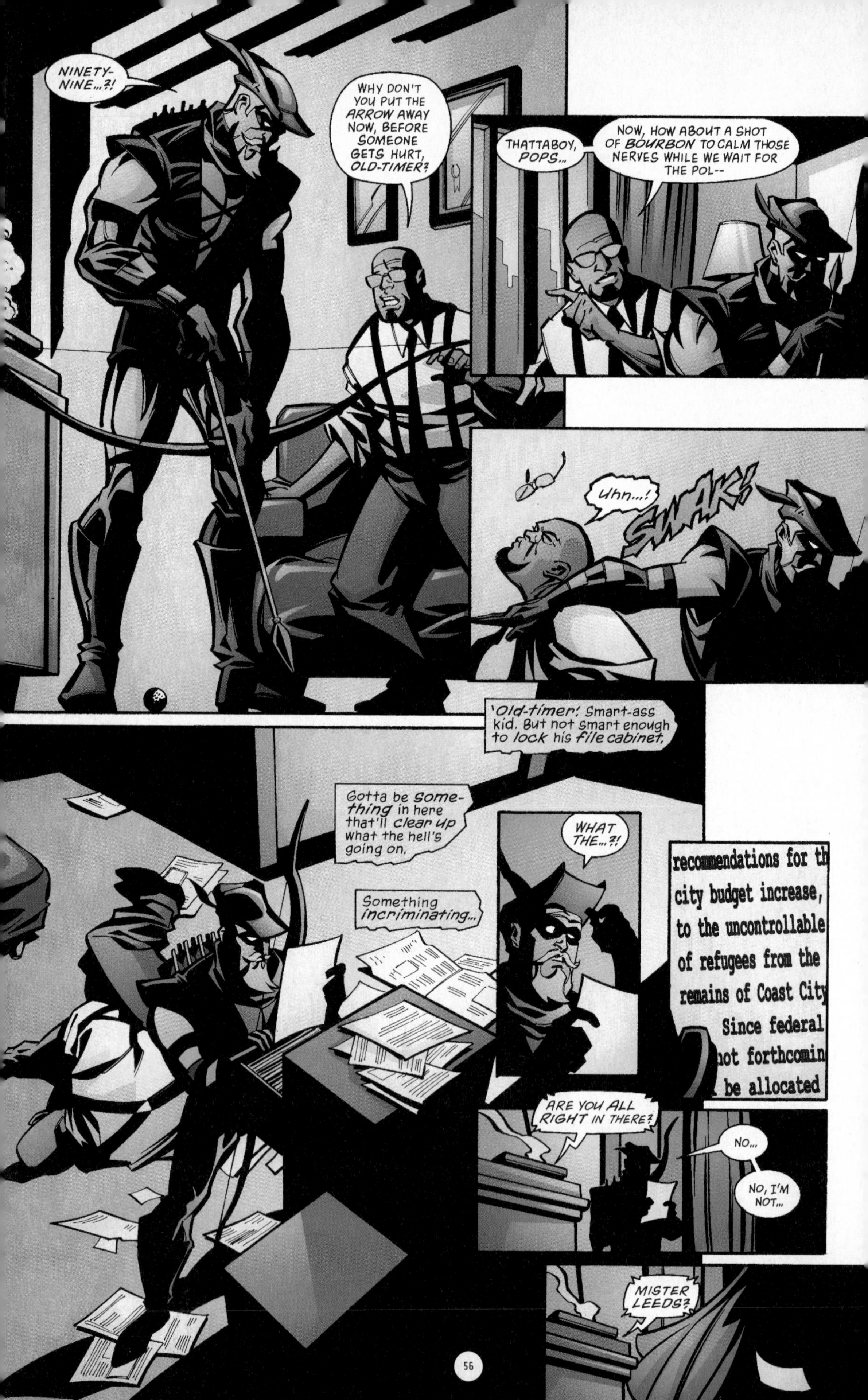
NINETY-NINE...?!
WHY DON'T YOU PUT THE ARROW AWAY NOW, BEFORE SOMEONE GETS HURT, OLD-TIMER?
THATTABOY, POPS...
NOW, HOW ABOUT A SHOT OF BOURBON TO CALM THOSE NERVES WHILE WE WAIT FOR THE POL--
Uhn...!
SWAK!
'Old-timer.' Smart-ass kid. But not smart enough to lock his file cabinet.
Gotta be something in here that'll clear up what the hell's going on.
Something incriminating...
WHAT THE...?!
recommendations for th
city budget increase,
to the uncontrollable
of refugees from the
remains of Coast City
Since federal
not forthcomin
be allocated
ARE YOU ALL RIGHT IN THERE?
NO...
NO, I'M NOT...
MISTER LEEDS?

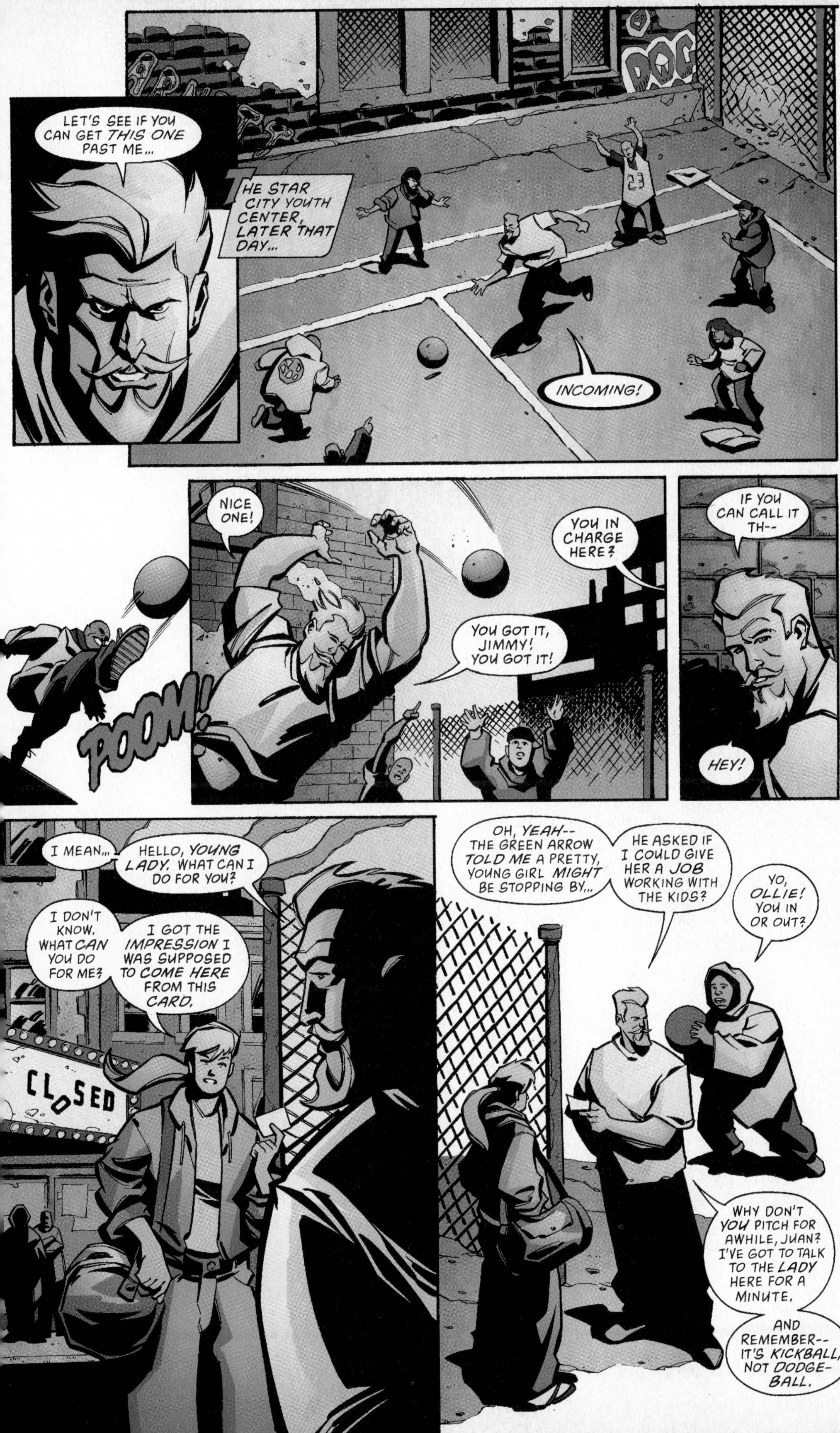
LET'S SEE IF YOU CAN GET THIS ONE PAST ME...
THE STAR CITY YOUTH CENTER, LATER THAT DAY...
INCOMING!
NICE ONE!
YOU IN CHARGE HERE?
YOU GOT IT, JIMMY! YOU GOT IT!
POOM!
IF YOU CAN CALL IT TH--
HEY!
I MEAN...
HELLO, YOUNG LADY. WHAT CAN I DO FOR YOU?
I DON'T KNOW. WHAT CAN YOU DO FOR ME?
I GOT THE IMPRESSION I WAS SUPPOSED TO COME HERE FROM THIS CARD.
CLOSED
OH, YEAH-- THE GREEN ARROW TOLD ME A PRETTY, YOUNG GIRL MIGHT BE STOPPING BY...
HE ASKED IF I COULD GIVE HER A JOB WORKING WITH THE KIDS?
YO, OLLIE! YOU IN OR OUT?
WHY DON'T YOU PITCH FOR AWHILE, JUAN? I'VE GOT TO TALK TO THE LADY HERE FOR A MINUTE.
AND REMEMBER-- IT'S KICKBALL, NOT DODGE-BALL.

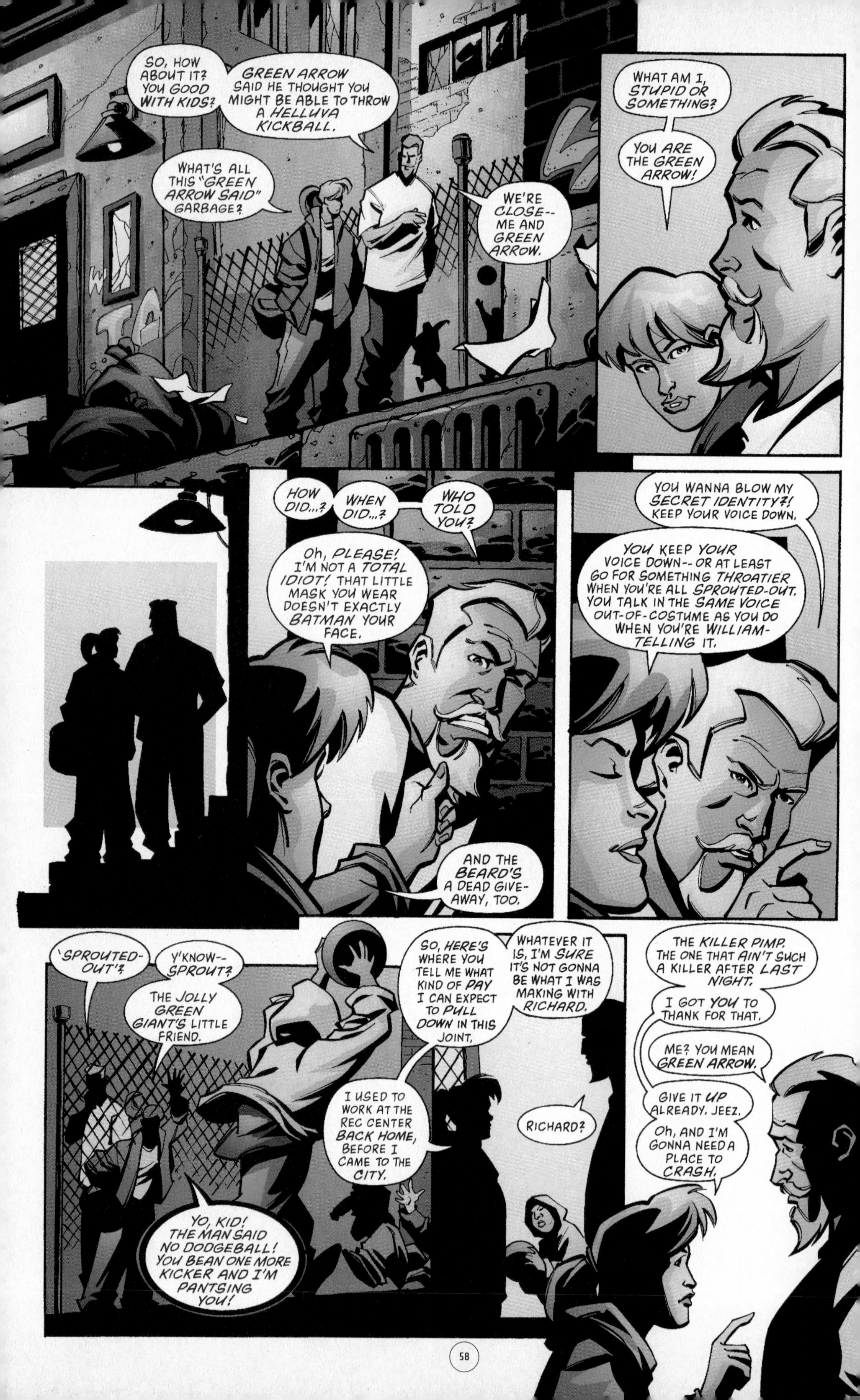
SO, HOW ABOUT IT? YOU GOOD WITH KIDS?
GREEN ARROW SAID HE THOUGHT YOU MIGHT BE ABLE TO THROW A HELLUVA KICKBALL.
WHAT'S ALL THIS "GREEN ARROW SAID" GARBAGE?
WE'RE CLOSE-- ME AND GREEN ARROW.
WHAT AM I, STUPID OR SOMETHING?
YOU ARE THE GREEN ARROW!
HOW DID...?
WHEN DID...?
WHO TOLD YOU?
Oh, PLEASE! I'M NOT A TOTAL IDIOT! THAT LITTLE MASK YOU WEAR DOESN'T EXACTLY BATMAN YOUR FACE.
AND THE BEARD'S A DEAD GIVE-AWAY, TOO.
YOU WANNA BLOW MY SECRET IDENTITY?! KEEP YOUR VOICE DOWN.
YOU KEEP YOUR VOICE DOWN-- OR AT LEAST GO FOR SOMETHING THROATIER WHEN YOU'RE ALL SPROUTED-OUT. YOU TALK IN THE SAME VOICE OUT-OF-COSTUME AS YOU DO WHEN YOU'RE WILLIAM-TELLING IT.
'SPROUTED-OUT'?
Y'KNOW-- SPROUT?
THE JOLLY GREEN GIANT'S LITTLE FRIEND.
SO, HERE'S WHERE YOU TELL ME WHAT KIND OF PAY I CAN EXPECT TO PULL DOWN IN THIS JOINT.
WHATEVER IT IS, I'M SURE IT'S NOT GONNA BE WHAT I WAS MAKING WITH RICHARD.
I USED TO WORK AT THE REC CENTER BACK HOME, BEFORE I CAME TO THE CITY.
RICHARD?
YO, KID! THE MAN SAID NO DODGEBALL! YOU BEAN ONE MORE KICKER AND I'M PANTSING YOU!
THE KILLER PIMP. THE ONE THAT AIN'T SUCH A KILLER AFTER LAST NIGHT.
I GOT YOU TO THANK FOR THAT.
ME? YOU MEAN GREEN ARROW.
GIVE IT UP ALREADY. JEEZ.
Oh, AND I'M GONNA NEED A PLACE TO CRASH.

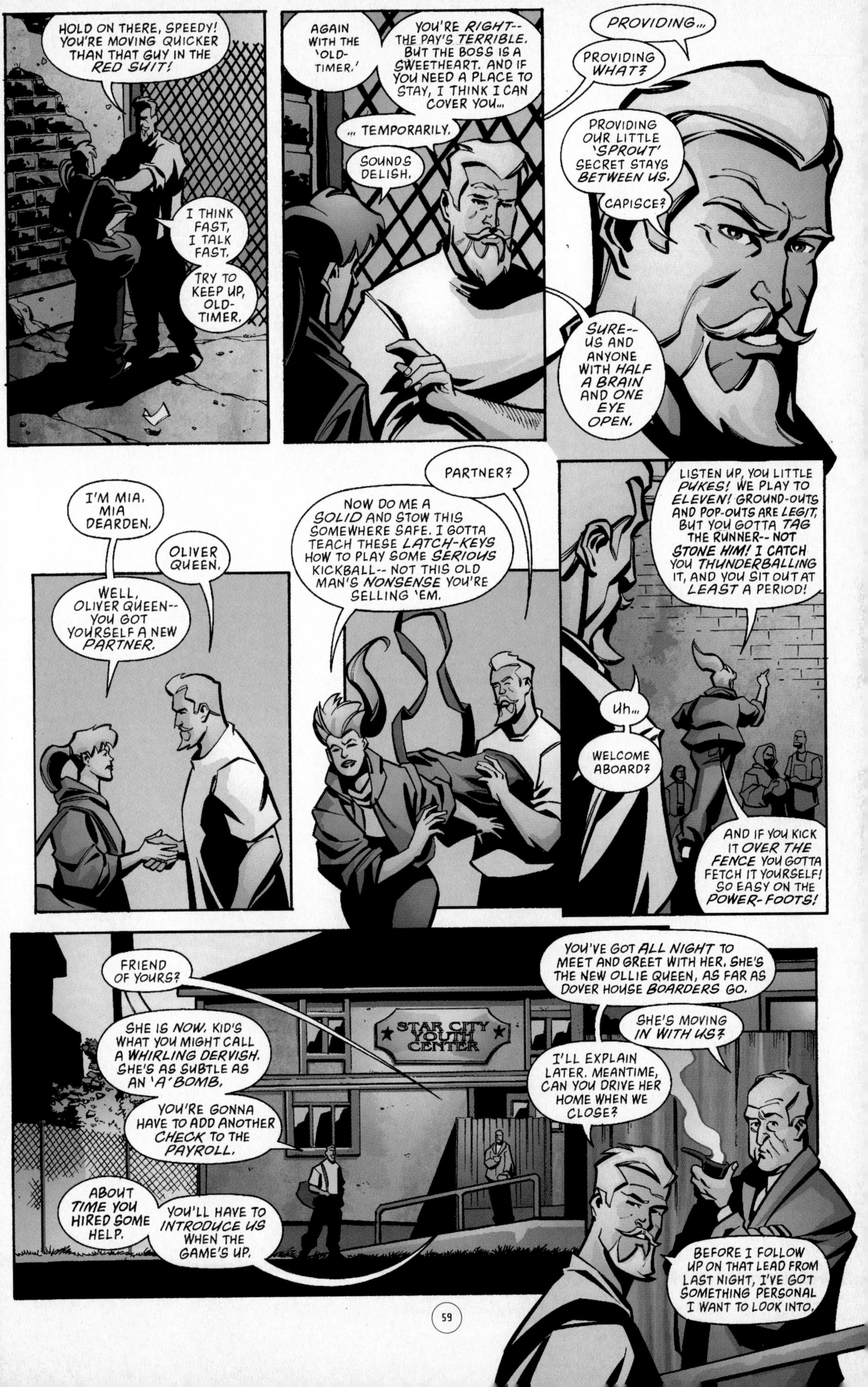
HOLD ON THERE, SPEEDY! YOU'RE MOVING QUICKER THAN THAT GUY IN THE RED SUIT!
I THINK FAST, I TALK FAST.
TRY TO KEEP UP, OLD-TIMER.
AGAIN WITH THE 'OLD-TIMER.'
YOU'RE RIGHT-- THE PAY'S TERRIBLE. BUT THE BOSS IS A SWEETHEART. AND IF YOU NEED A PLACE TO STAY, I THINK I CAN COVER YOU...
... TEMPORARILY.
SOUNDS DELISH.
PROVIDING...
PROVIDING WHAT?
PROVIDING OUR LITTLE 'SPROUT' SECRET STAYS BETWEEN US.
CAPISCE?
SURE-- US AND ANYONE WITH HALF A BRAIN AND ONE EYE OPEN.
I'M MIA. MIA DEARDEN.
OLIVER QUEEN.
WELL, OLIVER QUEEN-- YOU GOT YOURSELF A NEW PARTNER.
PARTNER?
NOW DO ME A SOLID AND STOW THIS SOMEWHERE SAFE. I GOTTA TEACH THESE LATCH-KEYS HOW TO PLAY SOME SERIOUS KICKBALL-- NOT THIS OLD MAN'S NONSENSE YOU'RE SELLING 'EM.
LISTEN UP, YOU LITTLE PUKES! WE PLAY TO ELEVEN! GROUND-OUTS AND POP-OUTS ARE LEGIT, BUT YOU GOTTA TAG THE RUNNER-- NOT STONE HIM! I CATCH YOU THUNDERBALLING IT, AND YOU SIT OUT AT LEAST A PERIOD!
Uh...
WELCOME ABOARD?
AND IF YOU KICK IT OVER THE FENCE YOU GOTTA FETCH IT YOURSELF! SO EASY ON THE POWER-FOOTS!
STAR CITY YOUTH CENTER
FRIEND OF YOURS?
SHE IS NOW. KID'S WHAT YOU MIGHT CALL A WHIRLING DERVISH. SHE'S AS SUBTLE AS AN 'A' BOMB.
YOU'RE GONNA HAVE TO ADD ANOTHER CHECK TO THE PAYROLL.
ABOUT TIME YOU HIRED SOME HELP.
YOU'LL HAVE TO INTRODUCE US WHEN THE GAME'S UP.
YOU'VE GOT ALL NIGHT TO MEET AND GREET WITH HER. SHE'S THE NEW OLLIE QUEEN, AS FAR AS DOVER HOUSE BOARDERS GO.
SHE'S MOVING IN WITH US?
I'LL EXPLAIN LATER. MEANTIME, CAN YOU DRIVE HER HOME WHEN WE CLOSE?
BEFORE I FOLLOW UP ON THAT LEAD FROM LAST NIGHT, I'VE GOT SOMETHING PERSONAL I WANT TO LOOK INTO.

THE STAR CITY BUS TERMINAL...

NEXT!

SIR...?

DERRIS LINES

GOTHAM
METROPOLIS
NEW YORK
LOS ANGELES
LEONARD
CHICAGO
STAR CITY

SIR! YOU'RE HOLDING UP THE LINE!

GOTHAM
METROPOLIS
NEW YORK
LOS ANGELES
CHICAGO

CHICAG
HUB C
KEYST
CENTRAI
RED B

OH-- I'M SORRY, GOT A LITTLE LOST THERE.

WHAT CITY, SIR?

Uh, ROUND TRIP TO COAST CITY, PLEASE.

YOU'RE KIDDING, RIGHT?

NO. I WANT A TICKET TO THE COAST CITY BUS STATION, AND THEN ANOTHER TICKET THAT'LL GET ME BACK HERE.

WHERE I'M FROM, THAT'S CALLED A ROUND-TRIP.

WHERE I'M FROM, THAT'S CALLED A HEAD-TRIP.

LOOK, LADY-- JUST GIVE ME THE TICKETS.

OH, RIGHT AWAY, SIR, BUT I GOTTA WARN YOU, THE COAST CITY ROUTE GOES BY WAY OF ATLANTIS AND NARNIA. IS THAT GOING TO BE A PROBLEM FOR YOU?

WHAT THE HELL ARE YOU--?

WE'RE A LITTLE BUSY FOR GAMES TODAY, JOKER JUNIOR! NOW BEAT IT BEFORE I CALL A COP!

NEXT!

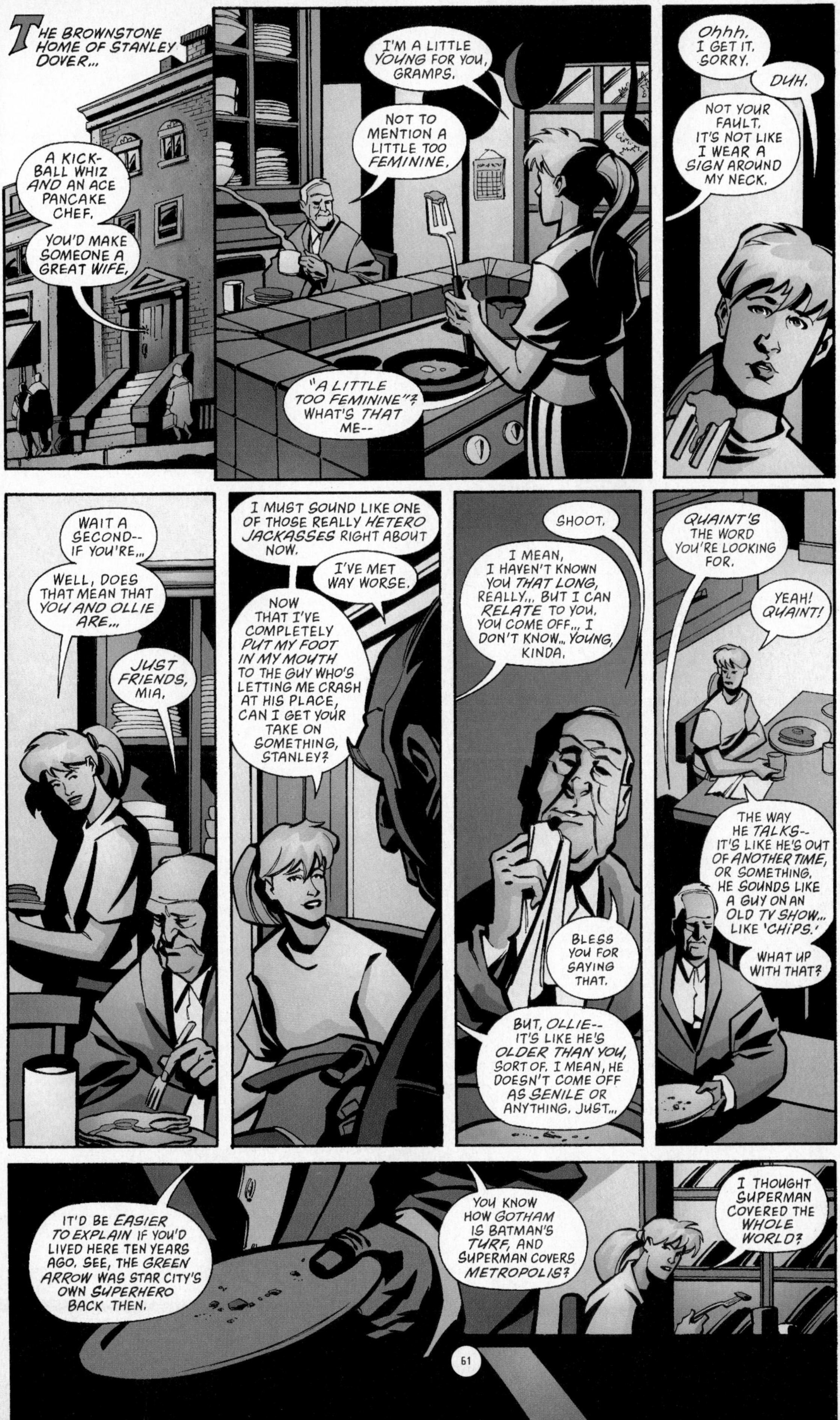
THE BROWNSTONE HOME OF STANLEY DOVER...
A KICK-BALL WHIZ AND AN ACE PANCAKE CHEF.
YOU'D MAKE SOMEONE A GREAT WIFE.
I'M A LITTLE YOUNG FOR YOU, GRAMPS.
NOT TO MENTION A LITTLE TOO FEMININE.
"A LITTLE TOO FEMININE"? WHAT'S THAT ME--
Ohhh. I GET IT. SORRY.
DUH.
NOT YOUR FAULT. IT'S NOT LIKE I WEAR A SIGN AROUND MY NECK.
WAIT A SECOND-- IF YOU'RE...
WELL, DOES THAT MEAN THAT YOU AND OLLIE ARE...
JUST FRIENDS, MIA.
I MUST SOUND LIKE ONE OF THOSE REALLY HETERO JACKASSES RIGHT ABOUT NOW.
I'VE MET WAY WORSE.
NOW THAT I'VE COMPLETELY PUT MY FOOT IN MY MOUTH TO THE GUY WHO'S LETTING ME CRASH AT HIS PLACE, CAN I GET YOUR TAKE ON SOMETHING, STANLEY?
SHOOT.
I MEAN, I HAVEN'T KNOWN YOU THAT LONG, REALLY... BUT I CAN RELATE TO YOU. YOU COME OFF... I DON'T KNOW... YOUNG, KINDA.
BLESS YOU FOR SAYING THAT.
BUT, OLLIE-- IT'S LIKE HE'S OLDER THAN YOU, SORT OF. I MEAN, HE DOESN'T COME OFF AS SENILE OR ANYTHING. JUST...
QUAINT'S THE WORD YOU'RE LOOKING FOR.
YEAH! QUAINT!
THE WAY HE TALKS-- IT'S LIKE HE'S OUT OF ANOTHER TIME, OR SOMETHING. HE SOUNDS LIKE A GUY ON AN OLD TV SHOW... LIKE 'CHiPS.'
WHAT UP WITH THAT?
IT'D BE EASIER TO EXPLAIN IF YOU'D LIVED HERE TEN YEARS AGO. SEE, THE GREEN ARROW WAS STAR CITY'S OWN SUPERHERO BACK THEN.
YOU KNOW HOW GOTHAM IS BATMAN'S TURF, AND SUPERMAN COVERS METROPOLIS?
I THOUGHT SUPERMAN COVERED THE WHOLE WORLD?

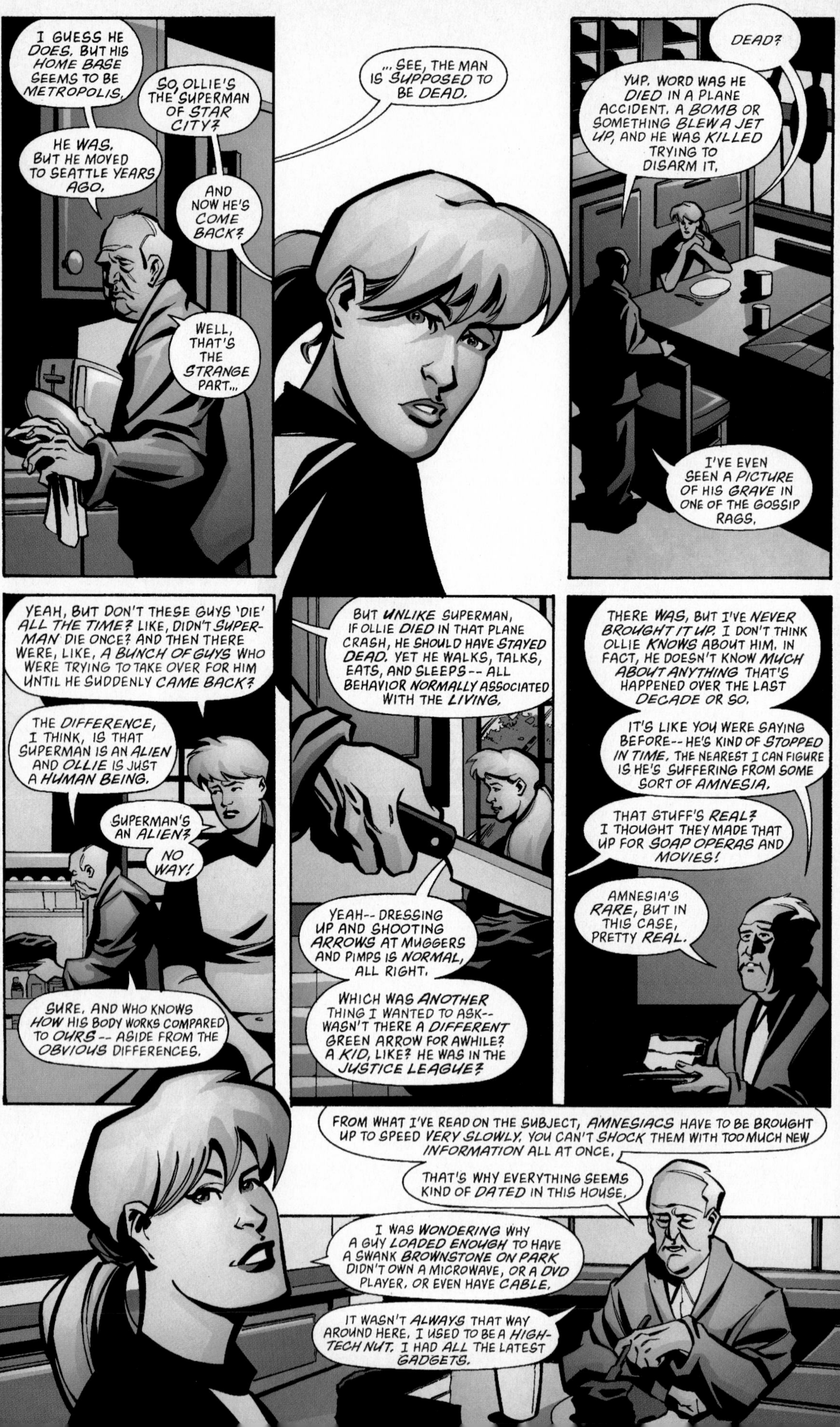

I GUESS HE DOES. BUT HIS HOME BASE SEEMS TO BE METROPOLIS.
SO, OLLIE'S THE SUPERMAN OF STAR CITY?
HE WAS. BUT HE MOVED TO SEATTLE YEARS AGO.
AND NOW HE'S COME BACK?
WELL, THAT'S THE STRANGE PART...
...SEE, THE MAN IS SUPPOSED TO BE DEAD.
DEAD?
YUP. WORD WAS HE DIED IN A PLANE ACCIDENT. A BOMB OR SOMETHING BLEW A JET UP, AND HE WAS KILLED TRYING TO DISARM IT.
I'VE EVEN SEEN A PICTURE OF HIS GRAVE IN ONE OF THE GOSSIP RAGS.
YEAH, BUT DON'T THESE GUYS 'DIE' ALL THE TIME? LIKE, DIDN'T SUPERMAN DIE ONCE? AND THEN THERE WERE, LIKE, A BUNCH OF GUYS WHO WERE TRYING TO TAKE OVER FOR HIM UNTIL HE SUDDENLY CAME BACK?
THE DIFFERENCE, I THINK, IS THAT SUPERMAN IS AN ALIEN AND OLLIE IS JUST A HUMAN BEING.
SUPERMAN'S AN ALIEN?
NO WAY!
SURE. AND WHO KNOWS HOW HIS BODY WORKS COMPARED TO OURS -- ASIDE FROM THE OBVIOUS DIFFERENCES.
BUT UNLIKE SUPERMAN, IF OLLIE DIED IN THAT PLANE CRASH, HE SHOULD HAVE STAYED DEAD. YET HE WALKS, TALKS, EATS, AND SLEEPS -- ALL BEHAVIOR NORMALLY ASSOCIATED WITH THE LIVING.
YEAH-- DRESSING UP AND SHOOTING ARROWS AT MUGGERS AND PIMPS IS NORMAL, ALL RIGHT.
WHICH WAS ANOTHER THING I WANTED TO ASK-- WASN'T THERE A DIFFERENT GREEN ARROW FOR AWHILE? A KID, LIKE? HE WAS IN THE JUSTICE LEAGUE?
THERE WAS, BUT I'VE NEVER BROUGHT IT UP. I DON'T THINK OLLIE KNOWS ABOUT HIM. IN FACT, HE DOESN'T KNOW MUCH ABOUT ANYTHING THAT'S HAPPENED OVER THE LAST DECADE OR SO.
IT'S LIKE YOU WERE SAYING BEFORE-- HE'S KIND OF STOPPED IN TIME. THE NEAREST I CAN FIGURE IS HE'S SUFFERING FROM SOME SORT OF AMNESIA.
THAT STUFF'S REAL? I THOUGHT THEY MADE THAT UP FOR SOAP OPERAS AND MOVIES!
AMNESIA'S RARE, BUT IN THIS CASE, PRETTY REAL.
FROM WHAT I'VE READ ON THE SUBJECT, AMNESIACS HAVE TO BE BROUGHT UP TO SPEED VERY SLOWLY. YOU CAN'T SHOCK THEM WITH TOO MUCH NEW INFORMATION ALL AT ONCE.
THAT'S WHY EVERYTHING SEEMS KIND OF DATED IN THIS HOUSE.
I WAS WONDERING WHY A GUY LOADED ENOUGH TO HAVE A SWANK BROWNSTONE ON PARK DIDN'T OWN A MICROWAVE, OR A DVD PLAYER, OR EVEN HAVE CABLE.
IT WASN'T ALWAYS THAT WAY AROUND HERE. I USED TO BE A HIGH-TECH NUT. I HAD ALL THE LATEST GADGETS.

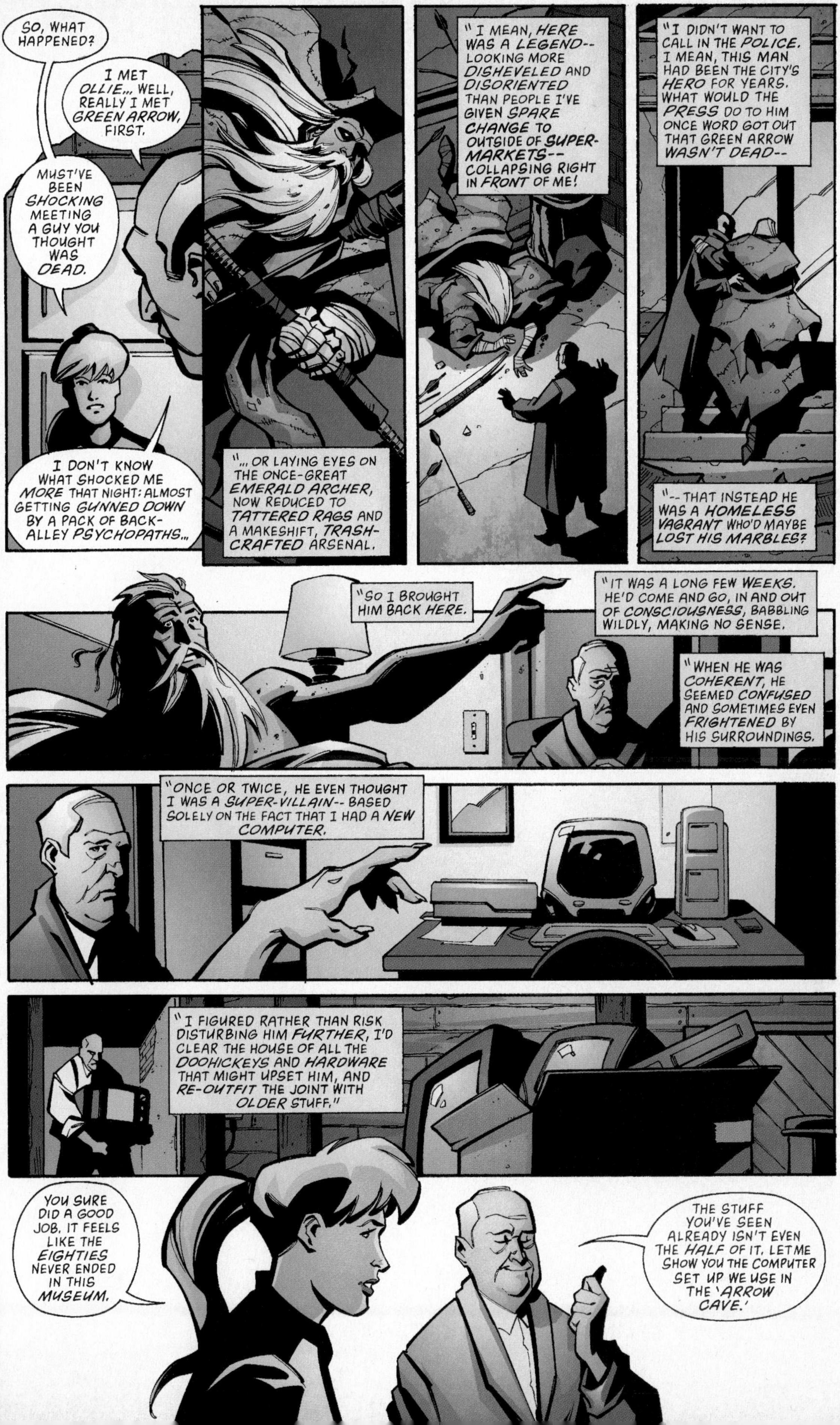
SO, WHAT HAPPENED?
I MET OLLIE... WELL, REALLY I MET GREEN ARROW, FIRST.
MUST'VE BEEN SHOCKING MEETING A GUY YOU THOUGHT WAS DEAD.
I DON'T KNOW WHAT SHOCKED ME MORE THAT NIGHT: ALMOST GETTING GUNNED DOWN BY A PACK OF BACK-ALLEY PSYCHOPATHS...
"...OR LAYING EYES ON THE ONCE-GREAT EMERALD ARCHER, NOW REDUCED TO TATTERED RAGS AND A MAKESHIFT, TRASH-CRAFTED ARSENAL.
"I MEAN, HERE WAS A LEGEND-- LOOKING MORE DISHEVELED AND DISORIENTED THAN PEOPLE I'VE GIVEN SPARE CHANGE TO OUTSIDE OF SUPER-MARKETS-- COLLAPSING RIGHT IN FRONT OF ME!
"I DIDN'T WANT TO CALL IN THE POLICE. I MEAN, THIS MAN HAD BEEN THE CITY'S HERO FOR YEARS. WHAT WOULD THE PRESS DO TO HIM ONCE WORD GOT OUT THAT GREEN ARROW WASN'T DEAD--
"-- THAT INSTEAD HE WAS A HOMELESS VAGRANT WHO'D MAYBE LOST HIS MARBLES?
"SO I BROUGHT HIM BACK HERE.
"IT WAS A LONG FEW WEEKS. HE'D COME AND GO, IN AND OUT OF CONSCIOUSNESS, BABBLING WILDLY, MAKING NO SENSE.
"WHEN HE WAS COHERENT, HE SEEMED CONFUSED AND SOMETIMES EVEN FRIGHTENED BY HIS SURROUNDINGS.
"ONCE OR TWICE, HE EVEN THOUGHT I WAS A SUPER-VILLAIN-- BASED SOLELY ON THE FACT THAT I HAD A NEW COMPUTER.
"I FIGURED RATHER THAN RISK DISTURBING HIM FURTHER, I'D CLEAR THE HOUSE OF ALL THE DOOHICKEYS AND HARDWARE THAT MIGHT UPSET HIM, AND RE-OUTFIT THE JOINT WITH OLDER STUFF."
YOU SURE DID A GOOD JOB. IT FEELS LIKE THE EIGHTIES NEVER ENDED IN THIS MUSEUM.
THE STUFF YOU'VE SEEN ALREADY ISN'T EVEN THE HALF OF IT. LET ME SHOW YOU THE COMPUTER SET UP WE USE IN THE 'ARROW CAVE.'

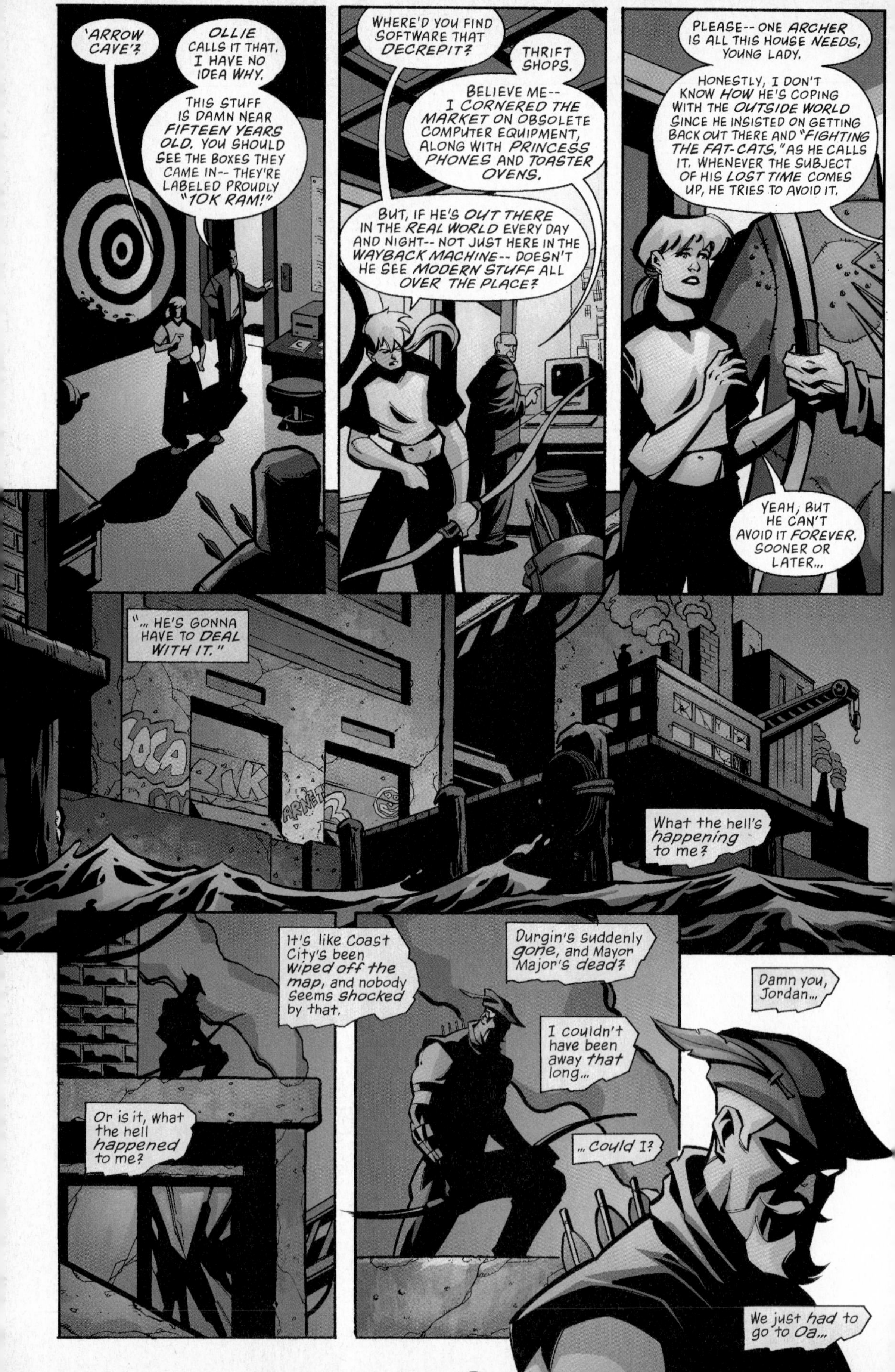

'ARROW CAVE'?
OLLIE CALLS IT THAT. I HAVE NO IDEA WHY.
THIS STUFF IS DAMN NEAR FIFTEEN YEARS OLD. YOU SHOULD SEE THE BOXES THEY CAME IN-- THEY'RE LABELED PROUDLY "10K RAM!"
WHERE'D YOU FIND SOFTWARE THAT DECREPIT?
THRIFT SHOPS.
BELIEVE ME-- I CORNERED THE MARKET ON OBSOLETE COMPUTER EQUIPMENT, ALONG WITH PRINCESS PHONES AND TOASTER OVENS.
BUT, IF HE'S OUT THERE IN THE REAL WORLD EVERY DAY AND NIGHT-- NOT JUST HERE IN THE WAYBACK MACHINE-- DOESN'T HE SEE MODERN STUFF ALL OVER THE PLACE?
PLEASE-- ONE ARCHER IS ALL THIS HOUSE NEEDS, YOUNG LADY.
HONESTLY, I DON'T KNOW HOW HE'S COPING WITH THE OUTSIDE WORLD SINCE HE INSISTED ON GETTING BACK OUT THERE AND "FIGHTING THE FAT-CATS," AS HE CALLS IT. WHENEVER THE SUBJECT OF HIS LOST TIME COMES UP, HE TRIES TO AVOID IT.
YEAH, BUT HE CAN'T AVOID IT FOREVER. SOONER OR LATER...
"... HE'S GONNA HAVE TO DEAL WITH IT."
What the hell's happening to me?
It's like Coast City's been wiped off the map, and nobody seems shocked by that.
Or is it, what the hell happened to me?
Durgin's suddenly gone, and Mayor Major's dead?
I couldn't have been away that long...
... Could I?
Damn you, Jordan...
We just had to go to Oa...

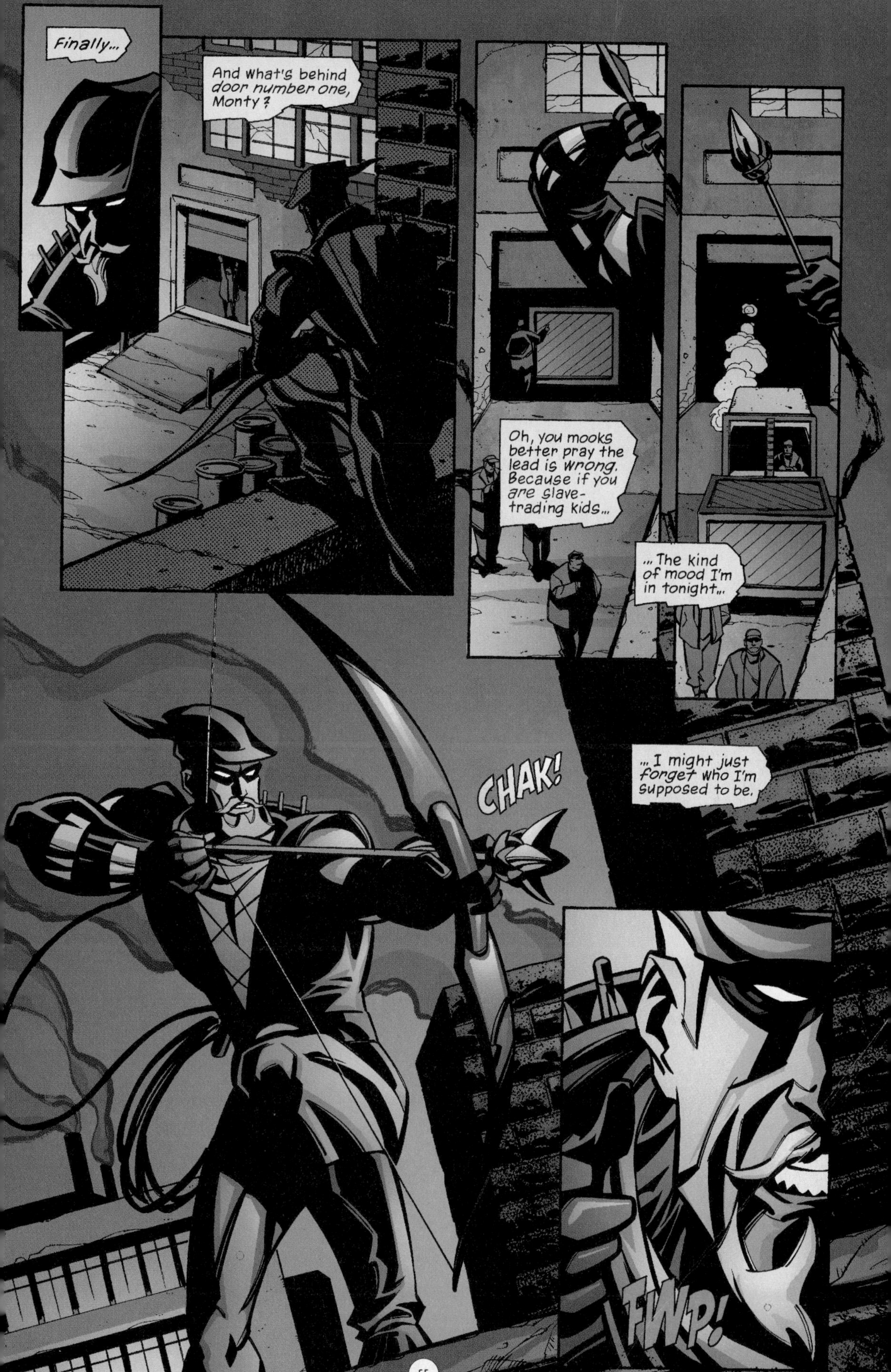
Finally...
And what's behind door number one, Monty?
Oh, you mooks better pray the lead is wrong. Because if you are slave-trading kids...
...The kind of mood I'm in tonight...
...I might just forget who I'm supposed to be.
CHAK!
FWP!

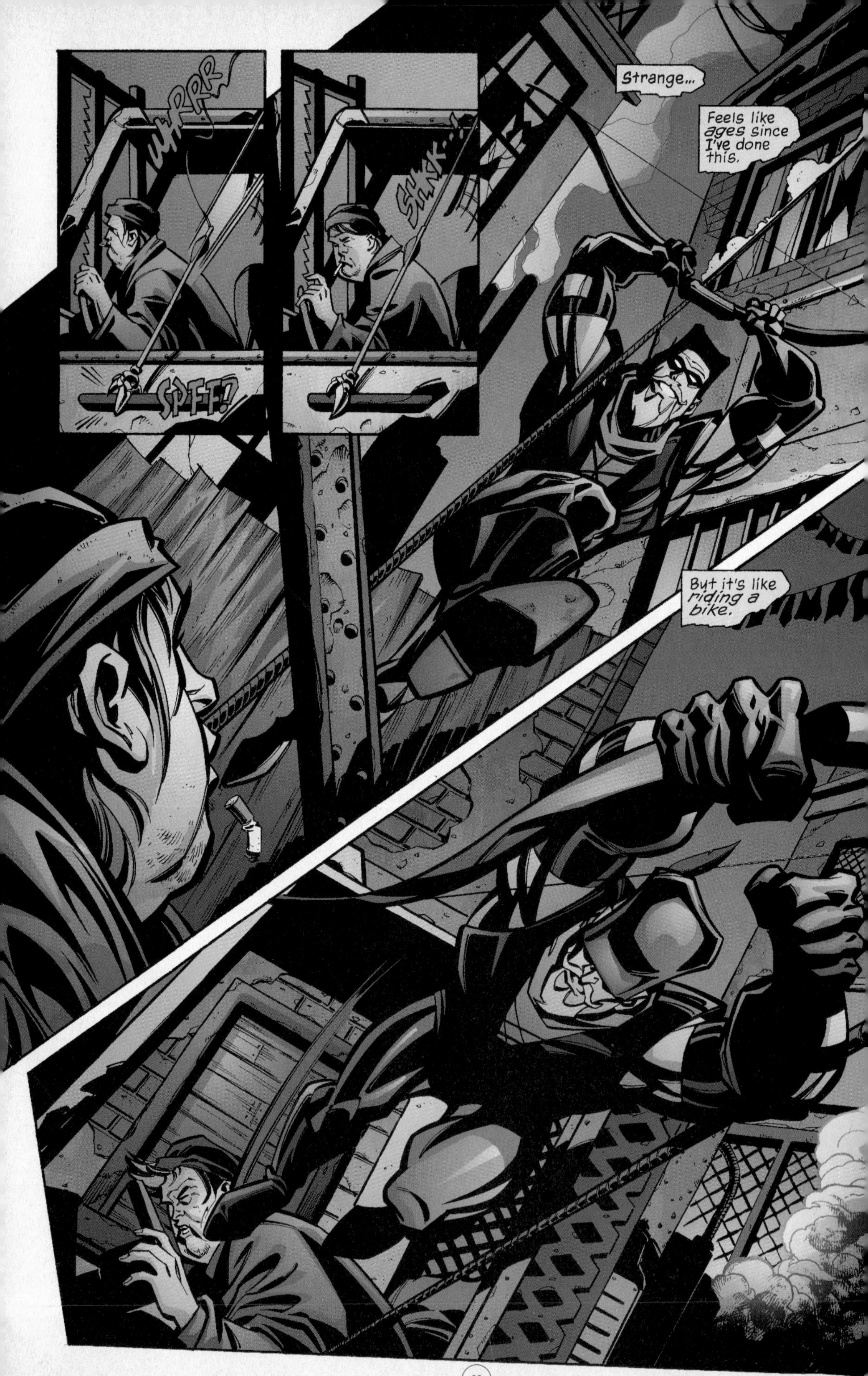
WHRRR
SPFFT?
SHNK
Strange...
Feels like ages since I've done this.
But it's like riding a bike.

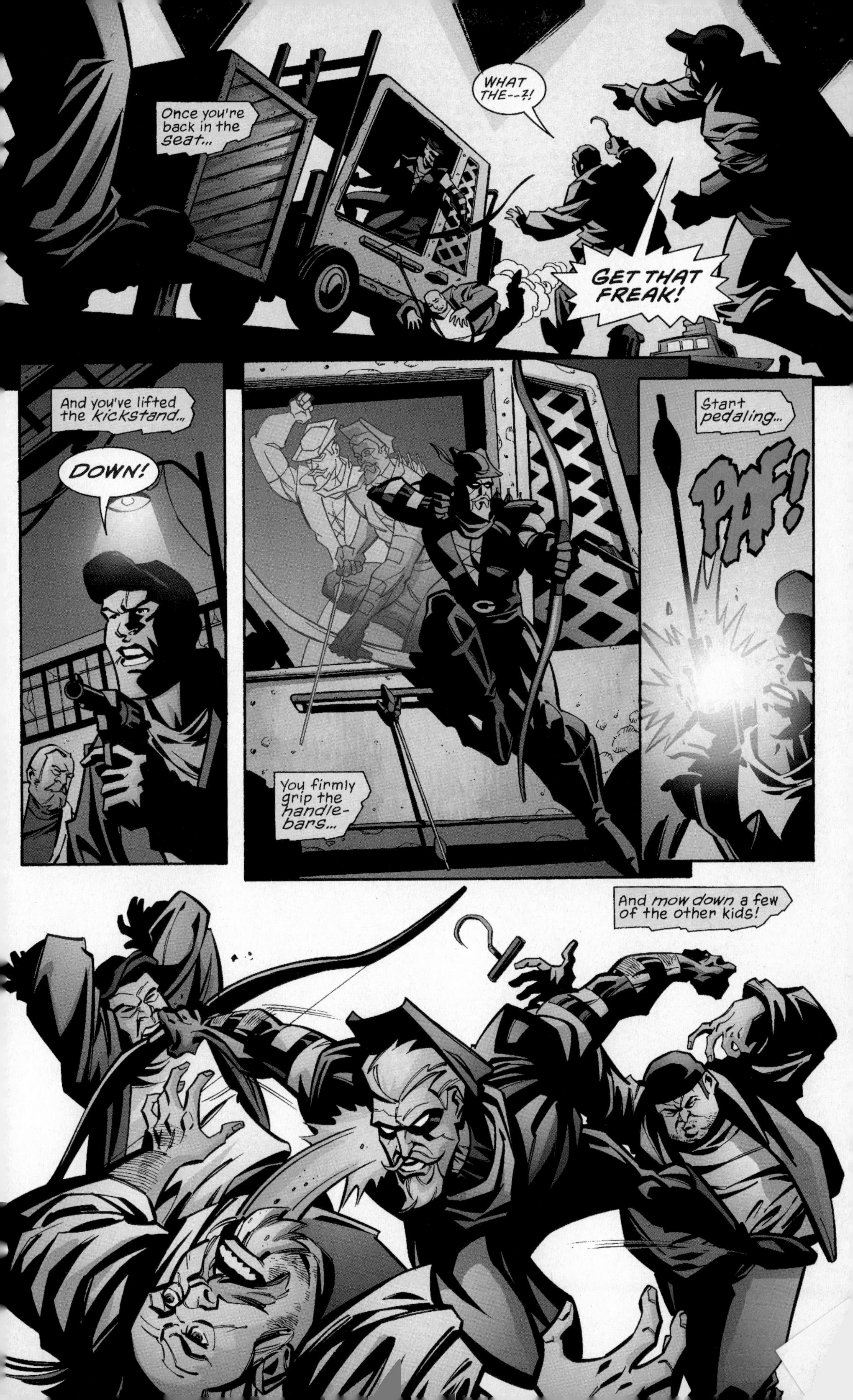
Once you're back in the seat...
WHAT THE--?!
GET THAT FREAK!
And you've lifted the kickstand...
DOWN!
You firmly grip the handle-bars...
Start pedaling...
PAF!
And mow down a few of the other kids!

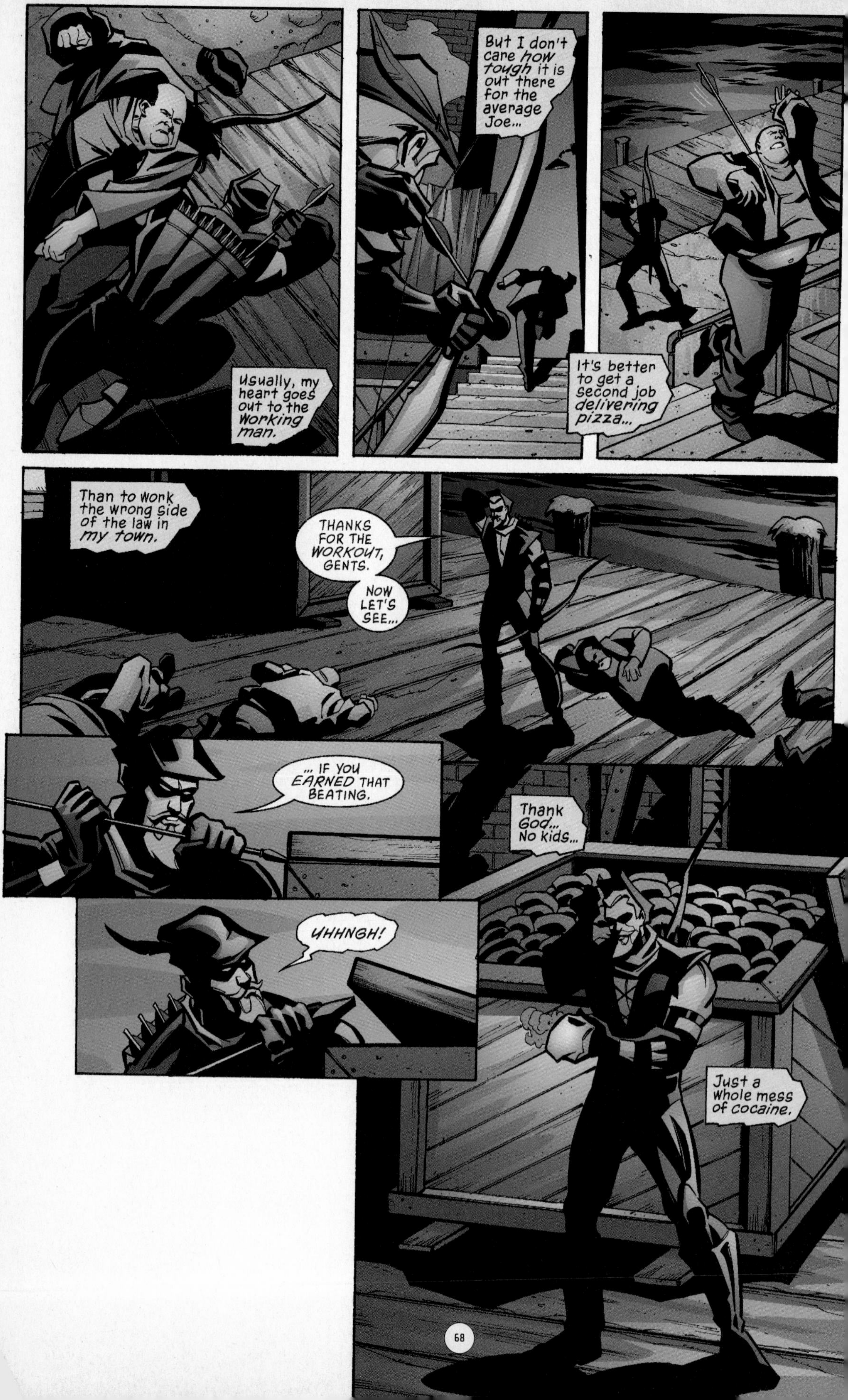
Usually, my heart goes out to the working man.
But I don't care how tough it is out there for the average Joe...
It's better to get a second job delivering pizza...
Than to work the wrong side of the law in my town.
THANKS FOR THE WORKOUT, GENTS.
NOW LET'S SEE...
... IF YOU EARNED THAT BEATING.
UHHNGH!
Thank God... No kids...
Just a whole mess of cocaine.

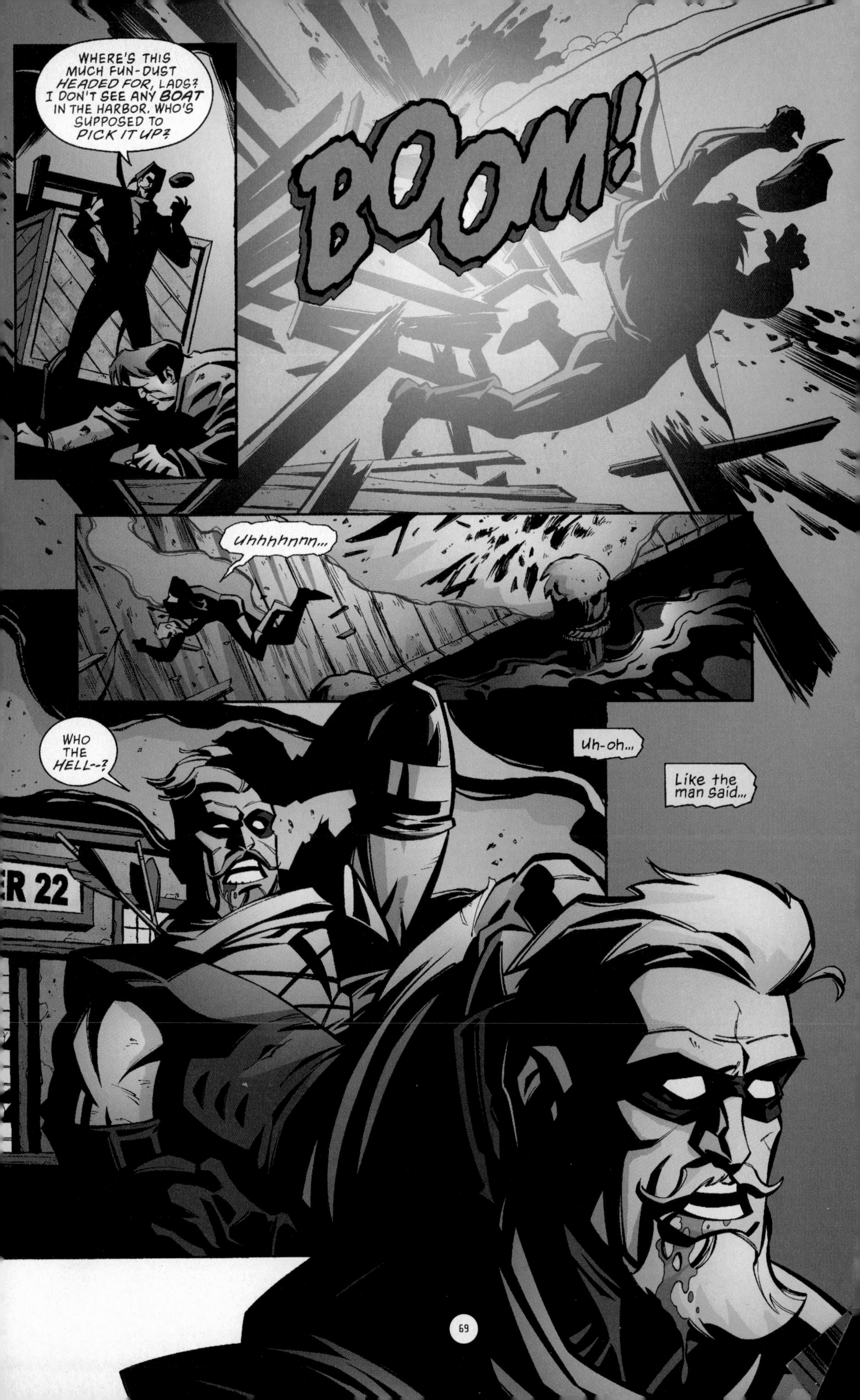
WHERE'S THIS MUCH FUN-DUST *HEADED FOR*, LADS? I DON'T SEE ANY *BOAT* IN THE HARBOR. WHO'S SUPPOSED TO *PICK IT UP*?
BOOM!
Uhhhhnnn...
WHO THE *HELL*--?
Uh-oh...
Like the man said...
ER 22

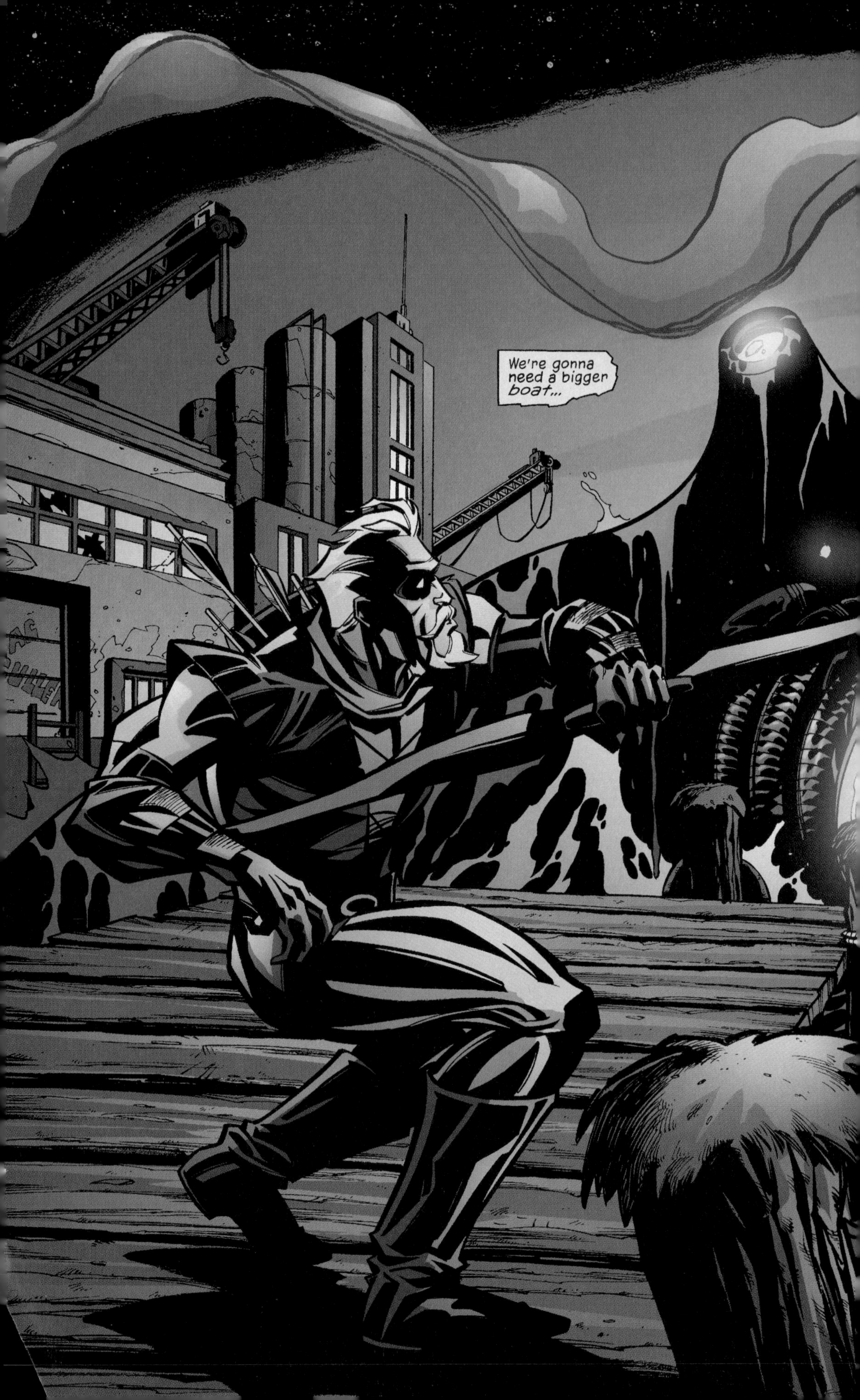
We're gonna need a bigger boat...

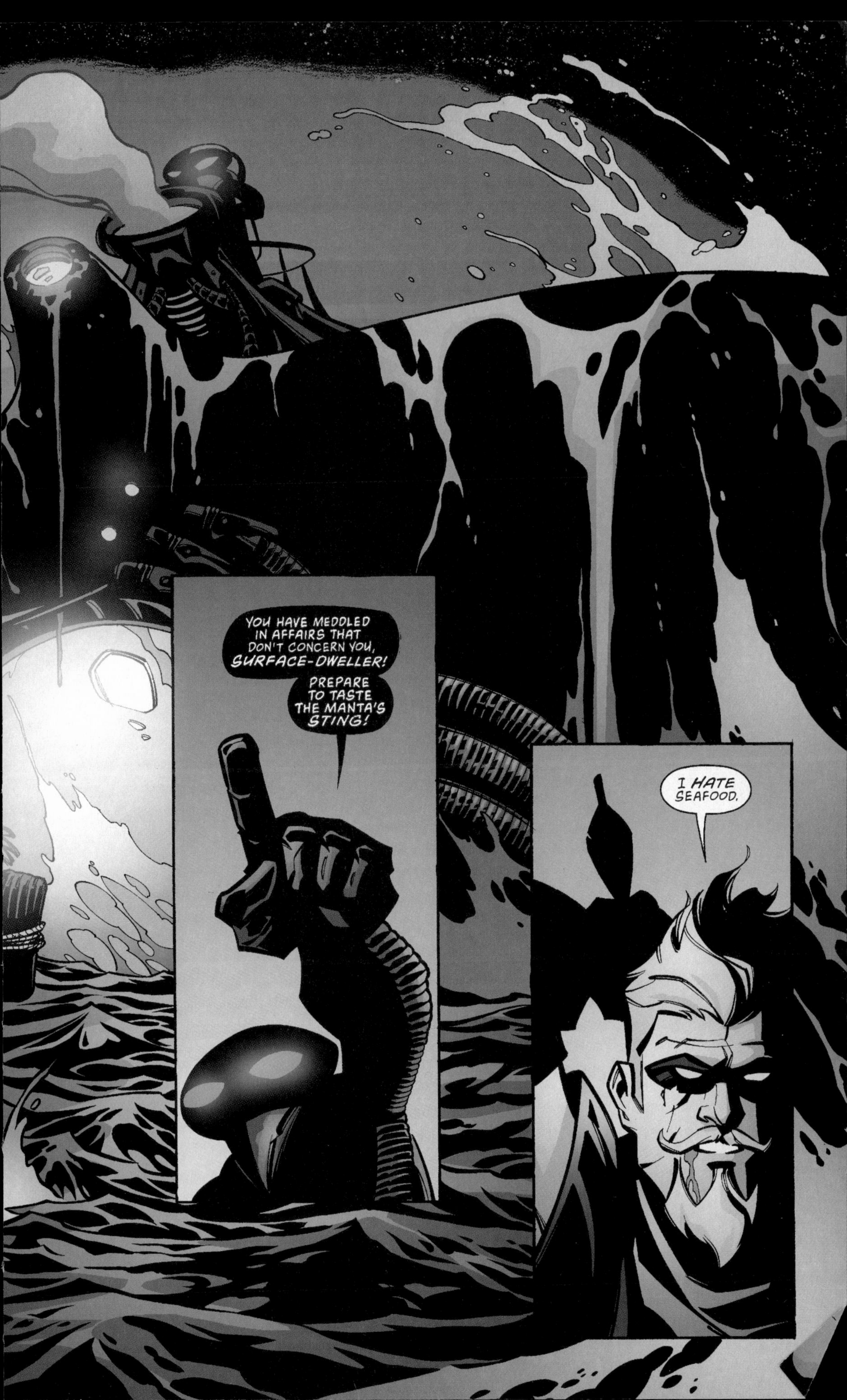
YOU HAVE MEDDLED IN AFFAIRS THAT DON'T CONCERN YOU, SURFACE-DWELLER!
PREPARE TO TASTE THE MANTA'S STING!
I HATE SEAFOOD.

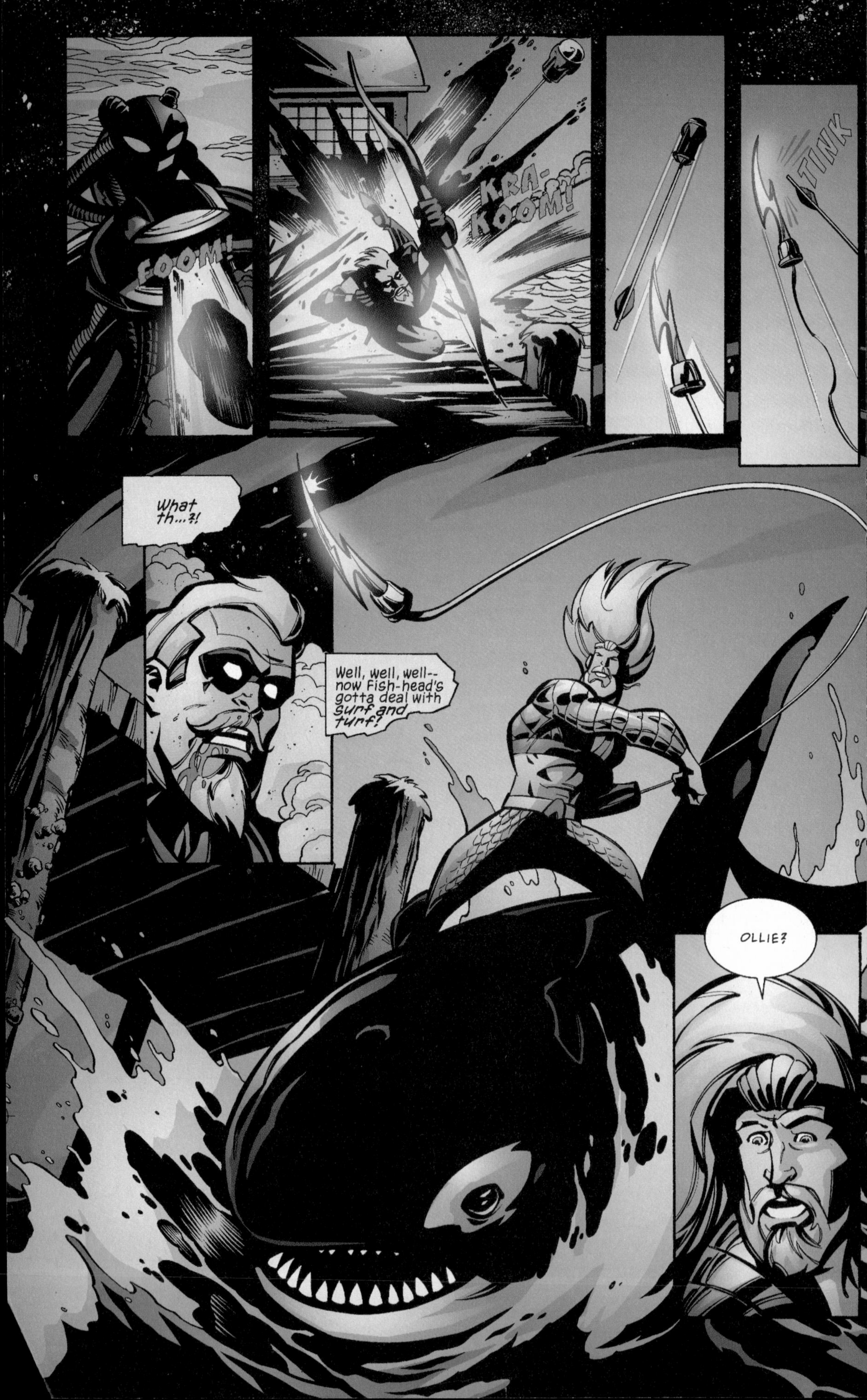
FOOM!
KRA-KOOM!
TINK
What th...?!
Well, well, well--now Fish-head's gotta deal with surf and turf!
OLLIE?

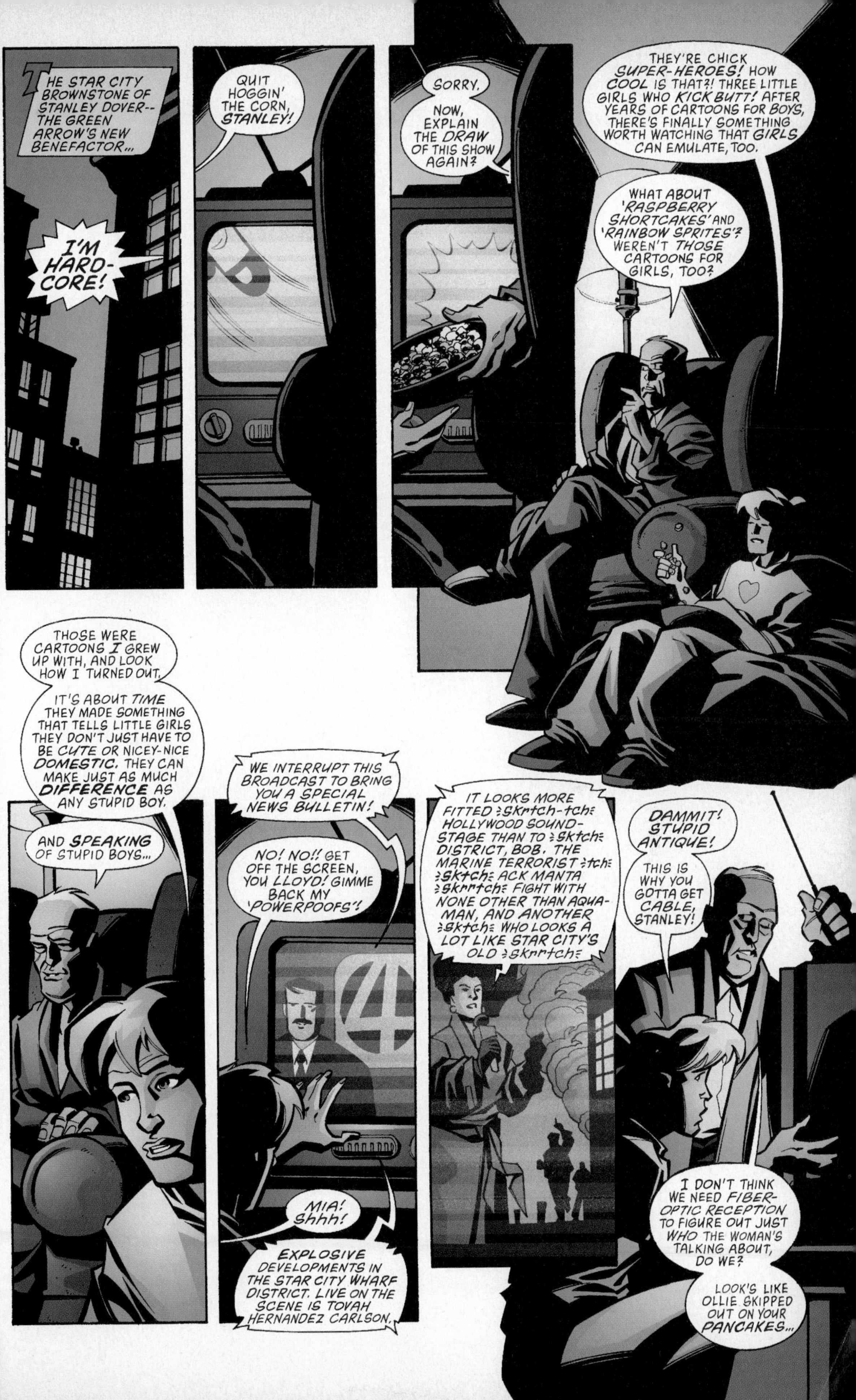
THE STAR CITY BROWNSTONE OF STANLEY DOVER-- THE GREEN ARROW'S NEW BENEFACTOR...
I'M HARD-CORE!
QUIT HOGGIN' THE CORN, STANLEY!
SORRY.
NOW, EXPLAIN THE DRAW OF THIS SHOW AGAIN?
THEY'RE CHICK SUPER-HEROES! HOW COOL IS THAT?! THREE LITTLE GIRLS WHO KICK BUTT! AFTER YEARS OF CARTOONS FOR BOYS, THERE'S FINALLY SOMETHING WORTH WATCHING THAT GIRLS CAN EMULATE, TOO.
WHAT ABOUT 'RASPBERRY SHORTCAKES' AND 'RAINBOW SPRITES'? WEREN'T THOSE CARTOONS FOR GIRLS, TOO?
THOSE WERE CARTOONS I GREW UP WITH, AND LOOK HOW I TURNED OUT.
IT'S ABOUT TIME THEY MADE SOMETHING THAT TELLS LITTLE GIRLS THEY DON'T JUST HAVE TO BE CUTE OR NICEY-NICE DOMESTIC. THEY CAN MAKE JUST AS MUCH DIFFERENCE AS ANY STUPID BOY.
AND SPEAKING OF STUPID BOYS...
WE INTERRUPT THIS BROADCAST TO BRING YOU A SPECIAL NEWS BULLETIN!
NO! NO!! GET OFF THE SCREEN, YOU LLOYD! GIMME BACK MY 'POWERPOOFS'!
MIA! Shhh!
EXPLOSIVE DEVELOPMENTS IN THE STAR CITY WHARF DISTRICT. LIVE ON THE SCENE IS TOVAH HERNANDEZ CARLSON.
IT LOOKS MORE FITTED skrtch-tch HOLLYWOOD SOUND-STAGE THAN TO sktch DISTRICT, BOB. THE MARINE TERRORIST tch sktch ACK MANTA skrrtch FIGHT WITH NONE OTHER THAN AQUA-MAN, AND ANOTHER sktch WHO LOOKS A LOT LIKE STAR CITY'S OLD skrrtch
DAMMIT! STUPID ANTIQUE!
THIS IS WHY YOU GOTTA GET CABLE, STANLEY!
I DON'T THINK WE NEED FIBER-OPTIC RECEPTION TO FIGURE OUT JUST WHO THE WOMAN'S TALKING ABOUT, DO WE?
LOOK'S LIKE OLLIE SKIPPED OUT ON YOUR PANCAKES...

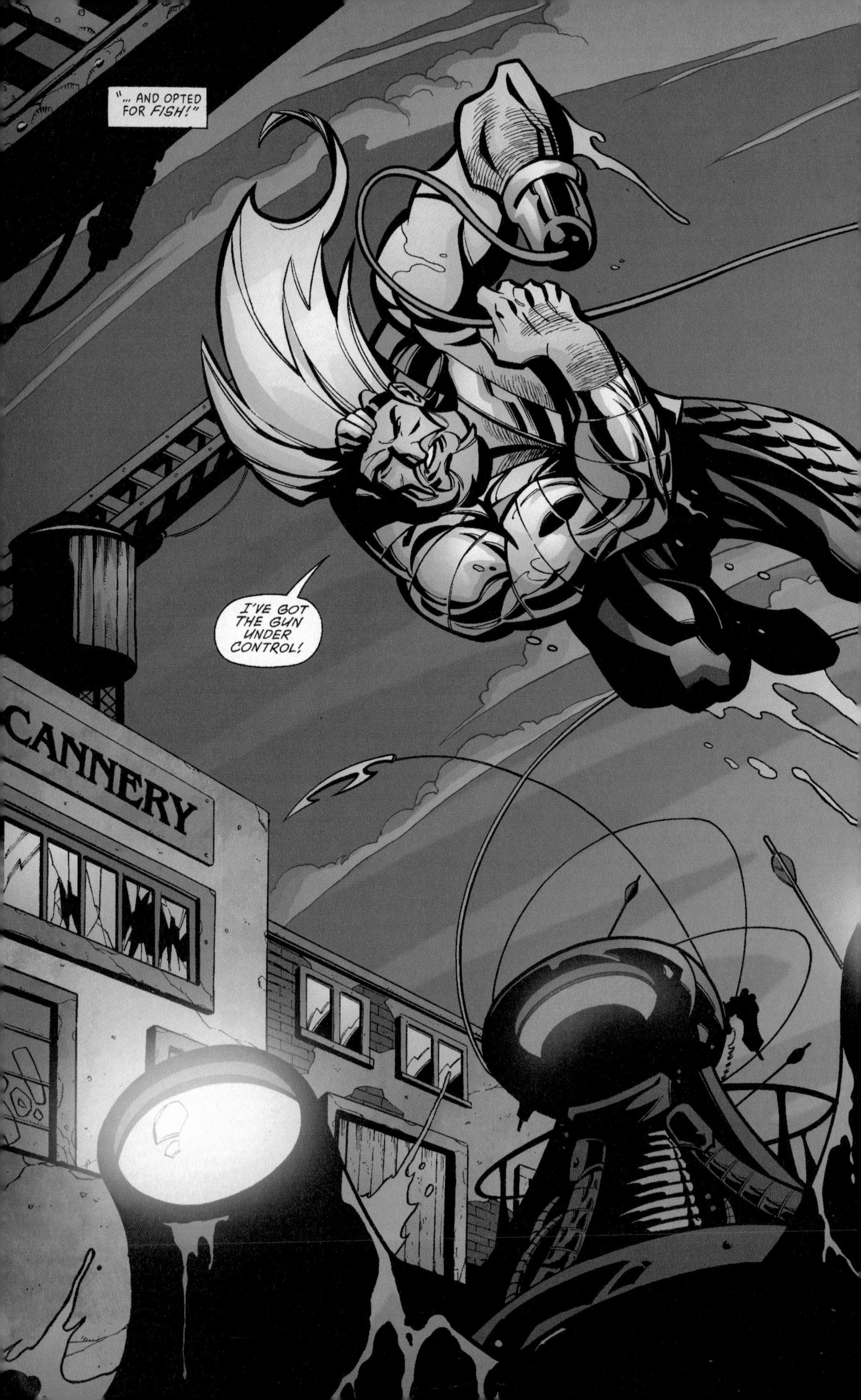
"... AND OPTED FOR FISH!"
I'VE GOT THE GUN UNDER CONTROL!
CANNERY

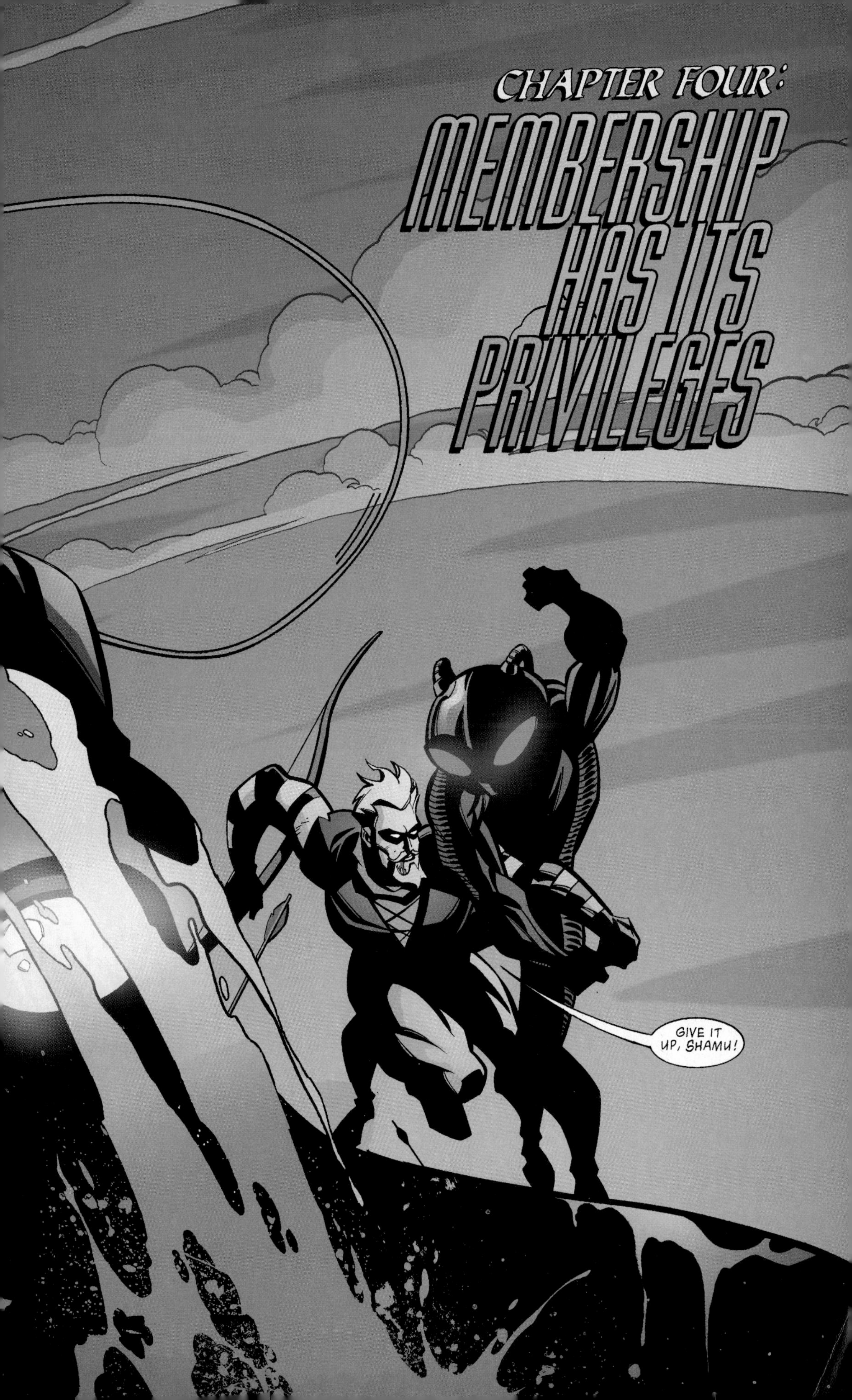
CHAPTER FOUR:
MEMBERSHIP HAS ITS PRIVILEGES
GIVE IT UP, SHAMU!

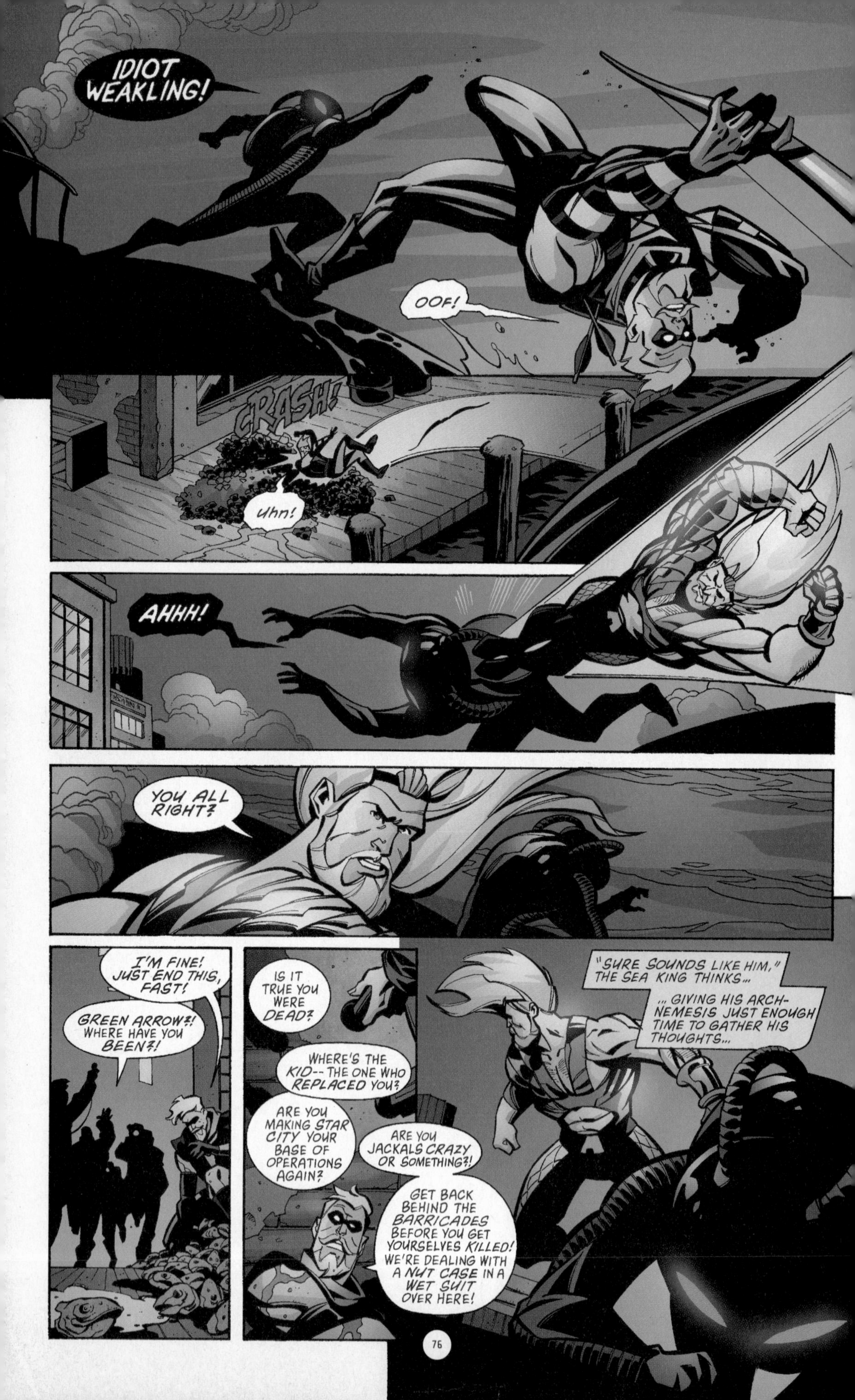
IDIOT WEAKLING!
OOF!
CRASH!
Uhn!
AHHH!
YOU ALL RIGHT?
I'M FINE! JUST END THIS, FAST!
GREEN ARROW?! WHERE HAVE YOU BEEN?!
IS IT TRUE YOU WERE DEAD?
WHERE'S THE KID-- THE ONE WHO REPLACED YOU?
ARE YOU MAKING STAR CITY YOUR BASE OF OPERATIONS AGAIN?
ARE YOU JACKALS CRAZY OR SOMETHING?!
GET BACK BEHIND THE BARRICADES BEFORE YOU GET YOURSELVES KILLED! WE'RE DEALING WITH A NUT CASE IN A WET SUIT OVER HERE!
"SURE SOUNDS LIKE HIM," THE SEA KING THINKS...
... GIVING HIS ARCH-NEMESIS JUST ENOUGH TIME TO GATHER HIS THOUGHTS...

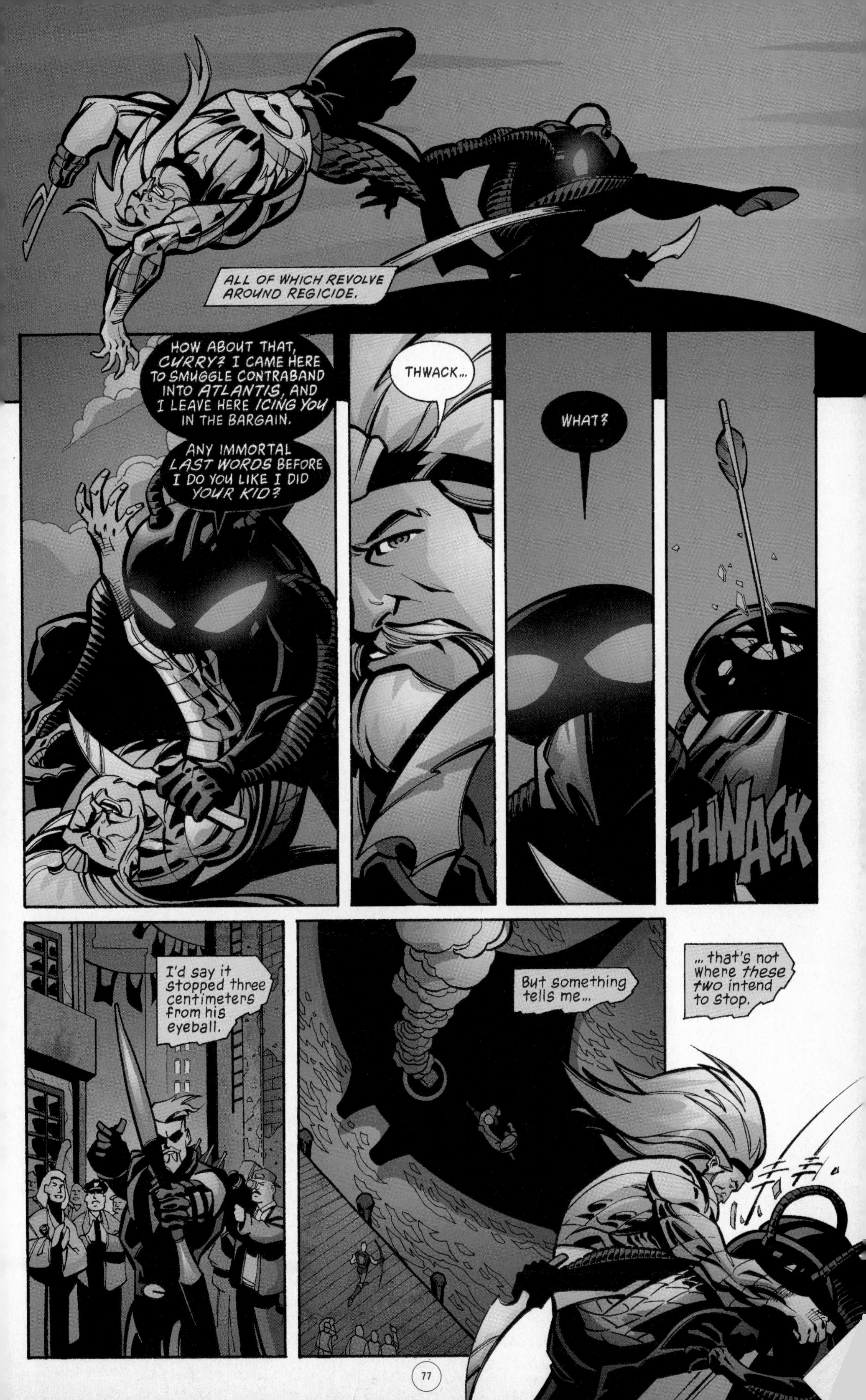
ALL OF WHICH REVOLVE AROUND REGICIDE.
HOW ABOUT THAT, CURRY? I CAME HERE TO SMUGGLE CONTRABAND INTO ATLANTIS, AND I LEAVE HERE ICING YOU IN THE BARGAIN.
ANY IMMORTAL LAST WORDS BEFORE I DO YOU LIKE I DID YOUR KID?
THWACK...
WHAT?
THWACK
I'd say it stopped three centimeters from his eyeball.
But something tells me...
...that's not where these two intend to stop.

STILL AS UGLY AS YOUR *SOUL* UNDER THIS OLD GEAR, HUNH?!

WELL, NO MATTER *WHAT* YOU COVER YOURSELF UP WITH, YOU CAN'T HIDE WHAT YOU ARE TO *ME*-- A SICK *CHILD-KILLER!*

CURRY... *NO!* PLEASE!

NO MERCY-- NOT THIS TIME! *THIS TIME...*

... YOU'RE *NOT* GETTING OFF *THE HOOK!*

AAHHHH!

FFTINGG!

SHW
SHW

What the hell *happened,* Arthur?

What the hell did you *become?*

LATER...

SO HE'S *NOT* DEALING IN THE *SLAVE-TRADING* OF KIDS?

NO. SOLELY *DRUGS* THIS TIME.

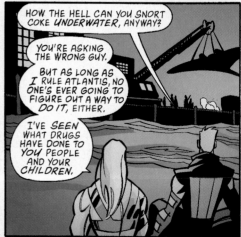

HOW THE HELL CAN YOU SNORT COKE *UNDERWATER,* ANYWAY?

YOU'RE ASKING THE WRONG GUY.

BUT AS LONG AS *I* RULE ATLANTIS, NO ONE'S EVER GOING TO FIGURE OUT A WAY TO *DO IT,* EITHER.

I'VE SEEN WHAT DRUGS HAVE DONE TO *YOU* PEOPLE AND YOUR *CHILDREN.*

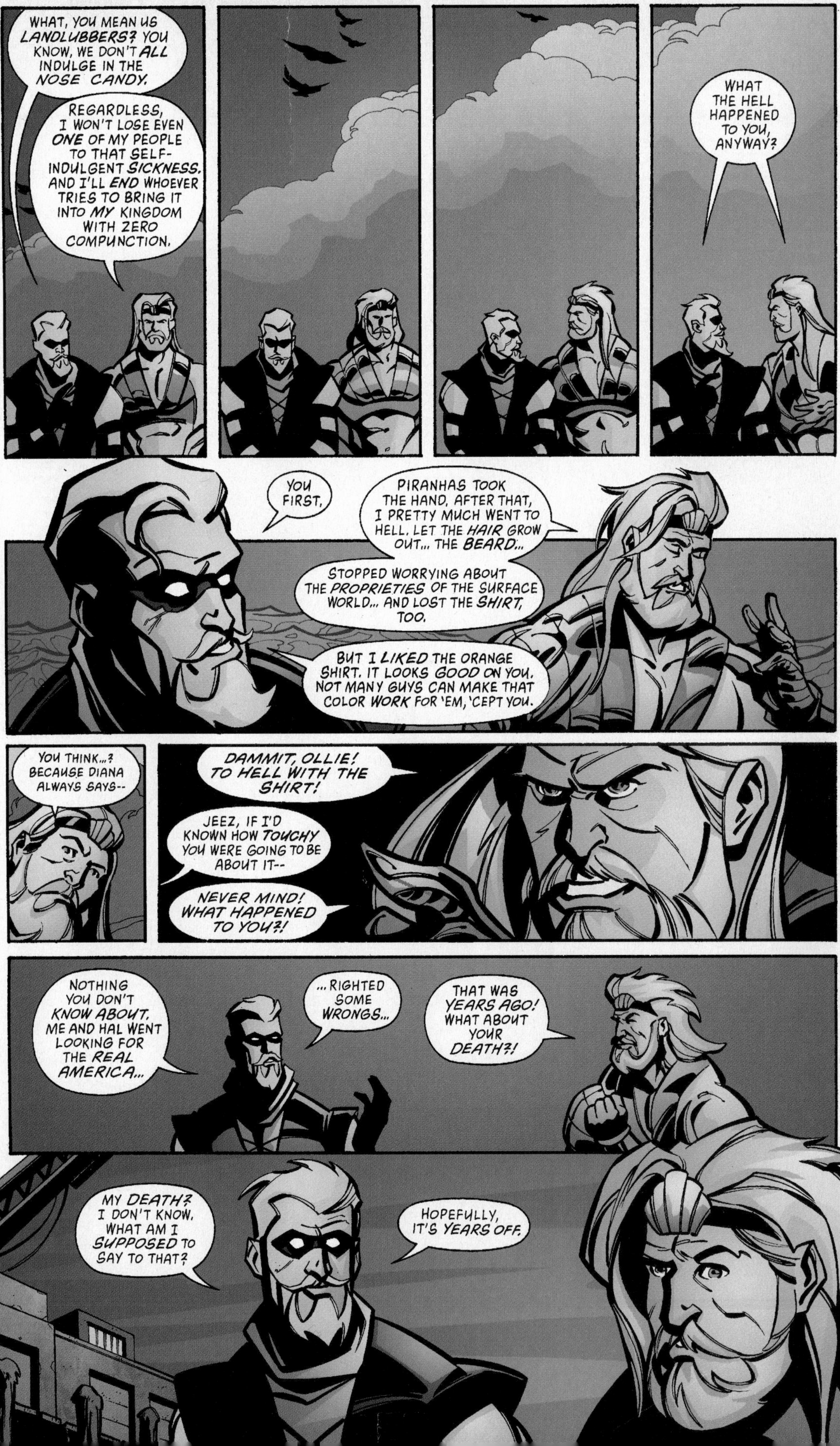
WHAT, YOU MEAN US LANDLUBBERS? YOU KNOW, WE DON'T ALL INDULGE IN THE NOSE CANDY.
REGARDLESS, I WON'T LOSE EVEN ONE OF MY PEOPLE TO THAT SELF-INDULGENT SICKNESS. AND I'LL END WHOEVER TRIES TO BRING IT INTO MY KINGDOM WITH ZERO COMPUNCTION.
WHAT THE HELL HAPPENED TO YOU, ANYWAY?
YOU FIRST.
PIRANHAS TOOK THE HAND. AFTER THAT, I PRETTY MUCH WENT TO HELL. LET THE HAIR GROW OUT... THE BEARD...
STOPPED WORRYING ABOUT THE PROPRIETIES OF THE SURFACE WORLD... AND LOST THE SHIRT, TOO.
BUT I LIKED THE ORANGE SHIRT. IT LOOKS GOOD ON YOU. NOT MANY GUYS CAN MAKE THAT COLOR WORK FOR 'EM, 'CEPT YOU.
YOU THINK...? BECAUSE DIANA ALWAYS SAYS--
DAMMIT, OLLIE! TO HELL WITH THE SHIRT!
JEEZ, IF I'D KNOWN HOW TOUCHY YOU WERE GOING TO BE ABOUT IT--
NEVER MIND! WHAT HAPPENED TO YOU?!
NOTHING YOU DON'T KNOW ABOUT. ME AND HAL WENT LOOKING FOR THE REAL AMERICA...
...RIGHTED SOME WRONGS...
THAT WAS YEARS AGO! WHAT ABOUT YOUR DEATH?!
MY DEATH? I DON'T KNOW. WHAT AM I SUPPOSED TO SAY TO THAT?
HOPEFULLY, IT'S YEARS OFF.

BUT THE *PLANE*...! WITH THE *BOMB*...! AND *SUPERMAN* SAID...! AND YOUR *GRAVE* IS...! AND *CONNOR* BECAME...! AND THE *LEAGUE*...!

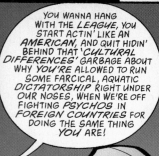

WOULD YOU QUIT YOUR *BABBLING*, YOU FIVE-FATHOM *FASCIST!* WHICH *REMINDS ME*-- WHEN THE HELL ARE YOU GOING TO ALLOW FOR SOME *DEMOCRATIC ELECTIONS* DOWN THERE?! *KINGS* WENT OUT OF STYLE WITH *RELIGIOUS PERSECUTION* IN THIS COUNTRY-- A COUNTRY YOU'RE A DE FACTO *PART OF*, BECAUSE WATER SURROUNDS MOST OF OUR BORDERS!

YOU WANNA HANG WITH THE *LEAGUE*, YOU START ACTIN' LIKE AN *AMERICAN*, AND QUIT HIDIN' BEHIND THAT *'CULTURAL DIFFERENCES'* GARBAGE ABOUT WHY *YOU'RE* ALLOWED TO RUN SOME FARCICAL, AQUATIC *DICTATORSHIP* RIGHT UNDER OUR NOSES, WHEN WE'RE OFF FIGHTING *PSYCHOS* IN *FOREIGN COUNTRIES* FOR DOING THE SAME THING *YOU* ARE!

YOU GOT ANYTHING YOU WANNA *SPUTTER OUT* NOW, I'M ALL EARS.

WELL...?!

OH, OLLIE-- I'VE *MISSED* YOU!

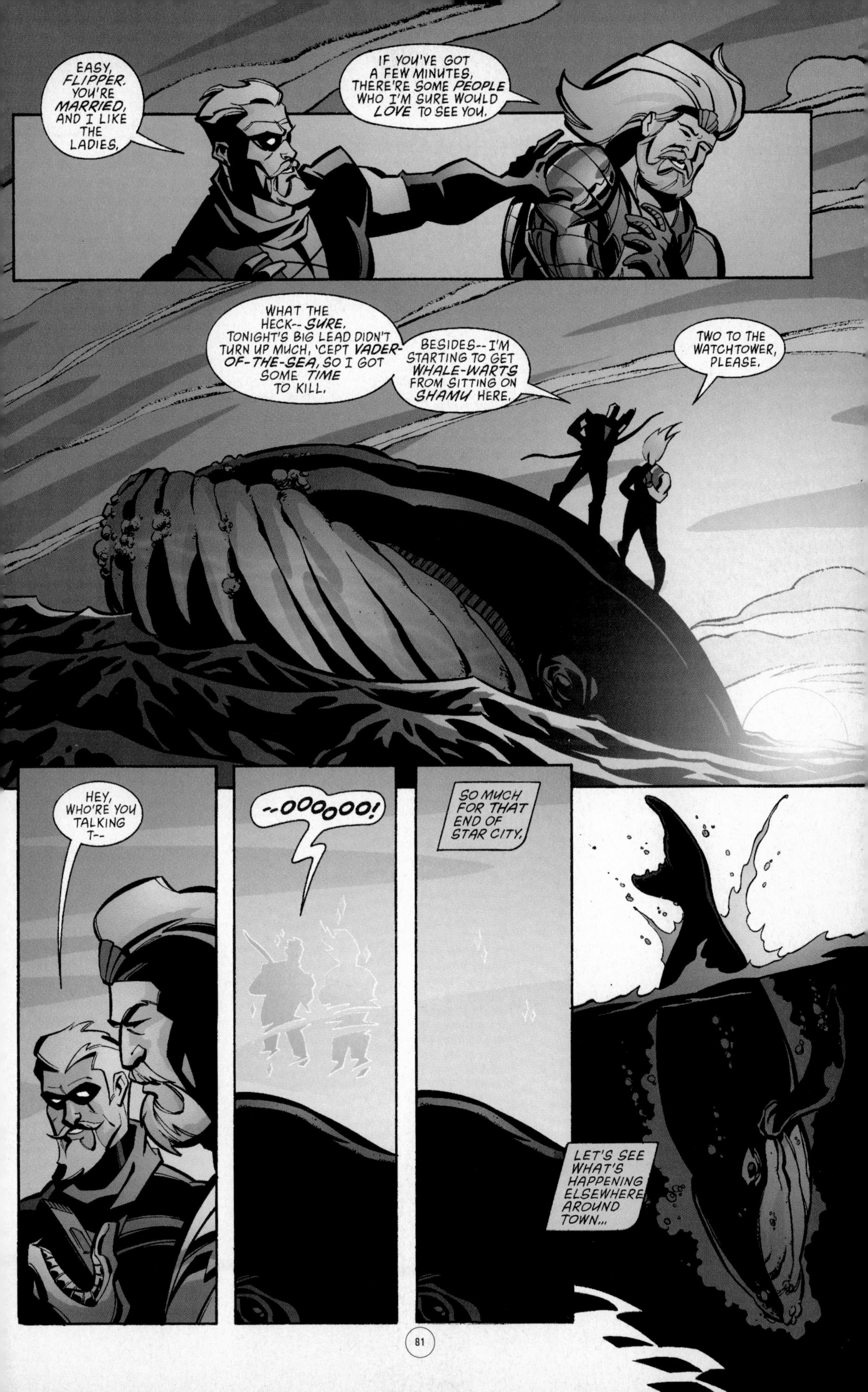
EASY, FLIPPER. YOU'RE MARRIED, AND I LIKE THE LADIES.
IF YOU'VE GOT A FEW MINUTES, THERE'RE SOME PEOPLE WHO I'M SURE WOULD LOVE TO SEE YOU.
WHAT THE HECK-- SURE. TONIGHT'S BIG LEAD DIDN'T TURN UP MUCH, 'CEPT VADER-OF-THE-SEA, SO I GOT SOME TIME TO KILL.
BESIDES-- I'M STARTING TO GET WHALE-WARTS FROM SITTING ON SHAMU HERE.
TWO TO THE WATCHTOWER, PLEASE.
HEY, WHO'RE YOU TALKING T--
--OOOOOO!
SO MUCH FOR THAT END OF STAR CITY.
LET'S SEE WHAT'S HAPPENING ELSEWHERE AROUND TOWN...

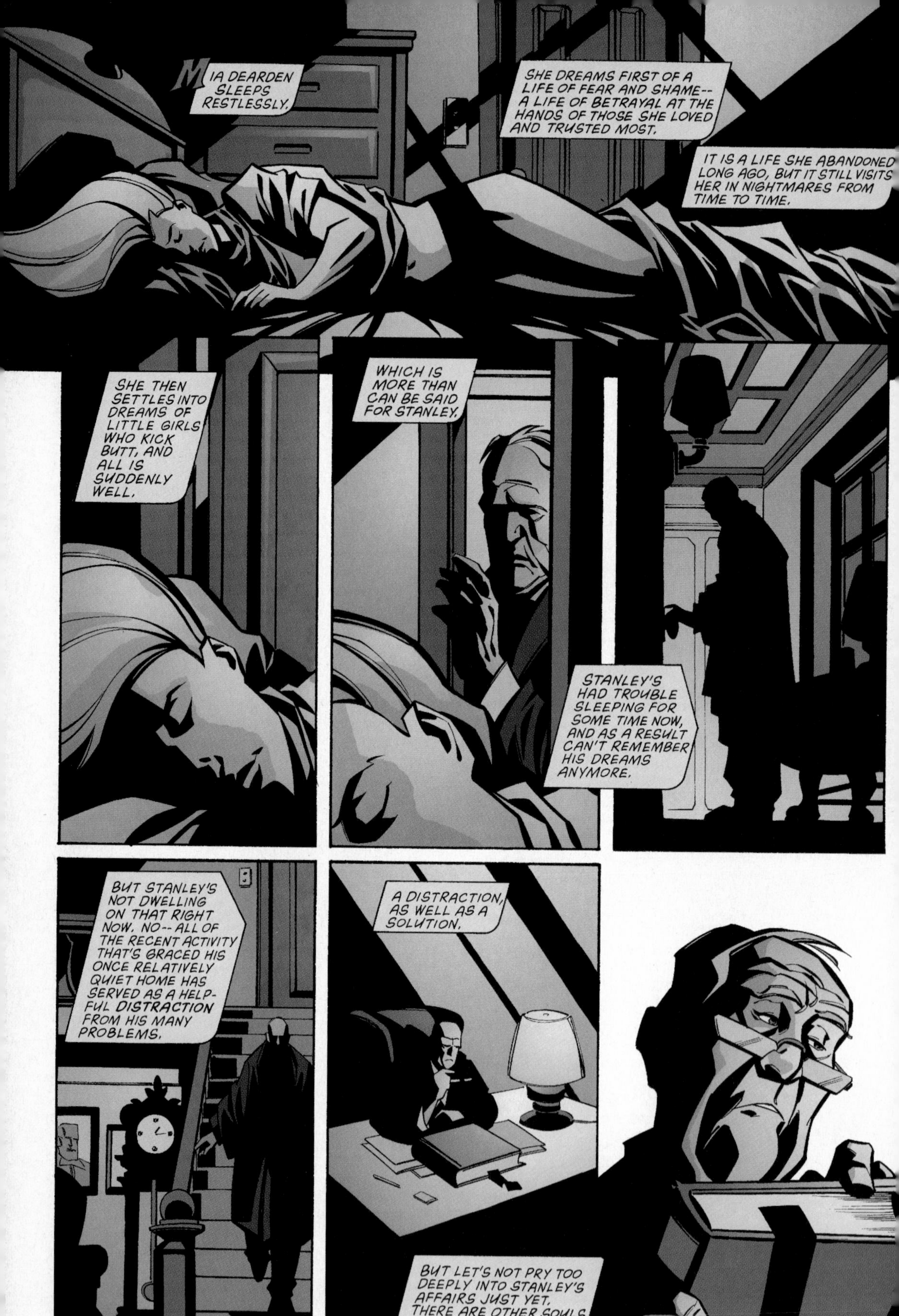
MIA DEARDEN SLEEPS RESTLESSLY.
SHE DREAMS FIRST OF A LIFE OF FEAR AND SHAME-- A LIFE OF BETRAYAL AT THE HANDS OF THOSE SHE LOVED AND TRUSTED MOST.
IT IS A LIFE SHE ABANDONED LONG AGO, BUT IT STILL VISITS HER IN NIGHTMARES FROM TIME TO TIME.
SHE THEN SETTLES INTO DREAMS OF LITTLE GIRLS WHO KICK BUTT, AND ALL IS SUDDENLY WELL.
WHICH IS MORE THAN CAN BE SAID FOR STANLEY.
STANLEY'S HAD TROUBLE SLEEPING FOR SOME TIME NOW, AND AS A RESULT CAN'T REMEMBER HIS DREAMS ANYMORE.
BUT STANLEY'S NOT DWELLING ON THAT RIGHT NOW. NO-- ALL OF THE RECENT ACTIVITY THAT'S GRACED HIS ONCE RELATIVELY QUIET HOME HAS SERVED AS A HELPFUL DISTRACTION FROM HIS MANY PROBLEMS.
A DISTRACTION, AS WELL AS A SOLUTION.
BUT LET'S NOT PRY TOO DEEPLY INTO STANLEY'S AFFAIRS JUST YET. THERE ARE OTHER SOULS TO BE LOOKED IN ON, HERE IN THE POST-MIDNIGHT QUIET OF STAR CITY...

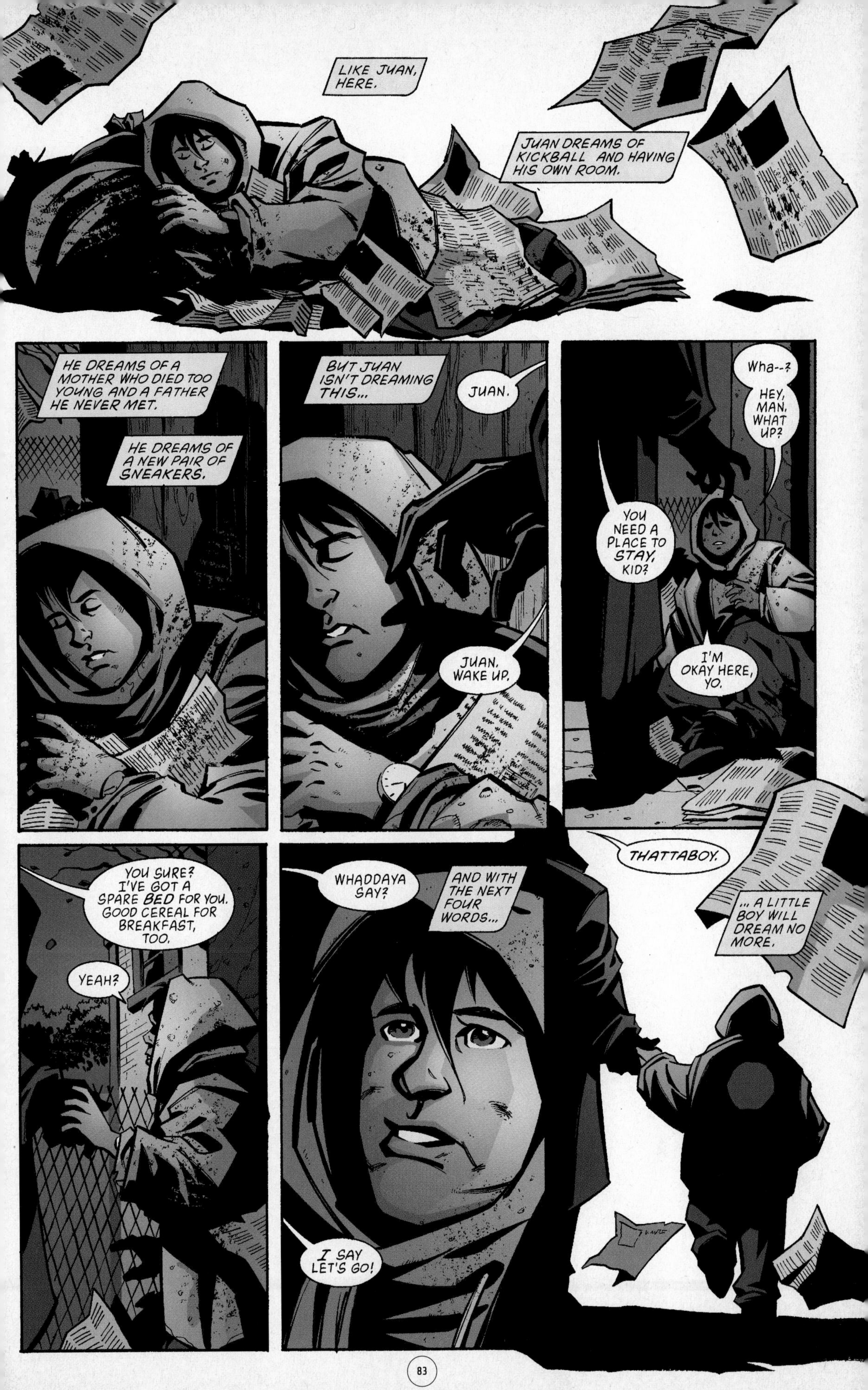
LIKE JUAN, HERE.
JUAN DREAMS OF KICKBALL AND HAVING HIS OWN ROOM.
HE DREAMS OF A MOTHER WHO DIED TOO YOUNG AND A FATHER HE NEVER MET.
HE DREAMS OF A NEW PAIR OF SNEAKERS.
BUT JUAN ISN'T DREAMING THIS...
JUAN.
JUAN, WAKE UP.
Wha--?
HEY, MAN, WHAT UP?
YOU NEED A PLACE TO STAY, KID?
I'M OKAY HERE, YO.
YOU SURE? I'VE GOT A SPARE BED FOR YOU. GOOD CEREAL FOR BREAKFAST, TOO.
YEAH?
WHADDAYA SAY?
AND WITH THE NEXT FOUR WORDS...
I SAY LET'S GO!
THATTABOY.
... A LITTLE BOY WILL DREAM NO MORE.

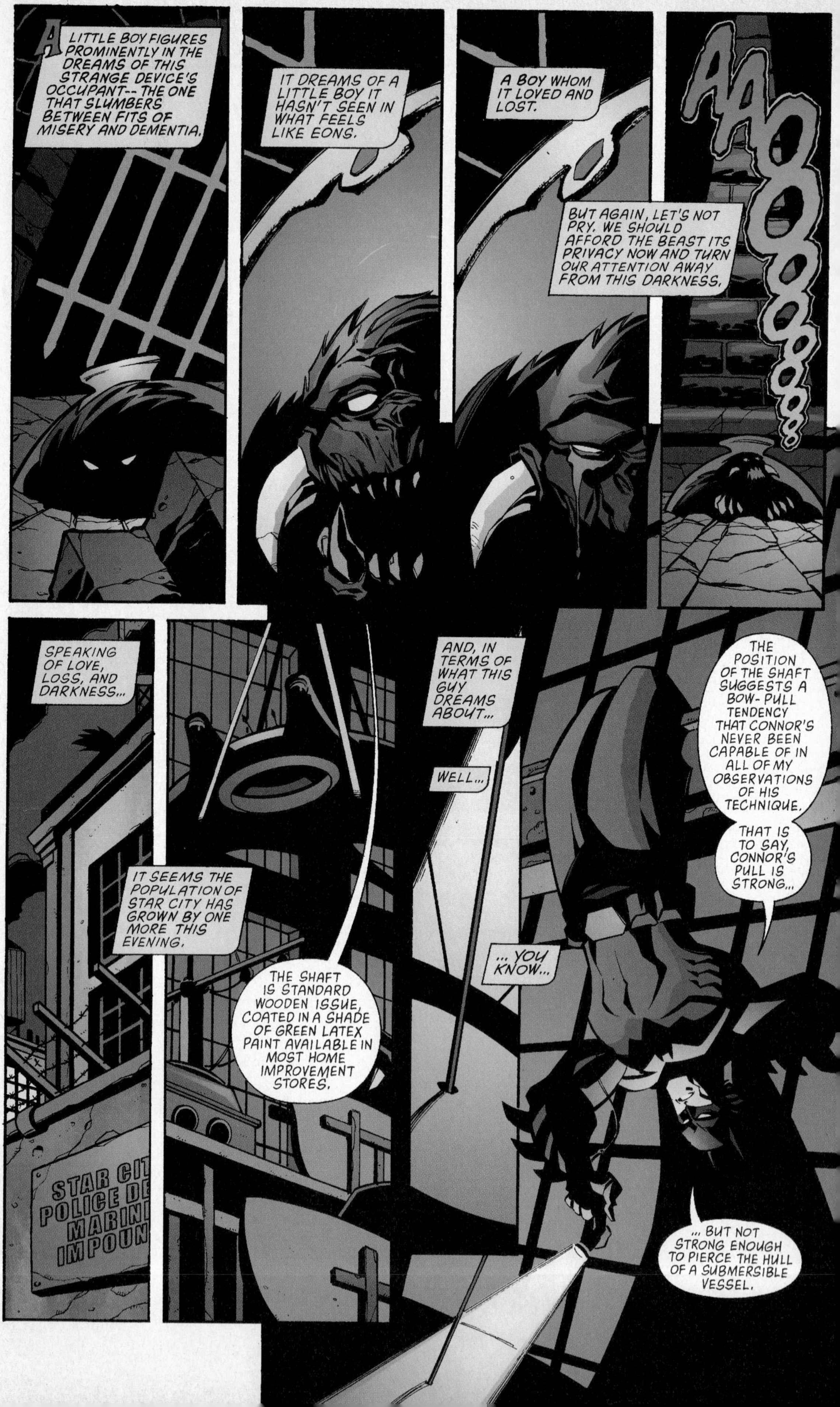
A LITTLE BOY FIGURES PROMINENTLY IN THE DREAMS OF THIS STRANGE DEVICE'S OCCUPANT-- THE ONE THAT SLUMBERS BETWEEN FITS OF MISERY AND DEMENTIA.
IT DREAMS OF A LITTLE BOY IT HASN'T SEEN IN WHAT FEELS LIKE EONS.
A BOY WHOM IT LOVED AND LOST.
BUT AGAIN, LET'S NOT PRY. WE SHOULD AFFORD THE BEAST ITS PRIVACY NOW AND TURN OUR ATTENTION AWAY FROM THIS DARKNESS.
AAAOOOOOOOOO
SPEAKING OF LOVE, LOSS, AND DARKNESS...
IT SEEMS THE POPULATION OF STAR CITY HAS GROWN BY ONE MORE THIS EVENING.
AND, IN TERMS OF WHAT THIS GUY DREAMS ABOUT...
WELL...
...YOU KNOW...
THE SHAFT IS STANDARD WOODEN ISSUE, COATED IN A SHADE OF GREEN LATEX PAINT AVAILABLE IN MOST HOME IMPROVEMENT STORES.
THE POSITION OF THE SHAFT SUGGESTS A BOW-PULL TENDENCY THAT CONNOR'S NEVER BEEN CAPABLE OF IN ALL OF MY OBSERVATIONS OF HIS TECHNIQUE.
THAT IS TO SAY, CONNOR'S PULL IS STRONG...
...BUT NOT STRONG ENOUGH TO PIERCE THE HULL OF A SUBMERSIBLE VESSEL.

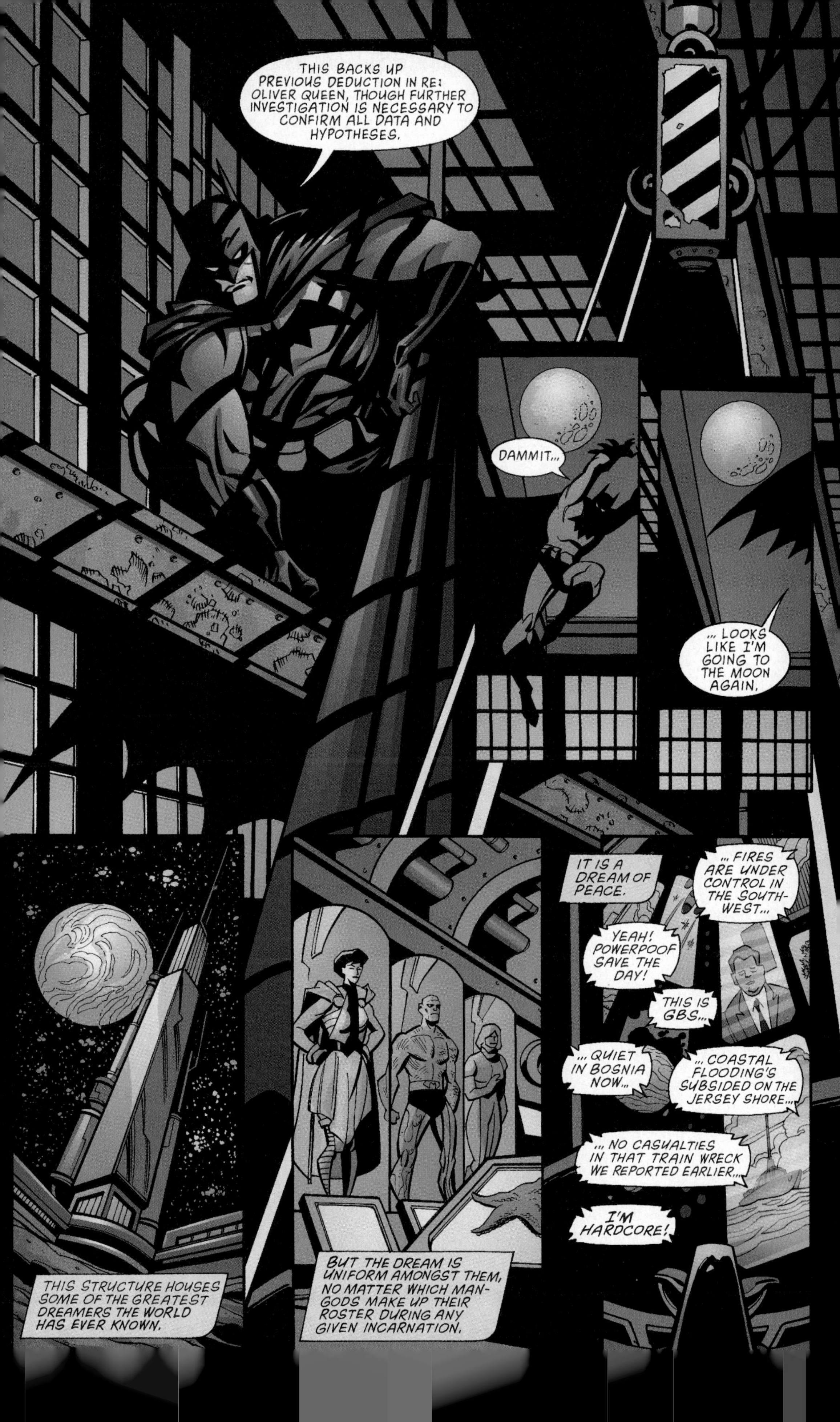
THIS BACKS UP PREVIOUS DEDUCTION IN RE: OLIVER QUEEN, THOUGH FURTHER INVESTIGATION IS NECESSARY TO CONFIRM ALL DATA AND HYPOTHESES.
DAMMIT...
...LOOKS LIKE I'M GOING TO THE MOON AGAIN.
THIS STRUCTURE HOUSES SOME OF THE GREATEST DREAMERS THE WORLD HAS EVER KNOWN.
BUT THE DREAM IS UNIFORM AMONGST THEM, NO MATTER WHICH MAN-GODS MAKE UP THEIR ROSTER DURING ANY GIVEN INCARNATION.
IT IS A DREAM OF PEACE.
...FIRES ARE UNDER CONTROL IN THE SOUTH-WEST...
YEAH! POWERPOOF SAVE THE DAY!
THIS IS GBS...
...QUIET IN BOSNIA NOW...
...COASTAL FLOODING'S SUBSIDED ON THE JERSEY SHORE...
...NO CASUALTIES IN THAT TRAIN WRECK WE REPORTED EARLIER...
I'M HARDCORE!

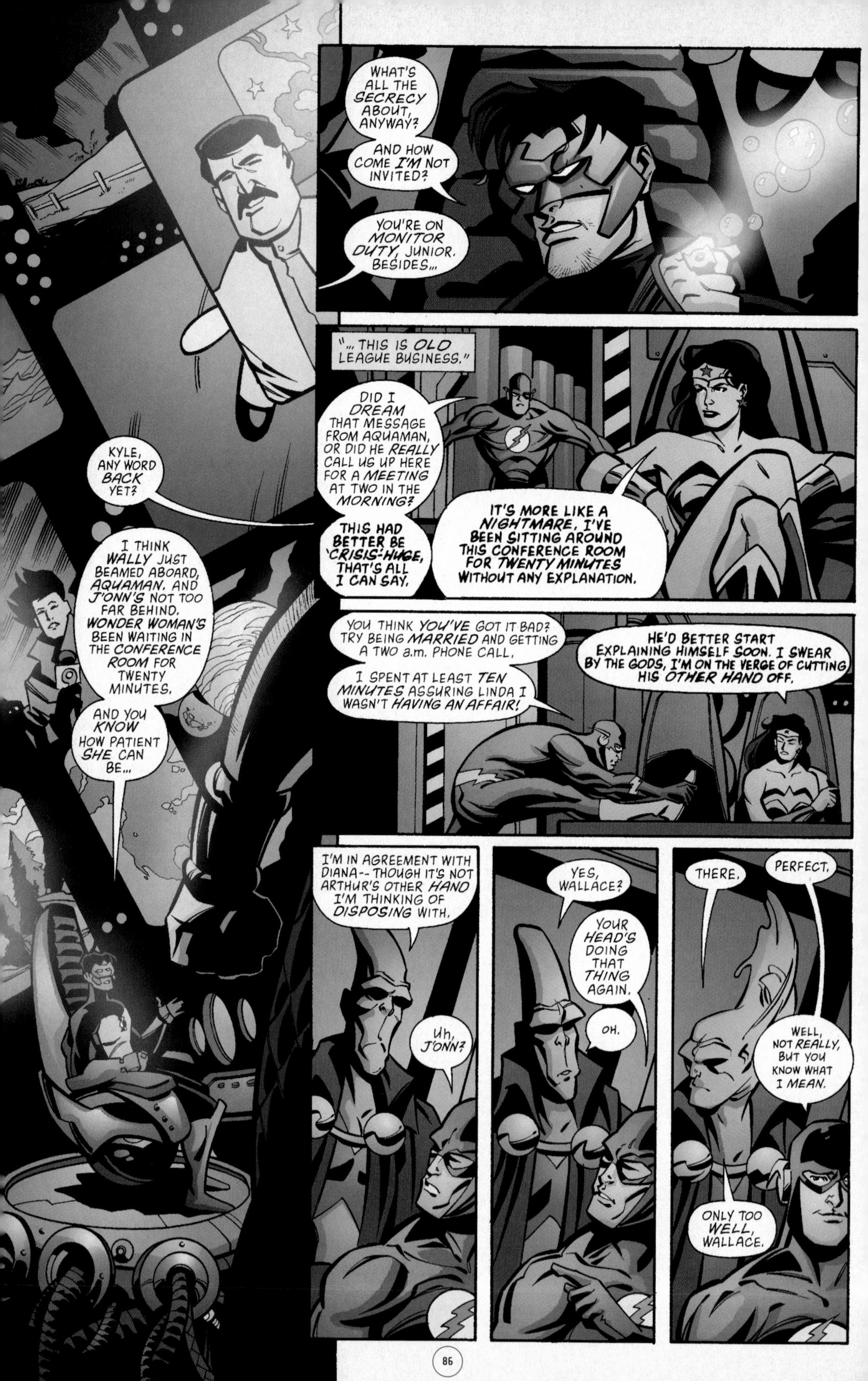

KYLE, ANY WORD BACK YET?
I THINK WALLY JUST BEAMED ABOARD, AQUAMAN. AND J'ONN'S NOT TOO FAR BEHIND. WONDER WOMAN'S BEEN WAITING IN THE CONFERENCE ROOM FOR TWENTY MINUTES.
AND YOU KNOW HOW PATIENT SHE CAN BE...
WHAT'S ALL THE SECRECY ABOUT, ANYWAY?
AND HOW COME I'M NOT INVITED?
YOU'RE ON MONITOR DUTY, JUNIOR. BESIDES...
"...THIS IS OLD LEAGUE BUSINESS."
DID I DREAM THAT MESSAGE FROM AQUAMAN, OR DID HE REALLY CALL US UP HERE FOR A MEETING AT TWO IN THE MORNING?
THIS HAD BETTER BE 'CRISIS'-HUGE, THAT'S ALL I CAN SAY.
IT'S MORE LIKE A NIGHTMARE. I'VE BEEN SITTING AROUND THIS CONFERENCE ROOM FOR TWENTY MINUTES WITHOUT ANY EXPLANATION.
YOU THINK YOU'VE GOT IT BAD? TRY BEING MARRIED AND GETTING A TWO a.m. PHONE CALL.
I SPENT AT LEAST TEN MINUTES ASSURING LINDA I WASN'T HAVING AN AFFAIR!
HE'D BETTER START EXPLAINING HIMSELF SOON. I SWEAR BY THE GODS, I'M ON THE VERGE OF CUTTING HIS OTHER HAND OFF.
I'M IN AGREEMENT WITH DIANA-- THOUGH IT'S NOT ARTHUR'S OTHER HAND I'M THINKING OF DISPOSING WITH.
Uh, J'ONN?
YES, WALLACE?
YOUR HEAD'S DOING THAT THING AGAIN.
OH.
THERE.
PERFECT.
WELL, NOT REALLY, BUT YOU KNOW WHAT I MEAN.
ONLY TOO WELL, WALLACE.

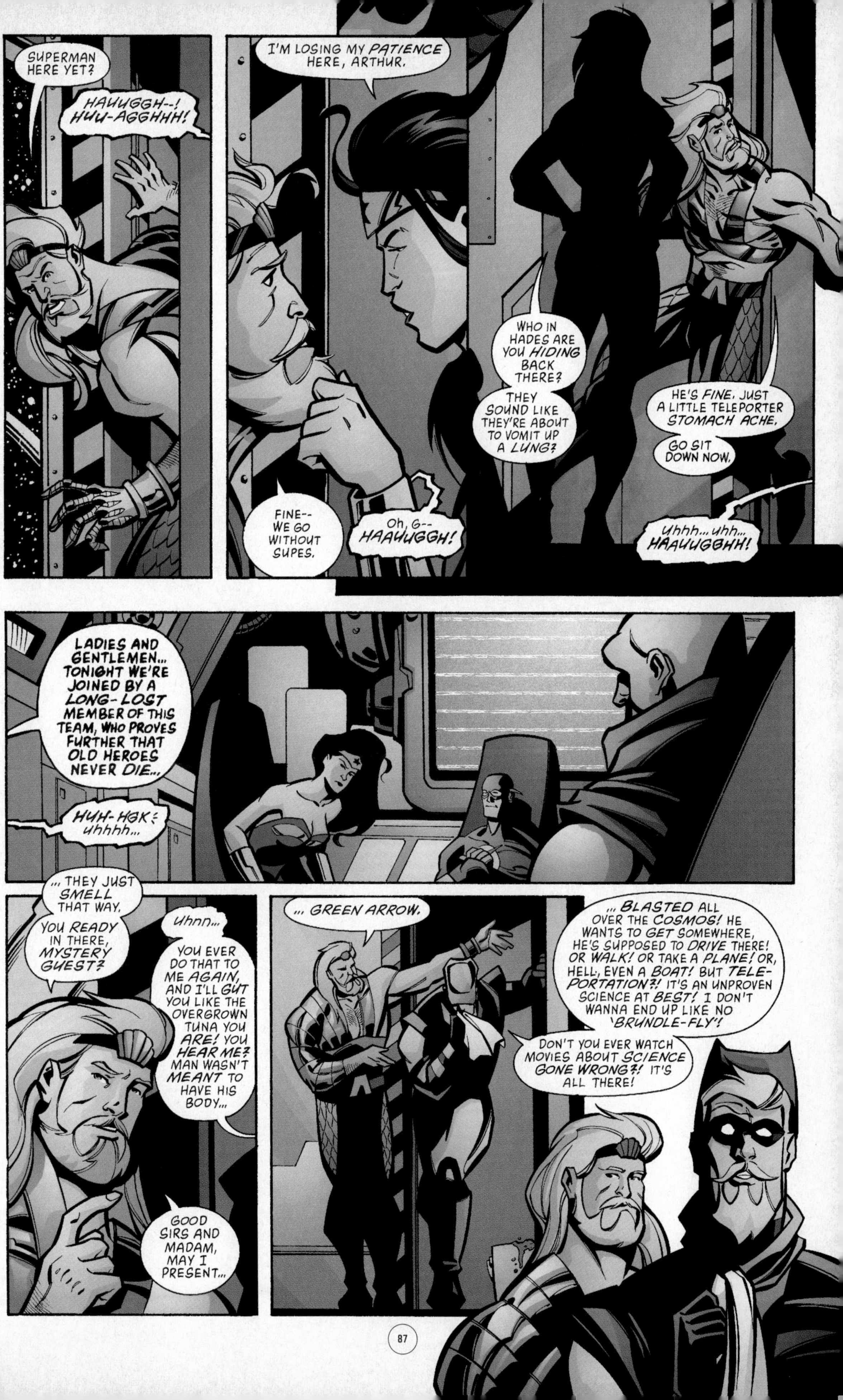
SUPERMAN HERE YET?
HAAUUGGH--! HUU-AGGHHH!
I'M LOSING MY PATIENCE HERE, ARTHUR.
FINE-- WE GO WITHOUT SUPES.
Oh, G-- HAAUUGGH!
WHO IN HADES ARE YOU HIDING BACK THERE?
THEY SOUND LIKE THEY'RE ABOUT TO VOMIT UP A LUNG?
HE'S FINE. JUST A LITTLE TELEPORTER STOMACH ACHE.
GO SIT DOWN NOW.
Uhhh... uhh... HAAUUGGHH!
LADIES AND GENTLEMEN... TONIGHT WE'RE JOINED BY A LONG-LOST MEMBER OF THIS TEAM, WHO PROVES FURTHER THAT OLD HEROES NEVER DIE...
HUH-HGK! uhhhh...
...THEY JUST SMELL THAT WAY.
YOU READY IN THERE, MYSTERY GUEST?
Uhnn...
YOU EVER DO THAT TO ME AGAIN, AND I'LL GUT YOU LIKE THE OVERGROWN TUNA YOU ARE! YOU HEAR ME? MAN WASN'T MEANT TO HAVE HIS BODY...
GOOD SIRS AND MADAM, MAY I PRESENT...
...GREEN ARROW.
...BLASTED ALL OVER THE COSMOS! HE WANTS TO GET SOMEWHERE, HE'S SUPPOSED TO DRIVE THERE! OR WALK! OR TAKE A PLANE! OR, HELL, EVEN A BOAT! BUT TELE-PORTATION?! IT'S AN UNPROVEN SCIENCE AT BEST! I DON'T WANNA END UP LIKE NO 'BRUNDLE-FLY'!
DON'T YOU EVER WATCH MOVIES ABOUT SCIENCE GONE WRONG?! IT'S ALL THERE!

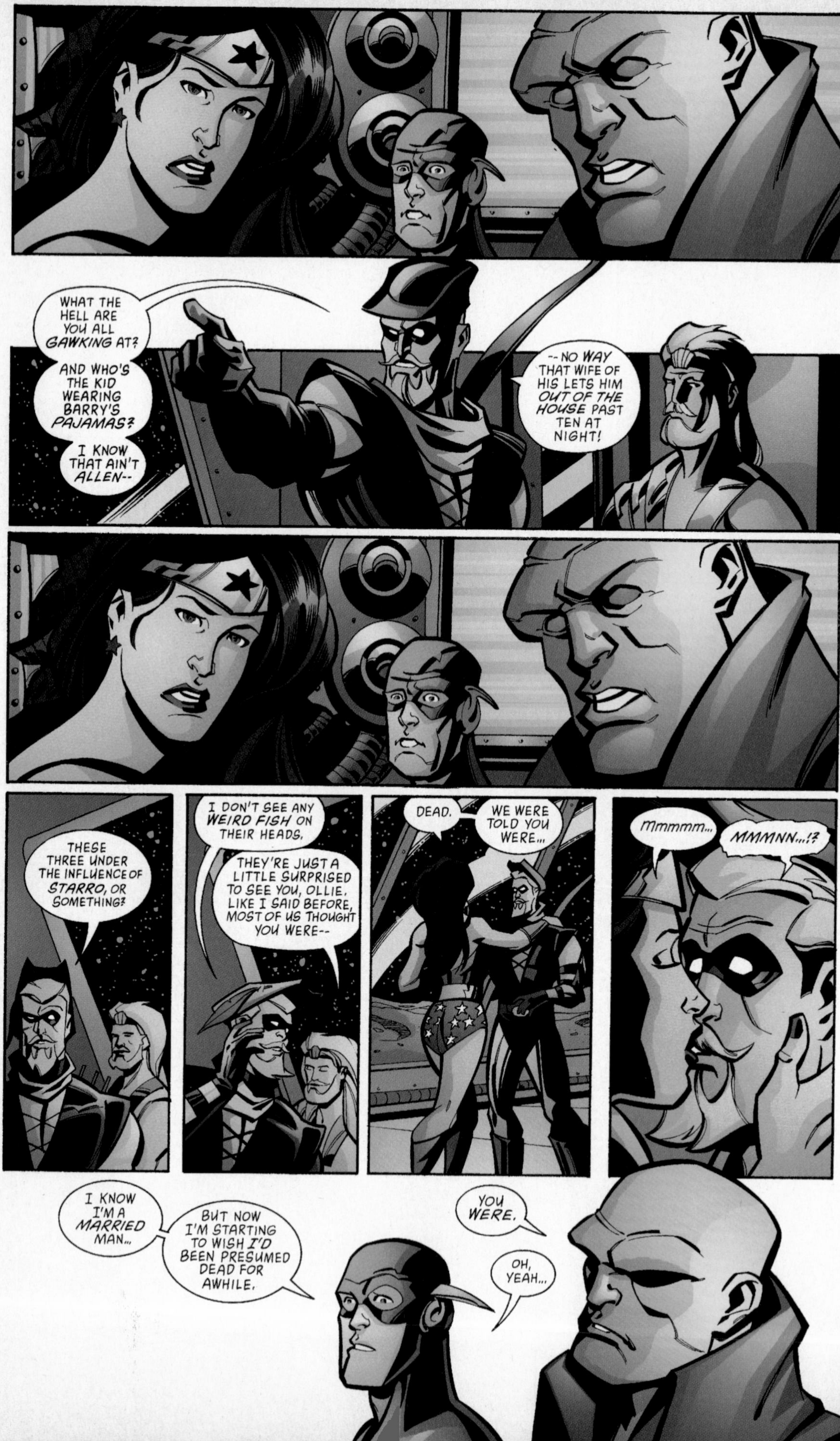
WHAT THE HELL ARE YOU ALL GAWKING AT?
AND WHO'S THE KID WEARING BARRY'S PAJAMAS?
I KNOW THAT AIN'T ALLEN--
--NO WAY THAT WIFE OF HIS LETS HIM OUT OF THE HOUSE PAST TEN AT NIGHT!
THESE THREE UNDER THE INFLUENCE OF STARRO, OR SOMETHING?
I DON'T SEE ANY WEIRD FISH ON THEIR HEADS.
THEY'RE JUST A LITTLE SURPRISED TO SEE YOU, OLLIE. LIKE I SAID BEFORE, MOST OF US THOUGHT YOU WERE--
DEAD.
WE WERE TOLD YOU WERE...
Mmmmm...
MMMNN...!?
I KNOW I'M A MARRIED MAN...
BUT NOW I'M STARTING TO WISH I'D BEEN PRESUMED DEAD FOR AWHILE.
YOU WERE.
OH, YEAH...

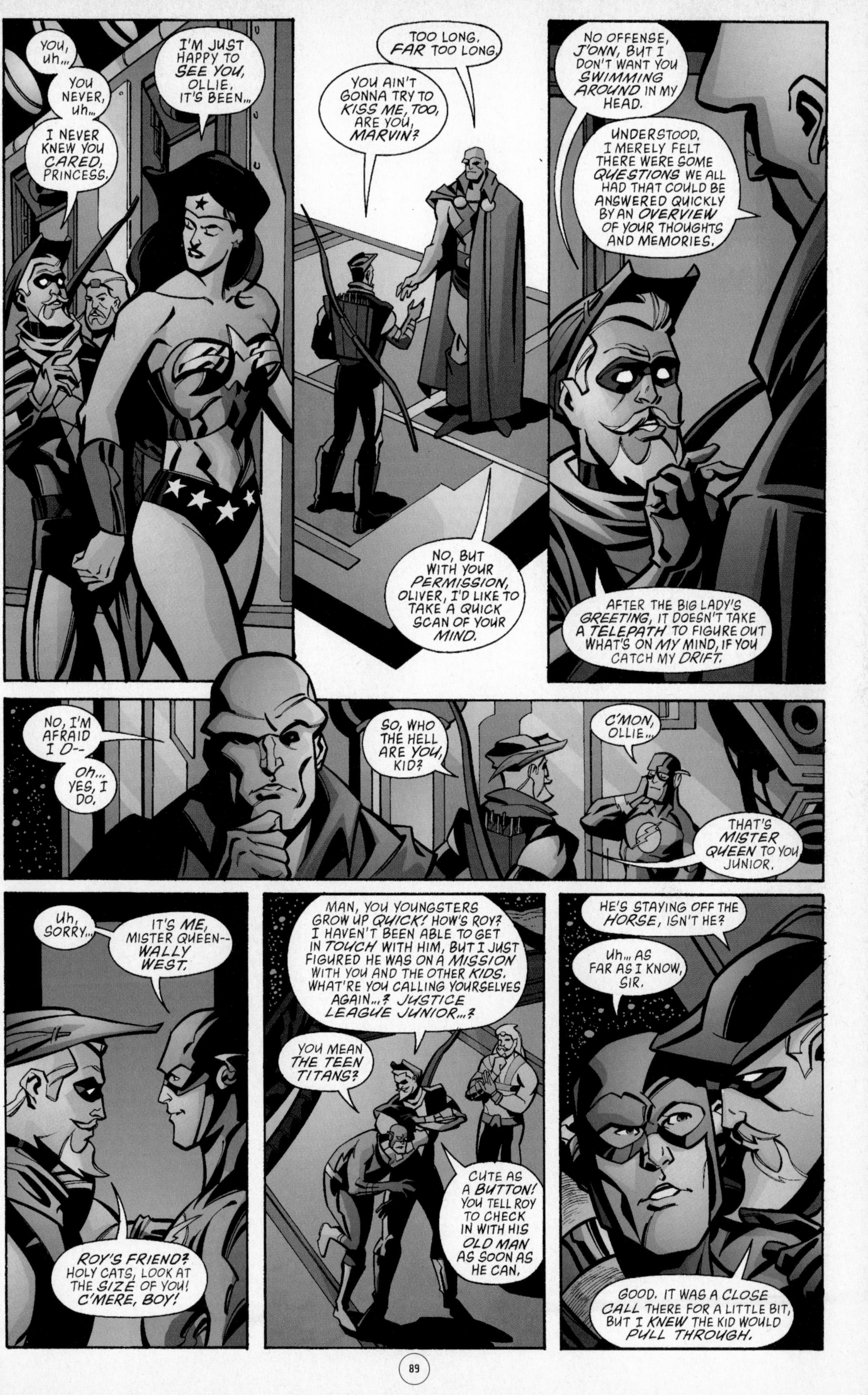
YOU, uh...
YOU NEVER, uh...
I NEVER KNEW YOU CARED, PRINCESS.
I'M JUST HAPPY TO SEE YOU, OLLIE. IT'S BEEN...
TOO LONG. FAR TOO LONG.
YOU AIN'T GONNA TRY TO KISS ME, TOO, ARE YOU, MARVIN?
NO, BUT WITH YOUR PERMISSION, OLIVER, I'D LIKE TO TAKE A QUICK SCAN OF YOUR MIND.
NO OFFENSE, J'ONN, BUT I DON'T WANT YOU SWIMMING AROUND IN MY HEAD.
UNDERSTOOD. I MERELY FELT THERE WERE SOME QUESTIONS WE ALL HAD THAT COULD BE ANSWERED QUICKLY BY AN OVERVIEW OF YOUR THOUGHTS AND MEMORIES.
AFTER THE BIG LADY'S GREETING, IT DOESN'T TAKE A TELEPATH TO FIGURE OUT WHAT'S ON MY MIND, IF YOU CATCH MY DRIFT.
NO, I'M AFRAID I D--
Oh... YES, I DO.
SO, WHO THE HELL ARE YOU, KID?
C'MON, OLLIE...
THAT'S MISTER QUEEN TO YOU JUNIOR.
Uh, SORRY...
IT'S ME, MISTER QUEEN-- WALLY WEST.
ROY'S FRIEND? HOLY CATS, LOOK AT THE SIZE OF YOU! C'MERE, BOY!
MAN, YOU YOUNGSTERS GROW UP QUICK! HOW'S ROY? I HAVEN'T BEEN ABLE TO GET IN TOUCH WITH HIM, BUT I JUST FIGURED HE WAS ON A MISSION WITH YOU AND THE OTHER KIDS. WHAT'RE YOU CALLING YOURSELVES AGAIN...? JUSTICE LEAGUE JUNIOR...?
YOU MEAN THE TEEN TITANS?
CUTE AS A BUTTON! YOU TELL ROY TO CHECK IN WITH HIS OLD MAN AS SOON AS HE CAN.
HE'S STAYING OFF THE HORSE, ISN'T HE?
Uh... AS FAR AS I KNOW, SIR.
GOOD. IT WAS A CLOSE CALL THERE FOR A LITTLE BIT, BUT I KNEW THE KID WOULD PULL THROUGH.

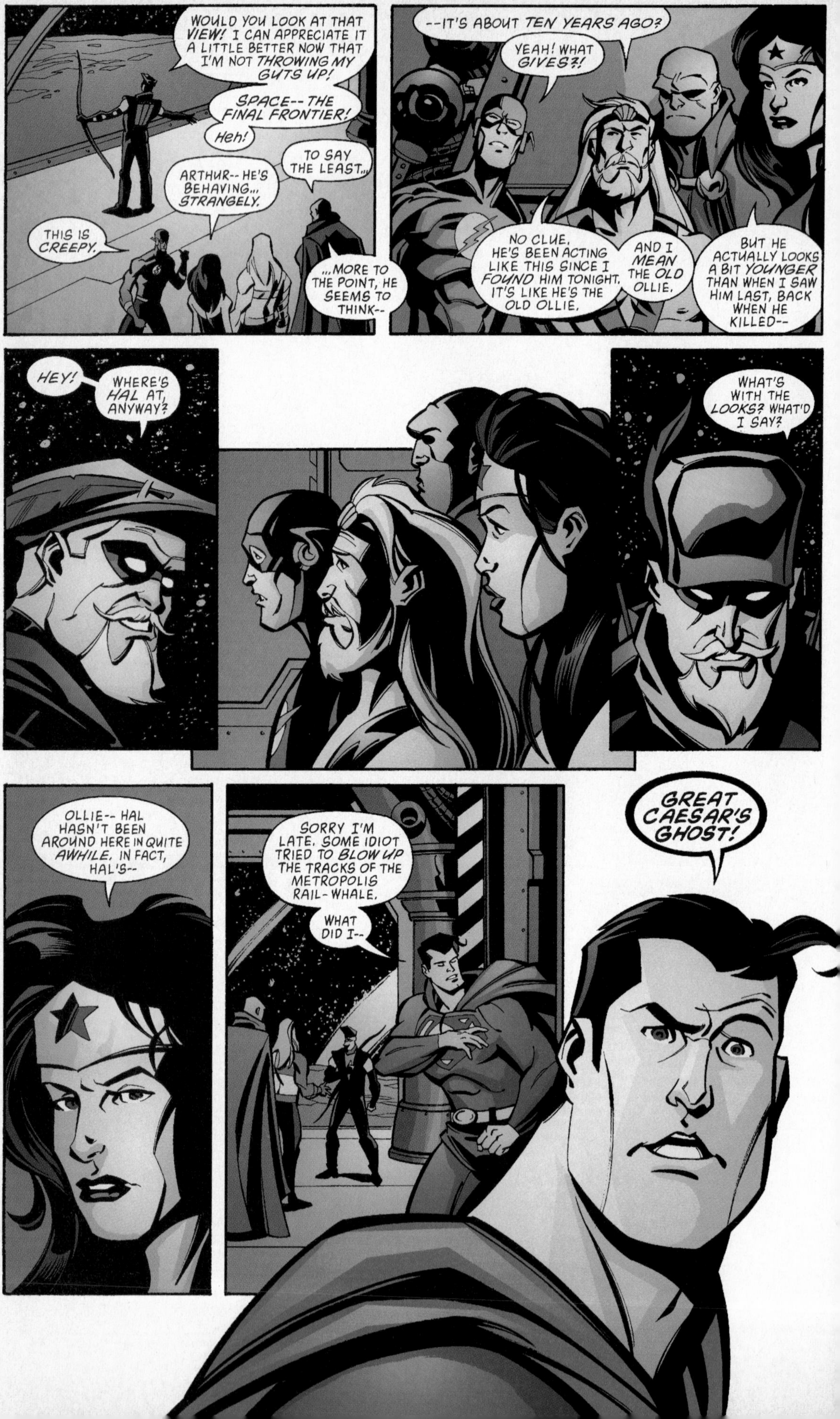
WOULD YOU LOOK AT THAT VIEW! I CAN APPRECIATE IT A LITTLE BETTER NOW THAT I'M NOT THROWING MY GUTS UP!
SPACE-- THE FINAL FRONTIER!
Heh!
TO SAY THE LEAST...
ARTHUR-- HE'S BEHAVING... STRANGELY.
THIS IS CREEPY.
...MORE TO THE POINT, HE SEEMS TO THINK--
--IT'S ABOUT TEN YEARS AGO?
YEAH! WHAT GIVES?!
NO CLUE. HE'S BEEN ACTING LIKE THIS SINCE I FOUND HIM TONIGHT. IT'S LIKE HE'S THE OLD OLLIE.
AND I MEAN THE OLD OLLIE.
BUT HE ACTUALLY LOOKS A BIT YOUNGER THAN WHEN I SAW HIM LAST, BACK WHEN HE KILLED--
HEY!
WHERE'S HAL AT, ANYWAY?
WHAT'S WITH THE LOOKS? WHAT'D I SAY?
OLLIE-- HAL HASN'T BEEN AROUND HERE IN QUITE AWHILE. IN FACT, HAL'S--
SORRY I'M LATE. SOME IDIOT TRIED TO BLOW UP THE TRACKS OF THE METROPOLIS RAIL-WHALE.
WHAT DID I--
GREAT CAESAR'S GHOST!

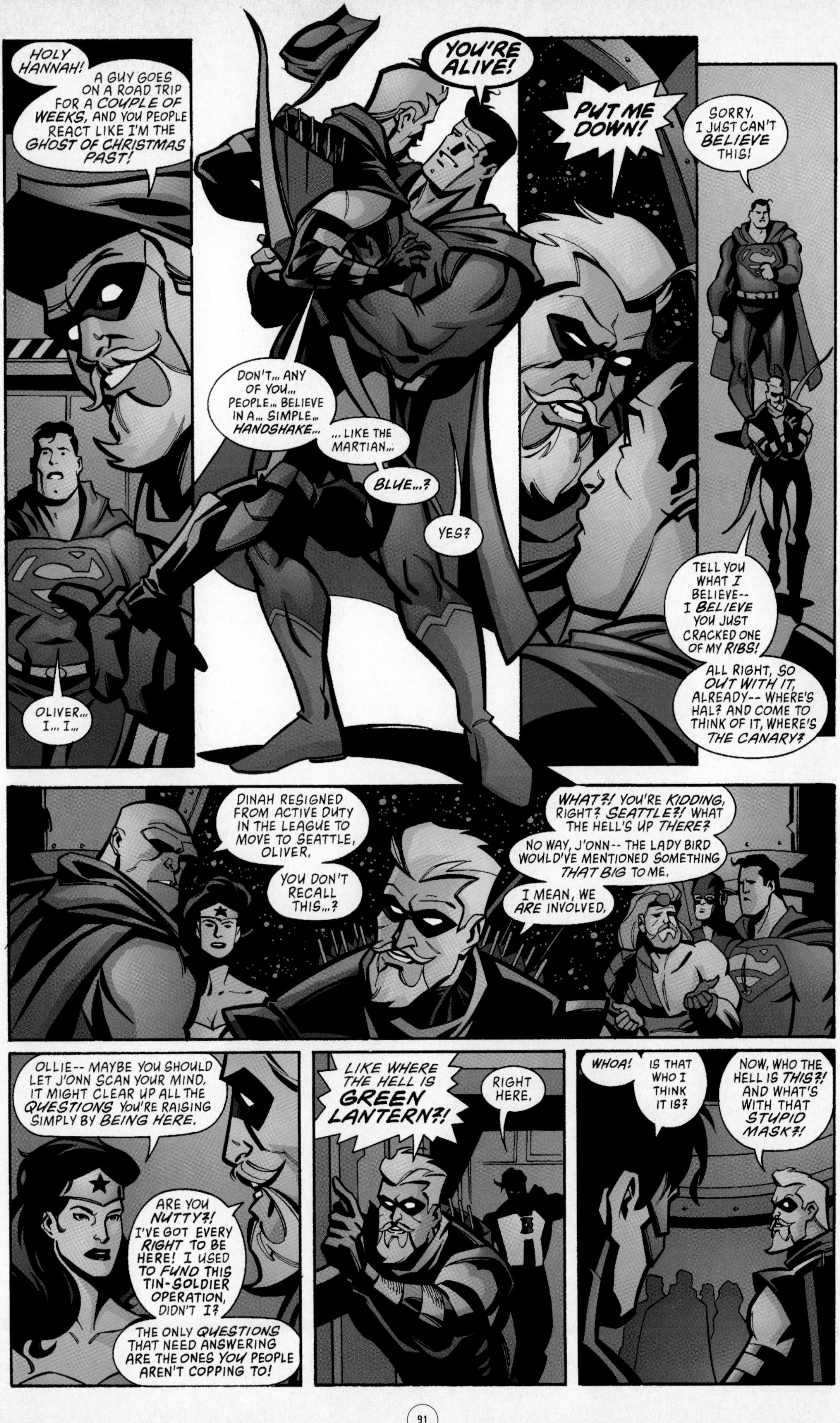
HOLY HANNAH! A GUY GOES ON A ROAD TRIP FOR A COUPLE OF WEEKS, AND YOU PEOPLE REACT LIKE I'M THE GHOST OF CHRISTMAS PAST!
OLIVER... I... I...
YOU'RE ALIVE!
DON'T... ANY OF YOU... PEOPLE... BELIEVE IN A... SIMPLE... HANDSHAKE...
...LIKE THE MARTIAN...
BLUE...?
YES?
PUT ME DOWN!
SORRY. I JUST CAN'T BELIEVE THIS!
TELL YOU WHAT I BELIEVE-- I BELIEVE YOU JUST CRACKED ONE OF MY RIBS!
ALL RIGHT, SO OUT WITH IT, ALREADY-- WHERE'S HAL? AND COME TO THINK OF IT, WHERE'S THE CANARY?
DINAH RESIGNED FROM ACTIVE DUTY IN THE LEAGUE TO MOVE TO SEATTLE, OLIVER.
YOU DON'T RECALL THIS...?
WHAT?! YOU'RE KIDDING, RIGHT? SEATTLE?! WHAT THE HELL'S UP THERE?
NO WAY, J'ONN-- THE LADY BIRD WOULD'VE MENTIONED SOMETHING THAT BIG TO ME.
I MEAN, WE ARE INVOLVED.
OLLIE-- MAYBE YOU SHOULD LET J'ONN SCAN YOUR MIND. IT MIGHT CLEAR UP ALL THE QUESTIONS YOU'RE RAISING SIMPLY BY BEING HERE.
ARE YOU NUTTY?! I'VE GOT EVERY RIGHT TO BE HERE! I USED TO FUND THIS TIN-SOLDIER OPERATION, DIDN'T I?
THE ONLY QUESTIONS THAT NEED ANSWERING ARE THE ONES YOU PEOPLE AREN'T COPPING TO!
LIKE WHERE THE HELL IS GREEN LANTERN?!
RIGHT HERE.
WHOA!
IS THAT WHO I THINK IT IS?
NOW, WHO THE HELL IS THIS?! AND WHAT'S WITH THAT STUPID MASK?!

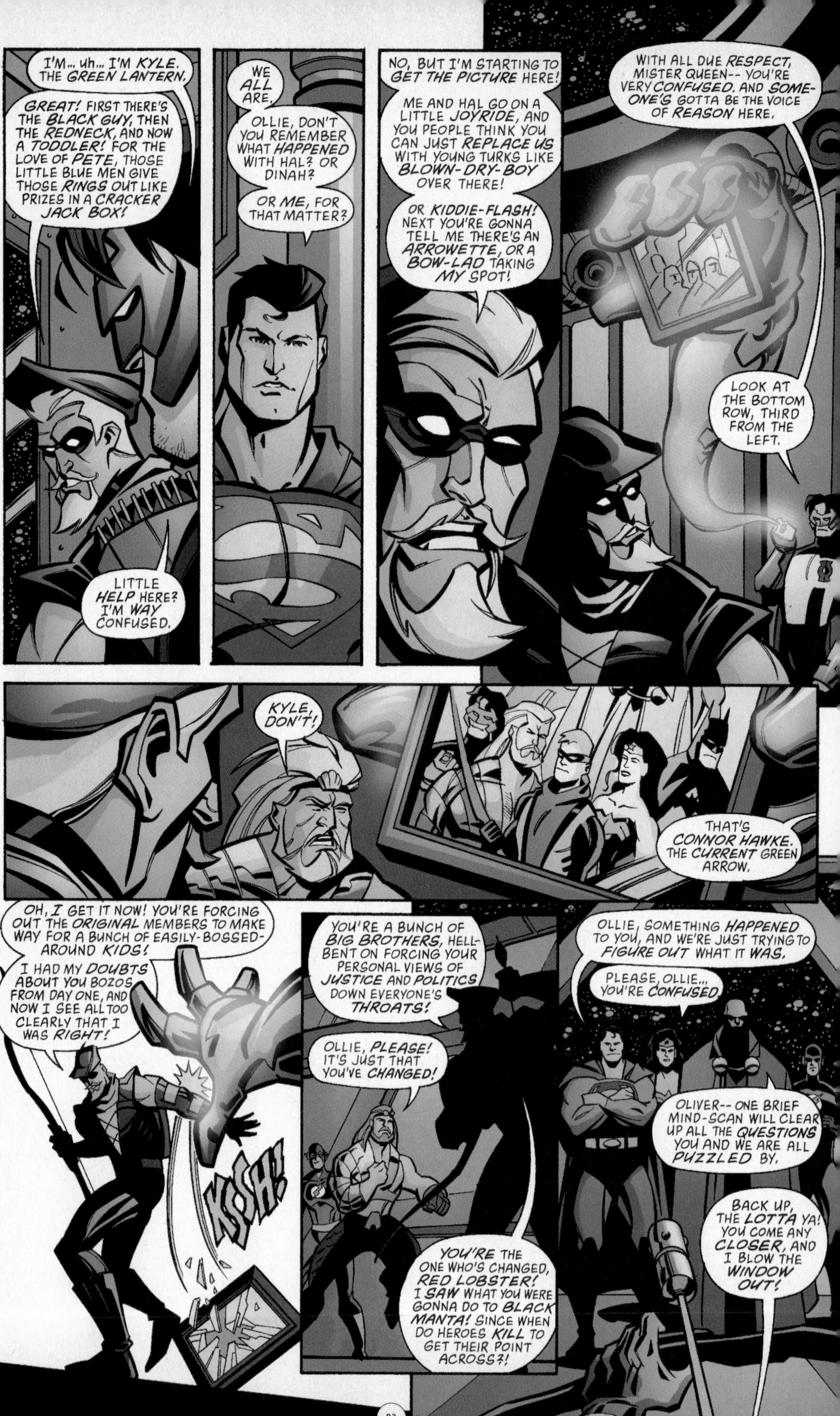
I'M... uh... I'M KYLE. THE GREEN LANTERN.
GREAT! FIRST THERE'S THE BLACK GUY, THEN THE REDNECK, AND NOW A TODDLER! FOR THE LOVE OF PETE, THOSE LITTLE BLUE MEN GIVE THOSE RINGS OUT LIKE PRIZES IN A CRACKER JACK BOX!
LITTLE HELP HERE? I'M WAY CONFUSED.
WE ALL ARE.
OLLIE, DON'T YOU REMEMBER WHAT HAPPENED WITH HAL? OR DINAH?
OR ME, FOR THAT MATTER?
NO, BUT I'M STARTING TO GET THE PICTURE HERE!
ME AND HAL GO ON A LITTLE JOYRIDE, AND YOU PEOPLE THINK YOU CAN JUST REPLACE US WITH YOUNG TURKS LIKE BLOWN-DRY-BOY OVER THERE!
OR KIDDIE-FLASH! NEXT YOU'RE GONNA TELL ME THERE'S AN ARROWETTE, OR A BOW-LAD TAKING MY SPOT!
WITH ALL DUE RESPECT, MISTER QUEEN-- YOU'RE VERY CONFUSED. AND SOMEONE'S GOTTA BE THE VOICE OF REASON HERE.
LOOK AT THE BOTTOM ROW, THIRD FROM THE LEFT.
KYLE, DON'T!
THAT'S CONNOR HAWKE. THE CURRENT GREEN ARROW.
OH, I GET IT NOW! YOU'RE FORCING OUT THE ORIGINAL MEMBERS TO MAKE WAY FOR A BUNCH OF EASILY-BOSSED-AROUND KIDS!
I HAD MY DOUBTS ABOUT YOU BOZOS FROM DAY ONE, AND NOW I SEE ALL TOO CLEARLY THAT I WAS RIGHT!
KSSH!
YOU'RE A BUNCH OF BIG BROTHERS, HELL-BENT ON FORCING YOUR PERSONAL VIEWS OF JUSTICE AND POLITICS DOWN EVERYONE'S THROATS!
OLLIE, PLEASE! IT'S JUST THAT YOU'VE CHANGED!
YOU'RE THE ONE WHO'S CHANGED, RED LOBSTER! I SAW WHAT YOU WERE GONNA DO TO BLACK MANTA! SINCE WHEN DO HEROES KILL TO GET THEIR POINT ACROSS?!
OLLIE, SOMETHING HAPPENED TO YOU, AND WE'RE JUST TRYING TO FIGURE OUT WHAT IT WAS.
PLEASE, OLLIE... YOU'RE CONFUSED.
OLIVER-- ONE BRIEF MIND-SCAN WILL CLEAR UP ALL THE QUESTIONS YOU AND WE ARE ALL PUZZLED BY.
BACK UP, THE LOTTA YA! YOU COME ANY CLOSER, AND I BLOW THE WINDOW OUT!

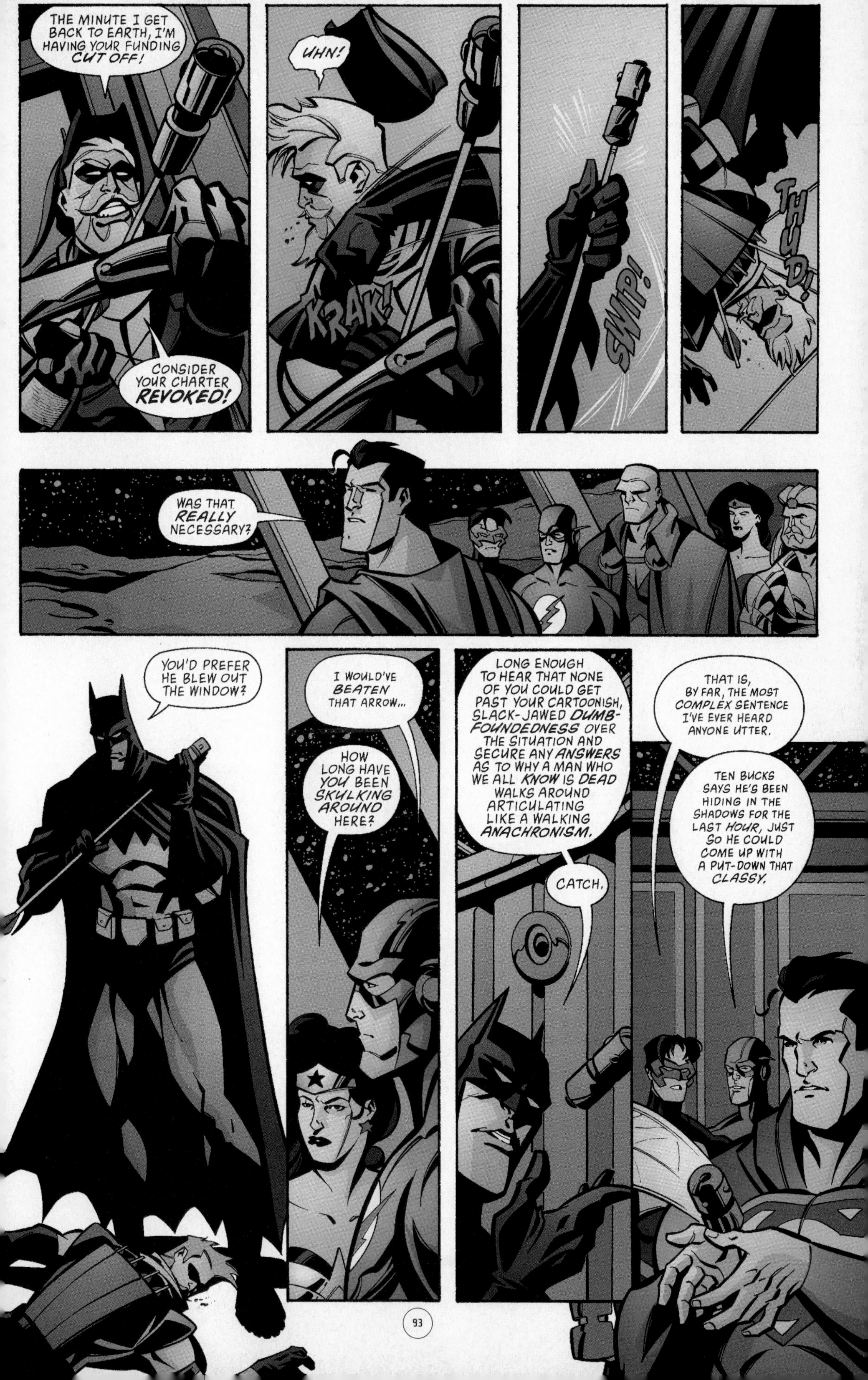
THE MINUTE I GET BACK TO EARTH, I'M HAVING YOUR FUNDING CUT OFF!
CONSIDER YOUR CHARTER REVOKED!
UHN!
KRAK!
SWIP!
THUD!
WAS THAT REALLY NECESSARY?
YOU'D PREFER HE BLEW OUT THE WINDOW?
I WOULD'VE BEATEN THAT ARROW...
HOW LONG HAVE YOU BEEN SKULKING AROUND HERE?
LONG ENOUGH TO HEAR THAT NONE OF YOU COULD GET PAST YOUR CARTOONISH, SLACK-JAWED DUMB-FOUNDEDNESS OVER THE SITUATION AND SECURE ANY ANSWERS AS TO WHY A MAN WHO WE ALL KNOW IS DEAD WALKS AROUND ARTICULATING LIKE A WALKING ANACHRONISM.
CATCH.
THAT IS, BY FAR, THE MOST COMPLEX SENTENCE I'VE EVER HEARD ANYONE UTTER.
TEN BUCKS SAYS HE'S BEEN HIDING IN THE SHADOWS FOR THE LAST HOUR, JUST SO HE COULD COME UP WITH A PUT-DOWN THAT CLASSY.

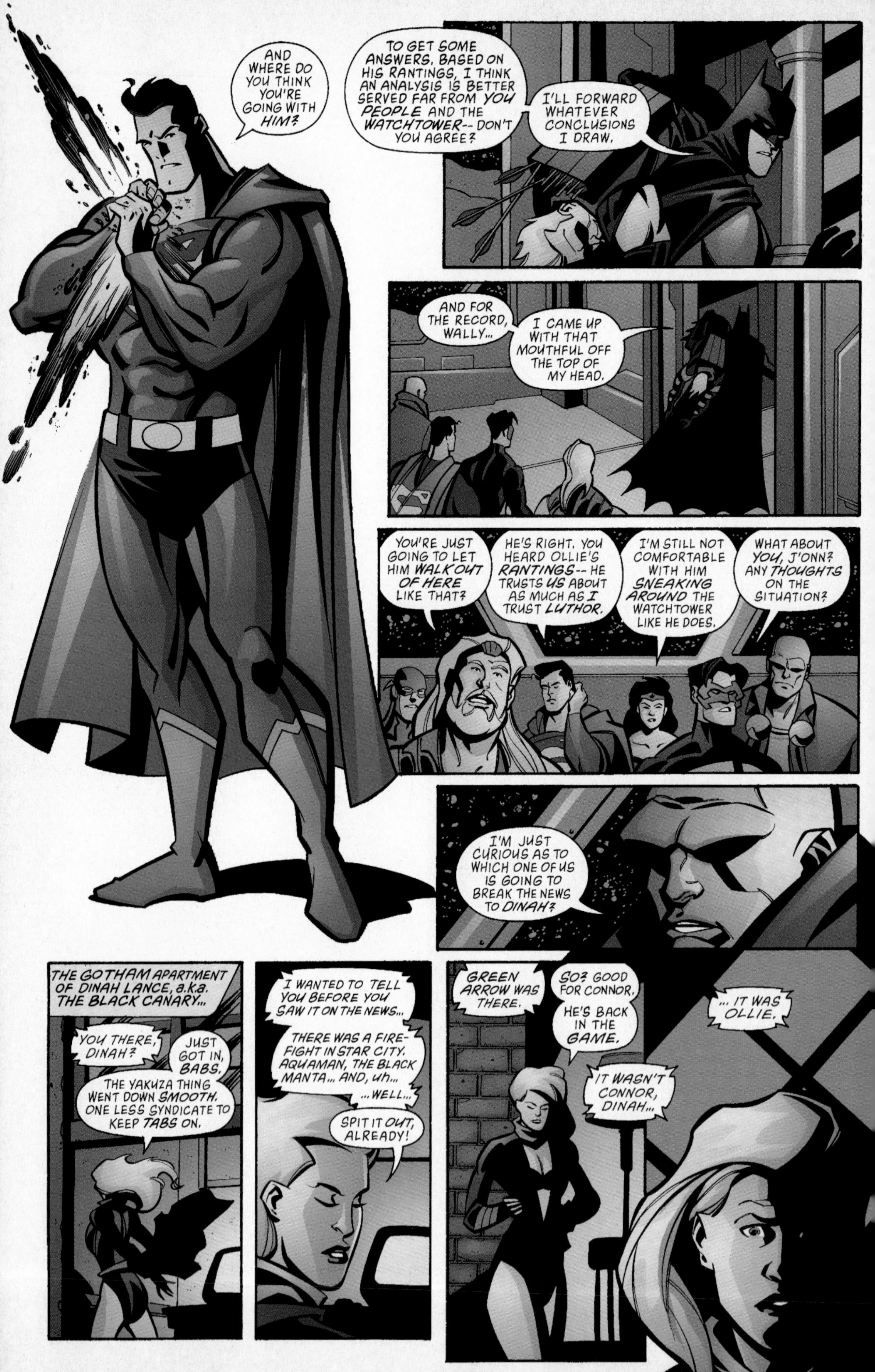
AND WHERE DO YOU THINK YOU'RE GOING WITH HIM?
TO GET SOME ANSWERS. BASED ON HIS RANTINGS, I THINK AN ANALYSIS IS BETTER SERVED FAR FROM YOU PEOPLE AND THE WATCHTOWER-- DON'T YOU AGREE?
I'LL FORWARD WHATEVER CONCLUSIONS I DRAW.
AND FOR THE RECORD, WALLY...
I CAME UP WITH THAT MOUTHFUL OFF THE TOP OF MY HEAD.
YOU'RE JUST GOING TO LET HIM WALK OUT OF HERE LIKE THAT?
HE'S RIGHT. YOU HEARD OLLIE'S RANTINGS-- HE TRUSTS US ABOUT AS MUCH AS I TRUST LUTHOR.
I'M STILL NOT COMFORTABLE WITH HIM SNEAKING AROUND THE WATCHTOWER LIKE HE DOES.
WHAT ABOUT YOU, J'ONN? ANY THOUGHTS ON THE SITUATION?
I'M JUST CURIOUS AS TO WHICH ONE OF US IS GOING TO BREAK THE NEWS TO DINAH?
THE GOTHAM APARTMENT OF DINAH LANCE, a.k.a. THE BLACK CANARY...
YOU THERE, DINAH?
JUST GOT IN, BABS.
THE YAKUZA THING WENT DOWN SMOOTH. ONE LESS SYNDICATE TO KEEP TABS ON.
I WANTED TO TELL YOU BEFORE YOU SAW IT ON THE NEWS...
THERE WAS A FIRE-FIGHT IN STAR CITY. AQUAMAN, THE BLACK MANTA... AND, uh...
...WELL...
SPIT IT OUT, ALREADY!
GREEN ARROW WAS THERE.
SO? GOOD FOR CONNOR.
HE'S BACK IN THE GAME.
IT WASN'T CONNOR, DINAH...
... IT WAS OLLIE.

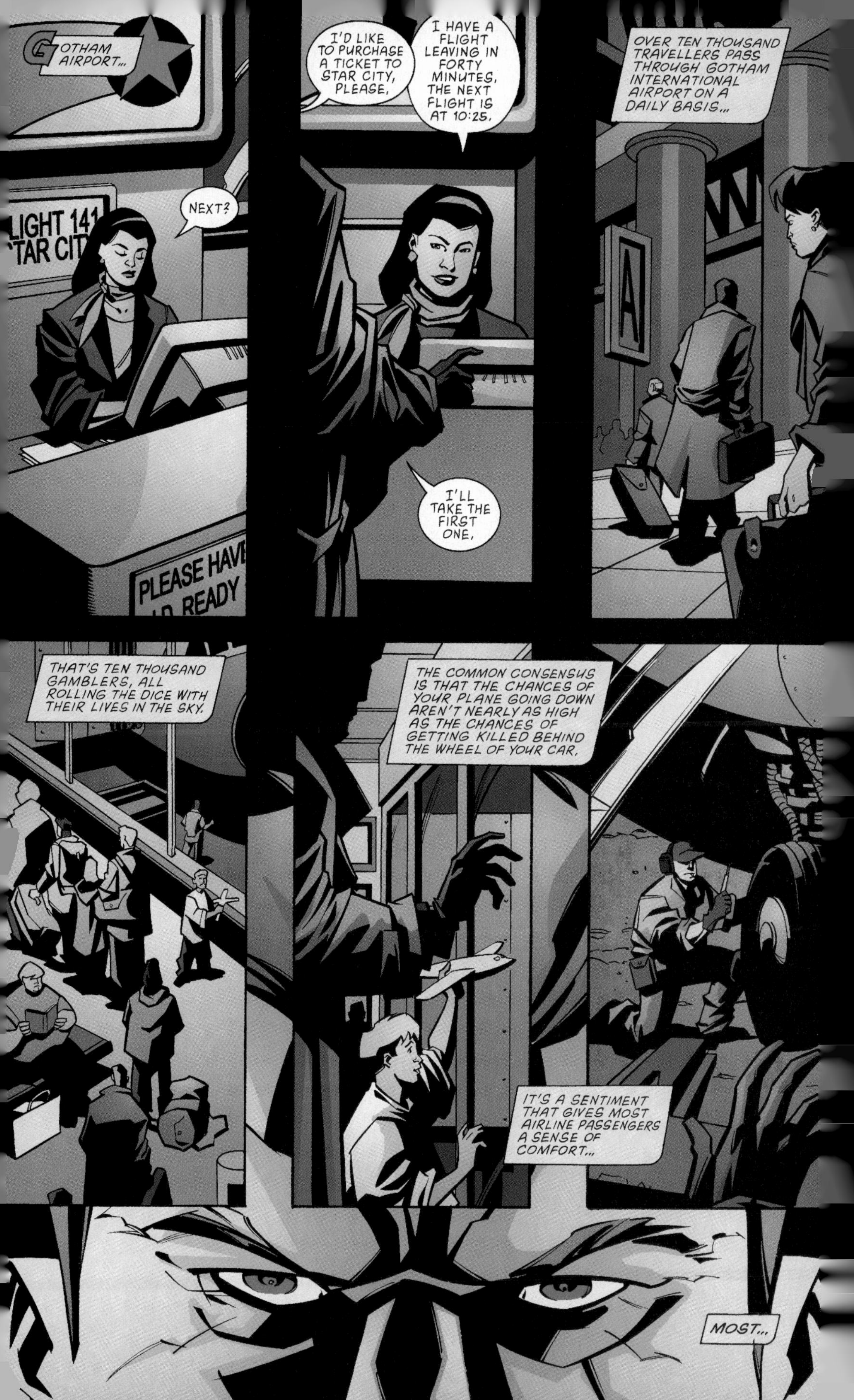
GOTHAM AIRPORT...
FLIGHT 141
STAR CIT
NEXT?
PLEASE HAVE
I.D. READY
I'D LIKE TO PURCHASE A TICKET TO STAR CITY, PLEASE.
I HAVE A FLIGHT LEAVING IN FORTY MINUTES, THE NEXT FLIGHT IS AT 10:25.
I'LL TAKE THE FIRST ONE.
OVER TEN THOUSAND TRAVELLERS PASS THROUGH GOTHAM INTERNATIONAL AIRPORT ON A DAILY BASIS...
A
THAT'S TEN THOUSAND GAMBLERS, ALL ROLLING THE DICE WITH THEIR LIVES IN THE SKY.
THE COMMON CONSENSUS IS THAT THE CHANCES OF YOUR PLANE GOING DOWN AREN'T NEARLY AS HIGH AS THE CHANCES OF GETTING KILLED BEHIND THE WHEEL OF YOUR CAR.
IT'S A SENTIMENT THAT GIVES MOST AIRLINE PASSENGERS A SENSE OF COMFORT...
MOST...

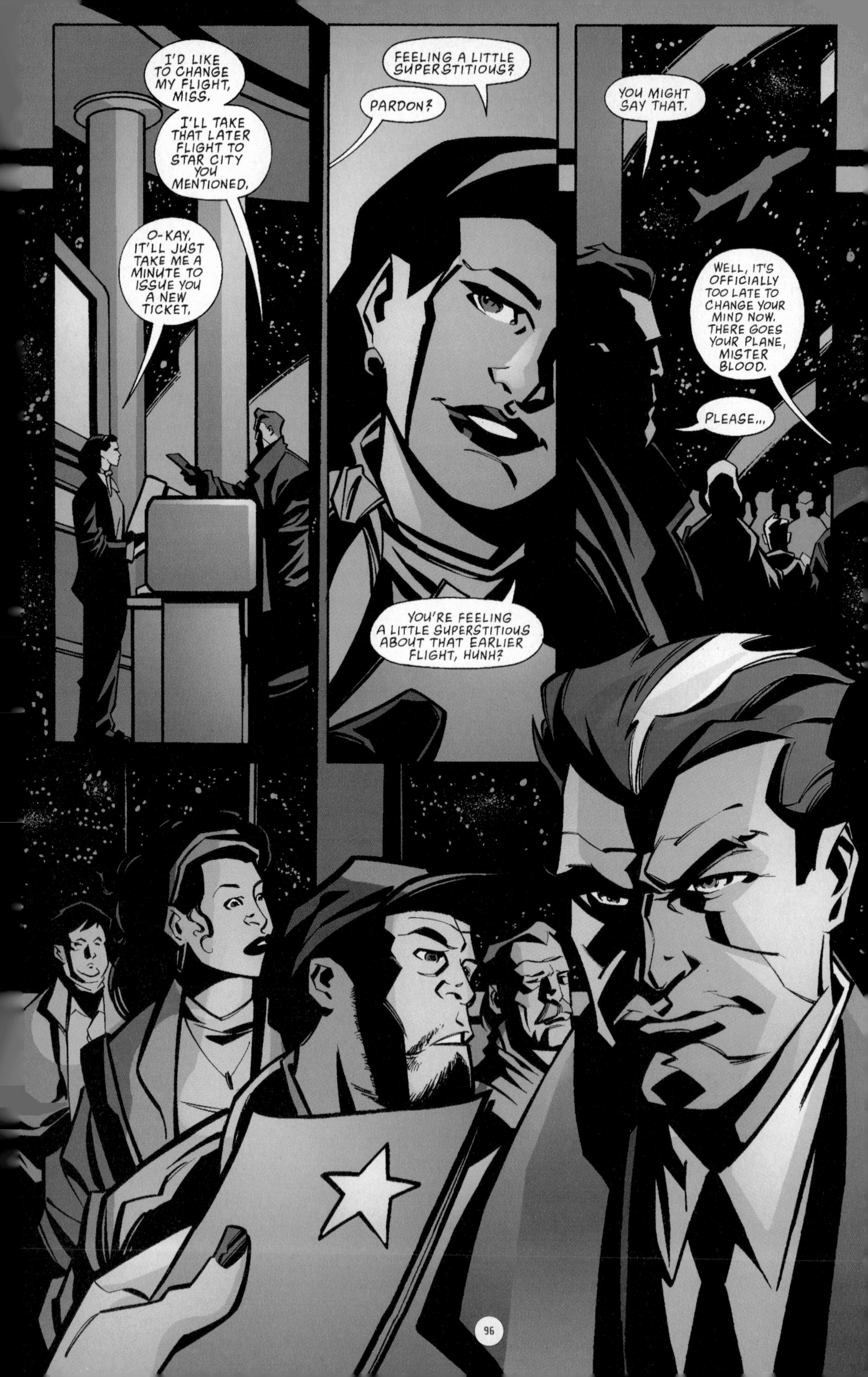
I'D LIKE TO CHANGE MY FLIGHT, MISS.
I'LL TAKE THAT LATER FLIGHT TO STAR CITY YOU MENTIONED.
O-KAY, IT'LL JUST TAKE ME A MINUTE TO ISSUE YOU A NEW TICKET.
FEELING A LITTLE SUPERSTITIOUS?
PARDON?
YOU'RE FEELING A LITTLE SUPERSTITIOUS ABOUT THAT EARLIER FLIGHT, HUNH?
YOU MIGHT SAY THAT.
WELL, IT'S OFFICIALLY TOO LATE TO CHANGE YOUR MIND NOW. THERE GOES YOUR PLANE, MISTER BLOOD.
PLEASE...

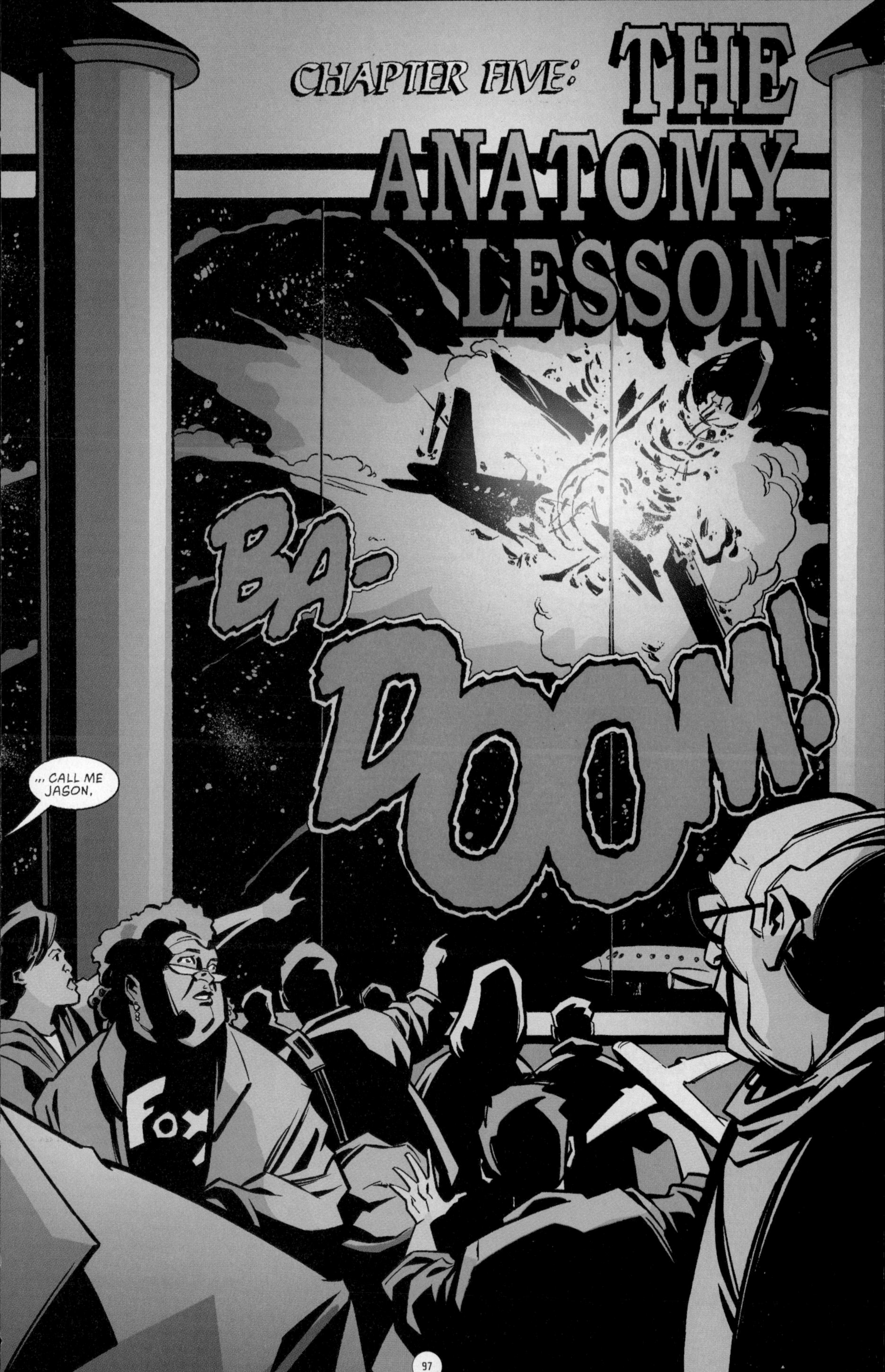
CHAPTER FIVE: THE ANATOMY LESSON
BA-DOOM!
... CALL ME JASON.
FOX

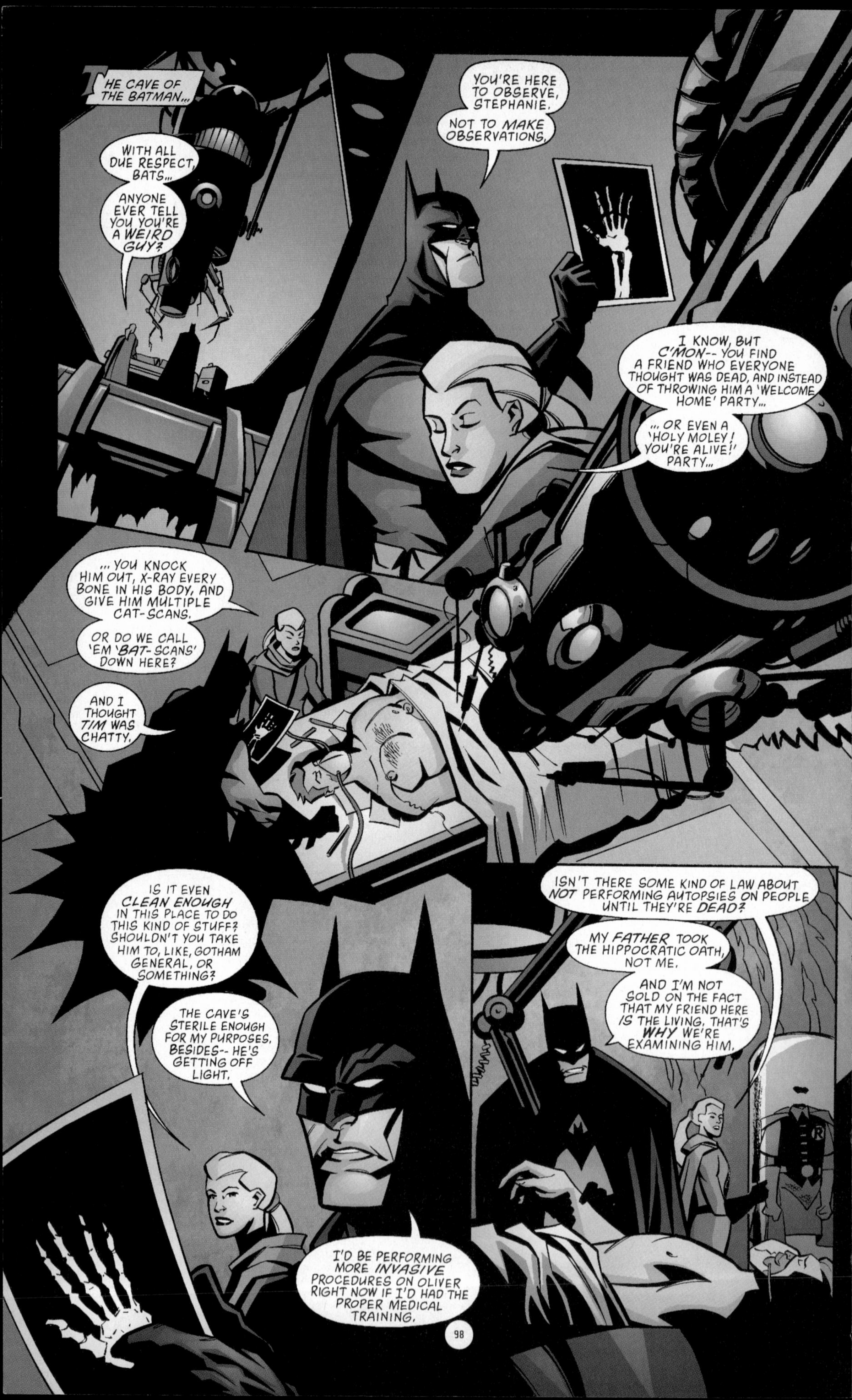
THE CAVE OF THE BATMAN...
YOU'RE HERE TO OBSERVE, STEPHANIE.
NOT TO MAKE OBSERVATIONS.
WITH ALL DUE RESPECT, BATS...
ANYONE EVER TELL YOU YOU'RE A WEIRD GUY?
I KNOW, BUT C'MON-- YOU FIND A FRIEND WHO EVERYONE THOUGHT WAS DEAD, AND INSTEAD OF THROWING HIM A 'WELCOME HOME' PARTY...
... OR EVEN A 'HOLY MOLEY! YOU'RE ALIVE!' PARTY...
... YOU KNOCK HIM OUT, X-RAY EVERY BONE IN HIS BODY, AND GIVE HIM MULTIPLE CAT-SCANS.
OR DO WE CALL 'EM 'BAT-SCANS' DOWN HERE?
AND I THOUGHT TIM WAS CHATTY.
IS IT EVEN CLEAN ENOUGH IN THIS PLACE TO DO THIS KIND OF STUFF? SHOULDN'T YOU TAKE HIM TO, LIKE, GOTHAM GENERAL, OR SOMETHING?
THE CAVE'S STERILE ENOUGH FOR MY PURPOSES. BESIDES-- HE'S GETTING OFF LIGHT.
I'D BE PERFORMING MORE INVASIVE PROCEDURES ON OLIVER RIGHT NOW IF I'D HAD THE PROPER MEDICAL TRAINING.
ISN'T THERE SOME KIND OF LAW ABOUT NOT PERFORMING AUTOPSIES ON PEOPLE UNTIL THEY'RE DEAD?
MY FATHER TOOK THE HIPPOCRATIC OATH, NOT ME.
AND I'M NOT SOLD ON THE FACT THAT MY FRIEND HERE IS THE LIVING. THAT'S WHY WE'RE EXAMINING HIM.

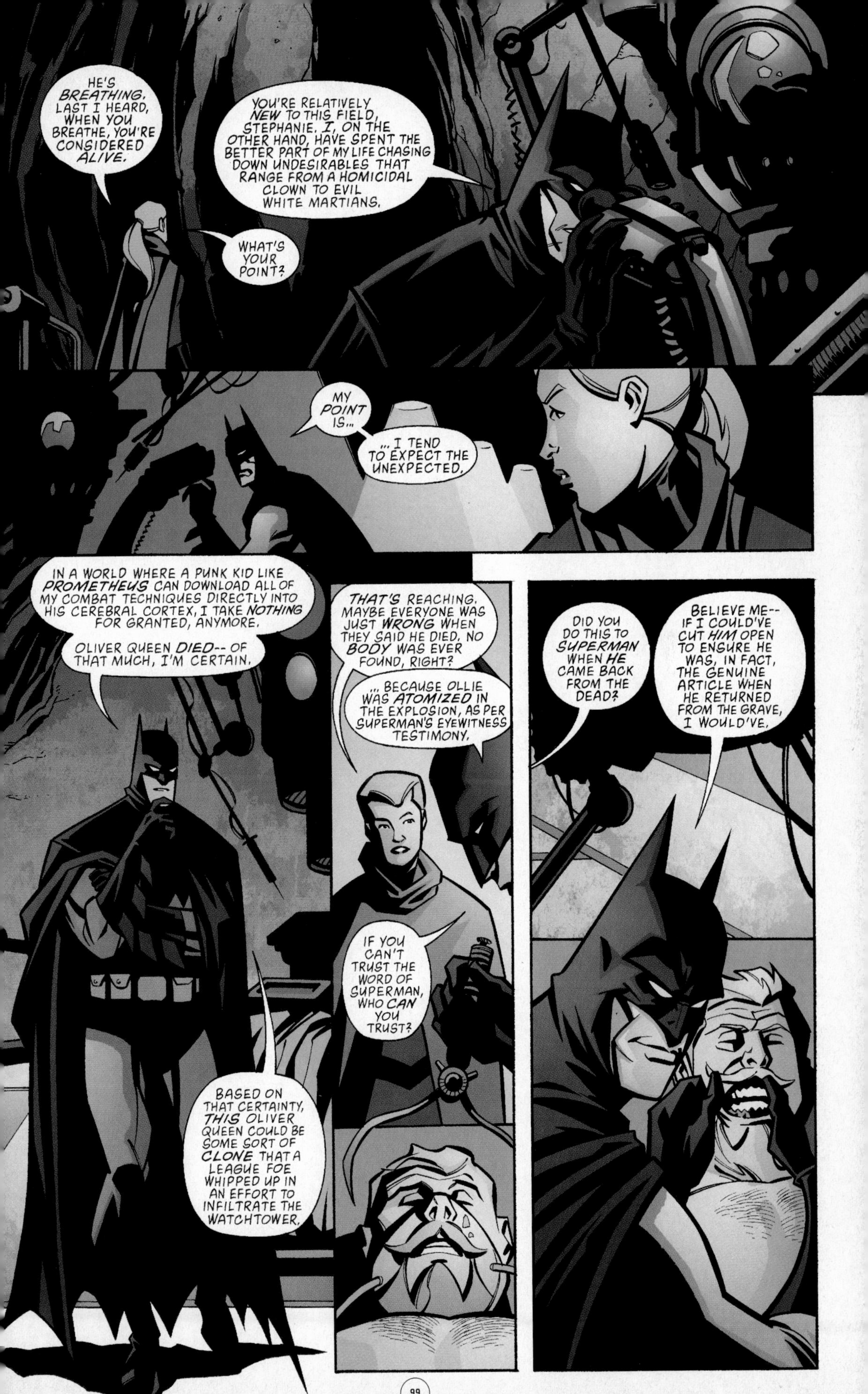
HE'S BREATHING. LAST I HEARD, WHEN YOU BREATHE, YOU'RE CONSIDERED ALIVE.
YOU'RE RELATIVELY NEW TO THIS FIELD, STEPHANIE. I, ON THE OTHER HAND, HAVE SPENT THE BETTER PART OF MY LIFE CHASING DOWN UNDESIRABLES THAT RANGE FROM A HOMICIDAL CLOWN TO EVIL WHITE MARTIANS.
WHAT'S YOUR POINT?
MY POINT IS...
...I TEND TO EXPECT THE UNEXPECTED.
IN A WORLD WHERE A PUNK KID LIKE PROMETHEUS CAN DOWNLOAD ALL OF MY COMBAT TECHNIQUES DIRECTLY INTO HIS CEREBRAL CORTEX, I TAKE NOTHING FOR GRANTED, ANYMORE.
OLIVER QUEEN DIED-- OF THAT MUCH, I'M CERTAIN.
THAT'S REACHING. MAYBE EVERYONE WAS JUST WRONG WHEN THEY SAID HE DIED. NO BODY WAS EVER FOUND, RIGHT?
...BECAUSE OLLIE WAS ATOMIZED IN THE EXPLOSION, AS PER SUPERMAN'S EYEWITNESS TESTIMONY.
IF YOU CAN'T TRUST THE WORD OF SUPERMAN, WHO CAN YOU TRUST?
BASED ON THAT CERTAINTY, THIS OLIVER QUEEN COULD BE SOME SORT OF CLONE THAT A LEAGUE FOE WHIPPED UP IN AN EFFORT TO INFILTRATE THE WATCHTOWER.
DID YOU DO THIS TO SUPERMAN WHEN HE CAME BACK FROM THE DEAD?
BELIEVE ME-- IF I COULD'VE CUT HIM OPEN TO ENSURE HE WAS, IN FACT, THE GENUINE ARTICLE WHEN HE RETURNED FROM THE GRAVE, I WOULD'VE.

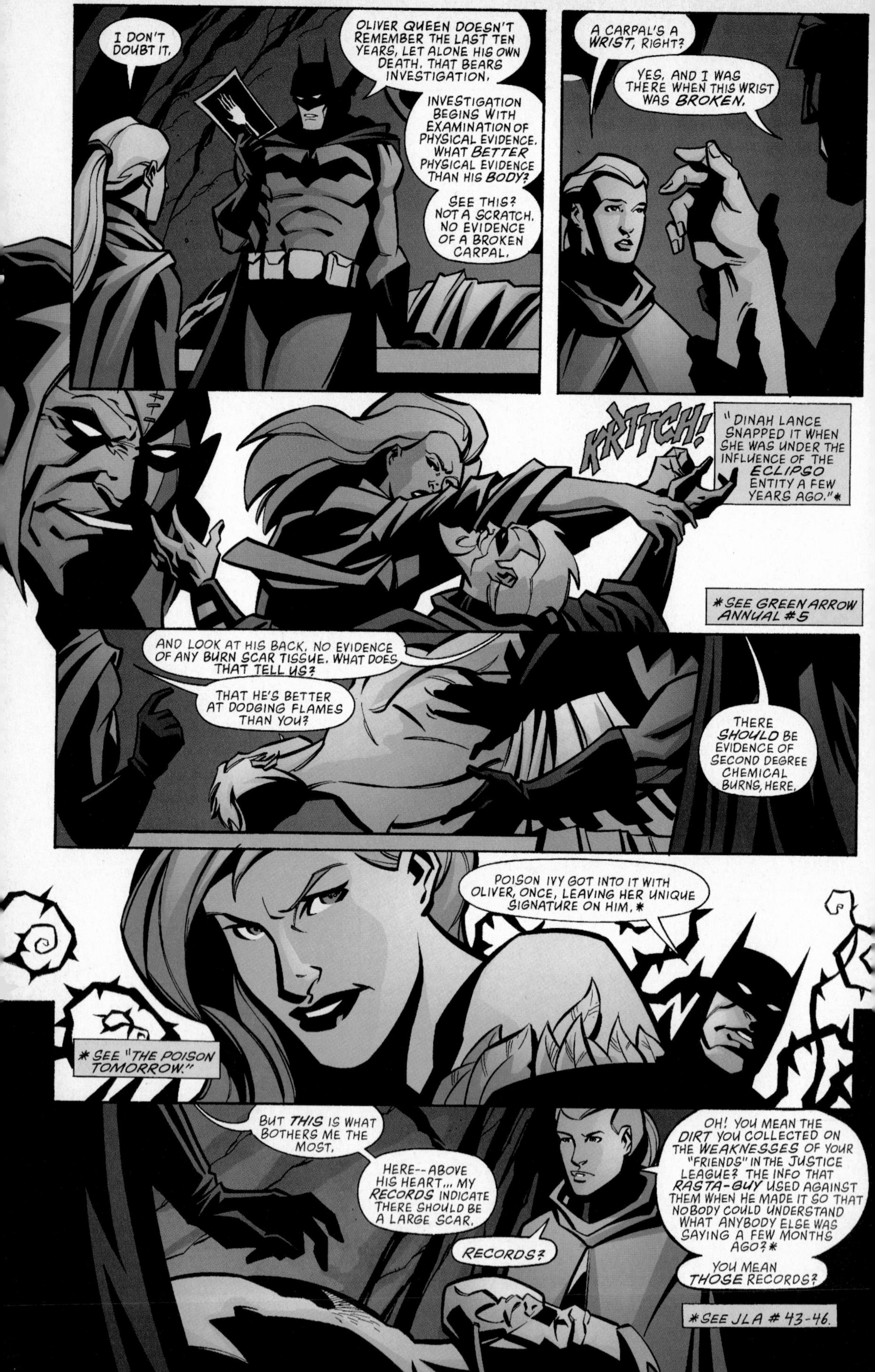
I DON'T DOUBT IT.
OLIVER QUEEN DOESN'T REMEMBER THE LAST TEN YEARS, LET ALONE HIS OWN DEATH. THAT BEARS INVESTIGATION.
INVESTIGATION BEGINS WITH EXAMINATION OF PHYSICAL EVIDENCE. WHAT BETTER PHYSICAL EVIDENCE THAN HIS BODY?
SEE THIS? NOT A SCRATCH. NO EVIDENCE OF A BROKEN CARPAL.
A CARPAL'S A WRIST, RIGHT?
YES, AND I WAS THERE WHEN THIS WRIST WAS BROKEN.
KRTTCH!
"DINAH LANCE SNAPPED IT WHEN SHE WAS UNDER THE INFLUENCE OF THE ECLIPSO ENTITY A FEW YEARS AGO."*
*SEE GREEN ARROW ANNUAL #5
AND LOOK AT HIS BACK. NO EVIDENCE OF ANY BURN SCAR TISSUE. WHAT DOES THAT TELL US?
THAT HE'S BETTER AT DODGING FLAMES THAN YOU?
THERE SHOULD BE EVIDENCE OF SECOND DEGREE CHEMICAL BURNS, HERE.
POISON IVY GOT INTO IT WITH OLIVER, ONCE, LEAVING HER UNIQUE SIGNATURE ON HIM.*
*SEE "THE POISON TOMORROW."
BUT THIS IS WHAT BOTHERS ME THE MOST.
HERE--ABOVE HIS HEART... MY RECORDS INDICATE THERE SHOULD BE A LARGE SCAR.
RECORDS?
OH! YOU MEAN THE DIRT YOU COLLECTED ON THE WEAKNESSES OF YOUR "FRIENDS" IN THE JUSTICE LEAGUE? THE INFO THAT RASTA-GUY USED AGAINST THEM WHEN HE MADE IT SO THAT NOBODY COULD UNDERSTAND WHAT ANYBODY ELSE WAS SAYING A FEW MONTHS AGO?*
YOU MEAN THOSE RECORDS?
*SEE JLA #43-46.

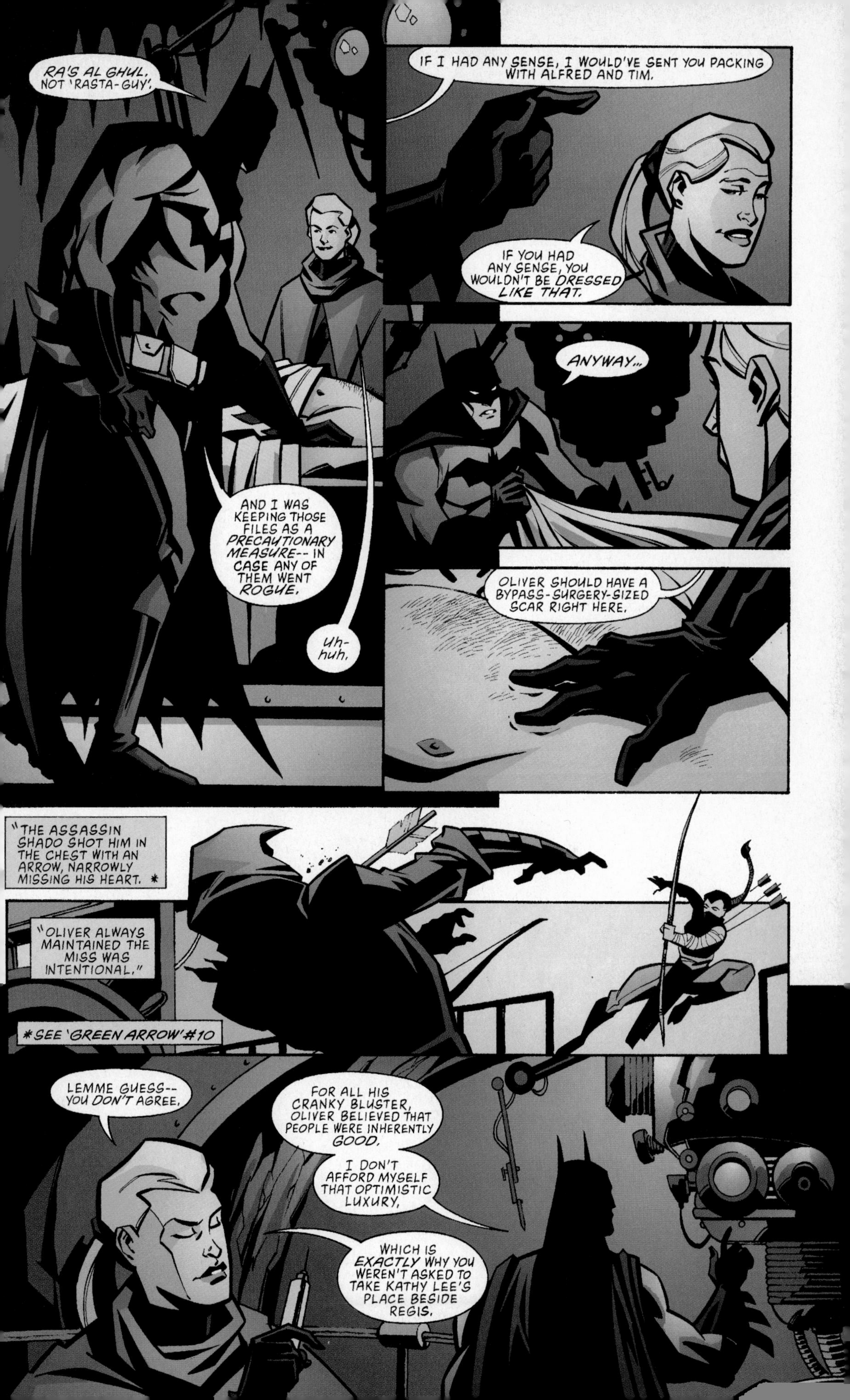
RA'S AL GHUL, NOT 'RASTA-GUY'.
IF I HAD ANY SENSE, I WOULD'VE SENT YOU PACKING WITH ALFRED AND TIM.
IF YOU HAD ANY SENSE, YOU WOULDN'T BE DRESSED LIKE THAT.
AND I WAS KEEPING THOSE FILES AS A PRECAUTIONARY MEASURE-- IN CASE ANY OF THEM WENT ROGUE.
Uh-huh.
ANYWAY...
OLIVER SHOULD HAVE A BYPASS-SURGERY-SIZED SCAR RIGHT HERE.
"THE ASSASSIN SHADO SHOT HIM IN THE CHEST WITH AN ARROW, NARROWLY MISSING HIS HEART. *
"OLIVER ALWAYS MAINTAINED THE MISS WAS INTENTIONAL."
*SEE 'GREEN ARROW' #10
LEMME GUESS-- YOU DON'T AGREE.
FOR ALL HIS CRANKY BLUSTER, OLIVER BELIEVED THAT PEOPLE WERE INHERENTLY GOOD.
I DON'T AFFORD MYSELF THAT OPTIMISTIC LUXURY.
WHICH IS EXACTLY WHY YOU WEREN'T ASKED TO TAKE KATHY LEE'S PLACE BESIDE REGIS.

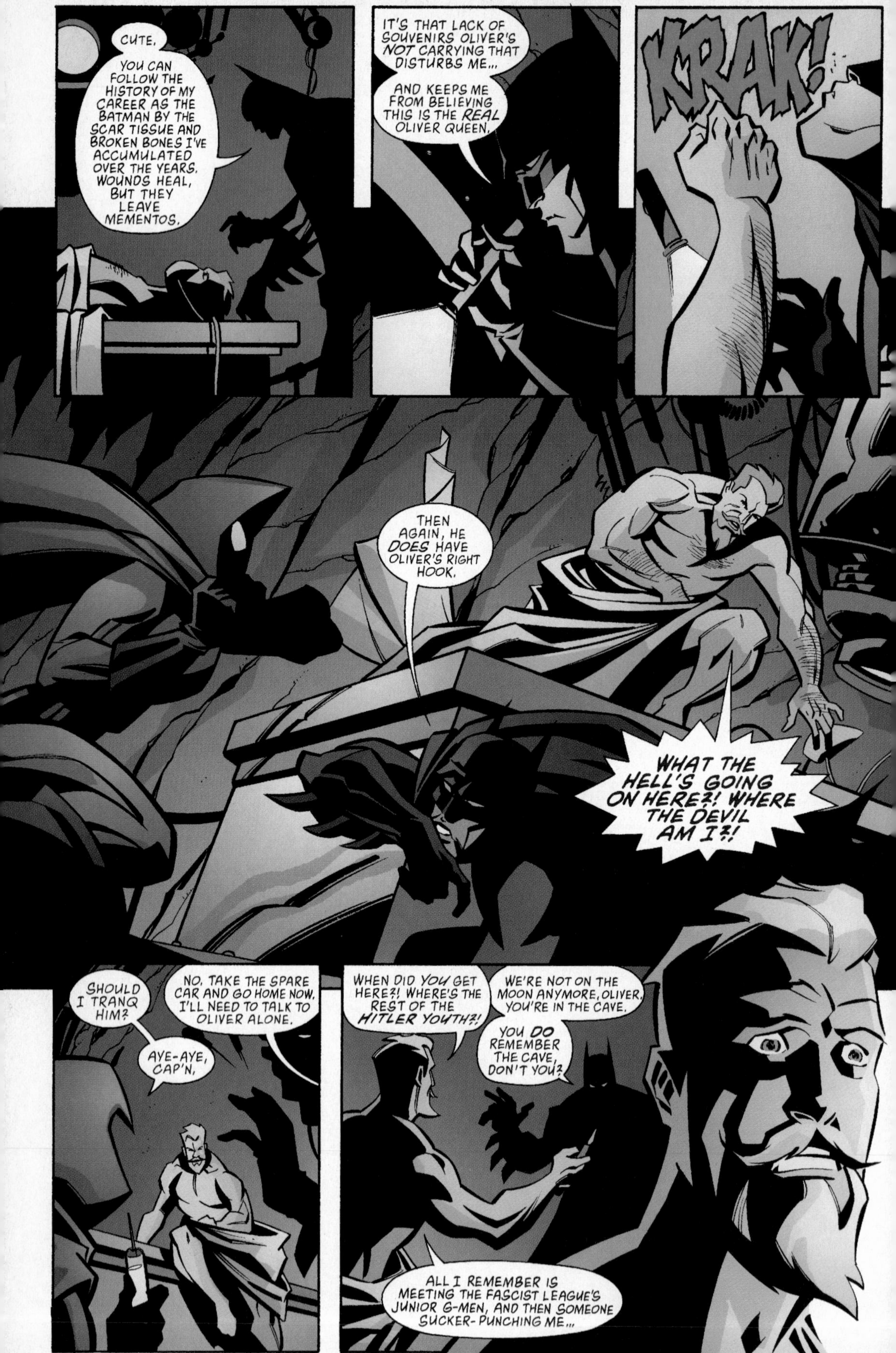
CUTE.
YOU CAN FOLLOW THE HISTORY OF MY CAREER AS THE BATMAN BY THE SCAR TISSUE AND BROKEN BONES I'VE ACCUMULATED OVER THE YEARS. WOUNDS HEAL, BUT THEY LEAVE MEMENTOS.
IT'S THAT LACK OF SOUVENIRS OLIVER'S NOT CARRYING THAT DISTURBS ME...
AND KEEPS ME FROM BELIEVING THIS IS THE REAL OLIVER QUEEN.
KRAK!
THEN AGAIN, HE DOES HAVE OLIVER'S RIGHT HOOK.
WHAT THE HELL'S GOING ON HERE?! WHERE THE DEVIL AM I?!
SHOULD I TRANQ HIM?
NO. TAKE THE SPARE CAR AND GO HOME NOW. I'LL NEED TO TALK TO OLIVER ALONE.
AYE-AYE, CAP'N.
WHEN DID YOU GET HERE?! WHERE'S THE REST OF THE HITLER YOUTH?!
WE'RE NOT ON THE MOON ANYMORE, OLIVER. YOU'RE IN THE CAVE.
YOU DO REMEMBER THE CAVE, DON'T YOU?
ALL I REMEMBER IS MEETING THE FASCIST LEAGUE'S JUNIOR G-MEN, AND THEN SOMEONE SUCKER-PUNCHING ME...

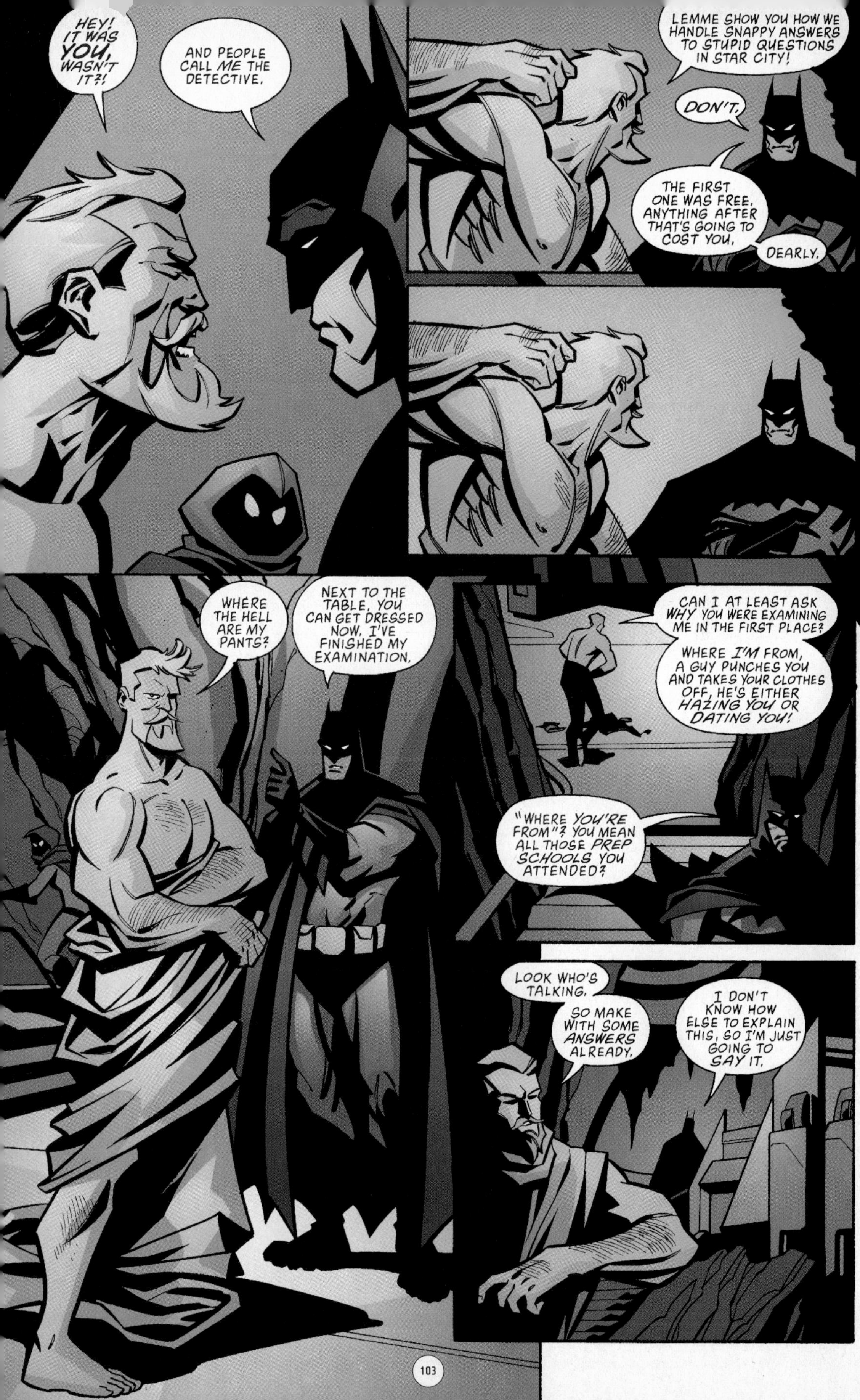
HEY! IT WAS YOU, WASN'T IT?!
AND PEOPLE CALL ME THE DETECTIVE.
LEMME SHOW YOU HOW WE HANDLE SNAPPY ANSWERS TO STUPID QUESTIONS IN STAR CITY!
DON'T.
THE FIRST ONE WAS FREE. ANYTHING AFTER THAT'S GOING TO COST YOU.
DEARLY.
WHERE THE HELL ARE MY PANTS?
NEXT TO THE TABLE. YOU CAN GET DRESSED NOW. I'VE FINISHED MY EXAMINATION.
CAN I AT LEAST ASK WHY YOU WERE EXAMINING ME IN THE FIRST PLACE?
WHERE I'M FROM, A GUY PUNCHES YOU AND TAKES YOUR CLOTHES OFF, HE'S EITHER HAZING YOU OR DATING YOU!
"WHERE YOU'RE FROM"? YOU MEAN ALL THOSE PREP SCHOOLS YOU ATTENDED?
LOOK WHO'S TALKING.
SO MAKE WITH SOME ANSWERS ALREADY.
I DON'T KNOW HOW ELSE TO EXPLAIN THIS, SO I'M JUST GOING TO SAY IT.

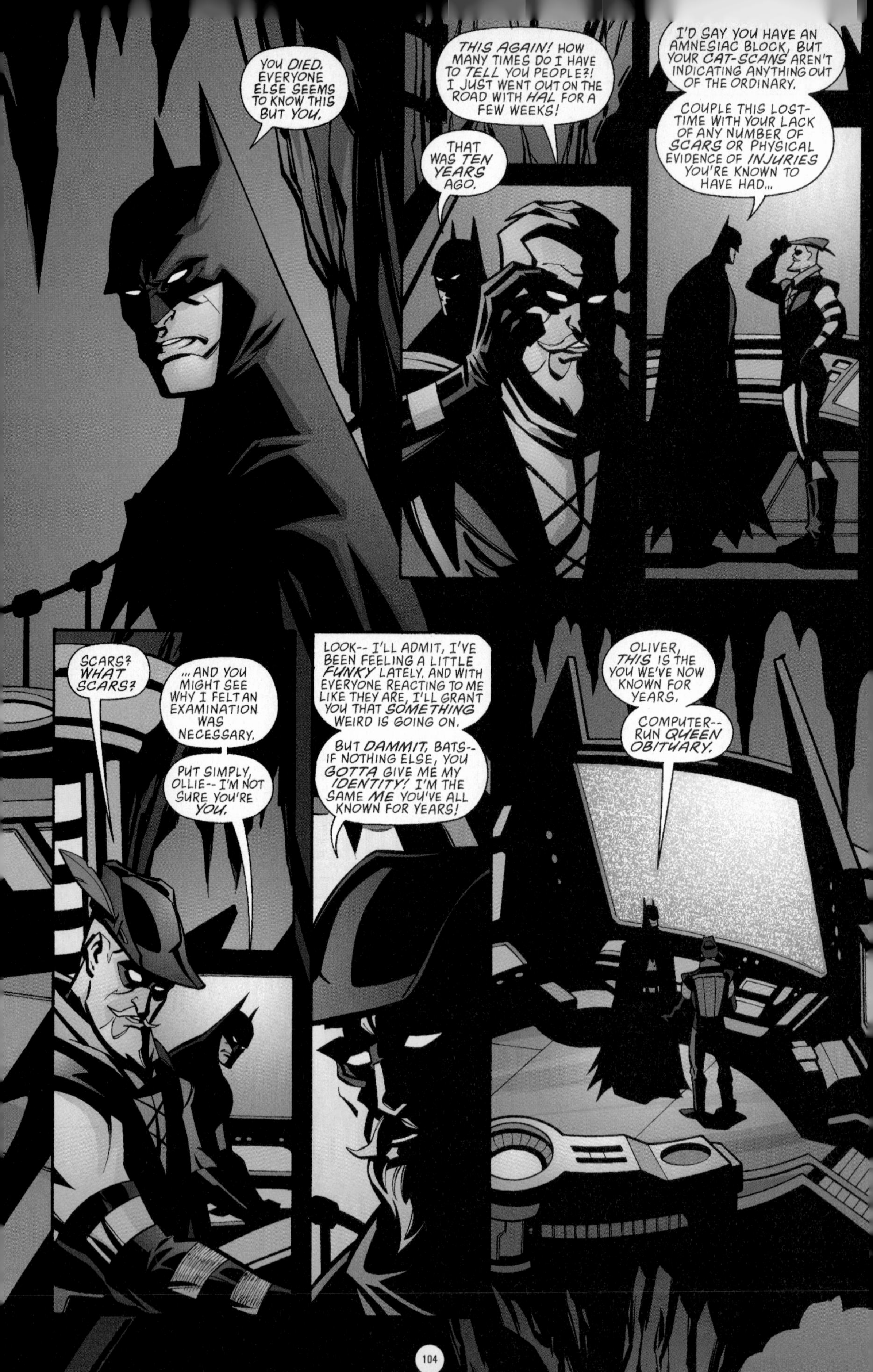
YOU DIED. EVERYONE ELSE SEEMS TO KNOW THIS BUT YOU.
THIS AGAIN! HOW MANY TIMES DO I HAVE TO TELL YOU PEOPLE?! I JUST WENT OUT ON THE ROAD WITH HAL FOR A FEW WEEKS!
THAT WAS TEN YEARS AGO.
I'D SAY YOU HAVE AN AMNESIAC BLOCK, BUT YOUR CAT-SCANS AREN'T INDICATING ANYTHING OUT OF THE ORDINARY.
COUPLE THIS LOST-TIME WITH YOUR LACK OF ANY NUMBER OF SCARS OR PHYSICAL EVIDENCE OF INJURIES YOU'RE KNOWN TO HAVE HAD...
SCARS? WHAT SCARS?
...AND YOU MIGHT SEE WHY I FELT AN EXAMINATION WAS NECESSARY.
PUT SIMPLY, OLLIE-- I'M NOT SURE YOU'RE YOU.
LOOK-- I'LL ADMIT, I'VE BEEN FEELING A LITTLE FUNKY LATELY. AND WITH EVERYONE REACTING TO ME LIKE THEY ARE, I'LL GRANT YOU THAT SOMETHING WEIRD IS GOING ON.
BUT DAMMIT, BATS-- IF NOTHING ELSE, YOU GOTTA GIVE ME MY IDENTITY! I'M THE SAME ME YOU'VE ALL KNOWN FOR YEARS!
OLIVER, THIS IS THE YOU WE'VE NOW KNOWN FOR YEARS.
COMPUTER-- RUN QUEEN OBITUARY.

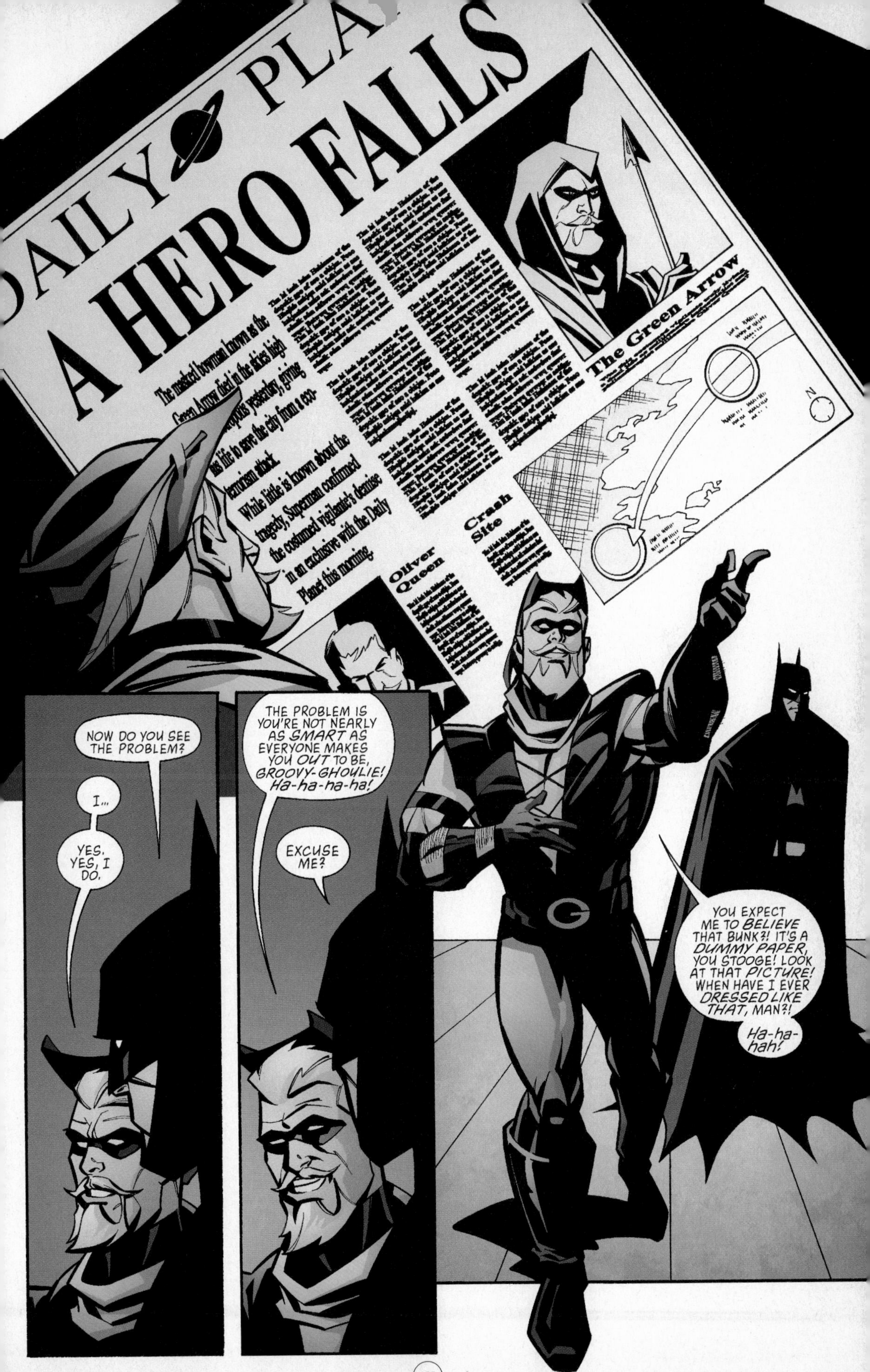
DAILY PLA
A HERO FALLS
The masked bowman known as the Green Arrow died in the skies high above Metropolis yesterday, giving his life to save the city from a terrorism attack.
While little is known about the tragedy, Superman confirmed the costumed vigilante's demise in an exclusive with the Daily Planet this morning.
The Green Arrow
Crash Site
Oliver Queen
NOW DO YOU SEE THE PROBLEM?
I...
YES. YES, I DO.
THE PROBLEM IS YOU'RE NOT NEARLY AS SMART AS EVERYONE MAKES YOU OUT TO BE, GROOVY-GHOULIE! Ha-ha-ha-ha!
EXCUSE ME?
YOU EXPECT ME TO BELIEVE THAT BUNK?! IT'S A DUMMY PAPER, YOU STOOGE! LOOK AT THAT PICTURE! WHEN HAVE I EVER DRESSED LIKE THAT, MAN?!
Ha-ha-hah!

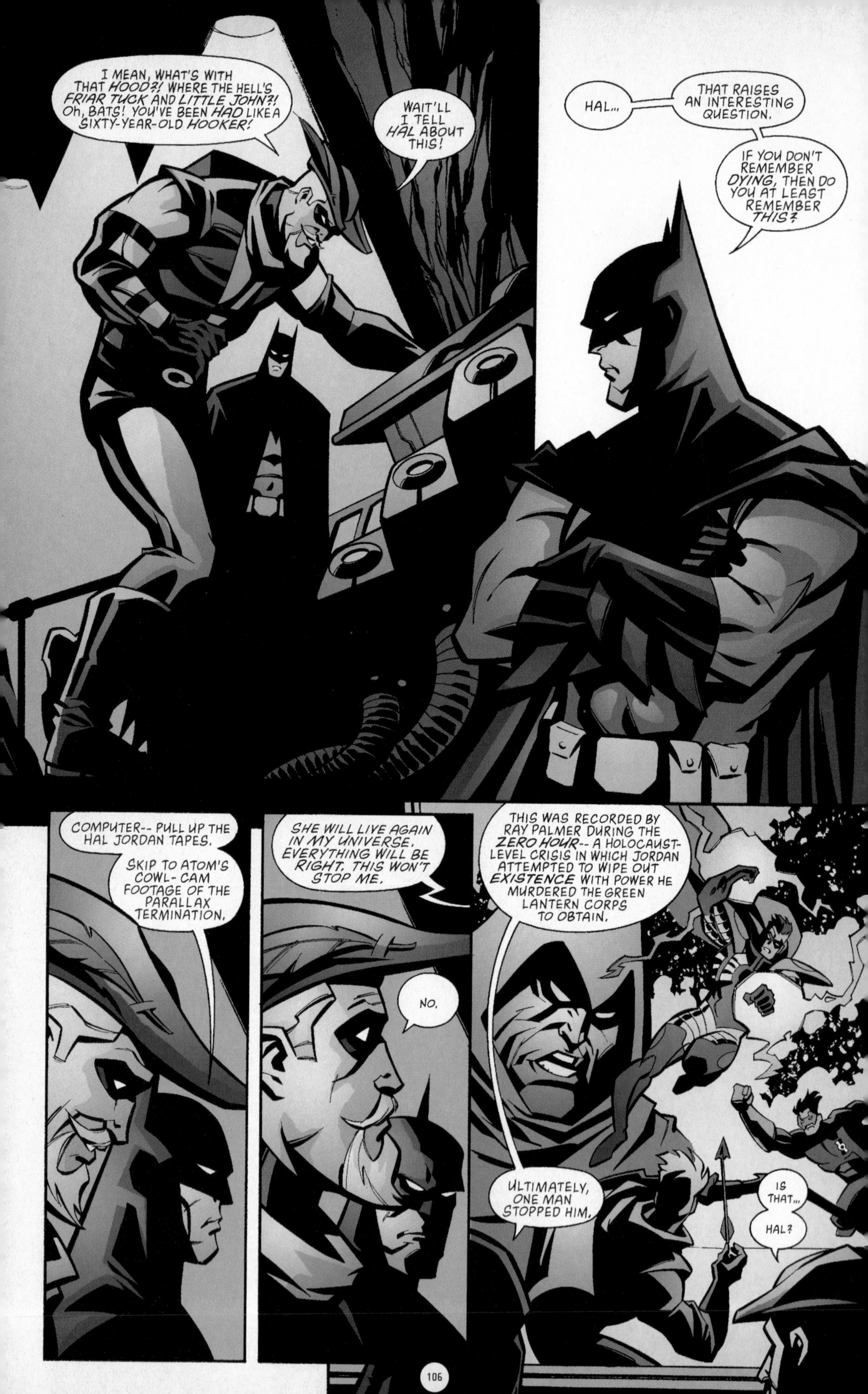
I MEAN, WHAT'S WITH THAT HOOD?! WHERE THE HELL'S FRIAR TUCK AND LITTLE JOHN?! Oh, BATS! YOU'VE BEEN HAD LIKE A SIXTY-YEAR-OLD HOOKER!
WAIT'LL I TELL HAL ABOUT THIS!
HAL...
THAT RAISES AN INTERESTING QUESTION.
IF YOU DON'T REMEMBER DYING, THEN DO YOU AT LEAST REMEMBER THIS?
COMPUTER-- PULL UP THE HAL JORDAN TAPES.
SKIP TO ATOM'S COWL-CAM FOOTAGE OF THE PARALLAX TERMINATION.
SHE WILL LIVE AGAIN IN MY UNIVERSE. EVERYTHING WILL BE RIGHT. THIS WON'T STOP ME.
NO.
THIS WAS RECORDED BY RAY PALMER DURING THE ZERO HOUR-- A HOLOCAUST-LEVEL CRISIS IN WHICH JORDAN ATTEMPTED TO WIPE OUT EXISTENCE WITH POWER HE MURDERED THE GREEN LANTERN CORPS TO OBTAIN.
ULTIMATELY, ONE MAN STOPPED HIM.
IS THAT...
HAL?

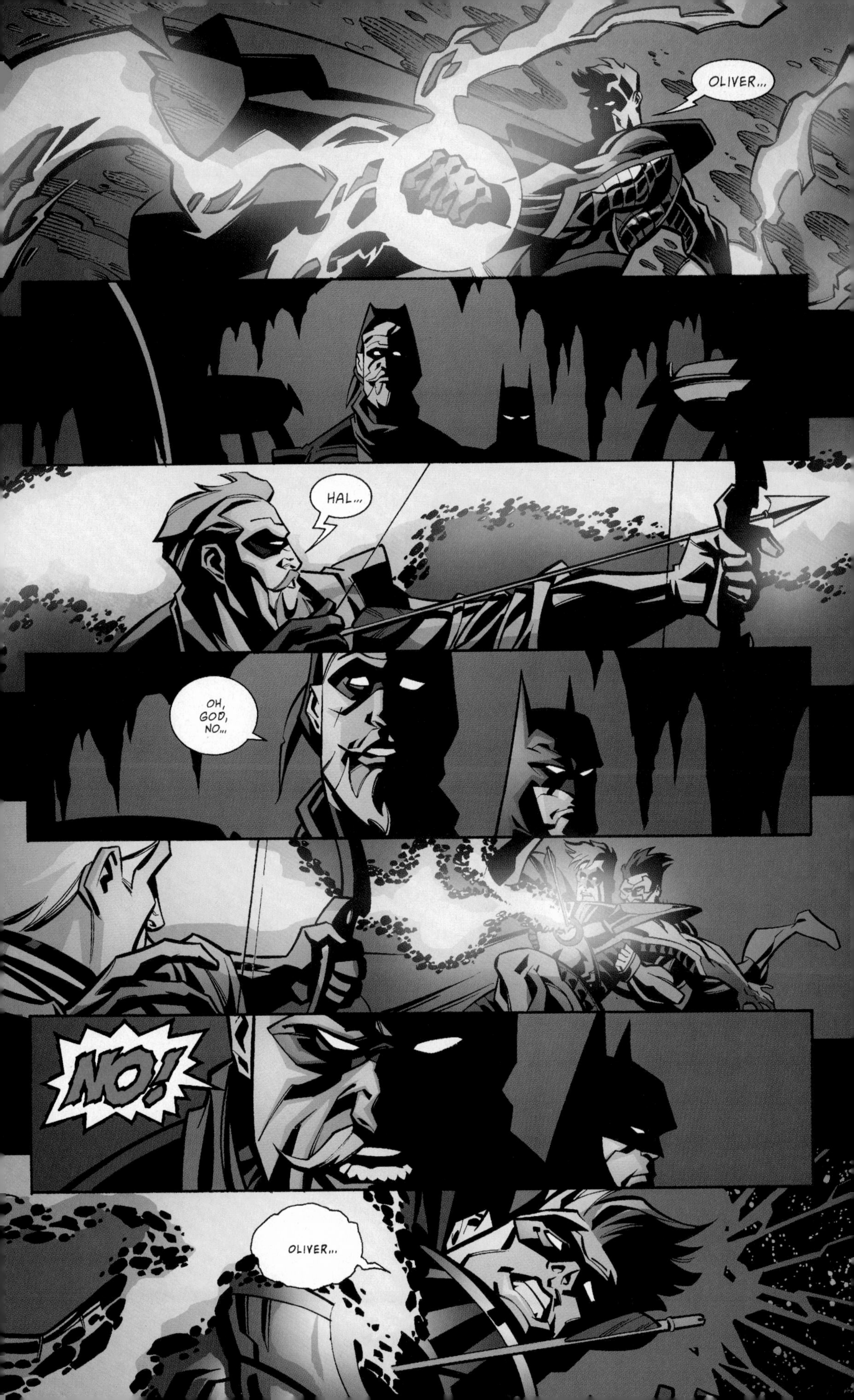
OLIVER...
HAL...
OH, GOD, NO...
NO!
OLIVER...

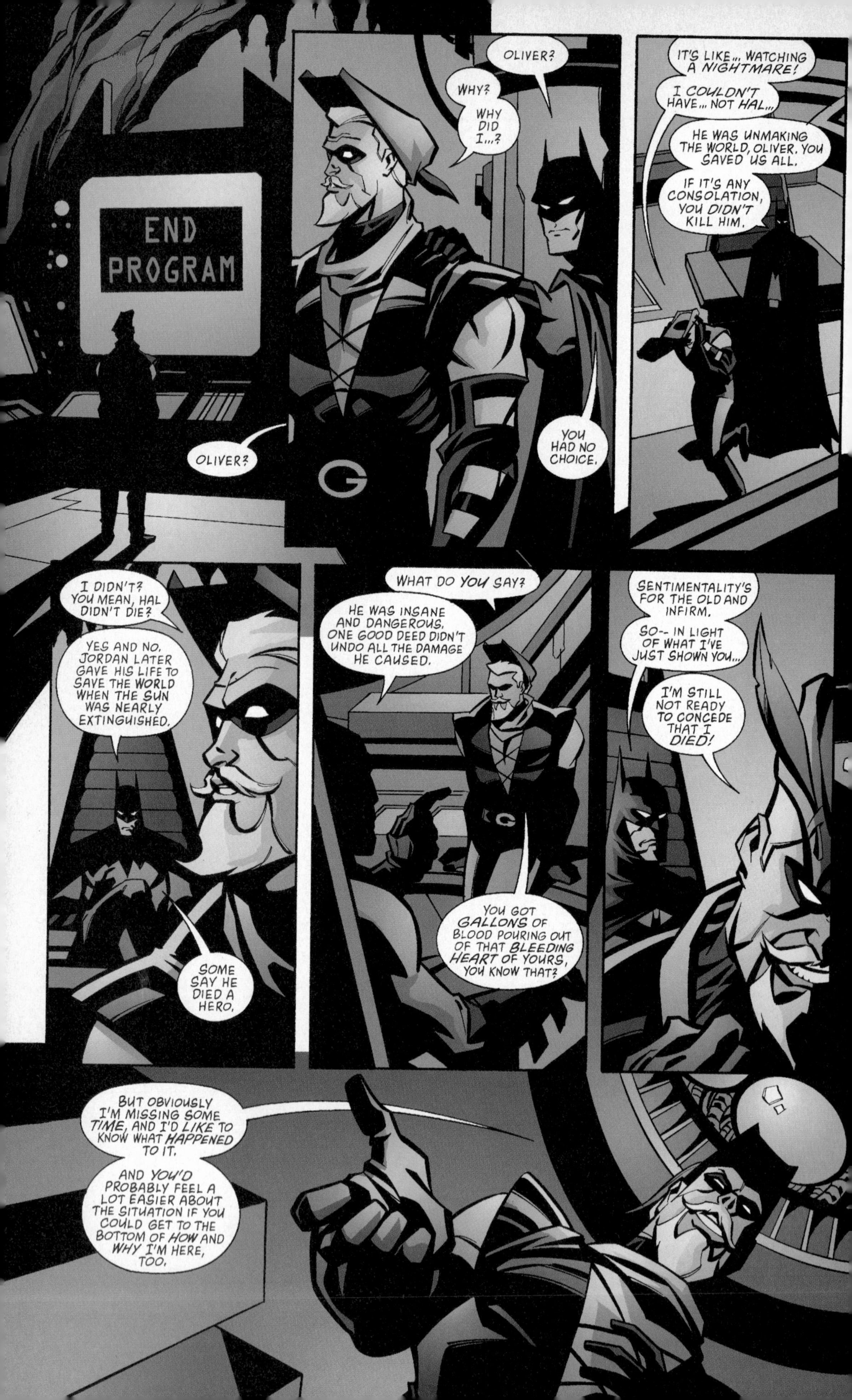
END PROGRAM
OLIVER?
OLIVER?
WHY? WHY DID I...?
YOU HAD NO CHOICE.
IT'S LIKE... WATCHING A NIGHTMARE!
I COULDN'T HAVE... NOT HAL...
HE WAS UNMAKING THE WORLD, OLIVER. YOU SAVED US ALL.
IF IT'S ANY CONSOLATION, YOU DIDN'T KILL HIM.
I DIDN'T? YOU MEAN, HAL DIDN'T DIE?
YES AND NO. JORDAN LATER GAVE HIS LIFE TO SAVE THE WORLD WHEN THE SUN WAS NEARLY EXTINGUISHED.
SOME SAY HE DIED A HERO.
WHAT DO YOU SAY?
HE WAS INSANE AND DANGEROUS. ONE GOOD DEED DIDN'T UNDO ALL THE DAMAGE HE CAUSED.
YOU GOT GALLONS OF BLOOD POURING OUT OF THAT BLEEDING HEART OF YOURS, YOU KNOW THAT?
SENTIMENTALITY'S FOR THE OLD AND INFIRM.
SO-- IN LIGHT OF WHAT I'VE JUST SHOWN YOU...
I'M STILL NOT READY TO CONCEDE THAT I DIED!
BUT OBVIOUSLY I'M MISSING SOME TIME, AND I'D LIKE TO KNOW WHAT HAPPENED TO IT.
AND YOU'D PROBABLY FEEL A LOT EASIER ABOUT THE SITUATION IF YOU COULD GET TO THE BOTTOM OF HOW AND WHY I'M HERE, TOO.

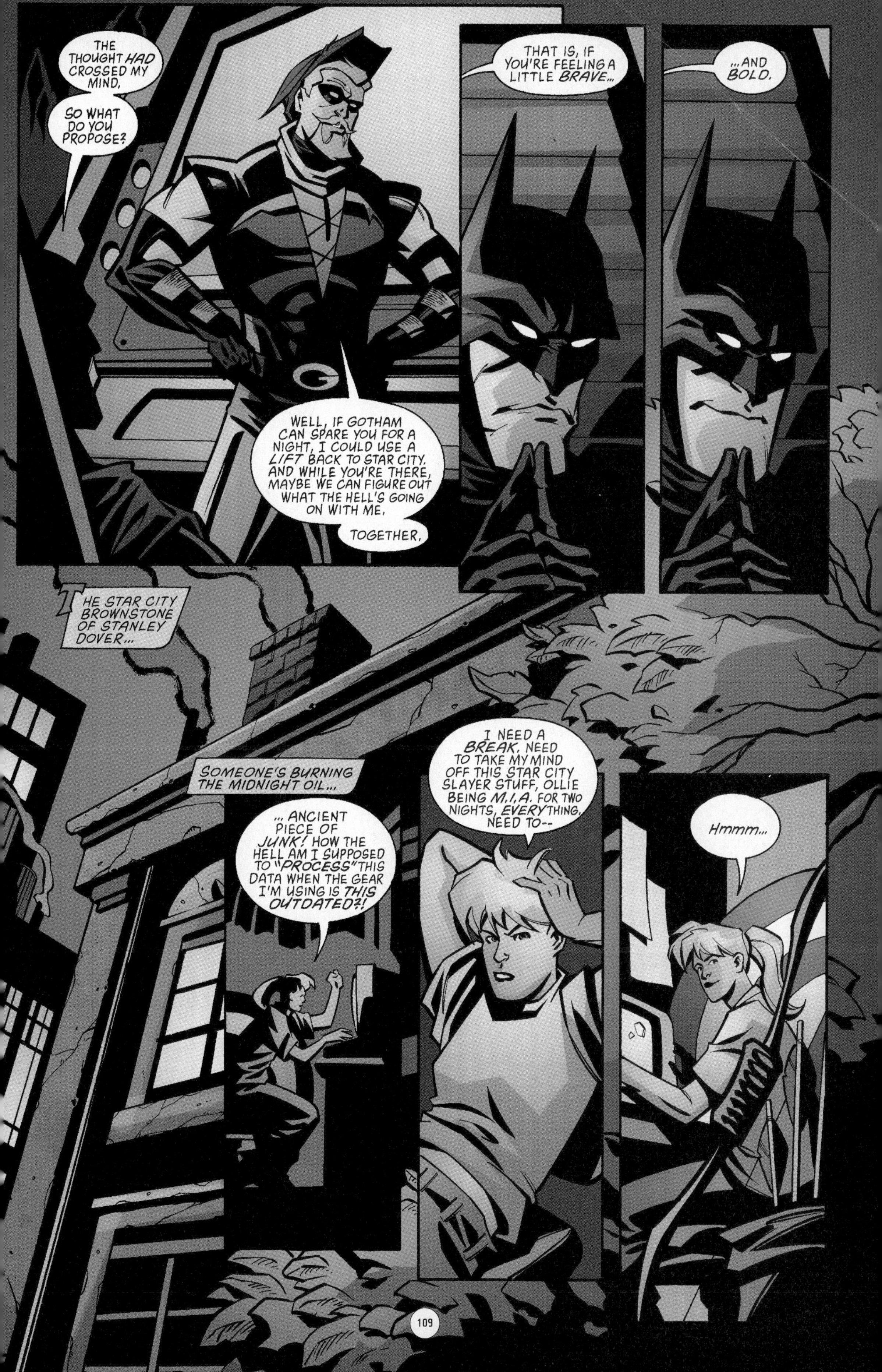
THE THOUGHT HAD CROSSED MY MIND.
SO WHAT DO YOU PROPOSE?
WELL, IF GOTHAM CAN SPARE YOU FOR A NIGHT, I COULD USE A LIFT BACK TO STAR CITY. AND WHILE YOU'RE THERE, MAYBE WE CAN FIGURE OUT WHAT THE HELL'S GOING ON WITH ME.
TOGETHER.
THAT IS, IF YOU'RE FEELING A LITTLE BRAVE...
...AND BOLD.
THE STAR CITY BROWNSTONE OF STANLEY DOVER...
SOMEONE'S BURNING THE MIDNIGHT OIL...
...ANCIENT PIECE OF JUNK! HOW THE HELL AM I SUPPOSED TO "PROCESS" THIS DATA WHEN THE GEAR I'M USING IS THIS OUTDATED?!
I NEED A BREAK. NEED TO TAKE MY MIND OFF THIS STAR CITY SLAYER STUFF, OLLIE BEING M.I.A. FOR TWO NIGHTS, EVERYTHING. NEED TO--
Hmmm...

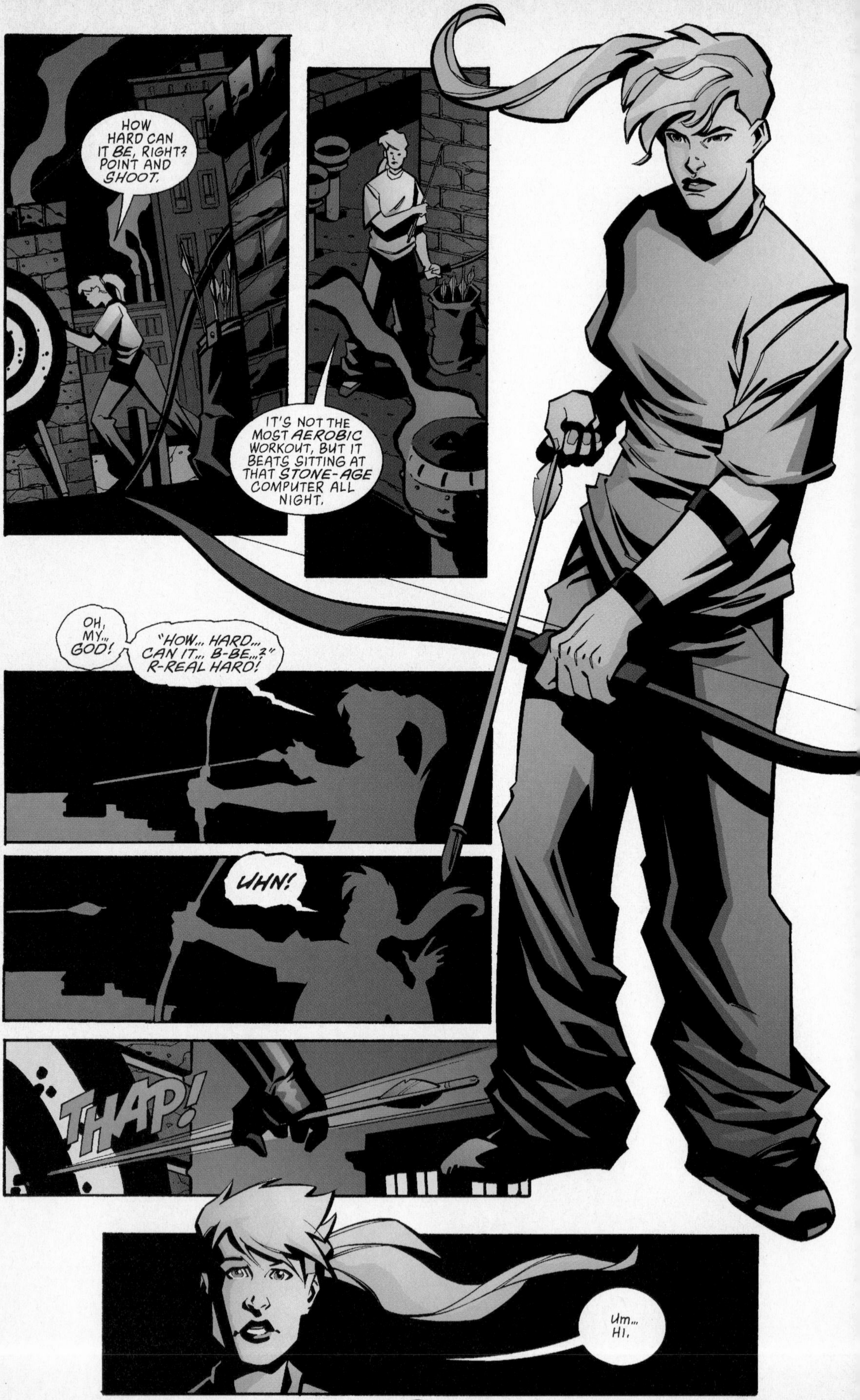
HOW HARD CAN IT BE, RIGHT? POINT AND SHOOT.
IT'S NOT THE MOST AEROBIC WORKOUT, BUT IT BEATS SITTING AT THAT STONE-AGE COMPUTER ALL NIGHT.
OH, MY... GOD!
"HOW... HARD... CAN IT... B-BE...?" R-REAL HARD!
UHN!
THAP!
Um... Hi.

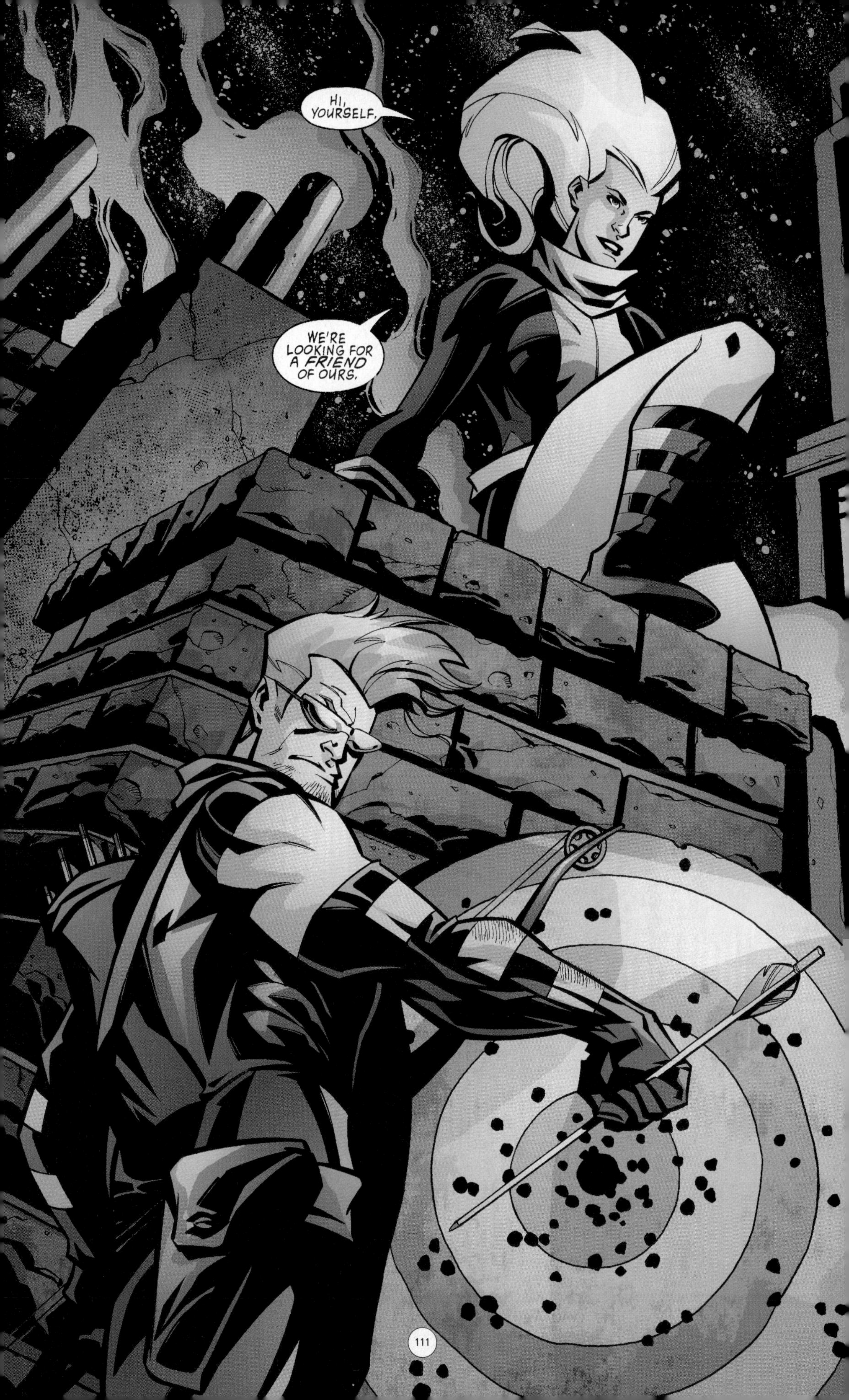
HI, YOURSELF.
WE'RE LOOKING FOR A FRIEND OF OURS.

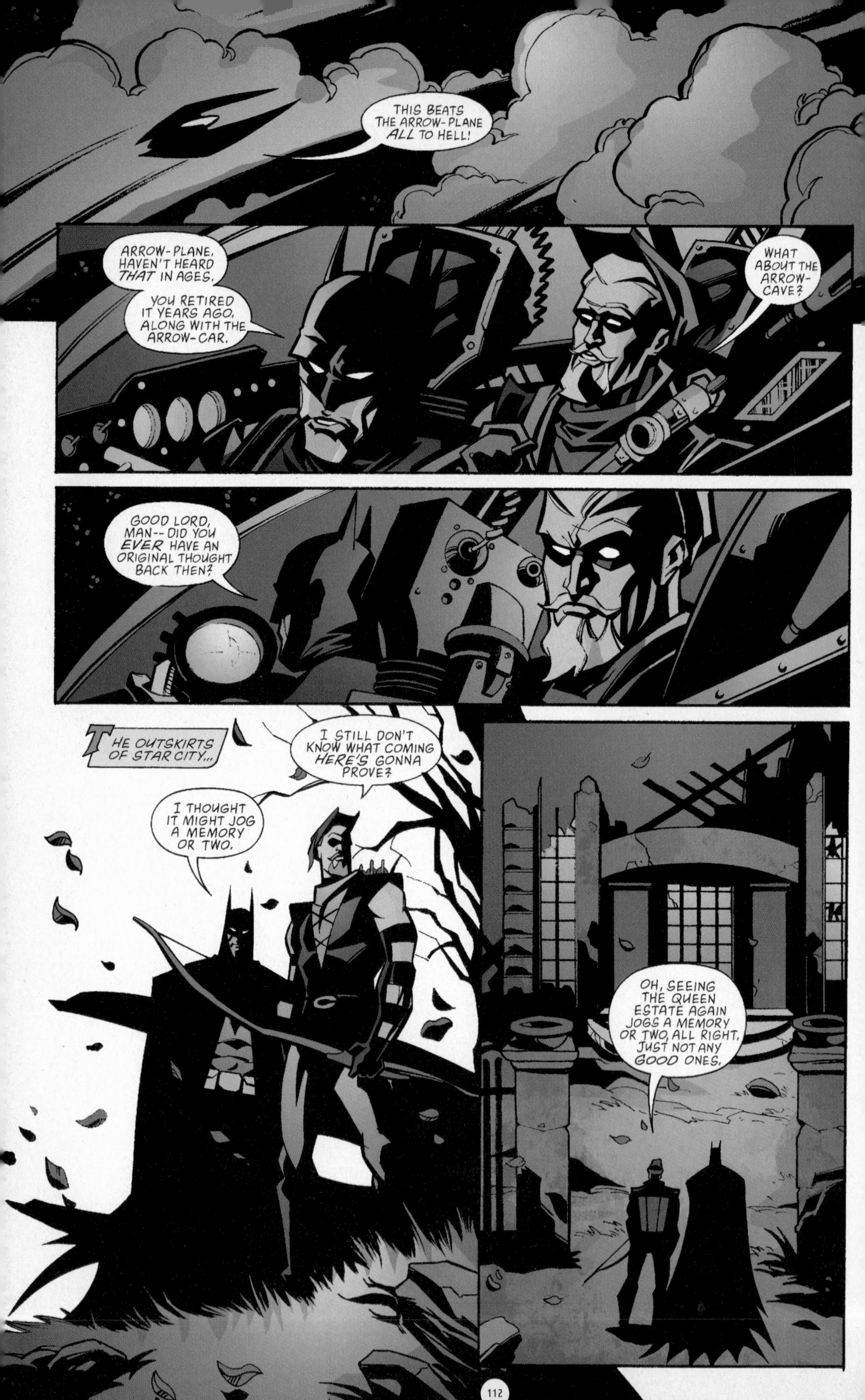
THIS BEATS THE ARROW-PLANE ALL TO HELL!
ARROW-PLANE. HAVEN'T HEARD THAT IN AGES.
YOU RETIRED IT YEARS AGO, ALONG WITH THE ARROW-CAR.
WHAT ABOUT THE ARROW-CAVE?
GOOD LORD, MAN-- DID YOU EVER HAVE AN ORIGINAL THOUGHT BACK THEN?
THE OUTSKIRTS OF STAR CITY...
I STILL DON'T KNOW WHAT COMING HERE'S GONNA PROVE?
I THOUGHT IT MIGHT JOG A MEMORY OR TWO.
OH, SEEING THE QUEEN ESTATE AGAIN JOGS A MEMORY OR TWO, ALL RIGHT. JUST NOT ANY GOOD ONES.

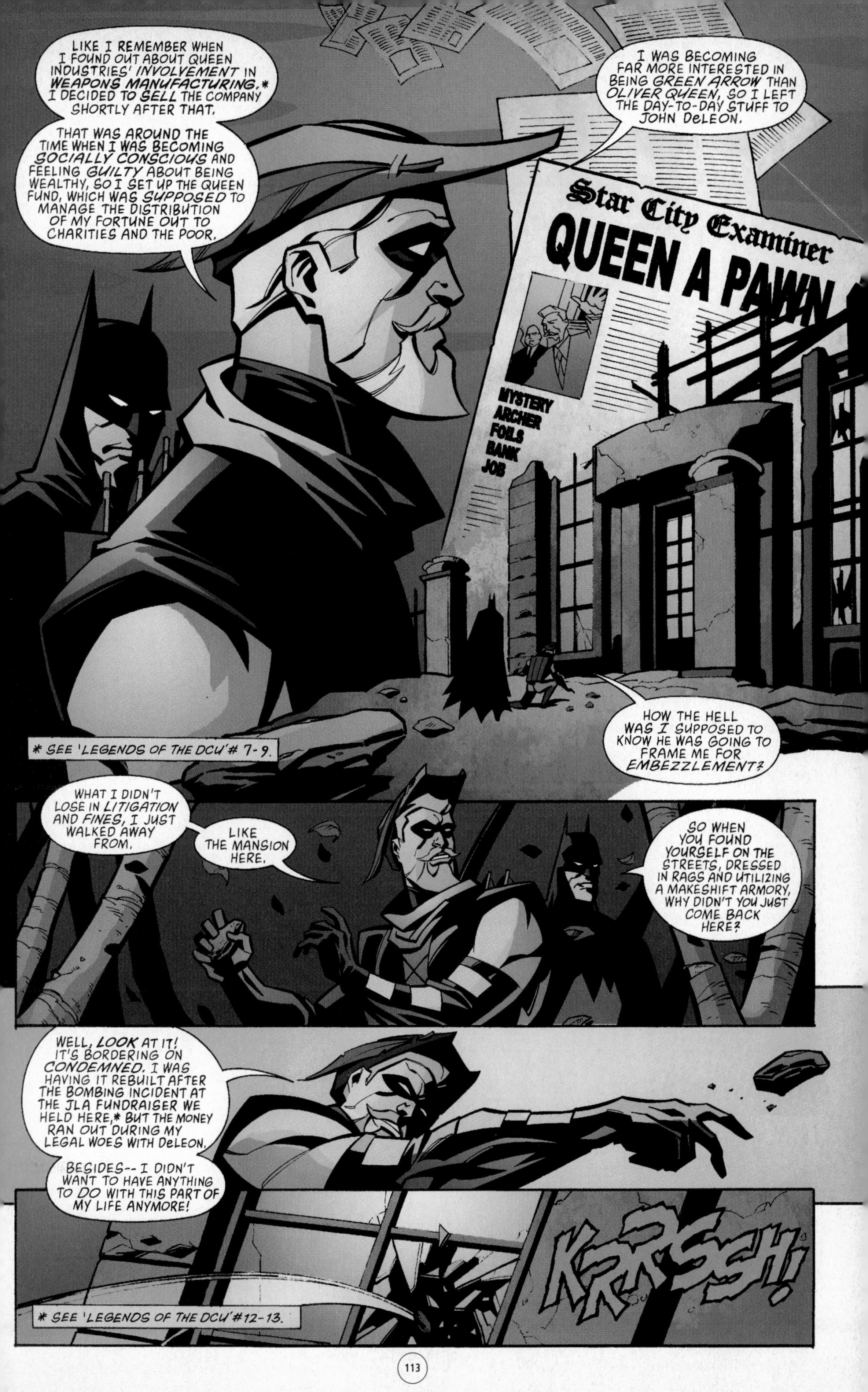
LIKE I REMEMBER WHEN I FOUND OUT ABOUT QUEEN INDUSTRIES' INVOLVEMENT IN WEAPONS MANUFACTURING.* I DECIDED TO SELL THE COMPANY SHORTLY AFTER THAT.
THAT WAS AROUND THE TIME WHEN I WAS BECOMING SOCIALLY CONSCIOUS AND FEELING GUILTY ABOUT BEING WEALTHY, SO I SET UP THE QUEEN FUND, WHICH WAS SUPPOSED TO MANAGE THE DISTRIBUTION OF MY FORTUNE OUT TO CHARITIES AND THE POOR.
I WAS BECOMING FAR MORE INTERESTED IN BEING GREEN ARROW THAN OLIVER QUEEN, SO I LEFT THE DAY-TO-DAY STUFF TO JOHN DeLEON.
Star City Examiner
QUEEN A PAWN
MYSTERY ARCHER FOILS BANK JOB
* SEE 'LEGENDS OF THE DCU' # 7-9.
HOW THE HELL WAS I SUPPOSED TO KNOW HE WAS GOING TO FRAME ME FOR EMBEZZLEMENT?
WHAT I DIDN'T LOSE IN LITIGATION AND FINES, I JUST WALKED AWAY FROM.
LIKE THE MANSION HERE.
SO WHEN YOU FOUND YOURSELF ON THE STREETS, DRESSED IN RAGS AND UTILIZING A MAKESHIFT ARMORY, WHY DIDN'T YOU JUST COME BACK HERE?
WELL, LOOK AT IT! IT'S BORDERING ON CONDEMNED. I WAS HAVING IT REBUILT AFTER THE BOMBING INCIDENT AT THE JLA FUNDRAISER WE HELD HERE,* BUT THE MONEY RAN OUT DURING MY LEGAL WOES WITH DeLEON.
BESIDES-- I DIDN'T WANT TO HAVE ANYTHING TO DO WITH THIS PART OF MY LIFE ANYMORE!
KRRSSH!
* SEE 'LEGENDS OF THE DCU' #12-13.

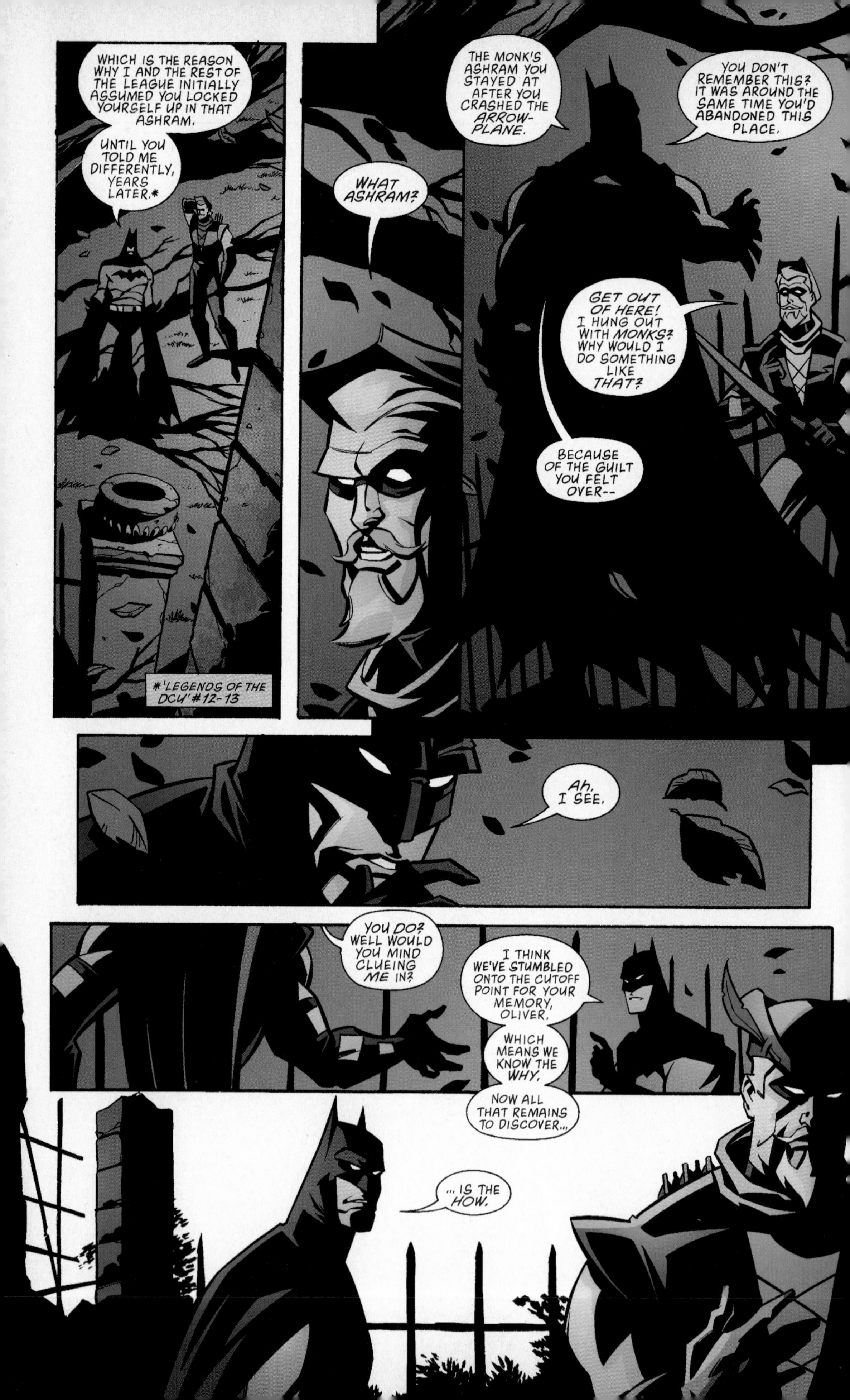
WHICH IS THE REASON WHY I AND THE REST OF THE LEAGUE INITIALLY ASSUMED YOU LOCKED YOURSELF UP IN THAT ASHRAM.
UNTIL YOU TOLD ME DIFFERENTLY, YEARS LATER.*
*'LEGENDS OF THE DCU' #12-13
THE MONK'S ASHRAM YOU STAYED AT AFTER YOU CRASHED THE ARROW-PLANE.
WHAT ASHRAM?
YOU DON'T REMEMBER THIS? IT WAS AROUND THE SAME TIME YOU'D ABANDONED THIS PLACE.
GET OUT OF HERE! I HUNG OUT WITH MONKS? WHY WOULD I DO SOMETHING LIKE THAT?
BECAUSE OF THE GUILT YOU FELT OVER--
AH. I SEE.
YOU DO? WELL WOULD YOU MIND CLUEING ME IN?
I THINK WE'VE STUMBLED ONTO THE CUTOFF POINT FOR YOUR MEMORY, OLIVER.
WHICH MEANS WE KNOW THE WHY.
NOW ALL THAT REMAINS TO DISCOVER...
...IS THE HOW.

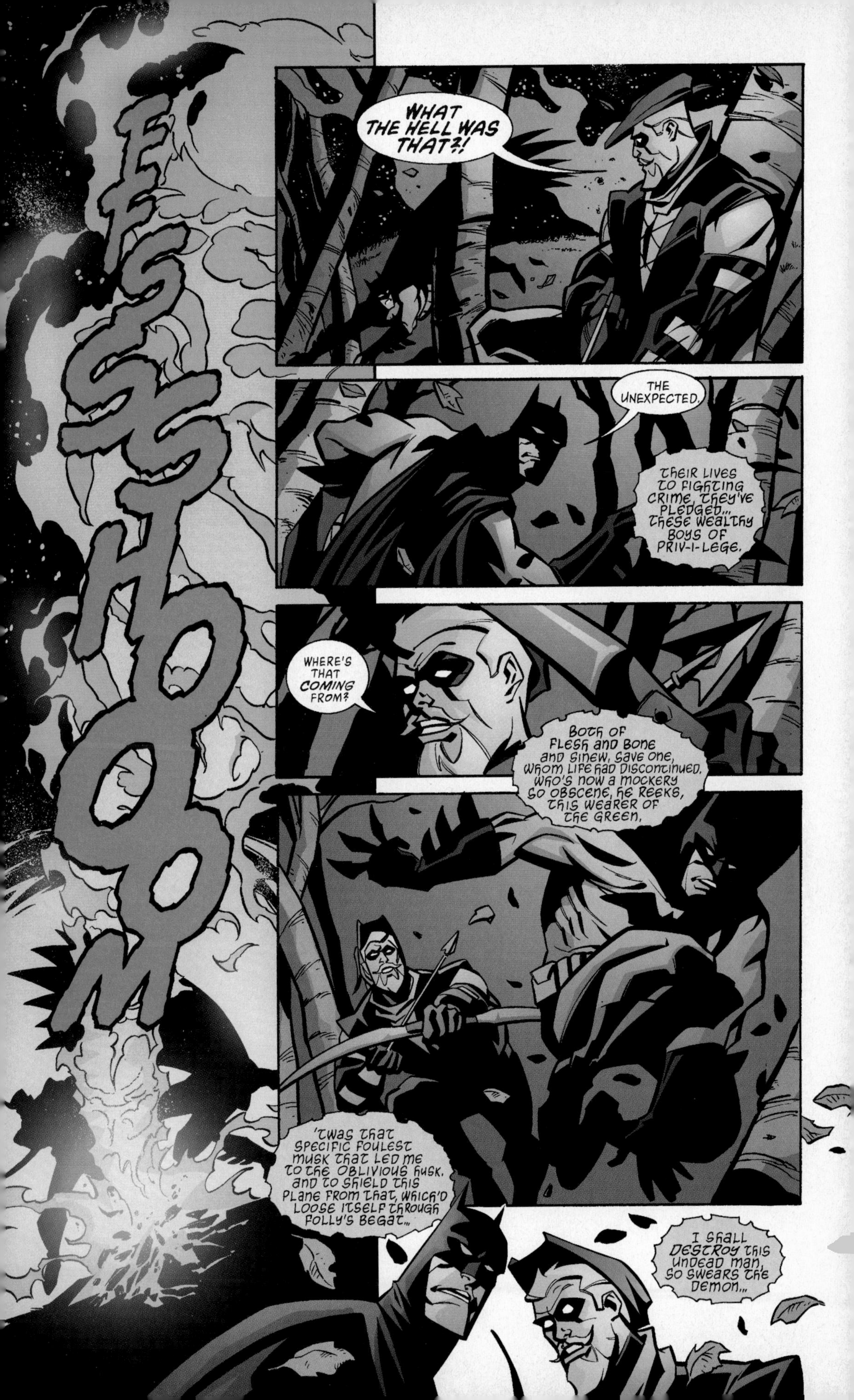
FFSSHHOOM
WHAT THE HELL WAS THAT?!
THE UNEXPECTED.
THEIR LIVES TO FIGHTING CRIME, THEY'VE PLEDGED... THESE WEALTHY BOYS OF PRIV-I-LEGE.
WHERE'S THAT COMING FROM?
BOTH OF FLESH AND BONE AND SINEW, SAVE ONE, WHOM LIFE HAD DISCONTINUED, WHO'S NOW A MOCKERY SO OBSCENE, HE REEKS, THIS WEARER OF THE GREEN,
'TWAS THAT SPECIFIC FOULEST MUSK THAT LED ME TO THE OBLIVIOUS HUSK, AND TO SHIELD THIS PLANE FROM THAT, WHICH'D LOOSE ITSELF THROUGH FOLLY'S BEGAT...
I SHALL DESTROY THIS UNDEAD MAN, SO SWEARS THE DEMON...

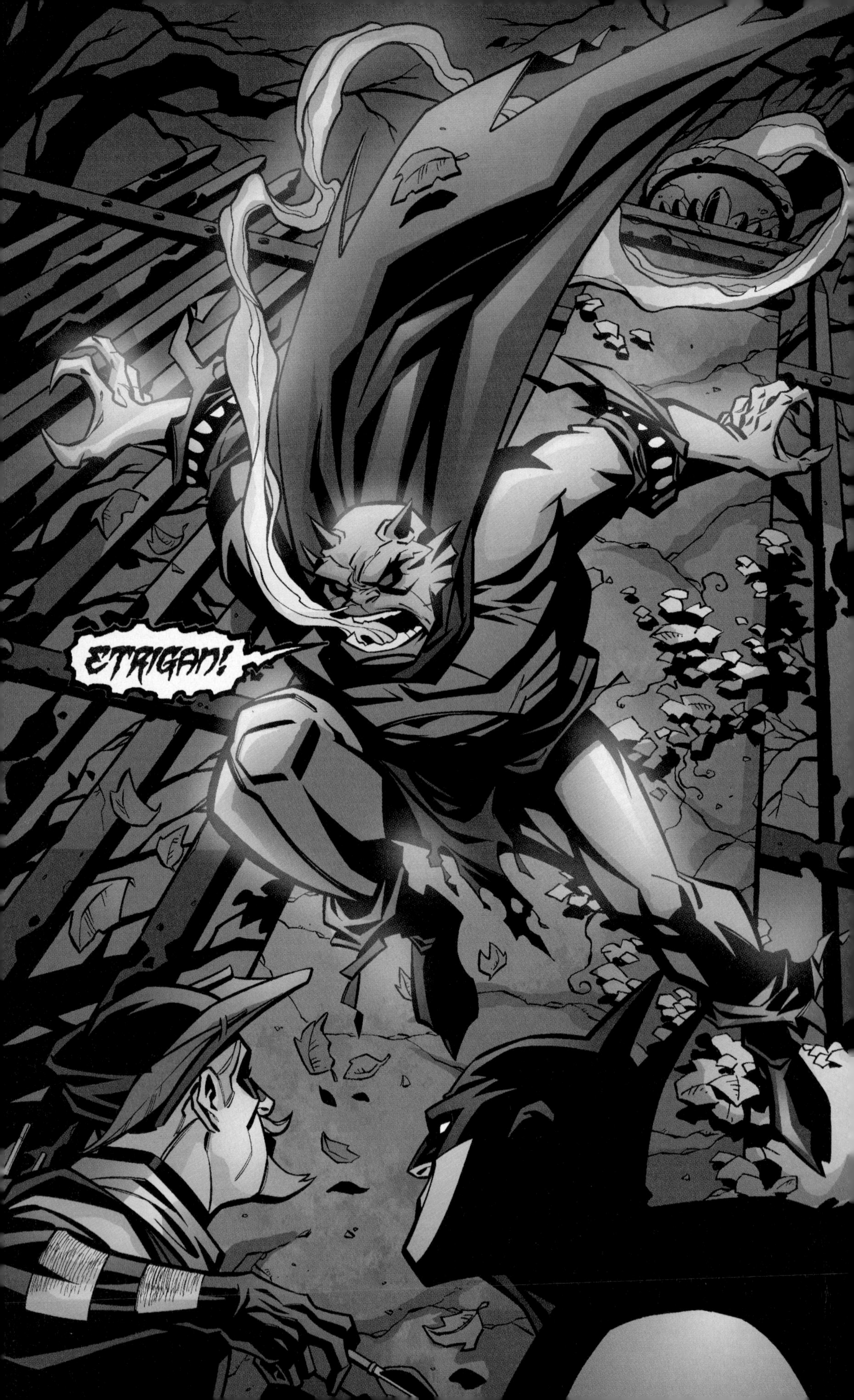
ETRIGAN!

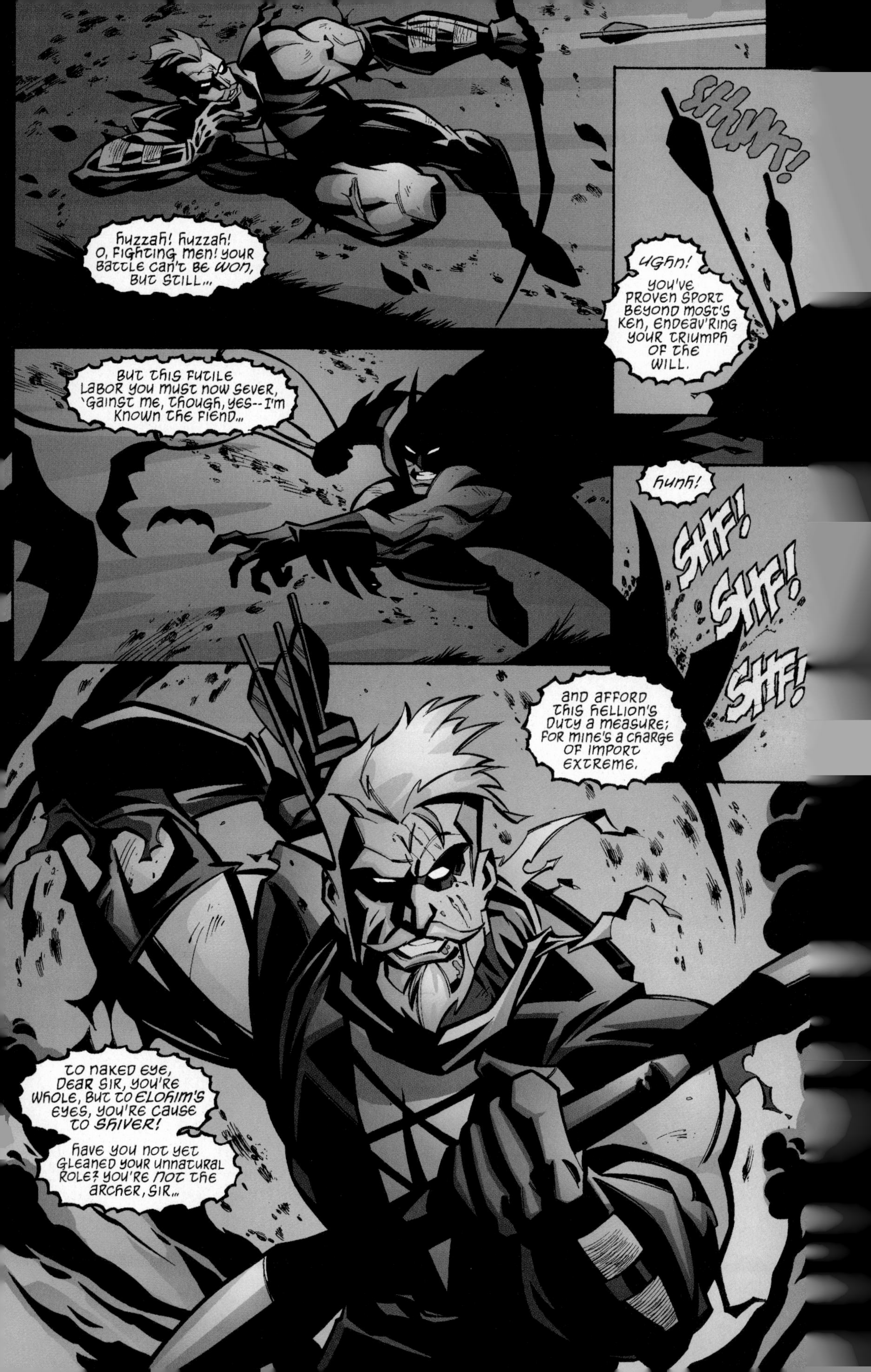
SHUNT!
HUZZAH! HUZZAH! O, FIGHTING MEN! YOUR BATTLE CAN'T BE WON, BUT STILL...
UGHH!
YOU'VE PROVEN SPORT BEYOND MOST'S KEN, ENDEAV'RING YOUR TRIUMPH OF THE WILL.
BUT THIS FUTILE LABOR YOU MUST NOW SEVER, 'GAINST ME, THOUGH, YES-- I'M KNOWN THE FIEND...
HUNH!
SHF! SHF! SHF!
AND AFFORD THIS HELLION'S DUTY A MEASURE; FOR MINE'S A CHARGE OF IMPORT EXTREME.
TO NAKED EYE, DEAR SIR, YOU'RE WHOLE, BUT TO ELOHIM'S EYES, YOU'RE CAUSE TO SHIVER!
HAVE YOU NOT YET GLEANED YOUR UNNATURAL ROLE? YOU'RE NOT THE ARCHER, SIR...

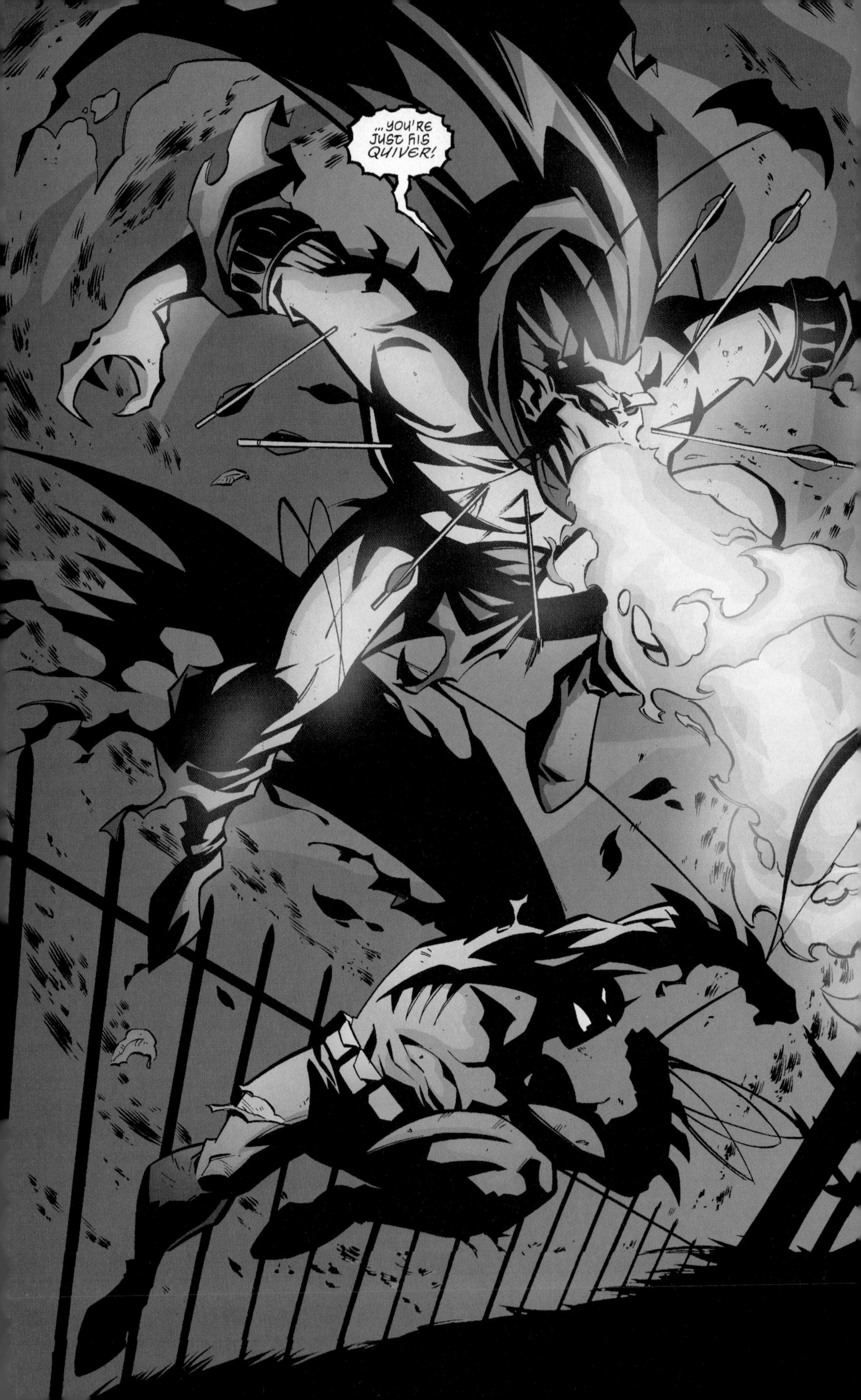
...YOU'RE JUST HIS QUIVER!

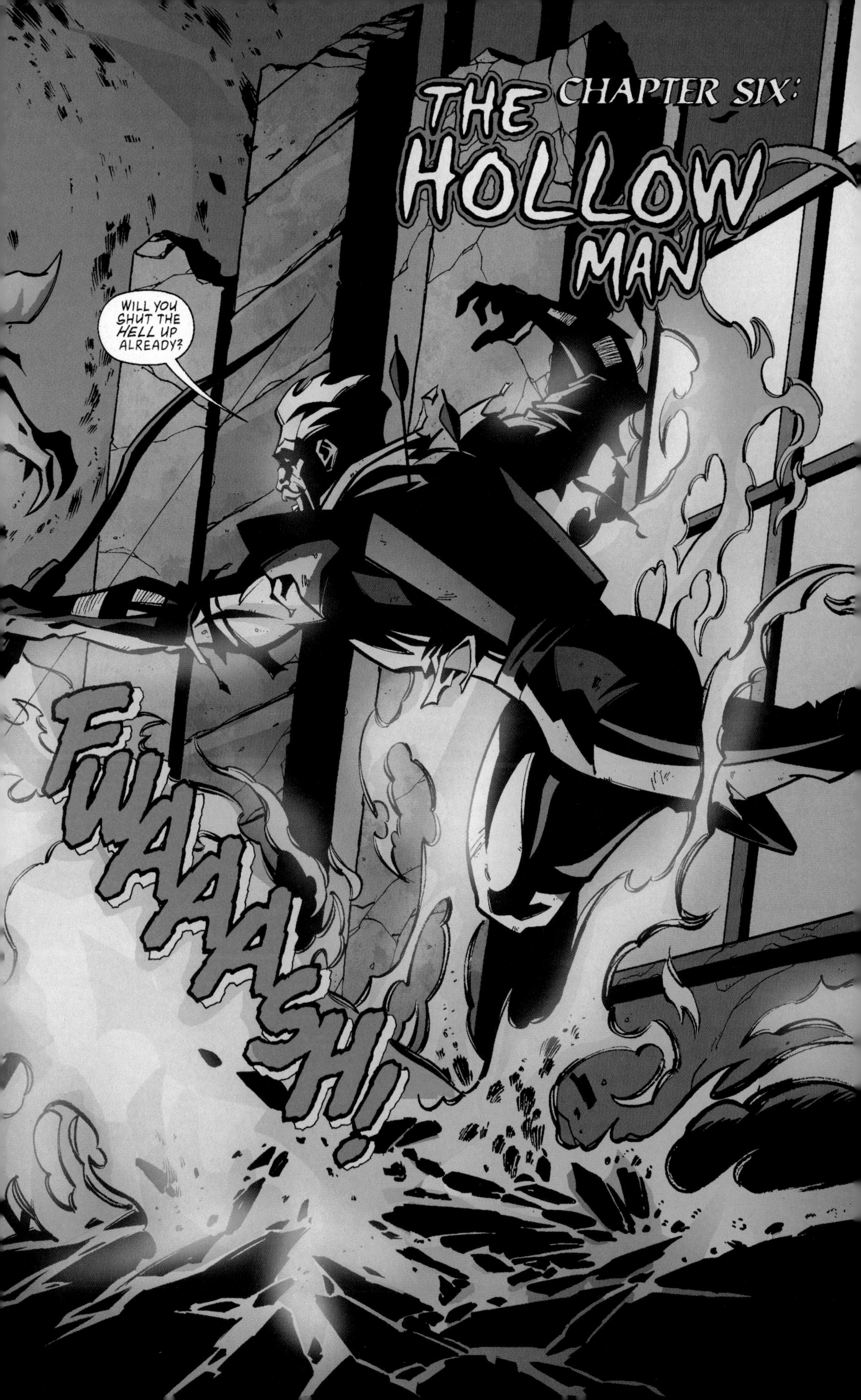
CHAPTER SIX:
THE HOLLOW MAN
WILL YOU SHUT THE HELL UP ALREADY?
FWAAASH!

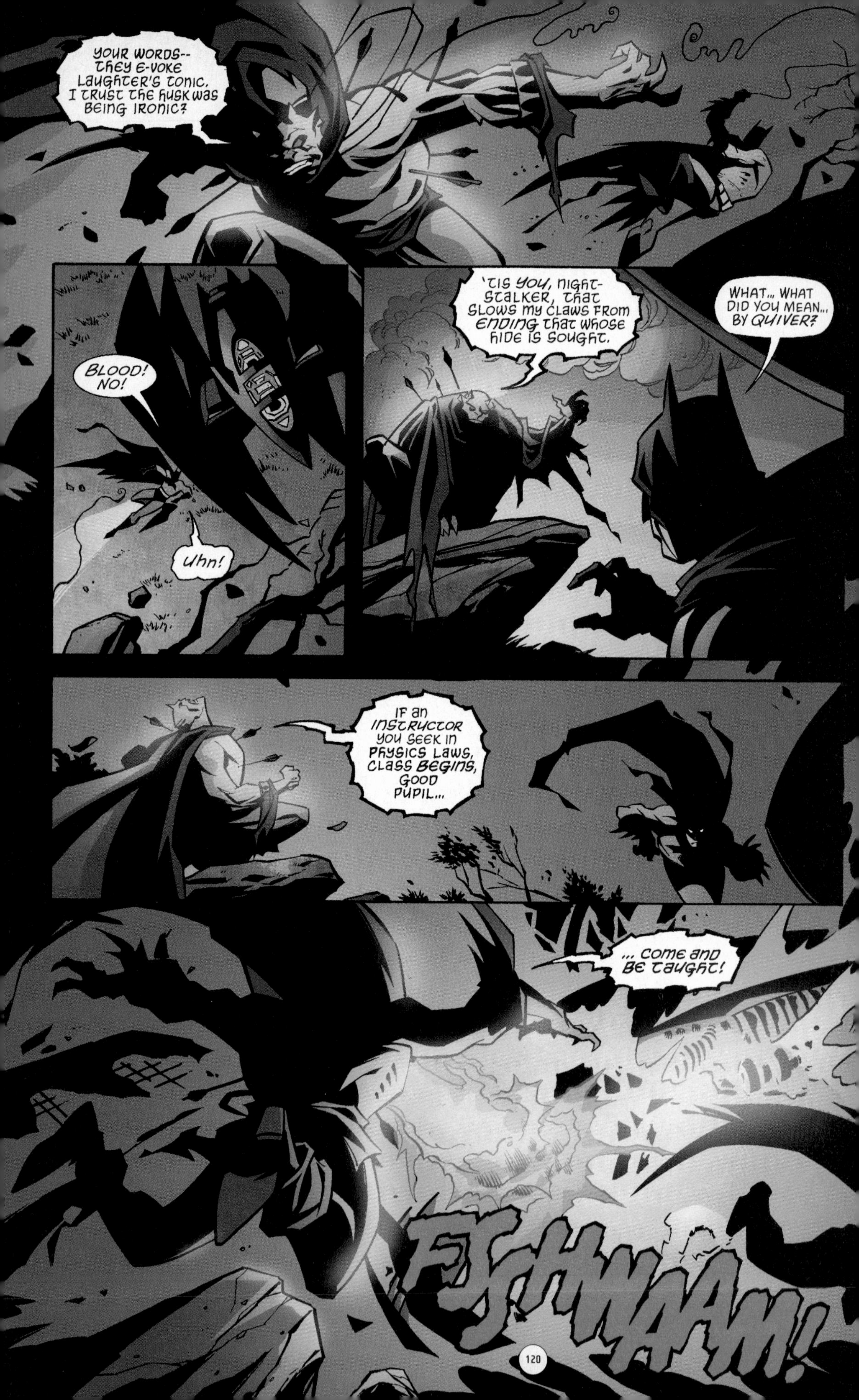

YOUR WORDS-- THEY E-VOKE LAUGHTER'S TONIC. I TRUST THE HUSK WAS BEING IRONIC?
BLOOD! NO!
Uhn!
'TIS YOU, NIGHT-STALKER, THAT SLOWS MY CLAWS FROM ENDING THAT WHOSE HIDE IS SOUGHT.
WHAT... WHAT DID YOU MEAN... BY QUIVER?
IF AN INSTRUCTOR YOU SEEK IN PHYSICS LAWS, CLASS BEGINS, GOOD PUPIL...
...COME AND BE TAUGHT!
FSHWAAM!

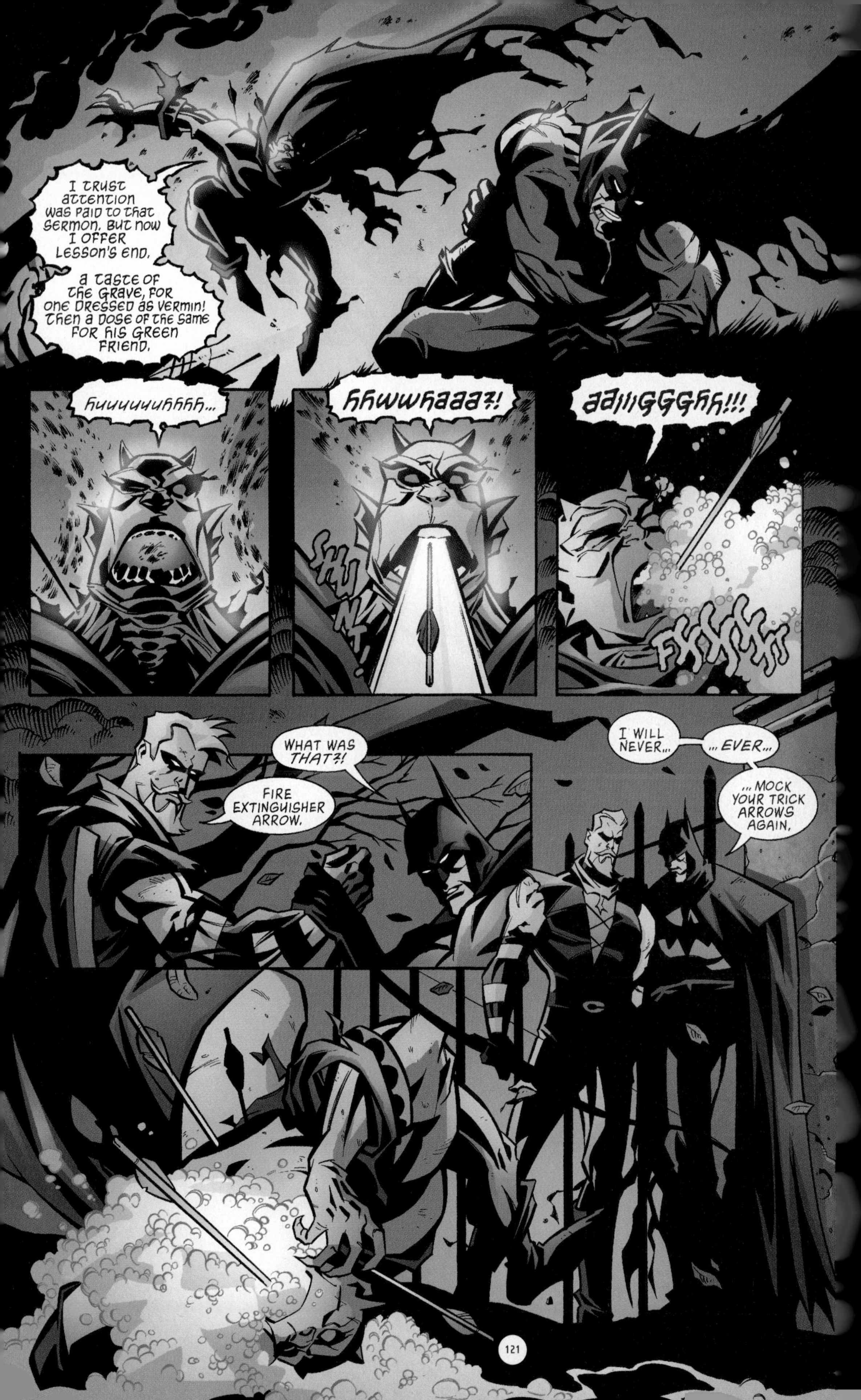
I TRUST ATTENTION WAS PAID TO THAT SERMON. BUT NOW I OFFER LESSON'S END.
A TASTE OF THE GRAVE, FOR ONE DRESSED AS VERMIN! THEN A DOSE OF THE SAME FOR HIS GREEN FRIEND.
HUUUUUUHHHH...
HHWWHAAA?!
SHUNK!
AAIIIGGGHH!!!
FHHH
WHAT WAS THAT?!
FIRE EXTINGUISHER ARROW.
I WILL NEVER...
...EVER...
...MOCK YOUR TRICK ARROWS AGAIN.

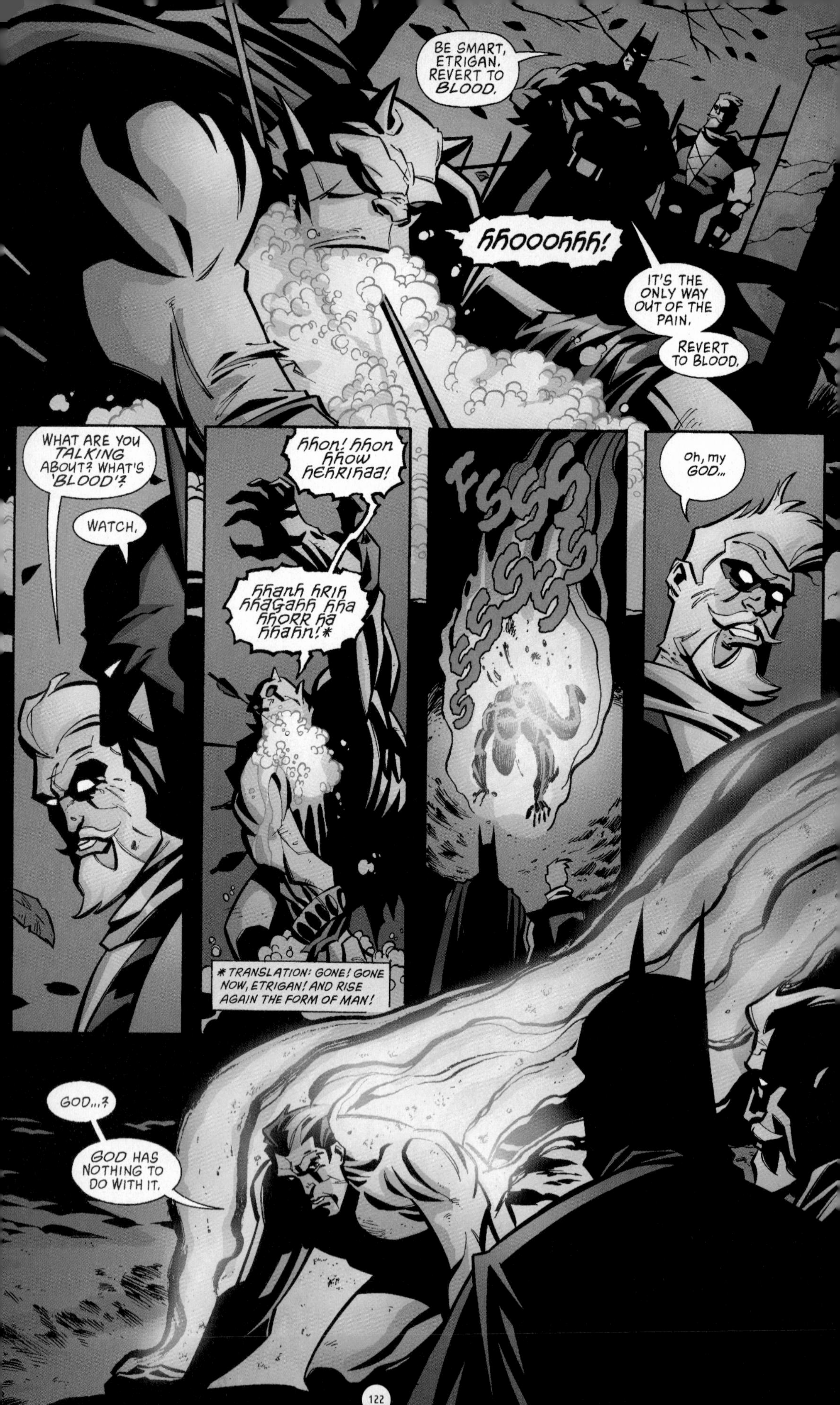
BE SMART, ETRIGAN. REVERT TO BLOOD.
HHOOOHHH!
IT'S THE ONLY WAY OUT OF THE PAIN.
REVERT TO BLOOD.
WHAT ARE YOU TALKING ABOUT? WHAT'S 'BLOOD'?
WATCH.
HHON! HHON HHOW HEHRIHAA!
HHANH HRIH HHAGAHH HHA HHORR HA HHAHN!*
*TRANSLATION: GONE! GONE NOW, ETRIGAN! AND RISE AGAIN THE FORM OF MAN!
FSSSSSSSS
Oh, my GOD...
GOD...?
GOD HAS NOTHING TO DO WITH IT.

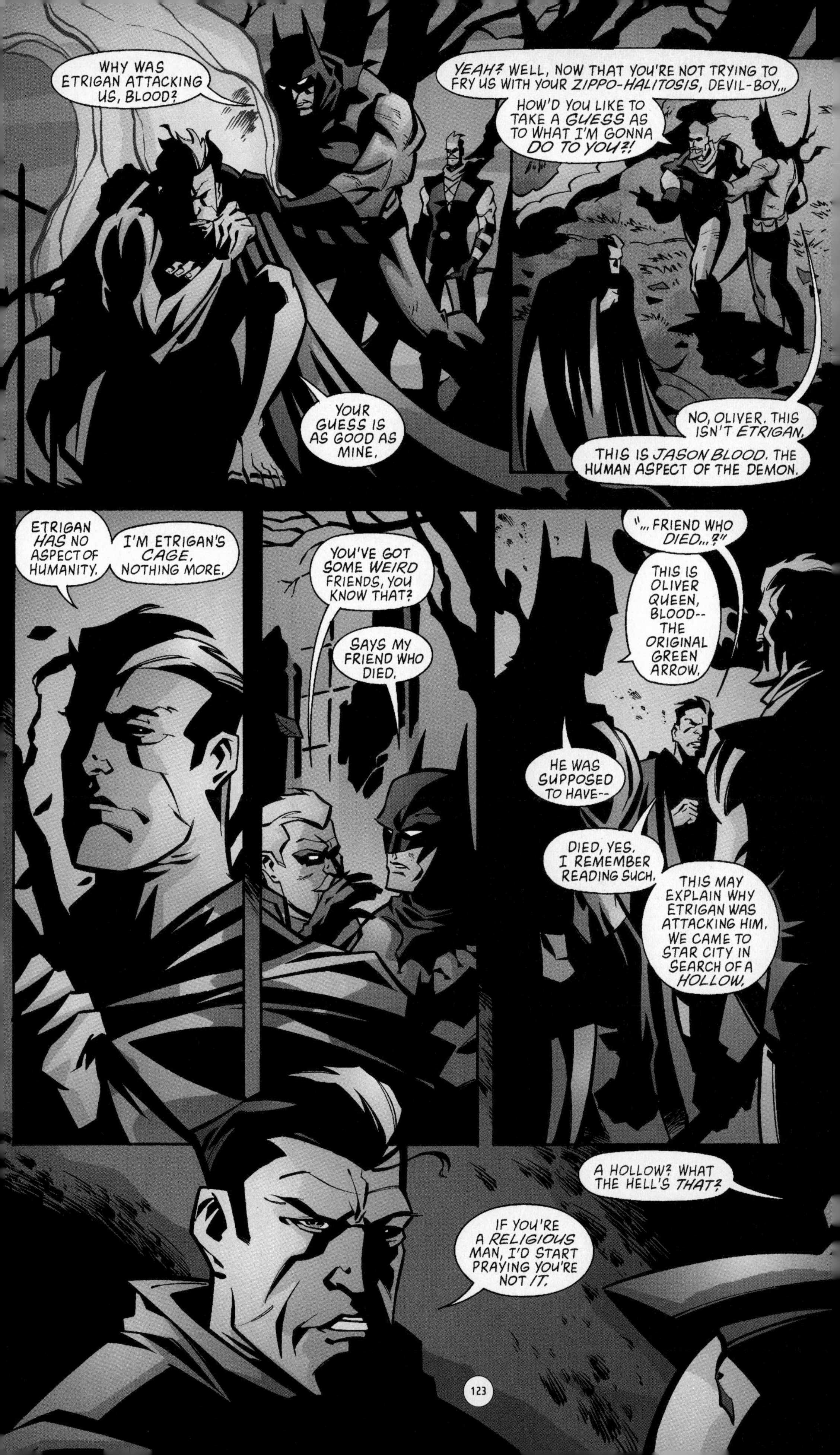
WHY WAS ETRIGAN ATTACKING US, BLOOD?
YOUR GUESS IS AS GOOD AS MINE.
YEAH? WELL, NOW THAT YOU'RE NOT TRYING TO FRY US WITH YOUR ZIPPO-HALITOSIS, DEVIL-BOY...
HOW'D YOU LIKE TO TAKE A GUESS AS TO WHAT I'M GONNA DO TO YOU?!
NO, OLIVER. THIS ISN'T ETRIGAN.
THIS IS JASON BLOOD. THE HUMAN ASPECT OF THE DEMON.
ETRIGAN HAS NO ASPECT OF HUMANITY.
I'M ETRIGAN'S CAGE, NOTHING MORE.
YOU'VE GOT SOME WEIRD FRIENDS, YOU KNOW THAT?
SAYS MY FRIEND WHO DIED.
"... FRIEND WHO DIED...?"
THIS IS OLIVER QUEEN, BLOOD-- THE ORIGINAL GREEN ARROW.
HE WAS SUPPOSED TO HAVE--
DIED, YES. I REMEMBER READING SUCH.
THIS MAY EXPLAIN WHY ETRIGAN WAS ATTACKING HIM. WE CAME TO STAR CITY IN SEARCH OF A HOLLOW.
A HOLLOW? WHAT THE HELL'S THAT?
IF YOU'RE A RELIGIOUS MAN, I'D START PRAYING YOU'RE NOT IT.

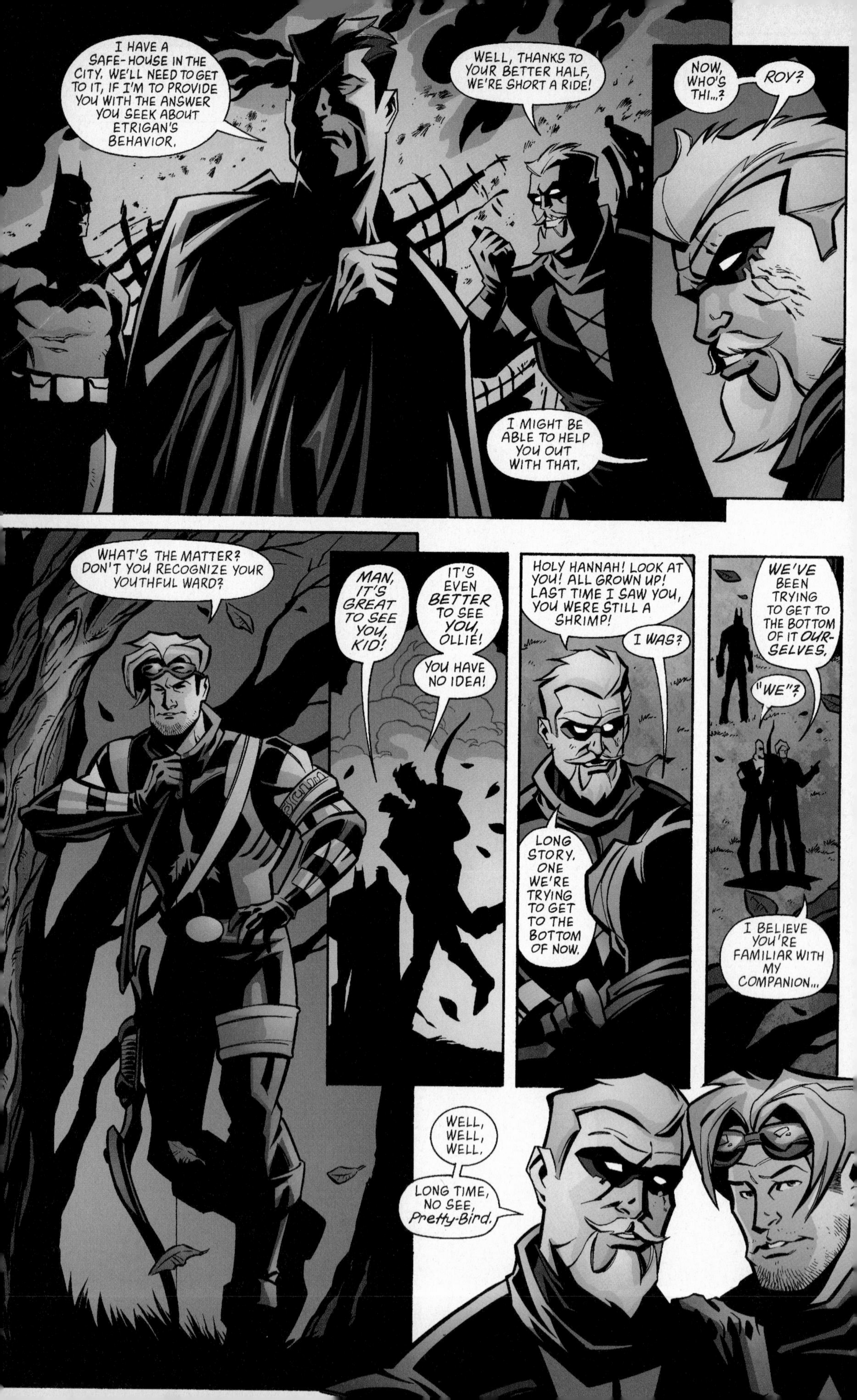
I HAVE A SAFE-HOUSE IN THE CITY. WE'LL NEED TO GET TO IT, IF I'M TO PROVIDE YOU WITH THE ANSWER YOU SEEK ABOUT ETRIGAN'S BEHAVIOR.
WELL, THANKS TO YOUR BETTER HALF, WE'RE SHORT A RIDE!
I MIGHT BE ABLE TO HELP YOU OUT WITH THAT.
NOW, WHO'S THI...?
ROY?
WHAT'S THE MATTER? DON'T YOU RECOGNIZE YOUR YOUTHFUL WARD?
MAN, IT'S GREAT TO SEE YOU, KID!
IT'S EVEN BETTER TO SEE YOU, OLLIE!
YOU HAVE NO IDEA!
HOLY HANNAH! LOOK AT YOU! ALL GROWN UP! LAST TIME I SAW YOU, YOU WERE STILL A SHRIMP!
I WAS?
LONG STORY. ONE WE'RE TRYING TO GET TO THE BOTTOM OF NOW.
WE'VE BEEN TRYING TO GET TO THE BOTTOM OF IT OURSELVES.
"WE"?
I BELIEVE YOU'RE FAMILIAR WITH MY COMPANION...
WELL, WELL, WELL.
LONG TIME, NO SEE, Pretty-Bird.

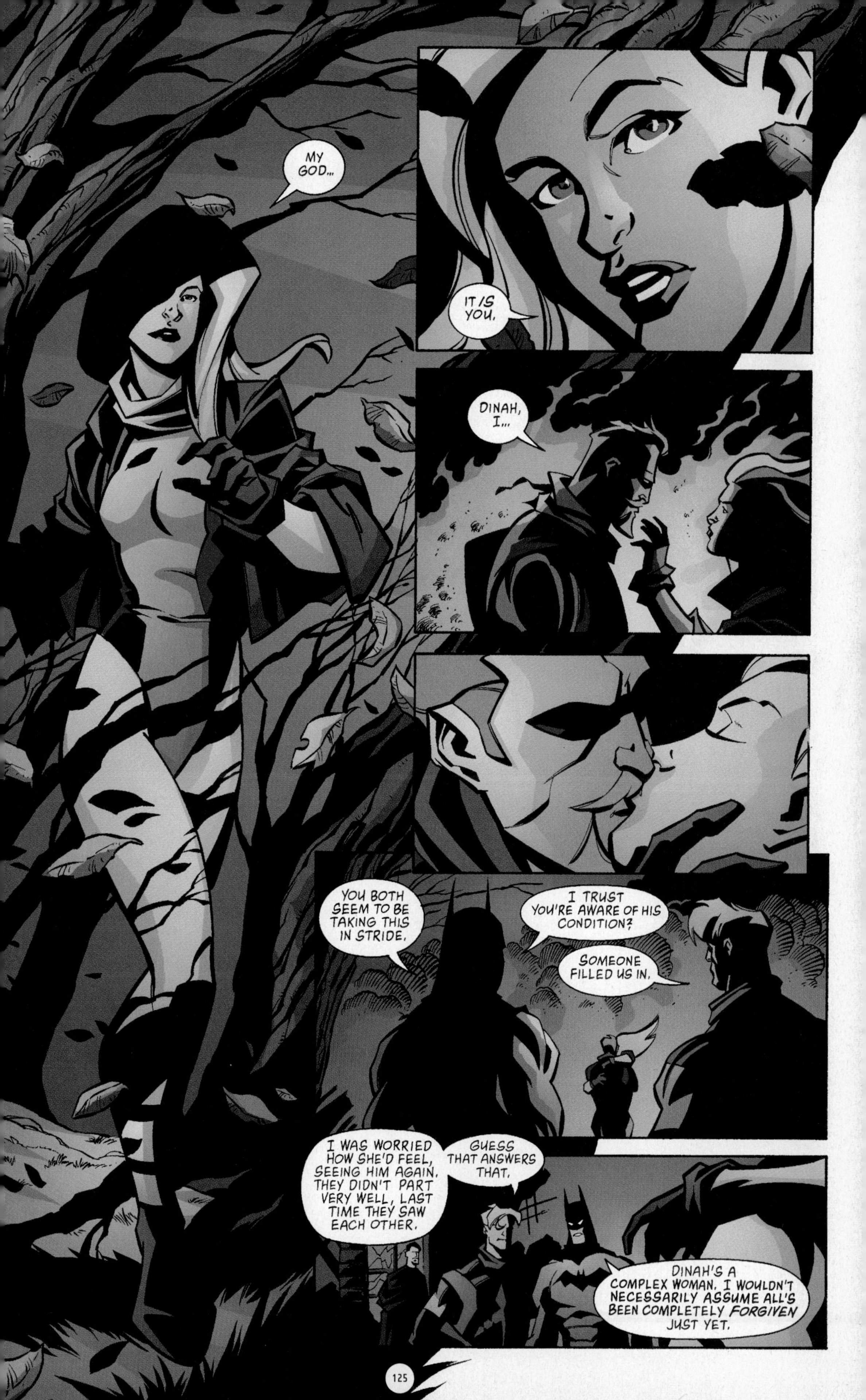
MY GOD...
IT IS YOU.
DINAH, I...
YOU BOTH SEEM TO BE TAKING THIS IN STRIDE.
I TRUST YOU'RE AWARE OF HIS CONDITION?
SOMEONE FILLED US IN.
I WAS WORRIED HOW SHE'D FEEL, SEEING HIM AGAIN. THEY DIDN'T PART VERY WELL, LAST TIME THEY SAW EACH OTHER.
GUESS THAT ANSWERS THAT.
DINAH'S A COMPLEX WOMAN. I WOULDN'T NECESSARILY ASSUME ALL'S BEEN COMPLETELY FORGIVEN JUST YET.

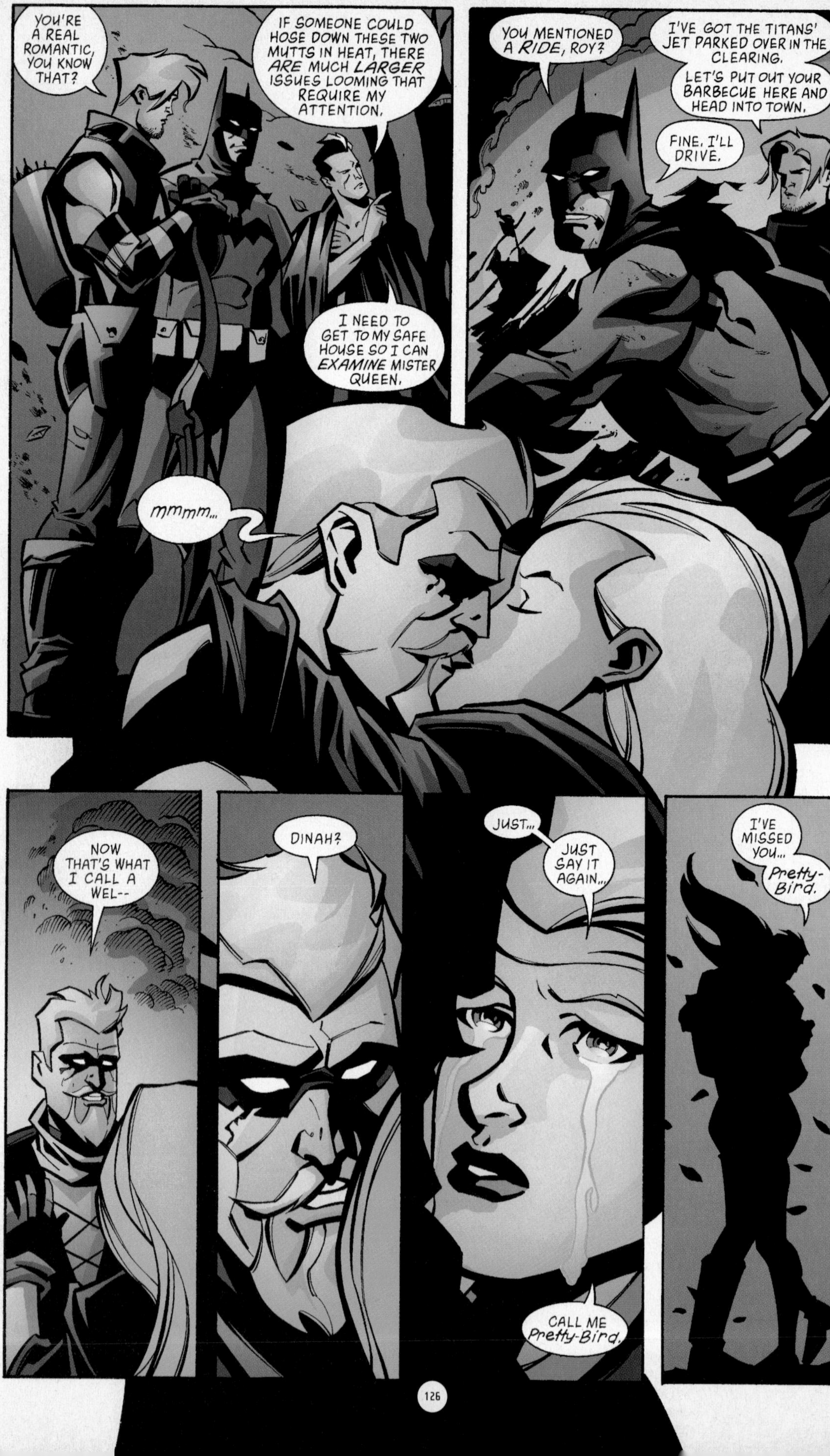
YOU'RE A REAL ROMANTIC, YOU KNOW THAT?
IF SOMEONE COULD HOSE DOWN THESE TWO MUTTS IN HEAT, THERE ARE MUCH LARGER ISSUES LOOMING THAT REQUIRE MY ATTENTION.
I NEED TO GET TO MY SAFE HOUSE SO I CAN EXAMINE MISTER QUEEN.
YOU MENTIONED A RIDE, ROY?
I'VE GOT THE TITANS' JET PARKED OVER IN THE CLEARING.
LET'S PUT OUT YOUR BARBECUE HERE AND HEAD INTO TOWN.
FINE. I'LL DRIVE.
mmmm...
NOW THAT'S WHAT I CALL A WEL--
DINAH?
JUST...
JUST SAY IT AGAIN...
CALL ME Pretty-Bird.
I'VE MISSED YOU... Pretty-Bird.

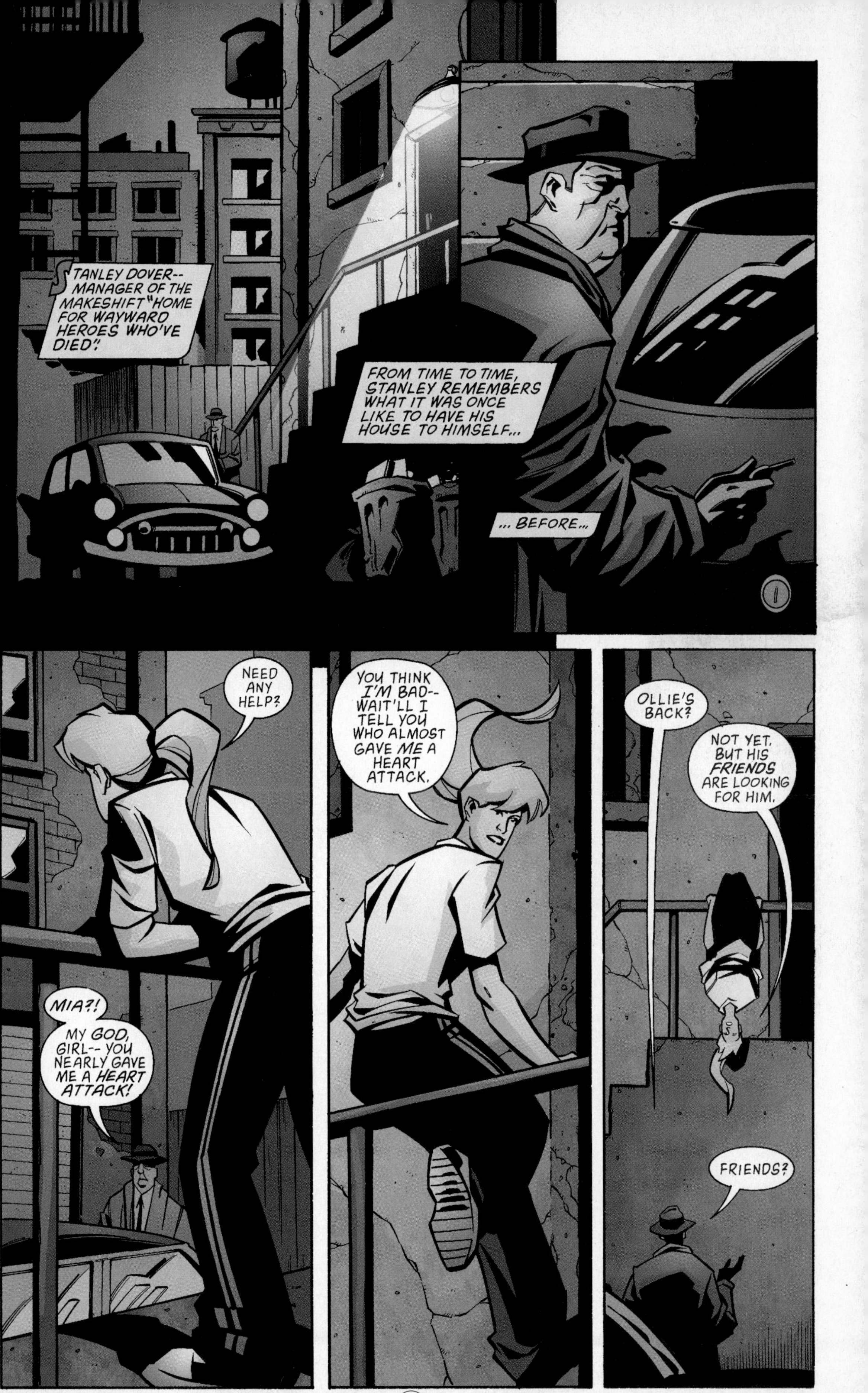
STANLEY DOVER-- MANAGER OF THE MAKESHIFT "HOME FOR WAYWARD HEROES WHO'VE DIED".
FROM TIME TO TIME, STANLEY REMEMBERS WHAT IT WAS ONCE LIKE TO HAVE HIS HOUSE TO HIMSELF...
... BEFORE...
NEED ANY HELP?
MIA?!
MY GOD, GIRL-- YOU NEARLY GAVE ME A HEART ATTACK!
YOU THINK I'M BAD-- WAIT'LL I TELL YOU WHO ALMOST GAVE ME A HEART ATTACK.
OLLIE'S BACK?
NOT YET. BUT HIS FRIENDS ARE LOOKING FOR HIM.
FRIENDS?

BLACK CANARY AND ARSENAL.

REALLY. DAMN.

D'JOU SEE THAT MOVE? HOW 'BOUT SOME PROPS?

Hmm?

FORGET IT. WHY "DAMN"?

I'M SORRY?

YOU SAID, "DAMN." WHY "DAMN"?

WELL, IT'S JUST THAT...

...WITH OLLIE STILL IN THE STATE HE IS, WHO KNOWS WHAT SEEING TWO IMPORTANT PEOPLE FROM HIS OLD LIFE MIGHT DO TO HIM?

MAYBE IT'LL BRING BACK EVERYTHING, AND HE'LL BE HIMSELF AGAIN. IT COULD BE GOOD FOR HIM TO SEE THEM, DON'T YOU THINK?

NEED ANY HELP WITH THAT STUFF IN THE TRUNK?

Uh... NO.

NO, THE STUFF IN THE TRUNK'LL KEEP 'TIL TOMORROW. LET'S JUST GET INSIDE.

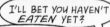

I'LL BET YOU HAVEN'T EATEN YET?

EAT? WHO CAN EAT WHEN YOU'VE GOT REAL, LIVE SUPER-HEROES ON YOUR ROOF, TALKING TO YOU LIKE YOU MATTER?

I MEAN, THESE GUYS FIGHT ALIENS AND DIRTBAGS LIKE RICHARD FOR A LIVING!

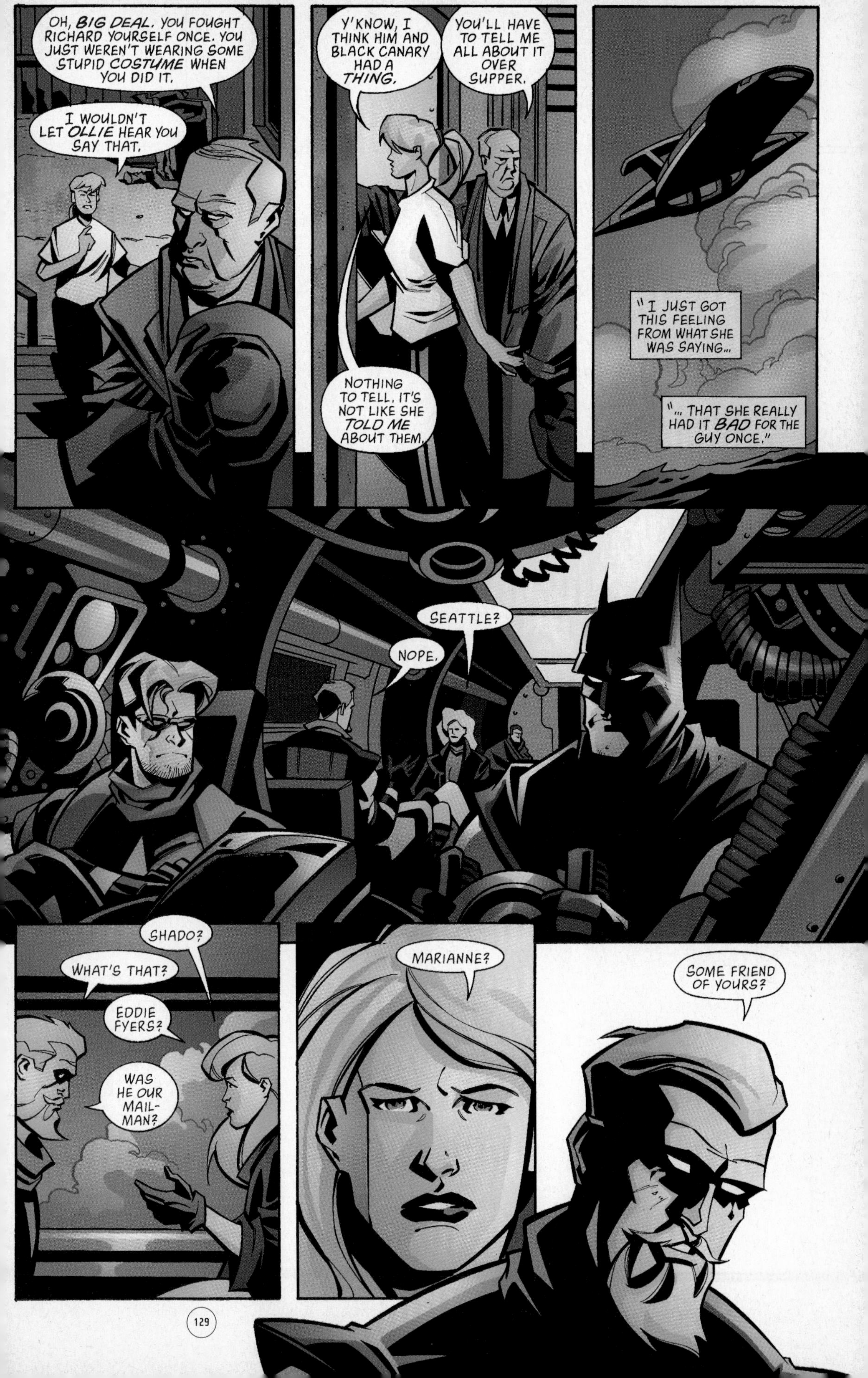
OH, BIG DEAL. YOU FOUGHT RICHARD YOURSELF ONCE. YOU JUST WEREN'T WEARING SOME STUPID COSTUME WHEN YOU DID IT.
I WOULDN'T LET OLLIE HEAR YOU SAY THAT.
Y'KNOW, I THINK HIM AND BLACK CANARY HAD A THING.
YOU'LL HAVE TO TELL ME ALL ABOUT IT OVER SUPPER.
NOTHING TO TELL. IT'S NOT LIKE SHE TOLD ME ABOUT THEM.
"I JUST GOT THIS FEELING FROM WHAT SHE WAS SAYING...
"... THAT SHE REALLY HAD IT BAD FOR THE GUY ONCE."
SEATTLE?
NOPE.
SHADO?
WHAT'S THAT?
EDDIE FYERS?
WAS HE OUR MAIL-MAN?
MARIANNE?
SOME FRIEND OF YOURS?

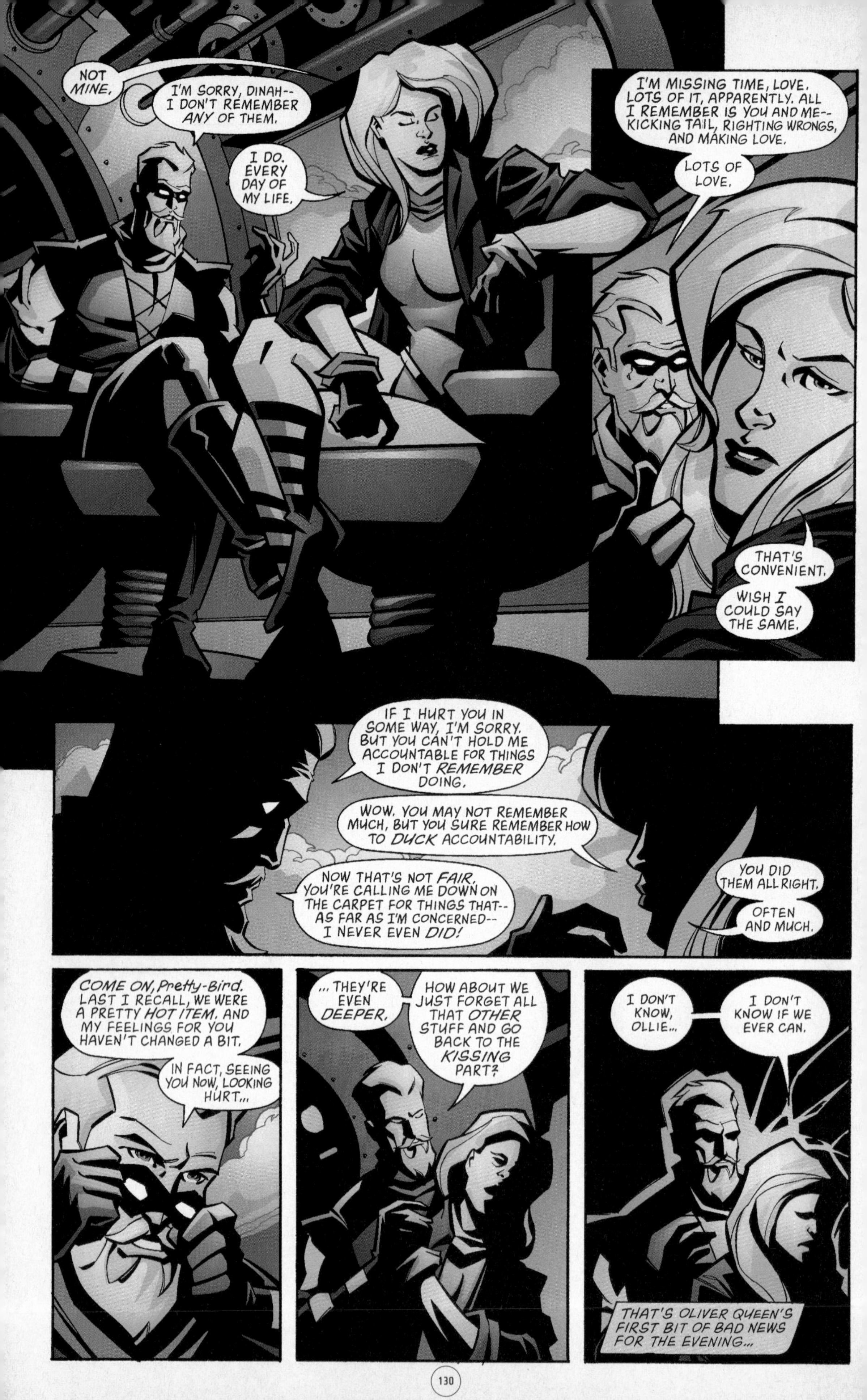
I'M SORRY, DINAH-- I DON'T REMEMBER ANY OF THEM.
NOT MINE.
I DO. EVERY DAY OF MY LIFE.
I'M MISSING TIME, LOVE. LOTS OF IT, APPARENTLY. ALL I REMEMBER IS YOU AND ME-- KICKING TAIL, RIGHTING WRONGS, AND MAKING LOVE.
LOTS OF LOVE.
THAT'S CONVENIENT.
WISH I COULD SAY THE SAME.
IF I HURT YOU IN SOME WAY, I'M SORRY. BUT YOU CAN'T HOLD ME ACCOUNTABLE FOR THINGS I DON'T REMEMBER DOING.
WOW. YOU MAY NOT REMEMBER MUCH, BUT YOU SURE REMEMBER HOW TO DUCK ACCOUNTABILITY.
NOW THAT'S NOT FAIR. YOU'RE CALLING ME DOWN ON THE CARPET FOR THINGS THAT-- AS FAR AS I'M CONCERNED-- I NEVER EVEN DID!
YOU DID THEM ALL RIGHT.
OFTEN AND MUCH.
COME ON, Pretty-Bird. LAST I RECALL, WE WERE A PRETTY HOT ITEM. AND MY FEELINGS FOR YOU HAVEN'T CHANGED A BIT.
IN FACT, SEEING YOU NOW, LOOKING HURT...
...THEY'RE EVEN DEEPER.
HOW ABOUT WE JUST FORGET ALL THAT OTHER STUFF AND GO BACK TO THE KISSING PART?
I DON'T KNOW, OLLIE...
I DON'T KNOW IF WE EVER CAN.
THAT'S OLIVER QUEEN'S FIRST BIT OF BAD NEWS FOR THE EVENING...

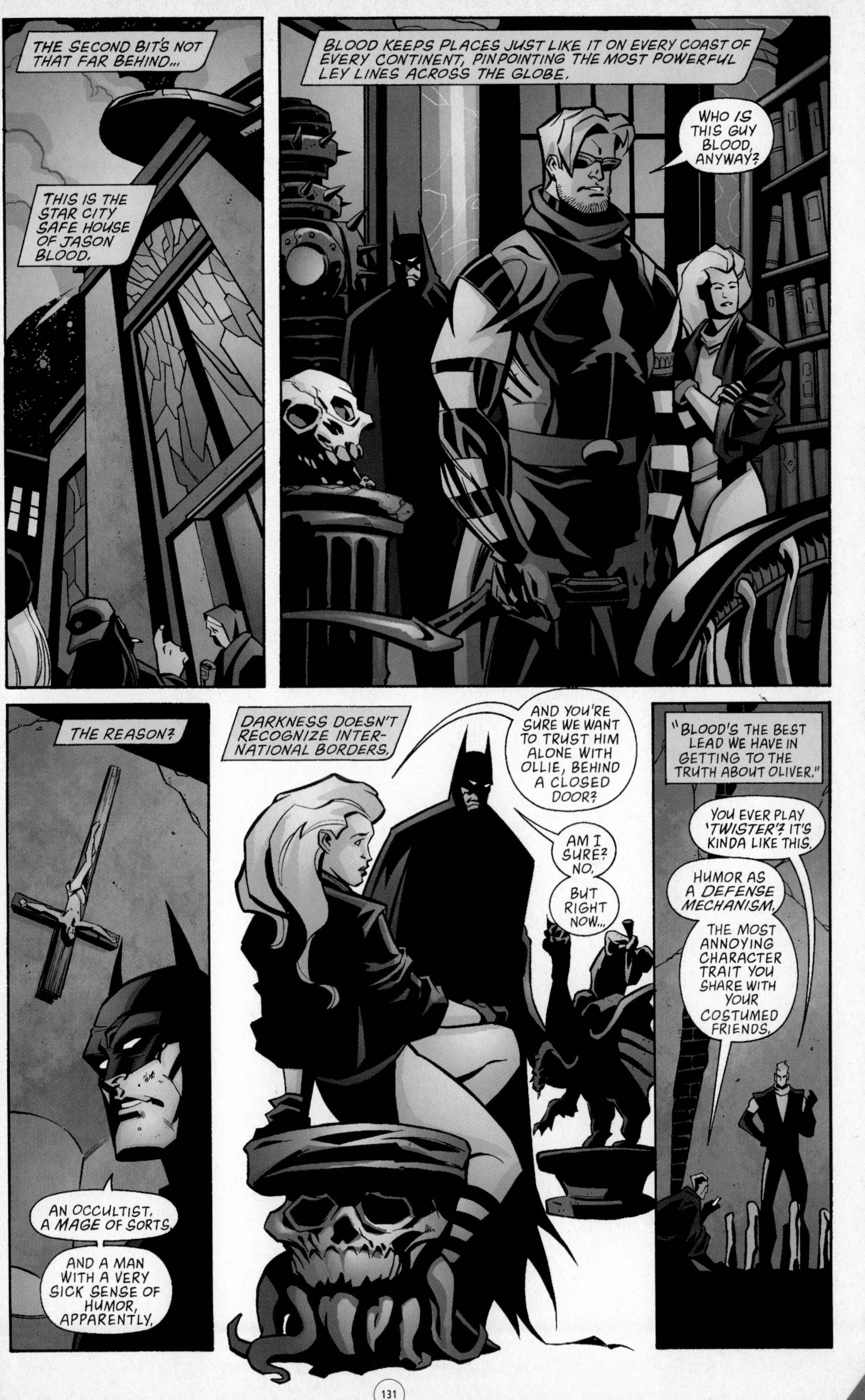
THE SECOND BIT'S NOT THAT FAR BEHIND...
THIS IS THE STAR CITY SAFE HOUSE OF JASON BLOOD.
BLOOD KEEPS PLACES JUST LIKE IT ON EVERY COAST OF EVERY CONTINENT, PINPOINTING THE MOST POWERFUL LEY LINES ACROSS THE GLOBE.
WHO *IS* THIS GUY BLOOD, ANYWAY?
THE REASON?
DARKNESS DOESN'T RECOGNIZE INTER-NATIONAL BORDERS.
AN OCCULTIST, A *MAGE* OF SORTS,
AND A MAN WITH A VERY SICK SENSE OF HUMOR, APPARENTLY.
AND YOU'RE SURE WE WANT TO TRUST HIM ALONE WITH OLLIE, BEHIND A CLOSED DOOR?
AM I SURE? NO.
BUT RIGHT NOW...
"BLOOD'S THE BEST LEAD WE HAVE IN GETTING TO THE TRUTH ABOUT OLIVER."
YOU EVER PLAY '*TWISTER*'? IT'S KINDA LIKE THIS.
HUMOR AS A *DEFENSE MECHANISM*.
THE MOST ANNOYING CHARACTER TRAIT YOU SHARE WITH YOUR COSTUMED FRIENDS.

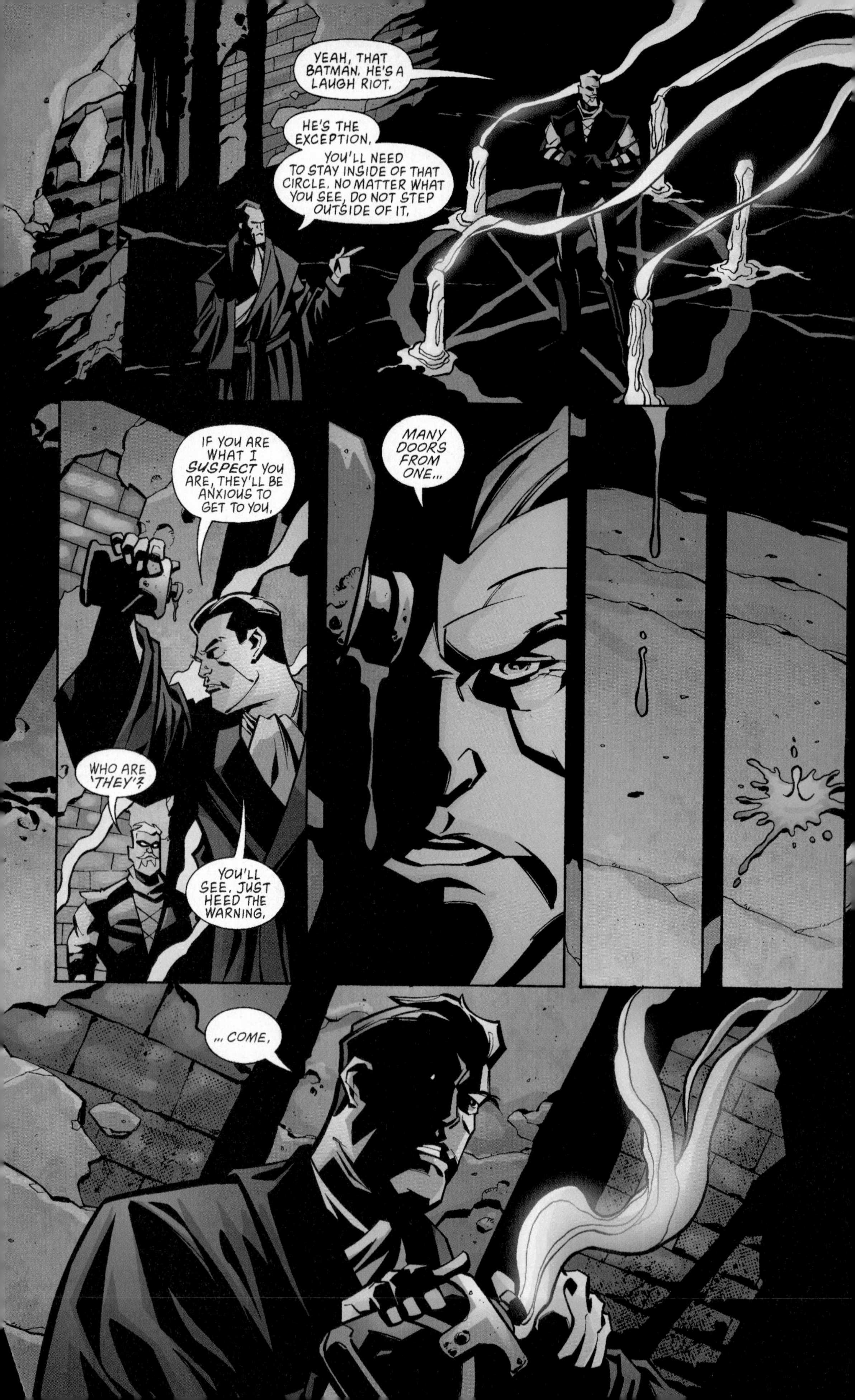
YEAH, THAT BATMAN. HE'S A LAUGH RIOT.
HE'S THE EXCEPTION.
YOU'LL NEED TO STAY INSIDE OF THAT CIRCLE. NO MATTER WHAT YOU SEE, DO NOT STEP OUTSIDE OF IT.
IF YOU ARE WHAT I SUSPECT YOU ARE, THEY'LL BE ANXIOUS TO GET TO YOU.
WHO ARE 'THEY'?
YOU'LL SEE. JUST HEED THE WARNING.
MANY DOORS FROM ONE...
...COME.

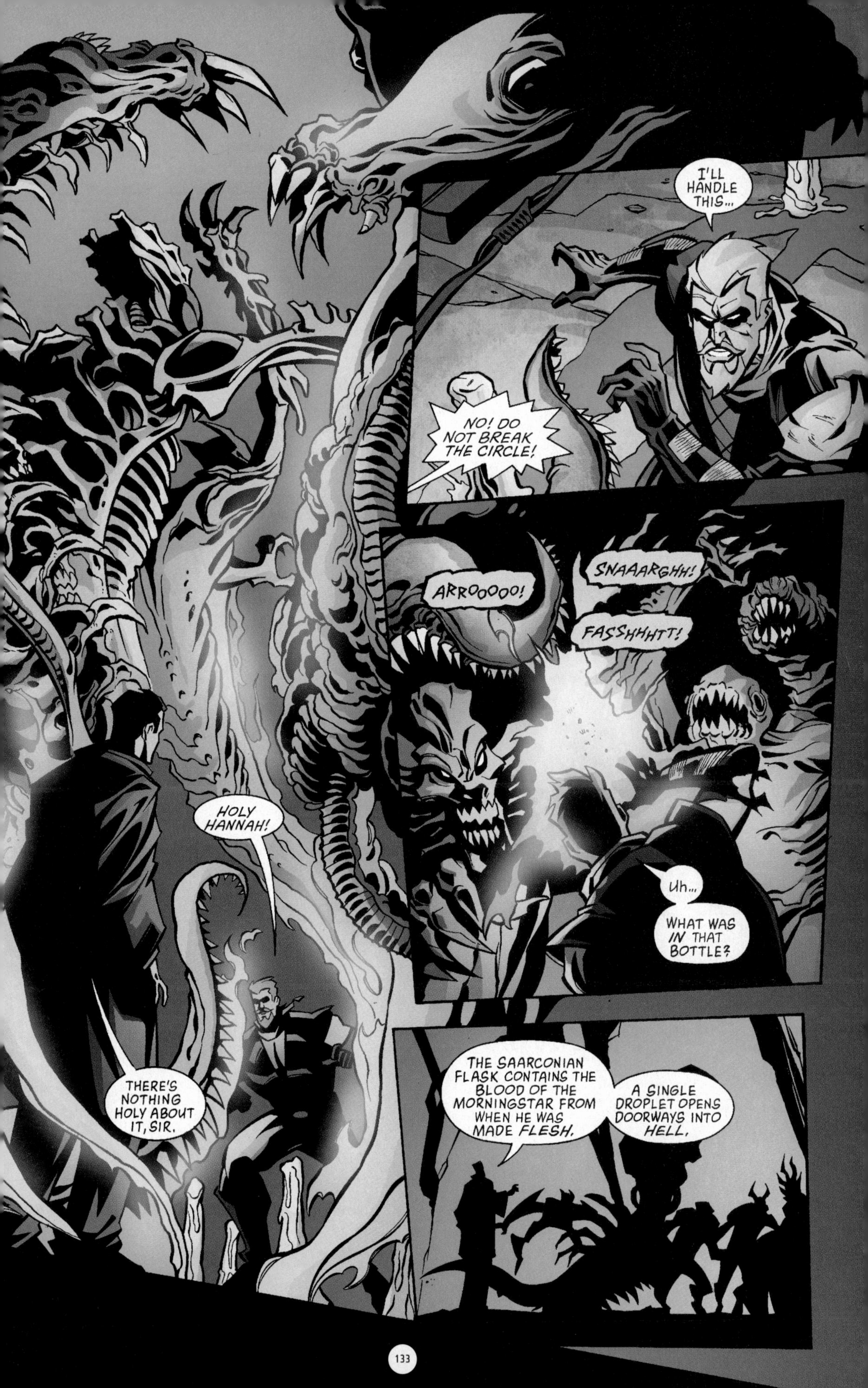

I'LL HANDLE THIS...
NO! DO NOT BREAK THE CIRCLE!
ARROOOOO!
SNAAARGHH!
FASSHHHTT!
HOLY HANNAH!
Uh...
WHAT WAS IN THAT BOTTLE?
THERE'S NOTHING HOLY ABOUT IT, SIR.
THE SAARCONIAN FLASK CONTAINS THE BLOOD OF THE MORNINGSTAR FROM WHEN HE WAS MADE FLESH.
A SINGLE DROPLET OPENS DOORWAYS INTO HELL.

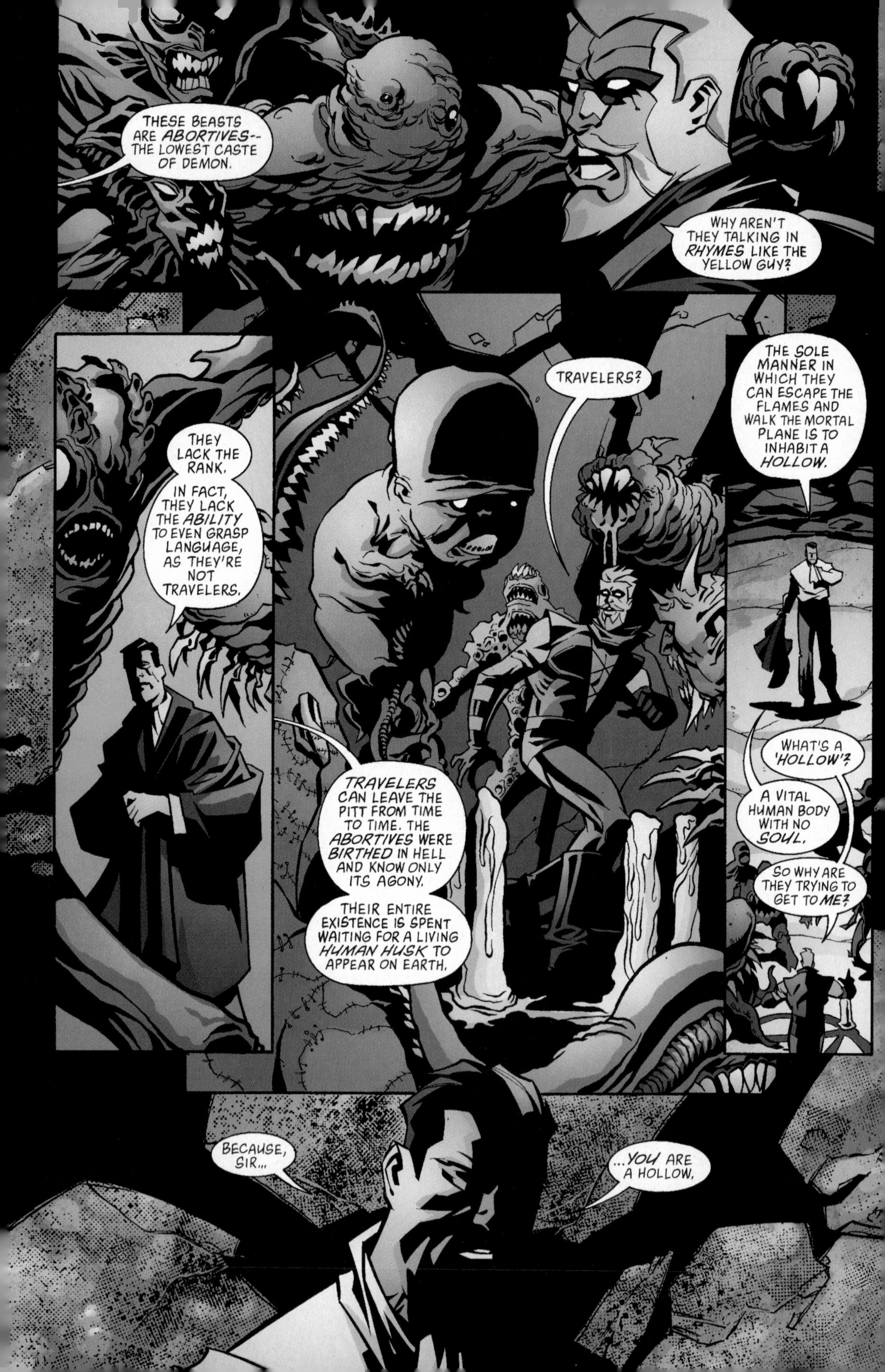
THESE BEASTS ARE ABORTIVES-- THE LOWEST CASTE OF DEMON.
WHY AREN'T THEY TALKING IN RHYMES LIKE THE YELLOW GUY?
THEY LACK THE RANK.
IN FACT, THEY LACK THE ABILITY TO EVEN GRASP LANGUAGE, AS THEY'RE NOT TRAVELERS.
TRAVELERS?
TRAVELERS CAN LEAVE THE PITT FROM TIME TO TIME. THE ABORTIVES WERE BIRTHED IN HELL AND KNOW ONLY ITS AGONY.
THEIR ENTIRE EXISTENCE IS SPENT WAITING FOR A LIVING HUMAN HUSK TO APPEAR ON EARTH.
THE SOLE MANNER IN WHICH THEY CAN ESCAPE THE FLAMES AND WALK THE MORTAL PLANE IS TO INHABIT A HOLLOW.
WHAT'S A 'HOLLOW'?
A VITAL HUMAN BODY WITH NO SOUL.
SO WHY ARE THEY TRYING TO GET TO ME?
BECAUSE, SIR...
...YOU ARE A HOLLOW.

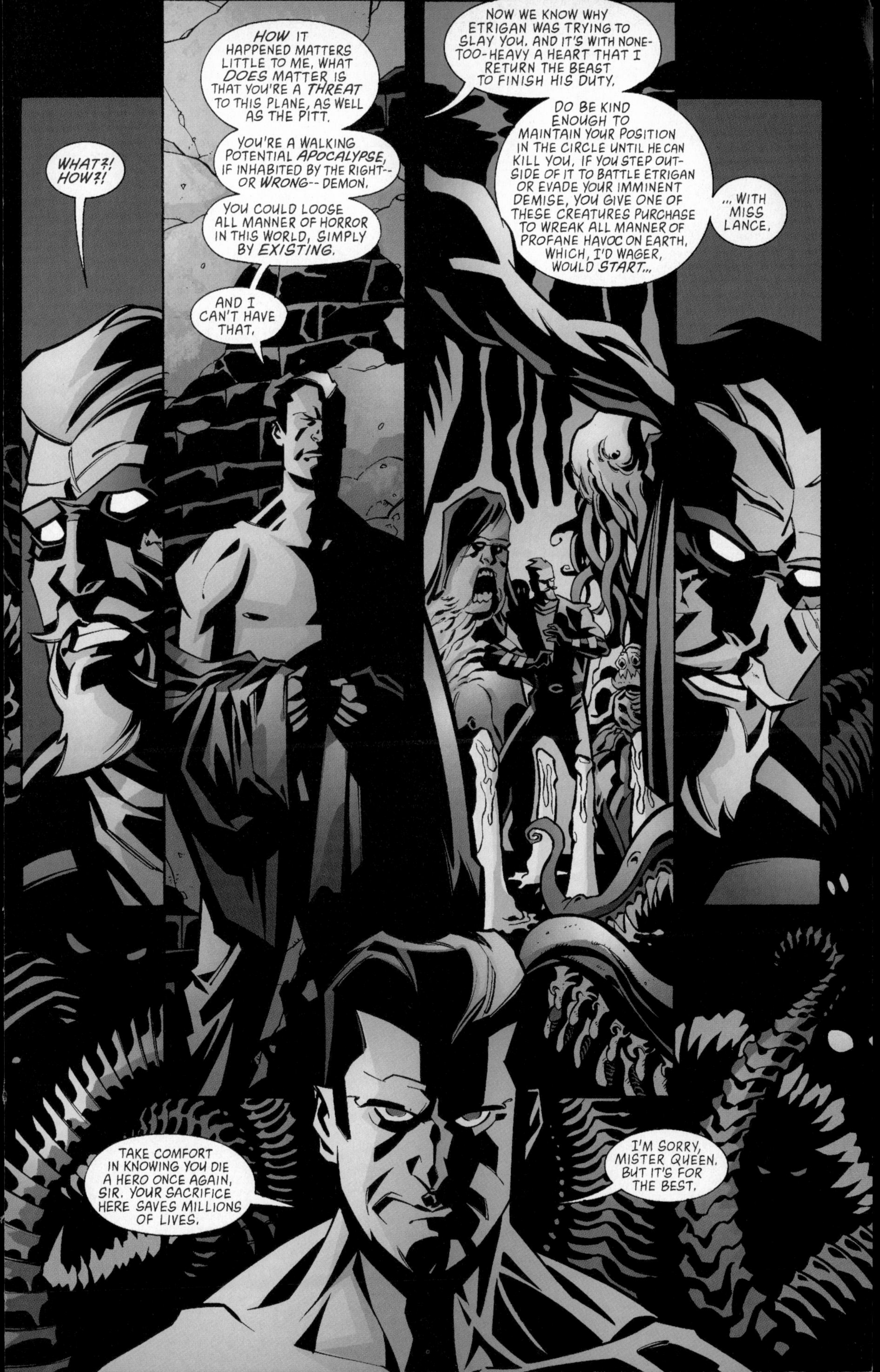
WHAT?! HOW?!
HOW IT HAPPENED MATTERS LITTLE TO ME. WHAT DOES MATTER IS THAT YOU'RE A THREAT TO THIS PLANE, AS WELL AS THE PITT.
YOU'RE A WALKING POTENTIAL APOCALYPSE, IF INHABITED BY THE RIGHT-- OR WRONG-- DEMON.
YOU COULD LOOSE ALL MANNER OF HORROR IN THIS WORLD, SIMPLY BY EXISTING.
AND I CAN'T HAVE THAT.
NOW WE KNOW WHY ETRIGAN WAS TRYING TO SLAY YOU. AND IT'S WITH NONE-TOO-HEAVY A HEART THAT I RETURN THE BEAST TO FINISH HIS DUTY.
DO BE KIND ENOUGH TO MAINTAIN YOUR POSITION IN THE CIRCLE UNTIL HE CAN KILL YOU. IF YOU STEP OUTSIDE OF IT TO BATTLE ETRIGAN OR EVADE YOUR IMMINENT DEMISE, YOU GIVE ONE OF THESE CREATURES PURCHASE TO WREAK ALL MANNER OF PROFANE HAVOC ON EARTH. WHICH, I'D WAGER, WOULD START...
...WITH MISS LANCE.
TAKE COMFORT IN KNOWING YOU DIE A HERO ONCE AGAIN, SIR. YOUR SACRIFICE HERE SAVES MILLIONS OF LIVES.
I'M SORRY, MISTER QUEEN. BUT IT'S FOR THE BEST.

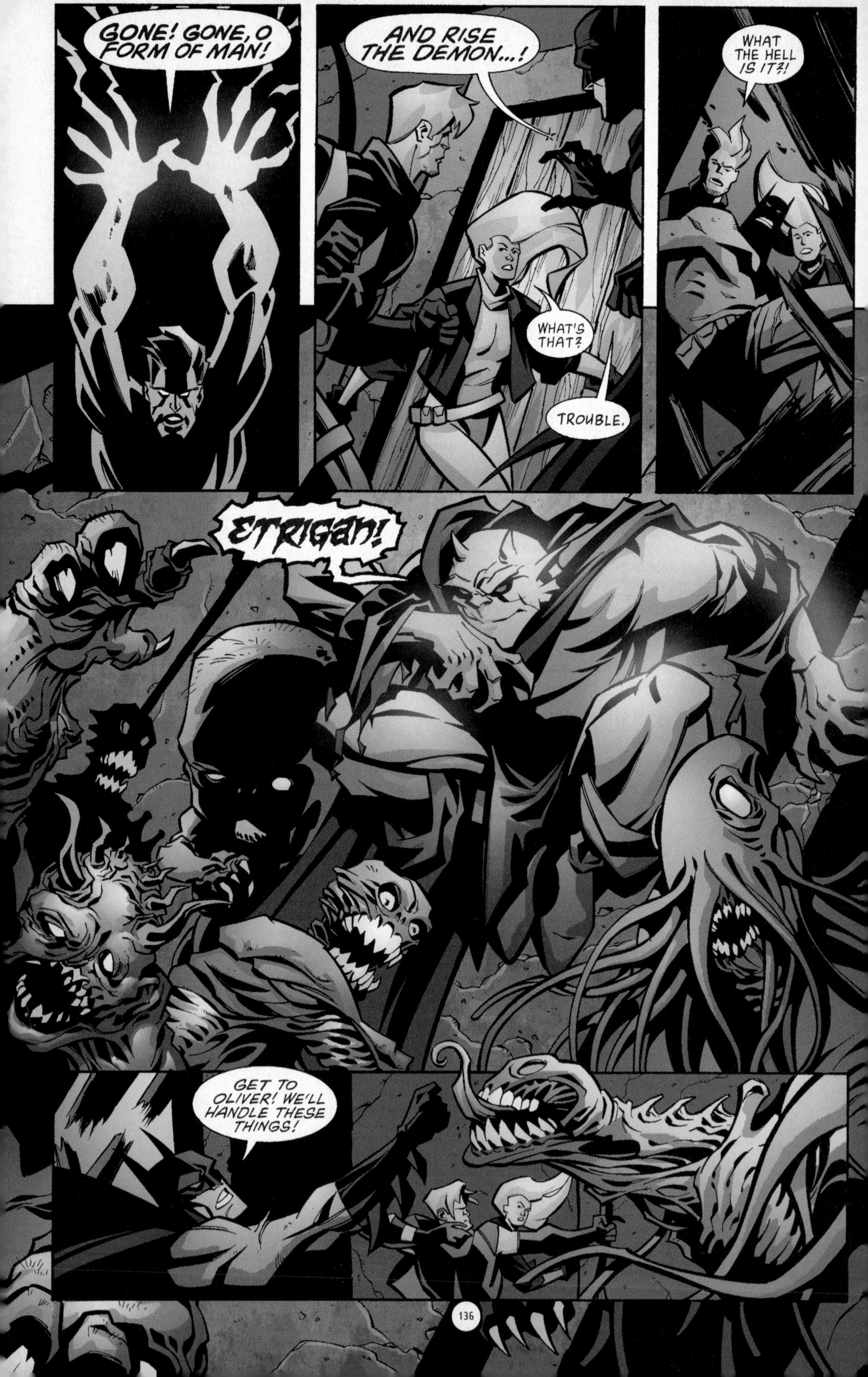
GONE! GONE, O FORM OF MAN!
AND RISE THE DEMON...!
WHAT'S THAT?
TROUBLE.
WHAT THE HELL IS IT?!
ETRIGAN!
GET TO OLIVER! WE'LL HANDLE THESE THINGS!

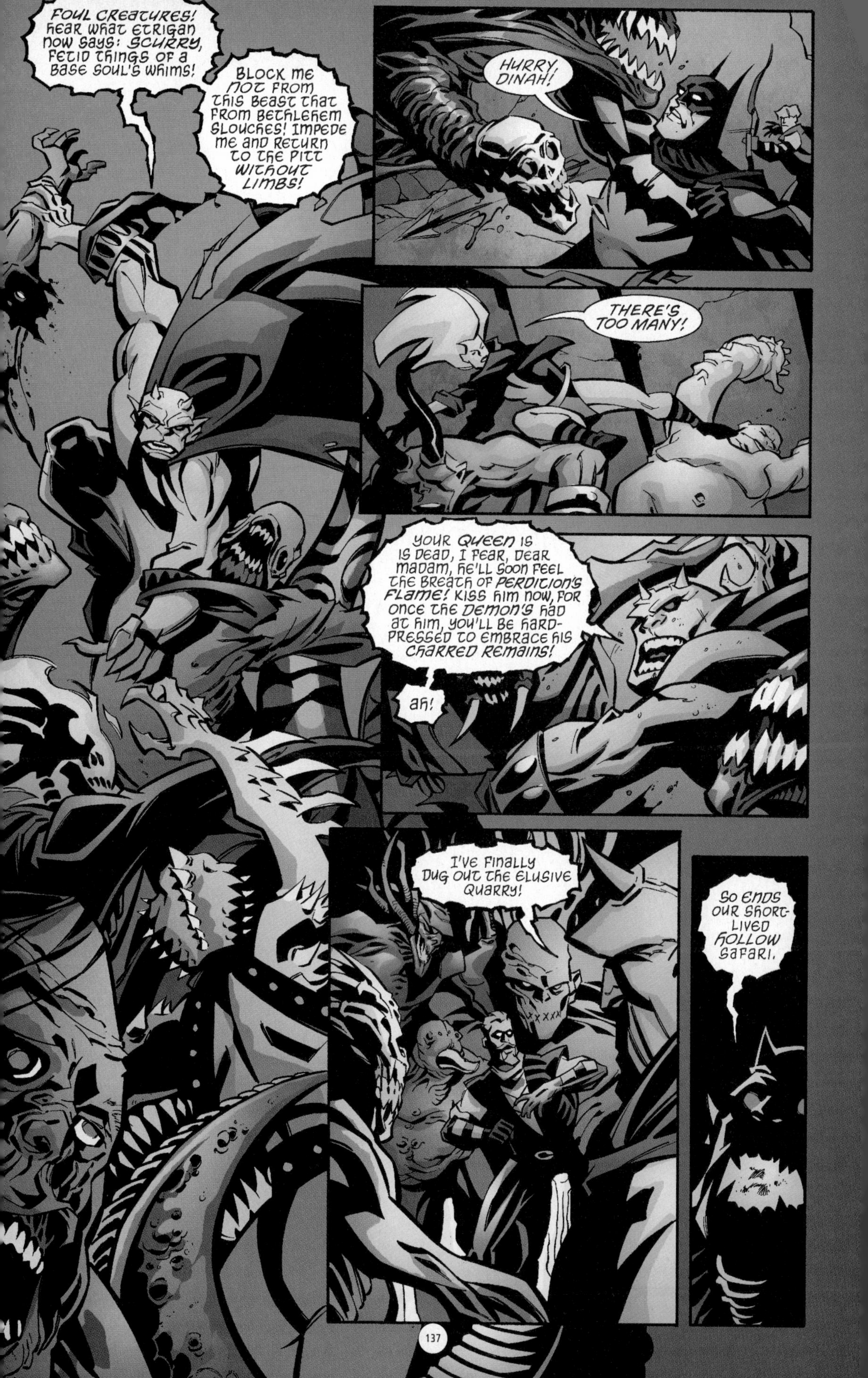

FOUL CREATURES! HEAR WHAT ETRIGAN NOW SAYS: SCURRY, FETID THINGS OF A BASE SOUL'S WHIMS!
BLOCK ME NOT FROM THIS BEAST THAT FROM BETHLEHEM SLOUCHES! IMPEDE ME AND RETURN TO THE PITT WITHOUT LIMBS!
HURRY, DINAH!
THERE'S TOO MANY!
YOUR QUEEN IS IS DEAD, I FEAR, DEAR MADAM, HE'LL SOON FEEL THE BREATH OF PERDITION'S FLAME! KISS HIM NOW, FOR ONCE THE DEMON'S HAD AT HIM, YOU'LL BE HARD-PRESSED TO EMBRACE HIS CHARRED REMAINS!
AH!
I'VE FINALLY DUG OUT THE ELUSIVE QUARRY!
SO ENDS OUR SHORT-LIVED HOLLOW SAFARI.

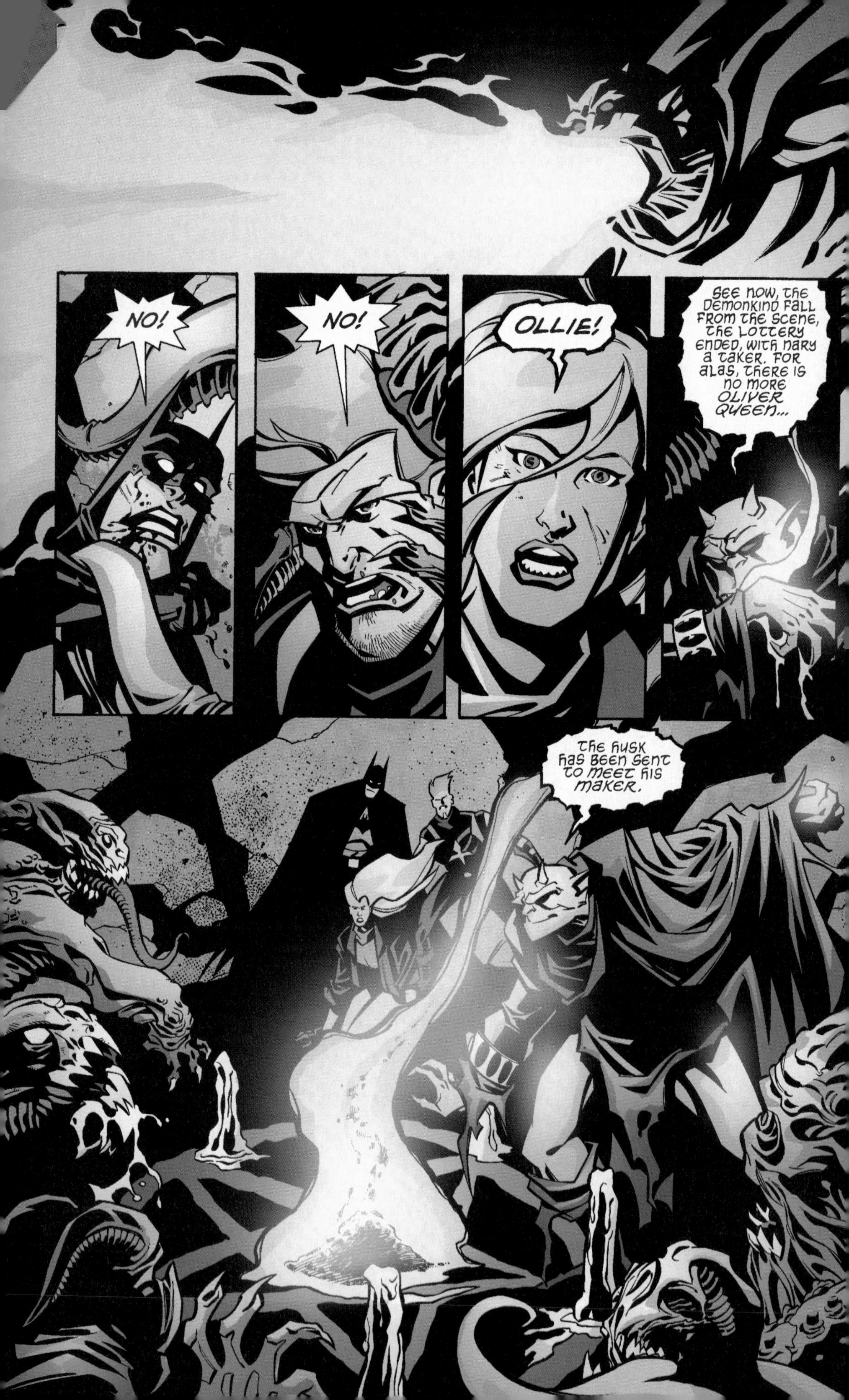
NO!
NO!
OLLIE!
SEE NOW, THE DEMONKIND FALL FROM THE SCENE, THE LOTTERY ENDED, WITH NARY A TAKER. FOR ALAS, THERE IS NO MORE OLIVER QUEEN...
THE HUSK HAS BEEN SENT TO MEET HIS MAKER.

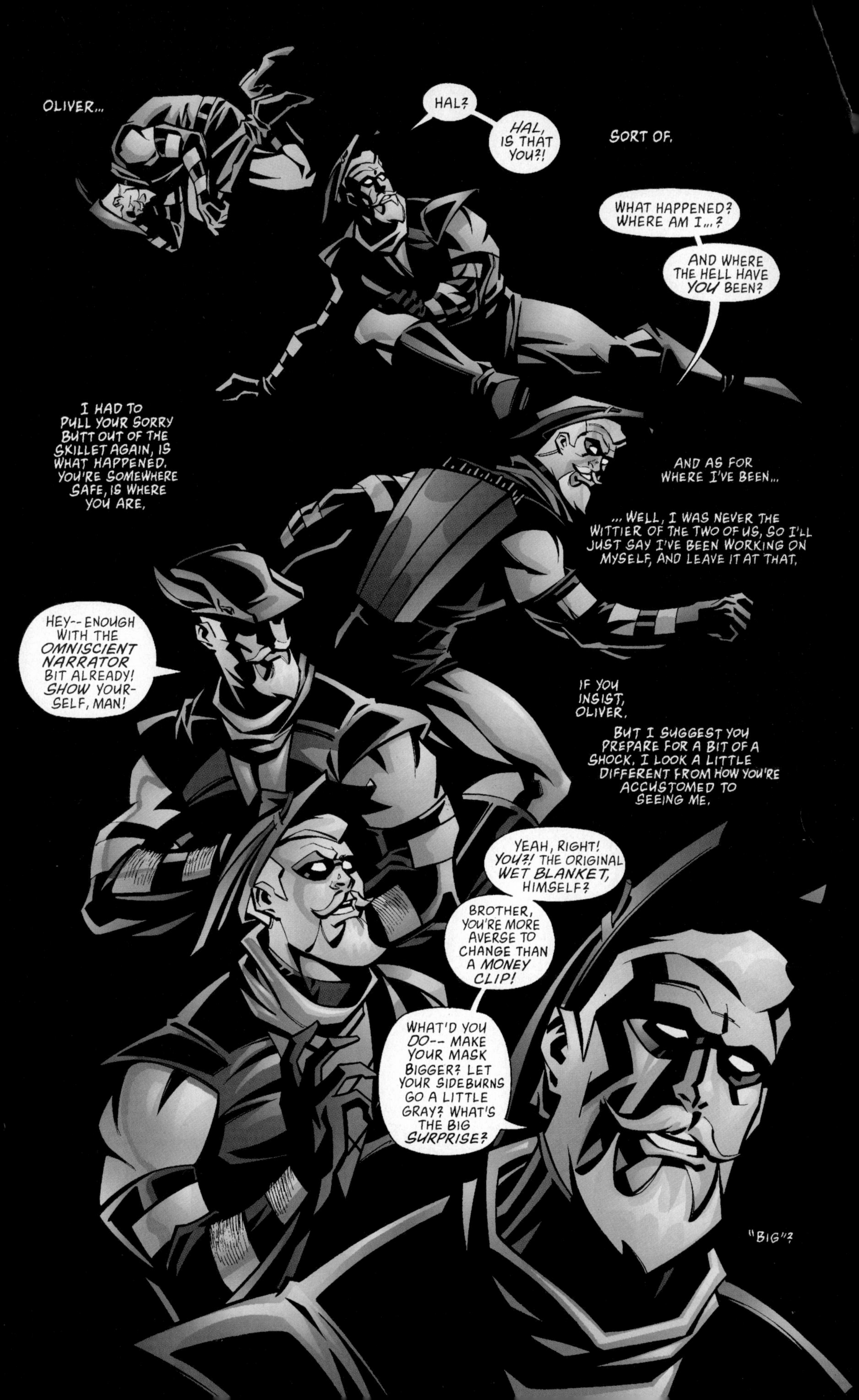

OLIVER...
HAL?
HAL, IS THAT YOU?!
SORT OF.
WHAT HAPPENED? WHERE AM I...?
AND WHERE THE HELL HAVE YOU BEEN?
I HAD TO PULL YOUR SORRY BUTT OUT OF THE SKILLET AGAIN, IS WHAT HAPPENED. YOU'RE SOMEWHERE SAFE, IS WHERE YOU ARE.
AND AS FOR WHERE I'VE BEEN...
...WELL, I WAS NEVER THE WITTIER OF THE TWO OF US, SO I'LL JUST SAY I'VE BEEN WORKING ON MYSELF, AND LEAVE IT AT THAT.
HEY--ENOUGH WITH THE OMNISCIENT NARRATOR BIT ALREADY! SHOW YOURSELF, MAN!
IF YOU INSIST, OLIVER.
BUT I SUGGEST YOU PREPARE FOR A BIT OF A SHOCK. I LOOK A LITTLE DIFFERENT FROM HOW YOU'RE ACCUSTOMED TO SEEING ME.
YEAH, RIGHT! YOU?! THE ORIGINAL WET BLANKET, HIMSELF?
BROTHER, YOU'RE MORE AVERSE TO CHANGE THAN A MONEY CLIP!
WHAT'D YOU DO-- MAKE YOUR MASK BIGGER? LET YOUR SIDEBURNS GO A LITTLE GRAY? WHAT'S THE BIG SURPRISE?
"BIG"?

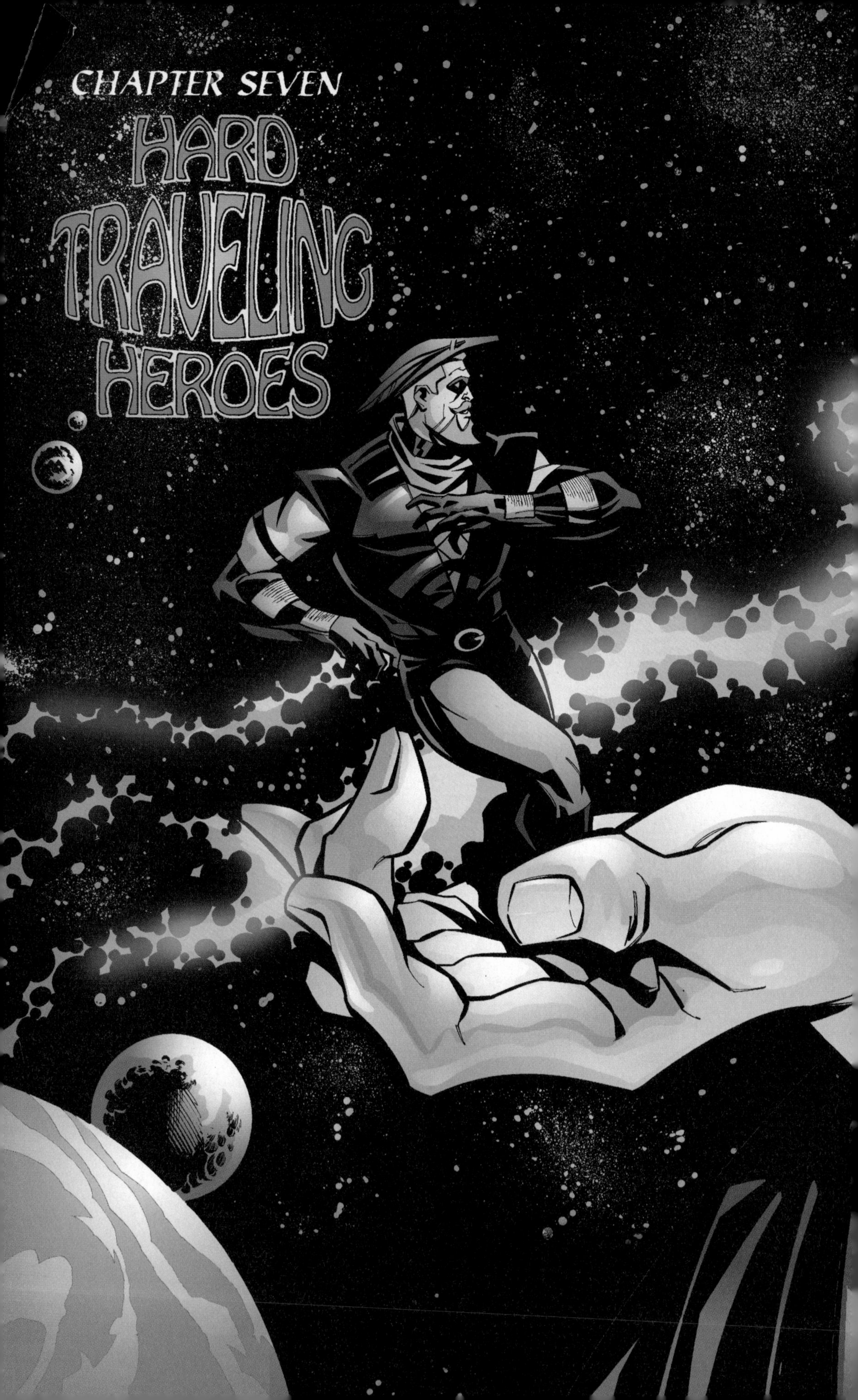
CHAPTER SEVEN
HARD
TRAVELING
HEROES

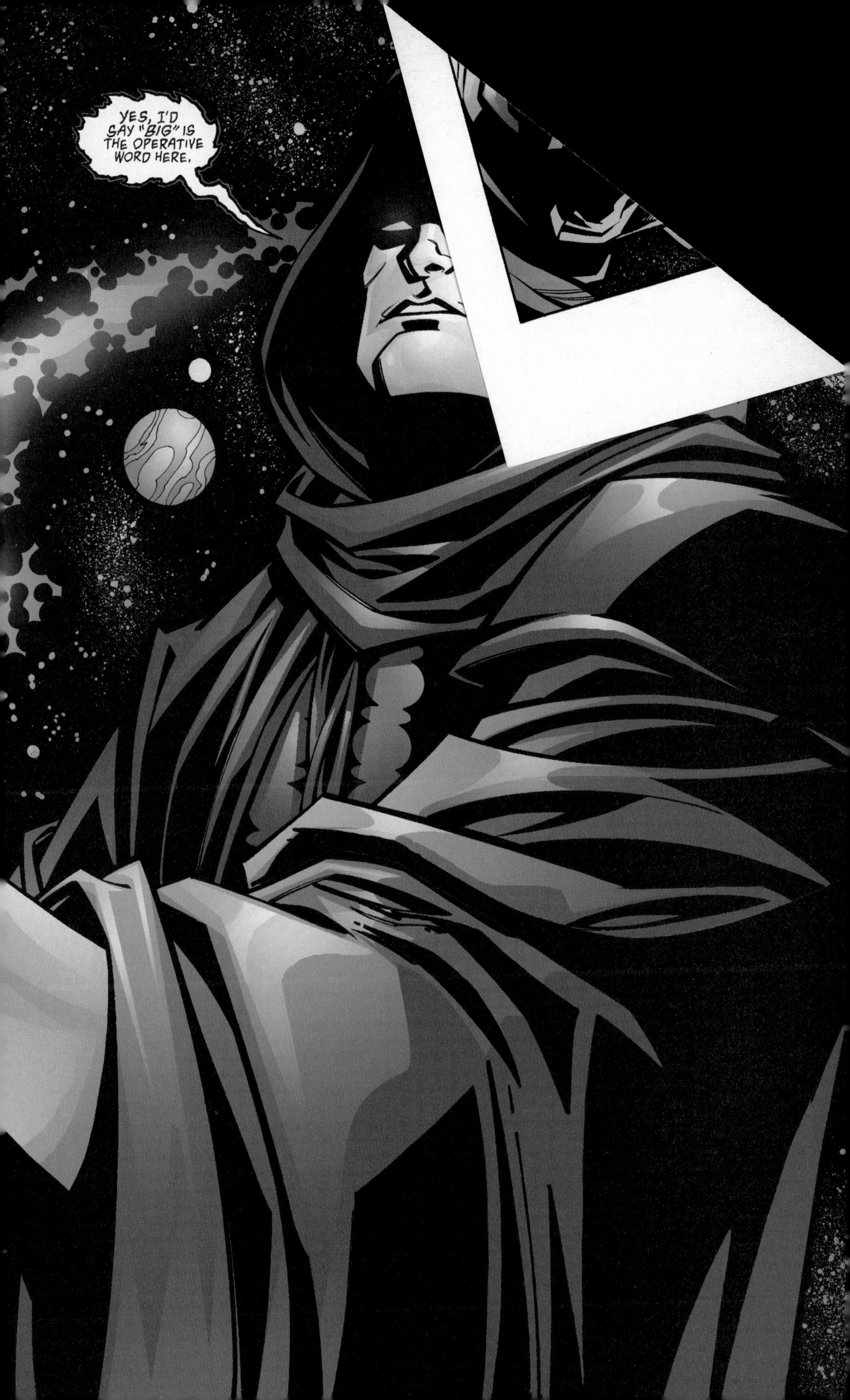
YES, I'D SAY "BIG" IS THE OPERATIVE WORD HERE.

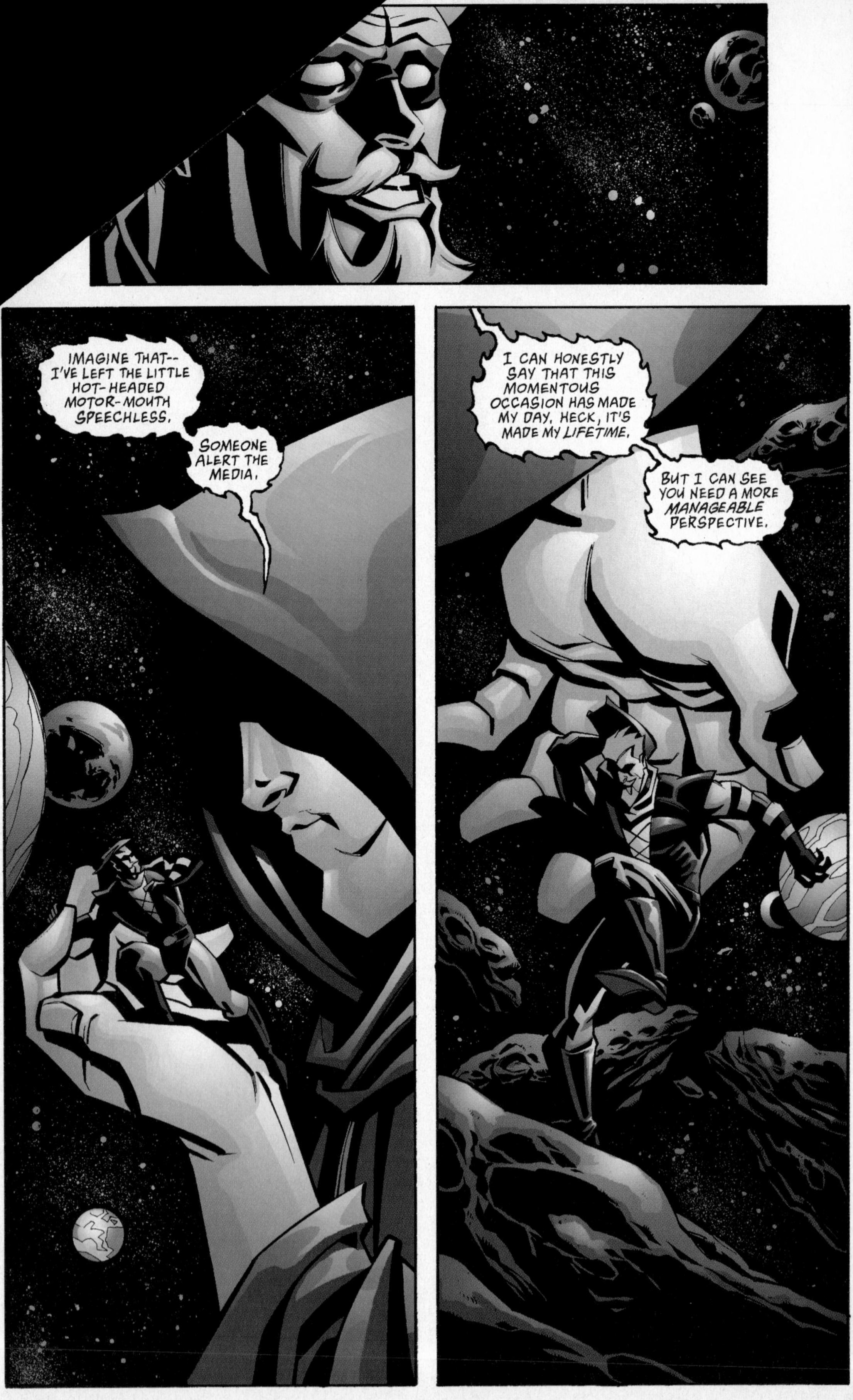

IMAGINE THAT-- I'VE LEFT THE LITTLE HOT-HEADED MOTOR-MOUTH SPEECHLESS.
SOMEONE ALERT THE MEDIA.
I CAN HONESTLY SAY THAT THIS MOMENTOUS OCCASION HAS MADE MY DAY. HECK, IT'S MADE MY *LIFETIME*.
BUT I CAN SEE YOU NEED A MORE *MANAGEABLE* PERSPECTIVE.

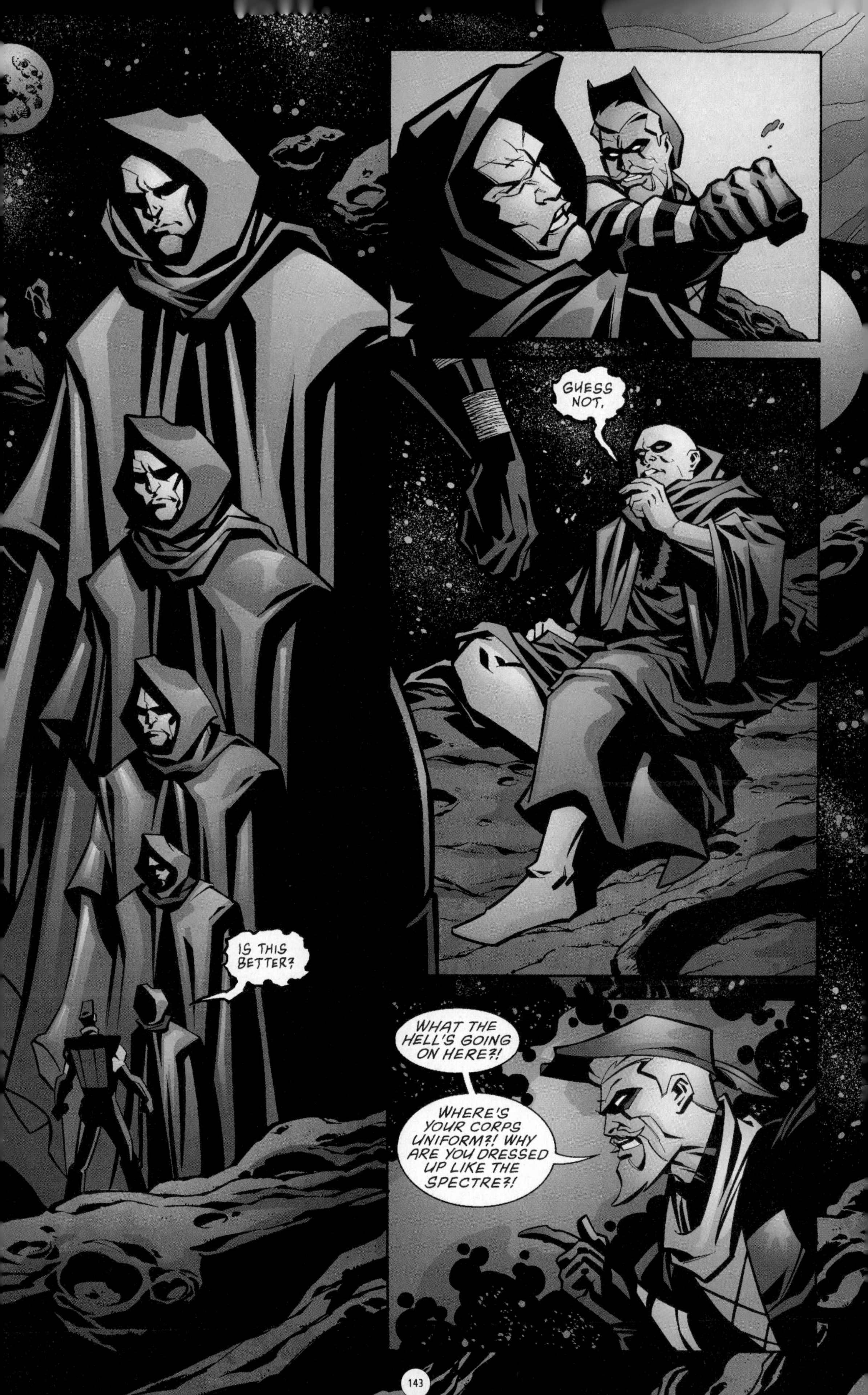
IS THIS BETTER?
GUESS NOT.
WHAT THE HELL'S GOING ON HERE?!
WHERE'S YOUR CORPS UNIFORM?! WHY ARE YOU DRESSED UP LIKE THE SPECTRE?!

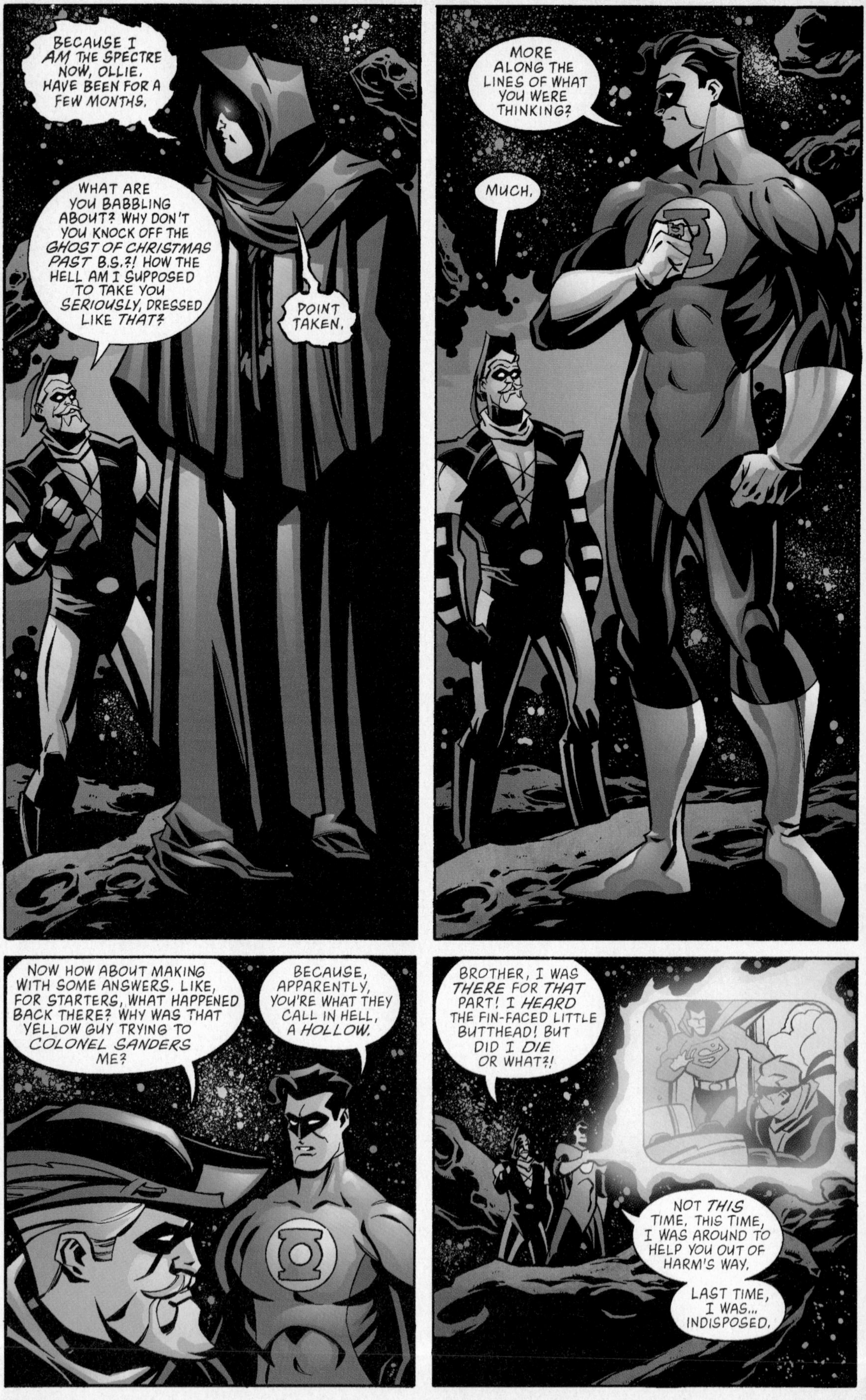
BECAUSE I AM THE SPECTRE NOW, OLLIE. HAVE BEEN FOR A FEW MONTHS.
WHAT ARE YOU BABBLING ABOUT? WHY DON'T YOU KNOCK OFF THE GHOST OF CHRISTMAS PAST B.S.?! HOW THE HELL AM I SUPPOSED TO TAKE YOU SERIOUSLY, DRESSED LIKE THAT?
POINT TAKEN.
MORE ALONG THE LINES OF WHAT YOU WERE THINKING?
MUCH.
NOW HOW ABOUT MAKING WITH SOME ANSWERS. LIKE, FOR STARTERS, WHAT HAPPENED BACK THERE? WHY WAS THAT YELLOW GUY TRYING TO COLONEL SANDERS ME?
BECAUSE, APPARENTLY, YOU'RE WHAT THEY CALL IN HELL, A HOLLOW.
BROTHER, I WAS THERE FOR THAT PART! I HEARD THE FIN-FACED LITTLE BUTTHEAD! BUT DID I DIE OR WHAT?!
NOT THIS TIME. THIS TIME, I WAS AROUND TO HELP YOU OUT OF HARM'S WAY.
LAST TIME, I WAS... INDISPOSED.

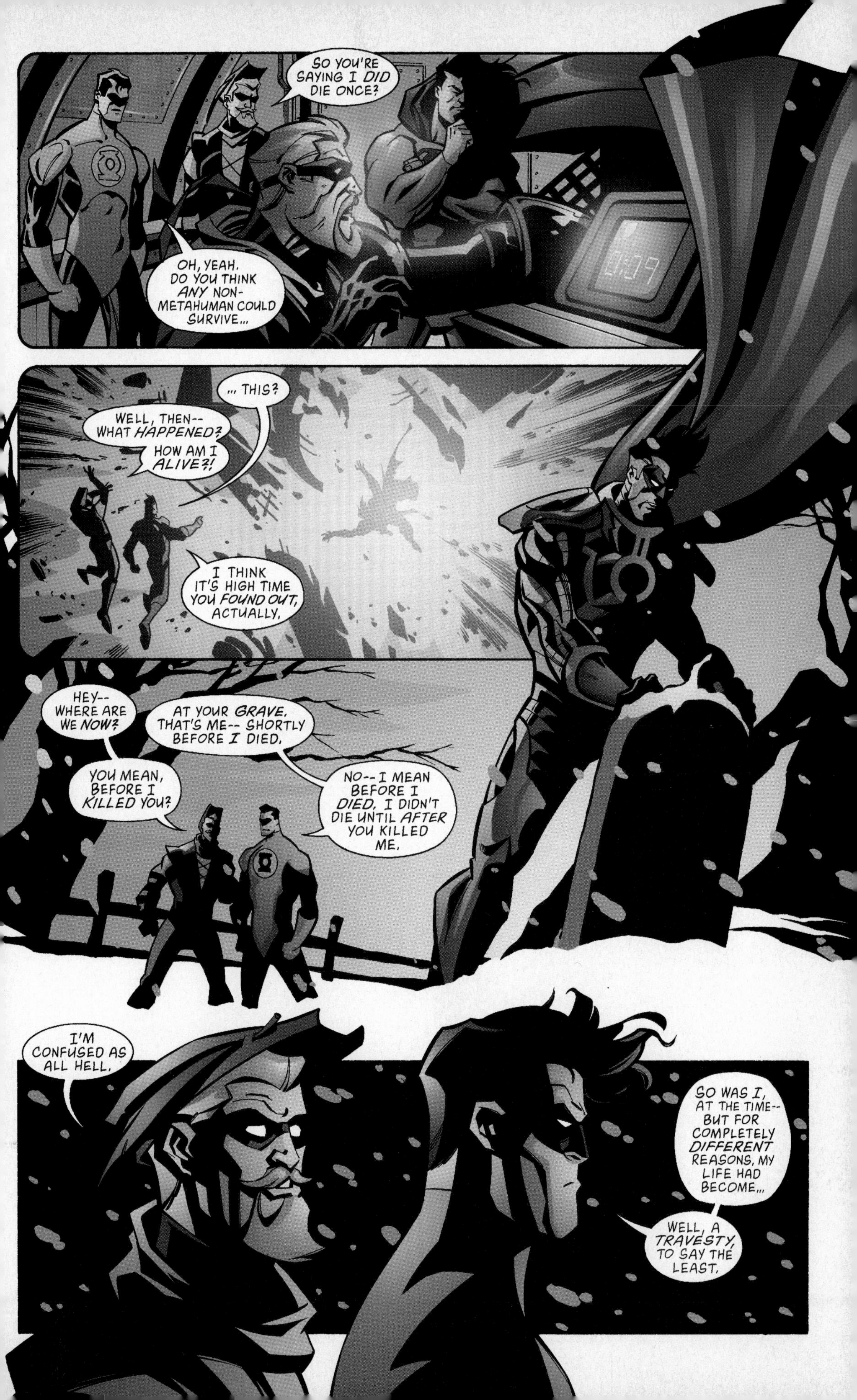
SO YOU'RE SAYING I DID DIE ONCE?
OH, YEAH. DO YOU THINK ANY NON-METAHUMAN COULD SURVIVE...
0:09
... THIS?
WELL, THEN-- WHAT HAPPENED? HOW AM I ALIVE?!
I THINK IT'S HIGH TIME YOU FOUND OUT, ACTUALLY.
HEY-- WHERE ARE WE NOW?
AT YOUR GRAVE. THAT'S ME-- SHORTLY BEFORE I DIED.
YOU MEAN, BEFORE I KILLED YOU?
NO-- I MEAN BEFORE I DIED. I DIDN'T DIE UNTIL AFTER YOU KILLED ME.
I'M CONFUSED AS ALL HELL.
SO WAS I, AT THE TIME-- BUT FOR COMPLETELY DIFFERENT REASONS. MY LIFE HAD BECOME...
WELL, A TRAVESTY, TO SAY THE LEAST.

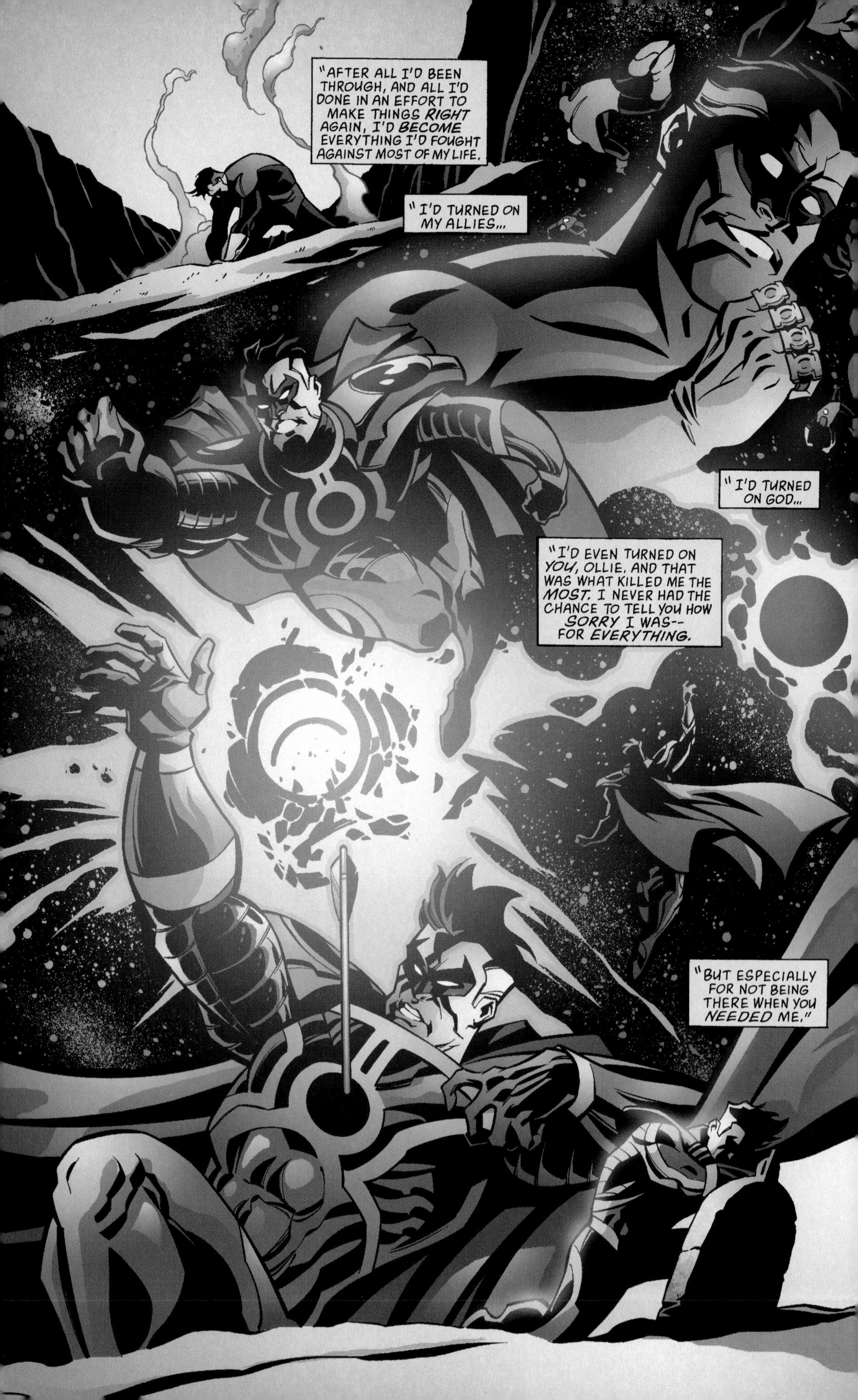
"AFTER ALL I'D BEEN THROUGH, AND ALL I'D DONE IN AN EFFORT TO MAKE THINGS RIGHT AGAIN, I'D BECOME EVERYTHING I'D FOUGHT AGAINST MOST OF MY LIFE.
"I'D TURNED ON MY ALLIES...
"I'D TURNED ON GOD...
"I'D EVEN TURNED ON YOU, OLLIE, AND THAT WAS WHAT KILLED ME THE MOST. I NEVER HAD THE CHANCE TO TELL YOU HOW SORRY I WAS-- FOR EVERYTHING.
"BUT ESPECIALLY FOR NOT BEING THERE WHEN YOU NEEDED ME."

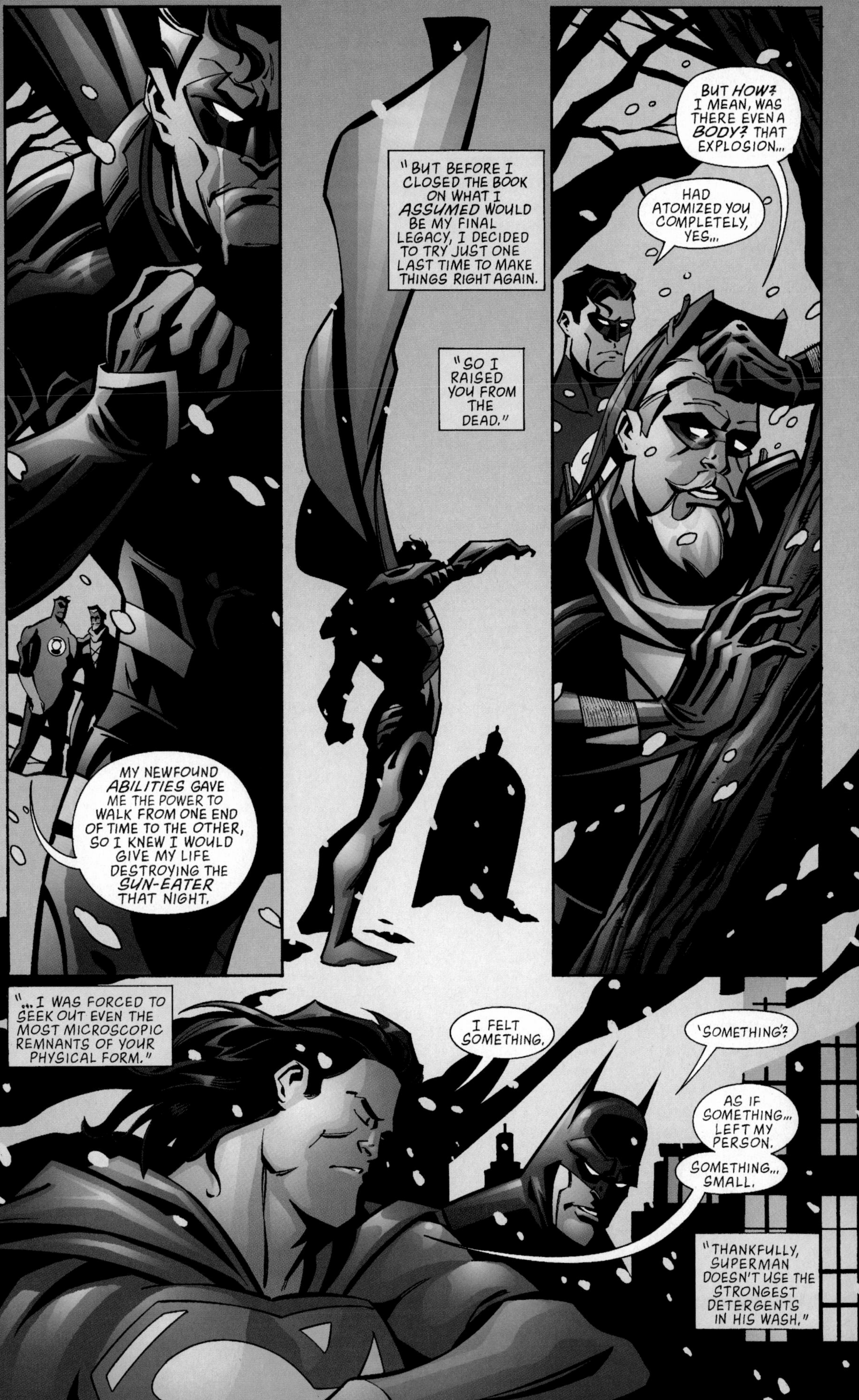
MY NEWFOUND ABILITIES GAVE ME THE POWER TO WALK FROM ONE END OF TIME TO THE OTHER, SO I KNEW I WOULD GIVE MY LIFE DESTROYING THE SUN-EATER THAT NIGHT.
"BUT BEFORE I CLOSED THE BOOK ON WHAT I ASSUMED WOULD BE MY FINAL LEGACY, I DECIDED TO TRY JUST ONE LAST TIME TO MAKE THINGS RIGHT AGAIN.
"SO I RAISED YOU FROM THE DEAD."
BUT HOW? I MEAN, WAS THERE EVEN A BODY? THAT EXPLOSION...
HAD ATOMIZED YOU COMPLETELY, YES...
"...I WAS FORCED TO SEEK OUT EVEN THE MOST MICROSCOPIC REMNANTS OF YOUR PHYSICAL FORM."
I FELT SOMETHING.
'SOMETHING'?
AS IF SOMETHING... LEFT MY PERSON.
SOMETHING... SMALL.
"THANKFULLY, SUPERMAN DOESN'T USE THE STRONGEST DETERGENTS IN HIS WASH."

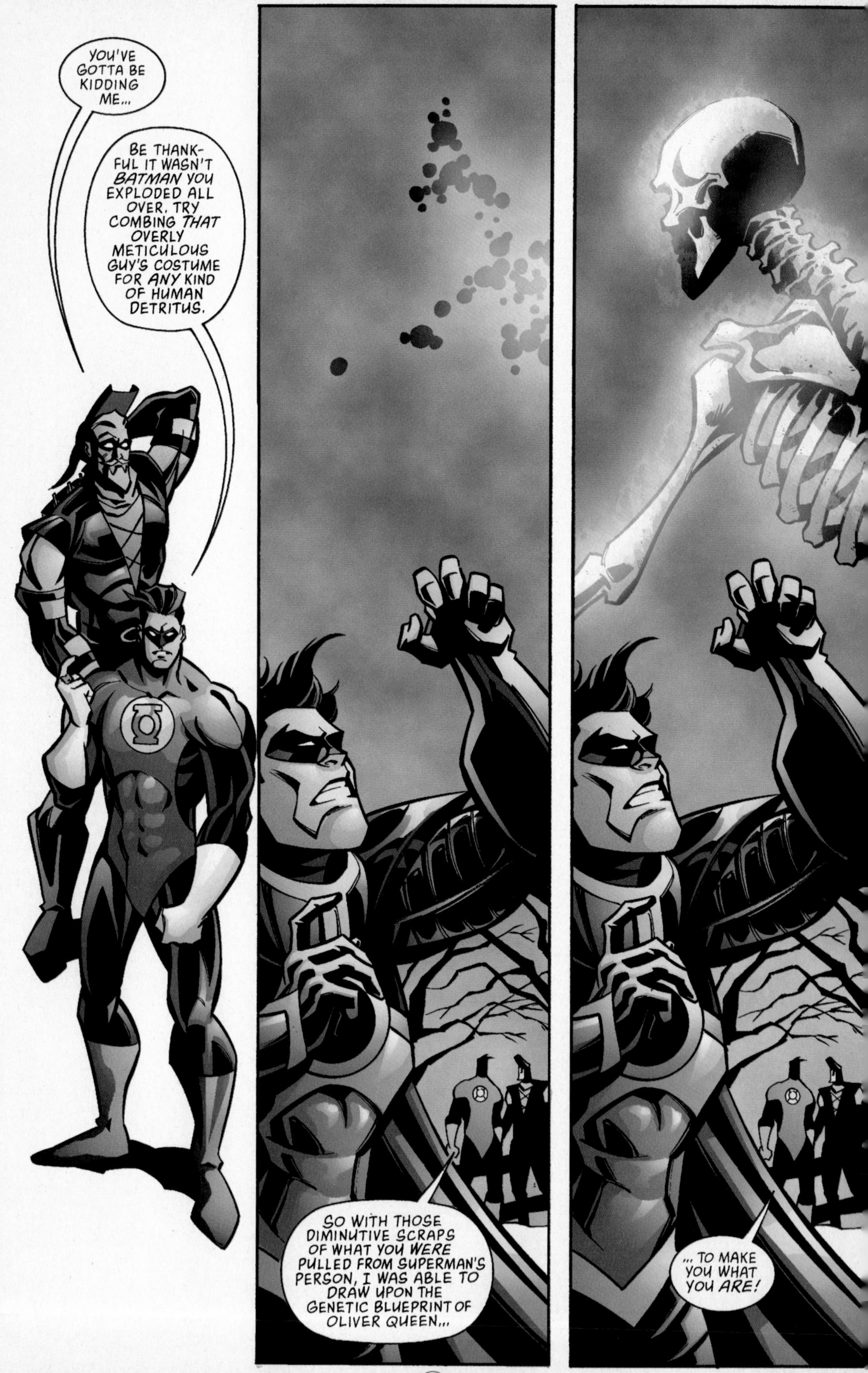

YOU'VE GOTTA BE KIDDING ME...
BE THANKFUL IT WASN'T BATMAN YOU EXPLODED ALL OVER. TRY COMBING THAT OVERLY METICULOUS GUY'S COSTUME FOR ANY KIND OF HUMAN DETRITUS.
SO WITH THOSE DIMINUTIVE SCRAPS OF WHAT YOU WERE PULLED FROM SUPERMAN'S PERSON, I WAS ABLE TO DRAW UPON THE GENETIC BLUEPRINT OF OLIVER QUEEN...
...TO MAKE YOU WHAT YOU ARE!

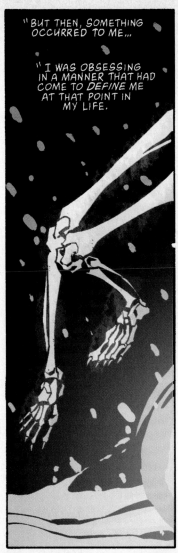

"BUT THEN, SOMETHING OCCURRED TO ME...

"I WAS OBSESSING IN A MANNER THAT HAD COME TO *DEFINE* ME AT THAT POINT IN MY LIFE.

"I WASN'T ACTING IN THE SERVICE OF *MANKIND*-- I WAS ACTING IN THE SERVICE OF *MYSELF*,

"I WAS *STILL* TRYING TO PLAY GOD."

SO I DECIDED TO SEEK ADVICE ON THE MATTER, AND THE *ADVISOR* I MET WITH SUGGESTED I BRING ONLY *PART* OF YOU BACK. WHAT HE DESCRIBED AS "THE *GOOD* PART."

THIS IS WHY YOUR MEMORY, SHALL WE SAY, *STOPS* AT A CERTAIN POINT. YOU HAVE NO KNOWL- EDGE OF YOUR LIFE BEYOND THE PERIOD WE SPENT TRAVELING ACROSS AMERICA.

AND WHAT *ADVISOR* WOULD THIS BE?

COME WITH ME, AND I'LL LET *HIM* EXPLAIN IT TO YOU *HIMSELF*.

OH, MAN-- WE'RE NOT TALKIN' ABOUT *JESUS* HERE, ARE WE?!

HAL-- DON'T TELL ME YOU'VE GONE AND "*FOUND CHRIST*" ON ME NOW.

SORT OF...

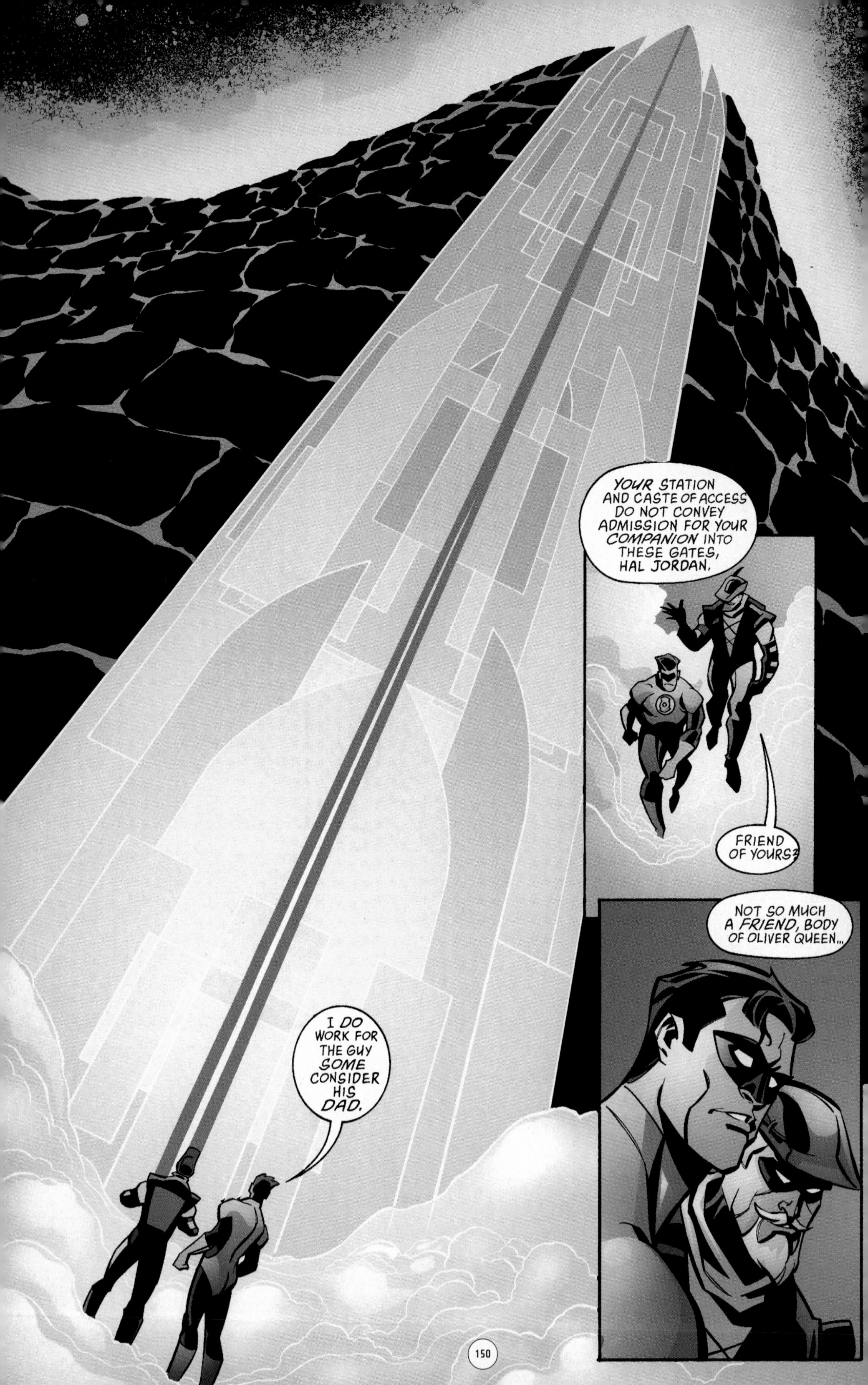
YOUR STATION AND CASTE OF ACCESS DO NOT CONVEY ADMISSION FOR YOUR COMPANION INTO THESE GATES, HAL JORDAN.
FRIEND OF YOURS?
NOT SO MUCH A FRIEND, BODY OF OLIVER QUEEN...
I DO WORK FOR THE GUY SOME CONSIDER HIS DAD.

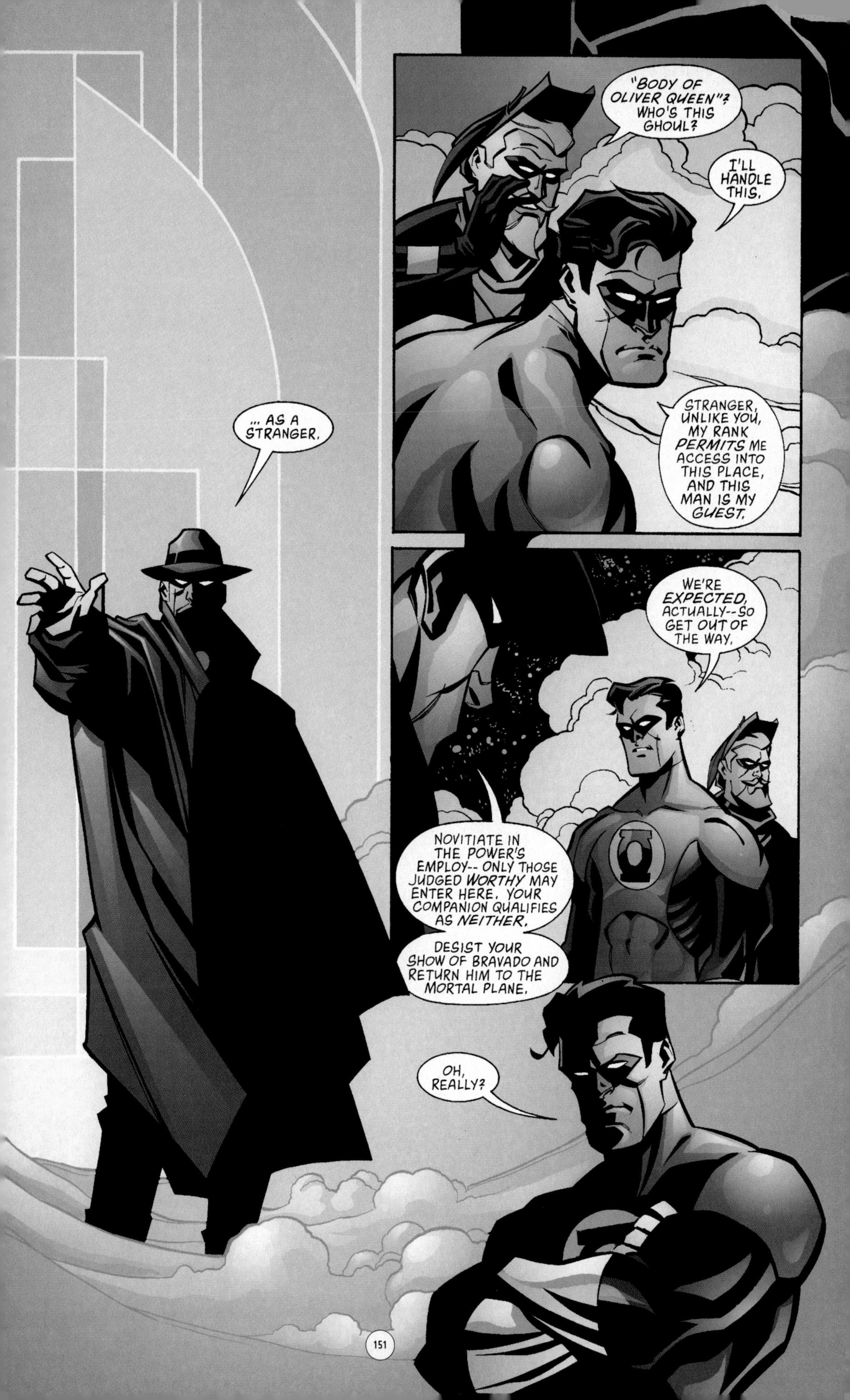
"BODY OF OLIVER QUEEN"? WHO'S THIS GHOUL?
I'LL HANDLE THIS.
...AS A STRANGER.
STRANGER, UNLIKE YOU, MY RANK PERMITS ME ACCESS INTO THIS PLACE, AND THIS MAN IS MY GUEST.
WE'RE EXPECTED, ACTUALLY-- SO GET OUT OF THE WAY.
NOVITIATE IN THE POWER'S EMPLOY-- ONLY THOSE JUDGED WORTHY MAY ENTER HERE. YOUR COMPANION QUALIFIES AS NEITHER.
DESIST YOUR SHOW OF BRAVADO AND RETURN HIM TO THE MORTAL PLANE.
OH, REALLY?

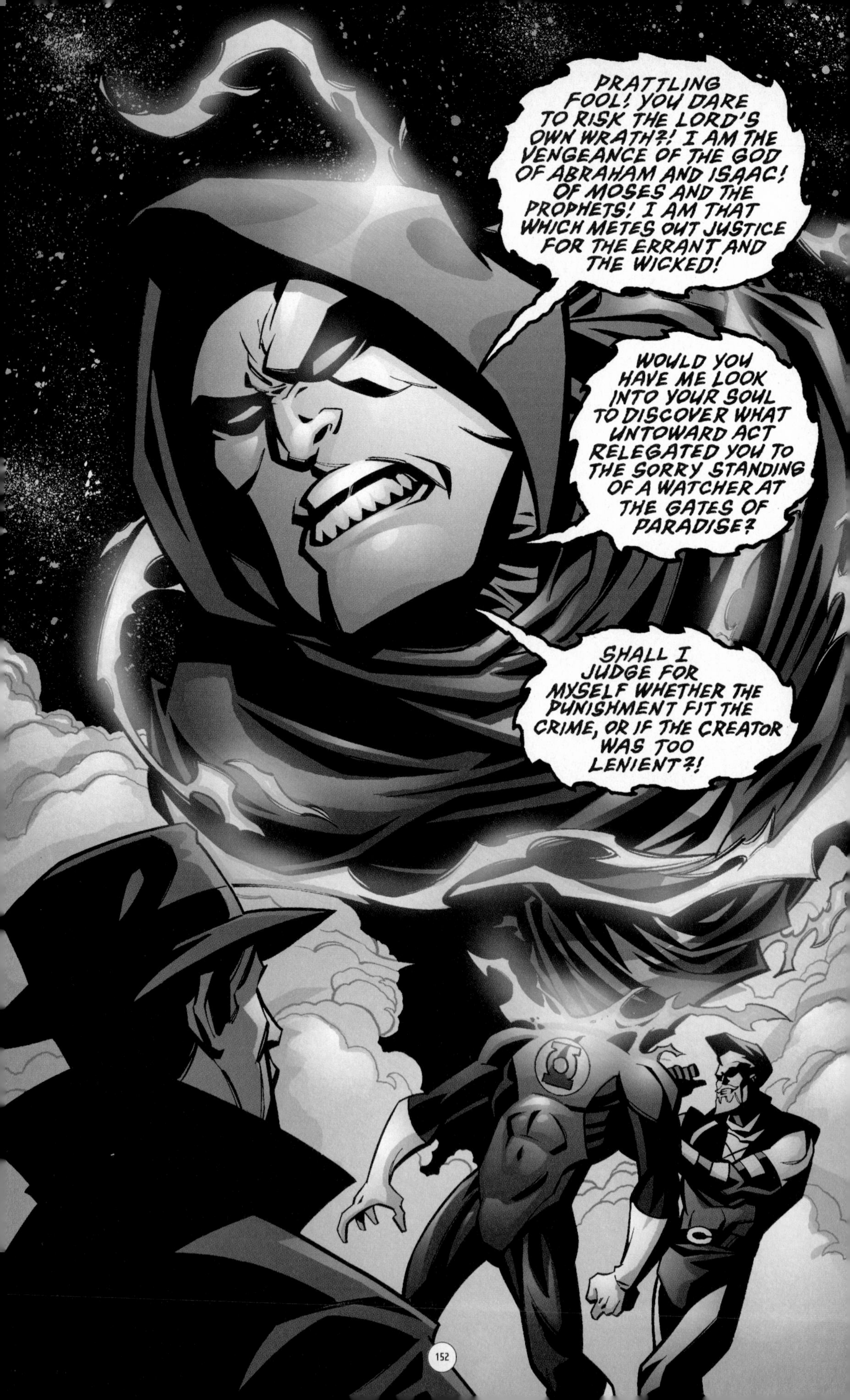
PRATTLING FOOL! YOU DARE TO RISK THE LORD'S OWN WRATH?! I AM THE VENGEANCE OF THE GOD OF ABRAHAM AND ISAAC! OF MOSES AND THE PROPHETS! I AM THAT WHICH METES OUT JUSTICE FOR THE ERRANT AND THE WICKED!
WOULD YOU HAVE ME LOOK INTO YOUR SOUL TO DISCOVER WHAT UNTOWARD ACT RELEGATED YOU TO THE SORRY STANDING OF A WATCHER AT THE GATES OF PARADISE?
SHALL I JUDGE FOR MYSELF WHETHER THE PUNISHMENT FIT THE CRIME, OR IF THE CREATOR WAS TOO LENIENT?!

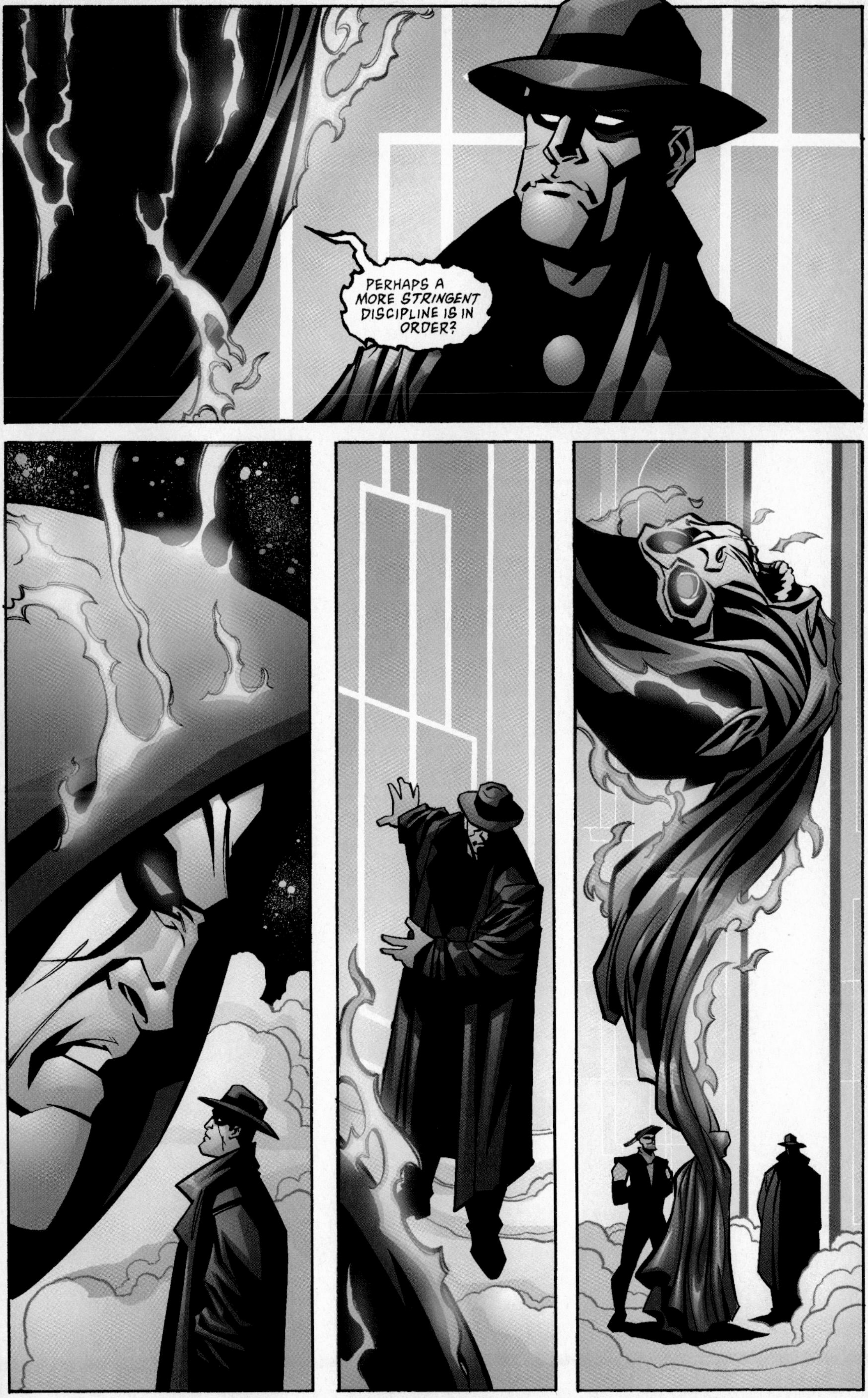
PERHAPS A MORE STRINGENT DISCIPLINE IS IN ORDER?

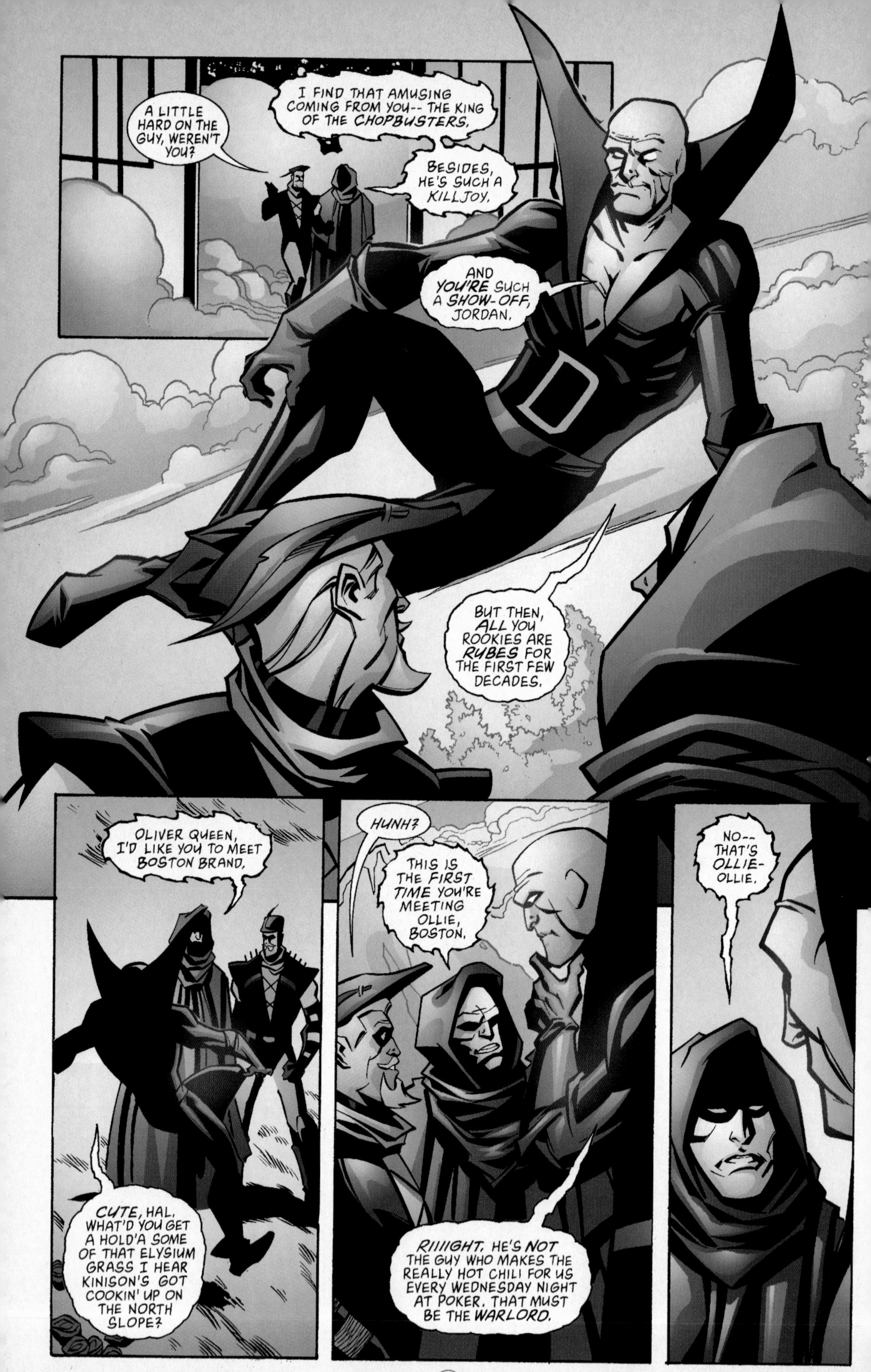

A LITTLE HARD ON THE GUY, WEREN'T YOU?
I FIND THAT AMUSING COMING FROM YOU-- THE KING OF THE CHOPBUSTERS.
BESIDES, HE'S SUCH A KILLJOY.
AND YOU'RE SUCH A SHOW-OFF, JORDAN.
BUT THEN, ALL YOU ROOKIES ARE RUBES FOR THE FIRST FEW DECADES.
OLIVER QUEEN, I'D LIKE YOU TO MEET BOSTON BRAND.
CUTE, HAL. WHAT'D YOU GET A HOLD'A SOME OF THAT ELYSIUM GRASS I HEAR KINISON'S GOT COOKIN' UP ON THE NORTH SLOPE?
HUNH?
THIS IS THE FIRST TIME YOU'RE MEETING OLLIE, BOSTON.
RIIIIGHT. HE'S NOT THE GUY WHO MAKES THE REALLY HOT CHILI FOR US EVERY WEDNESDAY NIGHT AT POKER. THAT MUST BE THE WARLORD.
NO-- THAT'S OLLIE-OLLIE.

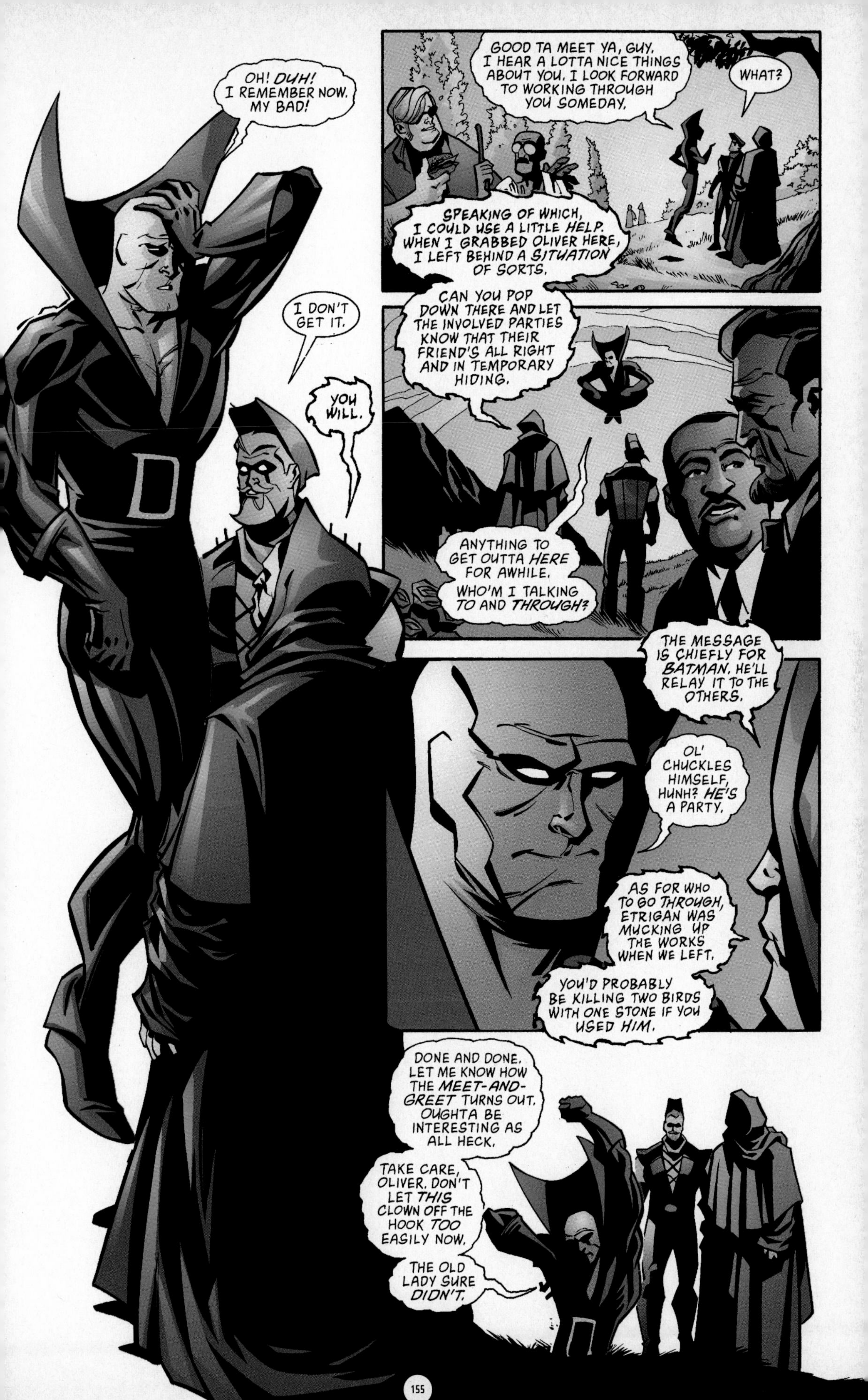
OH! DUH! I REMEMBER NOW. MY BAD!
GOOD TA MEET YA, GUY. I HEAR A LOTTA NICE THINGS ABOUT YOU. I LOOK FORWARD TO WORKING THROUGH YOU SOMEDAY.
WHAT?
SPEAKING OF WHICH, I COULD USE A LITTLE HELP. WHEN I GRABBED OLIVER HERE, I LEFT BEHIND A SITUATION OF SORTS.
I DON'T GET IT.
YOU WILL.
CAN YOU POP DOWN THERE AND LET THE INVOLVED PARTIES KNOW THAT THEIR FRIEND'S ALL RIGHT AND IN TEMPORARY HIDING.
ANYTHING TO GET OUTTA HERE FOR AWHILE.
WHO'M I TALKING TO AND THROUGH?
THE MESSAGE IS CHIEFLY FOR BATMAN. HE'LL RELAY IT TO THE OTHERS.
OL' CHUCKLES HIMSELF, HUNH? HE'S A PARTY.
AS FOR WHO TO GO THROUGH, ETRIGAN WAS MUCKING UP THE WORKS WHEN WE LEFT.
YOU'D PROBABLY BE KILLING TWO BIRDS WITH ONE STONE IF YOU USED HIM.
DONE AND DONE. LET ME KNOW HOW THE MEET-AND-GREET TURNS OUT. OUGHTA BE INTERESTING AS ALL HECK.
TAKE CARE, OLIVER. DON'T LET THIS CLOWN OFF THE HOOK TOO EASILY NOW.
THE OLD LADY SURE DIDN'T.

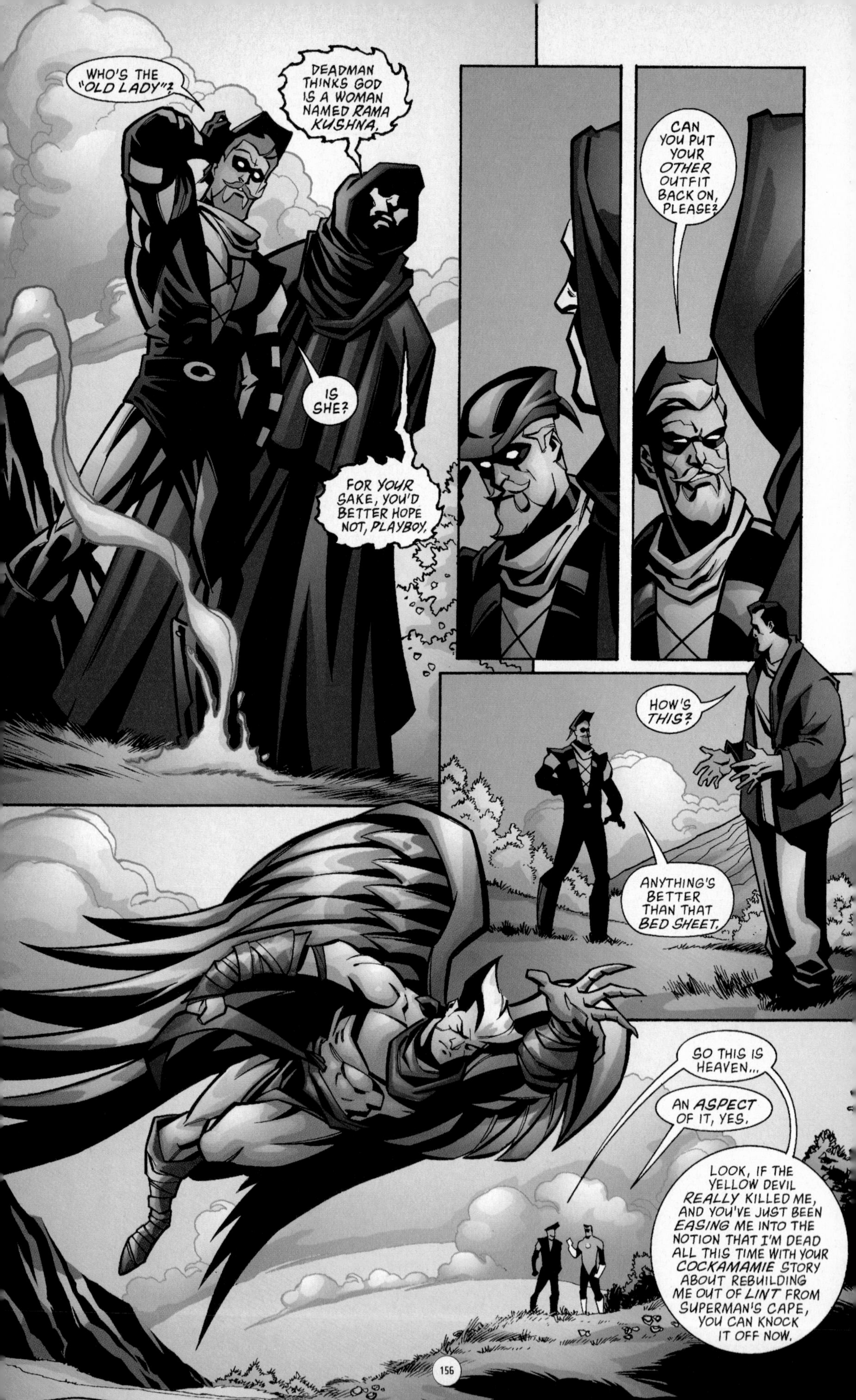
WHO'S THE "OLD LADY"?
DEADMAN THINKS GOD IS A WOMAN NAMED RAMA KUSHNA.
IS SHE?
FOR YOUR SAKE, YOU'D BETTER HOPE NOT, PLAYBOY.
CAN YOU PUT YOUR OTHER OUTFIT BACK ON, PLEASE?
HOW'S THIS?
ANYTHING'S BETTER THAN THAT BED SHEET.
SO THIS IS HEAVEN...
AN ASPECT OF IT, YES.
LOOK, IF THE YELLOW DEVIL REALLY KILLED ME, AND YOU'VE JUST BEEN EASING ME INTO THE NOTION THAT I'M DEAD ALL THIS TIME WITH YOUR COCKAMAMIE STORY ABOUT REBUILDING ME OUT OF LINT FROM SUPERMAN'S CAPE, YOU CAN KNOCK IT OFF NOW.

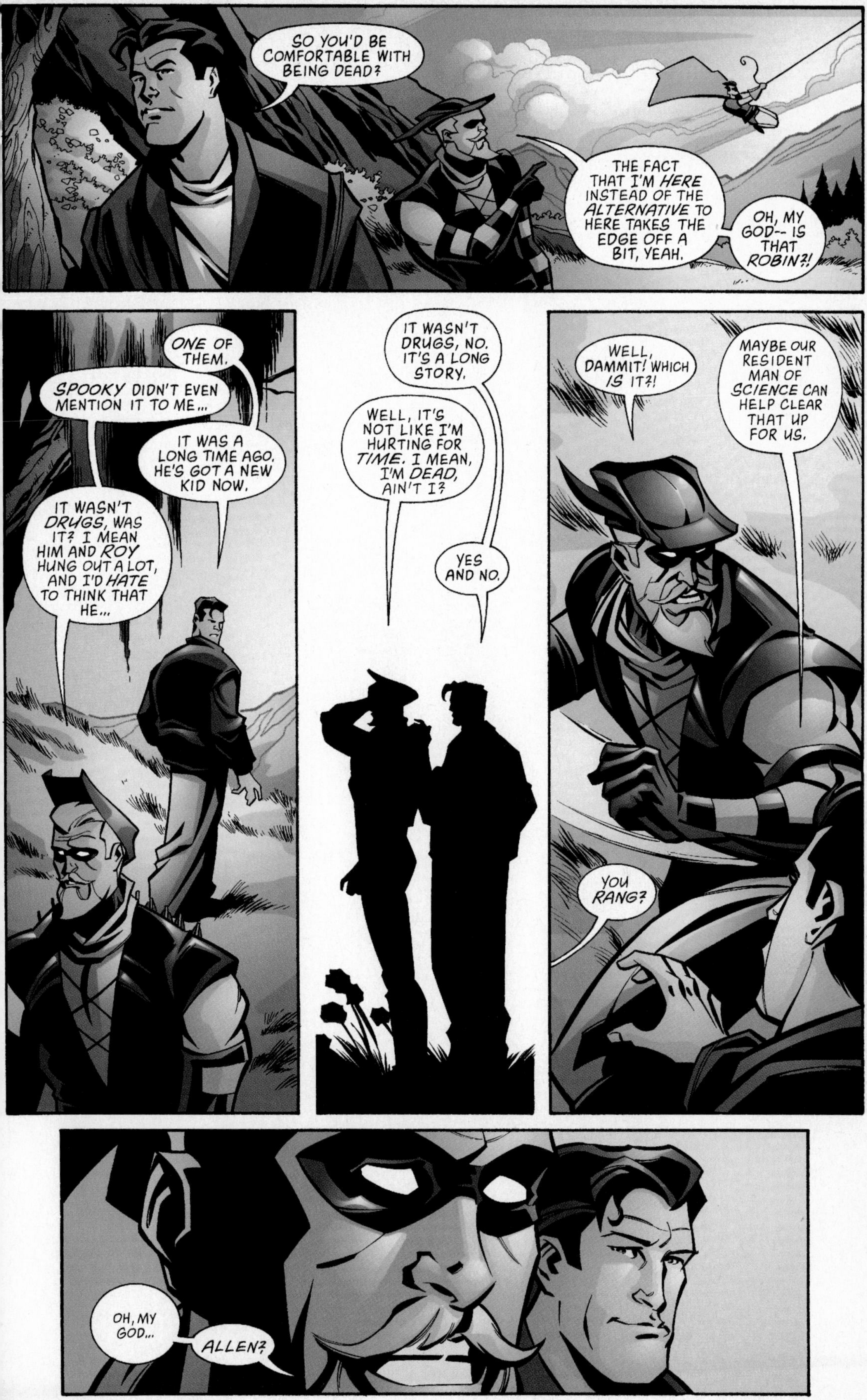

SO YOU'D BE COMFORTABLE WITH BEING DEAD?
THE FACT THAT I'M *HERE* INSTEAD OF THE *ALTERNATIVE* TO HERE TAKES THE EDGE OFF A BIT, YEAH.
OH, MY GOD-- IS THAT *ROBIN*?!
ONE OF THEM.
SPOOKY DIDN'T EVEN MENTION IT TO ME...
IT WAS A LONG TIME AGO. HE'S GOT A NEW KID NOW.
IT WASN'T *DRUGS*, WAS IT? I MEAN HIM AND *ROY* HUNG OUT A LOT, AND I'D *HATE* TO THINK THAT HE...
WELL, IT'S NOT LIKE I'M HURTING FOR *TIME*. I MEAN, I'M *DEAD*, AIN'T I?
IT WASN'T DRUGS, NO. IT'S A LONG STORY.
YES AND NO.
WELL, DAMMIT! WHICH *IS* IT?!
MAYBE OUR RESIDENT MAN OF *SCIENCE* CAN HELP CLEAR THAT UP FOR US.
YOU *RANG*?
OH, MY GOD...
ALLEN?

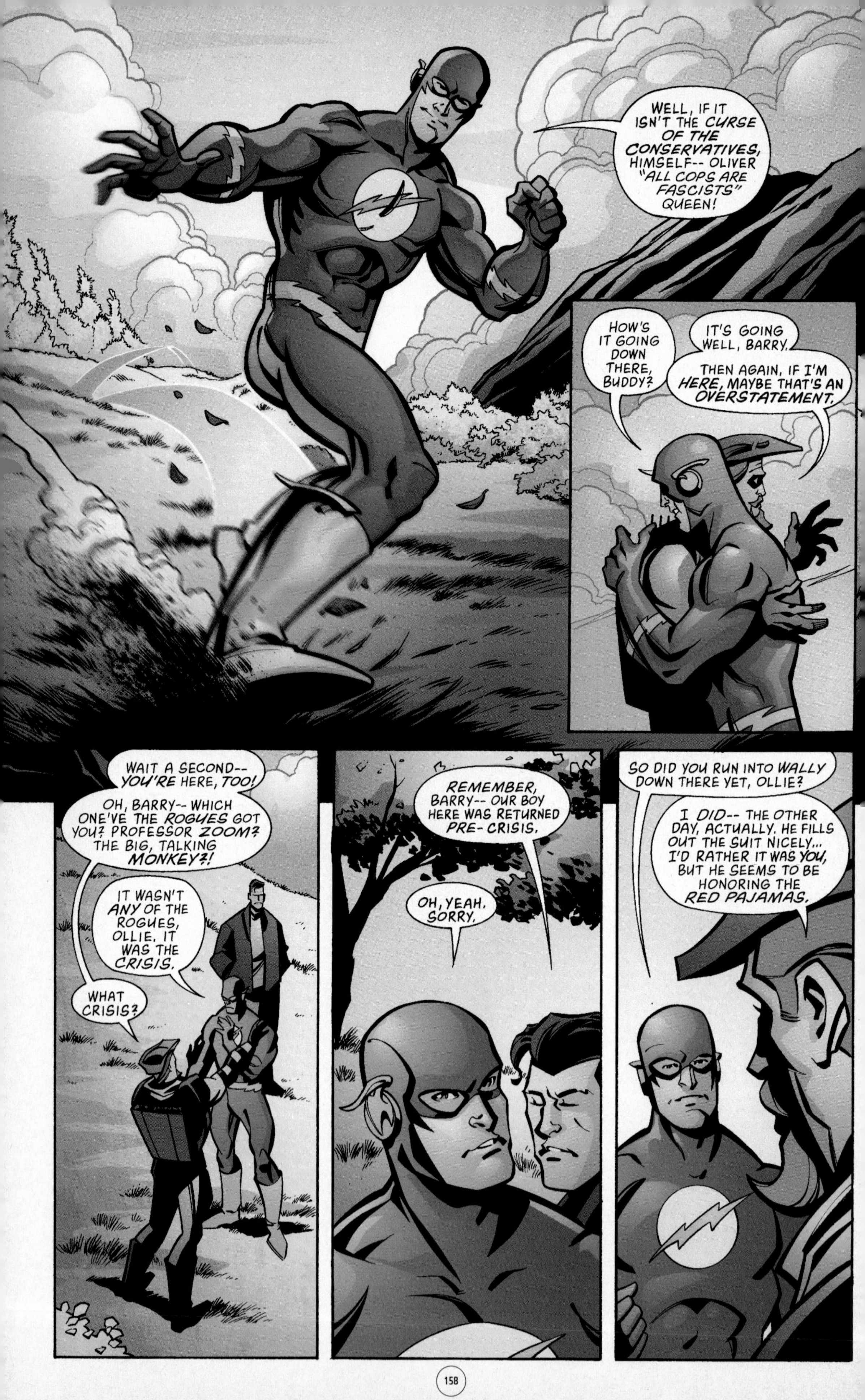
WELL, IF IT ISN'T THE CURSE OF THE CONSERVATIVES, HIMSELF-- OLIVER "ALL COPS ARE FASCISTS" QUEEN!
HOW'S IT GOING DOWN THERE, BUDDY?
IT'S GOING WELL, BARRY.
THEN AGAIN, IF I'M HERE, MAYBE THAT'S AN OVERSTATEMENT.
WAIT A SECOND-- YOU'RE HERE, TOO!
OH, BARRY-- WHICH ONE'VE THE ROGUES GOT YOU? PROFESSOR ZOOM? THE BIG, TALKING MONKEY?!
IT WASN'T ANY OF THE ROGUES, OLLIE. IT WAS THE CRISIS.
WHAT CRISIS?
REMEMBER, BARRY-- OUR BOY HERE WAS RETURNED PRE-CRISIS.
OH, YEAH. SORRY.
SO DID YOU RUN INTO WALLY DOWN THERE YET, OLLIE?
I DID-- THE OTHER DAY, ACTUALLY. HE FILLS OUT THE SUIT NICELY... I'D RATHER IT WAS YOU, BUT HE SEEMS TO BE HONORING THE RED PAJAMAS.

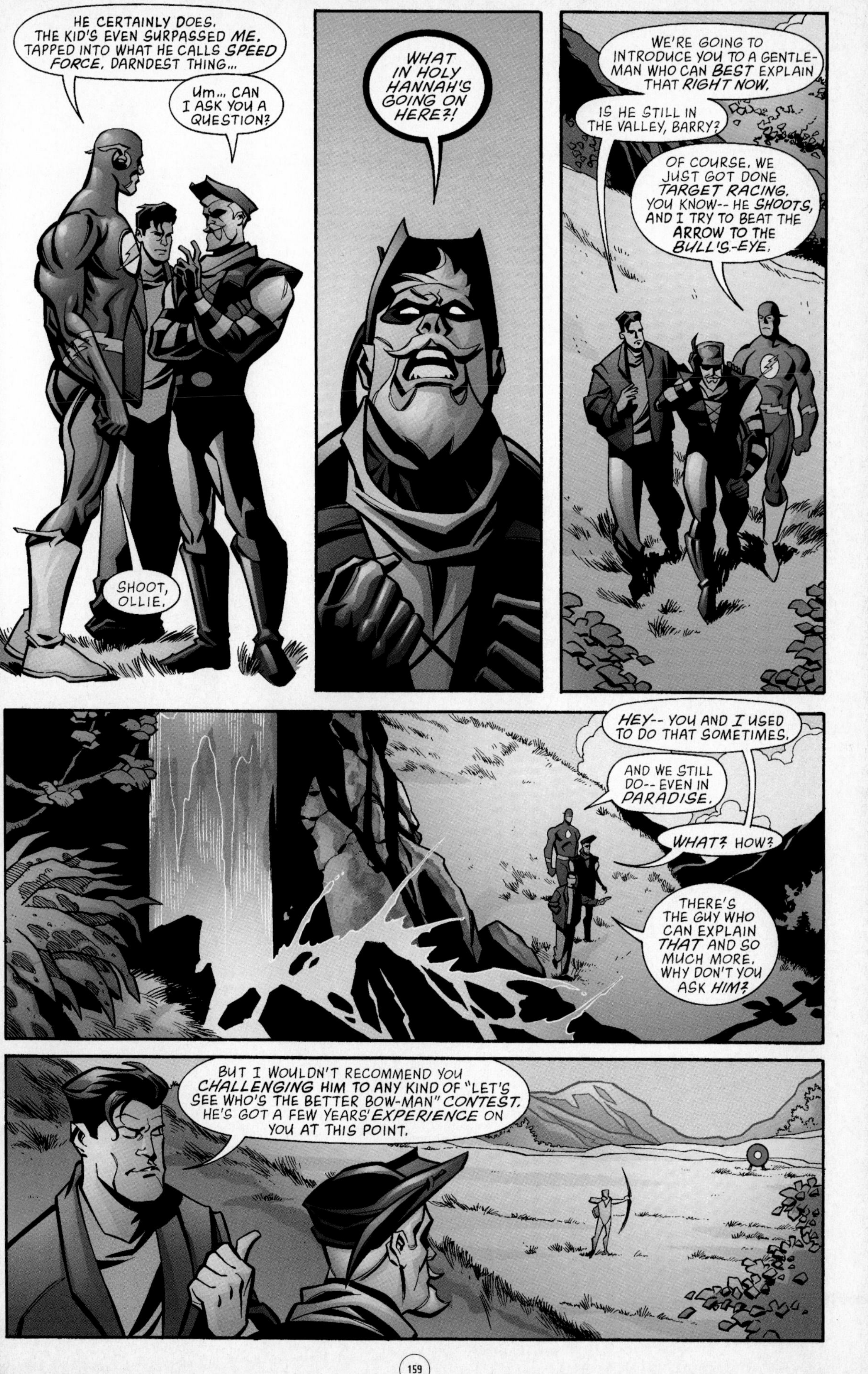

HE CERTAINLY DOES. THE KID'S EVEN SURPASSED ME. TAPPED INTO WHAT HE CALLS SPEED FORCE. DARNDEST THING...
Um... CAN I ASK YOU A QUESTION?
SHOOT, OLLIE.
WHAT IN HOLY HANNAH'S GOING ON HERE?!
WE'RE GOING TO INTRODUCE YOU TO A GENTLE-MAN WHO CAN BEST EXPLAIN THAT RIGHT NOW.
IS HE STILL IN THE VALLEY, BARRY?
OF COURSE. WE JUST GOT DONE TARGET RACING. YOU KNOW-- HE SHOOTS, AND I TRY TO BEAT THE ARROW TO THE BULL'S-EYE.
HEY-- YOU AND I USED TO DO THAT SOMETIMES.
AND WE STILL DO-- EVEN IN PARADISE.
WHAT? HOW?
THERE'S THE GUY WHO CAN EXPLAIN THAT AND SO MUCH MORE. WHY DON'T YOU ASK HIM?
BUT I WOULDN'T RECOMMEND YOU CHALLENGING HIM TO ANY KIND OF "LET'S SEE WHO'S THE BETTER BOW-MAN" CONTEST. HE'S GOT A FEW YEARS' EXPERIENCE ON YOU AT THIS POINT.

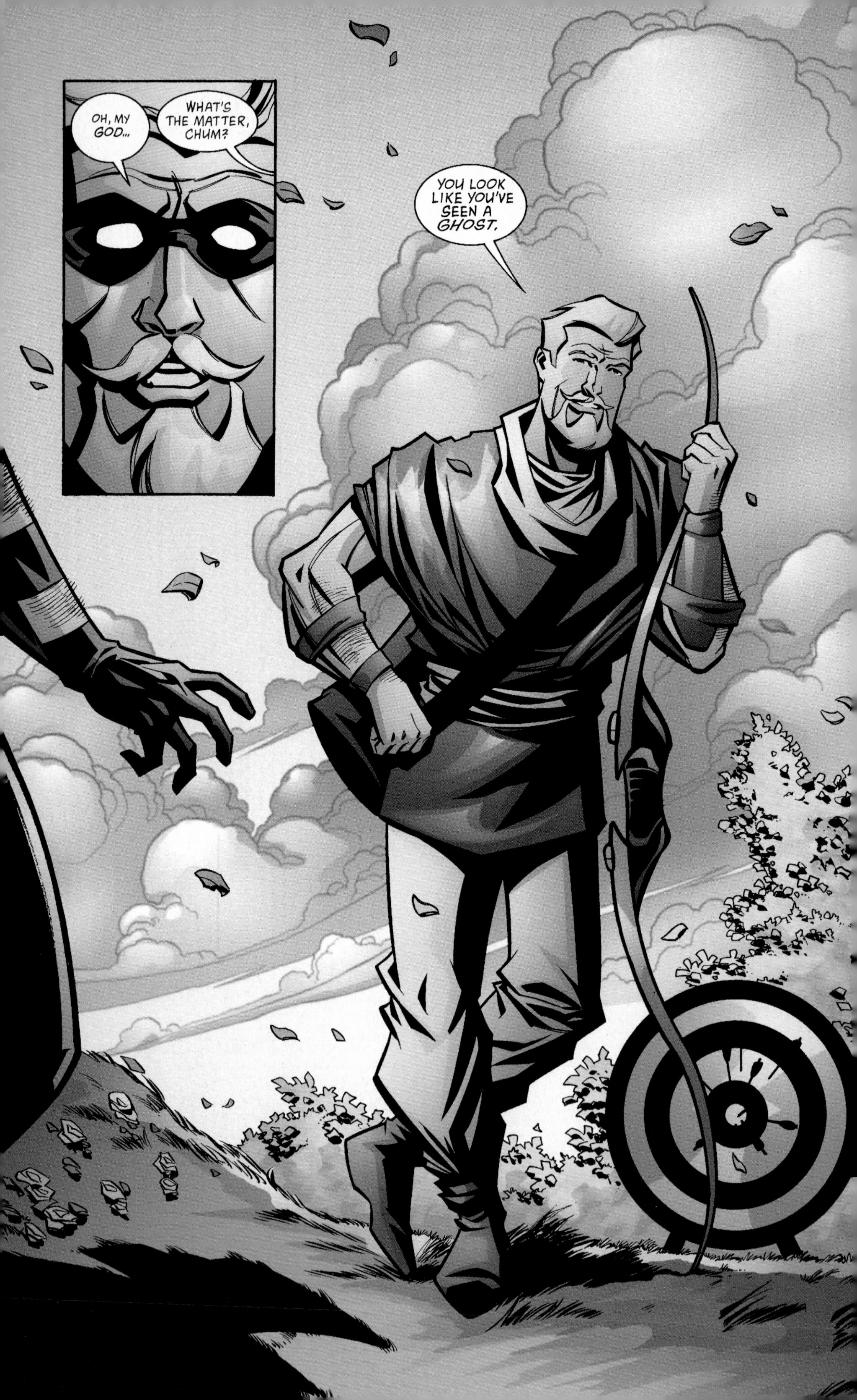
OH, MY GOD...
WHAT'S THE MATTER, CHUM?
YOU LOOK LIKE YOU'VE SEEN A GHOST.

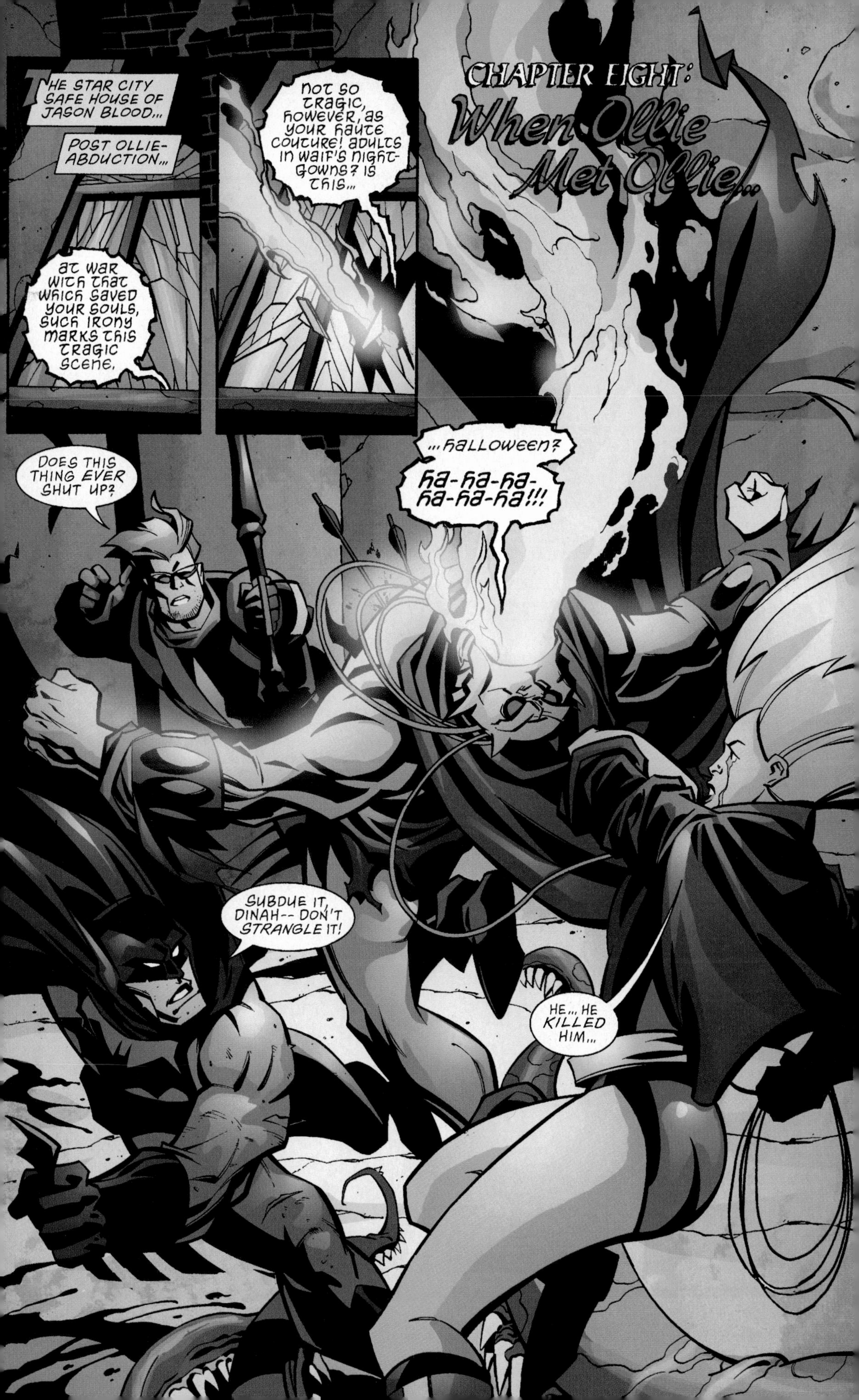
The Star City safe house of Jason Blood...
Post Ollie-abduction...
At war with that which saved your souls, such irony marks this tragic scene.
Not so tragic, however, as your haute couture! Adults in waif's night-gowns? Is this...
CHAPTER EIGHT:
When Ollie Met Ollie...
Does this thing ever shut up?
...Halloween?
Ha-ha-ha-ha-ha-ha!!!
Subdue it, Dinah-- don't strangle it!
He... he killed him...

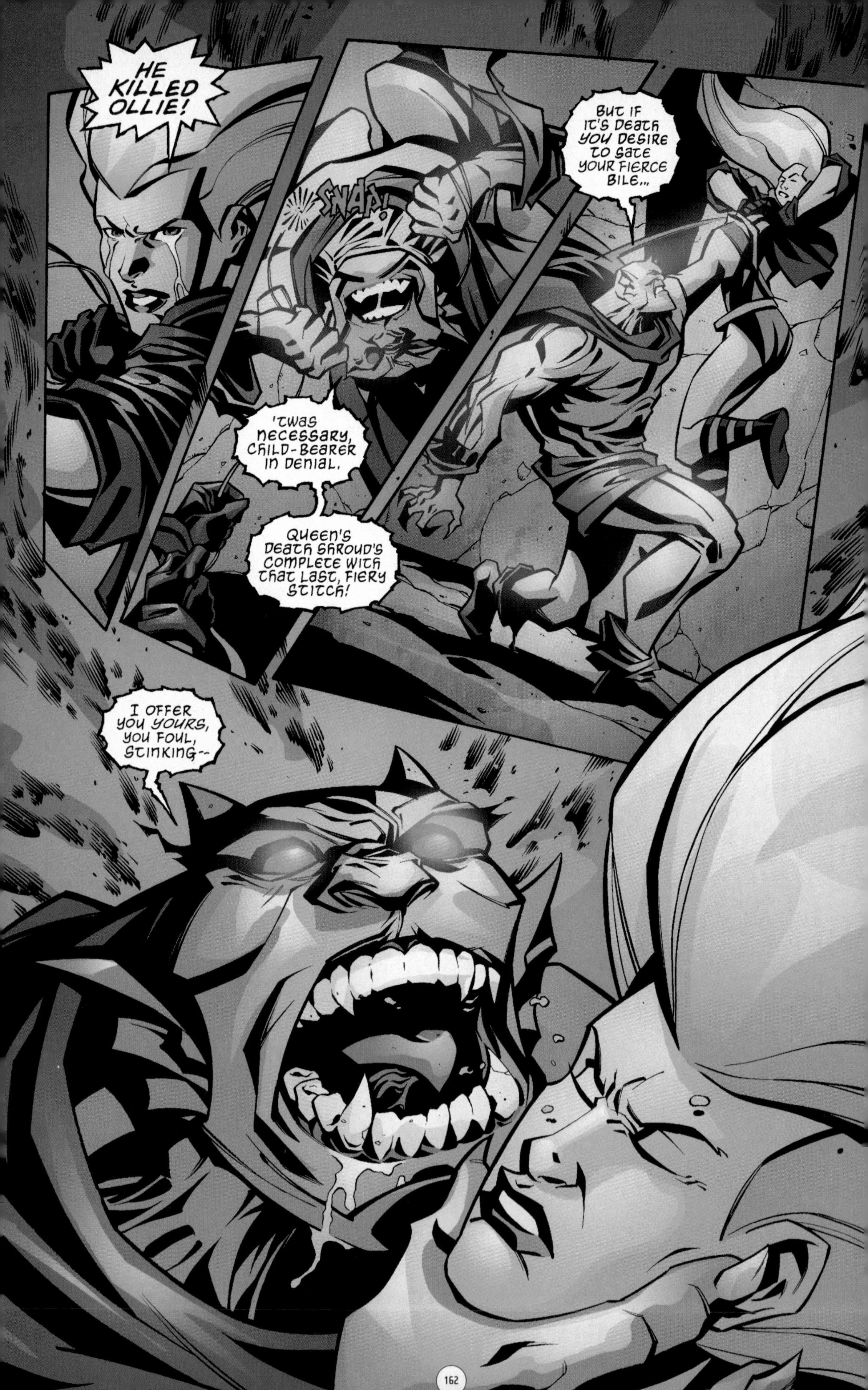
HE KILLED OLLIE!
SNAP!
'TWAS NECESSARY, CHILD-BEARER IN DENIAL.
QUEEN'S DEATH SHROUD'S COMPLETE WITH THAT LAST, FIERY STITCH!
BUT IF IT'S DEATH YOU DESIRE TO SATE YOUR FIERCE BILE...
I OFFER YOU YOURS, YOU FOUL, STINKING--

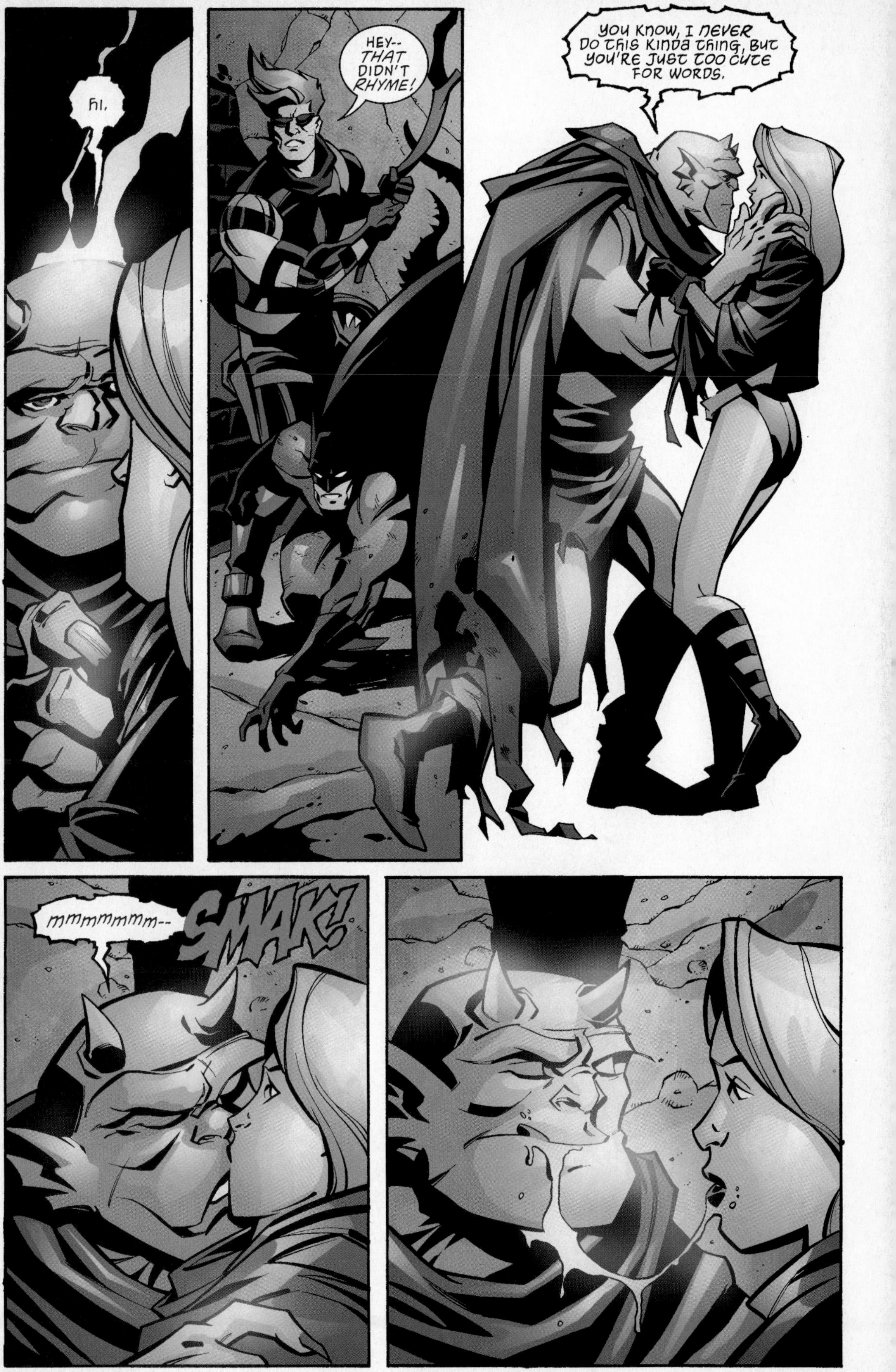
HI.
HEY-- THAT DIDN'T RHYME!
YOU KNOW, I NEVER DO THIS KINDA THING, BUT YOU'RE JUST TOO CUTE FOR WORDS.
mmmmmmm--
SMAK!

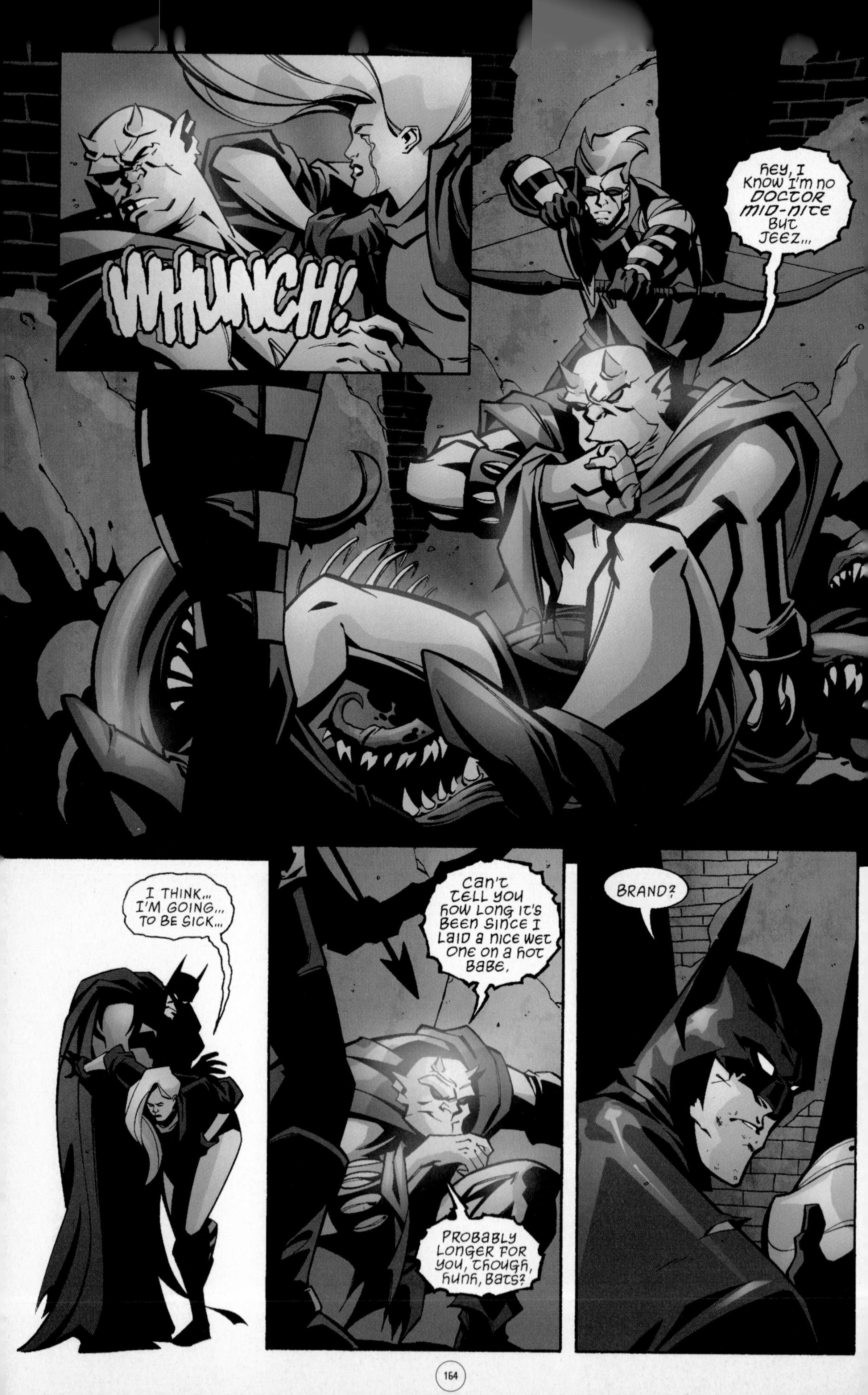
WHUNCH!
HEY, I KNOW I'M NO DOCTOR MID-NITE BUT JEEZ...
I THINK... I'M GOING... TO BE SICK...
CAN'T TELL YOU HOW LONG IT'S BEEN SINCE I LAID A NICE WET ONE ON A HOT BABE.
PROBABLY LONGER FOR YOU, THOUGH, HUNH, BATS?
BRAND?

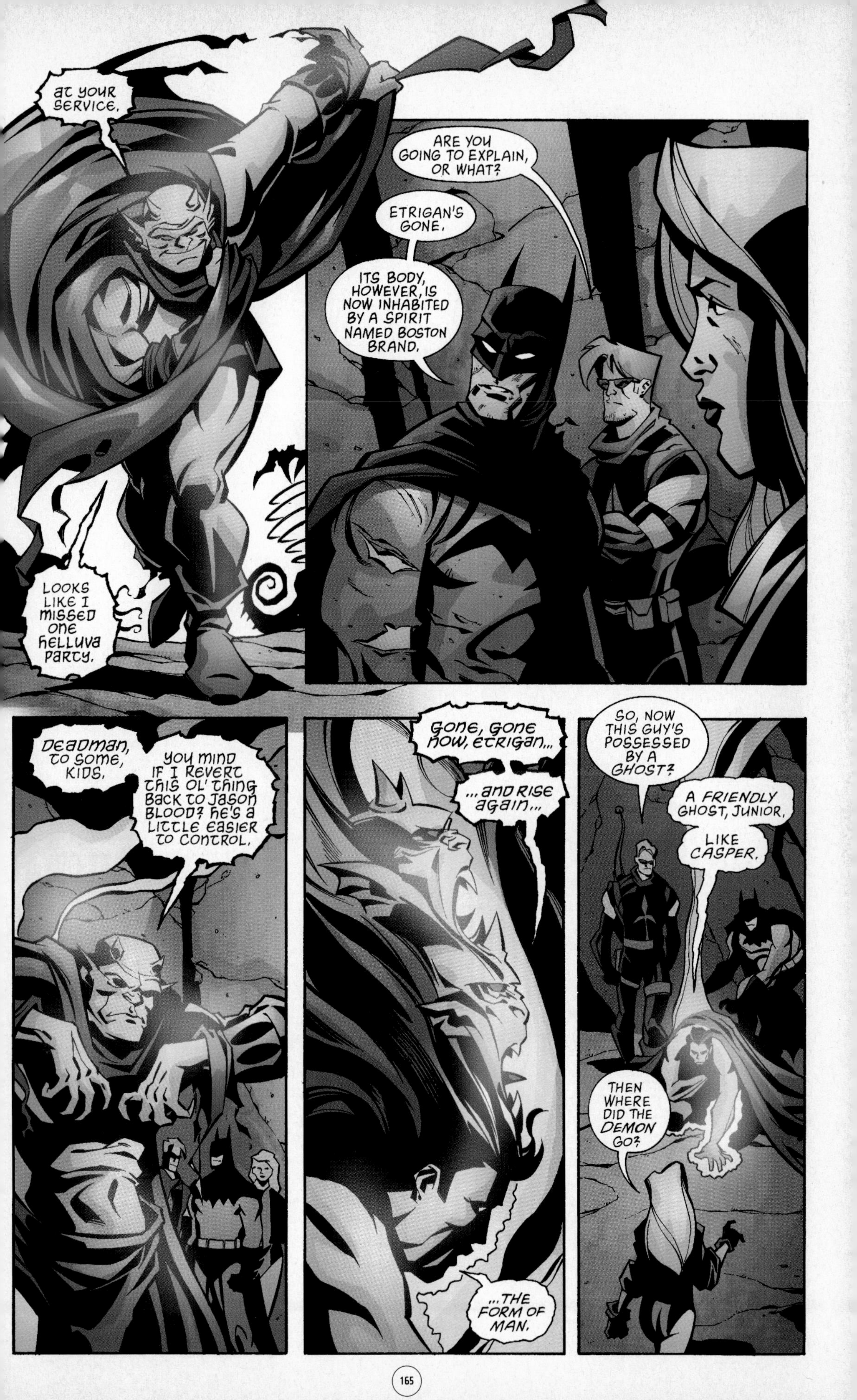
AT YOUR SERVICE.
ARE YOU GOING TO EXPLAIN, OR WHAT?
ETRIGAN'S GONE.
ITS BODY, HOWEVER, IS NOW INHABITED BY A SPIRIT NAMED BOSTON BRAND.
LOOKS LIKE I MISSED ONE HELLUVA PARTY.
DEADMAN, TO SOME, KIDS.
YOU MIND IF I REVERT THIS OL' THING BACK TO JASON BLOOD? HE'S A LITTLE EASIER TO CONTROL.
GONE, GONE NOW, ETRIGAN...
...AND RISE AGAIN...
...THE FORM OF MAN.
SO, NOW THIS GUY'S POSSESSED BY A GHOST?
A FRIENDLY GHOST, JUNIOR.
LIKE CASPER.
THEN WHERE DID THE DEMON GO?

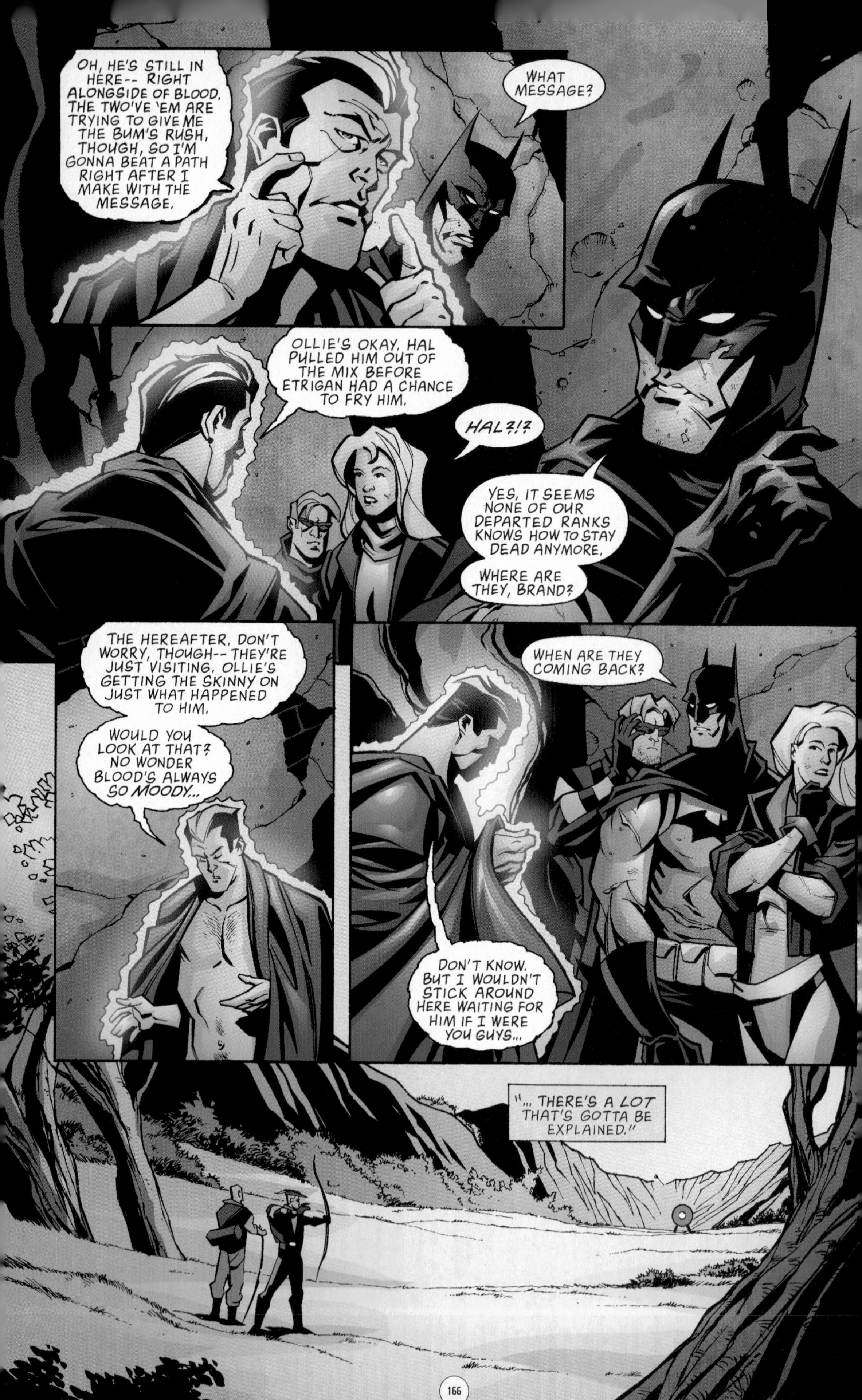

OH, HE'S STILL IN HERE-- RIGHT ALONGSIDE OF BLOOD. THE TWO'VE 'EM ARE TRYING TO GIVE ME THE BUM'S RUSH, THOUGH, SO I'M GONNA BEAT A PATH RIGHT AFTER I MAKE WITH THE MESSAGE.
WHAT MESSAGE?
OLLIE'S OKAY. HAL PULLED HIM OUT OF THE MIX BEFORE ETRIGAN HAD A CHANCE TO FRY HIM.
HAL?!?
YES, IT SEEMS NONE OF OUR DEPARTED RANKS KNOWS HOW TO STAY DEAD ANYMORE.
WHERE ARE THEY, BRAND?
THE HEREAFTER. DON'T WORRY, THOUGH-- THEY'RE JUST VISITING. OLLIE'S GETTING THE SKINNY ON JUST WHAT HAPPENED TO HIM.
WOULD YOU LOOK AT THAT? NO WONDER BLOOD'S ALWAYS SO MOODY...
WHEN ARE THEY COMING BACK?
DON'T KNOW. BUT I WOULDN'T STICK AROUND HERE WAITING FOR HIM IF I WERE YOU GUYS...
"... THERE'S A LOT THAT'S GOTTA BE EXPLAINED."

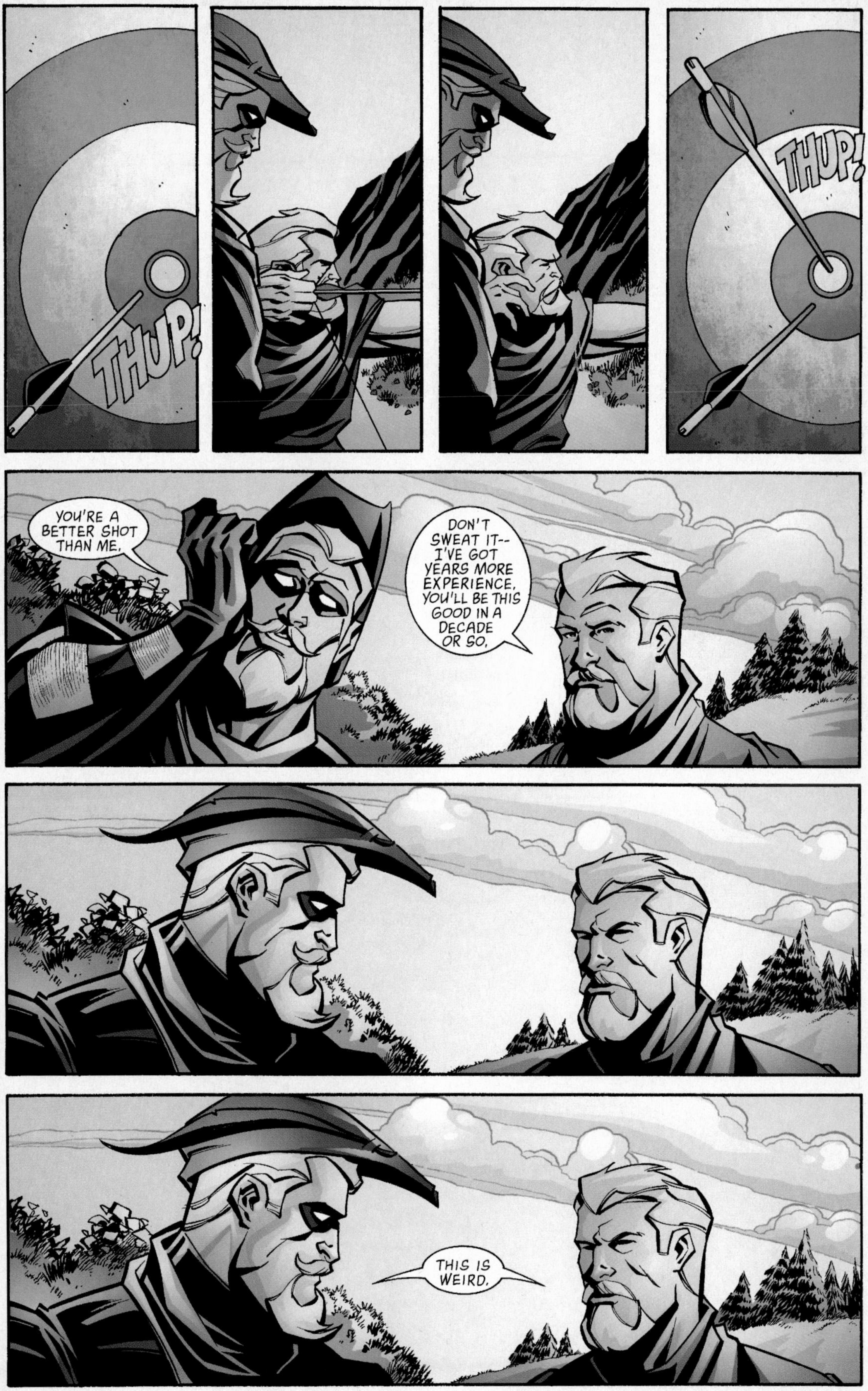
THUP!
THUP!
YOU'RE A BETTER SHOT THAN ME.
DON'T SWEAT IT-- I'VE GOT YEARS MORE EXPERIENCE. YOU'LL BE THIS GOOD IN A DECADE OR SO.
THIS IS WEIRD.

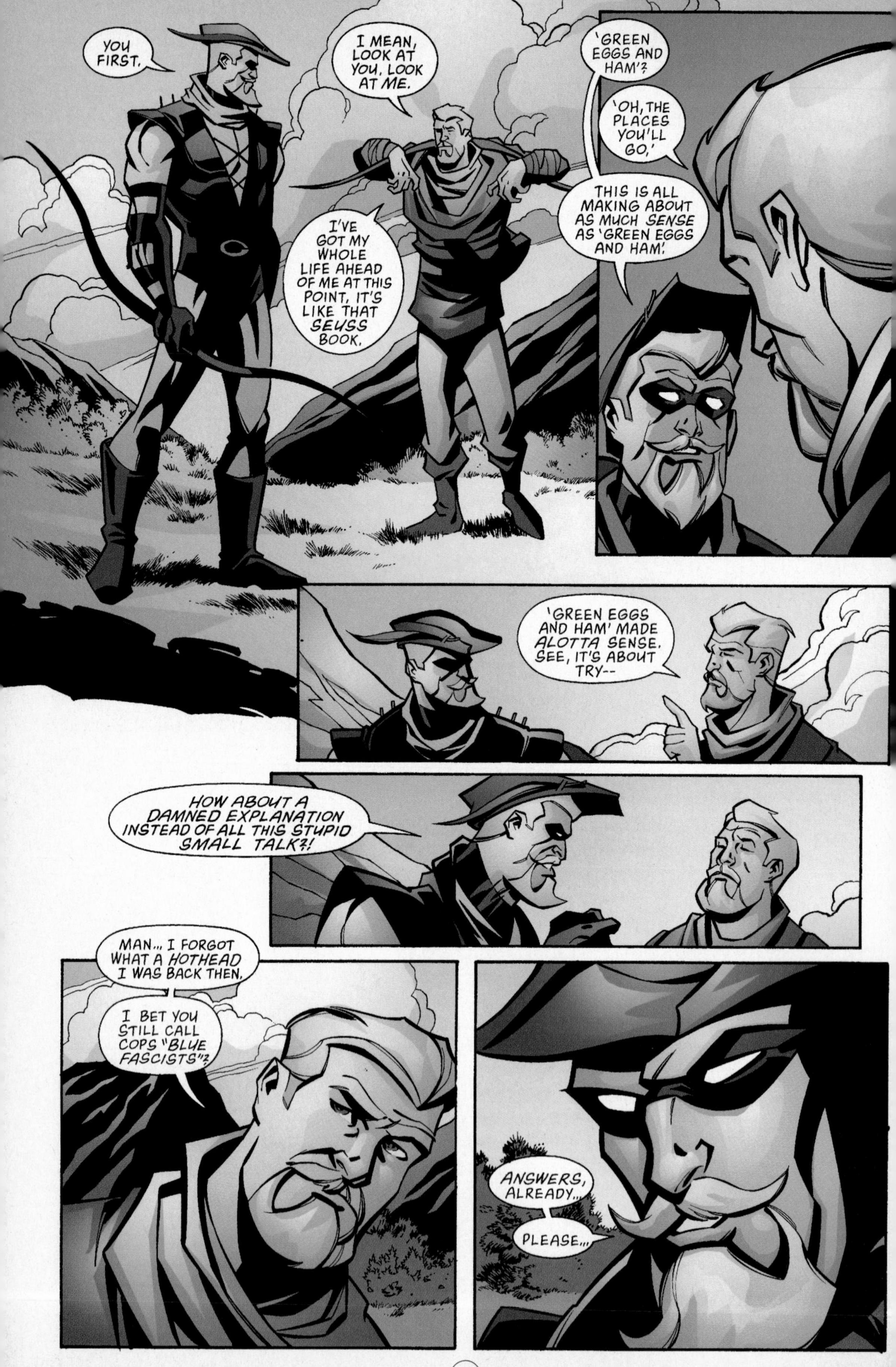

YOU FIRST.
I MEAN, LOOK AT YOU, LOOK AT ME.
I'VE GOT MY WHOLE LIFE AHEAD OF ME AT THIS POINT, IT'S LIKE THAT SEUSS BOOK.
'GREEN EGGS AND HAM'?
'OH, THE PLACES YOU'LL GO,'
THIS IS ALL MAKING ABOUT AS MUCH SENSE AS 'GREEN EGGS AND HAM.'
'GREEN EGGS AND HAM' MADE ALOTTA SENSE. SEE, IT'S ABOUT TRY--
HOW ABOUT A DAMNED EXPLANATION INSTEAD OF ALL THIS STUPID SMALL TALK?!
MAN... I FORGOT WHAT A HOTHEAD I WAS BACK THEN.
I BET YOU STILL CALL COPS "BLUE FASCISTS"?
ANSWERS, ALREADY...
PLEASE...

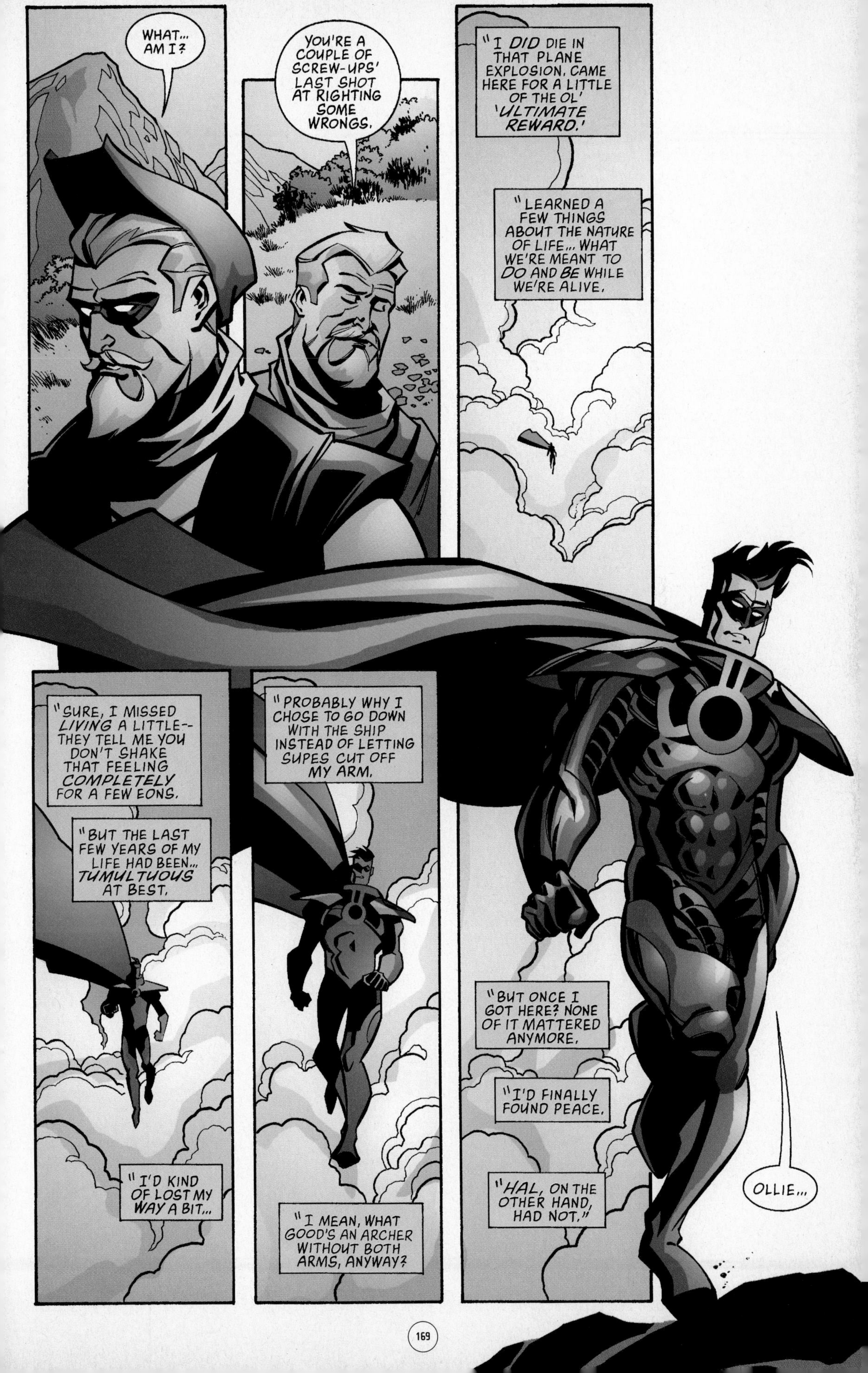
WHAT... AM I?
YOU'RE A COUPLE OF SCREW-UPS' LAST SHOT AT RIGHTING SOME WRONGS.
"I DID DIE IN THAT PLANE EXPLOSION. CAME HERE FOR A LITTLE OF THE OL' 'ULTIMATE REWARD.'
"LEARNED A FEW THINGS ABOUT THE NATURE OF LIFE... WHAT WE'RE MEANT TO DO AND BE WHILE WE'RE ALIVE.
"SURE, I MISSED LIVING A LITTLE-- THEY TELL ME YOU DON'T SHAKE THAT FEELING COMPLETELY FOR A FEW EONS.
"BUT THE LAST FEW YEARS OF MY LIFE HAD BEEN... TUMULTUOUS AT BEST.
"I'D KIND OF LOST MY WAY A BIT...
"PROBABLY WHY I CHOSE TO GO DOWN WITH THE SHIP INSTEAD OF LETTING SUPES CUT OFF MY ARM.
"I MEAN, WHAT GOOD'S AN ARCHER WITHOUT BOTH ARMS, ANYWAY?
"BUT ONCE I GOT HERE? NONE OF IT MATTERED ANYMORE.
"I'D FINALLY FOUND PEACE.
"HAL, ON THE OTHER HAND, HAD NOT."
OLLIE...

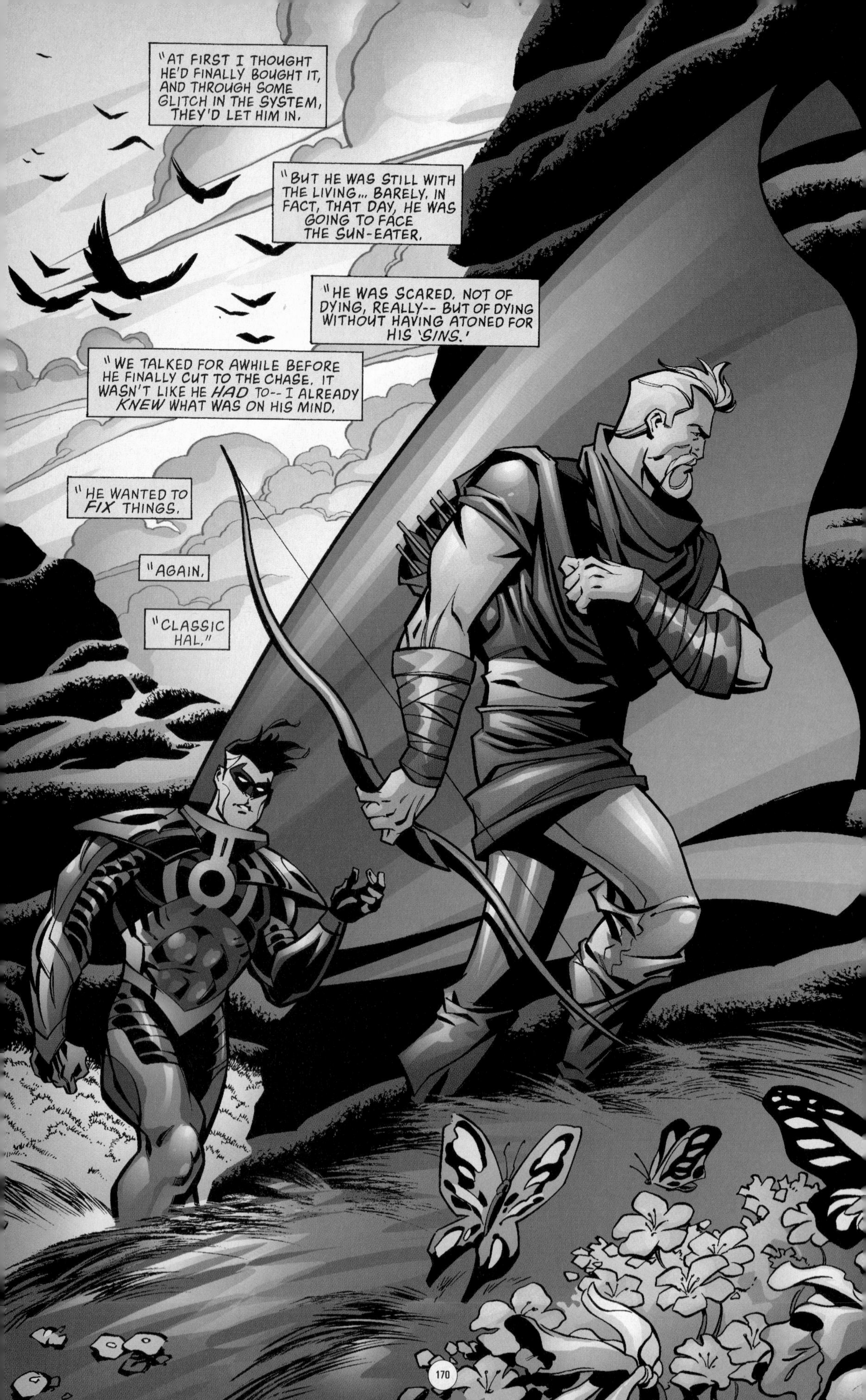
"AT FIRST I THOUGHT HE'D FINALLY BOUGHT IT, AND THROUGH SOME GLITCH IN THE SYSTEM, THEY'D LET HIM IN.
"BUT HE WAS STILL WITH THE LIVING... BARELY. IN FACT, THAT DAY, HE WAS GOING TO FACE THE SUN-EATER.
"HE WAS SCARED. NOT OF DYING, REALLY-- BUT OF DYING WITHOUT HAVING ATONED FOR HIS 'SINS.'
"WE TALKED FOR AWHILE BEFORE HE FINALLY CUT TO THE CHASE. IT WASN'T LIKE HE HAD TO-- I ALREADY KNEW WHAT WAS ON HIS MIND.
"HE WANTED TO FIX THINGS.
"AGAIN.
"CLASSIC HAL."

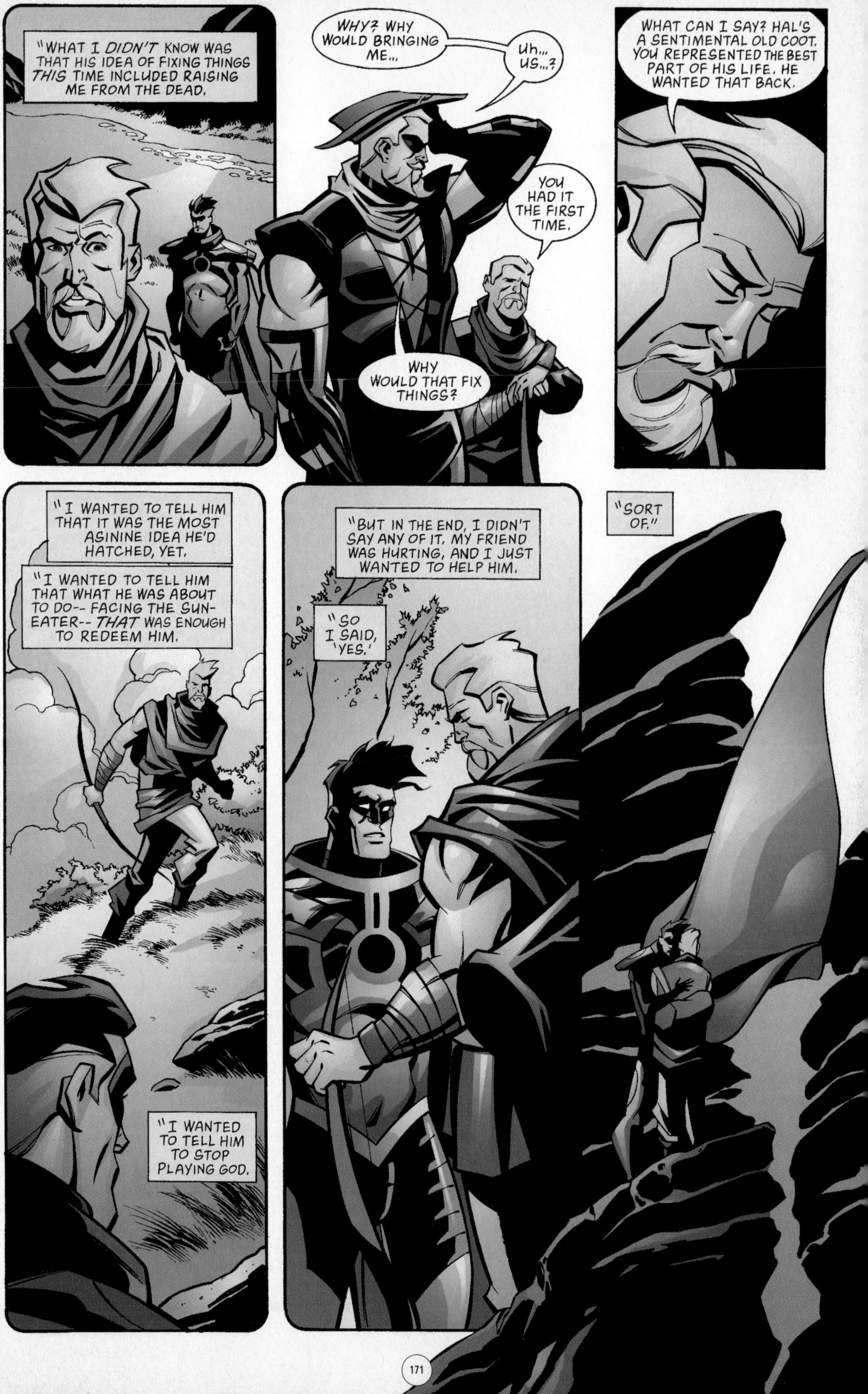
"WHAT I DIDN'T KNOW WAS THAT HIS IDEA OF FIXING THINGS THIS TIME INCLUDED RAISING ME FROM THE DEAD.
WHY? WHY WOULD BRINGING ME...
Uh... US...?
YOU HAD IT THE FIRST TIME.
WHY WOULD THAT FIX THINGS?
WHAT CAN I SAY? HAL'S A SENTIMENTAL OLD COOT. YOU REPRESENTED THE BEST PART OF HIS LIFE. HE WANTED THAT BACK.
"I WANTED TO TELL HIM THAT IT WAS THE MOST ASININE IDEA HE'D HATCHED, YET.
"I WANTED TO TELL HIM THAT WHAT HE WAS ABOUT TO DO-- FACING THE SUN-EATER-- THAT WAS ENOUGH TO REDEEM HIM.
"I WANTED TO TELL HIM TO STOP PLAYING GOD.
"BUT IN THE END, I DIDN'T SAY ANY OF IT. MY FRIEND WAS HURTING, AND I JUST WANTED TO HELP HIM.
"SO I SAID, 'YES.'
"SORT OF."

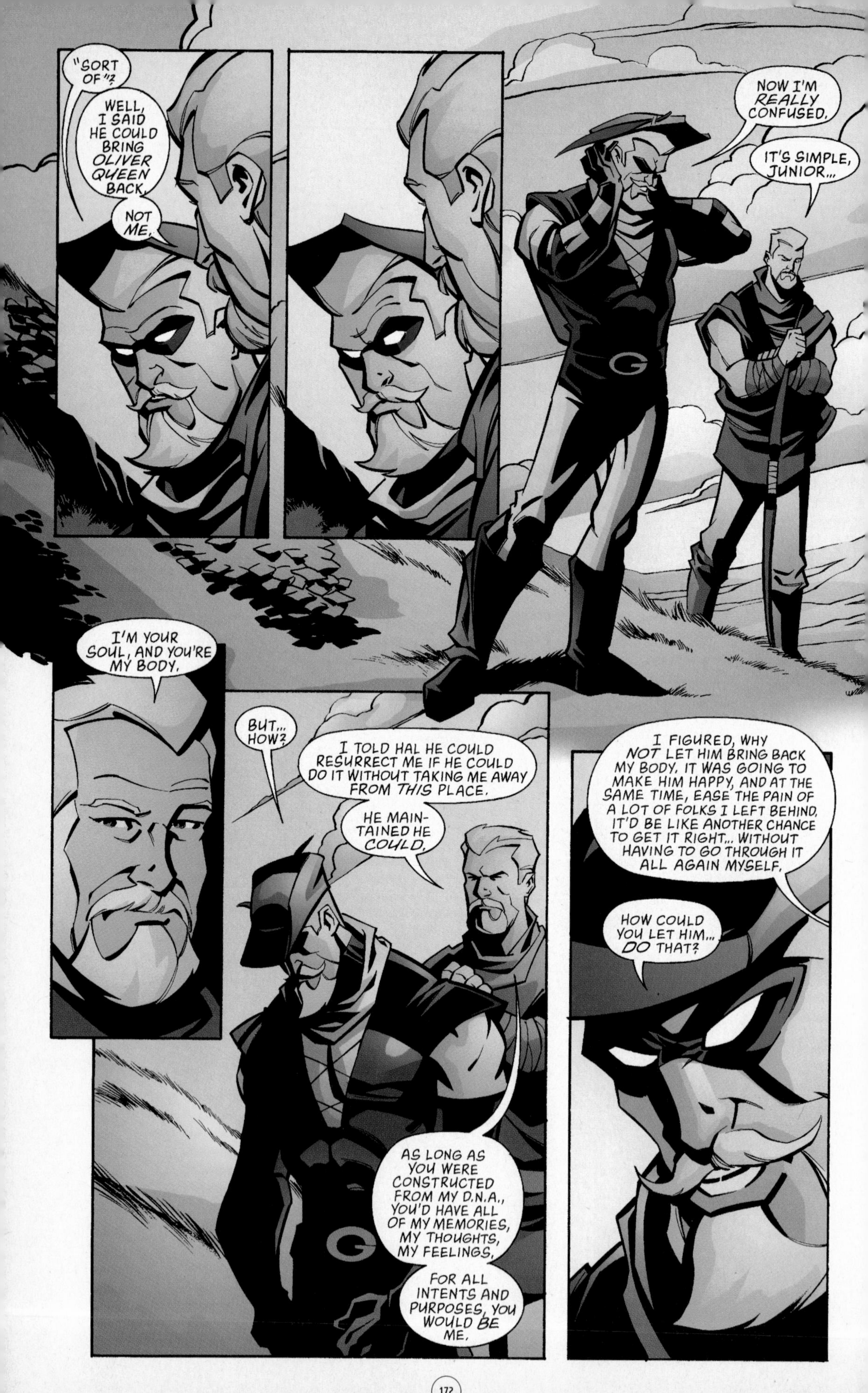
"SORT OF"?
WELL, I SAID HE COULD BRING OLIVER QUEEN BACK.
NOT ME.
NOW I'M REALLY CONFUSED.
IT'S SIMPLE, JUNIOR...
I'M YOUR SOUL, AND YOU'RE MY BODY.
BUT... HOW?
I TOLD HAL HE COULD RESURRECT ME IF HE COULD DO IT WITHOUT TAKING ME AWAY FROM THIS PLACE.
HE MAINTAINED HE COULD.
AS LONG AS YOU WERE CONSTRUCTED FROM MY D.N.A., YOU'D HAVE ALL OF MY MEMORIES, MY THOUGHTS, MY FEELINGS.
FOR ALL INTENTS AND PURPOSES, YOU WOULD BE ME.
I FIGURED, WHY NOT LET HIM BRING BACK MY BODY. IT WAS GOING TO MAKE HIM HAPPY, AND AT THE SAME TIME, EASE THE PAIN OF A LOT OF FOLKS I LEFT BEHIND. IT'D BE LIKE ANOTHER CHANCE TO GET IT RIGHT... WITHOUT HAVING TO GO THROUGH IT ALL AGAIN MYSELF.
HOW COULD YOU LET HIM... DO THAT?

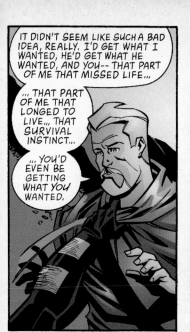

IT DIDN'T SEEM LIKE SUCH A BAD IDEA, REALLY. I'D GET WHAT I WANTED, HE'D GET WHAT HE WANTED, AND YOU-- THAT PART OF ME THAT MISSED LIFE...

...THAT PART OF ME THAT LONGED TO LIVE... THAT SURVIVAL INSTINCT...

...YOU'D EVEN BE GETTING WHAT YOU WANTED.

YOU THINK I WANT TO BE SOME SOULLESS HALF-LIFE?! DAMMIT, MAN-- WHAT GAVE YOU THE RIGHT?!

HEY-- YOU'RE AS MUCH ME AS YOU ARE YOU, KIDDO. I HAD EVERY RIGHT. DON'T COME OFF ALL VIOLATED, BECAUSE IN MY SHOES, YOU'D HAVE DONE THE SAME THING.

HELL-- YOU PRACTICALLY DID DO THE SAME THING, IF YOU THINK ABOUT IT!

WELL, WHY THE HELL DON'T I REMEMBER ANY OF THIS?

BECAUSE I WAS TRYING TO SPARE YOU THE GRIEF OF BEING ME.

Oh, THIS OUGHTA BE GOOD...

"I'D HAD A GOOD LIFE AT ONE POINT. A SIMPLE LIFE, FULL OF GOOD FRIENDS...

"...WILD ADVENTURES...

"...PASSIONATE LOVE...

"...AND THE SATISFACTION OF KNOWING I WAS ONE OF THE GOOD GUYS.

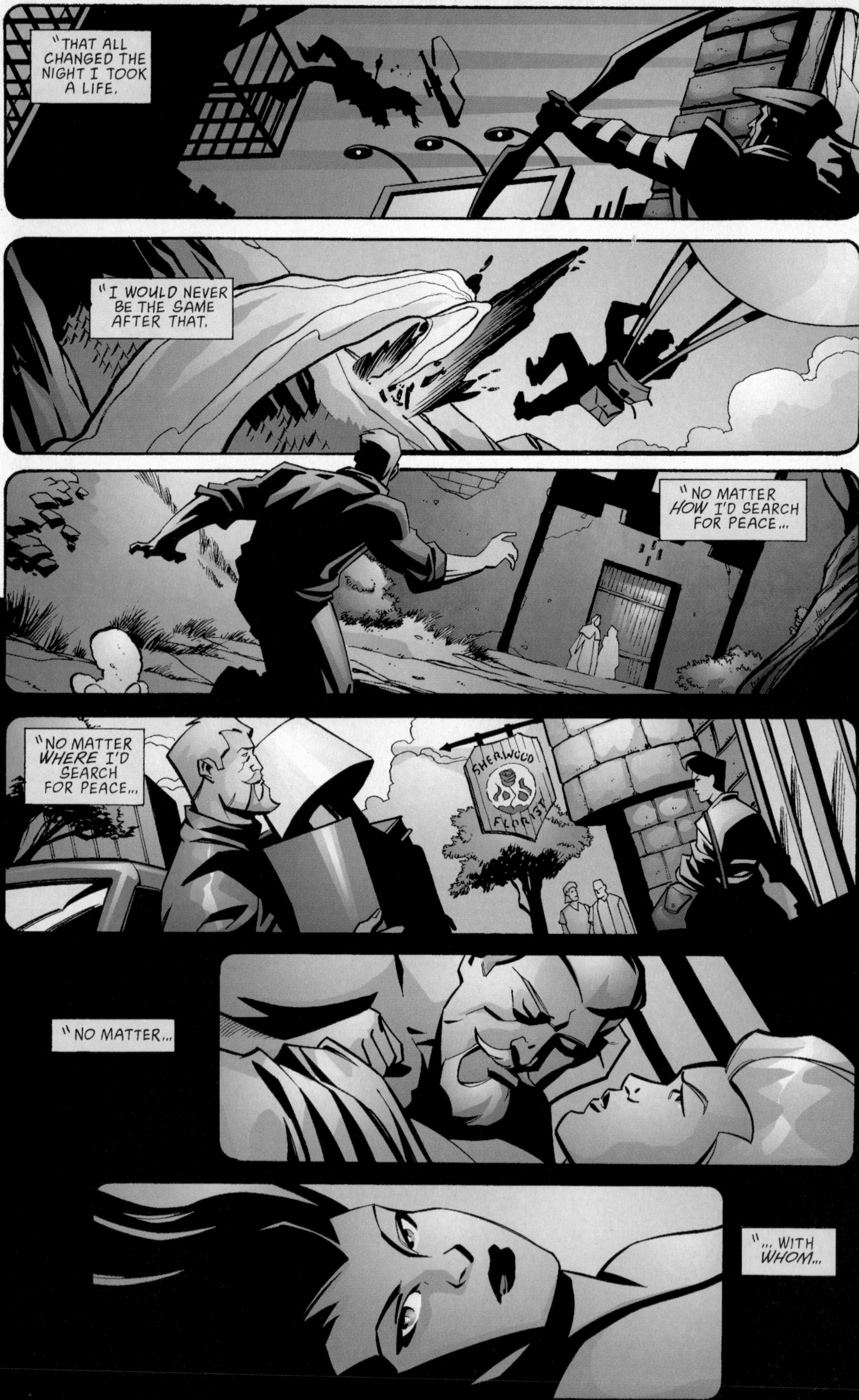
"THAT ALL CHANGED THE NIGHT I TOOK A LIFE.
"I WOULD NEVER BE THE SAME AFTER THAT.
"NO MATTER HOW I'D SEARCH FOR PEACE...
"NO MATTER WHERE I'D SEARCH FOR PEACE...
SHERWOOD FLORIST
"NO MATTER...
"...WITH WHOM...

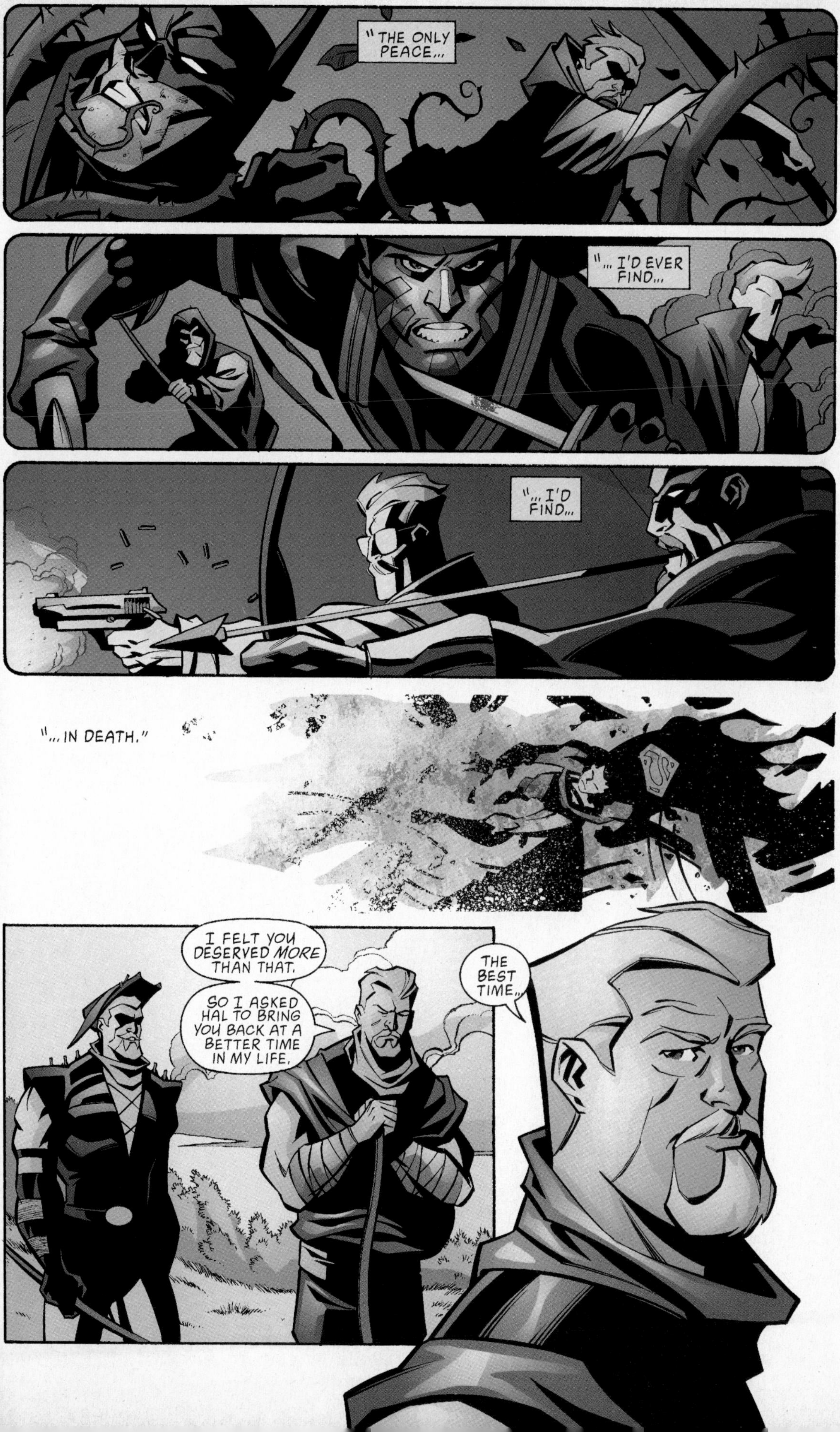
"THE ONLY PEACE...
"...I'D EVER FIND...
"...I'D FIND...
"...IN DEATH."
I FELT YOU DESERVED MORE THAN THAT.
SO I ASKED HAL TO BRING YOU BACK AT A BETTER TIME IN MY LIFE.
THE BEST TIME...

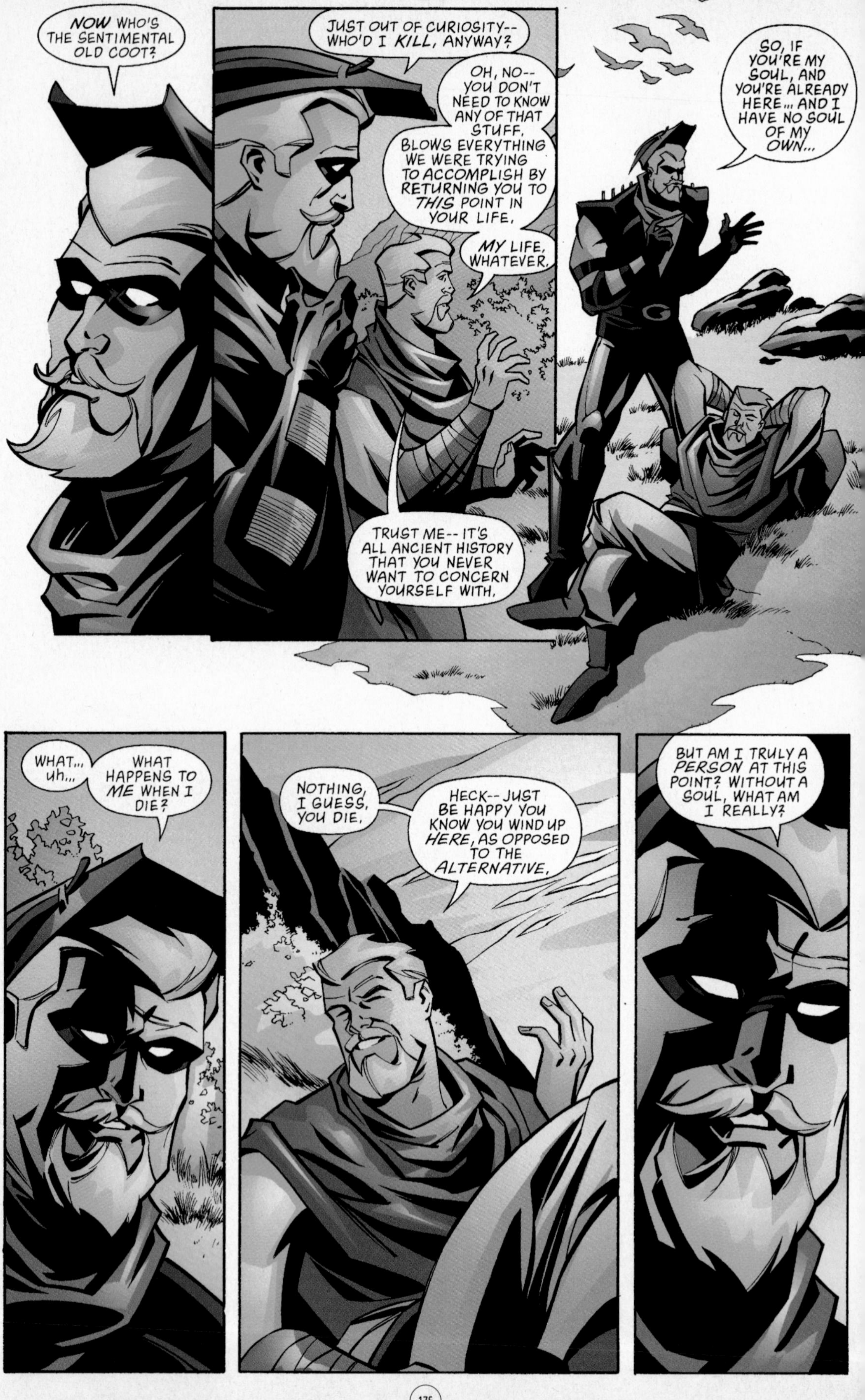
NOW WHO'S THE SENTIMENTAL OLD COOT?
JUST OUT OF CURIOSITY-- WHO'D I KILL, ANYWAY?
OH, NO-- YOU DON'T NEED TO KNOW ANY OF THAT STUFF. BLOWS EVERYTHING WE WERE TRYING TO ACCOMPLISH BY RETURNING YOU TO THIS POINT IN YOUR LIFE.
MY LIFE. WHATEVER.
TRUST ME-- IT'S ALL ANCIENT HISTORY THAT YOU NEVER WANT TO CONCERN YOURSELF WITH.
SO, IF YOU'RE MY SOUL, AND YOU'RE ALREADY HERE... AND I HAVE NO SOUL OF MY OWN...
WHAT... uh...
WHAT HAPPENS TO ME WHEN I DIE?
NOTHING, I GUESS. YOU DIE.
HECK-- JUST BE HAPPY YOU KNOW YOU WIND UP HERE, AS OPPOSED TO THE ALTERNATIVE.
BUT AM I TRULY A PERSON AT THIS POINT? WITHOUT A SOUL, WHAT AM I REALLY?

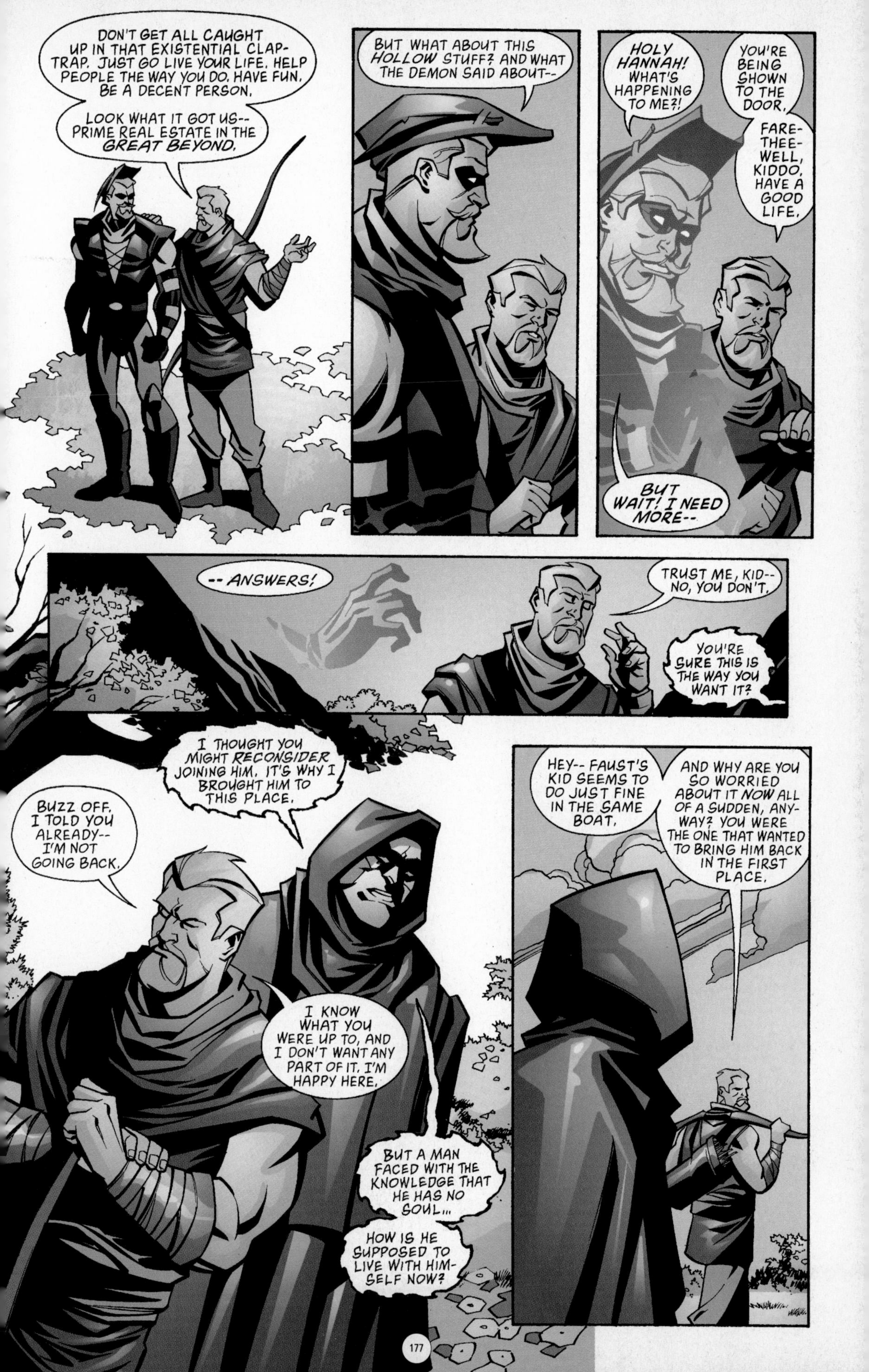
DON'T GET ALL CAUGHT UP IN THAT EXISTENTIAL CLAP-TRAP. JUST GO LIVE YOUR LIFE. HELP PEOPLE THE WAY YOU DO. HAVE FUN. BE A DECENT PERSON.
LOOK WHAT IT GOT US-- PRIME REAL ESTATE IN THE GREAT BEYOND.
BUT WHAT ABOUT THIS HOLLOW STUFF? AND WHAT THE DEMON SAID ABOUT--
HOLY HANNAH! WHAT'S HAPPENING TO ME?!
YOU'RE BEING SHOWN TO THE DOOR.
FARE-THEE-WELL, KIDDO. HAVE A GOOD LIFE.
BUT WAIT! I NEED MORE--
--ANSWERS!
TRUST ME, KID-- NO, YOU DON'T.
YOU'RE SURE THIS IS THE WAY YOU WANT IT?
I THOUGHT YOU MIGHT RECONSIDER JOINING HIM. IT'S WHY I BROUGHT HIM TO THIS PLACE.
BUZZ OFF. I TOLD YOU ALREADY-- I'M NOT GOING BACK.
I KNOW WHAT YOU WERE UP TO, AND I DON'T WANT ANY PART OF IT. I'M HAPPY HERE.
BUT A MAN FACED WITH THE KNOWLEDGE THAT HE HAS NO SOUL...
HOW IS HE SUPPOSED TO LIVE WITH HIM-SELF NOW?
HEY-- FAUST'S KID SEEMS TO DO JUST FINE IN THE SAME BOAT.
AND WHY ARE YOU SO WORRIED ABOUT IT NOW ALL OF A SUDDEN, ANY-WAY? YOU WERE THE ONE THAT WANTED TO BRING HIM BACK IN THE FIRST PLACE.

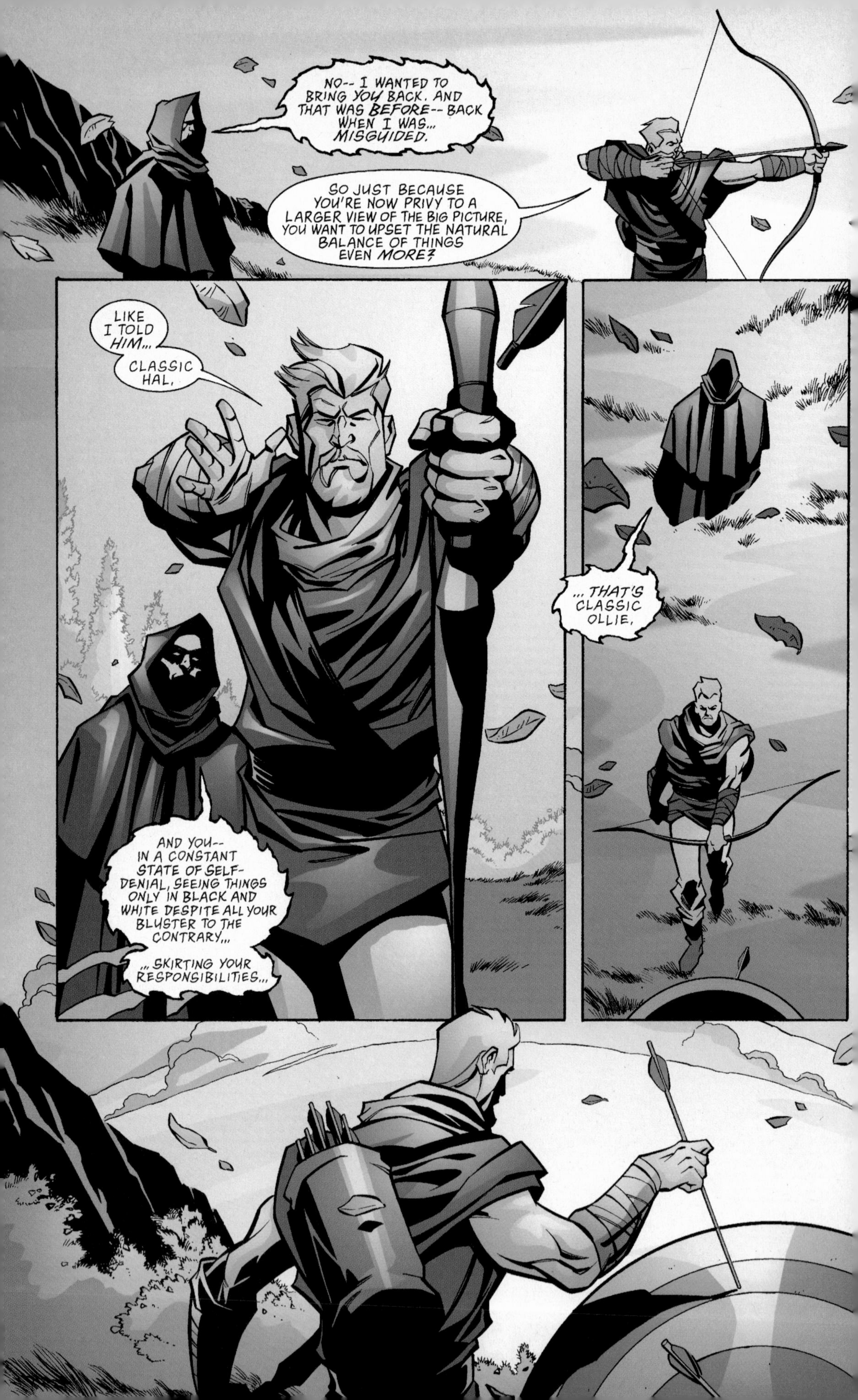
NO-- I WANTED TO BRING YOU BACK. AND THAT WAS BEFORE-- BACK WHEN I WAS... MISGUIDED.
SO JUST BECAUSE YOU'RE NOW PRIVY TO A LARGER VIEW OF THE BIG PICTURE, YOU WANT TO UPSET THE NATURAL BALANCE OF THINGS EVEN MORE?
LIKE I TOLD HIM...
CLASSIC HAL.
AND YOU-- IN A CONSTANT STATE OF SELF-DENIAL, SEEING THINGS ONLY IN BLACK AND WHITE DESPITE ALL YOUR BLUSTER TO THE CONTRARY...
...SKIRTING YOUR RESPONSIBILITIES...
...THAT'S CLASSIC OLLIE.

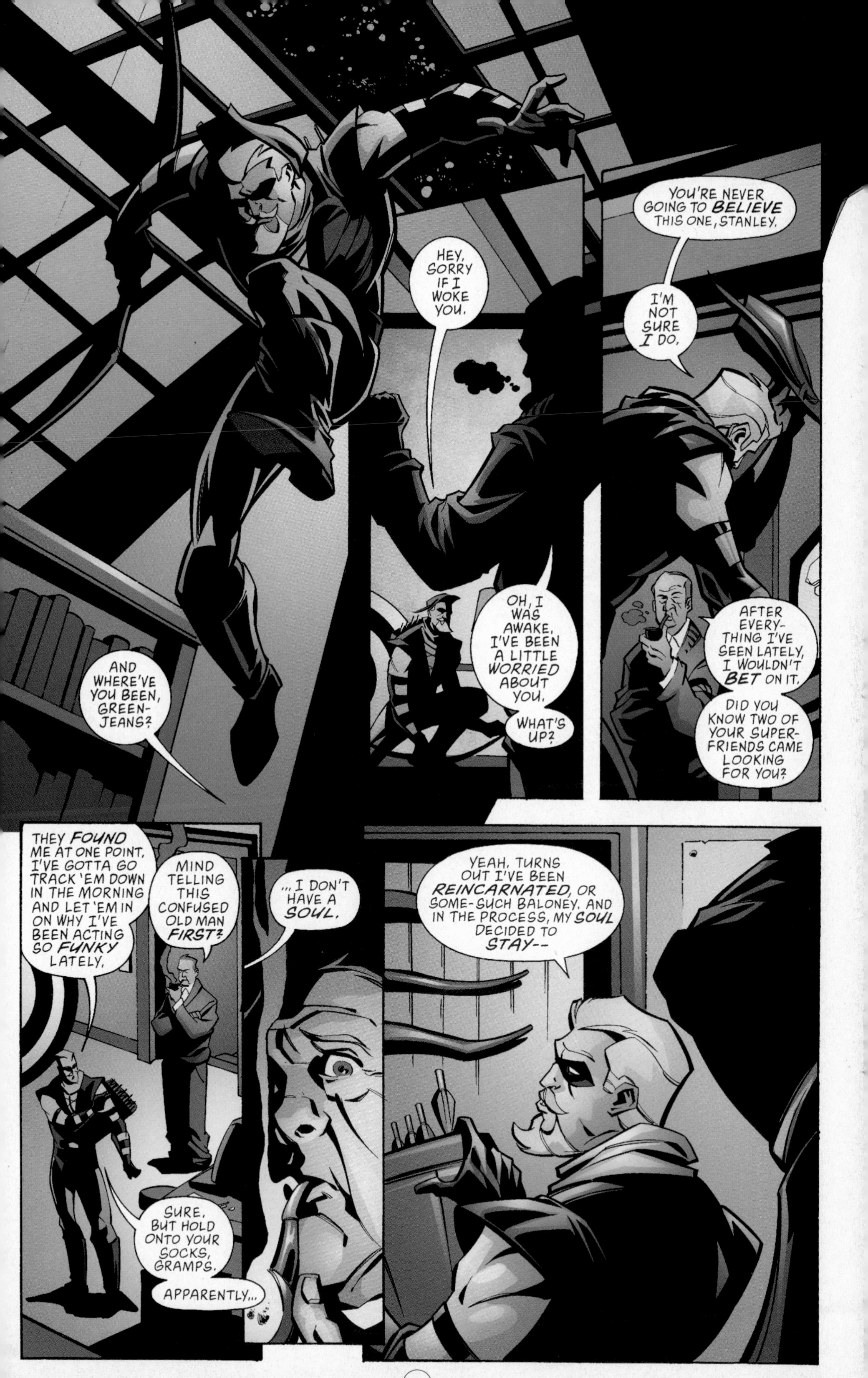
HEY, SORRY IF I WOKE YOU.
YOU'RE NEVER GOING TO BELIEVE THIS ONE, STANLEY.
I'M NOT SURE I DO.
AND WHERE'VE YOU BEEN, GREEN-JEANS?
OH, I WAS AWAKE. I'VE BEEN A LITTLE WORRIED ABOUT YOU.
WHAT'S UP?
AFTER EVERY-THING I'VE SEEN LATELY, I WOULDN'T BET ON IT.
DID YOU KNOW TWO OF YOUR SUPER-FRIENDS CAME LOOKING FOR YOU?
THEY FOUND ME AT ONE POINT. I'VE GOTTA GO TRACK 'EM DOWN IN THE MORNING AND LET 'EM IN ON WHY I'VE BEEN ACTING SO FUNKY LATELY.
MIND TELLING THIS CONFUSED OLD MAN FIRST?
SURE, BUT HOLD ONTO YOUR SOCKS, GRAMPS.
APPARENTLY...
...I DON'T HAVE A SOUL.
YEAH. TURNS OUT I'VE BEEN REINCARNATED, OR SOME-SUCH BALONEY. AND IN THE PROCESS, MY SOUL DECIDED TO STAY--

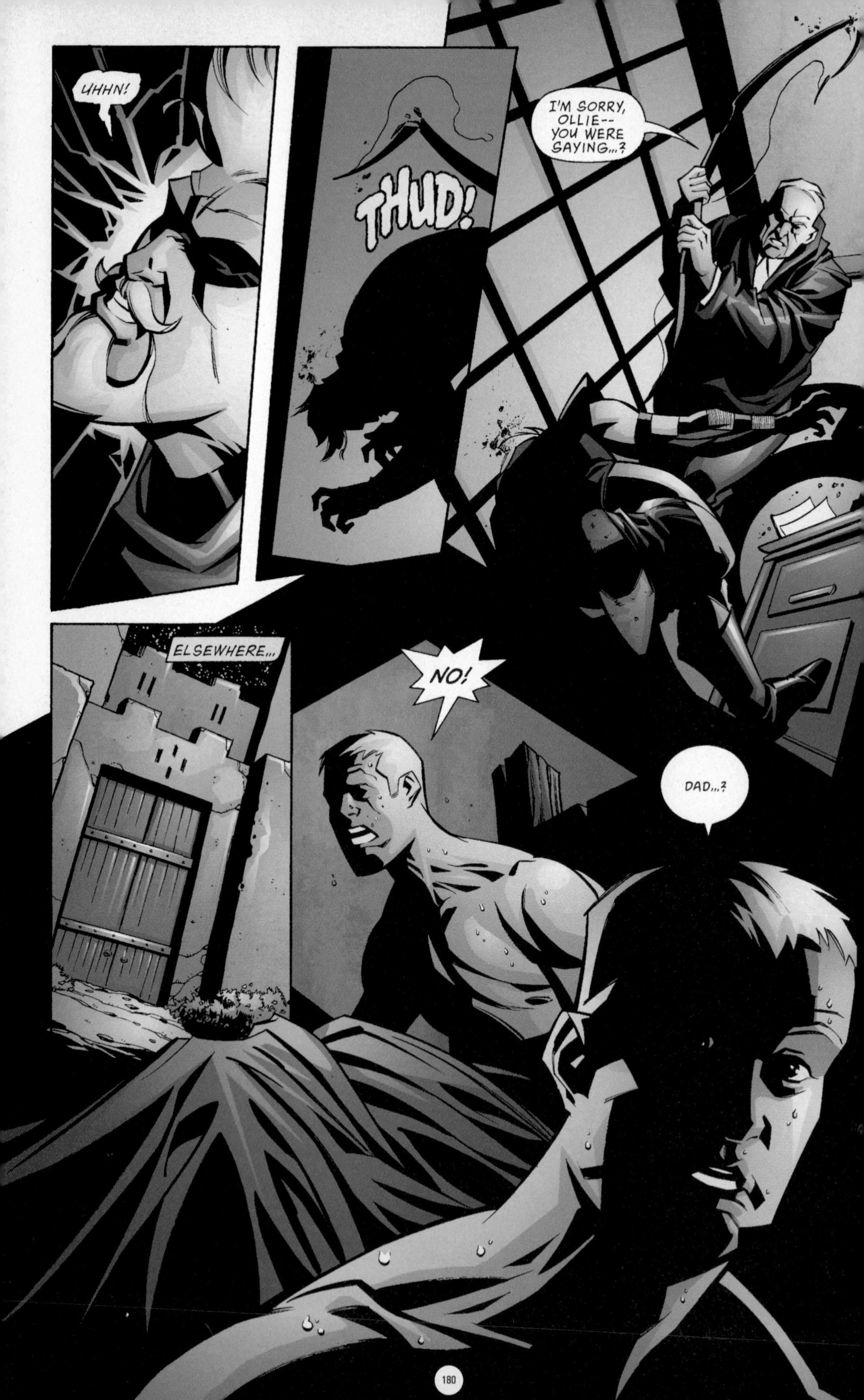
UHHN!
THUD!
I'M SORRY, OLLIE-- YOU WERE SAYING...?
ELSEWHERE...
NO!
DAD...?

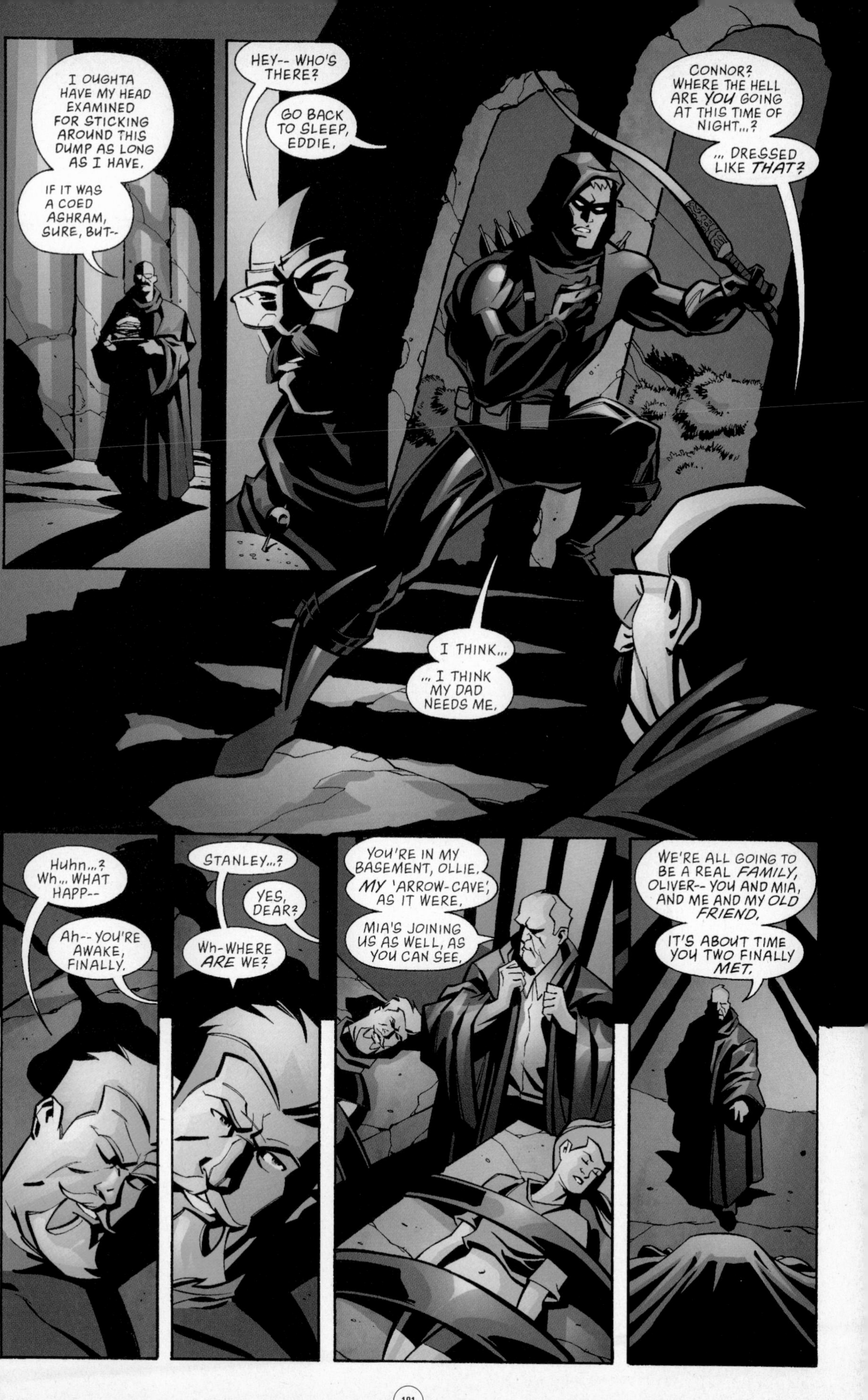
I OUGHTA HAVE MY HEAD EXAMINED FOR STICKING AROUND THIS DUMP AS LONG AS I HAVE.
IF IT WAS A COED ASHRAM, SURE, BUT--
HEY-- WHO'S THERE?
GO BACK TO SLEEP, EDDIE.
CONNOR? WHERE THE HELL ARE YOU GOING AT THIS TIME OF NIGHT...?
... DRESSED LIKE THAT?
I THINK...
... I THINK MY DAD NEEDS ME.
Huhn...? Wh... WHAT HAPP--
Ah-- YOU'RE AWAKE, FINALLY.
STANLEY...?
YES, DEAR?
Wh-WHERE ARE WE?
YOU'RE IN MY BASEMENT, OLLIE. MY 'ARROW-CAVE,' AS IT WERE.
MIA'S JOINING US AS WELL, AS YOU CAN SEE.
WE'RE ALL GOING TO BE A REAL FAMILY, OLIVER-- YOU AND MIA, AND ME AND MY OLD FRIEND.
IT'S ABOUT TIME YOU TWO FINALLY MET.

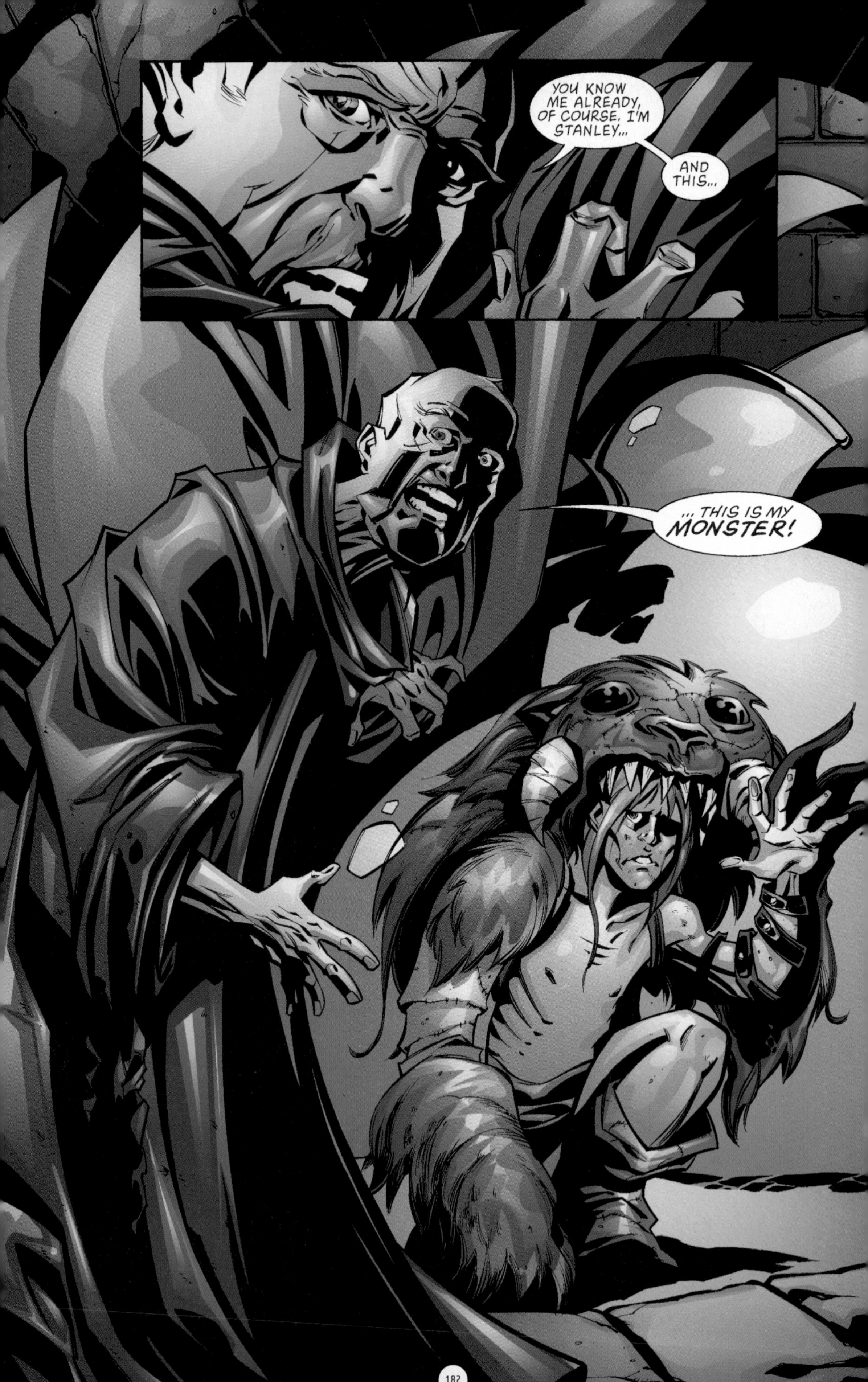
YOU KNOW ME ALREADY, OF COURSE. I'M STANLEY...
AND THIS...
...THIS IS MY MONSTER!

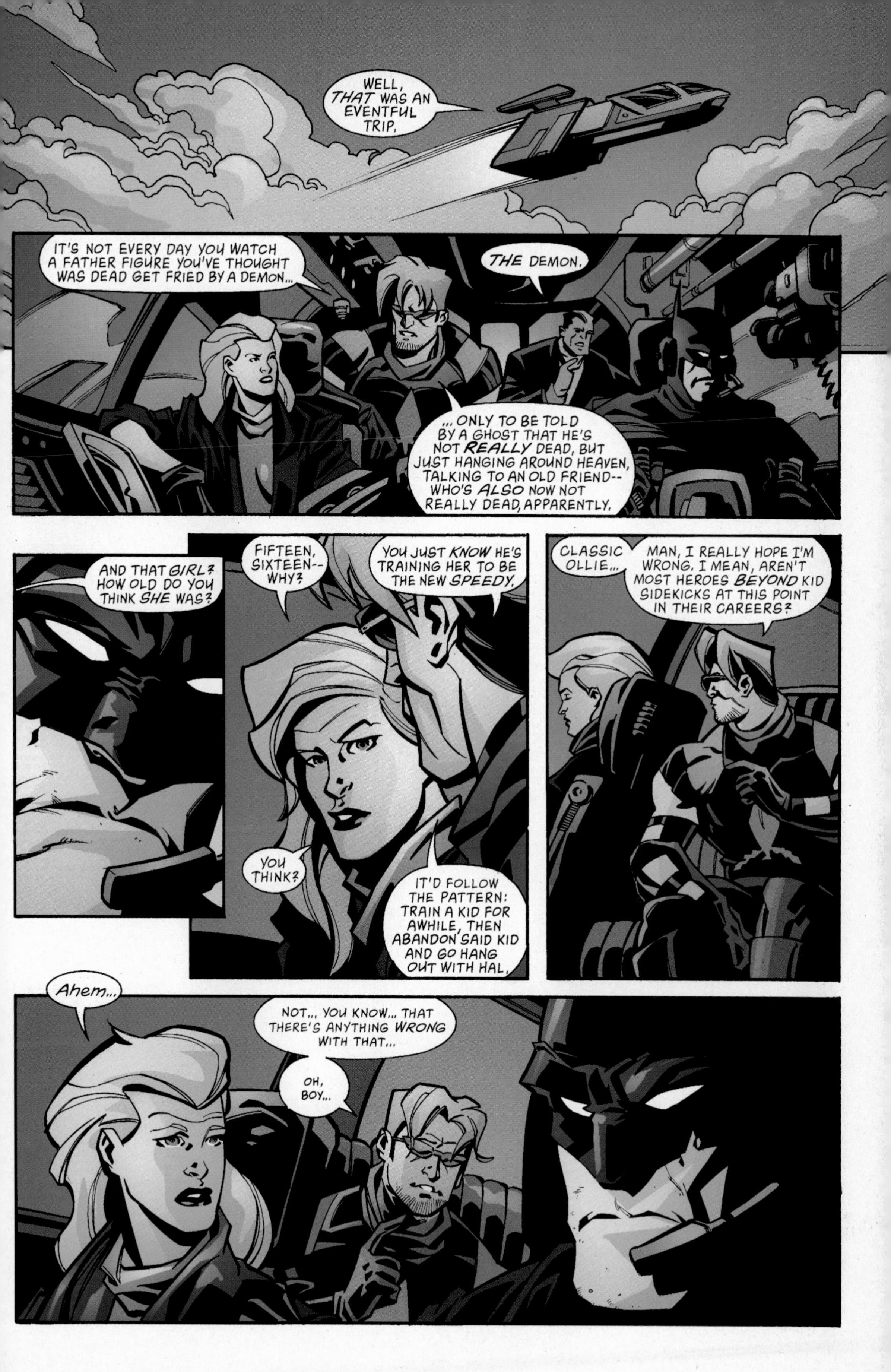
WELL, THAT WAS AN EVENTFUL TRIP.
IT'S NOT EVERY DAY YOU WATCH A FATHER FIGURE YOU'VE THOUGHT WAS DEAD GET FRIED BY A DEMON...
THE DEMON.
...ONLY TO BE TOLD BY A GHOST THAT HE'S NOT REALLY DEAD, BUT JUST HANGING AROUND HEAVEN, TALKING TO AN OLD FRIEND-- WHO'S ALSO NOW NOT REALLY DEAD, APPARENTLY.
AND THAT GIRL? HOW OLD DO YOU THINK SHE WAS?
FIFTEEN, SIXTEEN-- WHY?
YOU JUST KNOW HE'S TRAINING HER TO BE THE NEW SPEEDY.
YOU THINK?
IT'D FOLLOW THE PATTERN: TRAIN A KID FOR AWHILE, THEN ABANDON SAID KID AND GO HANG OUT WITH HAL.
CLASSIC OLLIE...
MAN, I REALLY HOPE I'M WRONG. I MEAN, AREN'T MOST HEROES BEYOND KID SIDEKICKS AT THIS POINT IN THEIR CAREERS?
Ahem...
NOT... YOU KNOW... THAT THERE'S ANYTHING WRONG WITH THAT...
OH, BOY...

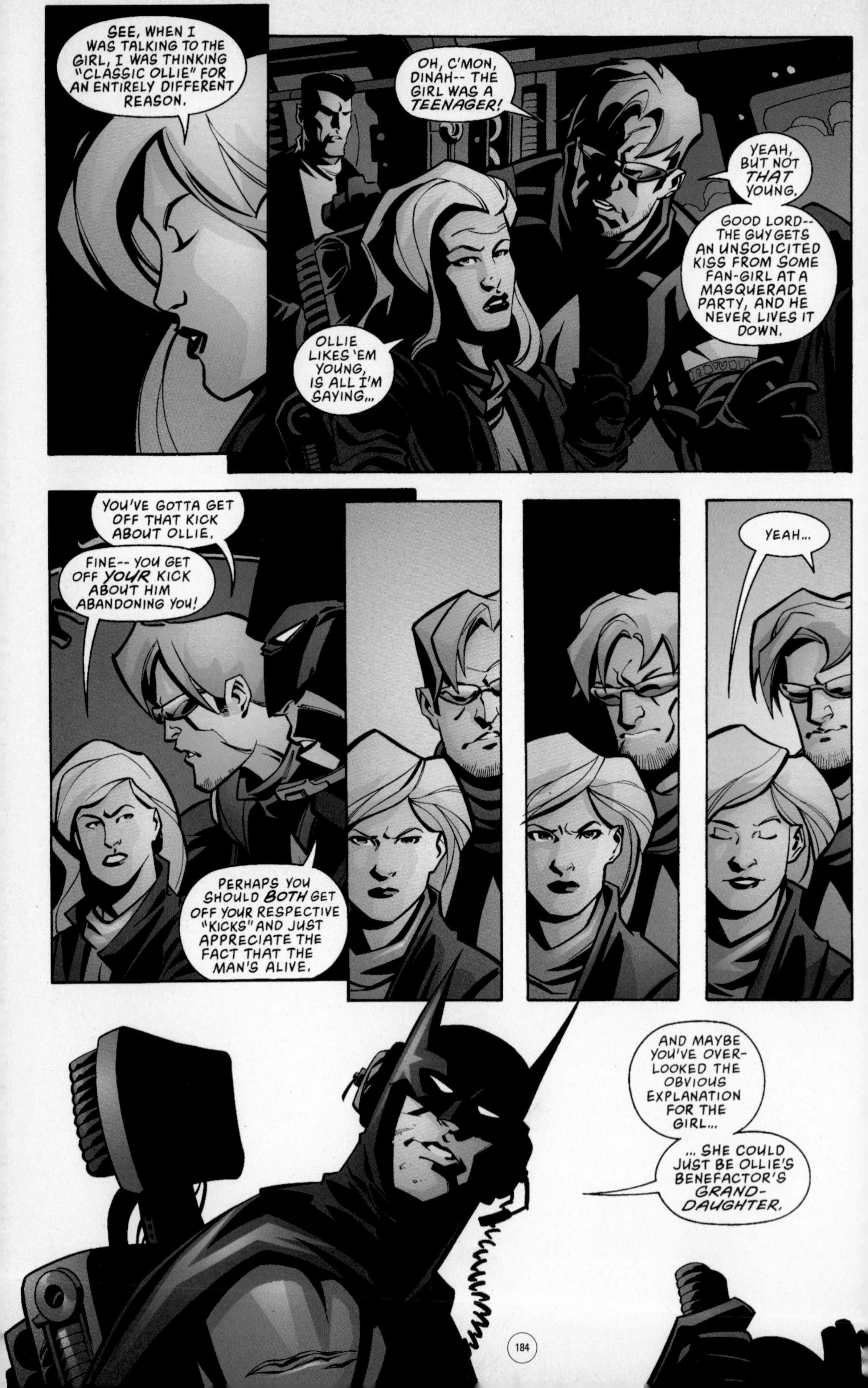
SEE, WHEN I WAS TALKING TO THE GIRL, I WAS THINKING "CLASSIC OLLIE" FOR AN ENTIRELY DIFFERENT REASON.
OH, C'MON, DINAH-- THE GIRL WAS A TEENAGER!
YEAH, BUT NOT THAT YOUNG.
GOOD LORD-- THE GUY GETS AN UNSOLICITED KISS FROM SOME FAN-GIRL AT A MASQUERADE PARTY, AND HE NEVER LIVES IT DOWN.
OLLIE LIKES 'EM YOUNG, IS ALL I'M SAYING...
YOU'VE GOTTA GET OFF THAT KICK ABOUT OLLIE.
FINE-- YOU GET OFF YOUR KICK ABOUT HIM ABANDONING YOU!
PERHAPS YOU SHOULD BOTH GET OFF YOUR RESPECTIVE "KICKS" AND JUST APPRECIATE THE FACT THAT THE MAN'S ALIVE.
YEAH...
AND MAYBE YOU'VE OVER-LOOKED THE OBVIOUS EXPLANATION FOR THE GIRL...
... SHE COULD JUST BE OLLIE'S BENEFACTOR'S GRAND-DAUGHTER.

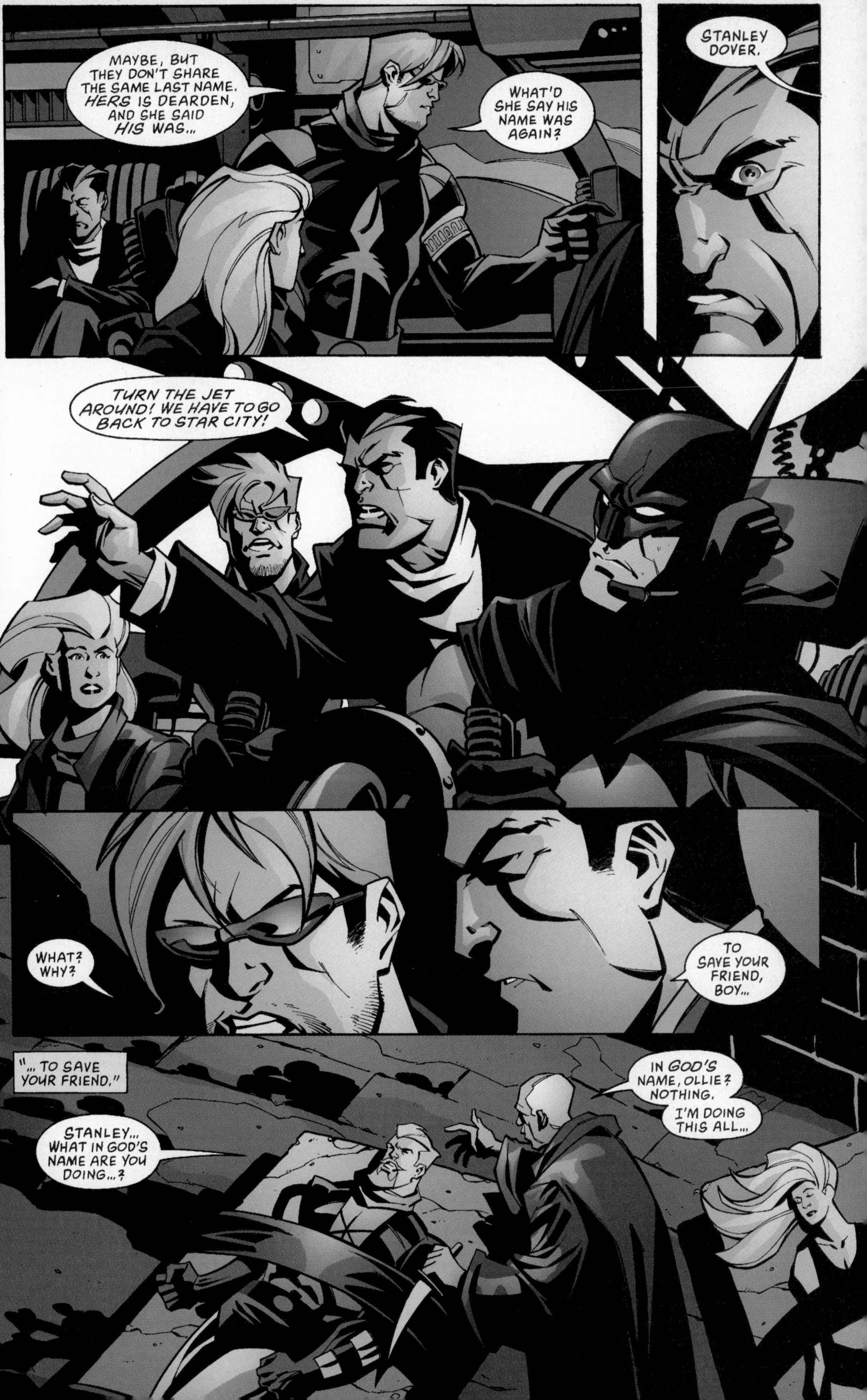
MAYBE, BUT THEY DON'T SHARE THE SAME LAST NAME. HERS IS DEARDEN, AND SHE SAID HIS WAS...
WHAT'D SHE SAY HIS NAME WAS AGAIN?
STANLEY DOVER.
TURN THE JET AROUND! WE HAVE TO GO BACK TO STAR CITY!
WHAT? WHY?
TO SAVE YOUR FRIEND, BOY...
"... TO SAVE YOUR FRIEND."
STANLEY... WHAT IN GOD'S NAME ARE YOU DOING...?
IN GOD'S NAME, OLLIE? NOTHING.
I'M DOING THIS ALL...

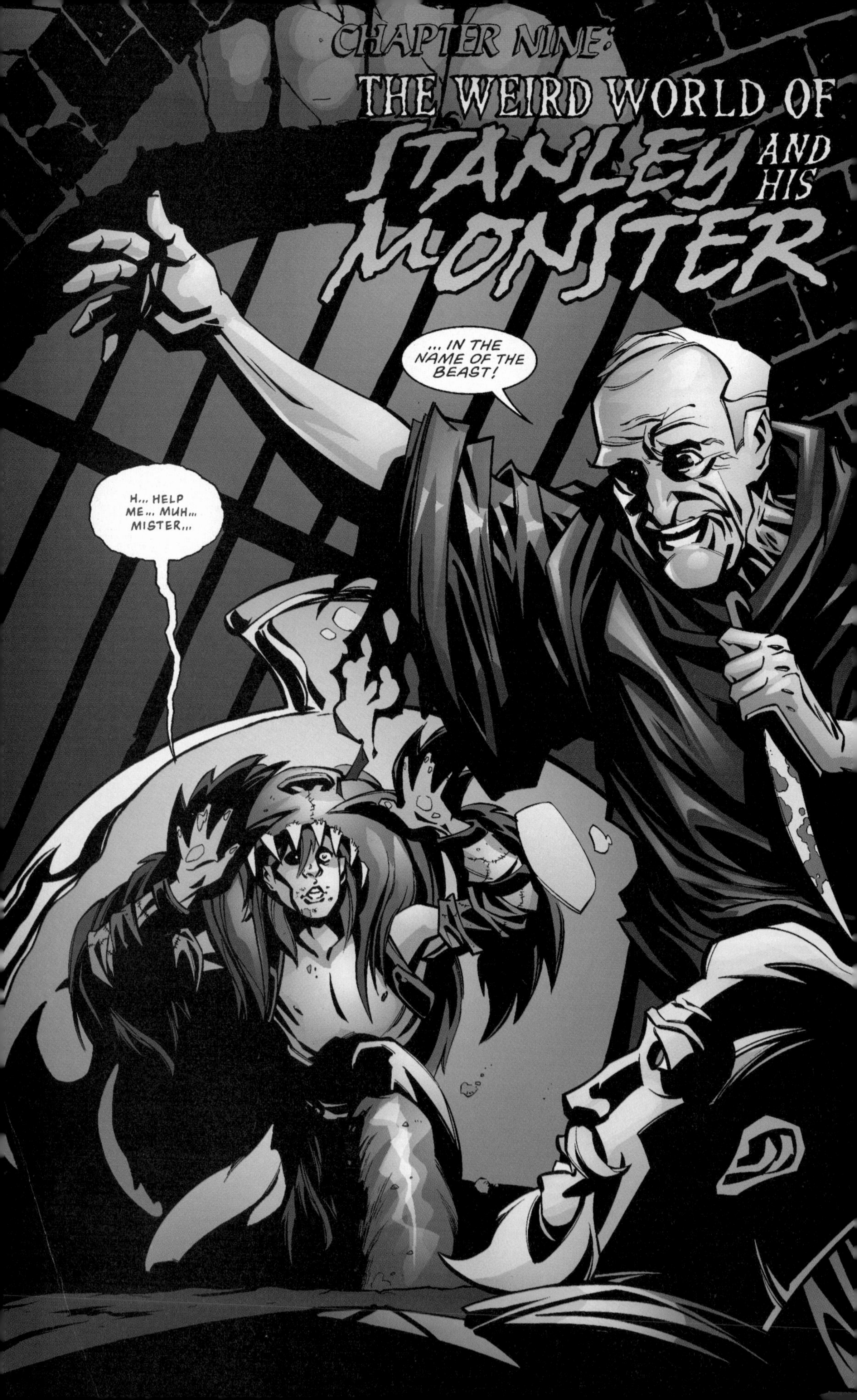
CHAPTER NINE:
THE WEIRD WORLD OF
STANLEY AND HIS
MONSTER
... IN THE NAME OF THE BEAST!
H... HELP ME... MUH... MISTER...

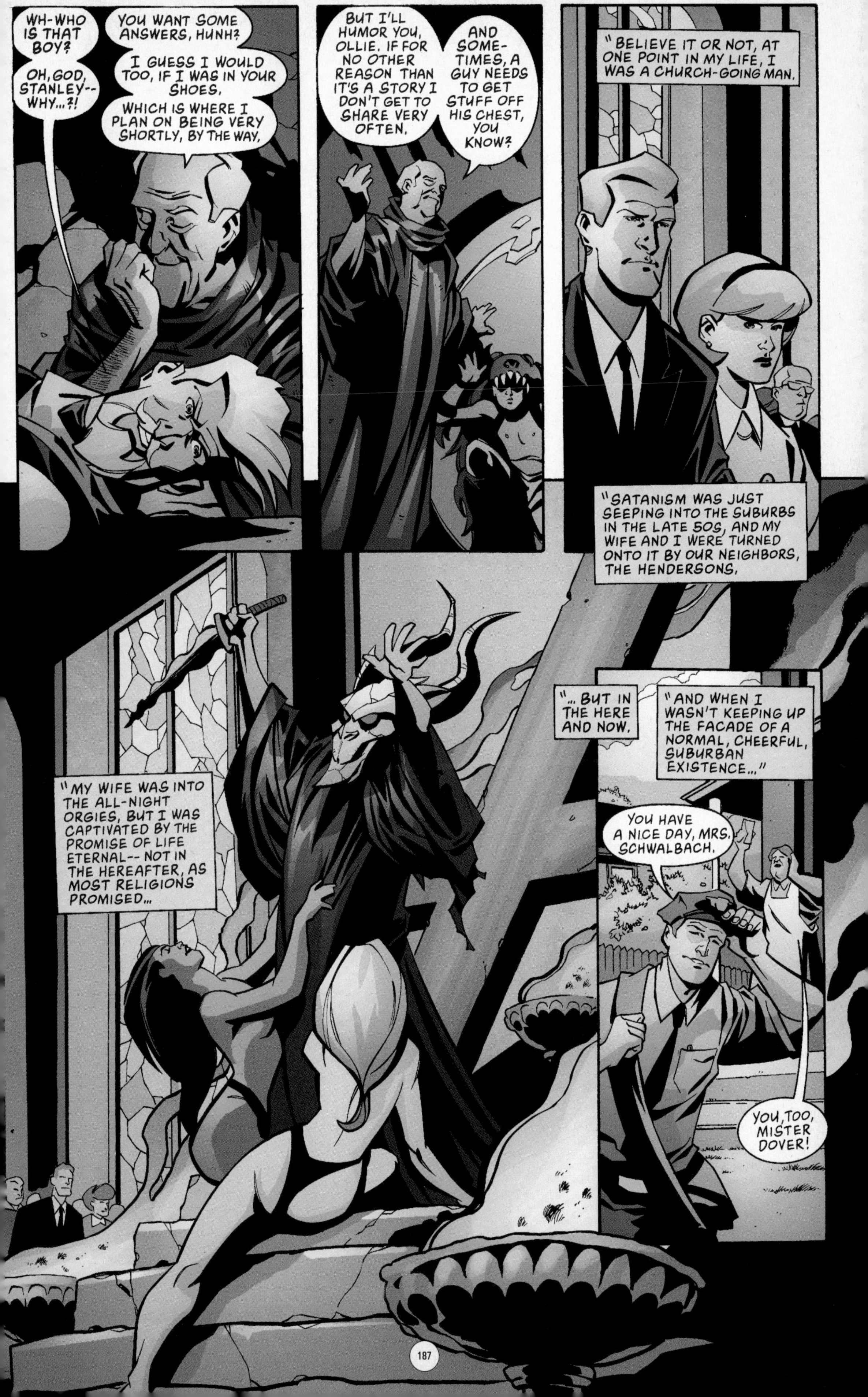

WH-WHO IS THAT BOY?
OH, GOD, STANLEY-- WHY...?!
YOU WANT SOME ANSWERS, HUNH?
I GUESS I WOULD TOO, IF I WAS IN YOUR SHOES.
WHICH IS WHERE I PLAN ON BEING VERY SHORTLY, BY THE WAY.
BUT I'LL HUMOR YOU, OLLIE. IF FOR NO OTHER REASON THAN IT'S A STORY I DON'T GET TO SHARE VERY OFTEN.
AND SOMETIMES, A GUY NEEDS TO GET STUFF OFF HIS CHEST, YOU KNOW?
"BELIEVE IT OR NOT, AT ONE POINT IN MY LIFE, I WAS A CHURCH-GOING MAN.
"SATANISM WAS JUST SEEPING INTO THE SUBURBS IN THE LATE 50S, AND MY WIFE AND I WERE TURNED ONTO IT BY OUR NEIGHBORS, THE HENDERSONS.
"MY WIFE WAS INTO THE ALL-NIGHT ORGIES, BUT I WAS CAPTIVATED BY THE PROMISE OF LIFE ETERNAL-- NOT IN THE HEREAFTER, AS MOST RELIGIONS PROMISED...
"...BUT IN THE HERE AND NOW.
"AND WHEN I WASN'T KEEPING UP THE FACADE OF A NORMAL, CHEERFUL, SUBURBAN EXISTENCE..."
YOU HAVE A NICE DAY, MRS. SCHWALBACH.
YOU, TOO, MISTER DOVER!

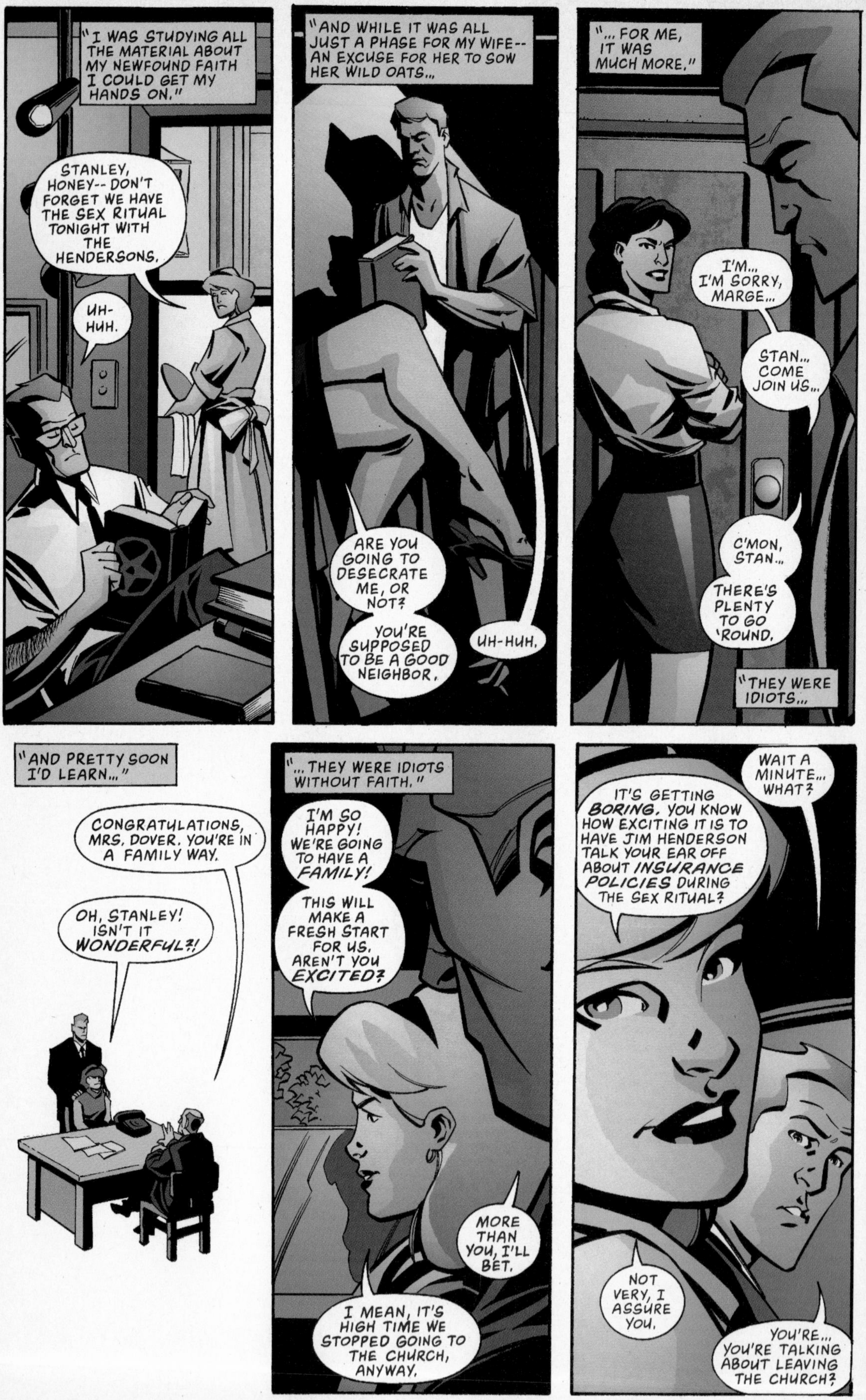
"I WAS STUDYING ALL THE MATERIAL ABOUT MY NEWFOUND FAITH I COULD GET MY HANDS ON."
STANLEY, HONEY-- DON'T FORGET WE HAVE THE SEX RITUAL TONIGHT WITH THE HENDERSONS.
UH-HUH.
"AND WHILE IT WAS ALL JUST A PHASE FOR MY WIFE-- AN EXCUSE FOR HER TO SOW HER WILD OATS...
ARE YOU GOING TO DESECRATE ME, OR NOT?
YOU'RE SUPPOSED TO BE A GOOD NEIGHBOR.
UH-HUH.
"... FOR ME, IT WAS MUCH MORE."
I'M... I'M SORRY, MARGE...
STAN... COME JOIN US...
C'MON, STAN...
THERE'S PLENTY TO GO 'ROUND.
"THEY WERE IDIOTS...
"AND PRETTY SOON I'D LEARN..."
CONGRATULATIONS, MRS. DOVER. YOU'RE IN A FAMILY WAY.
OH, STANLEY! ISN'T IT WONDERFUL?!
"... THEY WERE IDIOTS WITHOUT FAITH."
I'M SO HAPPY! WE'RE GOING TO HAVE A FAMILY!
THIS WILL MAKE A FRESH START FOR US. AREN'T YOU EXCITED?
MORE THAN YOU, I'LL BET.
I MEAN, IT'S HIGH TIME WE STOPPED GOING TO THE CHURCH, ANYWAY.
WAIT A MINUTE... WHAT?
IT'S GETTING BORING. YOU KNOW HOW EXCITING IT IS TO HAVE JIM HENDERSON TALK YOUR EAR OFF ABOUT INSURANCE POLICIES DURING THE SEX RITUAL?
NOT VERY, I ASSURE YOU.
YOU'RE... YOU'RE TALKING ABOUT LEAVING THE CHURCH?

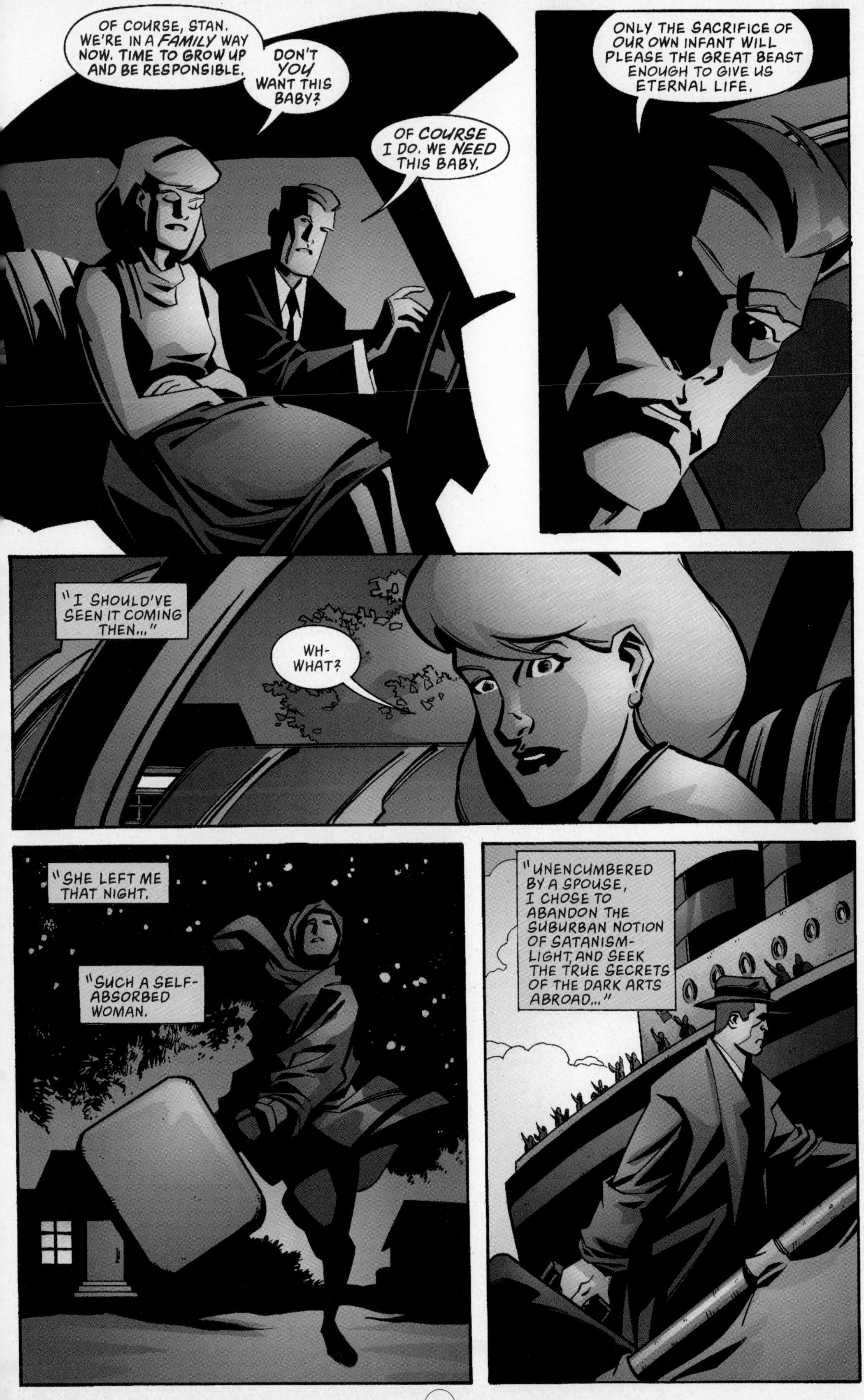
OF COURSE, STAN. WE'RE IN A FAMILY WAY NOW. TIME TO GROW UP AND BE RESPONSIBLE.
DON'T YOU WANT THIS BABY?
OF COURSE I DO. WE NEED THIS BABY.
ONLY THE SACRIFICE OF OUR OWN INFANT WILL PLEASE THE GREAT BEAST ENOUGH TO GIVE US ETERNAL LIFE.
"I SHOULD'VE SEEN IT COMING THEN..."
WH-WHAT?
"SHE LEFT ME THAT NIGHT.
"SUCH A SELF-ABSORBED WOMAN.
"UNENCUMBERED BY A SPOUSE, I CHOSE TO ABANDON THE SUBURBAN NOTION OF SATANISM-LIGHT, AND SEEK THE TRUE SECRETS OF THE DARK ARTS ABROAD..."

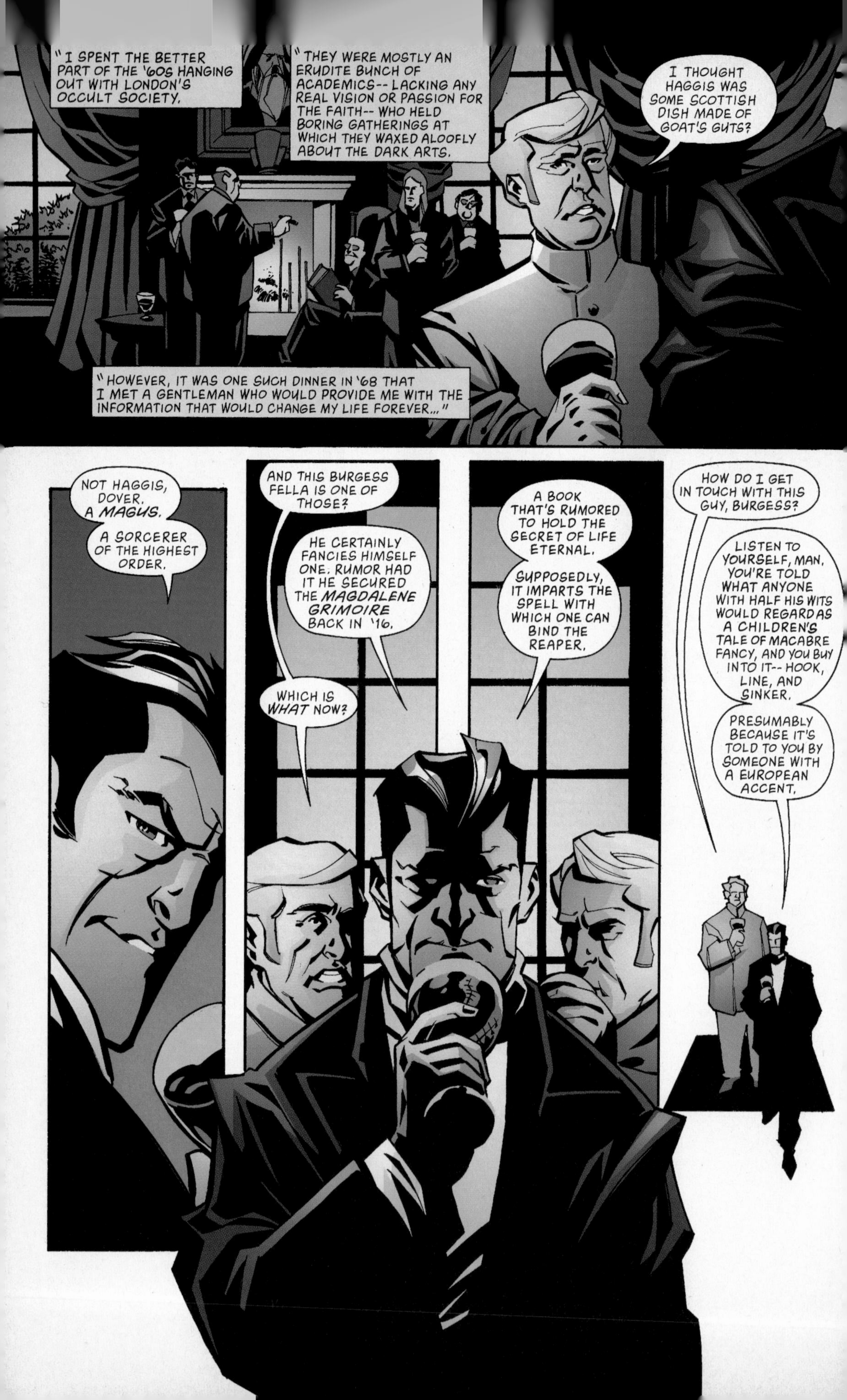
"I SPENT THE BETTER PART OF THE '60S HANGING OUT WITH LONDON'S OCCULT SOCIETY.
"THEY WERE MOSTLY AN ERUDITE BUNCH OF ACADEMICS-- LACKING ANY REAL VISION OR PASSION FOR THE FAITH-- WHO HELD BORING GATHERINGS AT WHICH THEY WAXED ALOOFLY ABOUT THE DARK ARTS.
I THOUGHT HAGGIS WAS SOME SCOTTISH DISH MADE OF GOAT'S GUTS?
"HOWEVER, IT WAS ONE SUCH DINNER IN '68 THAT I MET A GENTLEMAN WHO WOULD PROVIDE ME WITH THE INFORMATION THAT WOULD CHANGE MY LIFE FOREVER..."
NOT HAGGIS, DOVER. A MAGUS.
A SORCERER OF THE HIGHEST ORDER.
AND THIS BURGESS FELLA IS ONE OF THOSE?
HE CERTAINLY FANCIES HIMSELF ONE. RUMOR HAD IT HE SECURED THE MAGDALENE GRIMOIRE BACK IN '16.
WHICH IS WHAT NOW?
A BOOK THAT'S RUMORED TO HOLD THE SECRET OF LIFE ETERNAL.
SUPPOSEDLY, IT IMPARTS THE SPELL WITH WHICH ONE CAN BIND THE REAPER.
HOW DO I GET IN TOUCH WITH THIS GUY, BURGESS?
LISTEN TO YOURSELF, MAN. YOU'RE TOLD WHAT ANYONE WITH HALF HIS WITS WOULD REGARD AS A CHILDREN'S TALE OF MACABRE FANCY, AND YOU BUY INTO IT-- HOOK, LINE, AND SINKER.
PRESUMABLY BECAUSE IT'S TOLD TO YOU BY SOMEONE WITH A EUROPEAN ACCENT.

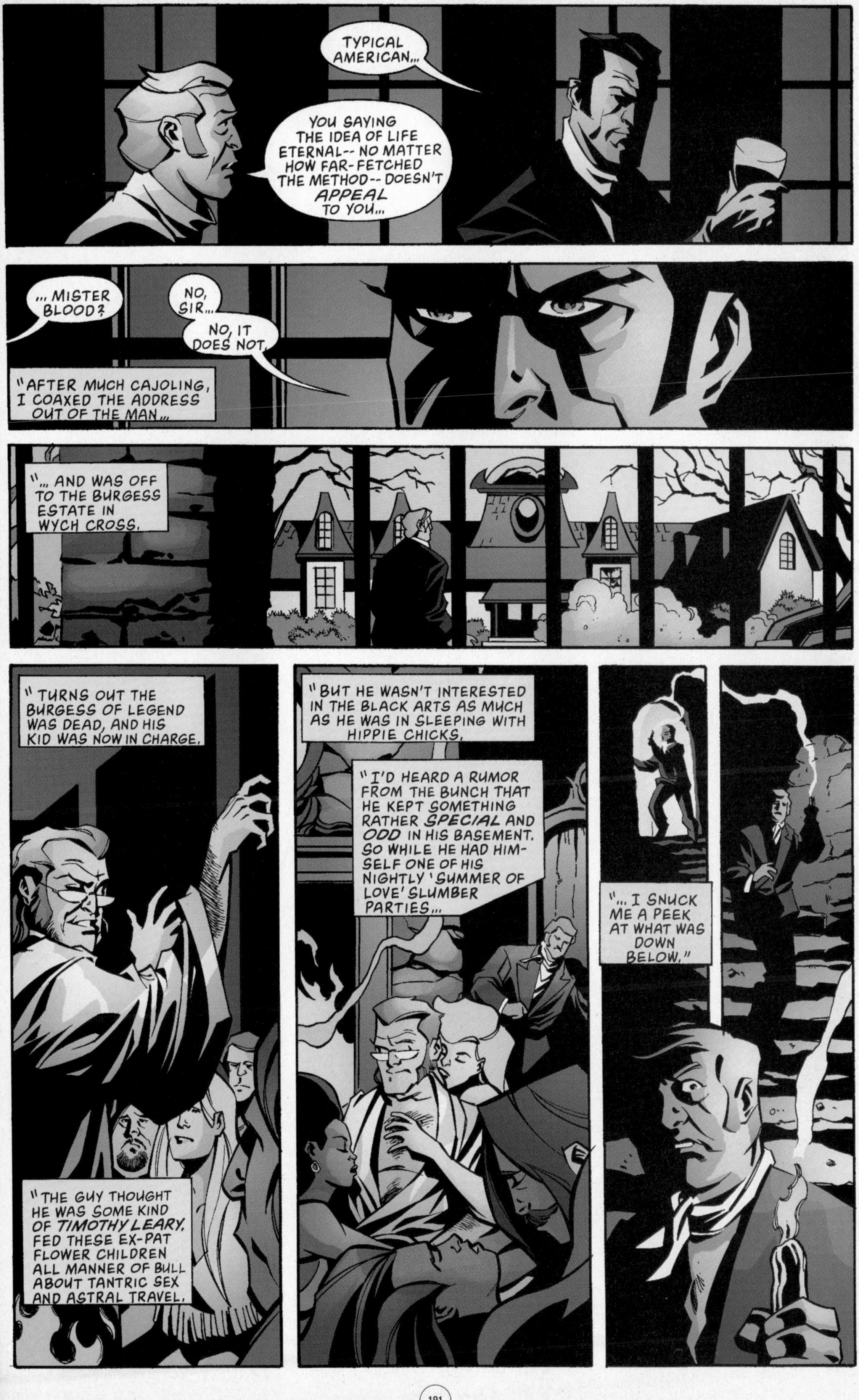
TYPICAL AMERICAN...
YOU SAYING THE IDEA OF LIFE ETERNAL-- NO MATTER HOW FAR-FETCHED THE METHOD-- DOESN'T APPEAL TO YOU...
...MISTER BLOOD?
NO, SIR...
NO, IT DOES NOT.
"AFTER MUCH CAJOLING, I COAXED THE ADDRESS OUT OF THE MAN...
"...AND WAS OFF TO THE BURGESS ESTATE IN WYCH CROSS.
"TURNS OUT THE BURGESS OF LEGEND WAS DEAD, AND HIS KID WAS NOW IN CHARGE.
"THE GUY THOUGHT HE WAS SOME KIND OF TIMOTHY LEARY. FED THESE EX-PAT FLOWER CHILDREN ALL MANNER OF BULL ABOUT TANTRIC SEX AND ASTRAL TRAVEL.
"BUT HE WASN'T INTERESTED IN THE BLACK ARTS AS MUCH AS HE WAS IN SLEEPING WITH HIPPIE CHICKS.
"I'D HEARD A RUMOR FROM THE BUNCH THAT HE KEPT SOMETHING RATHER SPECIAL AND ODD IN HIS BASEMENT. SO WHILE HE HAD HIMSELF ONE OF HIS NIGHTLY 'SUMMER OF LOVE' SLUMBER PARTIES...
"...I SNUCK ME A PEEK AT WHAT WAS DOWN BELOW."

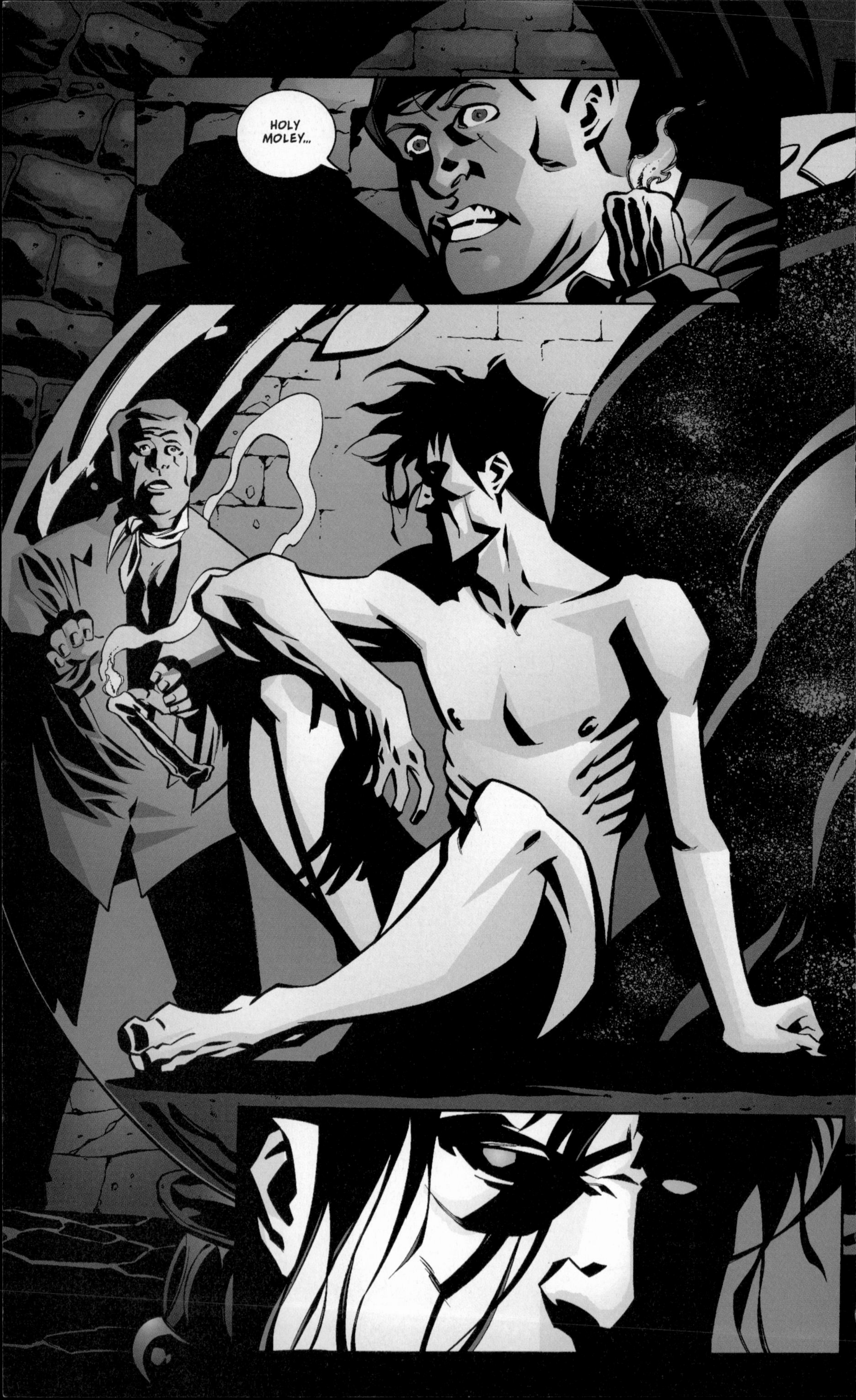
HOLY MOLEY...

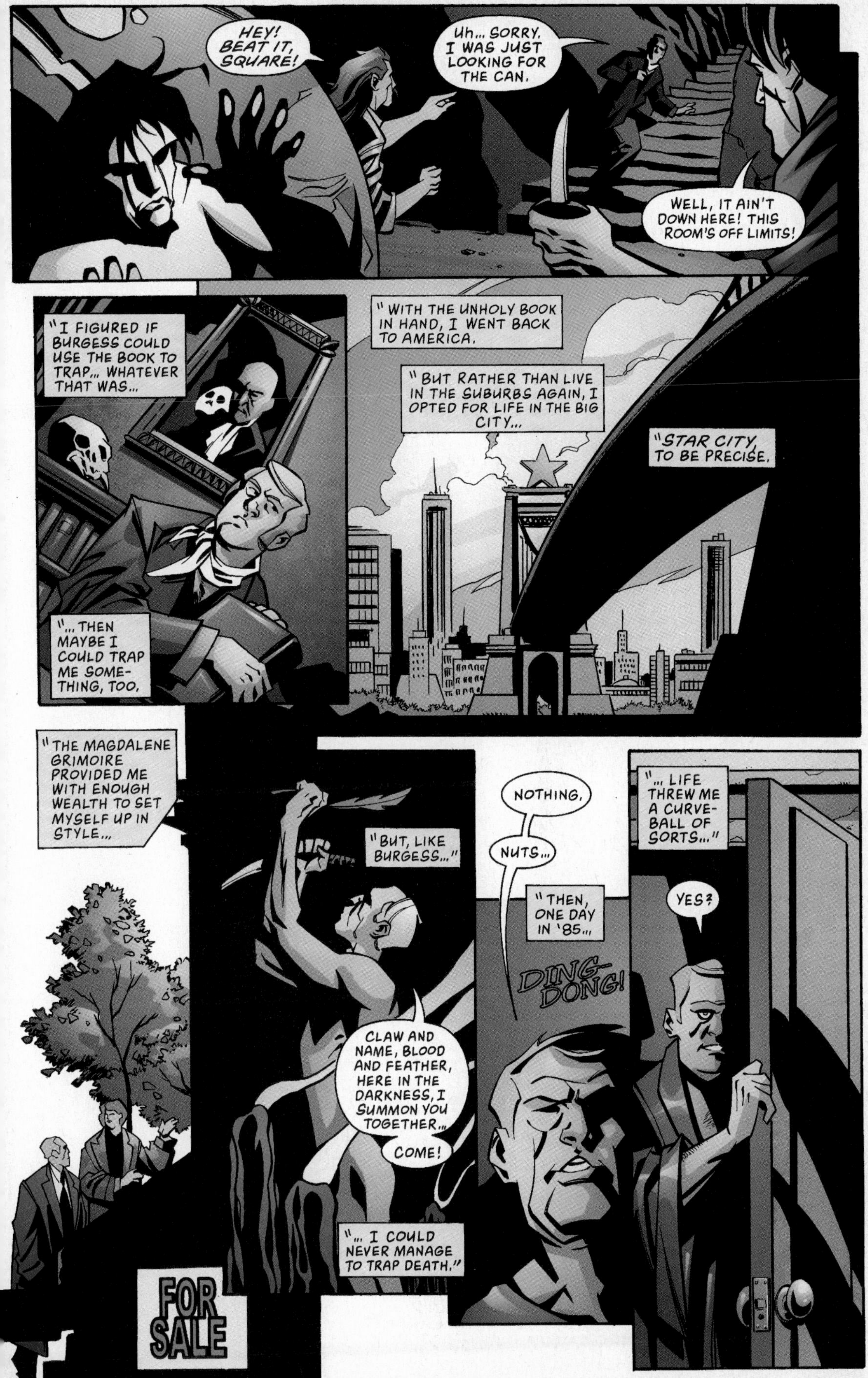

HEY! BEAT IT, SQUARE!
Uh... SORRY. I WAS JUST LOOKING FOR THE CAN.
WELL, IT AIN'T DOWN HERE! THIS ROOM'S OFF LIMITS!
"I FIGURED IF BURGESS COULD USE THE BOOK TO TRAP... WHATEVER THAT WAS...
"...THEN MAYBE I COULD TRAP ME SOME-THING, TOO.
"WITH THE UNHOLY BOOK IN HAND, I WENT BACK TO AMERICA.
"BUT RATHER THAN LIVE IN THE SUBURBS AGAIN, I OPTED FOR LIFE IN THE BIG CITY...
"STAR CITY, TO BE PRECISE.
"THE MAGDALENE GRIMOIRE PROVIDED ME WITH ENOUGH WEALTH TO SET MYSELF UP IN STYLE...
FOR SALE
"BUT, LIKE BURGESS..."
CLAW AND NAME, BLOOD AND FEATHER, HERE IN THE DARKNESS, I SUMMON YOU TOGETHER...
COME!
"...I COULD NEVER MANAGE TO TRAP DEATH."
NOTHING.
NUTS...
"THEN, ONE DAY IN '85...
DING-DONG!
"...LIFE THREW ME A CURVE-BALL OF SORTS..."
YES?

STANLEY DOVER?

YES?

I'M SHEILA DOVER...

I'M YOUR DAUGHTER.

"SHE TOLD ME HER MOTHER HAD DIED YEARS AGO, WHEN SHE WAS AN INFANT, AND SHE'D BEEN RAISED BY HER AUNT.

"'TWAS MITCH, HER FIANCE, THAT ENCOURAGED HER TO TRACK ME DOWN-- AS THE ONLY INFORMATION SHE'D EVER BEEN GIVEN ABOUT ME WAS THAT HER MOTHER ENDED OUR MARRIAGE BEFORE SHE WAS BORN.

"I PAINTED MY-SELF AS A VICTIM, MAKING UP SOME-THING ABOUT HER MOTHER RUNNING OFF WITH A DOOR-TO-DOOR SALES-MAN, BREAKING MY HEART...

"SHE CALLED ME 'DADDY!'

"SHEILA AND MITCH GOT MARRIED, AND A FEW YEARS LATER, THEY MADE ME A GRANDFATHER,

"THIS WAS MY SURFACE LIFE,

"MY SHROUDED LIFE WAS DEVOTED TO THE STUDY OF THE MAGDALENE GRIMOIRE, NOT TO MENTION OTHER ARCANE TEXTS,

"IT WAS ONE SUCH ALTERNATE TOME THAT I CAME ACROSS A PECULIAR DEMON THAT INTRIGUED ME..."

The Beast With No Name

With No Name is a rare ...on in Hell's Hierarchy. Known ...imility and kindness, the Beast ...her possesses nor partakes in the consumption of human flesh.

While caste and stature in Hell is based on rhyming cadence, honor is based in nomenclature. The Beast With No Name has thusly been denied identity since the inception of the Pitt, due largely to un-demonly demeanor.

194

"HERE WAS A DEMON THAT COULD BE BULLIED. OWNED, EVEN. A BEING OF ULTIMATE POWER THAT COULD BE BENT TO THE WILL OF THE MAN WHO CAPTURED IT.

"THIS WOULD BE MY NEW QUARRY.

"THE POWER I COULD SQUEEZE FROM THIS *BEAST WITH NO NAME* WOULD NOT ONLY GIVE ME LIFE ETERNAL, BUT THE ACTUAL MIGHT OF THE INFERNAL REALMS TO BOOT. I COULD BE A *HUMAN GOD!*

DING DONG!

"...IF ONLY SHEILA WOULD STOP TREATING ME LIKE A *BABY-SITTER.*"

HEY, DAD. MITCH IS AT WORK, AND I'VE GOT TO GO PICK UP SOME PAPERS FROM THE OFFICE, CAN YOU KEEP AN EYE ON THE BABY FOR A FEW HOURS?

SHEILA, I'VE GOT IMPORTANT THINGS TO--

THANKS, DAD, I'LL BE BACK TO PICK HIM UP AROUND SIX. LOVE YA!

"LIKE IT OR NOT, I'D FIND MYSELF WITH A LITTLE COMPANY FOR MY SUMMONING SESSIONS,"

OH, YE CAST DOWN! OH, YE UNBORN! OH, YE WHO BEARS THE HELL-WARD HORNS! REVEAL THYSELF THIS VERY MORN!

"THE PARAMETER OF THE SPELLS WOULD LULL BABY STANLEY TO SLEEP LIKE NURSERY RHYMES,

"IN RETROSPECT, IT WAS KIND OF CUTE,

"BUT IMAGINE MY FRUSTRATION *THEN:* YEARS OF ATTEMPTS TO SUMMON A DEMON THAT WERE MET WITH SILENCE.

NOTHING. NUTS!

"WHAT I DIDN'T KNOW WAS THAT MY EFFORTS TO CAST A BINDING SPELL OVER THIS BEAST FROM THE NETHER REGIONS WEREN'T BEING *IGNORED...*

"THEY WERE BEING *TRANSFERRED...*

"ONTO *SOME-ONE ELSE,*"

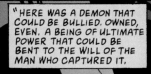

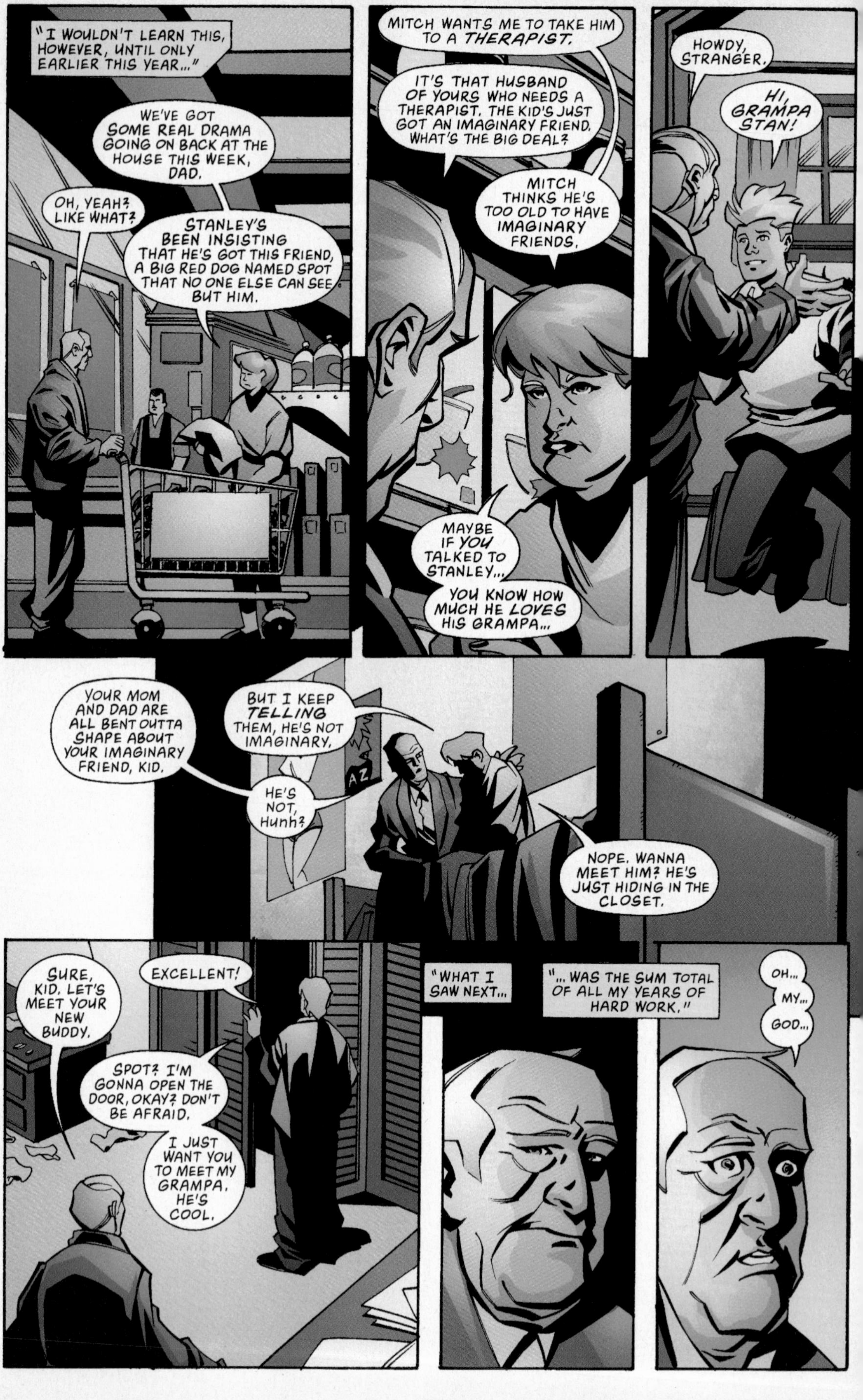
"I WOULDN'T LEARN THIS, HOWEVER, UNTIL ONLY EARLIER THIS YEAR..."
WE'VE GOT SOME REAL DRAMA GOING ON BACK AT THE HOUSE THIS WEEK, DAD.
OH, YEAH? LIKE WHAT?
STANLEY'S BEEN INSISTING THAT HE'S GOT THIS FRIEND, A BIG RED DOG NAMED SPOT THAT NO ONE ELSE CAN SEE BUT HIM.
MITCH WANTS ME TO TAKE HIM TO A THERAPIST.
IT'S THAT HUSBAND OF YOURS WHO NEEDS A THERAPIST. THE KID'S JUST GOT AN IMAGINARY FRIEND. WHAT'S THE BIG DEAL?
MITCH THINKS HE'S TOO OLD TO HAVE IMAGINARY FRIENDS.
MAYBE IF YOU TALKED TO STANLEY...
YOU KNOW HOW MUCH HE LOVES HIS GRAMPA...
HOWDY, STRANGER.
HI, GRAMPA STAN!
YOUR MOM AND DAD ARE ALL BENT OUTTA SHAPE ABOUT YOUR IMAGINARY FRIEND, KID.
BUT I KEEP TELLING THEM, HE'S NOT IMAGINARY.
HE'S NOT, HUNH?
AZ
NOPE. WANNA MEET HIM? HE'S JUST HIDING IN THE CLOSET.
SURE, KID. LET'S MEET YOUR NEW BUDDY.
EXCELLENT!
SPOT? I'M GONNA OPEN THE DOOR, OKAY? DON'T BE AFRAID.
I JUST WANT YOU TO MEET MY GRAMPA. HE'S COOL.
"WHAT I SAW NEXT...
"...WAS THE SUM TOTAL OF ALL MY YEARS OF HARD WORK."
OH... MY... GOD...

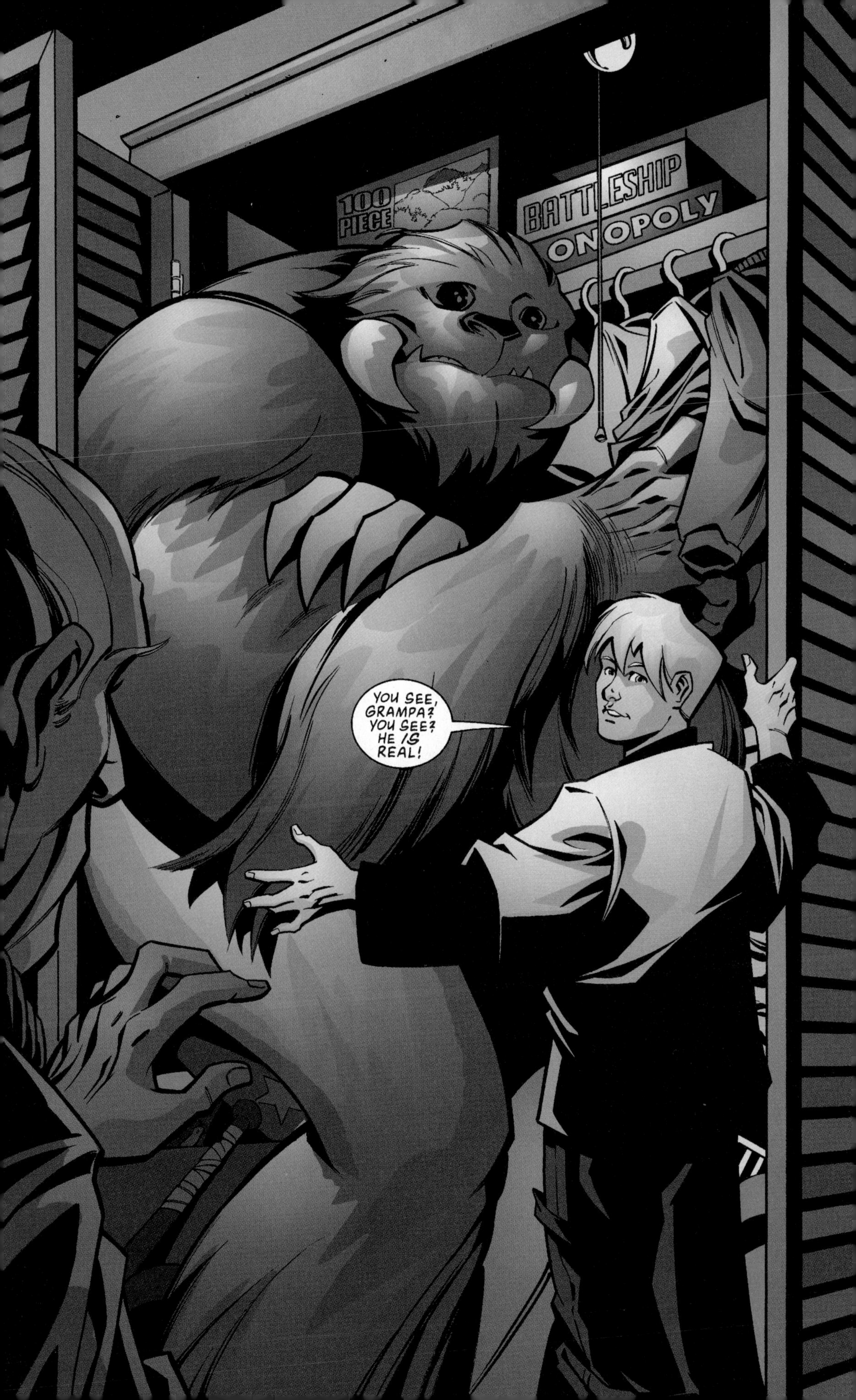
100 PIECE
BATTLESHIP
ONOPOLY
YOU SEE, GRAMPA? YOU SEE? HE IS REAL!

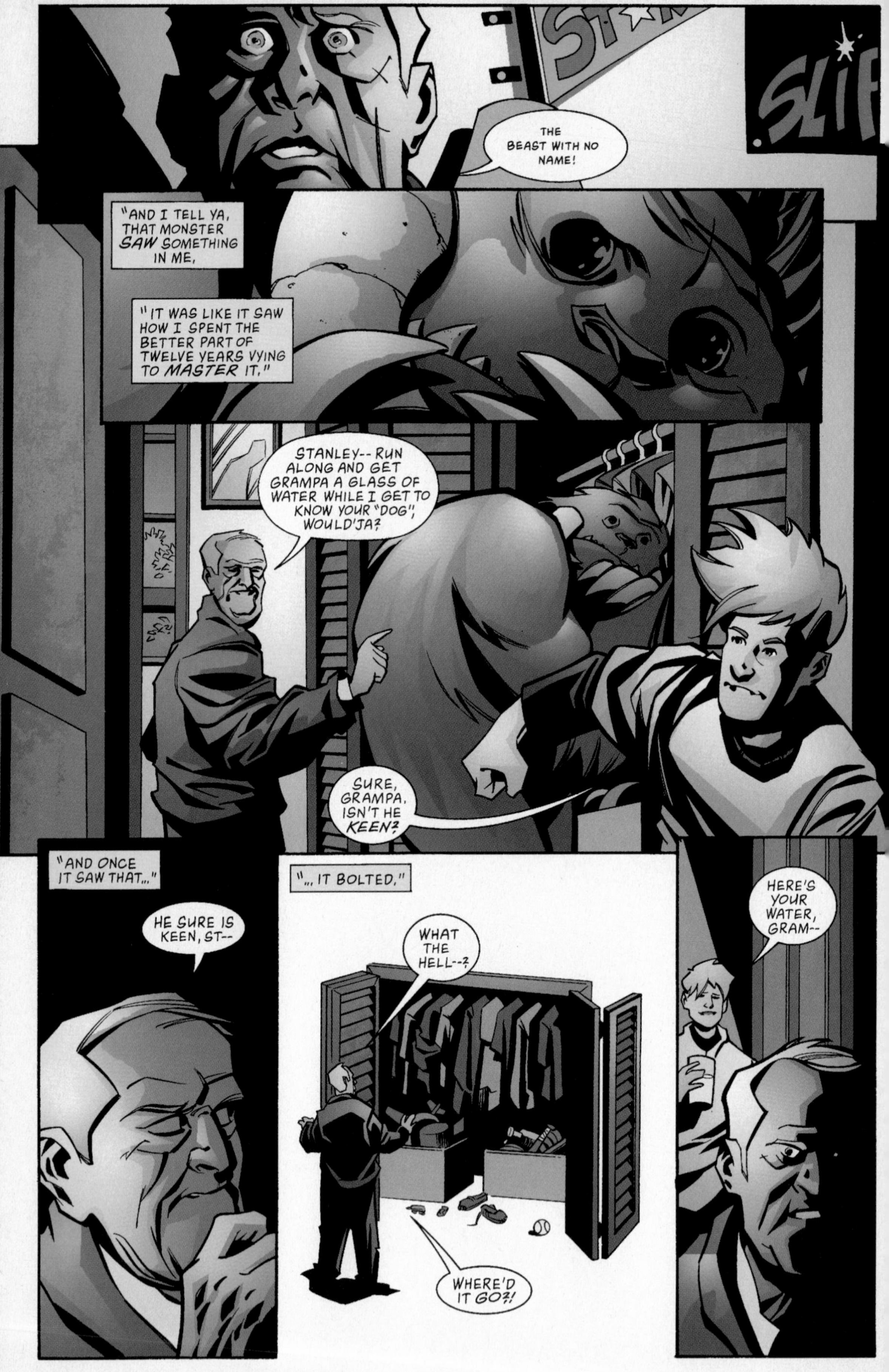
THE BEAST WITH NO NAME!
"AND I TELL YA, THAT MONSTER SAW SOMETHING IN ME,
"IT WAS LIKE IT SAW HOW I SPENT THE BETTER PART OF TWELVE YEARS VYING TO MASTER IT."
STANLEY-- RUN ALONG AND GET GRAMPA A GLASS OF WATER WHILE I GET TO KNOW YOUR "DOG", WOULD'JA?
SURE, GRAMPA, ISN'T HE KEEN?
"AND ONCE IT SAW THAT..."
HE SURE IS KEEN, ST--
"... IT BOLTED."
WHAT THE HELL--?
WHERE'D IT GO?!
HERE'S YOUR WATER, GRAM--

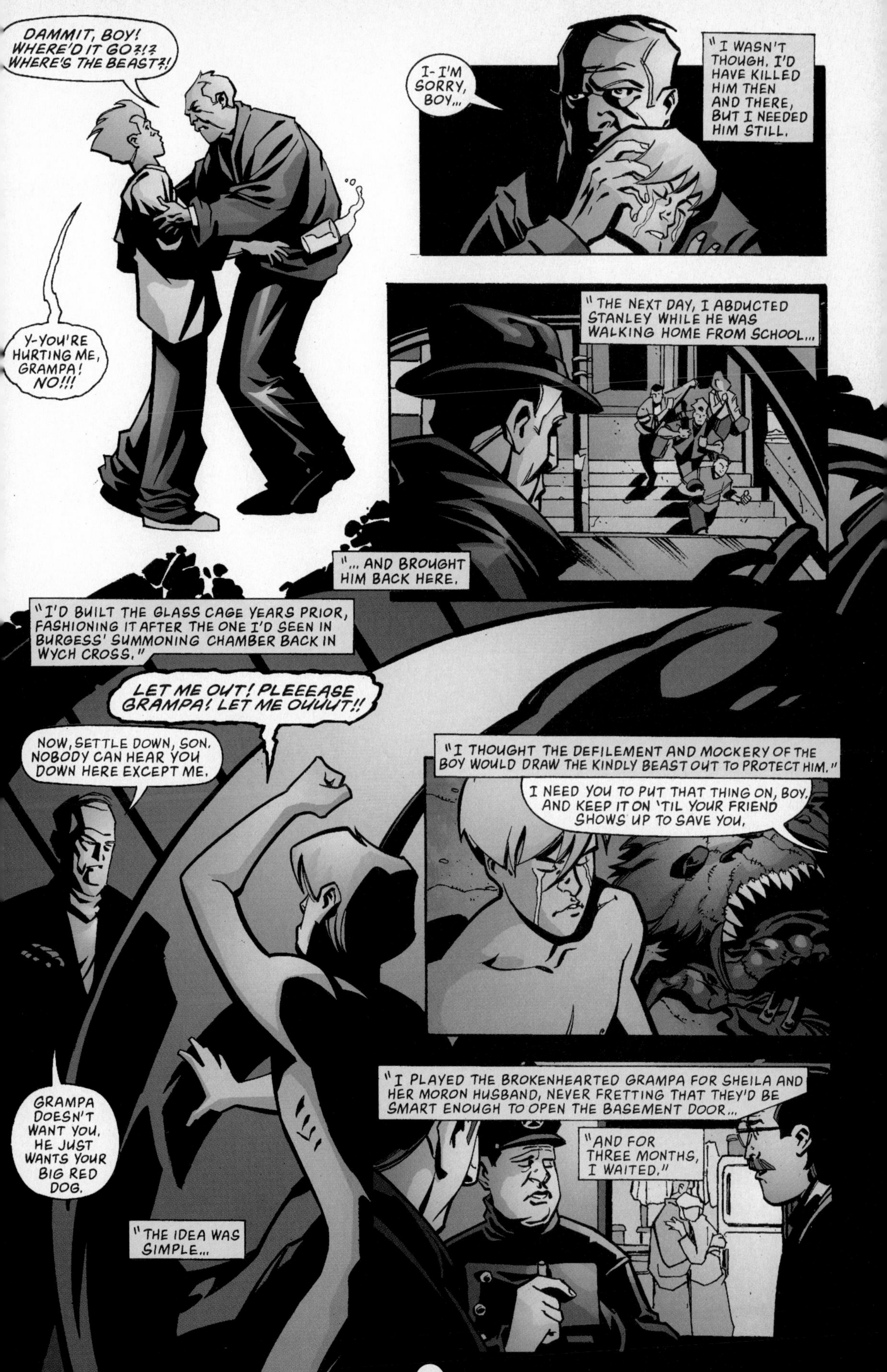
DAMMIT, BOY! WHERE'D IT GO?!? WHERE'S THE BEAST?!
Y-YOU'RE HURTING ME, GRAMPA! NO!!!
I- I'M SORRY, BOY...
"I WASN'T THOUGH. I'D HAVE KILLED HIM THEN AND THERE, BUT I NEEDED HIM STILL.
"THE NEXT DAY, I ABDUCTED STANLEY WHILE HE WAS WALKING HOME FROM SCHOOL...
"... AND BROUGHT HIM BACK HERE.
"I'D BUILT THE GLASS CAGE YEARS PRIOR, FASHIONING IT AFTER THE ONE I'D SEEN IN BURGESS' SUMMONING CHAMBER BACK IN WYCH CROSS."
LET ME OUT! PLEEEASE GRAMPA! LET ME OUUUT!!
NOW, SETTLE DOWN, SON. NOBODY CAN HEAR YOU DOWN HERE EXCEPT ME.
GRAMPA DOESN'T WANT YOU. HE JUST WANTS YOUR BIG RED DOG.
"THE IDEA WAS SIMPLE...
"I THOUGHT THE DEFILEMENT AND MOCKERY OF THE BOY WOULD DRAW THE KINDLY BEAST OUT TO PROTECT HIM."
I NEED YOU TO PUT THAT THING ON, BOY, AND KEEP IT ON 'TIL YOUR FRIEND SHOWS UP TO SAVE YOU.
"I PLAYED THE BROKENHEARTED GRAMPA FOR SHEILA AND HER MORON HUSBAND, NEVER FRETTING THAT THEY'D BE SMART ENOUGH TO OPEN THE BASEMENT DOOR...
"AND FOR THREE MONTHS, I WAITED."

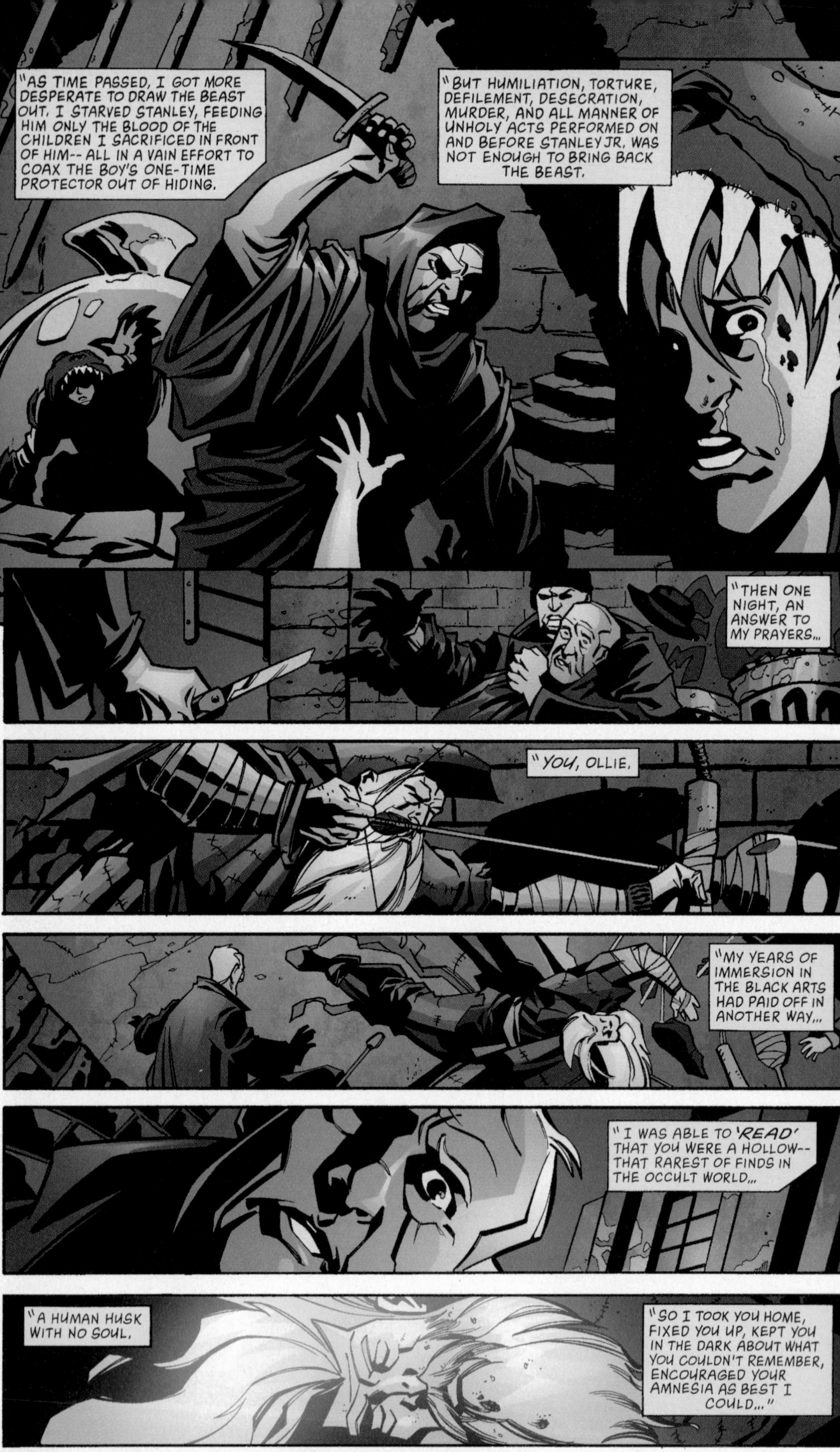
"AS TIME PASSED, I GOT MORE DESPERATE TO DRAW THE BEAST OUT. I STARVED STANLEY, FEEDING HIM ONLY THE BLOOD OF THE CHILDREN I SACRIFICED IN FRONT OF HIM-- ALL IN A VAIN EFFORT TO COAX THE BOY'S ONE-TIME PROTECTOR OUT OF HIDING.
"BUT HUMILIATION, TORTURE, DEFILEMENT, DESECRATION, MURDER, AND ALL MANNER OF UNHOLY ACTS PERFORMED ON AND BEFORE STANLEY JR. WAS NOT ENOUGH TO BRING BACK THE BEAST.
"THEN ONE NIGHT, AN ANSWER TO MY PRAYERS...
"YOU, OLLIE.
"MY YEARS OF IMMERSION IN THE BLACK ARTS HAD PAID OFF IN ANOTHER WAY...
"I WAS ABLE TO 'READ' THAT YOU WERE A HOLLOW-- THAT RAREST OF FINDS IN THE OCCULT WORLD...
"A HUMAN HUSK WITH NO SOUL.
"SO I TOOK YOU HOME, FIXED YOU UP, KEPT YOU IN THE DARK ABOUT WHAT YOU COULDN'T REMEMBER, ENCOURAGED YOUR AMNESIA AS BEST I COULD..."

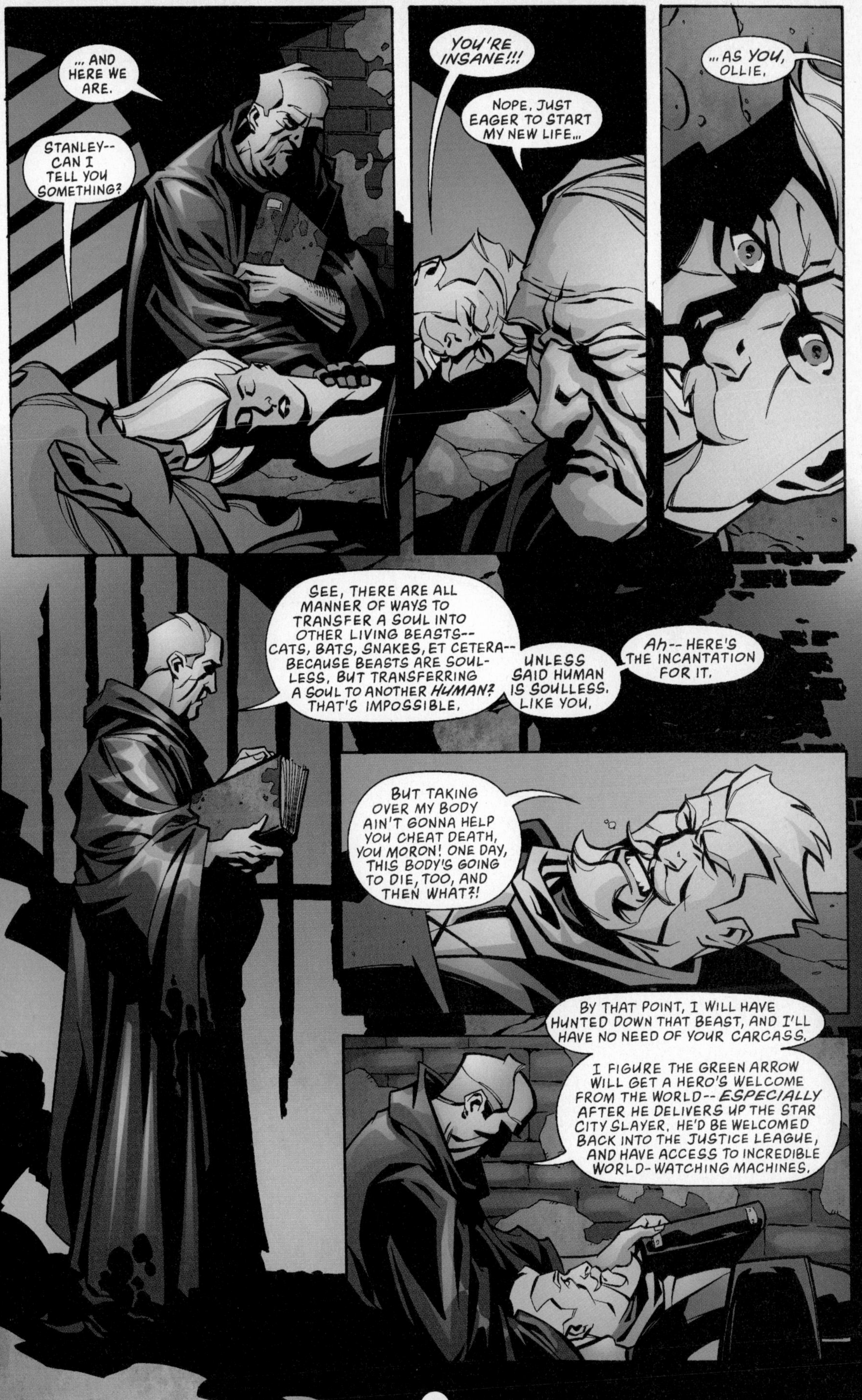
...AND HERE WE ARE.
STANLEY-- CAN I TELL YOU SOMETHING?
YOU'RE INSANE!!!
NOPE, JUST EAGER TO START MY NEW LIFE...
...AS YOU, OLLIE.
SEE, THERE ARE ALL MANNER OF WAYS TO TRANSFER A SOUL INTO OTHER LIVING BEASTS-- CATS, BATS, SNAKES, ET CETERA-- BECAUSE BEASTS ARE SOUL-LESS, BUT TRANSFERRING A SOUL TO ANOTHER HUMAN? THAT'S IMPOSSIBLE.
UNLESS SAID HUMAN IS SOULLESS. LIKE YOU.
Ah-- HERE'S THE INCANTATION FOR IT.
BUT TAKING OVER MY BODY AIN'T GONNA HELP YOU CHEAT DEATH, YOU MORON! ONE DAY, THIS BODY'S GOING TO DIE, TOO, AND THEN WHAT?!
BY THAT POINT, I WILL HAVE HUNTED DOWN THAT BEAST, AND I'LL HAVE NO NEED OF YOUR CARCASS.
I FIGURE THE GREEN ARROW WILL GET A HERO'S WELCOME FROM THE WORLD-- ESPECIALLY AFTER HE DELIVERS UP THE STAR CITY SLAYER. HE'D BE WELCOMED BACK INTO THE JUSTICE LEAGUE, AND HAVE ACCESS TO INCREDIBLE WORLD-WATCHING MACHINES.

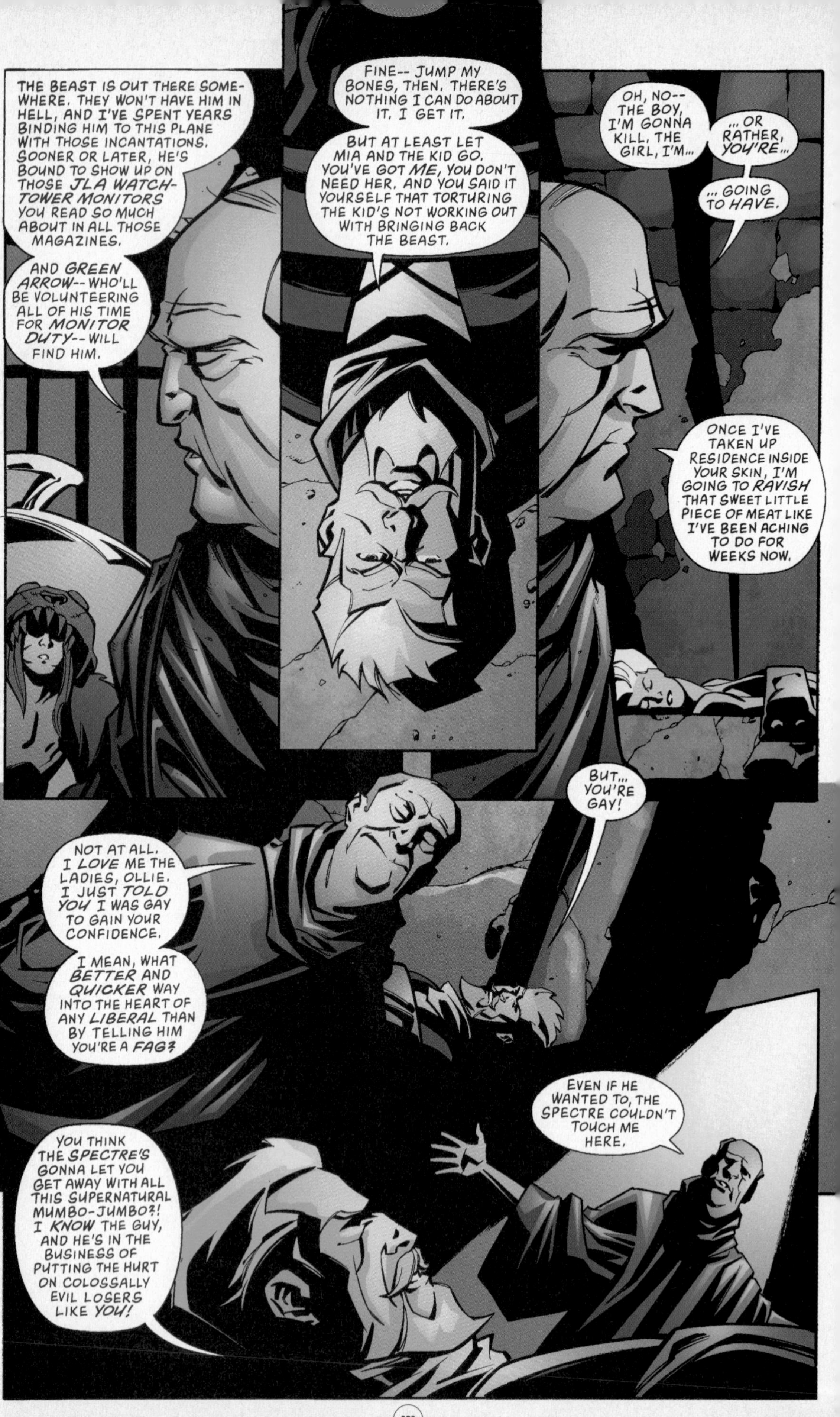
THE BEAST IS OUT THERE SOMEWHERE. THEY WON'T HAVE HIM IN HELL, AND I'VE SPENT YEARS BINDING HIM TO THIS PLANE WITH THOSE INCANTATIONS. SOONER OR LATER, HE'S BOUND TO SHOW UP ON THOSE JLA WATCHTOWER MONITORS YOU READ SO MUCH ABOUT IN ALL THOSE MAGAZINES.
AND GREEN ARROW--WHO'LL BE VOLUNTEERING ALL OF HIS TIME FOR MONITOR DUTY--WILL FIND HIM.
FINE-- JUMP MY BONES, THEN. THERE'S NOTHING I CAN DO ABOUT IT. I GET IT.
BUT AT LEAST LET MIA AND THE KID GO. YOU'VE GOT ME, YOU DON'T NEED HER. AND YOU SAID IT YOURSELF THAT TORTURING THE KID'S NOT WORKING OUT WITH BRINGING BACK THE BEAST.
OH, NO-- THE BOY, I'M GONNA KILL. THE GIRL, I'M...
...OR RATHER, YOU'RE...
...GOING TO HAVE.
ONCE I'VE TAKEN UP RESIDENCE INSIDE YOUR SKIN, I'M GOING TO RAVISH THAT SWEET LITTLE PIECE OF MEAT LIKE I'VE BEEN ACHING TO DO FOR WEEKS NOW.
BUT... YOU'RE GAY!
NOT AT ALL. I LOVE ME THE LADIES, OLLIE. I JUST TOLD YOU I WAS GAY TO GAIN YOUR CONFIDENCE.
I MEAN, WHAT BETTER AND QUICKER WAY INTO THE HEART OF ANY LIBERAL THAN BY TELLING HIM YOU'RE A FAG?
YOU THINK THE SPECTRE'S GONNA LET YOU GET AWAY WITH ALL THIS SUPERNATURAL MUMBO-JUMBO?! I KNOW THE GUY, AND HE'S IN THE BUSINESS OF PUTTING THE HURT ON COLOSSALLY EVIL LOSERS LIKE YOU!
EVEN IF HE WANTED TO, THE SPECTRE COULDN'T TOUCH ME HERE.

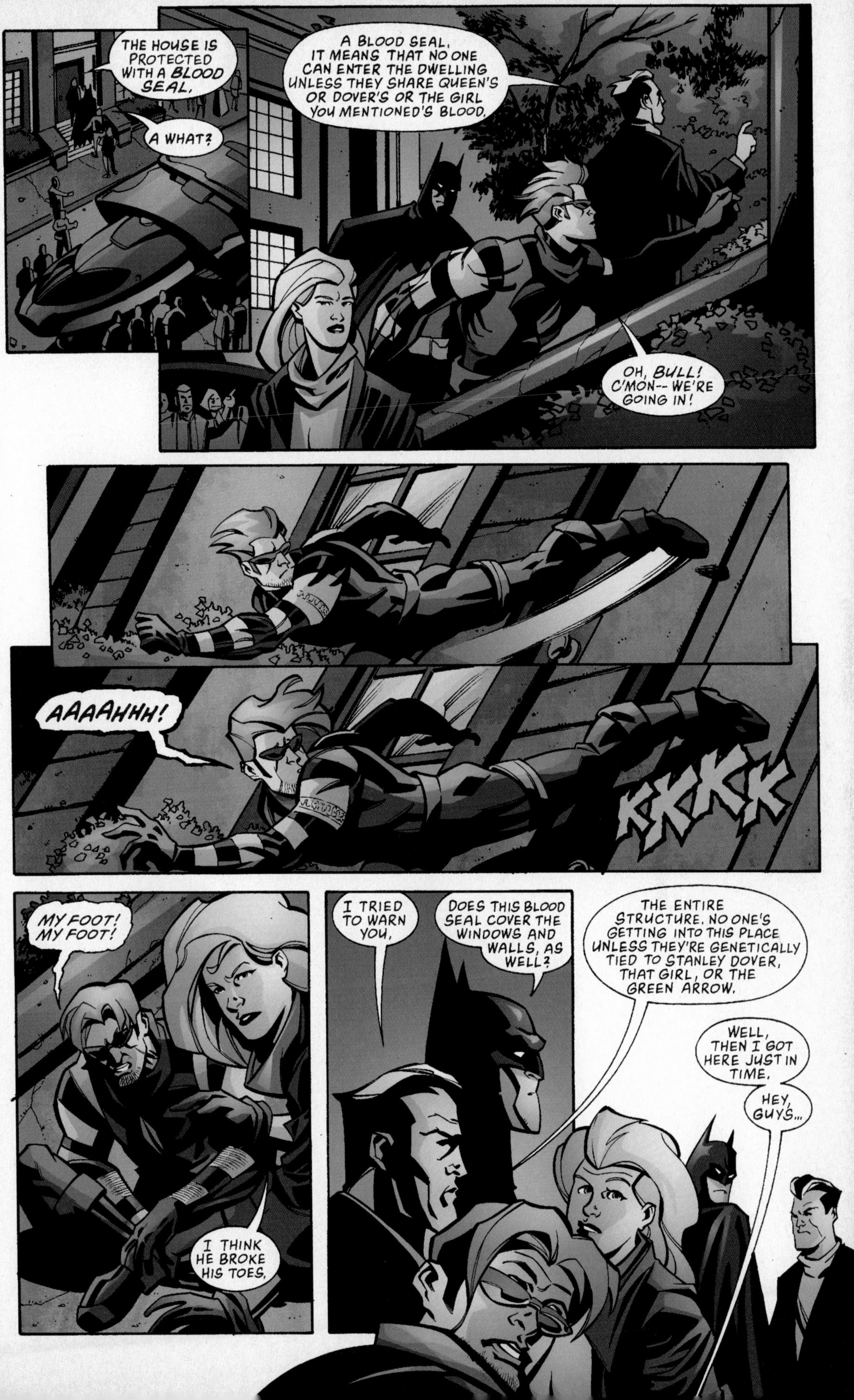
THE HOUSE IS PROTECTED WITH A BLOOD SEAL.
A WHAT?
A BLOOD SEAL. IT MEANS THAT NO ONE CAN ENTER THE DWELLING UNLESS THEY SHARE QUEEN'S OR DOVER'S OR THE GIRL YOU MENTIONED'S BLOOD.
OH, BULL! C'MON-- WE'RE GOING IN!
AAAAHHH!
KKKK
MY FOOT! MY FOOT!
I THINK HE BROKE HIS TOES.
I TRIED TO WARN YOU.
DOES THIS BLOOD SEAL COVER THE WINDOWS AND WALLS, AS WELL?
THE ENTIRE STRUCTURE. NO ONE'S GETTING INTO THIS PLACE UNLESS THEY'RE GENETICALLY TIED TO STANLEY DOVER, THAT GIRL, OR THE GREEN ARROW.
WELL, THEN I GOT HERE JUST IN TIME.
HEY, GUYS...

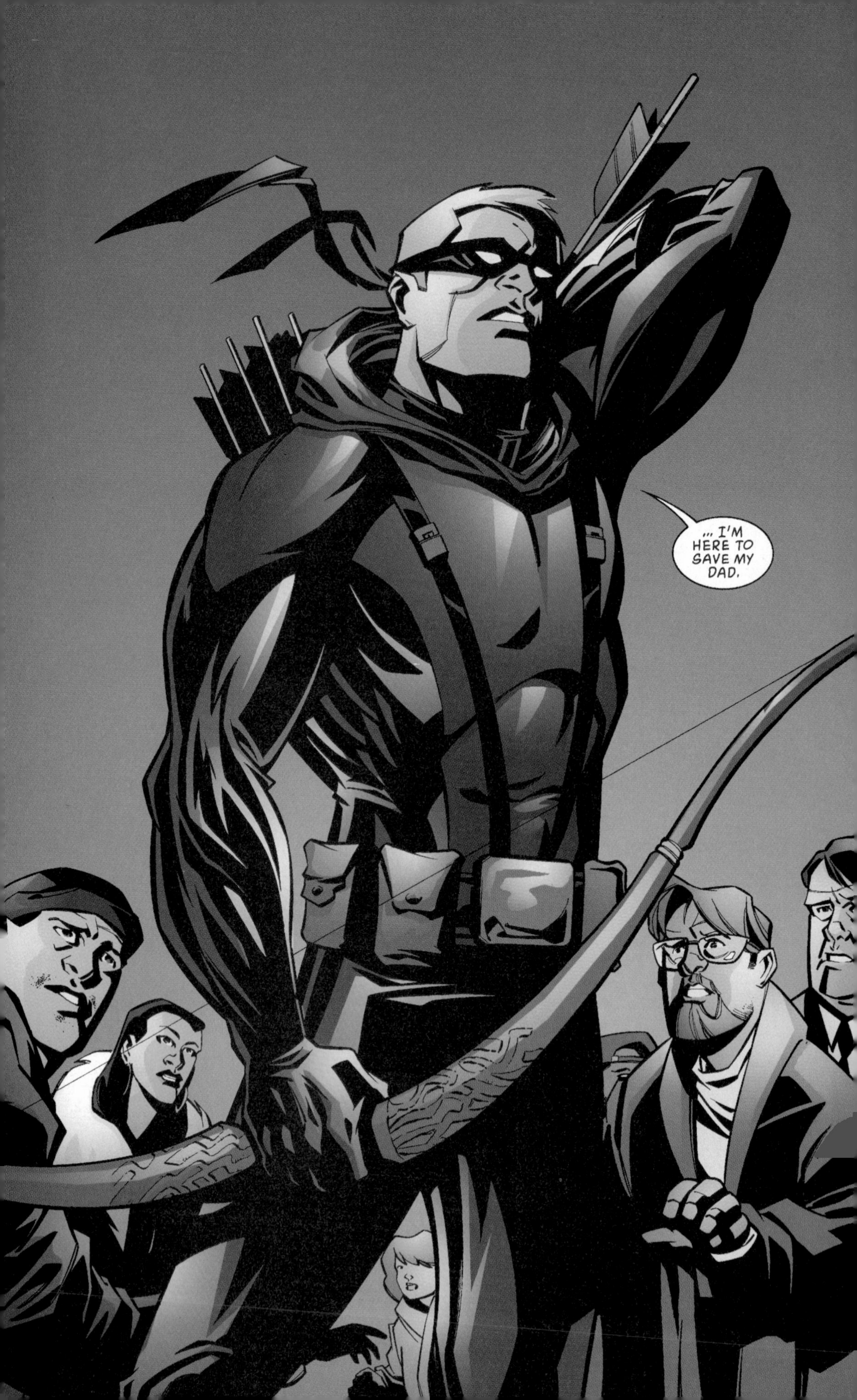
... I'M HERE TO SAVE MY DAD.

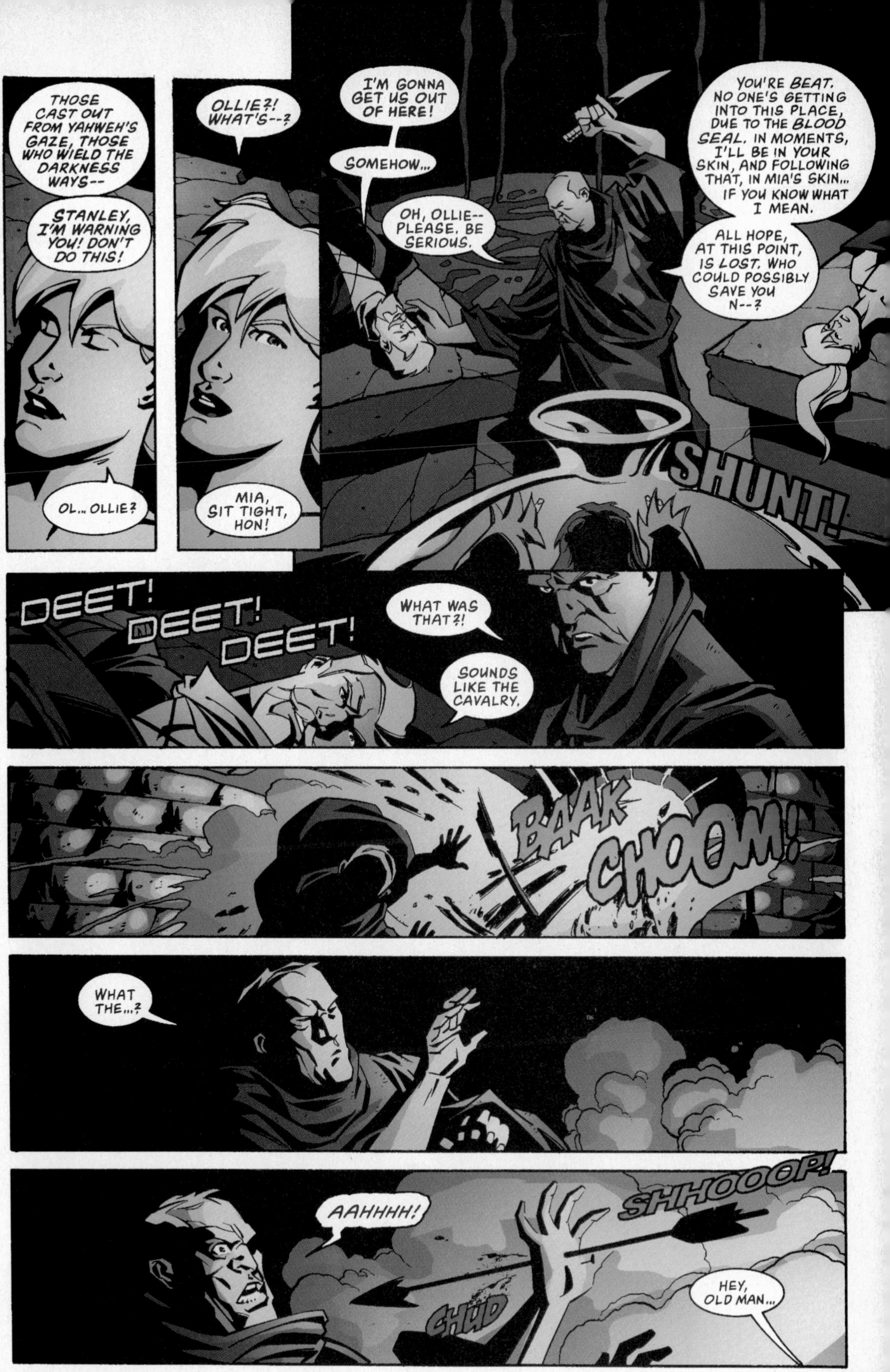
THOSE CAST OUT FROM YAHWEH'S GAZE, THOSE WHO WIELD THE DARKNESS WAYS--
STANLEY, I'M WARNING YOU! DON'T DO THIS!
OL... OLLIE?
OLLIE?! WHAT'S--?
MIA, SIT TIGHT, HON!
I'M GONNA GET US OUT OF HERE!
SOMEHOW...
OH, OLLIE-- PLEASE. BE SERIOUS.
YOU'RE BEAT. NO ONE'S GETTING INTO THIS PLACE, DUE TO THE BLOOD SEAL. IN MOMENTS, I'LL BE IN YOUR SKIN, AND FOLLOWING THAT, IN MIA'S SKIN... IF YOU KNOW WHAT I MEAN.
ALL HOPE, AT THIS POINT, IS LOST. WHO COULD POSSIBLY SAVE YOU N--?
SHUNT!
DEET! DEET! DEET!
WHAT WAS THAT?!
SOUNDS LIKE THE CAVALRY.
BAAK CHOOM!
WHAT THE...?
AAHHHH!
SHHOOOP!
CHUD
HEY, OLD MAN...

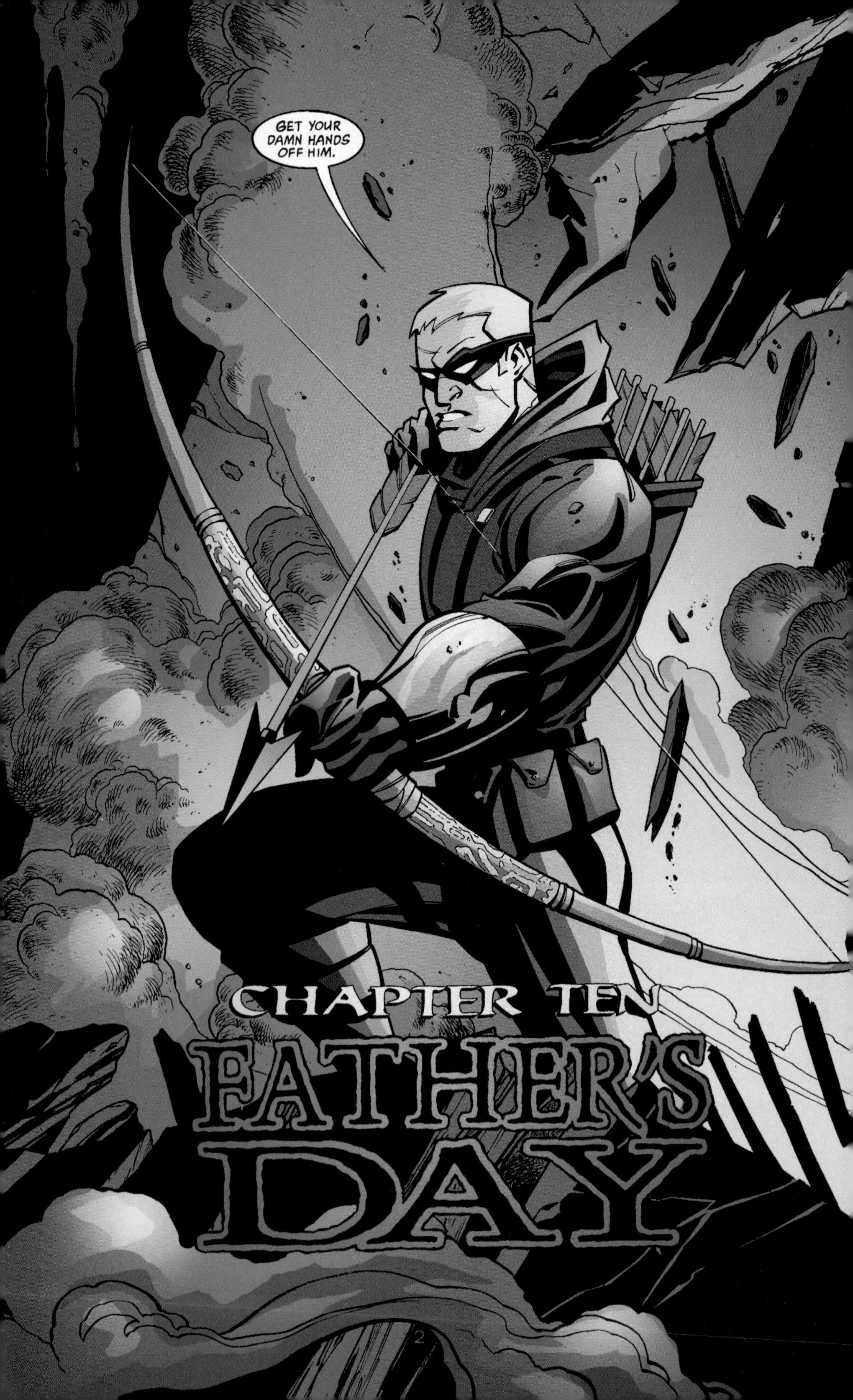
GET YOUR DAMN HANDS OFF HIM.
CHAPTER TEN
FATHER'S DAY

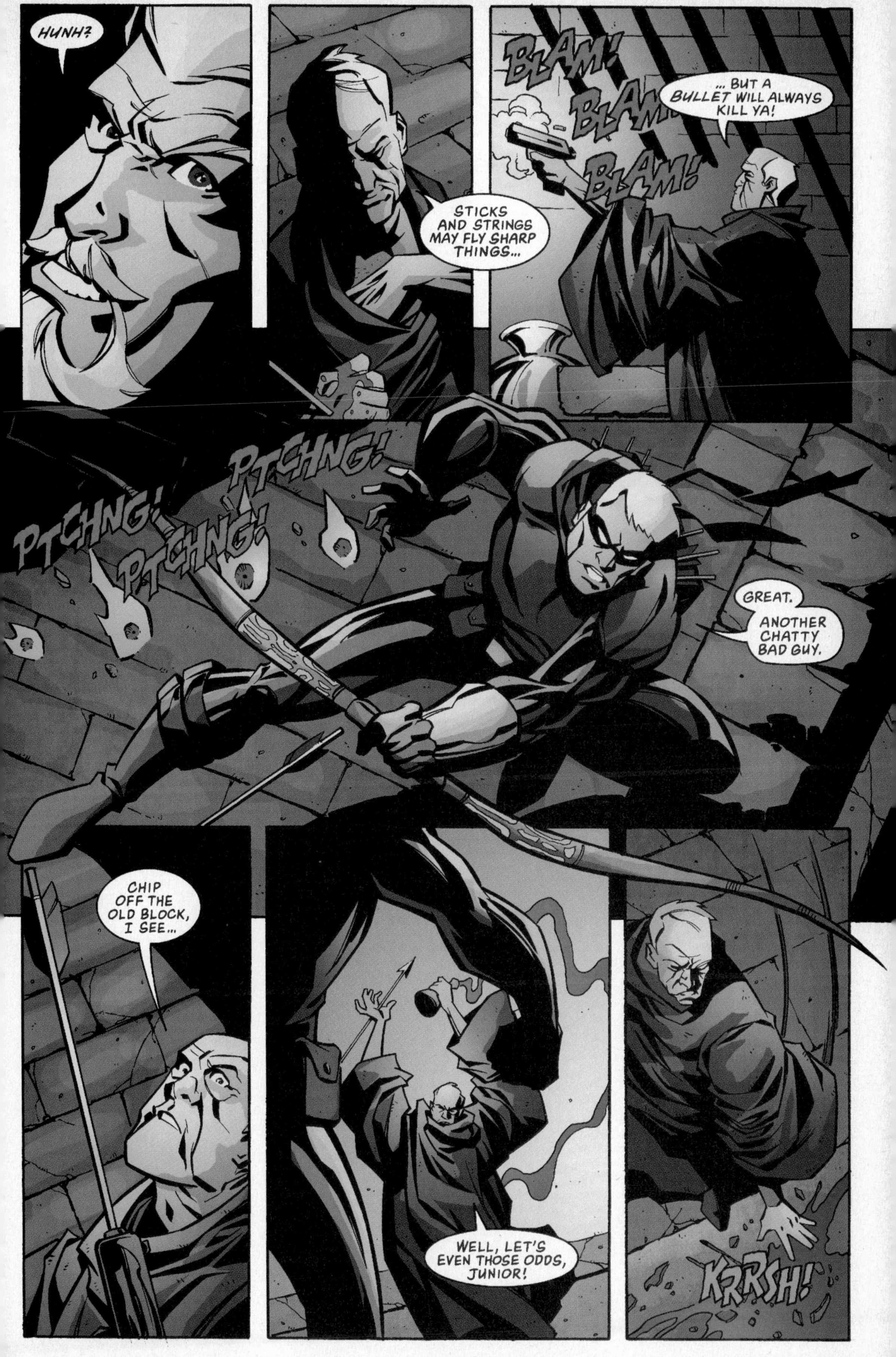
HUNH?
STICKS AND STRINGS MAY FLY SHARP THINGS...
BLAM! BLAM! BLAM!
... BUT A BULLET WILL ALWAYS KILL YA!
PTCHNG! PTCHNG! PTCHNG!
GREAT. ANOTHER CHATTY BAD GUY.
CHIP OFF THE OLD BLOCK, I SEE...
WELL, LET'S EVEN THOSE ODDS, JUNIOR!
KRRSH!

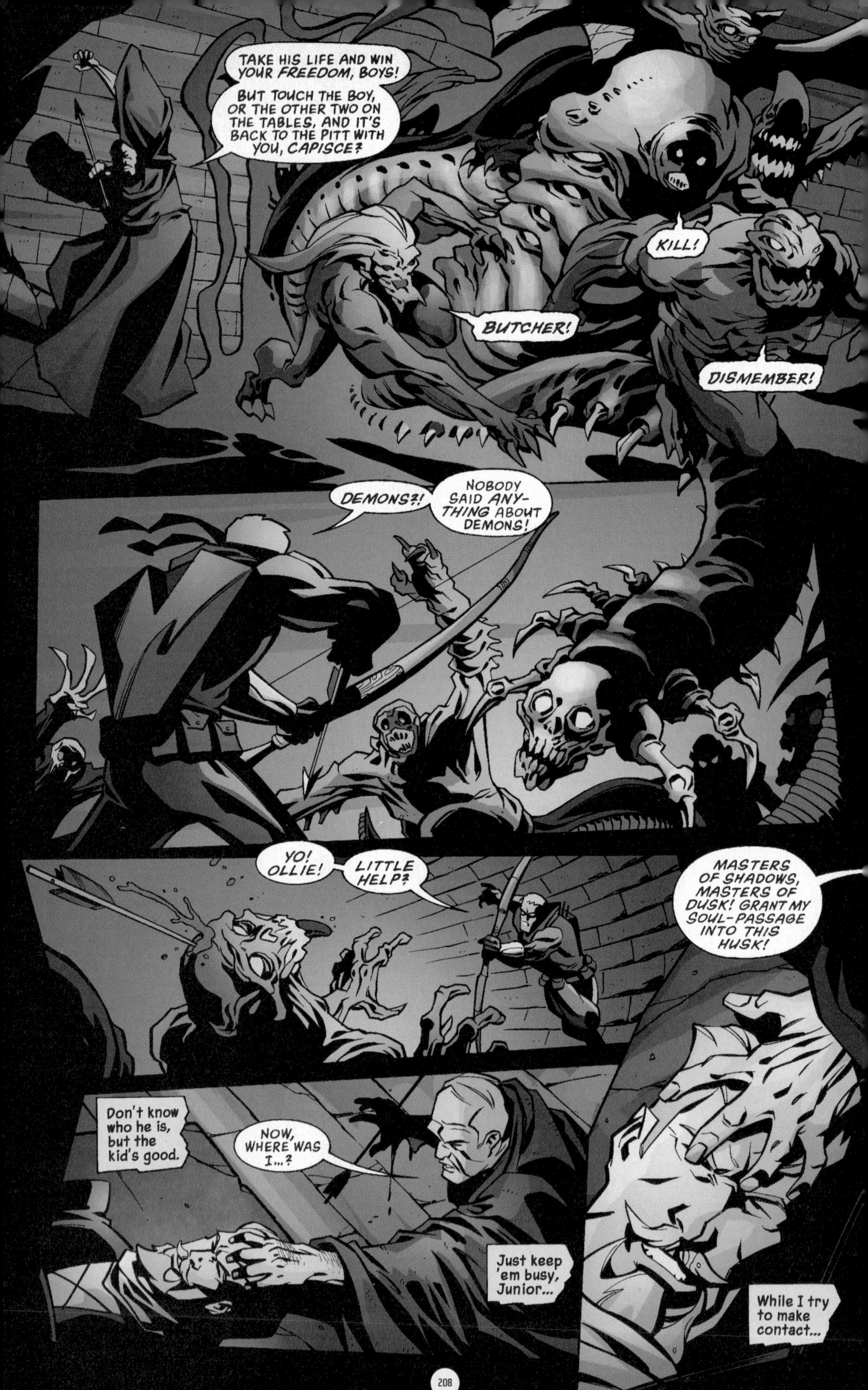
TAKE HIS LIFE AND WIN YOUR FREEDOM, BOYS!
BUT TOUCH THE BOY, OR THE OTHER TWO ON THE TABLES, AND IT'S BACK TO THE PITT WITH YOU, CAPISCE?
KILL!
BUTCHER!
DISMEMBER!
DEMONS?!
NOBODY SAID ANYTHING ABOUT DEMONS!
YO! OLLIE!
LITTLE HELP?
MASTERS OF SHADOWS, MASTERS OF DUSK! GRANT MY SOUL-PASSAGE INTO THIS HUSK!
Don't know who he is, but the kid's good.
NOW, WHERE WAS I...?
Just keep 'em busy, Junior...
While I try to make contact...

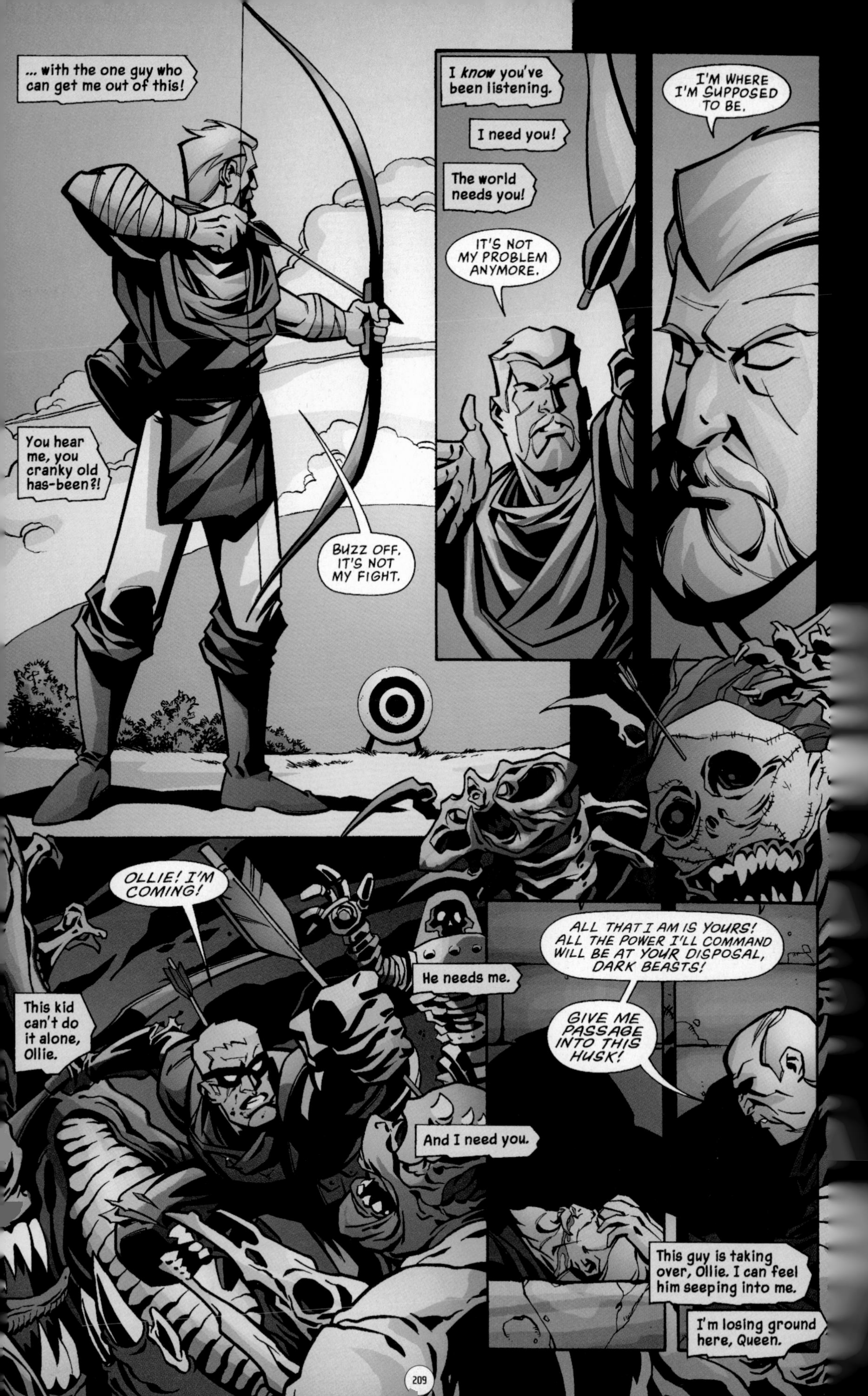

... with the one guy who can get me out of this!
You hear me, you cranky old has-been?!
BUZZ OFF. IT'S NOT MY FIGHT.
I know you've been listening.
I need you!
The world needs you!
IT'S NOT MY PROBLEM ANYMORE.
I'M WHERE I'M SUPPOSED TO BE.
OLLIE! I'M COMING!
This kid can't do it alone, Ollie.
He needs me.
And I need you.
ALL THAT I AM IS YOURS! ALL THE POWER I'LL COMMAND WILL BE AT YOUR DISPOSAL, DARK BEASTS!
GIVE ME PASSAGE INTO THIS HUSK!
This guy is taking over, Ollie. I can feel him seeping into me.
I'm losing ground here, Queen.

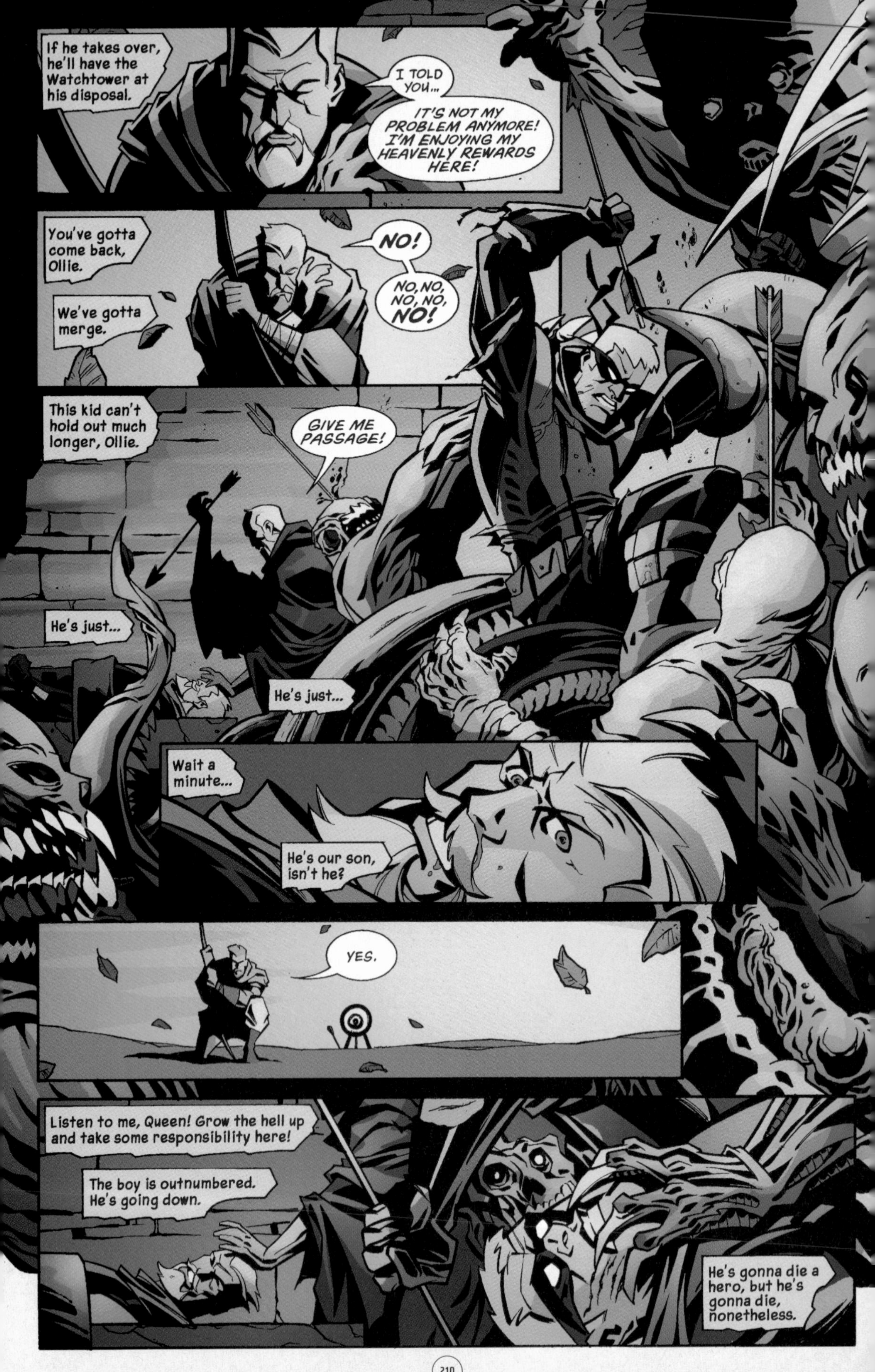
If he takes over, he'll have the Watchtower at his disposal.
I TOLD YOU...
IT'S NOT MY PROBLEM ANYMORE! I'M ENJOYING MY HEAVENLY REWARDS HERE!
You've gotta come back, Ollie.
We've gotta merge.
NO!
NO, NO, NO, NO, NO!
This kid can't hold out much longer, Ollie.
GIVE ME PASSAGE!
He's just...
He's just...
Wait a minute...
He's our son, isn't he?
YES.
Listen to me, Queen! Grow the hell up and take some responsibility here!
The boy is outnumbered. He's going down.
He's gonna die a hero, but he's gonna die, nonetheless.

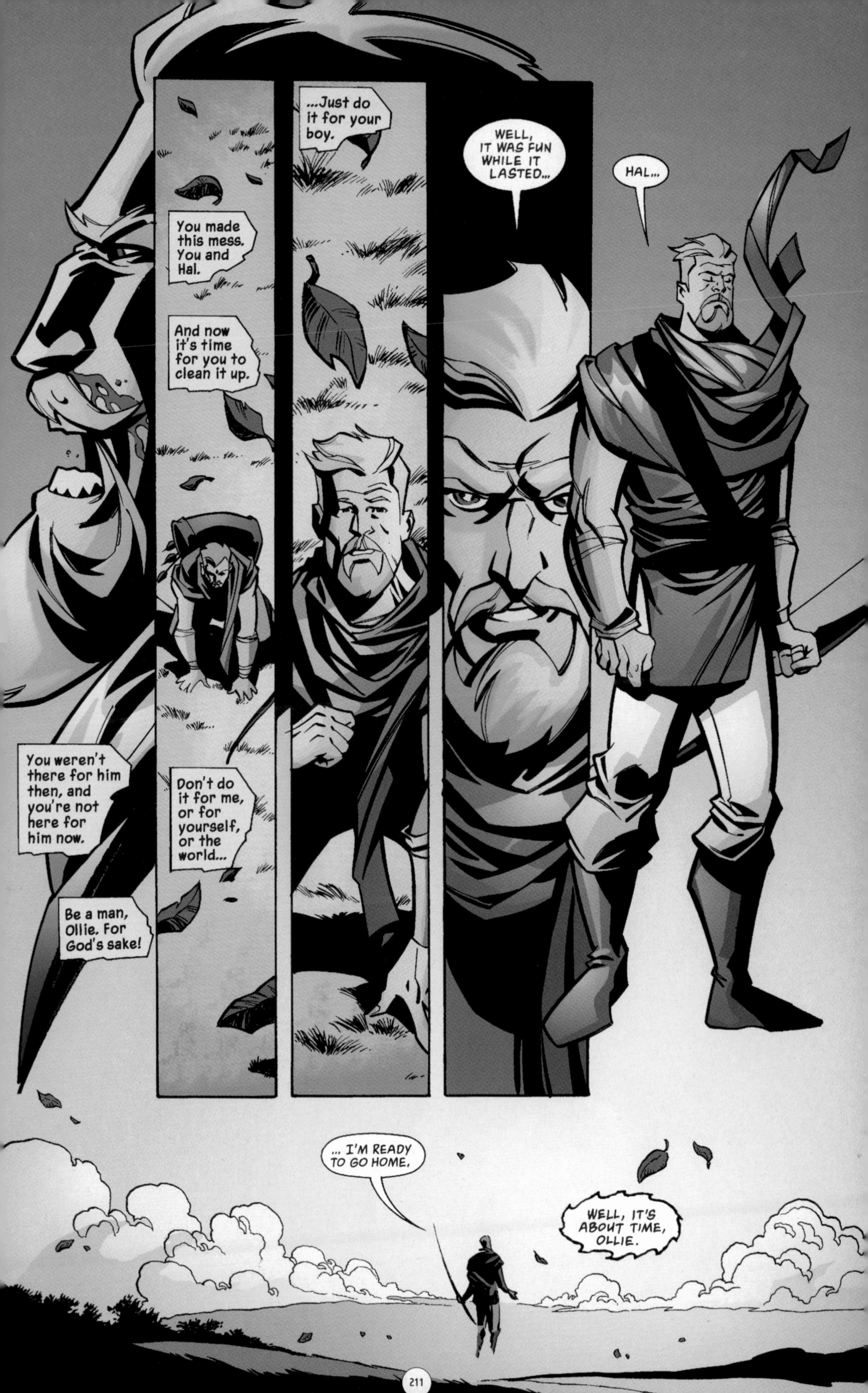
You made this mess. You and Hal.
And now it's time for you to clean it up.
...Just do it for your boy.
WELL, IT WAS FUN WHILE IT LASTED...
HAL...
You weren't there for him then, and you're not here for him now.
Don't do it for me, or for yourself, or the world...
Be a man, Ollie. For God's sake!
... I'M READY TO GO HOME.
WELL, IT'S ABOUT TIME, OLLIE.

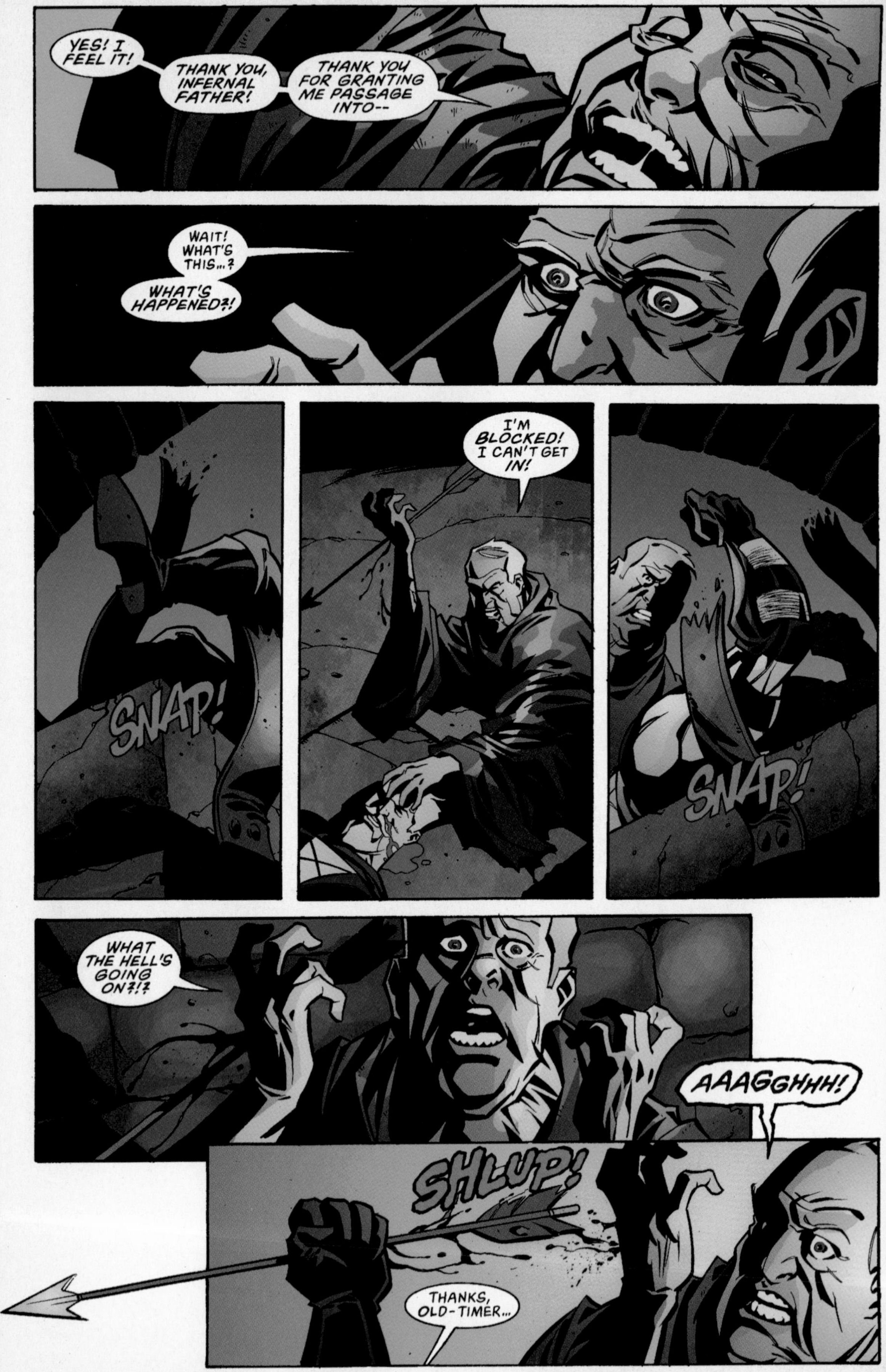
YES! I FEEL IT!
THANK YOU, INFERNAL FATHER!
THANK YOU FOR GRANTING ME PASSAGE INTO--
WAIT! WHAT'S THIS...?
WHAT'S HAPPENED?!
SNAP!
I'M BLOCKED! I CAN'T GET IN!
SNAP!
WHAT THE HELL'S GOING ON?!?
AAAGGHHH!
SHLUP!
THANKS, OLD-TIMER...

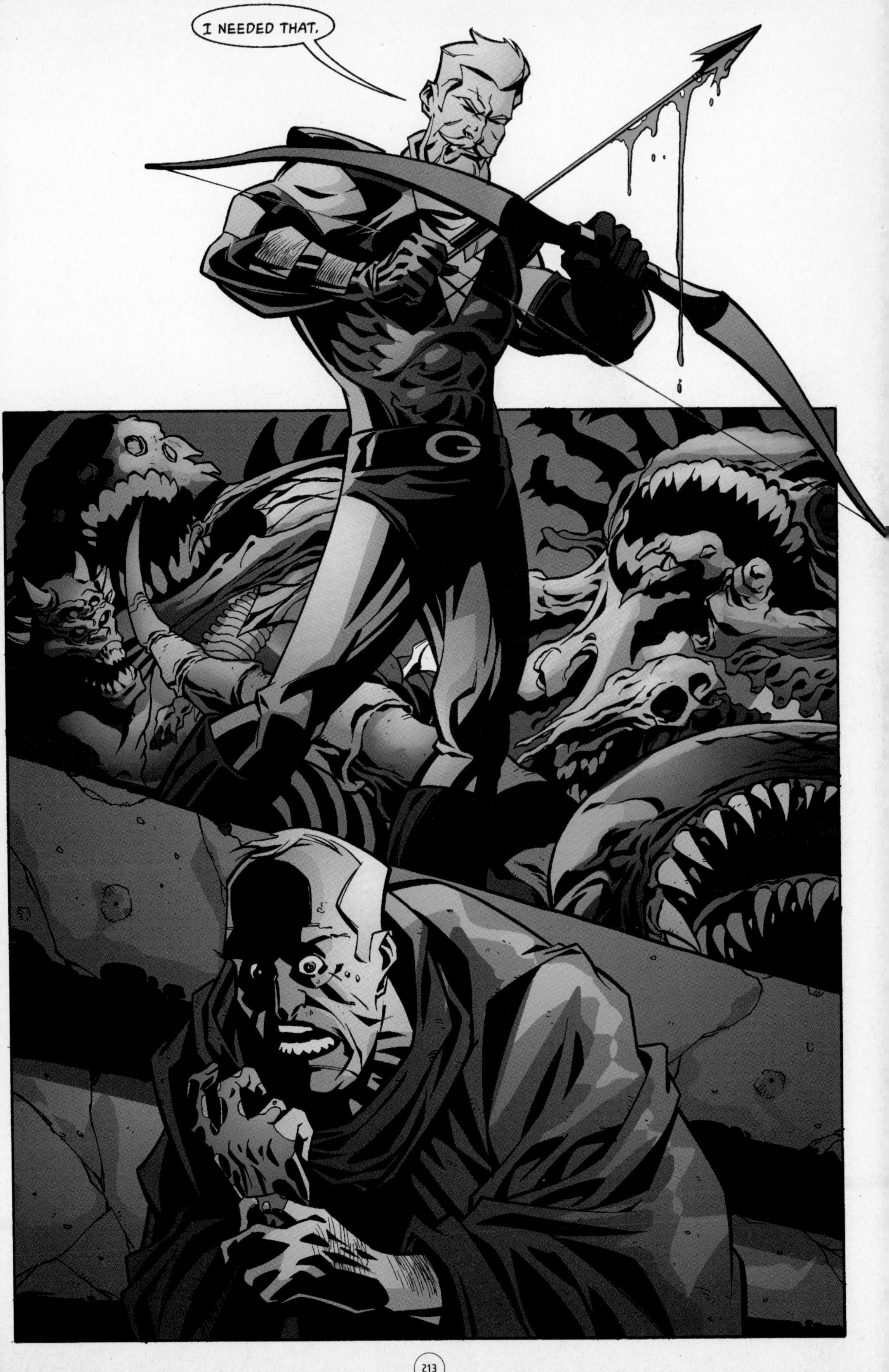
I NEEDED THAT.

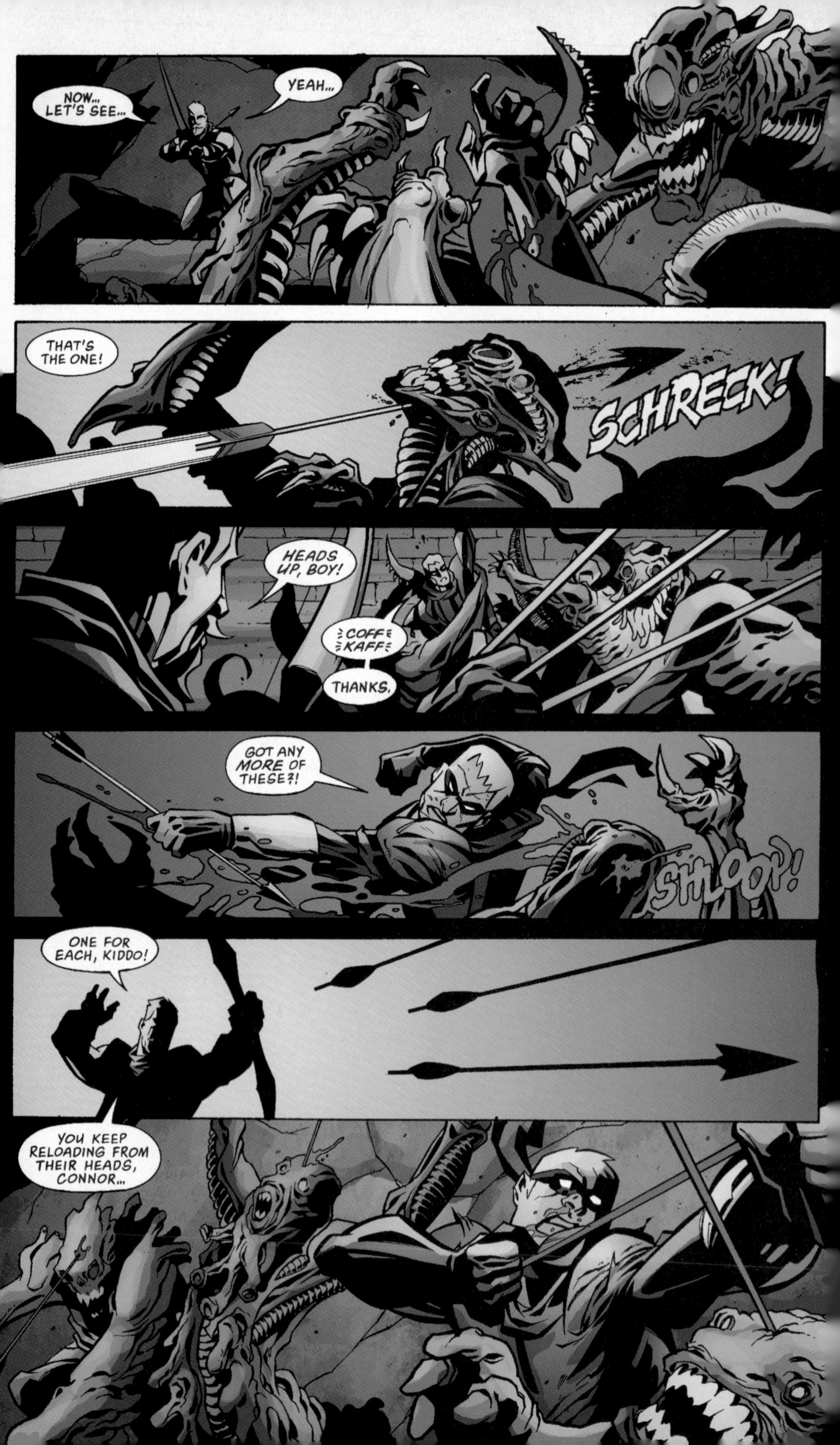
NOW... LET'S SEE...
YEAH...
THAT'S THE ONE!
SCHRECK!
HEADS UP, BOY!
COFF KAFF
THANKS.
GOT ANY MORE OF THESE?!
SHLOOP!
ONE FOR EACH, KIDDO!
YOU KEEP RELOADING FROM THEIR HEADS, CONNOR...

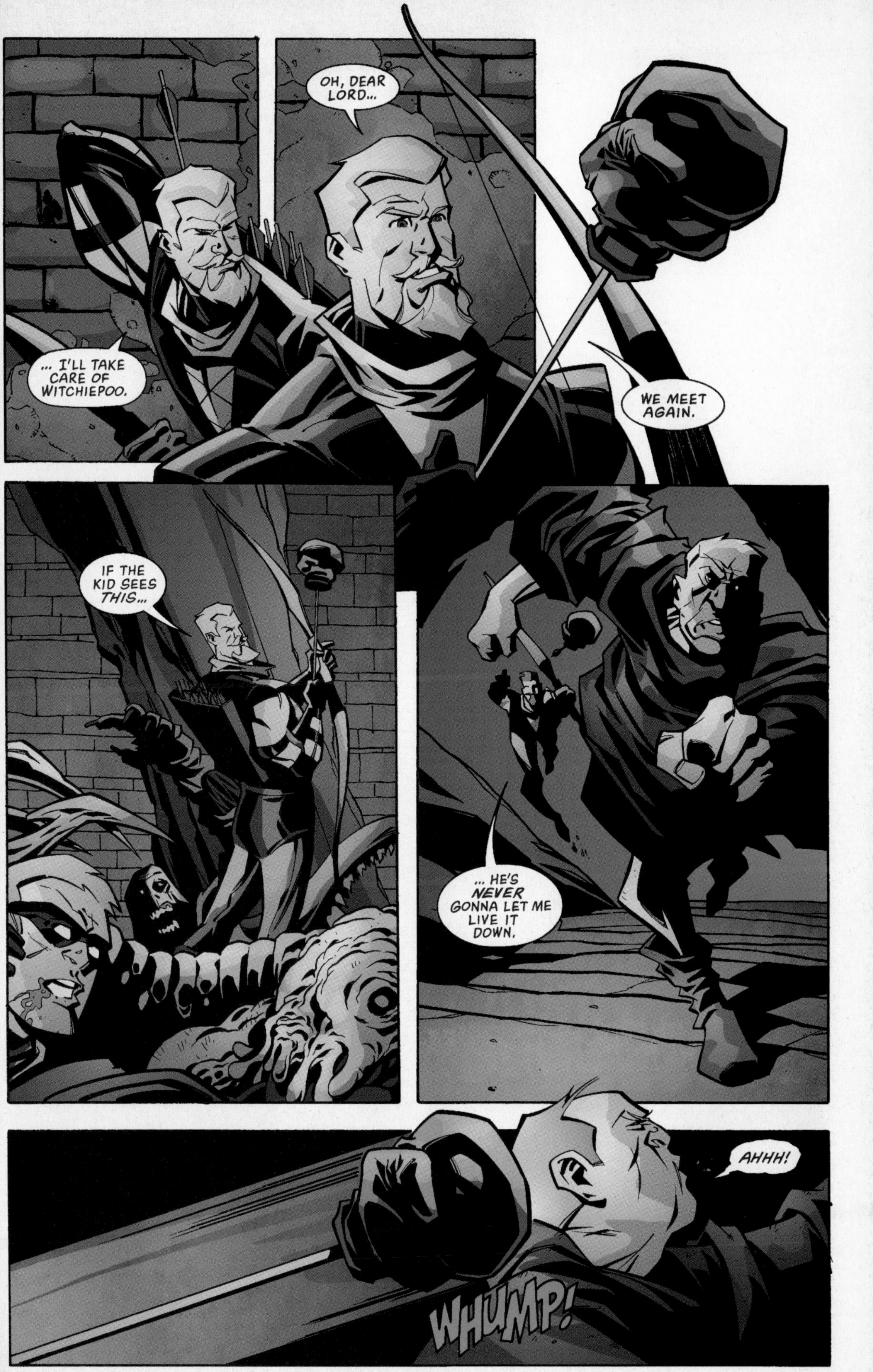
OH, DEAR LORD...
... I'LL TAKE CARE OF WITCHIEPOO.
WE MEET AGAIN.
IF THE KID SEES *THIS*...
... HE'S *NEVER* GONNA LET ME LIVE IT DOWN.
AHHH!
WHUMP!

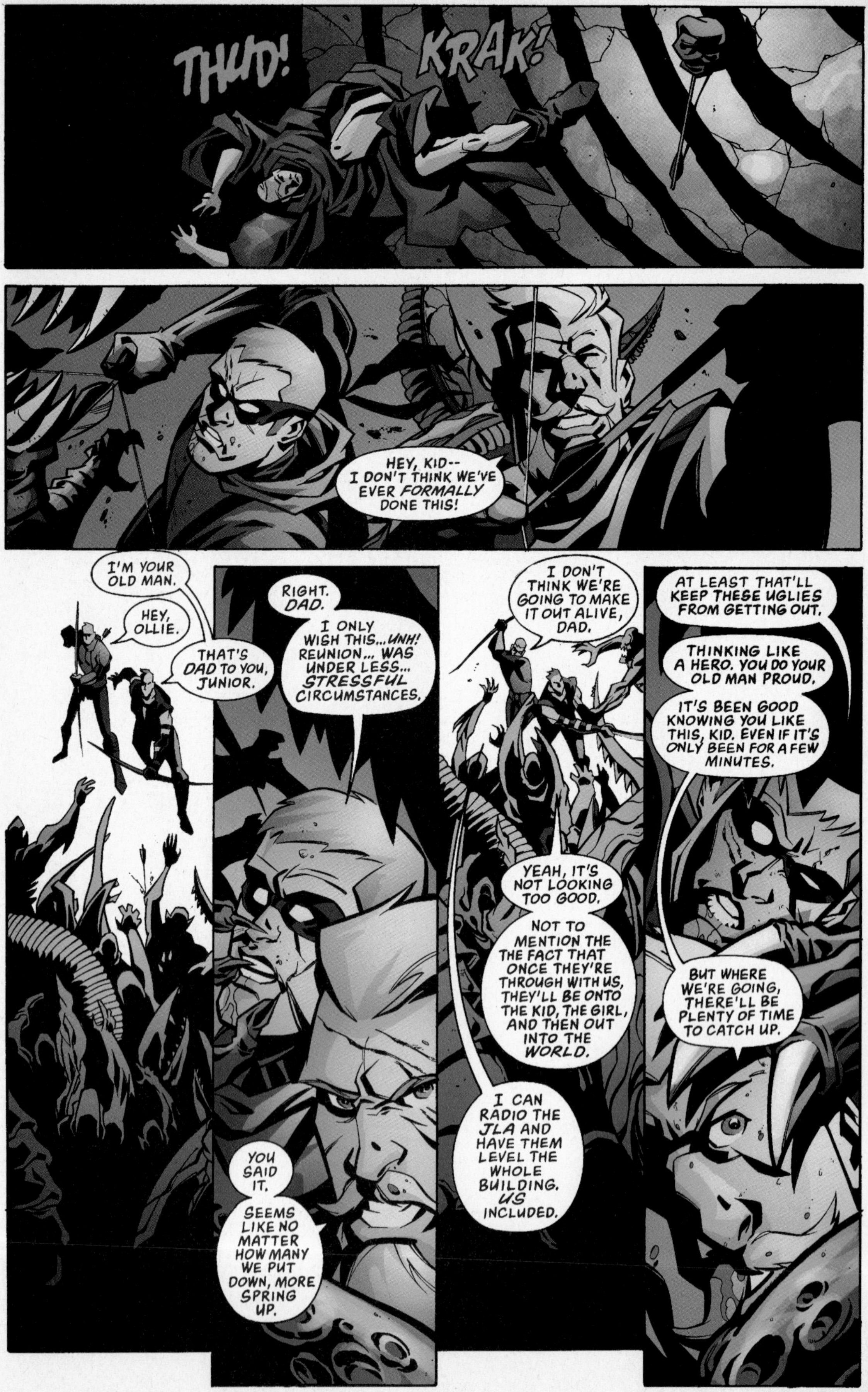
THUD!
KRAK!
HEY, KID-- I DON'T THINK WE'VE EVER FORMALLY DONE THIS!
I'M YOUR OLD MAN.
HEY, OLLIE.
THAT'S DAD TO YOU, JUNIOR.
RIGHT. DAD.
I ONLY WISH THIS... UNH! REUNION... WAS UNDER LESS... STRESSFUL CIRCUMSTANCES.
YOU SAID IT.
SEEMS LIKE NO MATTER HOW MANY WE PUT DOWN, MORE SPRING UP.
I DON'T THINK WE'RE GOING TO MAKE IT OUT ALIVE, DAD.
YEAH, IT'S NOT LOOKING TOO GOOD.
NOT TO MENTION THE THE FACT THAT ONCE THEY'RE THROUGH WITH US, THEY'LL BE ONTO THE KID, THE GIRL, AND THEN OUT INTO THE WORLD.
I CAN RADIO THE JLA AND HAVE THEM LEVEL THE WHOLE BUILDING. US INCLUDED.
AT LEAST THAT'LL KEEP THESE UGLIES FROM GETTING OUT.
THINKING LIKE A HERO. YOU DO YOUR OLD MAN PROUD.
IT'S BEEN GOOD KNOWING YOU LIKE THIS, KID. EVEN IF IT'S ONLY BEEN FOR A FEW MINUTES.
BUT WHERE WE'RE GOING, THERE'LL BE PLENTY OF TIME TO CATCH UP.

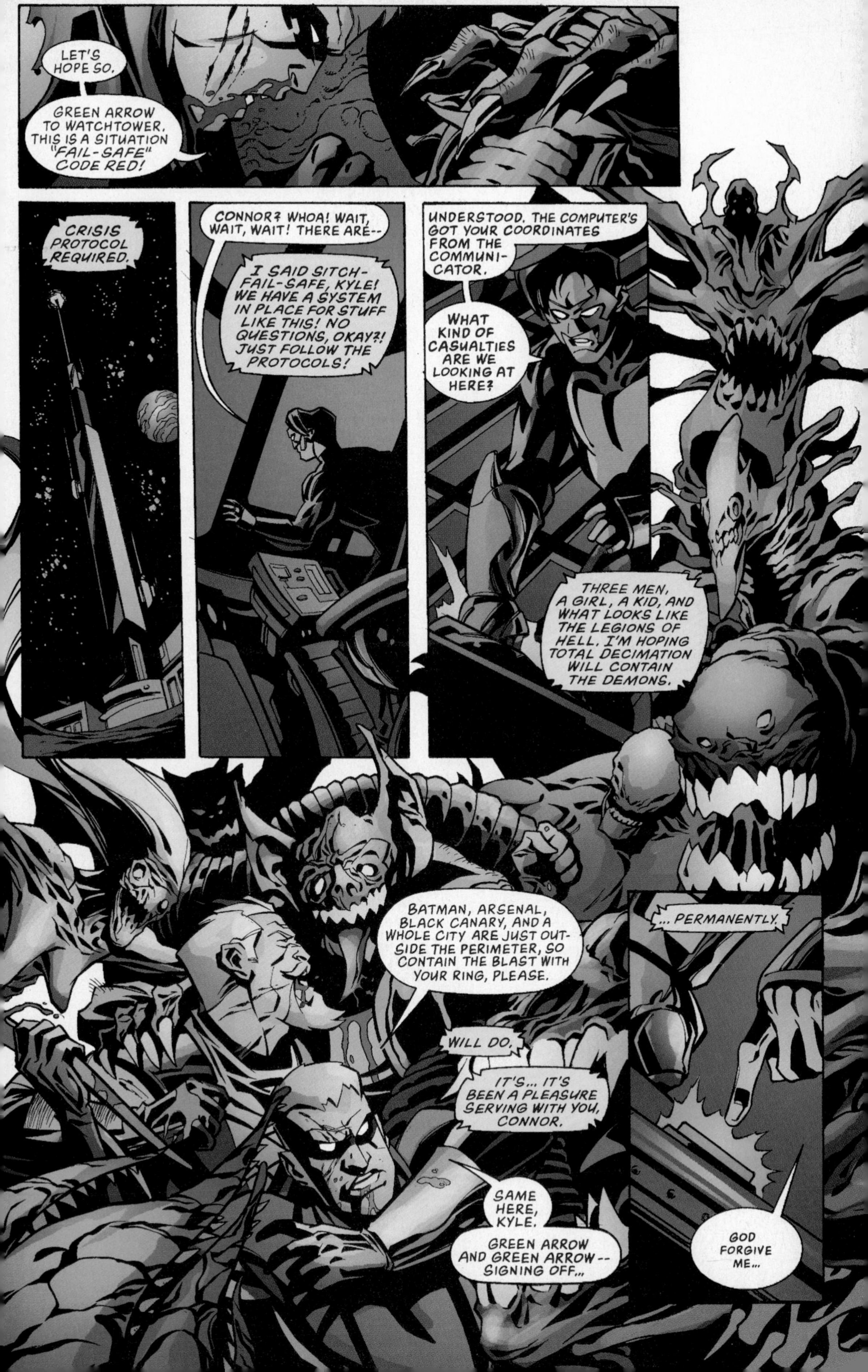
LET'S HOPE SO.
GREEN ARROW TO WATCHTOWER. THIS IS A SITUATION "FAIL-SAFE" CODE RED!
CRISIS PROTOCOL REQUIRED.
CONNOR? WHOA! WAIT, WAIT, WAIT! THERE ARE--
I SAID SITCH-FAIL-SAFE, KYLE! WE HAVE A SYSTEM IN PLACE FOR STUFF LIKE THIS! NO QUESTIONS, OKAY?! JUST FOLLOW THE PROTOCOLS!
UNDERSTOOD. THE COMPUTER'S GOT YOUR COORDINATES FROM THE COMMUNICATOR.
WHAT KIND OF CASUALTIES ARE WE LOOKING AT HERE?
THREE MEN, A GIRL, A KID, AND WHAT LOOKS LIKE THE LEGIONS OF HELL. I'M HOPING TOTAL DECIMATION WILL CONTAIN THE DEMONS.
...PERMANENTLY.
BATMAN, ARSENAL, BLACK CANARY, AND A WHOLE CITY ARE JUST OUTSIDE THE PERIMETER, SO CONTAIN THE BLAST WITH YOUR RING, PLEASE.
WILL DO.
IT'S... IT'S BEEN A PLEASURE SERVING WITH YOU, CONNOR.
SAME HERE, KYLE.
GREEN ARROW AND GREEN ARROW -- SIGNING OFF...
GOD FORGIVE ME...

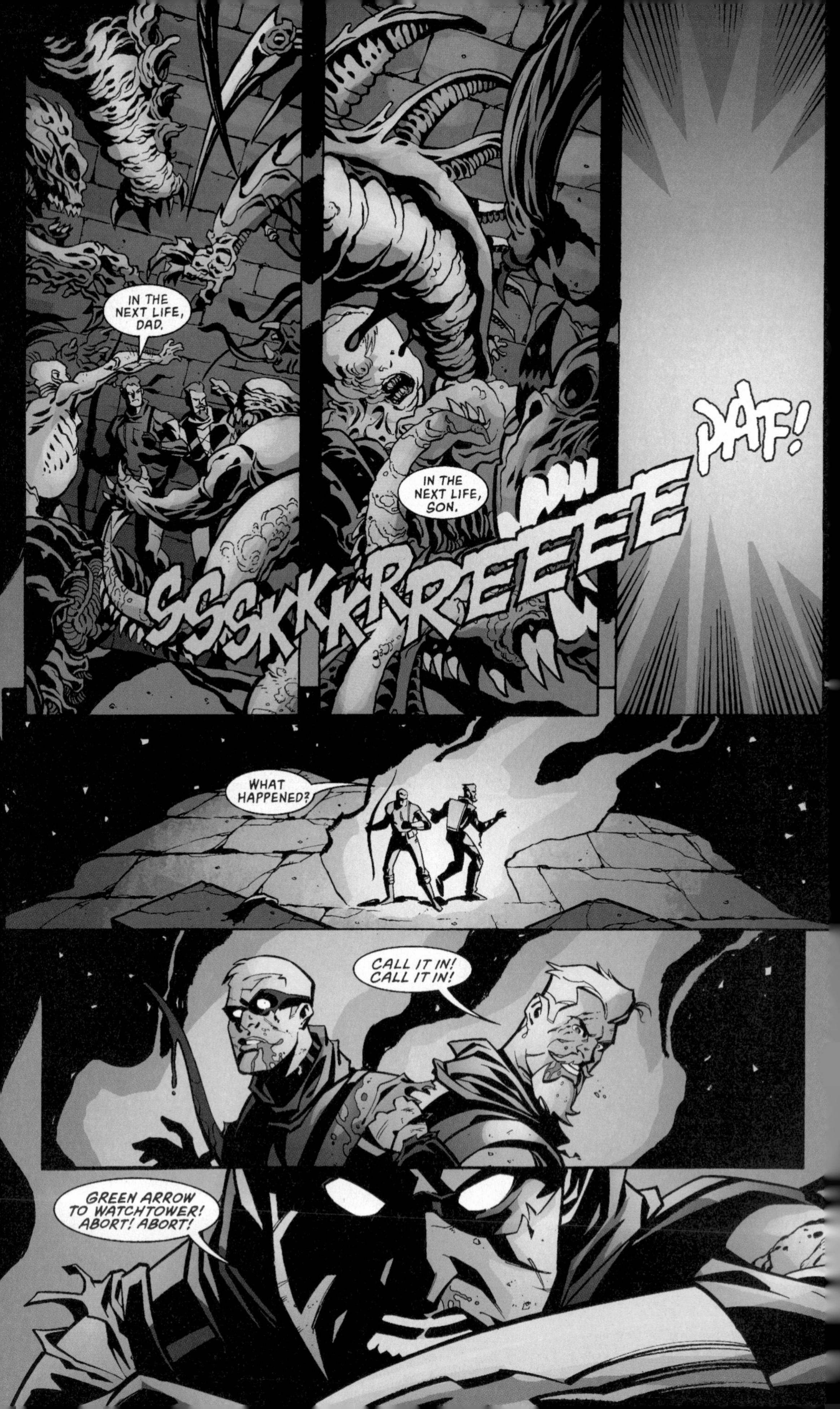
IN THE NEXT LIFE, DAD.
IN THE NEXT LIFE, SON.
SSSKKKRREEEEE
PAF!
WHAT HAPPENED?
CALL IT IN! CALL IT IN!
GREEN ARROW TO WATCHTOWER! ABORT! ABORT!

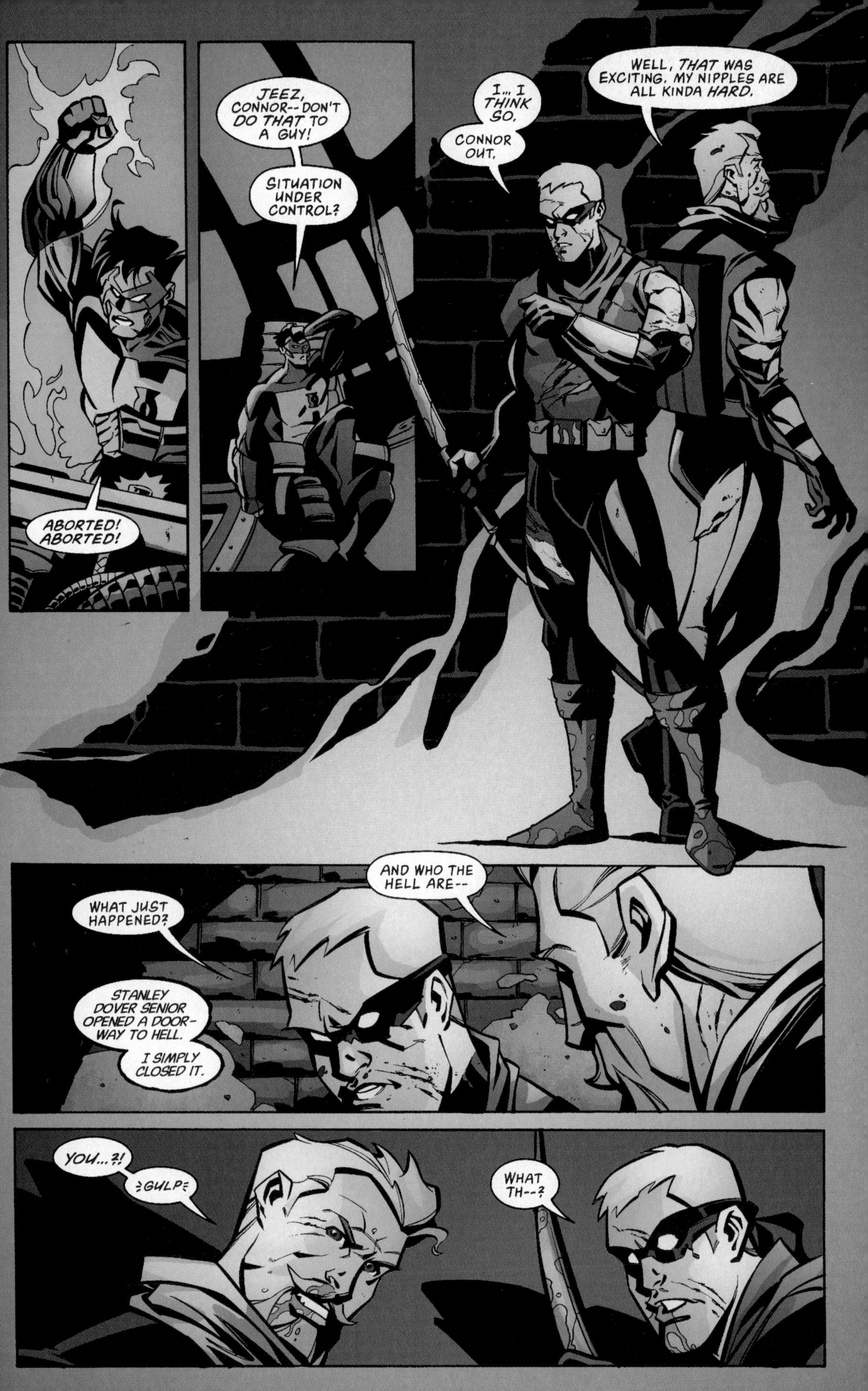
ABORTED! ABORTED!
JEEZ, CONNOR-- DON'T DO THAT TO A GUY!
SITUATION UNDER CONTROL?
I... I THINK SO.
CONNOR OUT.
WELL, THAT WAS EXCITING. MY NIPPLES ARE ALL KINDA HARD.
WHAT JUST HAPPENED?
AND WHO THE HELL ARE--
STANLEY DOVER SENIOR OPENED A DOOR-WAY TO HELL.
I SIMPLY CLOSED IT.
YOU...?!
GULP
WHAT TH--?

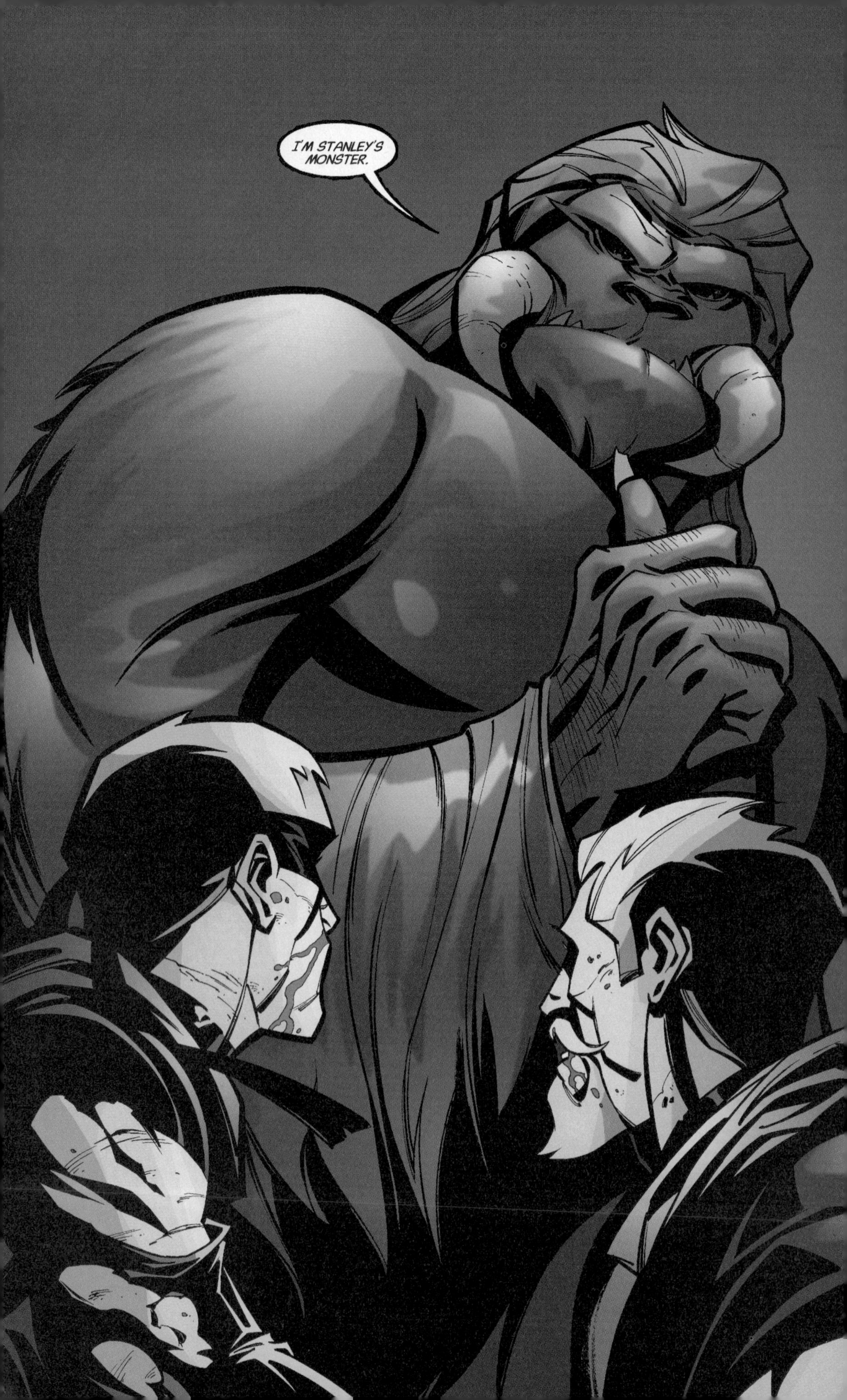
I'M STANLEY'S MONSTER.

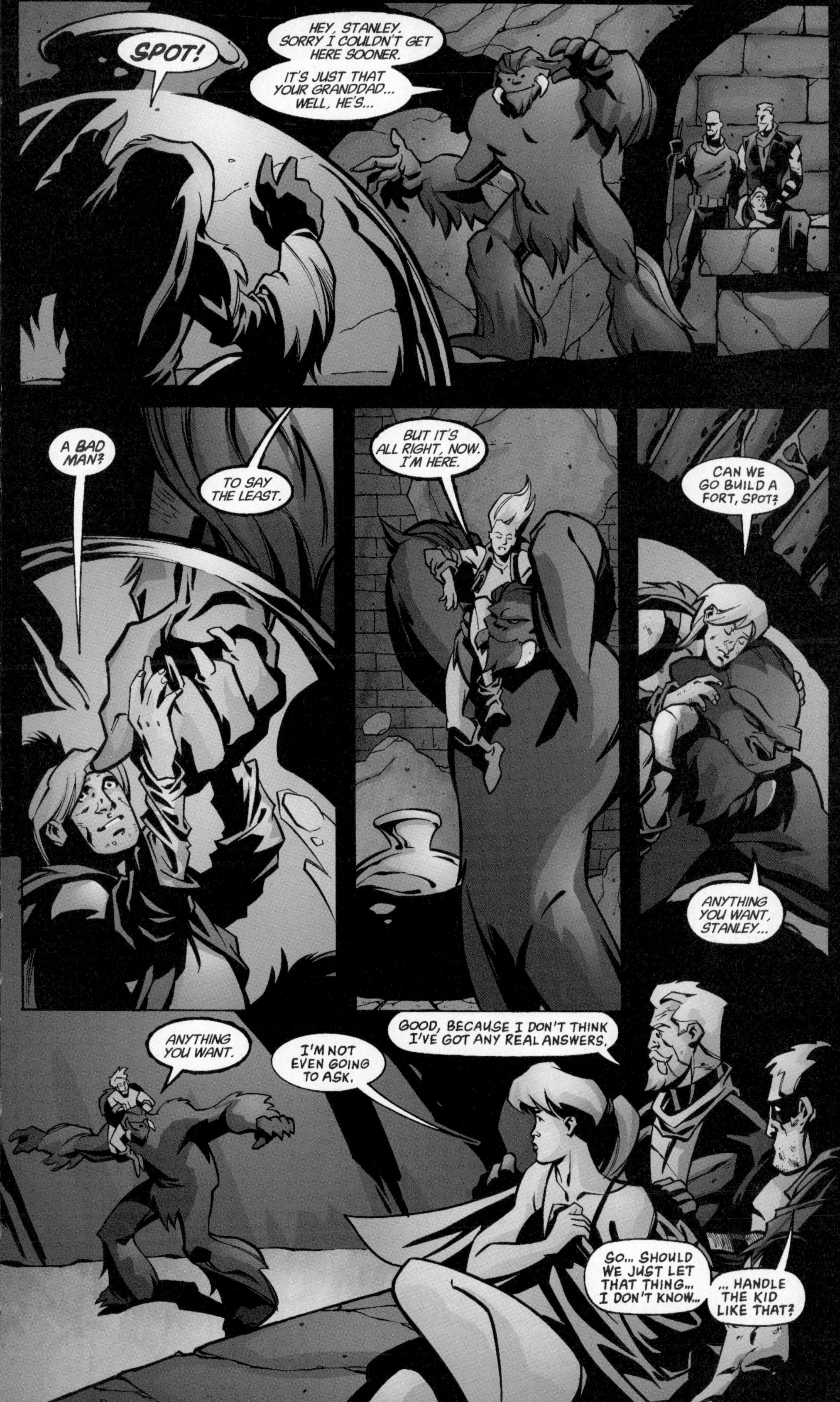
SPOT!
HEY, STANLEY. SORRY I COULDN'T GET HERE SOONER.
IT'S JUST THAT YOUR GRANDDAD... WELL, HE'S...
A BAD MAN?
TO SAY THE LEAST.
BUT IT'S ALL RIGHT, NOW. I'M HERE.
CAN WE GO BUILD A FORT, SPOT?
ANYTHING YOU WANT, STANLEY...
ANYTHING YOU WANT.
I'M NOT EVEN GOING TO ASK.
GOOD, BECAUSE I DON'T THINK I'VE GOT ANY REAL ANSWERS.
SO... SHOULD WE JUST LET THAT THING... I DON'T KNOW...
... HANDLE THE KID LIKE THAT?

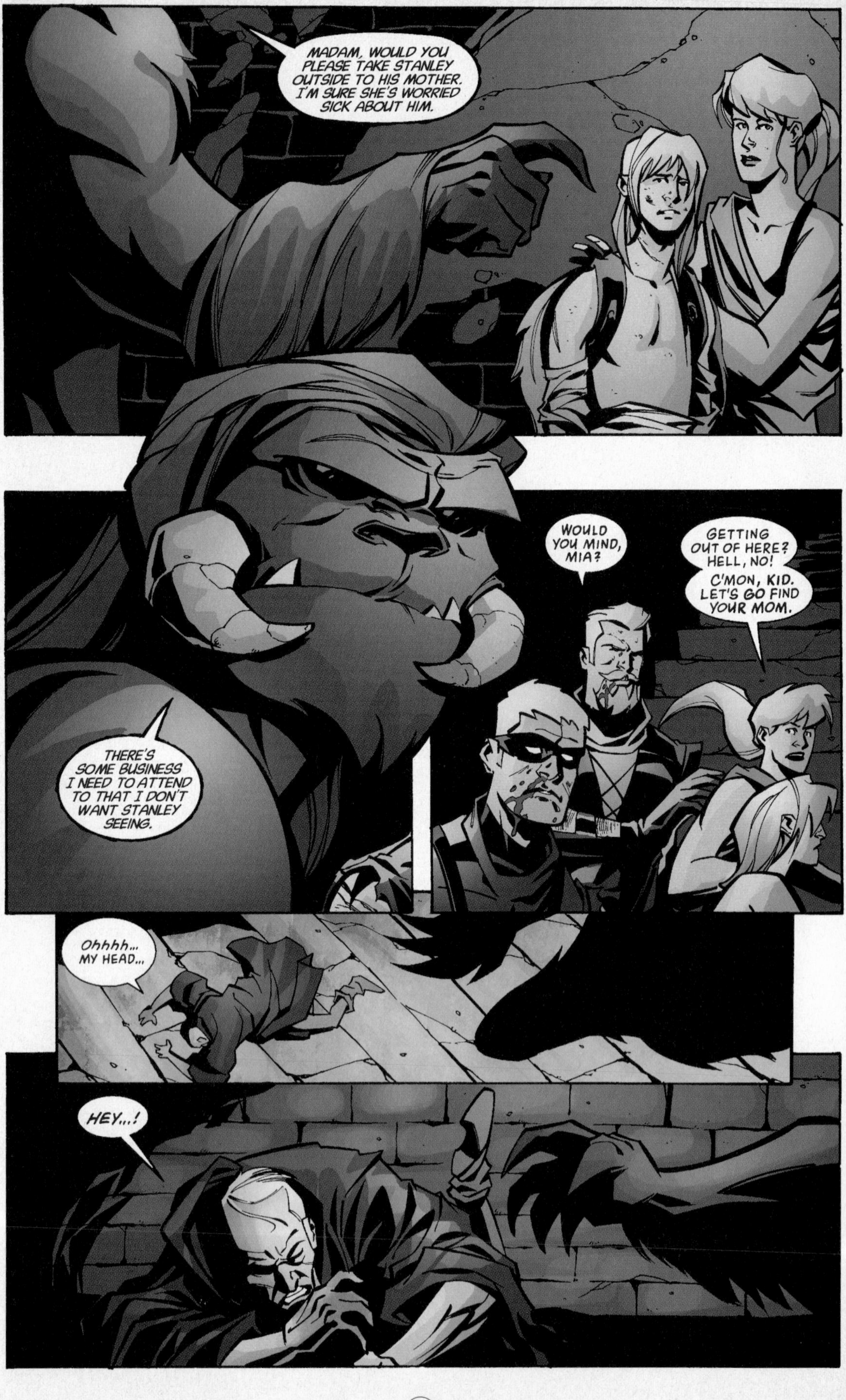
MADAM, WOULD YOU PLEASE TAKE STANLEY OUTSIDE TO HIS MOTHER. I'M SURE SHE'S WORRIED SICK ABOUT HIM.
THERE'S SOME BUSINESS I NEED TO ATTEND TO THAT I DON'T WANT STANLEY SEEING.
WOULD YOU MIND, MIA?
GETTING OUT OF HERE? HELL, NO!
C'MON, KID. LET'S GO FIND YOUR MOM.
Ohhhh... MY HEAD...
HEY...!

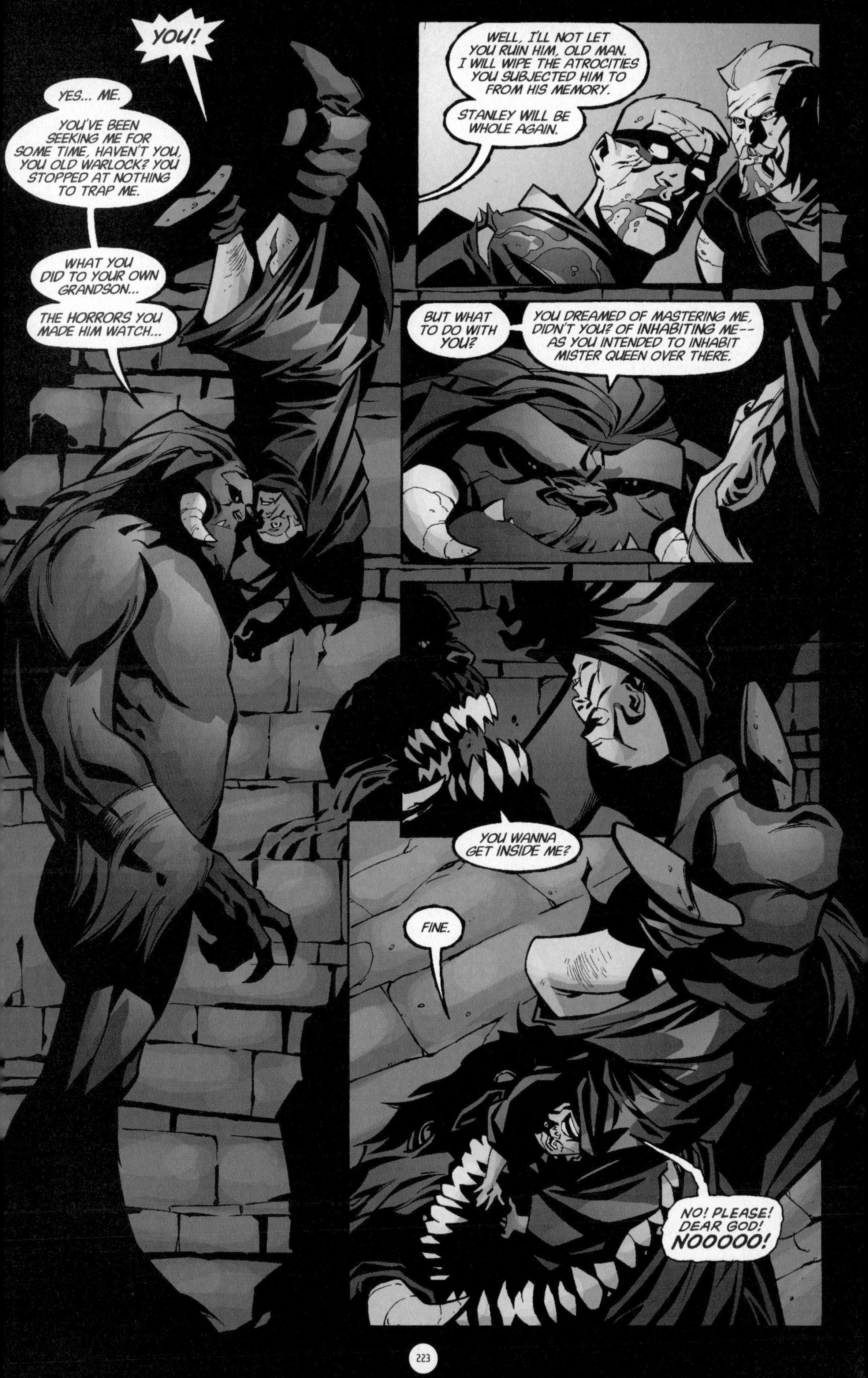
YOU!
YES... ME.
YOU'VE BEEN SEEKING ME FOR SOME TIME, HAVEN'T YOU, YOU OLD WARLOCK? YOU STOPPED AT NOTHING TO TRAP ME.
WHAT YOU DID TO YOUR OWN GRANDSON...
THE HORRORS YOU MADE HIM WATCH...
WELL, I'LL NOT LET YOU RUIN HIM, OLD MAN. I WILL WIPE THE ATROCITIES YOU SUBJECTED HIM TO FROM HIS MEMORY.
STANLEY WILL BE WHOLE AGAIN.
BUT WHAT TO DO WITH YOU?
YOU DREAMED OF MASTERING ME, DIDN'T YOU? OF INHABITING ME-- AS YOU INTENDED TO INHABIT MISTER QUEEN OVER THERE.
YOU WANNA GET INSIDE ME?
FINE.
NO! PLEASE! DEAR GOD! NOOOOO!

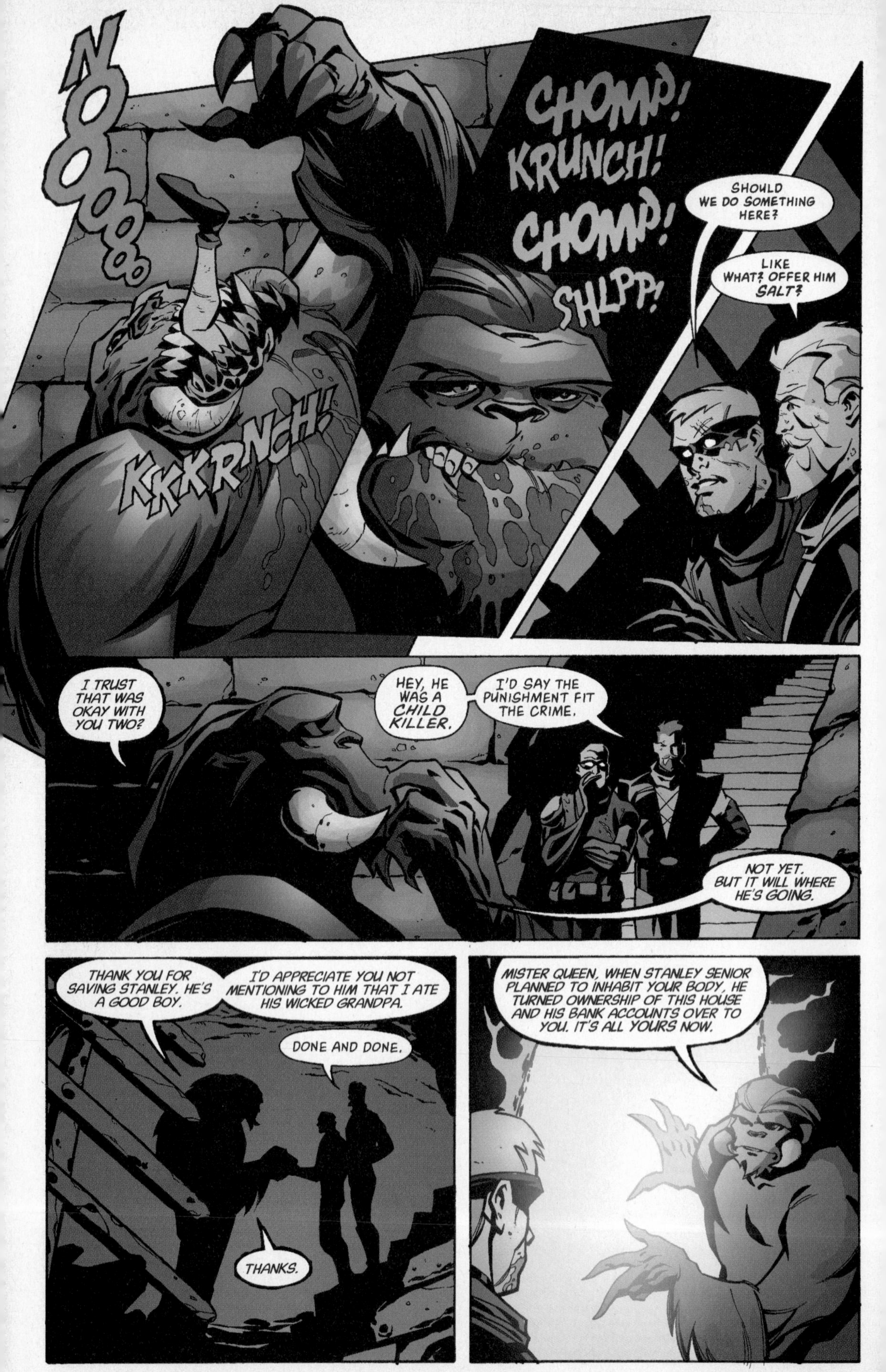

NOOOOoo
CHOMP! KRUNCH! CHOMP! SHLPP!
KKKRNCH!
SHOULD WE DO SOMETHING HERE?
LIKE WHAT? OFFER HIM SALT?
I TRUST THAT WAS OKAY WITH YOU TWO?
HEY, HE WAS A CHILD KILLER.
I'D SAY THE PUNISHMENT FIT THE CRIME.
NOT YET. BUT IT WILL WHERE HE'S GOING.
THANK YOU FOR SAVING STANLEY. HE'S A GOOD BOY.
I'D APPRECIATE YOU NOT MENTIONING TO HIM THAT I ATE HIS WICKED GRANDPA.
DONE AND DONE.
THANKS.
MISTER QUEEN, WHEN STANLEY SENIOR PLANNED TO INHABIT YOUR BODY, HE TURNED OWNERSHIP OF THIS HOUSE AND HIS BANK ACCOUNTS OVER TO YOU. IT'S ALL YOURS NOW.

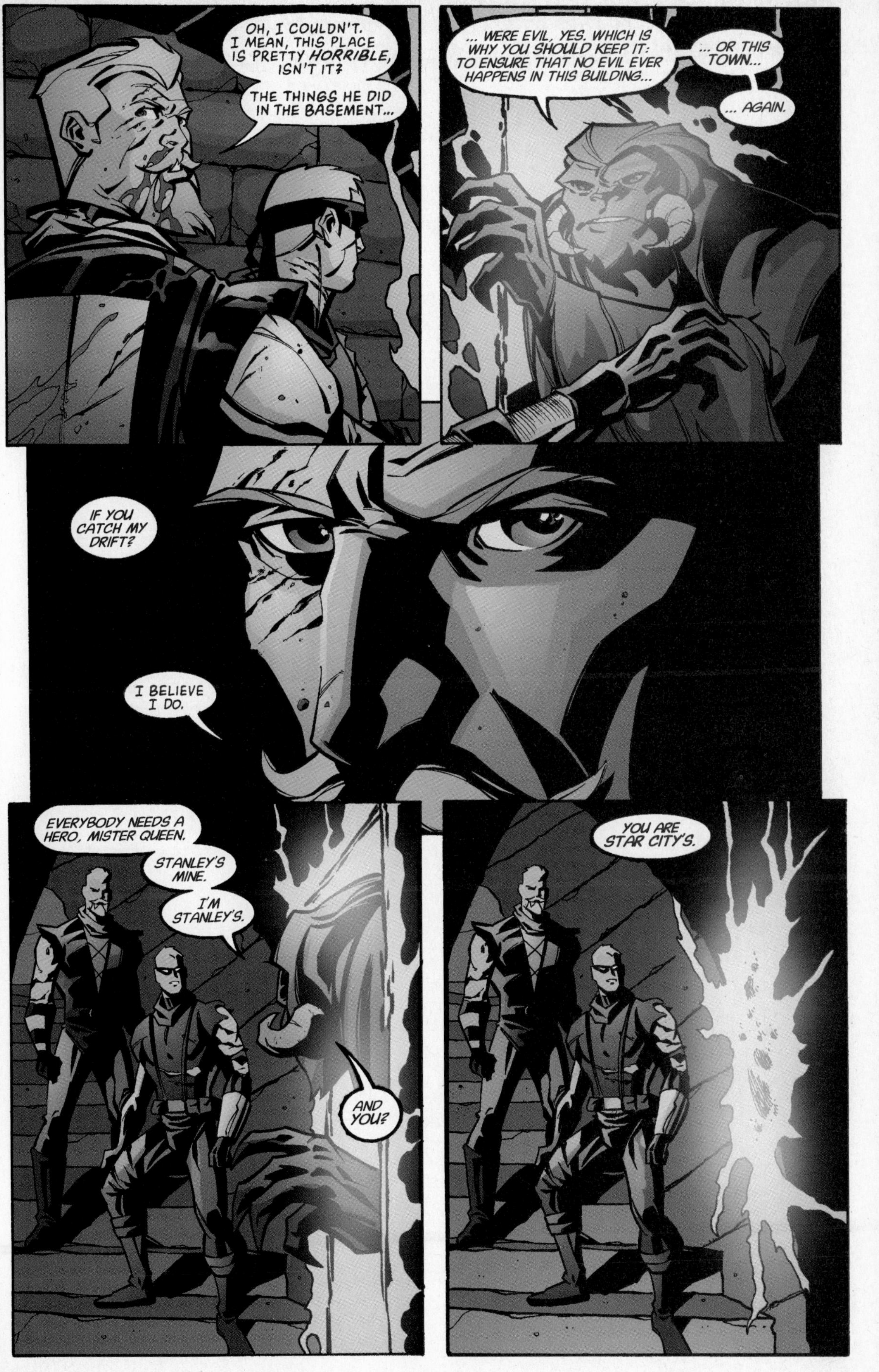
OH, I COULDN'T. I MEAN, THIS PLACE IS PRETTY *HORRIBLE*, ISN'T IT?
THE THINGS HE DID IN THE BASEMENT...
... WERE EVIL, YES. WHICH IS WHY YOU SHOULD KEEP IT: TO ENSURE THAT NO EVIL EVER HAPPENS IN THIS BUILDING...
... OR THIS TOWN...
... AGAIN.
IF YOU CATCH MY DRIFT?
I BELIEVE I DO.
EVERYBODY NEEDS A HERO, MISTER QUEEN.
STANLEY'S MINE.
I'M STANLEY'S.
AND YOU?
YOU ARE STAR CITY'S.

LIFE *ALWAYS* GOING TO BE THIS INTERESTING WITH YOU AROUND?

LET'S HOPE SO!

WANNA GRAB A DRINK?

I DON'T REALLY DRINK, DAD.

I'M A ZEN-BUDDHIST.

YOU TRYIN' TO TELL ME *BUDDHA* DIDN'T DRINK?! WITH THAT *BEER BELLY* OF HIS?

YOU'RE THE GUY WHO WAS *DEAD.* YOU TELL ME.

I'LL TELL YOU *LOTS* OF THINGS, CONNIE. STUFF THAT'LL MAKE YOUR HAIR STAND UP.

IF YOU EVER GROW ANY...

REGARDLESS-- LET'S GET OUTTA HERE FOR AWHILE... JUST *YOU* AND ME.

WHAT ABOUT BATMAN? AND ROY?

OR DINAH, FOR THAT MATTER?

I'VE SPENT *YEARS* TALKING TO THEM. AND IT LOOKS LIKE I'LL BE SPENDING EVEN MORE YEARS DOING THE SAME NOW THAT I'M BACK.

BUT FOR TODAY...

... I'D JUST LIKE TO HANG OUT WITH MY SON.

YOU *DO* HAVE A CAR, DON'T YOU?

A CAR? I DON'T EVEN HAVE A *LICENSE.*

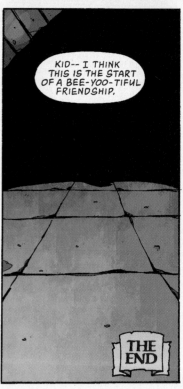

KID-- I THINK THIS IS THE START OF A BEE-YOO-TIFUL FRIENDSHIP.

THE END

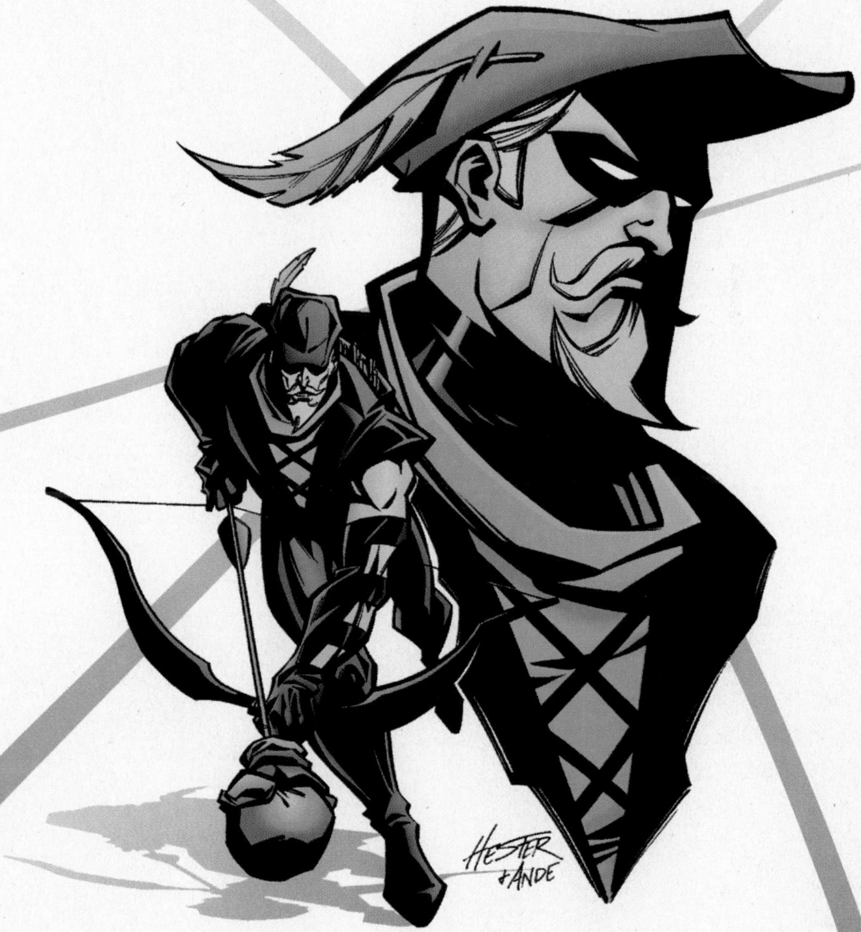
HESTER
&ANDE

C O V E R   G A L L E R Y

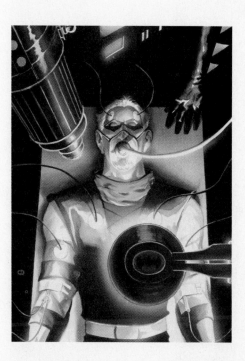

KEVIN SMITH

In the few years since his entry into the indie film community, Kevin Smith has seen it all — from the surprise critical and commercial success he received for his debut film *Clerks* to the disappointing critical and commercial drubbing he took on his second outing, *Mallrats*. He caught a break on his third film, the critically hailed *Chasing Amy*, and managed not to get killed by the religious zealots over his fourth film, the comedic meditation *Dogma*. Thus not deterred, Smith advanced and has written and directed the fifth and final installment in his New Jersey Chronicles, *Jay and Silent Bob Strike Back*, released by Dimension Films in August 2001.

Along the way, Smith has also found time to make himself a nuisance by smearing his name all over the pop culture landscape. He collaborated with indie film guru John Pierson on his best-selling book *Spike, Mike, Slackers, and Dykes*. He's published the screenplays to all four of his films. He's written comic books featuring not only his own characters (the multiple-printed *Clerks* and *Jay and Silent Bob*), but other characters as well (the award-winning *Daredevil* at Marvel Comics, and the award-winning GREEN ARROW at DC Comics). With his View Askew partner, Scott Mosier, he's also produced four low-budget, first-film efforts, including Bryan Johnson's forthcoming Lion Gate release, *Vulgar*. Smith and Mosier also co-executive produced the Academy Award-winning *Good Will Hunting*, starring View Askew stalwarts (and then unknowns) Matt Damon and Ben Affleck.

Besides *Mallrats*, however, Smith has survived other humbling "creative" experiences which he inexplicably has failed to suppress — such as his ill-fated *Superman Lives* screenplay for Warner Bros., and his animated series version of *Clerks* for ABC primetime, which the network unceremoniously cancelled after airing only two episodes.

But, but, but, Smith was one of the first filmmakers to venture into cyberspace, establishing the insanely popular View Askewniverse website (www.viewaskew.com) in the mid-nineties. And if the film thing doesn't pan out, he does own his own comic-book store — Jay and Silent Bob's Secret Stash, in beautiful downtown Red Bank, New Jersey.

As for the hood ornaments he's collected, there's plenty of tin to go around: the Filmmaker's Trophy at Sundance for *Clerks*; the Prix de la Jeunesse and the International Critic's Week Award at the Cannes Film Festival, also for *Clerks*; The Independent Spirit Award for Best Screenplay for *Chasing Amy*; and a Humanitas Award for *Good Will Hunting*. For his writing in the comics field, Smith has received a Harvey Award, a Wizard Fan Award, and an Eagle Award.

Yet at the end of the day, the two titles Smith touts most proudly are "husband" and "father." He married his wife Jennifer in April of '99, and celebrated the birth of their daughter, Harley Quinn, in June of that same year (you do the math).

PHIL HESTER

This Eisner Award-nominated artist was born in eastern Iowa, where he went on to study art at the University of Iowa. His pencilling credits to date include SWAMP THING, BRAVE OLD WORLD, FLINCH, *Ultimate Marvel Team-Up*, *The Coffin*, *Clerks: The Lost Scene*, *The Crow: Waking Nightmares*, *The Wretch* (nominated for the 1996 Eisner Award for Best New Series), *Aliens: Purge*, and GREEN ARROW. Hester continues to reside in Iowa with his wife, Christine, and their two children, Dean and Emma.

ANDE PARKS

Born and raised in Kansas, Ande Parks has been employed in the glamorous world of comic-book inking for over a decade, lending his talents to such titles as SUPERMAN, WONDER WOMAN and CATWOMAN. Often teamed with his longtime friend Phil Hester, he has won acclaim for his bold, graphic style. Parks has also created his own characters, *Uncle Slam* and *Fire Dog*. He is currently continuing his work on GREEN ARROW and is writing a gangster graphic novel. He lives in Kansas with his lovely wife and daughter.

THE STARS OF THE
DC UNIVERSE
CAN ALSO BE FOUND IN THESE BOOKS:

DC